AN INTRODUCTION TO
PHILOSOPHICAL ANALYSIS

ROUTLEDGE AND KEGAN PAUL
LONDON, MELBOURNE AND HENLEY

AN INTRODUCTION TO

SECOND EDITION

John Hospers

Professor of Philosophy
California State College at
Los Angeles

PHILOSOPHICAL ANALYSIS

First published in Great Britain 1956
by Routledge & Kegan Paul Limited
39 Store Street
London WC1E 7DD,
296, Beaconsfield Parade,
Middle Park, Melbourne,
3206, Australia.
Broadway House, Newtown Road
Henley-on-Thames, Oxon RG9 1EN

Reprinted six times

Second Edition published 1967
Reprinted 1970

Reprinted and first published as a paperback 1973

Reprinted 1976, 1978, 1981 and 1982

Printed in Great Britain
By Unwin Brothers Limited
The Gresham Press, Old Woking, Surrey, England
A member of the Staples Printing Group.

ISBN 0 7100 1560 7 (c)
ISBN 0 7100 7724 6 (p)

Preface

Those who approach philosophy for the first time do so from a variety of motives. Some are drawn into philosophy from their interest in the sciences, some from the arts, some from religion; others come to philosophy without any academic background, motivated by an uneasiness about "the meaning of things" or "what the world is all about"; still others have no motivation more specific than that of wanting to know what kind of thing people are talking about when they use the word "philosophy." Accordingly, the demands which different people make of philosophy, the questions they expect it to answer, are as diverse as the motives leading them to it; and as a result, the books which are written to satisfy these demands are similarly diverse. Often two books professing to introduce readers to philosophy contain little or none of the same material. For these reasons it is impossible to write a book that will satisfy all, or even (perhaps) a majority of, readers.

One might try to overcome this difficulty by writing a book so comprehensive that all the problems which anyone considered philosophical would be treated in it, and the reader would have only to select portions in which he was most interested. This, however, is hardly possible in practice: a book of a thousand pages would not begin to suffice. Nor would it be feasible to devote just a few pages to each problem: this would leave only outline summaries of the various issues, which would mean little to the reader; he might learn the meanings of some terms and absorb a few "general trends" from such a presentation, but he would not have been given enough material to make the problems come alive for him. The capsule method is even less successful in philosophy than it is elsewhere. The only apparent solution, then, would be to include not all, but only some, of the problems in the field. This method has its drawbacks, for no matter which problems are included and which are excluded, many readers are bound to object both to some of the inclusions and some of the exclusions. Yet this is the policy that has been followed in this book, as the one with the fewest all-round disadvantages.

This edition has been almost completely rewritten; very few pages of the first edition, written thirteen years ago, survive in the present one. Except for the title and the main structural outline of contents, it is virtually a new book. All the sections have been radically changed, and new sections have been added: on concepts, sources of knowledge, the problem of universals, and various other issues. The chapter on aesthetics has been omitted entirely, though with regret, since this topic is not usually treated in introductory courses, and the space has been used to make possible a fuller treatment of metaphysical and epistemological problems.

The author wishes to express his gratitude to the following publishers for permission to quote brief excerpts from works published by them: Open Court Publishing Co., *Analysis of Knowledge and Valuation* by C. I. Lewis and *Reason and Analysis* by Brand Blanshard; Macmillan & Co., London, The Macmillan Co., of Canada, and St. Martin's Press, Inc., New York, *The Critique of Pure Reason* by Immanuel Kant (Norman Kemp Smith translation) and *Foundations of Empirical Knowledge* by Alfred J. Ayer; George Allen & Unwin Ltd., *Some Main Problems of Philosophy* by G. E. Moore and *Social Principles and the Democratic State* by S. I. Benn and Richard Peters; *Mind*, "Empirical Propositions and Hypothetical Statements" by Sir Isaiah Berlin; Harcourt, Brace & World, *The Mind and Its Place in Nature* by C. D. Broad; Houghton Mifflin Co., *Invitation to Philosophy* by Durant Drake; University of California Press, *The Rise of Scientific Philosophy* by Hans Reichenbach; Harper & Row, Publishers, *A Philosophy of Science* by W. H. Werkmeister; Methuen & Co., London, *An Introduction to Metaphysics* by C. H. Whiteley and *Perception* by H. H. Price; Longmans, Green & Co., *Selected Papers on Philosophy* by William James; and Hutchinson Publishing Group Ltd., London, and Barnes & Noble, Inc., for *Theory of Knowledge* by A. D. Woozley.

The author's deep gratitude is acknowledged to his colleagues who were kind enough to read and comment on various portions of the manuscript: in particular, Professor Martin Lean, for chapters 1 and 8 (as well as the formulation of points made on pages 222–23 and 434–35); Professor Salvator Cannavo for chapters 2 through 4; Professor Paul Edwards for chapters 5 through 7; and Professor Stanley McDaniel for chapters 1, 2, 3, 5, 6, 8, and 9. Generous thanks are due also to Miss Janet Polish for assistance in the typing of the manuscript and to Miss Sharon Milan for assistance in the preparation of the Index.

Readings in Introductory Philosophical Analysis (Prentice-Hall, 1968), a paperback book of readings, has been designed to accompany this book.

John Hospers

Contents

1

MEANING AND DEFINITION, 1

2

KNOWLEDGE, 101

3

NECESSARY TRUTH, 160

9

ETHICAL PROBLEMS, 566

1
Meaning and Definition

At the beginning of any systematic discussion one is expected to define terms, and our principal term is "philosophy." But the term "philosophy" cannot be defined as easily as "chemistry," "biology," or "sociology." For one thing, people working in the field they call philosophy have offered very different, even conflicting, definitions of this term; and if we presented a definition at the outset, we would be running the great risk of making a premature judgment on a matter that should first be weighed as carefully as possible. It will be preferable to show, in the course of our investigations, *why* scholars in the field have suggested different definitions—and this will take time. Second, and more important, are special difficulties about the definition, which we shall not be in a position to understand until we have examined some problems about definition in general, and that is one of the things we shall endeavor to do in this chapter.

With or without a definition of "philosophy," there is a great advantage in approaching our subject by means of the topic of *semantics*—the study of the relation of the words in our language to the world we use language to talk about. There are numerous confusions and pitfalls to which almost every reader will fall victim if he is not first clear about some of the basic principles and problems of semantics—or in other words, the relation of language to what we talk about by means of language. A useful introduction to virtually any subject-matter would be a study of different phases of meaning, the nature and function of definition, the dangers (and sometimes advantages) of imprecise use of words, and the conditions under which sentences have meaning. For philosophy's highly abstract subject-matter, containing an unusually large number of pitfalls for the unwary, the preliminary survey of certain basic semantic problems is not only useful but indispensable. If we did not survey these problems first, we would have to backtrack and study them later. In our first chapter, then, we shall concern ourselves with the relation of language to the world—a topic that has come to be recognized as being within the proper domain of the very enterprise called "philosophy."

1. Word-meaning

Among human beings, *language* is the principal instrument of communication. Any language is composed of *words,* which are combined to form *sentences.* We encounter different problems in the study of each of these. Accordingly, we shall begin with a study of the nature and function of words, and reserve the discussion of sentences till later in the chapter.

What is a word? We could spend a great deal of time discussing competing definitions; but for our present purposes, it will be sufficient to suggest (though it is a bit of an oversimplification) that a word is the *smallest unit of meaning.* The word "cat" has a meaning, but the letters of which it is composed—"c," "a," and "t"—do not. The letters are only the building blocks of words, and they have no meaning by themselves except in rare cases in which a word is composed of a single letter ("a," "I").

It is true that some words are compound words whose components are other words: "switchman" is composed of "switch" and "man"; but even in these cases the word is the unit of meaning, not the parts of the word. You cannot infer what the meaning of the compound word is from the meanings of the component words. A switchman, for example, is not a man who is a switch. Letters are the constituents of written words, much as atoms are the constituents of molecules. (But do prefixes and suffixes have a meaning by themselves or only as a part of the words to which they are attached?)

Is a word merely a noise when it is spoken, or a set of marks on paper when it is written? A word is these things, but not *only* these things. A word is a spoken noise or set of written marks *with a meaning.* A meaning can also occur in sign language, which is neither spoken nor written but only a gesture or bodily movement, but a word in sign language is still a gesture with a meaning.

Our account thus far, however, is still not enough to distinguish words from other things. While it is true that all words have meanings, it is not true that all things that have meanings are words. Mathematical symbols have meanings, but they are not words. A twister in the sky means that a tornado is approaching; a fall in the barometric pressure means that a cold front is on the way; one kind of bell means that church services are about to be held, another that class is over, another that someone is at the door, still another that someone is on the phone. If someone moans and groans, this normally means (depending on the context) that he is in pain; if he screams, that he is in terror or excited by something or wants to call your immediate attention to something; tracks in the sand mean one thing (a bear has been this way), a dirty house another (the inhabitants haven't cleaned it recently). Yet none of these things are words.

All of these things are called *signs.* One thing, A, is a sign of another thing, B, if A *stands for* B in some way or other. But there are different ways in which one thing can stand for another. Words are *conventional* signs, as opposed to *natural* signs. When dark nimbus clouds are in the sky, we say "This means rain"; and this relation between clouds and rain makes the clouds a sign of rain—in this case a natural sign, for it exists in nature and is not of human invention. People discovered that certain kinds of clouds are followed by rain; they did not make it so. Clouds would still be indicators of rain even if people had not discovered this fact. It is a fact of nature, not of man's doing. When people try to discover the meaning of certain tracks in the mud, they are trying to find out what or who made them; and again this is a fact of nature. The meaning of the tracks (such as "A bear has been here") is something we discover, not something we make or which becomes true because of a decision on our part. We could *mis*interpret the tracks and thus not be properly on our guard. In doing this, we would be misinterpreting a fact of nature.

But isn't the fact that people use words also a fact of nature? Indeed it is, if the word "nature" is used in its widest sense to mean everything that exists in space and time; nevertheless, words have a kind of meaning that is different from that of clouds, bear tracks, and other things in nature. Human beings have *given* words their meanings; or more precisely, human beings have taken certain noises and given them meanings. People speaking different languages may utter different noises with the same meaning, such as "cat" in English, "chat" in French, and "Katze" in German. You and I have not established meanings for the noises; we have learned meanings that have developed, sometimes over centuries, or meanings that are intended by other people today when they use the noise. We learn the convention, the custom or practice of using this noise. When we learn the meaning of dark clouds, however, we are learning facts of nature that would exist if there were no human conventions. Bells, on the other hand, are conventional signs because human beings themselves have determined and established what they are to mean.

We are not saying that once upon a time a group of people sat down together and decided among themselves what was to be meant by various noises. (What words would they have used in communicating with one another, to decide among themselves what each noise was to mean?) The origin of language is lost in the mists of history, and we need not stop to speculate how it started. In whatever way it started, the fact is that a language is a system of words, a system of conventional signs whose meanings we have to learn if we are to know the language, and whose ingredients—words— would be noises without meaning if sometime, somewhere, they had not acquired these meanings for their human users.

But screams and groans are also noises made by human beings, and yet they are not words. Nor are they human conventions. A child may scream and groan before he learns a language. An adult may do so, and convey his meaning to others who have not learned the system of verbal conventions that constitute his language. One does not need to learn a language in order to know how to interpret another's groans, tears, and laughter; he learns their meanings as he learns natural signs—with this difference: often he does not have to be *taught* what they mean, since his awareness of his own behavior when he feels pain, anger, or joy may be enough to enable him to interpret this same behavior in others. But a man whose native tongue is German or Swahili will not say "Ouch!" when his finger is burned.

Usually the relation of a natural sign, A, to what it is a sign of, B, will be a *causal* relation (as in clouds meaning rain) or a relation of *resemblance* (as in a map of the city which stands for the city). But some signs may have *both* natural and conventional elements. A road sign that says "Curve" is entirely conventional—the word bears no resemblance to what it means. But the road sign may contain no word at all, just a *picture* of a leftward curve, and this means that there is a left curve ahead. There is a natural relation (resemblance) between the shape of the curve on the road sign and the shape of the curve ahead; but apart from a convention, which has to be *learned* by motorists, the road sign still wouldn't *mean* anything. Without the convention, how would you know it wasn't just an interesting shape that someone had drawn and posted; or assuming it meant something, that it didn't mean "curve behind" or "curve two miles to the east" or even "curves exist"? You have to learn in this case, just as you do with a word, that this shape has been devised by man to bear a specific meaning in this context, and this remains true even when there is a natural relation (resemblance) between the sign and what it means. The same holds true of the onomatopoetic words in a language (words that sound like their meaning): "buzz," "crack," "whir," "splash," etc. There is some resemblance, usually quite faint, between the noise and what it means, but not enough so that you could usually guess its meaning without having learned it first; and different languages have very different sounds for the same thing, even in the case of these words, which would indicate that the resemblance between the word and its meaning is not very great. (Would you be able to guess what "buzz" meant if you hadn't learned it?) Thus, even when there is a resemblance between a sign and what it is a sign of, we still have to learn the meaning that has been given it by convention.

A distinction is often made between signs and *symbols,* but it is not always made in the same way. (1) Sometimes the word "symbols" is made to mean the same as "conventional signs"; in this usage, bells ringing, musical notation, and words are all symbols. All have been devised by man and do not exist as signs in nature apart from man; but when something stands for something else in nature, apart from man's invention, then we have signs rather than symbols. (2) Sometimes the word "symbols" is used to stand for signs to which we respond by having a *concept.* (Concepts will be discussed in Chapter 2.) The appearance of meat causes the dog to salivate, and later, the word even without the food causes the dog to salivate. "Meat" remains a sign for the dog, because when you utter the word "meat" he *expects* meat.

But for human beings the word "meat" operates as a symbol and not a sign: when we hear the word "meat," we do not expect the appearance of meat but conceive of (have a concept of) meat. (See Susanne K. Langer, *Philosophy in a New Key*.) Since nothing in this chapter requires us to decide how to distinguish signs from symbols, we shall use the word "sign" as a generic term to mean *anything* that stands for something else (in whatever way), then distinguish different kinds of signs, leaving to others the thankless task of adjudicating the conflicting meanings of the term "symbol." (In other contexts when we talk about symbols, such as Freudian symbols or symbols in art—"the whale in *Moby Dick* is a symbol of evil"—the word "symbol" carries a still different meaning.)

The relation of words to things. It was long believed that there was some natural connection between words and what the words stand for. This is not to say that anybody ever thought that a word *is* a thing (as has been sometimes alleged when writers speak about "confusing the word with the thing"), or confused the word "cat" with the creature, cat; but primitive people did believe that the utterance of certain words would have *effects* on the thing meant by the word (for example, uttering the word "God" would evoke the wrath of God), and more particularly, that there was a "natural connection" between the word and the thing it stands for, so that the word could not "rightly" be used to stand for anything else.

But no such natural connection exists; words are *arbitrary* signs (arbitrary because another noise could have been used just as well), which became *conventional* signs once they were adopted by other users of the language. The meanings that words have were originally not discovered but *assigned*. The woman who admired the astronomers because, as she said, "they learned the names of all those stars," was mistaken: the astronomers *gave* names to the stars, and other people then learned the names that the astronomers gave them.

The relation of a word to its meaning is in some ways like that of a label to a bottle. The label tells you what is in the bottle (if you are able to read the label), but it has no natural relation either of causality or resemblance to the contents of the bottle. Different labels are written in different languages, but they are all equally understood by those who have learned what the writing on the label means. The label is only an indicator of what is in the bottle, and has no importance in itself—it is simply a set of written marks which bear no intrinsic relation to the contents of the bottle. The relation of the label to the contents of the bottle is different from the relation of the *aroma* coming from the bottle to the contents. If the bottle contains ammonia, the pungent smell is a natural sign of what is in the bottle, but the *word* "ammonia" is not a natural sign but a conventional one. (But let us not push this comparison too far: some words, such as "and," do not stand for things in the world, as we shall have occasion to notice shortly.)

Since words are conventional signs, there is no such thing as the right or wrong word for a thing. A word may be needlessly long or cumbersome or hard to pronounce or to spell, and it can be objected to for these reasons, but not because the noise used to stand for a thing is the *wrong* noise. Another noise could always have been used instead.

But aren't certain words the wrong ones? Suppose the name "Finns" has been used to stand for a certain people; then isn't the land they live in rightly called "Finland" and wrongly called anything else?

It would not be wrong to call it something else: some other noise might have been given instead, and it would not have been the wrong noise. But *once some names have already been given,* it is often most *convenient* to be guided in the rest of the name-giving process by those names which are already there. If the name "Finns" has already been given to a certain people, and the word "land" means what it does now, what is more convenient than to call the land "Finland," "land of the Finns"? Although it is easiest to remember that way, there are many cases where this has not been done, but other entirely unrelated names have been given, and these names are not wrong. The word "Finland" is still not a *natural* sign for that country: the "natural" relation here is not one of resemblance between the word and the country, but between the word "Finland" and the other *words* "Finn" and "land."

But surely it is inaccurate to call some things by certain names? If I called the thing on which I am sitting a lamp instead of a chair, surely that would be mistaken, wouldn't it?

Yes, it would be mistaken *if* we meant by the noise "lamp" what people who speak English already mean by it, something that (among other things) serves to give light You are surely not sitting on a thing that gives light, and to say that you are would be mistaken; more precisely, it would be false. But of course you could use the noise "lamp" to stand for it if you wanted to; to do so would only be extremely confusing to other people. We would then have *two* meanings for the noise "lamp," the one you just gave it and the conventional one which those who speak English have used for generations. In order not to mislead them, you would (if you wanted to stick to your new usage) have to tell them in advance that you were not using the noise "lamp" to mean the same thing that they were. Even so, the situation would be greatly complicated by your new usage: every time you used the noise "lamp," they would have to remember that you were using it to mean something different from the thing *they* had used the word to mean for many years. Such complication would be needless. There would be nothing to be said for it and everything to be said against it, but it would not be wrong—only unnecessarily confusing. It would only be wrong (false) if you said "I'm sit-ing on a lamp" and used the word "lamp" in this sentence in the conventional sense that you had just rejected. The error in it would be that of using a noise to stand for a thing which by convention had been referred to by a *different* noise, and then turning around and using this noise (perhaps unconsciously) in its conventional sense.

Freedom of stipulation.   "Anybody can use any noise he wants to refer to anything he wants, as long as he makes clear what he is using the noise to refer to." This is the rule of freedom of stipulation. Its results, as we have seen, would be confusing; however, you are always free to stipulate; the only question is whether it is practical or useful in any way to avail yourself of it.

If you want to avoid unnecessary confusion in the use of language, you had better refer to a thing by the same noise that other people already use in referring to it.

The rule of common usage.   Because of the unnecessary confusion and inconvenience that would be brought about if you tried to inflict a set of symbols of your own invention upon society and everyone else did the same, the rule that is usually suggested for your employment of words is that you *follow common usage.* This is what we ordinarily do without being told to do it, simply because it would be pointless to invent a new noise to stand for a thing when another noise is already being used by everyone around us. We find it easier simply to fall in line with a usage which is already established. When we *do* employ a word in a way contrary to common usage, we should inform our hearers of what we *are* using it to mean. Conversely, when we do not inform our hearers of what we are using our words to mean, they have a right to take for granted that we are using them in their conventional sense—in other words, that we are following common usage.

We do not ordinarily act as perversely and capriciously as in the above example of the word "lamp." Nevertheless, the rule of common usage can be of considerable practical importance, as the following example will illustrate:

In scientific or pseudo-scientific circles it is sometimes said that nothing is really solid. Even the table, which looks so solid, is really not solid at all. If we could look at it through ultra-microscopic eyes, we should find that it is a hurly-burly of atoms and electrons separated by distances which are enormous compared with their own sizes; thus the table consists mostly of empty space. No sample of matter that we would ever encounter on the earth, then, is "really solid."

But in common usage, things like tables, trees, boards, and sidewalks are spoken of as "solid," while puddles of water, melted butter, and hydrogen gas are not. Are all our statements about the solidity of tables then mistaken? No, for when we say that a table is solid we mean that if we put our hands on it they will not go through the surface, as they would through the surface of the water in a vessel, and perhaps also that unless subjected to great heat or pressure, it retains its shape, instead of spreading or assuming the shape of its container, as water does. If something fulfills these requirements, we call it solid; that is what "solid" means in ordinary usage. The scientist's account of the table is undoubtedly correct (at any rate this is not the place to discuss it); but if the scientist or anyone else says that the table is not really solid at all, his assertion is misleading unless he specifies how he is using the word. In daily life if someone said, "Be careful up there; the board is solid enough, but the plaster isn't," he would be easily understood, and the hearer would avoid stepping on the plaster for fear that it would give way. But if, referring to that same board, the speaker said, "Neither the board nor the plaster is solid," this would be misleading because the hearer would probably conclude that the board was as insecure as the plaster, and therefore he would not venture up on the rafters at all. (In this example, the ordinary usage of "solid" is "strong enough to hold your weight," rather than solid as opposed to liquid, or solid as opposed to perforated with holes. All these are common usages of the word "solid," but the pseudo-scientific meaning is not one of them.)

Exceptions to the rule of common usage.   Should one *always* stick to common usage of a word? There are several qualifications we might wish to add to the rule of common usage.

1. There may not be a word for what you want to talk about. Perhaps, then, you undertake to make one up: that is, to take a noise and use it to stand for something that has not been given a name in your language. This will be a new arbitrary symbol. If your usage catches on and other people adopt it, your noise will have become a conventional symbol; it will then have attained common usage. When the mathematician Kasner found that he wanted to refer frequently to the 100th power of ten, he asked his little grandson, "What would *you* call it?" "Googol," was the immediate response. And so the noise (now a word) "googol" has attained common usage in writings on popular mathematics.

2. Sometimes there is a common usage for a word, but you want to depart from it because the thing that the word stands for already has another word standing for it. For example, some persons now tend to use the word "God" to refer simply to nature as a whole. The word "God" already has a common usage, to refer to a supernatural Being. The word "nature" also has a common usage, to refer to the totality of things, events, and processes in the universe. Even though the word "God" were very commonly used in this new sense, you might want to resist this tendency; you would want to depart from this increasingly common usage because its results would be confusing. Word 1 stands for Thing 1; Word 2 stands for Thing 2; why complicate the matter by trying to make Word 1 also stand for Thing 2? Sometimes common usage may tend to do this, and when it does, it may well be in the interest of clarity to resist such usage.

Many people use the words "annoyed" and "aggravated" as if they were synonymous. This is probably a more common usage of these words than the usage that lexicographers would call the "correct" one. Why do they consider the less frequent usage incorrect? There are various reasons: etymology, "educated" use, linguistic purism. But the most important reason is that it *blurs* a distinction that the "correct" usage makes clear. Being aggravated is not at all the same as being annoyed—it means an increase or intensification of an undesired condition already present (as in "Her illness became aggravated by the cold that she contracted"). If we use "aggravated" to mean the same thing as "annoyed," we have a pointless *duplication* of language—two words for the same thing, and consequently a *vacuum* where a word ought to be, for we now have no single word with which to talk about the condition we correctly call "aggravation." Another example: many people say "jealous" when they should say "envious." There is a clear distinction here: people can experience jealousy in a triangular love-situation, and a man may be jealous of his reputation; but he is *envious* of others if he thinks they are better off than he is and wishes he were in their place. If we forget this, we blur an important distinction: if we say "I'm jealous of my boss because he has more money and power than I have," we have two words ("jealous" and "envious") for the same thing, and no word that uniquely labels the condition of jealousy. The same thing happens when we confuse "dumb" with "stupid," however common that confusion may be.

More often, however, when a word or phrase is used in violation of common usage, this is not done in the interest of clarity but in the interest of beguiling you into accepting an unwarranted conclusion. Thus, if someone said, "There are no democracies left in the world," you might be misled by his assertion, until you discovered that he was using the word "democracy" to apply only to governments in which every citizen is a voting member of a national legislature (instead of voting for representatives to do this). You and he may argue at cross purposes until you realize that he is using the word in this rather unusual sense. Similarly, if someone said to you, "There aren't really any material objects in the world—there are only spirits," you might be surprised, then skeptical, then inclined to deny it vehemently. But your surprise would vanish if you found that he was using the word "spirits" in such a broad way that it included trees, houses, planets, and so on—the very things to which common usage already assigns the phrase "material objects." Perhaps without knowing what they are doing, people will flaunt one of their assertions as a new discovery about the universe, whereas in reality they are merely manipulating words and employing them in violation of common usage without informing their hearers of the fact.

3. Sometimes, and this is perhaps the most important case of all, a word does stand for something in common usage, but is employed with such haziness and indefiniteness that you are not satisfied in following common usage by continuing to use the word. The word "liberal," for example, is considered (by some people) so indefinite in its present meaning that its continued use is confusing and unprofitable. They feel that the word as now used is simply a blanket term covering a nest of confusions, and they want to avoid this situation in the interest of clarity, even at the expense of ignoring common usage.

When it seems to you that you would be only perpetuating confusion by continuing to follow common usage of a word, you can do either of two things: (1) you can drop the word altogether and try to say what you want to say more precisely (but more lengthily) by using different words; or (2) you can keep on using the same word but try to purify it by using it in some special and more precise sense—generally by restricting it rather arbitrarily to some specific portion of the hazy area of reference which it now has. (If you were going to use it to mean something entirely different, there would be no point in continuing to use the same word at all: thus, there would be no point in using the word "liberal" to mean "two or more feet high.")

Common usage is a guide to meaning, not to truth.   With the above qualifications, common usage is a guide for determining what you shall use your words to mean. But it does not determine whether a statement in which you use these words is true or false. Common usage is recommended, with qualifications, as the most useful and convenient guide in your use of language. It does not guarantee that the statements you make are true. ("All cats bark" is false, when each word in this sentence is being employed in its usual sense.) Still less does the rule of common usage recommend that you follow common usage in the quite different sense of following tribal or national customs, or that you hold to beliefs which are commonly held. Neither, of course, does it recommend the opposite; it is simply irrelevant either way.

Words that stand for other words.   When we talk about cats, we use the word "cats" without quotation marks; but when we want to talk about the *word* "cats," what do we do? A *word* can be what a certain word stands for. Sometimes we want to talk about cats, and so we need a word for them; but sometimes (less frequently) we may want to talk about the word that we use to stand for cats—and we want a word for that too.

It would be possible for us to use one word to stand for the *animals,* cats, and a quite different word to stand for the *word,* "cats." But this would be very inconvenient and cumbersome, especially if we did the same thing with every word in the language. If we had 100,000 words for things, we would then need 100,000 more words to stand for those words. Then, if we wanted to talk about these words in turn, we would need 100,000 more—and so on ad infinitum. Instead, we adopt this policy: when we want to talk about the *word* "cats," we use the same word over again, only *in quotation marks*. Thus:

> Cats have tails.
> "Cats" has four letters.

This is the policy that is adopted in most philosophical writing and throughout this book—including this paragraph. And if we want to go further and talk about the word that we have just used to name the word "cats," we use the same word once more and place still another pair of quotation marks around it. Thus:

" 'Cats' " is a word which stands for the word "cats," which stands for cats.

Quotation marks are, however, used for other purposes as well: in directly quoting someone's remarks, for example, and in certain literary and colloquial words. One should not conclude that whenever quotation marks are used the writer is talking about the words rather than about the things referred to by the words.

Meanings of the word "meaning."   Whenever A is a sign of B, we say that A *means* B; but since A can be a sign of B in a number of different ways, A can mean B in a number of different ways. Words mean in a way different from that in which red sunsets mean fair weather tomorrow. There are many complexities involved in the question "What exactly is the relation of words to their meaning?" But before we examine these, let us notice some of the important ways in which the word "meaning" is used, which are not limited to word-meaning: in other words, some meanings of "meaning."

1. Indicator.   The appearance of A means (indicates) that B is coming. A twister in the sky indicates that a tornado is coming. (It is a sign of it; but the word "sign" is used much more broadly than this in semantics, to cover *any* kind of A-standing-for-B relation, not only the kind in which A is an indicator of B.) Similarly, nimbus clouds mean (indicate) that rain is on the way. (Let us note in passing that it is not the *word* "clouds" that stands for rain. The word "clouds" stands for the clouds; and the clouds stand for—are an indicator of—the rain.)

2. Cause.   What does A mean? That is, what caused it? What do the footprints in the sand mean—that is, who or what caused them? (Sometimes a sign of B is also a cause of B, or a part of the cause of B, but not always. Twisters do not cause tornadoes, but clouds can be considered one of the causes of rain, depending on the meaning of the word "cause," which we shall examine in Chapter 4.)

3. Effect.   In countless cases of the use of the word "meaning," "A means B" can be translated into "A has B as its result (effect)" or "B is the effect of A" or "A has B as its consequence." President Roosevelt's announcement after Pearl Harbor, "This means war" could be translated, "The effect of this will be war." This sense of the word "meaning" is extremely important, even when talking about word-meaning, as we shall see when we discuss emotive meaning later in the chapter.

4. Intention.   "I meant to wash the dishes" means the same as "I intended to wash the dishes." "My meaning in saying this was . . ." becomes "My intent in saying this was . . . ."

5. Explanation.   "What does it mean?" is often translatable into *"Why* did it occur?" ("Those are her footprints all right, but they're pointing the wrong way. What does it mean?") Explanations are given in answer to the question "Why?" A request for an explanation is not the same thing as a request for a cause, as we shall see in Chapter 4, although some explanations are causal in nature.

6. *Purpose.* Sometimes "purpose" means the same as "intention": "My intention in taking my vacation at this time was . . ." becomes "My purpose in taking my vacation at this time was . . . ." But we also say,, "It was a meaningless act"—it served no purpose. In addition, we also attribute purposes to inanimate things to which we do not attribute any intentions: for example, "What is the purpose of a hammer?" The word "purpose" has more than one meaning, as we shall see in Chapter 4.

7. *Implication.* "If you started the day with $10, and you spent $4 and took in nothing, that means you have $6 left"—in other words, the first statement implies the second. "Meaning" is often used in the sense of implication, where "means" is synonymous with "implies."

8. *Significance.* "Do you feel that your life has meaning?"—in other words, significance. "Significance" is itself a tricky word. Taken literally, it means that which is signified: a word has significance (in this sense) when it stands for something. But "significance" is more usually employed in the rather vague sense of *importance,* as in "This is a very significant development." In a question such as "What is the meaning of life?" the trouble lies with the question, for it is not clear without further inquiry what the questioner is asking: significance in the sense of importance? purpose (and in which sense)? If the questioner could phrase his question in different words, perhaps it would not perplex us so much. To have a clear answer, you first have to have a clear *question.*

"What is the meaning of . . . ?" questions. Because of these multiple meanings of the word "meaning," it is not always clear which meaning of the word "meaning" we have in mind when we ask a meaning-question. In particular, we should be extremely careful whether we are asking about the meaning of a *word* (i.e., what thing the word stands for) or about the meaning of the *thing* the word stands for in one of the senses of "meaning" that apply to things. Here are a few examples:

1. "What is the meaning of apogee?" Should the word have quotation marks around it here? It should, if it is intended as an inquiry into what the *word* "apogee" stands for; and in nine cases out of ten, this is probably what the person is asking. If the questioner already knew the meaning of the word, he would not be likely to ask the question.

2. "You don't appreciate what war means." Here it is unlikely that the speaker is accusing anyone of not knowing what the word "war" means. He is saying something about the thing, war. In all probability he is saying something about conditions that war causes or brings about—devastation, broken homes, poverty, and the like.

3. "What is the meaning of life?" Here again it is almost surely not the word "life" about which the person is inquiring. He knows what the *word*

means, and he is probably asking something (again, he may not clearly realize what) about an explanation of the thing, life. He knows that living things grow, reproduce, and so on; but he wants to know, in some sense of "explain" (see Chapter 4), how these remarkable processes are to be explained. Perhaps he means something like "What is the purpose of there being life (or human life) on earth?"—but in this case it is necessary to clarify the meaning of "purpose" (which we shall try to do in Chapter 4). At any rate, the question is not about the word, but about the thing named by the word, although what it is that he wants to know about the thing may not be clear even to himself.

"What is . . . ?" questions.   The same difficulties pervade a closely related group of questions, beginning with the words "what is." What is syzygy? What is matter? What is time? What is man? What is philosophy? Sometimes in asking these questions we want to know what thing a *word* is used to stand for: for example, "What is syzygy?" could be translated "What does the word 'syzygy' mean?" When the reply is given, "The point on the moon's orbit at which it is in direct line with the sun and the earth," our question has been answered. But if we ask, "What is time?" we are probably not asking what the *word* "time" means; we already know that (though we may not be able to define it, as we shall see later in this chapter). We may not be at all clear about *what* information about the thing, time, we are requesting. In very general questions like this, the difficulty often lies with the unclarity of a question and not with the impossibility of an answer: once again, to have a clear answer we must first have a clear question. At any rate, it seems evident that general "What is—?" questions of this type are meant to be about the thing rather than about the word.

Much confusion can result if we fail to keep this distinction in mind. Two persons may be arguing about the question "What is lightning?" One may say, "For hundreds of years, until Benjamin Franklin and others discovered that lightning was a form of electricity, nobody knew what lightning was." Another person may reply, "But people have known for thousands of years what lightning is. What they didn't know until less than 200 years ago is what the *explanation* of lightning is. But the ancients knew lightning when they saw it—you surely can't deny that." The two people are not really disagreeing at all; they are arguing at cross purposes, since they are not discussing the same question. One is talking about the word, the other about the thing. In one sense, people have always known what lightning is—they have known what the *word* "lightning" (or synonymous words in other languages) means or stands for. After all, words have no meanings except those that people give them, and knowing what a word means is simply knowing what meaning the users of a language have given to a certain noise. People who speak the English language usually know very well what the word "lightning" means. Perhaps they are not always able to give a strict *definition* of the word—we shall discuss this point in the next section—but they do know how to apply the word "lightning" to the world; they know which things to apply the word to and which not to, and in this important sense they do know the meaning of the word. What people have not always known is the physics of lightning, and in this sense people living 200 years ago and some people today do not know what lightning is.

Ambiguity.   Often a word is used with more than one meaning. Indeed, a brief look at a dictionary will show you that the majority of words are used with more than one meaning. If all such words were said to be ambiguous (the popular sense of "ambiguous"), then the vast majority of words would be ambiguous. But semanticists and philosophers usually call a word "ambiguous" only when there is some uncertainty about which meaning is being used in the particular instance. A word isn't ambiguous by itself, it is *used* ambiguously: it is ambiguous when one cannot tell from the context what sense is being used. Usually one *can* tell this from the context. For example, if you say "I'm going to the bank to deposit some money," I do not expect you to go to the river bank. The word "bank" has these two senses (and more), but it is not thereby ambiguous: the two senses are so unrelated that no one is likely to confuse them.

Usually, however, the senses of a word *are* related to one another; and, when you hear the word first in one meaning and then in another, you can often guess from the context what the second meaning is—an achievement which would have been very unlikely to occur if the words were utterly unrelated in meaning. If you first heard the word "sharp" when someone was describing a knife, then heard it when someone was describing the quality of a cheese, you would probably be able to guess the meaning of the word "sharp" in the second context: "sharp" describes the cutting power of the knife; similarly, sharp cheese seems to cut the tongue or palate. Later, when you heard someone described as "a sharp student" or "a sharp cookie," you would probably guess that too: the penetrating, cutting power of the intellect is sufficiently similar to the cutting power of the knife and the cheese. In such a case, it is *no accident* that the same word was used in all these senses; whereas the double sense of "bank" can be considered a linguistic accident. It just happened that the word "bank" developed from different languages in which it had different meanings, and our uses branched out from these origins. But it didn't just happen that the word "sharp" was used to describe a quality of knives, of cheeses, and of minds.

The meanings are *related,* but not the *same*—otherwise no ambiguity would arise. A knife is sharp when it cuts well, when it can literally divide a loaf of bread or a cold slab of butter. A sharp cheese does not have this characteristic; it does not literally even cut the palate—it only seems to; it gives that impression, at least enough to lead us to use the same word "sharp" in referring to it. But a knife that only seemed to cut bread would not be sharp. And still different characteristics are referred to in calling a student "sharp," but the senses of the word are related to one another.

Process-product ambiguity is one kind of ambiguity that is so pervasive, and *can* be so confusing, that it has received a distinctive name. We often use a word to stand for a process, and use the same word over again to stand for the product resulting from that process. When someone says, "They went to look at the construction," he may mean that they went to look at (1) people in the process of constructing something or (2) the thing which has been constructed. A person writing a poem expresses his feelings (process), and the poem he writes (product) is also said to express those feelings; the word "express" characterizes both the process and the product.

Type-token ambiguity is also a source of confusion. Suppose you write on a piece of paper, "Seven plus five equals twelve," and then you write the same words again on the next line. Have you written two sentences or one? You might say, "There are two sentences—one on the first line and one on the second"; but you might equally well say, "There is only one sentence—it's the same sentence written twice." The word "sentence" is ambiguous: in one sense of "sentence" we have one sentence; in another sense, two sentences. Each written or spoken occurrence of a certain word or sentence is a "token," and in this sense each one counts as a sentence. The boy whose teacher makes him stay after school and write "I am a bad boy" on the blackboard 100 times has written 100 sentences; and after all the effort expended, he would be quite indignant at the suggestion that he had written only one. But in another sense he has written only one sentence 100 times; that is, there has been only one sentence-*type,* of which he has written 100 tokens. Writing or speaking the same words in the same order is sufficient in the type-sense to make it one sentence, no matter how often repeated.[1]

Another example: one person says that there are slightly more than 60,000 words in the average novel, and another person says that Shakespeare had the largest vocabulary of any English writer, having used in his writings more than 14,000 words. "But how can this be?" one may ask. "Hasn't every novelist, then, used more words than Shakespeare did?" The trouble lies once again in the type-token ambiguity. In the token sense, every occurrence of a word counts as a word; thus if the word "the" is used 1,000 times in the novel, this counts as 1,000 words. But in the Shakespeare case, not the token but the type is meant: no matter how often the word "the" is used, it counts as only one word. Differently stated, Shakespeare used more than 14,000 *different* words.

Figurative language. The *figurative* use of language sometimes leads to ambiguity. We have already discussed different senses of the word "sharp": In "a sharp knife" the word was used literally: a sharp knife is one that cuts well; but in "a sharp cheese" the word was used figuratively: the sharp cheese only *feels* as if it is cutting the tongue. In the literal sense, only

---

[1] If one wrote "A is larger than B" and "B is smaller than A," he would have written two different sentence-types. Although these two have the same meaning— that is, they express the same proposition—they are different sentences.

organisms have necks, but we also speak figuratively of the neck of a bottle. In "He saw a fox in the forest," the word "fox" is used literally; but in "You're a sly fox," it is used figuratively. In each case there is some meaning in common between the literal and the figurative sense: the neck of a bottle is in some ways *like* the neck of an organism, hence we have come to use the same word for both; and a person who is called a fox is being described as having certain characteristics such as craft and cunning, which foxes are popularly supposed to have. Usually both the literal and the figurative sense of a word have a long-established use, and both are to be found in a dictionary; and when you know the literal meaning of a word and hear it used in a figurative sense, you can usually guess what that meaning is. Thus we speak of a kernel of grain, a grain of truth; your shadow, a shadow of your former self; a cool evening, a cool reception; a heavy weight, a heavy heart; a house on fire, on fire with anger; a warm temperature, a warm color. The tendency of words in a language is to proliferate figurative senses. From one basic sense, another (figurative) sense springs; and from this sense several more arise, blossoming out like the stems of a plant, until the meanings in the upper branches may have very little similarity left to the meaning in the trunk.[2]

One final caution: Do not assume that just because a word applies to different things, it therefore has different senses. There are willow trees and maple trees and many other *kinds* of trees, but this does not give the word "tree" many senses. The word "tree" has exactly the same meaning whether you are talking about elm trees, cypress trees, chestnut trees, or any other kind of tree. The fact that there are kinds of X does not make the word "X" ambiguous. But the word may have different senses for other reasons. When we speak of a family tree, we are not using the word "tree" to refer to a plant of any kind, but to an entirely different sort of thing, a recorded genealogy. Again there is a relation of the two meanings, for when you start with an ancestor, then trace his children and his children's children, and so on, and you record this on paper, you get a spreading effect (visually) like the branches of a tree, hence the term "family *tree*." So the word "tree" has several senses, but not because it can be used to talk about different kinds of tree.

Exercises

1. "Isn't the word 'cat' the *right* word for this pet of mine that meows and purrs? Surely it would be applying the wrong name to it if I called it a buffalo!" "Well, there aren't any right and wrong names for things, so it would be equally right if you called it a buffalo." Resolve the argument.

[2] See, for example, the many senses of the words "tap" and "pick" in Chartlon Laird, *The Miracle of Language* (Greenwich, Conn.: Fawcett Publications, Inc.), pp. 54–59.

2. When a child learns the meanings of words, he doesn't *invent words* for talking about things. What then is the point of saying that human beings give names rather than discover them?

3. Answer this objection: "Nothing can be determined by appealing to common usage of language. You can't decide on an issue by showing how people use words! *Common usage may be wrong.* Suppose we tried to settle the question whether the earth is round by this method. In the Middle Ages one might have used the rule to prove that the earth is flat. Yet, as we know, that wouldn't prove for a moment that the earth really is flat."

4. Place quotation marks where they belong in the following sentences:

    a. Chien is the French word which means the same as the English word dog.

    b. Chien is the French word referring to dogs.

    c. The word order is important in determining the meaning of a sentence: for example, Brutus killed Caesar does not mean the same as Caesar killed Brutus.

    d. The word order contains five letters.

    e. There are cars passing along Main Street is a true statement.

    f. The word cat names cats; and the name for the word cat is cat.

5. "Valor is courage." " 'Valor' means the same as 'courage'." Why are the following incorrect?

    a. "Valor" means "courage."

    b. "Valor" means the same as courage.

6. Which of the last words in the following sentences should have quotation marks around them? Explain why.

    a. What is the meaning of your behavior?

    b. What is the meaning of this piece of news?

    c. What is the meaning of scopophilia?

    d. You don't know the meaning of love.

    e. Nobody knows the true meaning of life.

    f. This is the true meaning of democracy.

7. Criticize the preceding exercise for the phrase "true meaning." In what sense can there be a true meaning of things? Can there be a true meaning of words? Explain. How would you interpret the phrase "the true meaning of the word 'democracy' "?

8. Analyze the following "what is" questions and assertions.

    a. Nobody knows what electricity is (we know only what it does).

    b. Nobody knows what a cold is (we know only what its symptoms are).

    c. What is telekinesis?

    d. What is democracy, really?

    e. Nobody in this group knows what this animal is.

    f. What is truth?

9. Try to translate the following sentences containing figurative expressions into sentences not containing these expressions. (Try not to substitute one figurative expression for another.)

    a. She was burned up with jealousy.

    b. That's a high note (on the piano).

    c. She has higher moral standards than he.

    d. I'm above all that.

    e. I want to have the matter firmly fixed in my mind.

    f. It didn't really happen; it's all in your mind.

    g. His mind is cluttered with all kinds of silly details.

     h. He dived into a sea of troubles.

     i. She was a shadow of her former self.

     j. Life's but a walking shadow, a poor player. . . .

     k. "All the world's a stage."

     l. Life is but a dream.

    m. "Architecture is frozen music."

     n. "Life, like a dome of many-colored glass,
        Stains the white radiance of eternity."

     o. Her personality radiated warmth; she positively glowed.

     p. A river takes the easiest way—downhill. So do most men.

     q. A king must have nerves of iron and a will of steel; he must be both
        a lion and a fox.

10. Can you construct a satisfactory definition of the following: "word," "phrase," "sentence"?

11. Is the word "color" ambiguous because it can denote red, green, and so forth? Is the word "pleasant" ambiguous because what is pleasant to me may not be to you? Is the word "fast" ambiguous because what is slow for an airplane is fast for an automobile and what is slow for an automobile is fast for a bicycle?

12. Show how the word "is" (together with all forms of the verb "to be") is ambiguous by means of these examples: "A yard is three feet"; "The chair is yellow"; "Water is H_2O."

13. Are these different kinds of X, or different senses of the word "X"?

     a. kitchen table, table of statistics

     b. collie dog, toy dog

     c. eating his breakfast, eating his words

     d. back of the room, back of his mind

     e. behind the house, behind his actions

     f. higher elevation, higher tones

     g. hard chair, hard examination

     h. easy chair, chair of philology

     i. tap on the shoulder, fixing the tap

14. Are these ambiguous words related in meaning, or is the use of the same word for both meanings a "linguistic accident"?

     a. top of the house, top of the morning

     b. mouth of an organism, mouth of a river

     c. distant hills, distant attitude

     d. add numbers, add ingredients in a recipe

     e. a point (in geometry), proving your point

     f. take a rest, the rest is easy

     g. chocolate bar, sit at the bar, bar examination, bar none

     h. state of the nation, state of California

     i. make a slip, buy a slip

     j. cut her cold, cut her finger

2. Definition

We have distinguished many senses of the ambiguous word "meaning," most of which have nothing to do specifically with words at all. Now let us examine word-meaning in particular. What is the relation between a word and what it means?

Let us first consider two of the possible but not very satisfactory views on this question. (1) One is that what a word means is the thoughts, feelings, or images that its utterance evokes in one's mind (ideational theory of meaning). But this will hardly suffice: the utterance of the word "cat" may evoke the most diverse set of mental pictures, attitudes, feelings, and thoughts. For example, when you hear the word you may imagine a cat and I may not. And yet there is surely some respect in which the word has the same meaning for all of us as long as it is used to talk about the same species of animal. The only mental state that seems to be always present in such a case is simply that of *understanding what the word means*. And this last phrase itself uses the word "meaning," so it cannot be used to tell us what meaning *is*.

Another view is that (2) what a word means is its tendency to produce in its hearers a certain type of behavior, or at least a tendency toward such behavior (behavioral theory of meaning). But this too will hardly suffice: different persons on hearing a word may behave in a vast variety of ways, and in many cases in no way at all. Does the word therefore have a different meaning for each of them? You and I may react quite differently to the word "snake," but don't we nevertheless mean the same thing by the word? And if we hear a hundred words to which we don't react (or tend to react) behaviorally at all, does this show that they convey no meaning at all?

One could state the behavioral theory in a more complex way: words are not normally used in isolation, but in sentences and still wider contexts in which the behavior of one who unders.ands the sentence is fairly constant. Even so, however, one could raise questions: Is the behavioral response to "There's a snake behind you" always the same, or even similar? And even if it were, what of more abstract sentences such as we constantly come across in philosophy—such as "All words have meaning of some kind," to which there is ordinarily no particular behavior-response at all? And even if there were, and it were uniform, would not the response be the *consequence* of understanding the meaning of the word or sentence, rather than what that meaning *consists* in?

A much more satisfactory account of meaning would seem to be that (3) words *refer* to the things in the world (the referential theory of meaning). We use the word "cat" to refer to cats, the word "run" to refer to various acts of running, and so on. To determine what a word means, find out what things we use it to refer to.

But this will not suffice either. Let us examine a very limited class of words to which the theory does apply—those words we call *proper names*. If you call your daughter "Margaret," your parrot "Polly," or your dog "Rover," you are referring to them by means of proper names, because they are used to label one thing only. "One word, one thing"—this formula applies only to proper names. "That's my house, Sunny Gables," you say, together with an act of pointing; you are using the words "Sunny Gables" as the *name* of your house, and you *refer* to the house by means of that name. Proper names are clearly used to refer to individual things. But they are the only words that are used solely to refer. Most words, as we shall see, do not refer to things at all, not even if we use the word "thing" in a very broad sense, to include material objects, animals, people, activities, qualities, and relations, as we do when we say "What sort of thing have you done?" and "Did anything happen yesterday?" and "What thing is there about her that I don't have?" Let us see why this is so.

1. There are many words that clearly do not refer in any way at all. Consider interjections—"oh," "aha," "hurrah," and so on—which do have a meaning of some sort (else they would not be words) but do not refer to any things, any qualities of things, any activities, or anything else that could be called things. These words are ordinarily used to express or evoke feelings and attitudes, but to express or evoke in others a feeling is not the same as to refer to a feeling.

Or consider conjunctions ("and," "as," "but," "or," "because"); these words are *connectives:* they are used to introduce phrases and clauses, but they do not refer to things. Yet they do have meanings, and their meanings make a difference to the sentences in which they occur: "I am going *and* you are going" has a meaning different from "I am going *or* you are going." These words function *syntactically* (in relation to other words in a sentence) but not *semantically;* they do not label any things or groups of things.

2. Some words refer, but their reference is not the same as their meaning. Consider personal pronouns: the word "I" changes its reference all the time; when Jones uses it, it refers to Jones; when Smith uses it, it refers to Smith; and so on for millions of users of the language. Yet the *meaning* of "I" does not change these millions of times; it always has the same meaning. A person who uses it is always talking about himself; reference to the speaker (whoever it is) is the one meaning of "I." Thus while "I" does refer, what it refers to constantly changes, so what it means cannot be the same as what it refers to. (The same is true of "this," "that," "here," "now," etc.)

3. The reverse also occurs: we may have two different meanings but the things referred to are the same. "Sir Walter Scott" and "the author of *Waverly*" have two different meanings, but they refer to the same person. One could understand what the phrase "the author of *Waverly*" means without knowing that Sir Walter Scott was the author, or even that such a person existed. "The President of the United States" and "the commander-in-chief of the armed forces of the United States" are phrases with two different meanings, and one could easily understand one phrase without understanding the other; yet the two phrases always refer to the same individual.

4. "But at least nouns refer to things, in a perfectly straightforward way." Do they? Even if we admit that the word "horse" refers to horses, since there are horses to which one can point, what does "unicorn" refer to, or

"gremlin," "dragon," "leprechaun," "centaur"? How can the word "unicorn" refer to unicorns when there *are* no unicorns to be referred to? Still, the word "unicorn" has a meaning: any horse with a horn in the middle of its head is a unicorn. It just happens that there aren't any such creatures, so there is nothing for "unicorn" to refer to. But this doesn't prevent the word "unicorn" from having a meaning.

5. We can go still further and question whether even the word "horse" refers to anything. Will pointing to any horse give the meaning of the word "horse"? The person might well think that the word "horse" was a proper name for that one particular animal, or he might think that "horse" meant the same as "animal." It would surely not be obvious to him that the word "horse" refers to an entire class of creatures, the class of (not animals, but) horses. And *does* the word "horse" refer to the class of things, horses? It would not seem so. One can say that the class of horses is very large (that is, there are many horses), but this isn't the same as saying, "Horse is very large." But if "horse" referred to the class horses, the sentence "Horse is very large" should mean the same as "The class of horses is very large." It is true that the word "horse" can be used to refer to many individual things, but this is not the same as saying that the meaning of the word "horse" *is* the reference. Indeed, we can know—as easily with "horse" as with "unicorn"—what the word means without knowing whether there are any such creatures for the word to refer to.

Words as tools. Instead of saying that all words refer, it would be preferable to say that each word functions as a *tool* that is used to do something or perform some job in communication. Just as each tool in a toolkit is used to do a different job, so too different kinds of words perform different kinds of jobs in a language: nouns perform one kind, pronouns another, verbs and adverbs and prepositions still others. "Cat" does one kind of job, "cattiness" another, and "catlike" a still different one. When, then, do we know the meaning of a word? When we know exactly what job it does, what function it has in the language. Sometimes the function may be that of referring to things, but more often it is not.

And when do we know what function it fulfills? We can answer this briefly in a formula that may later require some clarification: When we know *the rule for its use*—that is, when we know the rule that tells us under what conditions the word is to be used, which enables us to determine when the word is applicable to a given situation and when it is not. We know what the word "horse" means when we know in what circumstances the word "horse" can be used to apply to something—and also in what circumstances it is *not* applicable: it is as important not to call "horse" something that isn't a horse as it is to call "horse" everything that *is* a horse. The same applies to "unicorn"; even though this word applies to no animals in the world, we know the meaning of the word because we know what we *would* call a unicorn if we came across it. The same for "slowly" (we use it when something moves in a certain manner), "above" (when one thing is higher than another, we say it is above it), and "hurrah" (we use it when we feel triumphant, to *express* our feeling, not to *refer* to it). Every word in our language has a distinctive function or job—duplicated by other words only when two words are exact synonyms, which is rare—and we understand the meaning of a word (the same applies to phrases) when we know the rule which states the conditions in which that word is to be employed.

We must be quite careful here, for the word "use" is slippery. There are meanings of "use" that are quite irrelevant here, such as "The use of 'whomever' has virtually disappeared," "The use[3] of a swear word is sometimes very effective," "We do not use this word in polite society." You know nothing about the meaning of a word when you know that it isn't used in polite society; conditions of use in this sociological sense do not determine meaning. A person who didn't know a word of English might repeatedly hear two people say "Good luck!" to one another on leave-taking, and he would infer that this was the appropriate thing to say (noise to utter) in these circumstances—but he still wouldn't know what these words *mean*. We cannot simply say, "Meaning is use," and let it go at that.[4]

When you make explicit the rule that determines in what conditions a word or phrase is to be used (applied to a situation), you are *defining* the word or phrase. When you do this, you will then be using *other* words, and those other words must be equivalent in meaning to the word you are defining, so that the defining phrase can be substituted for the defined word without changing the meaning of the sentence in which it occurs. This, at any rate, is the most usual, most accepted, and most "standard" sense of the word "definition": definition by equivalent words. Usually, however, the word "definition" is used more broadly than this, to include *any way of indicating* what a word means (within a given language group); and in this sense, it is possible to define words without stating a rule; we can also define by (1) giving the denotation of a word and (2) giving an ostensive definition. These two will concern us later in this section; first let us consider the main sense, definition by equivalent words.

Definition by Equivalent Words

The word "yard" is equivalent in meaning to the phrase "three feet": that is, you can replace the word with the phrase and the sentence will not have changed its meaning. (The word "yard" is used in more than one sense. When we talk about the back yard of a house we cannot replace "yard" with "three feet"; of course "yard" can be replaced by "three feet" only in the

[3] Sometimes this kind of case is called "usage" rather than "use." See Gilbert Ryle, "Ordinary Language," in *Ordinary Language*, ed. V. C. Chappell.

[4] For an examination of these difficulties, see William P. Alston, "Meaning and Use," *Philosophical Quarterly*, XIII (April 1963), 107–24.

sense in which "yard" is used as a measure of length. In a word with more than one sense, there will be as many rules governing its application as there are senses of the word.) The word "father" is equivalent in meaning to "male parent." Sometimes a single word will suffice: for example, "courage" means the same as "valor"; but since there are very few exact synonyms in any language, this method is not very satisfactory—subtle differences in meaning are not brought out by simply giving a synonym. Usually a longer phrase is required to define the word precisely.

It is possible for a definition to be *logically* satisfactory (that is, the expressions are really interchangeable because they have the same meaning) but not *psychologically* satisfactory (that is, it may not convey any meaning to the hearer because he does not know the meanings of the words in the definition). Thus if you defined "brother" as "male sibling," this would be logically correct, but most people do not know that "sibling" means offspring of the same parents, and so the definition, though accurate enough, would be of no use to them. When you define a word, it is ordinarily one whose meaning your hearer is unfamiliar with, and he can understand the definition you give only if he *is* familiar with the meanings of the words in the definition.

As we have just noted, there is not often a *single* word in the language that is equivalent in meaning to the word being defined; exact synonyms are rare. But it also happens frequently that there may be no *group* of words in the language that is equivalent in meaning to the defined word. No matter how you try, you may be unable to find any string of words, however long, that is interchangeable in meaning with the word you are trying to define. Some of these words are used to label sensory experiences—"red," "pain," "pungent," "fear"—of which we cannot convey to others the specific experienced quality meant by the word unless we confront him with one or another of the experiences which the word labels: we have to produce a pain in him, for example, by sticking him with a pin, to make him understand what the word "pain" means. No word or combination of words, nothing but direct confrontation with the experience itself, will suffice. Such words have to be *ostensively* defined, and we shall discuss ostensive definition later in this section. But some of the words for which we can find no equivalent words are very abstract ones—like "time," "being," "relation"—words so broad in their meaning that we cannot find any broader categories in which to place them, and the problem of defining these words will be with us from now till the end of our study.

Defining characteristics.   One enormous help in clarifying the meanings of our words is to consider carefully which characteristics of a thing we consider to be *defining.*[5] A defining characteristic of a thing (not only a

---

[5] We cannot use this method for all words, since some words do not stand for things in any sense at all. There are no defining characteristics for "oh," since this word does not stand for any thing; the same is true of connective words like "and."

physical thing but a quality, an activity, a relation, etc.) is a characteristic *in the absence of which the word would not be applicable to the thing*. Being three-sided is a defining characteristic of triangles, since nothing would be (that is, would be *called* by our language-group) a triangle unless it had three sides; and having all points on the circumference equidistant from the center is a defining characteristic of circles, since nothing would be a circle that did not possess this characteristic. But being at least two inches in height or circumference is not a defining characteristic of a triangle or circle, since something can be a triangle or a circle and yet be smaller than this.

The test of whether a certain characteristic is defining is always this: would the same word still apply if the thing lacked the characteristic? If the answer is no, the characteristic is defining; if the answer is yes, it is merely accompanying. Can a triangle have unequal sides and still be a triangle? Yes. Then having equal sides is not a defining characteristic of triangles. Can a triangle have unequal sides and still be an equilateral triangle? No. Then having equal sides is defining of equilateral triangles. A defining characteristic is a *sine qua non* (literally "without which not"). Would this thing still be an X if it didn't have characteristic A? If it would not, then having A is a *sine qua non* of its being an X—it is defining.

This is not the same question as "Would it still have A if it weren't an X?" The answer to this last question might well be yes even if the answer to the first one was no. Would it still be a triangle if it weren't a plane figure? No. Would it still be a plane figure if it weren't a triangle? It very well might: it could be a square, a parallelogram, a pentagon, etc. Having A is essential to its being an X, but being an X is not essential to its having A. Y and Z may also have A. In other words, there are many classes of things in the world that have *some* defining characteristics in common. The characteristic of being solid is defining of many things—chairs, trees, ice, etc.

Clearly this does not mean (imply) that all these words have the same definition. Two words would not have the same definition unless *all* the defining characteristics were the same. The words "asteroid" and "planetoid" have the same definition and therefore designate the same total set of characteristics. But there are not many words like this; it would obviously be a pointless duplication of language. One word may be defined by characteristics A, B, and C, and another word by characteristics A, B, and D; but two words will not often have the same total set of defining characteristics, and hence the same definition.

A word is said to *designate* the sum of the characteristics a thing must have for the word to apply to it. Thus the word "triangle" designates the characteristics of being three-sided, closed, and two-dimensional. But none of these defining characteristics alone is sufficient, since there are many closed figures which are not triangles, plane figures which are not triangles, and three-sided figures (such as open ones) which are not triangles.

Scope of definitions.   When you try to formulate a definition for a word in common use, or evaluate a definition suggested by someone else, there are three important things to keep in mind:

1. The definition should not be too broad. If you defined "telephone" simply as "instrument for communication," your definition would be so broad as to include many things that no one would call telephones. You have to narrow or restrict the definition by *adding* one or more defining characteristics: you must say what kind of instrument for communication a telephone is, as distinguished from other such instruments.

2. The definition of the word should not be too narrow. If you defined "tree" as "plant with green leaves, at least 50 feet tall, growing vertically from the ground," your definition would be so narrow as to exclude many things that we now call trees. Many trees—that is, many things we call trees—are not so tall, some do not have green leaves nor any leaves at all, and so forth. You have to broaden this definition by *subtracting* these characteristics, so that all the things we call trees can still be denoted by the word "tree" according to your definition.

Sometimes a suggested definition is too broad and too narrow at the same time. Defining "telephone" as "instrument of long-distance communication" is too narrow, for the things we call telephones are often used for short-distance communication; at the same time it is too broad, for without this unsatisfactory restricting condition it covers many things which are not called telephones at all. The problem is to get all the defining characteristics into the definition, but none that are not defining.

3. Even if the definition of the word is neither too broad nor too narrow, it may be unsatisfactory. Two terms may have exactly the same range (denotation) and still have different meanings. Suppose that four characteristics, A, B, C, and D, *always* occurred together, so that there was nothing in the universe that had A without also having the other three, and vice versa. Suppose further that one person uses a word, "X," for characteristics A, B, and C; and that another person uses a word, "Y," for characteristics A, B, and D. The denotations of the two words will be exactly the same: everything having A, B, and C will also have D, and everything having A, B, and D will also have C. Yet their definitions are different.

Suppose that a definition of the word "elephant" is suggested: "an animal that draws water up its trunk and squirts it into its mouth." Let us assume for the sake of simplicity that every elephant does this, and that everything that does this is an elephant (that is, nothing *but* elephants do this). The definition is thus neither too broad nor too narrow as far as its denotation is concerned. But now let us ask: "Couldn't a creature do this and still not be an elephant? Some creature, perhaps, on another planet or a new creature yet to develop; or a zebra on which had been grafted a trunk which could be used in this way? Couldn't a thing *fail* to do this and still be an elephant? Perhaps one that had his trunk-mechanism stopped up, or one that eschews the use of water?" If we are to use the word "elephant" in any ordinary sense, the answer is surely yes. Such creatures may not actually exist; but that does not matter: a zebra who fulfilled the requirements of the definition would still not be an elephant, and an elephant who couldn't use his trunk would still be an elephant, and we can know this *without* knowing whether either of these creatures actually exists. It is enough to know that *if* the first existed it would not be an elephant, and if the second existed it would—just as we can know that *if* I had eaten a pound of arsenic I wouldn't be writing at this moment, even though I did not actually eat a pound of arsenic.[6]

In other words, a definition must be adequate to the *possible* as well as the actual cases. We want to know what are the characteristics, the presence of which would entitle something to be called an elephant and the absence of which would keep it from being called one. To know this, we must go beyond the range of the *actual* things to which the word is applied. "The practical test in fact, when we wish to know whether any proposed definition is a true one or not, is to try whether by conceivable variation of circumstances we can cause it to break down, by its exclusion of what we are resolved to retain or its inclusion of what we are resolved to reject."[7] If every round thing was red and every red thing was round, the words "red" and "round" would have the same range (denotation): everything on a complete list of red things would also be on a complete list of round things, and vice versa; nor could anyone ever point to a red thing that was not also a round thing, and vice versa. And yet the words "red" and "round" would not mean the same: "red" would still be a color-word and "round" a shape-word. No sameness of denotation could ever give them the same meaning.

When we are distinguishing defining from accompanying characteristics, we should be particularly careful about the *universally accompanying* characteristics: when D *always* accompanies A, B, and C, we may think that it belongs in the definition. But let us then ask ourselves, "Even though D always accompanies A, B, and C, *if* sometime D did *not* accompany A, B, and C, would the thing in question still be called an X?" If the answer is yes, the characteristic is still accompanying and not defining.

Shifts in defining characteristics. The tendency, however, is for a universally accompanying characteristic to become defining. This does not mean that one characteristic is both defining and accompanying at the same time; it means only that the designation of the word sometimes shifts gradually in the history of a language, so that the word does not designate the same characteristics at all times. The most usual direction of this shift is for universally accompanying characteristics to become incorporated (perhaps unconsciously) into the definition. Let us suppose that the word "whale" was

[6] Of course, if "elephant" is defined as a species of creatures that *normally* or *usually* uses its trunk in this way, a creature who didn't so use it could still be an elephant, as long as it was an abnormal member of the species.

[7] J. Venn, *Empirical Logic* (New York: The Macmillan Company, 1889), p. 304.

once used to apply to anything that had characteristics A, B, and C. But then it was discovered that the creatures that had A, B, and C also had another characteristic, D—they were mammals. This came to be added to the list of defining characteristics, for today nothing that was non-mammalian would be called a whale. (This is not to say that in discovering that whales were mammals we *found* the correct definition of the word "whale." We *could* have kept on using the word "whale" in the old way, so that if a creature having A, B, and C turned up without D, we would have called it a whale in spite of its non-mammalian character. But much zoological classification had already taken place on the basis of whether the creatures were mammalian or not, and it was most convenient simply to shift this definition a bit to accommodate the existing classification.)

Sometimes, in fact, D comes to *replace* the original A, B, and C as the one and only defining characteristic of X. Before the causes of various diseases were known, they were defined entirely by means of their symptoms: each disease had a different (but often overlapping) set of symptoms, and was identified and defined by reference to these. But when the spirochete was discovered through microscopes, and it was observed that *whenever* the spirochete was present the symptoms of syphilis also occurred, then the disease-entity "syphilis" came to be defined entirely in terms of the spirochete: if the spirochete was present, the patient had syphilis; if it wasn't, he didn't.

"Causal" definitions. This example illustrates another important point: in medicine and certain other technical fields, the cause of something is often included in its definition: "X is anything that is caused by A." But we should not assume that this is always the case: a headache is simply a pain in the head, no matter what it is that causes the headache (and headaches have a bewildering variety of causes). "Headache" is not a technical term in medicine, and its causes are not included in the definition of the term; but "syphilis" *is* such a term, and the sole criterion of its presence or absence is the spirochete that *causes* the symptoms to occur. As we see from this example, definitions change in the light of our advancing knowledge. Before the discovery of the spirochete, no definition of "syphilis" involving this microscopic creature could have been given.

That certain technical terms are defined causally should not, however, mislead us (as they mislead almost every introductory student) into believing that every word can be defined in this way. This is particularly the case with experience-words. "In the light of our present knowledge, 'red' may now be defined in terms of wave-lengths of light: red is any color within the range 4000–7000 Angstrom units." As a physicist's technical definition of "red," as he uses it in the laboratory, this is satisfactory. But there remains the ordinary sense of the word "red," as used by millions of people every day who know nothing about physics. They are able to identify red objects and use the word "red" correctly without ever knowing anything about light-waves; indeed, people did this for countless centuries before the rise of modern physics. We shall consider the case of red again when we discuss ostensive definition; meanwhile, it should be made quite clear that "red" (in its ordinary sense) cannot be defined by reference to wave-lengths of light. People see red in their dreams and hallucinations when there are no objects at all to emanate light-waves. The reverse also occurs: light-waves emanate from these objects but the observer, even with his eyes open, does not see red because he doesn't notice the red object. More radical still, the entire wave-theory of light might be scrapped in favor of another one at a later date (just as the wave-theory replaced the earlier corpuscular theory), but this would not change the appearance of the *shade of color* we call "red" in the slightest. The occurrence of these light-waves is (usually, not always) a causal condition for the seeing of red, but this is only to say that the light-waves are an accompanying and not a defining characteristic of "red" (in its ordinary sense). "Red" is the word we use for just *that* shade of color, and that shade is called "red" *regardless of what causes it.*

In the same way, "pain" cannot be defined as "stimulation of nerve-endings." One could talk till doomsday about stimulation of nerve-endings and yet have no idea what pain is—and millions of people know very well what pain is without knowing anything about nerve-endings. The scientific discovery is that *when* pain is experienced, there is *also* (immediately prior thereto) a stimulation of nerve-endings—usually, not always. But this is a discovery *about* pain, not a definition of the *word* "pain." You would *already* have to know what "pain" means to know what kind of experience the stimulation of nerve-endings leads to.

Some psychologists have defined "depression" as "repressed anger." It may well be the case (this is not the place to dispute it) that *when* a person experiences depression, it turns out (on psychological analysis) that he has repressed his anger about something; but this is a discovery about the causes of depression, not a definition of the word "depression." Indeed if one did not know beforehand what "depression" means, how could he or anyone else have discovered what it is that is brought on by repressed anger? The causal conditions of the thing X are not to be confused with the definition of the word "X."

Importance of the distinction between defining and accompanying characteristics.   In many cases when we attribute a characteristic to a thing, we do not make clear whether or not the characteristic we are mentioning is one we consider to be defining. Yet it is often of the utmost importance that we do this: for whether, and in what manner, our statement will be disputed depends entirely on which kind of characteristic it is. To state a defining characteristic is to state a part of the meaning (definition) of a term; but to state an accompanying characteristic is to state some fact, not about the term itself (for the accompanying characteristic is no part of its meaning), but about the thing named by the term. Thus:

> Steel is an alloy of iron.
> Steel is used for purposes of construction.

The first sentence states a defining characteristic, for if something were not an alloy of iron it would not be steel (that is, the word "steel" would not apply to it); but the second sentence states an accompanying characteristic, for if steel were no longer used for purposes of construction it would still be steel. The first sentence, then, states part of the meaning of the *word*, "steel"; on the other hand, the second sentence asserts a fact about the *thing*, steel. Often it is virtually impossible to tell from a sentence whether the speaker is stating the meaning of a *word* or stating a fact about the *thing* named by the word. "The good student is the one who gets the highest grades," someone says. Is he stating all or a part of what he *means* by the phrase "good student"? Is he defining the term, or is he taking for granted that we know what the phrase "good student" means and asserting that all good students *also* get the highest grades? Often the speaker himself is not clear about this. Yet if we want to dispute the statement, we shall have to know which it is, for in the first case we shall be disputing a *verbal usage,* and in the second case we shall be disputing an alleged *fact*. In the first case we might say, "You may use the phrase 'good student' to mean that, but most people would probably define the phrase differently." In the second case we might say, "But it isn't true that all good students get high grades; here is one who doesn't." The issue is verbal in the first case, factual in the second.

The situation is worsened further if the speaker shifts his ground during the course of the argument. For example:

> A: All swans are white.
> B: In Australia there are black swans.
> A: But those creatures are black—so they can't be swans!

Ordinarily A's first assertion would be taken as a factual statement (whether true or false) about swans—in other words, as a statement of an accompanying characteristic; being white is not considered a defining characteristic of swans. As a factual statement, however, A's assertion can be disputed, and is in fact disputed by B. So A makes his first statement invulnerable to disproof by any facts whatsoever; he does so by turning it from a factual statement into a statement about the *word* "swan," making whiteness defining of being a swan. Clearly, if that is what he had been stating in the first place, B would not have challenged the statement in the way he did; he would simply have commented on the unusual manner in which A was using the word "swan." B naturally took A's statement as a statement about the creatures, swans, not about the word. A then promptly switched the meaning of his first assertion from that of a factual statement into a definition.

Needless to say, A has not eliminated any black swans from the world by this verbal sleight of hand. Those creatures remain quite undisturbed by A's maneuver. He may succeed in preventing B from *calling* them by the *name* "swans," but black swans by any other name are just as black. True, B may be puzzled and not know how to answer A. "After all," he may think, "I can't say there are black swans if being white is a part of the very meaning of the word." Yet he will remain convinced that the black swans still exist. The puzzlement, of course, is needless: there would have been no trouble to begin with if A and B had been clear about defining and accompanying characteristics. (A may do the same thing, with greater effect, in a more abstract controversy: "The good students are those who get the highest grades." "Here is a good student who just doesn't get high grades." "He doesn't? Well, then, he can't be a good student.")

Definition and existence. When you have stated the defining characteristics of X, you have proved nothing one way or the other about whether an X exists. The word "horse" denotes many things, and the word "centaur" (a creature half man and half horse) denotes no things whatever, for there are no centaurs. (There are *pictures* of centaurs—centaur-pictures—and *images* of centaurs in our minds when we imagine them, but no centaurs.) But the meaning of the two words is equally clear; we know what characteristics something has to have to be labeled "centaur" just as well as we know what characteristics something has to have to be labeled "horse." When you are able to define a word in terms of characteristics A, B, and C, you have still not shown that there *exists* anything in the universe that has characteristics A, B, and C. You cannot legislate centaurs into existence by defining a word, any more than you can legislate black swans out of existence by redefining the word "swan." From defining "X," you can draw no conclusions whatever about whether there are any X's in the world; that is not a matter for definition but for scientific investigation.

It is interesting to observe in this connection that if the word "meaning" referred to denotation only, words such as "centaur," "brownie," "elf," "dragon," and "gremlin" (since they have no denotation) would all mean the same—namely nothing. But of course they do mean something, and they all have different meanings—that is, different designations. Each term designates a different set of characteristics, although nothing that has these characteristics happens to exist.

Attempts to make all characteristics defining. Another kind of difficulty in which people sometimes find themselves can be avoided if they keep clearly in mind the distinction between those characteristics which are defining and those which are not.

"How," we are sometimes asked, "can something be the same thing as before, and yet be subject to many changes? How can a human being change

from a boy to a man and still remain the same human being? Isn't everything
in the universe constantly changing? Heraclitus (500 B.C.) said that you
can't step into the same river twice, because the water you stepped into the
time before has already gone downstream. Similarly, scientists tell us that
there is not a single cell in your body that was there seven years ago. But how
then can I say I am the same person that I was then? Can't I say I am not
responsible for a debt I contracted then because I'm not the same person any
longer? Indeed, everything in the universe is in constant flux. Even things
that seem still, such as the table on which I am now writing, are congeries of
atoms and electrons, and are not in the same state for two split-seconds
together. How then am I entitled to speak of it as the same table for two split-
seconds together? But if I cannot speak of the same object existing for two
moments running, how can words be applicable to the world? How can
language, which consists of a comparatively static group of words, name
items in the shifting, ever-changing flux which is the world if the names don't
even apply from one moment to the next?"

It should not be difficult now to allay these fears, not by denying the
statements which scientists assert, but by remembering the principles we
have thus far learned. Doubtless changes are going on in the table every
moment, even though our eyes cannot detect them; but the object does not on
that account cease to be a table. Nor, for that matter, is it a different river at
this moment although no drop of water in it is any longer in the same place it
was before. It is not a *defining* characteristic of rivers that they always
contain the same drops of water, much less that these drops of water be at the
same place from moment to moment; and as long as this characteristic is not
defining, it can keep on being a river, and even the same river, even though
the water in it is always changing. The table can undergo any number of
changes and still be a table as long as it does not cease to have those
characteristics which *make* it a table, in other words its defining
characteristics. Many characteristics of a thing can change or disappear and
be replaced by others, and the thing in question will still be that kind of thing
as long as the defining characteristics continue to be present. Thus, tadpoles
change into frogs (they lose the defining characteristics of tadpoles), but
frogs, although they undergo changes also, always remain frogs (they do not
lose the defining characteristics of frogs). It is only if we foolishly take *every*
characteristic that a thing has as defining that we reach the conclusion that a
thing never persists even through the space of a second, for during the space
of a second it always loses *some* characteristic or other, such as the
characteristic of having some particular molecule in its body in some
particular place. This conclusion can be avoided if we take (as we normally
do) a *few* of the characteristics as defining and the rest of them as accompanying. The absence of a characteristic of the latter class in no way
prevents it from being "the same river," "the same table," "the same
person."

"It's still a table" is, of course, different from "It's still *the same* table." We shall say more about "the same X" on pp. 38–39.

Intrinsic v. relational characteristics.   Any characteristic of a thing can be a defining one. Often, for reasons of convenience, it is the *intrinsic* characteristics, or the characteristics of a thing that do not depend on the existence of other things, which are made defining. Thus in the case of chemical compounds it is the elements of which the thing is composed that are defining: "salt (ordinary table salt) is whatever is composed of one part sodium and one part chlorine." In the case of organisms it is usually the form or shape of the thing that is defining: thus horses and cows have much the same chemical composition but differ in shape and contour, and this is the distinguishing mark between them. In the case of inorganic objects, such as tables, again it is the shape that is defining: a wooden table would still be a table (that is, it would still be called "table") when petrified into stone, but it would no longer be a table if chopped up into kindling, even though the pile of kindling contained all the matter that was in the table.

But in the case of many words, it is not the intrinsic but the *relational* characteristics that are defining: in other words, characteristics which the thing has only in relation to other things. Thus what distinguishes the class of brothers from all other classes is not only an intrinsic characteristic, their sex, but their relation to other individuals—namely, their having the same parents. Hundreds of words are defined in terms of relational, not intrinsic, characteristics: "brother," "husband," "friend," "physician," "general," "superior," "younger," "larger," and so on.

One kind of relational characteristic which is sometimes defining is the object's *use*. Thus, words like "chair," "axe," "pen" are sometimes defined in terms of the object's use for sitting, chopping, and writing, rather than in terms of its appearance. Either way of defining these words would have some basis in common usage of them; and, once again, there is no "right" or "wrong" way of defining them. One should not say that there is only *one* right way of defining "axe," and that is in terms of the thing's use or function. (Ask yourself at this point: "How do *I* use the word 'axe'? Would I use the word 'axe' to label something used for chopping but which didn't look like the axes I've seen? Would I use the word 'axe' to label something which I'd call an axe on the basis of its appearance but which was neither designed nor used for chopping?")

Stipulative and reportive definitions.   When we define a word, we are indicating (presumably to someone else) what the word means. But this phrase should now sound suspicious. A word, as we have repeatedly observed, doesn't just "mean" something. A word is an arbitrary symbol which is given meaning by human beings. What, then, are we doing when we "indicate what a word means"? We are doing one of two things: either (1) we are stating what *we* are going to mean by it, or (2) we are reporting what people in general, more specifically those who use the language we are speaking, or sometimes some segment of those who use that language, already mean by it. In the first case we are stipulating a meaning, and we have a *stipulative* definition. In the second case we are reporting the usage of others, and we have a *reportive,* or *lexical,* definition.

Usually when we state definitions we state reportive definitions—the kind we generally get from a dictionary, which reports what meanings are actually attached to different words by the users of a language. (Only rarely does a dictionary try to stipulate or legislate meanings.) We do not usually invent new meanings for a word; we report those which the words already have—that is, have been given by others. Thus when we say "A triangle is a closed plane figure bounded by three straight lines" we are saying that English-speaking people use the noise "triangle" to mean the same as "closed plane figure bounded by three straight lines." We do not have to stipulate this meaning; we simply report the meaning that is already there and, presumably, follow this usage ourselves. When a word has an established meaning in our language we do not feel the need to stipulate one. As a rule we stipulate only when (1) a word is ambiguous, and we want to indicate which sense we mean—even here we do not usually stipulate a new meaning, but only point out which of the several meanings that are already attached to the word we are using on this occasion; or (2) we believe that a word already in existence has no clear meaning and we stipulate a more precise one than it already has—such as when we stipulate a meaning for "democracy," not implying thereby that this correctly reports how most people speaking English use the word, but only that it is a more precise one than people generally employ; or (3) we find no word in existence for some meaning we have in mind, so we invent one: this is pure stipulation, not a report at all, because no one has used this noise before to mean what we are now meaning (intending) by it.

Can definitions be true or false? It is sometimes said that a definition can be neither true nor false, because when you define a word you are simply putting into words a resolution as to how you are going to use the word, and a resolution cannot be true or false. To this it is sometimes responded, "But a definition *is* true or false. If someone said a triangle was a four-sided figure, or a horse, or a five-foot bookshelf, he would be wrong—those would be false definitions!"

You may be inclined to agree with both parties, and it should not take you long to figure out that both parties are right: the root of the difficulty is that the one is talking about stipulative definitions and the other about reportive definitions. A stipulative definition says, in effect, "I shall use this word to mean so-and-so." It does not imply that the word is or has been used by anyone else to mean this. It acts as a *notice* that from now on we are to expect that he will use this noise with this meaning. But he can stipulate *whatever meaning he wants* for the word, and his stipulation is neither true nor false. (What *is* true or false is whether he actually goes on to use the word in accordance with his stipulation.) On the other hand, a reportive definition is indeed true or false. If someone defines "triangle" as a four-sided figure, meaning by this that the word "triangle" is used in English to stand for figures with four sides, this would be a false statement: it would be a false report about how a word in the English language is used. Reportive definitions are reports of word-usage, and there can be true reports and false reports. In this sense, then, definitions not only can be, but are, true or false.

Fundamentality of definitions.   This, however, is not the end of the matter. Shall we merely say, "This is a true report of how 'pneumonia' was defined in the nineteenth century (before the virus was discovered)," and "That is a true report on how the same word is defined today," and let it go at that? Isn't the present definition *better* than the nineteenth-century one? We have already seen how definitions change in the light of advancing knowledge. Shouldn't we go on to say, then, that today's definition is *preferable* to the one of a hundred years ago? Indeed we can and we should, for defining is a human enterprise which always has a goal in view. In the case of experience-words like "red" (used in the ordinary sense), the goal is simply to enable us to *identify* as red the cases to which the word "red" applies. But in the case of scientific and technical terms, the definitions should reflect our advancing knowledge, since the acquisition of knowledge is one of our most important human goals.

Let us consider an unusually controversial example, in which this point—the preferability of one definition to another—is illustrated in another way: the definition of the word "man."

The definition of "man."   If we were asked to pick out, among the enormous quantity of organisms on this planet, which ones were men,[8] there would doubtless be universal, or nearly universal, agreement. We can say "That's a horse, that's a dog, that's a monkey, and that's a man" without making any mistakes in identification. There might be a few borderline cases (such as Neanderthal man and other species no longer existing), but in general people would agree which creatures are to count as human beings, that is, which creatures are *denoted* by the word "man." With this agreed denotation as our starting-point, how shall we *define* the term? Can we agree on a designation as well as a denotation? But here the dispute begins. "Man is a featherless biped"—but a plucked chicken is also a featherless biped. So this won't cover even the agreed-upon denotation. "Man is the laughing animal"—but do hyenas laugh? (Yes, unless laughing is defined in terms of an *intelligent* reaction to a situation.) But there are others that will do better: "Man is the animal with a sense of guilt"; "Man is the aesthetic animal"; and so on.

Now, even if these last-mentioned definitions apply to all human beings and *only* to human beings, we have the uncomfortable feeling that they are only universally accompanying characteristics, not defining ones. (1) They

---

[8] Men in the generic sense, meaning "human being," not men in the sense distinguished from women.

may cover the actual cases, but would they also cover the possible ones? Would *any* creature that exhibited a sense of guilt be called human, no matter what it looked like? And would any creature that never exhibited any sense of guilt be called a man? (According to some psychologists, psychopaths fulfill this description very well; are they then not human beings?) (2) But even if all men fulfilled the requirements in question and *only* men did so, we could still question whether "man" should be defined in these ways, because of the lack of *fundamentality* of the definition. We can explain this point by citing Aristotle's definition of "man."

"Man is the rational animal," said Aristotle (384–322 B.C.). This does not mean that all men exhibit rationality, but that they are *capable* of it—that man is the species that has the capacity for rationality, and no other animal has. Of course, "rationality" would in turn have to be defined, and this is a very complex issue indeed: rationality includes ability to reason, but this in turn presupposes the ability to form broad mental abstractions, or concepts. In any event, rationality is a more fundamental trait of man than the other qualities mentioned, since a creature without rational powers would be unable to have aesthetic experiences (dogs do not appreciate works of art) nor would he have a sense of shame or guilt (the dog puts his tail between his legs when he fears punishment, but this is not the same as feeling guilt).

Aristotle defined "man" as "rational animal" presumably because he considered man's rational nature to be more *fundamental* than the characteristics given in other definitions. The other characteristics are less fundamental because they *presuppose* this one—that is, they could not occur if this feature were not present. If B, C, and D would not be possible without A, then A is more fundamental than B, C, and D, and a definition in terms of A is consequently preferable to definition in terms of the others. (We have encountered a similar situation in the definition of names of diseases: we define "pneumonia" in terms of the virus, A, which causes the symptoms B, C, and D; the existence of the virus explains the symptoms, but not vice versa.)

But this is not the only way in which "man" has been defined. Aristotle's definition was in terms of man's rational capacities; and if this definition is accepted, a creature without rational capacities—for example, a Mongoloid idiot, who may have even less rational capacity than an ape—would not be counted as a man even though he looked like all the other creatures we call men. If this fact makes us uncomfortable, we might try a quite different kind of definition: a *biological* one. We distinguish dogs from cats, horses from cows, and countless other creatures by means of their general appearance; why not man also? But what characteristics would these be? Men have two eyes, one nose, two ears, one mouth, two arms, two legs, they stand upright, etc. But (1) many creatures other than man also have two eyes, etc.; and (2) many men have only one eye, one arm, one leg (or none at all), etc. There are many creatures we would all call men who lack one or more of these characteristics. Still, a biological definition of "man" may be possible; but before we can attempt this, we must study yet another aspect of the meaning of words (the "quorum" feature, pp. 70–72).

Another example of the point about fundamentality in definition: Suppose someone defines "noon" as the time of day when the shadows cast by the sun are the shortest. This may seem at first glance to be a wholly satisfactory definition. There may be cloudy days when there are no shadows at all, but this could be corrected by saying that the shadows *would* be the shortest *if* the sun were visible at that time. Astronomers, however, define "noon" as the time at which the sun crosses the meridian at any given longitude—the meridian being a great circle drawn through the sky intersecting the north and south points of the horizon and passing through the zenith (the point directly overhead). The definition is thus made independent of whether there are any objects on the earth to cast any shadows, and of whether there are cloudy days in which no shadows are cast. The position of the shadows at noon is a *consequence* of the sun's being at the midway point of its daily course. Accordingly, "noon" is defined in terms of the actual position of the sun in relation to points on the earth, not in terms of a consequence of this fact, that the shadows it casts are the shortest at that time. The first explains the second, but the second does not explain the first; so the first is accepted as the more satisfactory definition.

Verbal disputes.   It will be plain by now that giving a satisfactory definition is a difficult and tricky business. It is easy to stipulate a new definition for a word, but this is of very little interest to anyone unless you are in a position to make other users of the language follow your stipulation; otherwise you will only be adding a new meaning to a word that already has another meaning and will cause more confusion than you prevent. What is difficult to convey, by means of words, is exactly what a word *already* in the language means. It is often less difficult in the case of technical terms, whose meaning was originally stipulated by some innovator in the field in a precise way, and then was adopted by others. The task is most difficult in the case of the most familiar and everyday words in our language. Try to define "chair," "cat," "run," "car," "beyond," rapidly," and "space" in such a way that the definition you provide has exactly the same meaning as the word to be defined. You will see that the task is staggeringly difficult.

Fortunately, it is not always necessary to do this. Often we are unable to state a definition—say, for "cat"—but we do have a more or less vague criterion-in-mind for applying this word to things in the world. We cannot supply a definition, but we can distinguish cats from non-cats and never make mistakes about it. And when characteristics A, B, and C always go together, it is not necessary to state which of them are defining—until we come across A and B without C. Even so, most problems about meaning that arise revolve around just one characteristic of the X in question, and are resolved once we know whether that characteristic is or is not to be taken as defining.

Since people often do not mean the same thing by the words they use (and just as often have nothing very clearly in mind at all), they often get into disputes involving these words; and the dispute may drag on endlessly without being resolved, because the disputants are not careful to be clear about the meanings of the words they are using. The old dispute, "If a tree falls in the forest and nobody is there to hear it, is there a sound?" is a *verbal* dispute—one that could be settled by being clear about the meanings of the words involved. In this case the crucial word is "sound." If you are talking about sound *waves* (alternating condensations and rarefactions of air), such as can be recorded on instruments, then there are sounds regardless of whether anyone is there to hear the tree fall. But if you mean the *experience* of sound—the sound-*sensations*—then both disputants will agree that there can be no sound-experiences unless there is someone there to experience them. Once it has been made clear that the word "sound" is being used in two different senses, the dispute is resolved; there is nothing left to dispute about.

Not all disputes, of course, are verbal; most are *factual:* they can be resolved, not by being clearer about the meanings of our words but only by a further investigation of the facts. If two people disagree about how many planets there are in the solar system, or whether the majority of the people in the United States today prefer an aggressive foreign policy, or whether there are snakes in Ireland, there is no way to settle these matters except further investigation of the facts of the case—which may be long and difficult. No degree of clarity about the use of words will settle these disputes. Even here, however, verbal difficulties may enter: for example, the meaning of the word "planet" must be made clear (some might consider the asteroids to be very small planets); what exactly is to count as an "aggressive" foreign policy must be more precisely specified; and even in the last case, one must be clear whether Northern Ireland is to be included in the survey, and what exactly is to count as being a snake.

Here are two examples of strictly verbal disputes.

Example 1:

Some years ago, being with a camping party in the mountains, I returned from a solitary ramble to find everyone engaged in a ferocious metaphysical dispute. The *corpus* of the dispute was a squirrel—a live squirrel supposed to be clinging to one side of a tree trunk; while over against the tree's opposite side a human being was imagined to stand. This human witness tries to get sight of the squirrel by moving rapidly round the tree, but no matter how fast he goes, the squirrel moves as fast in the opposite direction, and always keeps the tree between himself and the man, so that never a glimpse of him is caught. The resultant metaphysical problem now is this: *Does the man go round the squirrel or not?* He goes round the tree, sure enough, and the squirrel is on the tree; but does he go round the squirrel? In the unlimited leisure of the wilderness discussion had been worn threadbare. Everyone had taken sides and was obstinate; and the numbers on both sides were even. Each side, when I appeared, therefore appealed to me to make it a majority. Mindful of the scholastic adage that whenever you meet a contradiction you must make a distinction, I immediately sought and found one, as follows: "Which party is right," I said, "depends on what you *practically mean* by 'going round' the squirrel. If you mean passing from the north of him to the east, then to the south, then to the west, and then to the north of him again, obviously the man does go round him, for he occupies these successive positions. But if on the contrary you mean being first in front of him, then on the right of him, then behind him, then on his left, and finally in front again, it is quite obvious that the man fails to go round him for by compensating movements the squirrel makes, he keeps his belly turned towards the man all the time, and his back turned away. Make the distinction, and there is no occasion for any further dispute. You are both right and both wrong, according as you conceive the verb 'to go round' in one practical fashion or the other."

Although one or two of the hotter disputants called my speech a shuffling evasion, saying they wanted no quibbling or scholastic hair-splitting, but meant just plain English "round," the majority seemed to think that the distinction had assuaged the dispute.[9]

The issue, of course, is a verbal one because its solution depends on how we define the preposition "round." This difficulty may never have faced us before because usually everything that goes round something else in the first sense also does so in the second, such as a planet going round the sun. But now, when the one occurs without the other, we have to decide which one we are going to take as defining.

Example 2. When can you be said to be in the same train as the one you were in last week? "This is the Twentieth Century Limited." "Oh, that's the same train I took to New York last week." But is it necessarily the same set of cars? Apparently not; for you might take the Twentieth Century Limited from Chicago yesterday and I might take it from Chicago today, although we are certainly not in the same set of cars, for the set of cars you took yesterday is today in New York.

Rather than argue, "It *is* the same train!" "It isn't!" let us ask what we mean by the phrase "same train." Do we call two sets of cars the same train if they have the same labels or signs (such as "Twentieth Century Limited") attached to them?

But this too does not seem to be our criterion. If someone went out on the sly and switched labels on every car of the Twentieth Century Limited, would it cease to be the Twentieth Century Limited at the moment when the signs were removed? Of course not; we would say that the *labels* are now the wrong ones. (Or suppose there were no labels on the cars at all; then it would still be the Twentieth Century Limited—it would just be ever so much harder to discover that it was.) Similarly, this would still be Spamm Street even though a prankster relabeled it "Spasm Street" or took the signs off entirely.

---

[9] William James, *Pragmatism* (New York: David McKay Co., Inc.), pp. 43–45.

What, then, makes this the Twentieth Century Limited and not another train? Surely the fact that the official in charge of naming and scheduling gave it that name; if the person in charge, in his official capacity, were to change the name, then it would no longer be the Twentieth Century Limited but, say, the Droit de Seigneur.

Once it is realized that the issue is a verbal one, we shall not argue the question as if it were an insoluble one (where "no one will ever know the right answer") or some deep mystery in the nature of things. There are many factual questions which are difficult enough to answer, for it is difficult and sometimes impossible to know what the facts are, particularly if they are facts outside the sphere of observation. But many questions that pose as factual questions are really *verbal* questions, such as the ones in these examples. These questions we can answer by clearing up the meanings of our words. There are enough difficult problems which are not verbal without unnecessarily adding the verbal ones to the list.

Just as many disputes can be resolved by clearing up words, so can *questions*. It is not always clear from the wording of a question whether it is information about *things* or about *words* that would answer it. The "what is" and "what is the meaning of" questions in Section 1 are examples. Questions beginning with "What *is the nature of* . . ." are usually (whether the questioners are aware of it or not) requests for defining characteristics. Sometimes, when we ask, "What is the nature of cats?" or "What is the nature of water?" we are asking for accompanying characteristics as well as defining ones: we want to know what some of the most usual or important characteristics of cats or water are, whether defining or not. But more often when we want to know about the nature of X, we want to know the defining characteristics of X, those characteristics in the absence of which we would not call the thing an X. The same holds for "essence-questions." "What *is the essence of* X?" is usually a disguised request for the definition, or at least some of the defining characteristics, of X. Those characteristics without which something would not be an X are the characteristics which constitute "the essence" of X.[10]

"Real definitions." Sometimes it is contended that in addition to stipulative definitions and reportive definitions, there is still a third type of definition-by-equivalent-words, namely "real" definition, which is said to be definition not of words, but of *things*. We have already considered what it is to define a word—either to give a new meaning to a word, or to report on a meaning that has already been given to a word. But what is it to define a thing? We have defined the word "triangle"; now what would it be, in addition, to define the thing, triangle?

[10] This is not the whole story about essence-questions. Sometimes a person who asks for "the essence" wants some *preferred* definition, or something he for various possible reasons *wants* the word to mean. See the discussion of persuasive definitions, pp. 53–54.

If the meaning of the word "define" itself is to remain fairly precise, it would seem that we should restrict the use of this word to verbal expressions: words and phrases. It is always words or phrases of which we ask, and give, definitions. If someone asks for the definition not of a word but of a thing which the word stands for, he is asking for something different, which for the sake of clarity we would do well not to call "definition" at all. What then would a person be asking for who asked for the definition of a thing, or class of things? He might say, "I am asking for the *essence* of thing"; but requests for essences, as we have already seen, are usually requests for the defining characteristics, that is, the characteristics which are used as defining within a language-group. The definition of the word "triangle" tells us what people who use this word mean by it; and this is the definition of a word, not of a thing. Sometimes what is being sought is the *analysis* of a thing—either the chemical analysis of a physical object (water is analyzable into H_2O) or the conceptual analysis of a certain idea or concept (concerning which we shall have much to say in Chapter 2). But whatever is involved in the analysis of a thing, it should be clearly distinguished from definition, which is concerned solely with the meanings of words and phrases.[11]

Definition by Denotation

When we are asked to define a word, we are not always in a position to give a set of words which are equivalent in meaning to the word being defined. Sometimes we may not be able to on the spur of the moment, though we could do so on further reflection; but sometimes there may be no set of words which are equivalent in meaning to the word for which a definition is requested. In either case, it is usually much easier to give a *denotation*. You may not be clear about what characteristics a creature must have in order to be a human being, but at least you can give some examples of human beings: John Jones, Mary Smith, and so on. Each example—each individual to which the word applies—is a denotation of the word. The entire denotation of a word is the complete list of all the things to which the word applies: the entire denotation of "tree" includes all the trees in the world. The word "tree" denotes each member of the class, trees, and the entire class of trees is the entire or complete denotation of the word "tree." (The things denoted do not have to exist now. The present denotation of "man" does not include George Washington, but the total denotation of the word does, for a complete list of human beings on the earth—past, present, and future—would include George Washington.)

Let us note that it is individual things that are denoted by a word; the word denotes each and every individual thing to which the word is applicable. (Strictly speaking, the word does not denote: *we* denote, that is, we use the

[11] On the various things that people may be seeking when they ask for a "real definition" or "the definition of a thing," see Richard Robinson, *Definition*, Chapter 6.

word to denote every individual . . . etc.) The word "tree" denotes (we use it to denote) this tree, that tree, and so on. Now, most of the individual things denoted by the word do not have names. Most people do, but most trees do not. A *proper name* is a word or phrase which is used to denote one individual thing only. "Abraham Lincoln" is a proper name denoting the sixteenth president of the United States; your own name, whatever it is, denotes you. Your dog has one proper name, "Rover," your cat "Tabby" has another, and so on. Sometimes collections of things or people (when regarded as a unit) are given proper names, for instance, your regiment, your club, your garden of flowers may each have a proper name.

It often happens that more than one person or thing has the same proper name. More than one town has been named "Knoxville," more than one person has been named "Robert Smith," more than one dog has been named "Fido." But these words are still proper names because there is no set of *common characteristics* underlying membership in the class. "Fido" is still a proper name for each dog that has been given that name. But the class of Fidos—that is, of the dogs who are named "Fido"—is a class and not an individual, and the basis for membership in the class is the possession of the name, just as being a feathered vertebrate is the basis for membership in the class of birds. It sometimes happens that what was once a proper name has come to be used as a class-word as well: "Dunkirk" is the name of a city in France, but since it became a symbol for heroic defeat in 1940, the word has come to designate this characteristic: thus, "Let's not make this a Dunkirk." (Calling it "*a* Dunkirk" already indicates that it is a class-word, not a proper name.) Similarly, "Quisling" is the name of a Nazi collaborator in World War II, but the word has come to symbolize all traitors, and so we speak of this or that person as *a* Quisling—and in this latter sense the word is no longer a proper name, any more than "traitor" is a proper name. No word is a proper name if there is some common characteristic which is the basis for membership in the class. In the absence of any such characteristic, the fact that two people or dogs or cities happen to have the same name is a "linguistic accident."

All the individual things in the world *could* be given proper names, but most of them *have not* been given proper names. Some dogs and cats, usually those which are pets, have proper names; there can also be proper names for inanimate objects, as when a person calls his car "Bouncing Belinda." But most non-human objects lack proper names: the general word—"tree," "house," "car"—still denotes every individual member of the class, but most of these individual members do not have names. Your pet bird may have a name, but the vast majority of birds which you see flying through the air have been given no name at all.

"But they do have names!" one may object; "this bird is a robin, that bird is a chickadee, and so on." But the words "robin" and "chickadee" are not proper names; they are class-words, not proper names. The word "wren" is not the name of an individual bird; it denotes many thousands of individual birds, namely, every wren there is, just as the more general word "bird" denotes every bird there is. It is misleading, therefore, to say that robins, wrens, and chickadees, etc., are all denotations of the word "bird"; for the denotation of a word is always an individual thing (whether we have a name for it or not), and not a *class* of things such as robins. Robins and wrens are *species* of birds, but only the individual creatures are denotations of the word "bird." Robins and wrens are *classes* of denotations of "bird."

What has all this to do with definition? Sometimes, when we are asked for the definition of a word, we simply mention denotations of the word (John Jones, Abraham Lincoln) or classes of denotations (sparrows, robins); and if the hearer already knows what these words mean, he has some idea of what the general word ("bird," "man") means. But only *some* idea: he would know what some of the things (or groups) are to which the word applies, but he would not yet know what is most important to know—what it is about these examples that makes them all examples of the kind of thing in question. In the case of "bird," even a long list of examples would be very misleading. You might decide on the basis of the examples given that what makes something a bird is that it flies, whereas this is not contained in the definition of "bird" at all: some things that fly (bats) aren't birds, and some birds (ostriches) don't fly. As a way of finding out what a word means, denotation will do as a first approximation only.

When you know what characteristics something has to have to be an X, you can figure out whether a certain thing is an X by discovering whether it has the defining characteristics. But if you know only a partial list—or even a complete list (impossible in most cases)—of the individuals denoted by the word, you still do not know why *this* collection of things is put together and labeled with this word. Or to put the matter more technically but also more precisely: if two words have the same designation, they have to have the same denotation; but if they have the same denotation, they may still have a different designation. "Crow" and "black crow" have different designations, for the characteristic of being black is included in the second but not the first; but they have the same denotation, for, since all crows are black, for every member of the class of crows there is also a member of the class of black crows, and vice versa.

Some words, such as "unicorn," *designate but do not denote;* there are no unicorns, hence no individual things for the word to denote. But there are also words which *denote but do not designate;* these are proper names. When you learn the proper name of something, you still do not know what characteristics it has: "Bessie" might be the name of a woman, a cow, a goat, a car, etc. Suppose you are in a railroad station asking where to make a train reservation, and you are told, "See Harry Jones." This information is of no use to you at all. But if you are told, "See the man with the badge at the window marked 'Reservations,' " you have been given the information you seek. But this information did not consist of any proper names, but of general words like "badge," "window," "man," and so on. When you need to know the characteristics of something or someone, proper names will not help you, for they do not designate any characteristics—they only denote. There are no characteristics which a thing has to have in order for the proper name "Clink" to apply to it, for you can apply this term as a proper name for anything you please.

The need for general words.   If it is true (as seems likely) that no two trees, chairs, or gallops, or anything else in the world, are exactly alike, why should we have one general word, such as "tree," to denote all of them? Since every thing in the world is different, why not avoid confusion by having a different word for each of them? In short, why not have nothing but proper names?

One answer is that it would be impossible even if it were desirable: it would place such a tax on our memory that we could not use language at all. Suppose you gave a different name to each of the two thousand chairs in an auditorium, and managed to remember them; then you would have to start all over again with different names when you entered the adjacent auditorium. You would soon have to give up the project as hopeless.

But even if our memory were up to the task, it would not be desirable. Suppose there were no general words, and Smith built himself a house and called it "N," then Jones built himself a house and called it "O," and then Black built one and called it "P." Now you come along; you cannot say you are going to build a "house," because there are no general words. You have no way of indicating in words the similarity between what you are going to build and what the others have built. Yet you want a word that covers them all (and future cases as well) on the basis of the similarity among them. But to do this is to have general words.

Moreover, general words remind us that however different individual things may be from one another, they do have common characteristics. They do not have to have many, only enough to entitle them all to the application of the same word. People differ enormously, but the Boston aristocrat and the African Hottentot both have certain characteristics in common that entitle them both to be called human beings. The word "above" applies not only to the relation that the chandelier in my dining room bears to the dining-room table but also to the relation that your upstairs bedroom has to your kitchen. And so on.

But general words also tend to obliterate the differences among things and overemphasize their similarities. Two things may be referred to by the same word, while they may be much more different than alike. One should not assume that two things with the same general word are identical; yet having the same word for both of them tends to make one assume this unconsciously. "Oh, another banker," says the shopgirl as she goes out on a new date. But bankers, like all other creatures, differ in many ways from each other. "One star differeth from another in glory," says the psalmist. We should guard against the tendency to make the inference, "Identical names, therefore identical things." Even the same thing is different at different times. General words may tend to *fossilize* our conception of the ever-changing, infinitely various world of things to make us conceive the world as being composed of static *types* rather than of different things, some of which are similar enough to each other to be given the same name.

Light passes through a solid crystal. This many persons deem a standing miracle. What we see excites no surprise. The passage through solid crystal is the marvel. We know the difficulty which would attend the passage of our hand through the crystal, and we deem the passage of the light identical with the passage of the hand. Nothing is more fallacious than thus to construe the word "passage" in these different uses of it. The two operations possess the requisite analogy to make the word "passage" applicable to both, but its meaning in each application is what our senses reveal, and not what the identity of the word implies.[12]

Classification.   Probably no two things in the universe are exactly alike in all respects. Consequently, no matter how much alike two things may be, we may still use the characteristics in which they differ as a basis for putting them in different classes. Thus, even if two icicles were exactly alike in shape, size, and chemical structure (even when examined under a very powerful microscope)—though doubtless this would never happen—we could call one, say, a "flep" and the other a "flup" because one was hanging from the north side of the house and the other from the west side. (We would be using "flep" to refer to any icicle of that very specific shape, size, and composition, hanging on the north side of such-and-such kinds of dwellings.) Or, if the two exactly similar icicles hung an inch apart, we could make the fact that the one was west of the other the basis for putting them into different classes and using different class words for them. We *could* make the criteria for membership in a class so detailed and specific that in the entire universe there would exist no more than one member of each class. In practice we do not do this, for language then would be just as unmanageable as it would be if all words were proper names. What we do is to use rather inclusive class words, such as "cow," and then, if the need arises, we can make differences within this class the basis for further distinctions, such as "Guernsey cow," "brindle cow," and so on, marking out as many sub-classes as we find convenient within the main class. (Every profession carries this process of subdivision further than laymen do. We talk vaguely about bones, nerves, and muscles, but medical men must speak of pituitary glands, ganglia, medulla oblongata, and the like.)

In the same way, there are probably no two things in the universe so different from one another that they do not have some characteristics in common which can be made the basis for membership in the same class. For

[12] Alexander B. Johnson, *A Treatise on Language*, p. 85.

example, a thought and a sandpile are vastly different, but both are "temporal entities," i.e., they occur in time. Triangles, trees, the square root of −1, running, and the relation of being above, though they belong in utterly different categories, have in common at least the fact that they have all been thought of by me in the last ten minutes. In practice this fact would hardly justify us in devising a general word to include all of them, but it could be done: we could use a noise, say "biltrus," and say that a biltrus is anything thought of by me. Often we do in fact build up wider and more inclusive classifications, such as "Guernsey," "cow," "mammal," "animal," "organism," physical thing," "existing thing," each successive word applying to more and more things because the requirements for membership in the class are progressively fewer and less restrictive.[13]

Are there natural classes of things?   The common characteristics which we take as criteria for the use of a general word are a matter of convenience. Our classifications depend on our interests and our need for recognizing both the similarities and the differences among things. Many overlapping classifications can be equally valid. Animals are classified in one way by the zoologist, in another way by the fur industry, in still another way by the leather industry. Houses are classified in one way by the architect, in another way by the gas inspector, and in still another by the fire department. Moreover, we could devise many special classes other than the present ones if we wished, but since there is no need for it, we do not bother. Doubtless there are tables in the world that have been painted twice, then taken upstairs after twenty-one years' use, then brought down again and sold as antiques. But we have not bothered to devise a word for tables that possess in common this rather peculiar set of characteristics.

There are as many possible classes in the world as there are common characteristics or combinations thereof which can be made the basis of classification. Those to which we may be most accustomed we often tend to think of as the "natural," the inevitable, the only correct classifications. This, of course, is a mistake. If we were more interested in the colors of creatures than in their shapes, or if animals always bred true to color but offspring of the same parents had a chaotic variety of shapes, sizes, number of legs, and so on, then, doubtless, we would consider classification by color more "natural" or more "right" than classification by any other means. If their being poisonous or non-poisonous, or their being capable or incapable of becoming domesticated, depended consistently upon their colors, then doubtless we would classify them according to their colors.

Nature guides us, but does not dictate to us, in the selection of classes. Nature guides us in the sense that we often find in nature certain *regularly*

---

[13] Sometimes the addition of further restrictions does not make the class smaller: "rational animal," "rational animal with thumb-forefinger apposition," "rational animal with thumb-forefinger apposition with articulated spine," etc.—all denote man. But the addition of further restrictions cannot, of course, make the class larger.

recurring combinations of characteristics, so that it seems useful to assign a name to the combination. Thus let us suppose (though this is an oversimplification) that we use the word "dog" for anything that is a mammal, barks, has long ears, has a long nose, and wags its tail when it is pleased or excited. The class of dogs is a natural class in the sense that these characteristics pretty regularly occur together (not with perfect regularity, however: there are "monsters" or freaks of nature). For example, we find that creatures having the other "doggish" characteristics also usually bark and do not meow or hiss. It is convenient, then, to lump all these individuals together under one class word, "dog." A different but overlapping combination of characteristics is employed for the use of the word "cat." Let us say that anything having characteristics A, B, C, and D is called "dog," and anything having A, E, F, and G is called "cat." We could, if we liked, devise another word and use it to refer to anything having characteristics B, E, H, and J—for example, any five-footed mammal, green in color, which has a long slender nose and purrs. But as far as we know there are no such creatures, so it is simply not useful to us to devise such a classification.

Are classes in nature or are they man-made? As so often happens, the answer depends on the meaning of the question. Classes are in nature in the sense that the *common characteristics* can be found in nature, waiting (as it were) to be made the basis for a classification. On the other hand, classes are man-made in the sense that the *act of classifying* is the work of human beings, depending on their interests and needs. We could have made classifications quite different from those we did make by selecting from the infinite reservoir of nature *different* groups of common characteristics (as bases for classification) from those we did select.

Extending a classification.   When we want to give a name to a class of things which is like but not exactly like a class for which we already have a name, we are faced by a choice: shall we extend the old name to include the different but related things, or shall we keep the old name as it is and devise a new name for the new class? Shall we call the new anti-tank weapons "guns" (with a qualifying adjective in front) on the basis of their similarity to the things we already call "guns," or shall we call them by a new name, "bazookas," on the basis of their differences from the things we call "guns"? Shall we call communism a religion, because of certain qualities of devotion, fanatical loyalty, and submergence of the self in a common cause which it shares with ways of life and thought we already refer to as religions, or shall we deny the term "religion" to it because it professes no belief in a supernatural Being? What of a chemical element possessing every characteristic usually associated with the name, except its atomic weight? Shall we consider it a different class and distinguish it with a new name, or shall we retain the old name and say that they all belong in the same class, perhaps distinguishing this group from the rest of the class by means of the word "isotope"?

If we use the old name, we shall be putting less of a tax on the memory because of the new word. More important, by using the same word for both, we shall be calling attention to the similarity between the new class and the old. But at the same time we shall be obscuring the differences between the new things and the old, tending to make others believe that the new thing is just like the old because it has the same name. On the other hand, if we use a new word we shall make the differences quite clear, but we may also tend to keep others (as well as ourselves) from being aware of genuine similarities between the two.

Which procedure we adopt in any particular case will depend largely on whether it is the likenesses or the differences that strike us as more important. And often the overriding consideration in estimating the importance is the preservation of an entire system of classification (as in the isotope example), such as the periodic table of the elements, with all its value for prediction and explaining countless facts about the chemical elements. We classify in such a way as to preserve the entire *system* of classification.

Denotation and definition.   In spite of its obvious disadvantages, defining by denotation is of some importance. In many words we seem to be at a loss for a definition, or are presented with a multitude of various and conflicting definitions, and yet the denotation of the word in question is agreed on by all parties to the dispute. People may agree that individuals M, N, and O are all X's, but they may not agree about what characteristics of M, N, and O are the ones that make them X's (what characteristics are defining). For example: Almost everyone would agree that Wordsworth, Coleridge, Keats, and Shelley are Romantic poets, and that Wagner, Brahms, Liszt, and Mahler are Romantic composers. They agree on the denotation (at least on these denotations; they might still dispute about borderline cases), but they do not agree, nor do scholars agree to this day, on exactly *what* features of the works of these artists entitle them to be called "Romantic." (Nor is it agreed whether "Romantic" has the same meaning when speaking of music or visual art as it does when speaking of literature.) Agreeing on the denotation of a term, then, at least provides us with some basis for further discussion. If the disputants did not agree even on the denotation, they would probably not be able to get even to first base in agreeing on the definition.

The word "philosophy," which many readers probably thought should have been defined in the very first paragraph of this book, is another of those terms whose denotation is more agreed upon than its definition. Virtually everyone who has studied the subject will agree that certain issues and problems are philosophical ones: the nature and extent of human knowledge; the relation of the knowing mind to the outside world; the problem of determinism and human freedom; the validation of statements about cause, about God, about the good, the beautiful, and many other things. But there is far from universal agreement on what all these problems have in common that entitles them to be called philosophical problems.

There is still another aspect of definition (persuasive definition) that we shall have to consider before we can make any more fruitful suggestions about the definition of "philosophy." Any further remarks about the difficult task of defining this term will have to be kept in abeyance until that time.

Connotation

In addition to designation and denotation, some words have *connotation*. The connotation of a word or phrase consists of the *associations* it has in the minds of the people who use it. Thus the word "snake" designates the characteristics of being legless and reptilian; it denotes all the snakes there are in the world; and it *connotes* (to most people, at any rate) the characteristics of being slimy and revolting.[14] (The connoted characteristics may not exist in the things to which they are attributed: snakes are not slimy.) The word "egghead" is an approximate synonym for "intellectual," but it has different associations, being used in some circles as a term of contempt. The word "square," used to describe a person, designates certain characteristics—having chiefly to do with being conservative, old-fashioned, hidebound, resistant to innovation—but as used by many of the younger set, it has a contemptuous ring. Many animal-words have connotations: consider Machiavelli's statement, "The prince must be both a lion and a fox" (both brave and crafty), and the facetious definition of an assistant dean, "A mouse training to be a rat."

The connotations of a word vary from person to person and group to group; but there are many connotations that are sufficiently uniform within a language-group that anyone who understands the words at all also knows what they connote. Even a man who likes snakes knows that he is not being complimented when his wife says to him, "You snake!"

One reason why it is so difficult to find exact synonyms in English or any other language is that even when two words have the same designation and the same denotation, they usually do not have the same connotation. The range of thoughts, images, attitudes, and feelings *suggested* by the word is different from those of even its close synonyms. Almost the only words that are exactly synonymous are technical terms that have little or no connotation at all, such as "planetoid" and "asteroid"; but most of the words we use in daily life are rich in connotations: consider the difference between "sweat" and "perspire," "earth" and "world," "father" and "daddy." Poetry, the

[14] Sometimes the word "connotation" has been used (by John Stuart Mill, for example) to mean the same as what we have here called "designation." But the usual meaning of "connotation" among the users of English is what we are describing here, and if the word were also used to mean designation, we would have two very different meanings for the same word, operating in very similar contexts.

effect of which depends on richness of connotation, must accordingly employ the language of daily life, and would be sterile if it employed to any great degree a scientific or technical vocabulary.

Connotation and meaning.   Assuming now that we include only those connotations that are fairly universal within a language-group, are the connotations of a word to be considered part of the word's meaning? The word "snake" designates certain characteristics and denotes a vast variety of organisms; but is the unfavorable connotation of this word also a part of its meaning?

We are certainly tempted to answer in the negative. The meaning of a word, we would say, is one thing, and its effects upon hearers or readers is quite another. The fact that the utterance of the word "snake" affects most people unpleasantly has nothing to do with the *semantics* of the word "snake." The semantics of a word is concerned with the relation of a word to its meaning, and the *pragmatics* of a word has to do with its effect upon its users, both speakers and hearers. Should not these two be kept quite clearly distinct? The word "communist" denotes anyone who adheres to an economic system involving state ownership of all property, whether one approves of this system or not. The word "sea" means a certain type of body of water, regardless of what associations people may have with this word or what thoughts or images may be evoked in one's mind when the word is uttered.

Meaning and effect are clearly not the same thing. Still, many persons, including some philosophers, have suggested various kinds of connotation and called them "meaning." A word may have so many kinds of connotation that it would be idle to attempt an exhaustive list, but it may be worth our while to consider several of the main types of connotation a word may have and inquire whether any of them have any title to be called "meaning."

1. "Pictorial meaning."   The "pictorial meaning" of a word, it has been said, consists of the mental pictures it evokes in the hearer's or reader's mind. Many words do have this type of effect: when someone utters the word "elephant" you may picture an elephant; and when someone says "chartreuse," you may conjure up a mental image of that color. But this, it would surely seem, is an *effect* that the utterance of the word has upon you, and not a part of its meaning. You know what "red" means when you can identify red things and distinguish them from all others, and you know what "elephant" means when you can do the same with elephants. Many people have very few mental pictures at all: they do not form a mental picture of an elephant when the word "elephant" is uttered; they use the word correctly, they can identify all the denotations of the word, and they may even be able to offer a definition-in-other-words of it, but they form no mental pictures. They may *think* of elephants when they utter the word, but thinking of an elephant is not the same thing as *picturing* an elephant. You may think about justice or irritability, but what do you picture when you think of these things?

And if you do have mental pictures, are they a part of the world's meaning? The mental picture is a part of the word's *effect* on you, but it is not what the word *means*. You and I both understand the meaning of the word "snake," even though you may picture a snake of some kind or other when you hear the word spoken and I do not picture anything at all. Even in poetry, many sensitive readers do not seem to form any mental pictures, and those who do have widely varying pictures.

> Freeze, freeze, thou bitter sky.
> Thou dost not bite so nigh
> As benefits forgot.

What do you picture when you read these lines of Shakespeare? Clouds hovering over a snow-clad landscape? Does it matter? Does your understanding of these words depend on forming mental pictures? It may be—though this is arguable—that you can appreciate poetry more if you do form mental pictures, but at least the mental pictures do not constitute any part of the meaning of the words themselves.

2. *"Poetic meaning."* Shakespeare's line "Canst thou not minister unto a mind diseased?" does not have the same effect as "Can't you help a lunatic?" And Macbeth's "To the last syllable of recorded time" is different from "To the last minute of recorded time." So is "[Life] is a tale told by an idiot, full of sound and fury, signifying nothing" different from "Life is meaningless." In each one of these pairs, is there a difference of meaning or only a difference of effect?

Here the situation is much less clear. It is easy to say, "Each of these pairs of lines has the same meaning, but they just have different effects." Is this true? Might it not be nearer the truth to say, "The lines have different effects *because* they have different meanings"?

Yet how do their meanings differ? Their *connotations* indeed differ, but if connotation is not to be included as meaning, how do their *meanings* differ? It's true that you couldn't translate "Canst thou not minister unto a mind diseased?" into "Can't you help a lunatic?" without ruining the poetic effect, but what difference is there in *meaning*? Doesn't "lunatic" mean approximately the same as "mind diseased," and "help" approximately the same as "minister unto," in spite of a difference in connotation? If both terms have the same designation and denotation, don't they have the same meaning? One who argues thus will say that the effect—in this case the aesthetic effect—of the two lines is very different but that their meaning is approximately the same.

On the other hand, some writers have made a distinction between *primary* meaning and *secondary* meaning, saying that in poetry it is the secondary meaning that counts. The primary meaning of a word or phrase is given in its definition—usually what the dictionary gives as its meaning (though the dictionary often gives much more as well, including accompanying characteristics, such as "Tigers are native to India"; examples; and pictorial illustrations, such as the picture of a tiger). But the secondary meaning of a word includes the full range of what it *suggests* to the hearer or reader.

The word "sea" *designates* certain characteristics, such as being a large body of salt water; this is its primary word-meaning. It also *connotes* certain other characteristics, such as being sometimes dangerous, being changeable in mood but endless in motion, being a thoroughfare, being a barrier, and so on. These are its *secondary word-meanings*.[15]

Are we still sure that "secondary meaning" should not be called meaning at all? that the effects of a word on its hearer or reader have nothing to do with its meaning?

3. *"Emotive meaning."* We now come to the most discussed, the most controversial, type of connotation. "The emotive meaning of a word," it has been said, consists of "the aura of favorable or unfavorable feeling that hovers about a word."[16] Surely, one may say, the aura of favorable or unfavorable feeling that "hovers about a word" (that is, that the word evokes in the hearer's or reader's mind) is a part of the *effect* of the word, and once again the question arises, what has this to do with its meaning?

Sometimes what we have called the meaning of a word (its definition) is called its *"cognitive* meaning," and the effects on listeners or readers (specifically, what attitudes and feelings it evokes) its "emotive meaning." Thus "German" and "Kraut" would have the same cognitive meaning, but they differ enormously in emotive meaning. (Let us observe, however, that the distinction, even if accepted, is not an exhaustive one: emotive meaning covers only a *part,* though an important part, of what is covered by "secondary meaning." The mental pictures people have associated with the word "sea" would not be part of its emotive meaning even if they were uniform among all users of the language, since they are not part of the favorable or unfavorable *attitudes* and *feelings* evoked by the word.)

What are we to say of this? Shall we say that the two terms have the same *meaning* but differ only in their effects on listeners, or shall we include their effects on listeners (perhaps even the intention of the speaker) as part of their meaning? The issue, of course, is a verbal one, depending on how widely we choose to use the word "meaning." But a verbal issue is not necessarily a trivial one; much may depend on where we draw our boundary-lines. In the case of "sea" we would be strongly tempted in the interests of clarity and simplicity to distinguish meaning from effect and say that a word's meaning is one thing and its effects another. On the other hand, we are tempted to say that "German" and "Kraut," "psychologist" and "headshrinker," *do* have different meanings. How shall we resolve this issue?

[15] Monroe C. Beardsley, *Aesthetics* (New York: Harcourt, Brace & World, Inc., 1958), p. 125. Last italics mine.
[16] Charles L. Stevenson, "The Emotive Meaning of Ethical Terms," *Mind,* 1937.

One thing is clear: not *every* difference in effect can count as a difference in meaning. The fact that when I say "I am leaving now" Jones is happy and Smith is unhappy does not indicate any difference in meaning: the meaning of the sentence is exactly the same for the two hearers but has different effects upon them. Similarly, the word "conservative" has an unfavorable aura about it in liberal circles (as does "liberal" in conservative circles), but again this does not constitute a difference in meaning: each term denotes those who adhere to a certain political economic theory, and it does this *regardless* of what the speaker's or hearer's attitude toward that theory is.

May we not say, nonetheless, that there *is* a difference between "German" and "Kraut" (and similar differences between words for other groups) because a person who referred to someone as a "Kraut" would not only be saying he was German, but would be construed as having an unfavorable attitude toward the person in question, as he would *not* in calling him "German"? The unfavorable attitude seems in this case to be built into the word-meaning itself because of the almost universal convention regarding its use. A person who referred to another as a "Kraut" would be communicating as much about his own attitude as about the other person's nationality, but this would not be the case with "conservative" or "liberal," for here the meaning of the words is quite *independent* of the attitude of speaker or hearer toward a person who is referred to by these words.

Consider the difference between "He's a communist" and "He's a stool pigeon."

The mere fact that "He's a stool pigeon," unlike "He's an informant for the police," tends to elicit unfavorable attitudes toward the person to whom the term is being applied does not suffice to show any difference of meaning between the two. . . . But there is a difference in meaning if in saying "He's a stool pigeon" one is taking responsibility for having an unfavorable attitude toward him and is not taking any such responsibility in saying "He's an informant for the police." In other words, there is a difference in meaning if, having said "He is a stool pigeon," I am prepared to recognize that a response like "What's wrong with what he is doing?" is not out of order. And it does seem that there is such a difference in the cases cited. . . . We can distinguish between the "emotive meaning" and the "cognitive meaning" of a sentence insofar as we can distinguish, within the class of conditions for which a speaker would take responsibility in uttering the sentence, between those that have to do with the feelings and attitudes of the speaker and those that have to do with other things. Thus, we might list the following conditions for "He's a stool pigeon":

1. Some particular male person is singled out by the context.
2. This person is an informant for a police organization.
3. S has an unfavorable attitude toward this sort of activity.

We can say that 1 and 2 contribute to the "cognitive meaning" of the sentence and 3 to the "emotive meaning." But we would not be justified in speaking of the emotive meaning of "communist" just on the grounds that it typically evokes unfavorable reactions, apart from any regular practice of using it in such a way as to take responsibility for the existence of unfavorable attitudes in the utterance of it.[17]

In short: it is no part of the meaning of "communist" that condition 3 is present, but it is a part of the meaning of "stool pigeon." Stated otherwise, we could say that the speaker's unfavorable attitude is a defining characteristic in the case of calling someone a stool pigeon but not in the case of calling someone a communist. And once a characteristic is defining, it *is* a part of the meaning of the word. A person could speak of a communist approvingly and still use the word correctly; but if he approved of someone who was an informant for a police organization he would not be entitled to use the word "stool pigeon": he would have to select some other word or phrase, for the very use of *this* one implies (as a part of its meaning) an unfavorable attitude toward the person who is being referred to.

Whether or not we accept "emotive meaning" as a genuine case of meaning or still prefer to call it "effect," it is worthwhile to observe that it is comparatively seldom that the "emotive meaning" of two terms is different without *some* corresponding difference in "cognitive meaning." "Horse" and "charger" have a different emotive meaning, but this is just because they also have different cognitive meanings: not every horse is a charger—a broken-down nag is still a horse, but not a charger. "Compromise" and "appease" differ in emotive meaning (the latter is usually unfavorable, the former not as much), but if we examine our word-usage closely we shall see that we do not attach the same cognitive significance to the two terms either: we might refer to the Founding Fathers of the American Republic as compromisers (they had to compromise in order to agree on a constitution) but not appeasers; an appeaser may sacrifice all his principles in giving in to someone else, but one who compromises will give in on details or matters he considers to be of less than fundamental importance but will not do so on the fundamental principles in which he believes.

Persuasive definition.   Still another type of definition has been suggested, based on the concept of "emotive meaning" (which is itself, we should remember, only one aspect of "secondary meaning"). When a word or phrase has already acquired a favorable emotive meaning, people often want to use the word or phrase to carry a cognitive meaning different from its ordinary one, so as to take advantage of the favorable emotive meaning that the word already has. Suppose that the word "cultured" has at a given time the following cognitive meaning: "acquainted with the arts." But now suppose that it is considered a mark of esteem (in the society in which the word is used) to be acquainted with the arts; gradually the word "cultured" acquires a favorable emotive meaning in addition to its cognitive meaning. Once this has occurred, the word "cultured" is subjected to all kinds of at-

[17] William P. Alston, *Philosophy of Language,* p. 47.

tempts at re-definition in order to make use of this favorable emotive meaning. Thus an after-dinner speaker may say, *"True* culture is not acquaintance with the arts but with science and technology." Of course there is no such thing as the *true* meaning of a word: there are only common and uncommon meanings, exact and inexact meanings. But his audience is not sensitive to these distinctions, and the speaker successfully makes use of the favorable emotive meaning the word "culture" already has in order to make them respond favorably to science and technology, which he wants them to prefer. He has now given a *persuasive definition* of "cultured": he has attached a different cognitive meaning to the word, while the emotive meaning has remained the same. He has performed a kind of sleight-of-hand trick (perhaps without realizing it himself), shifting the cognitive meaning while the emotive meaning remains constant, hoping perhaps that his audience won't notice the switch.

The same thing can happen, of course, with *un*favorable emotive meaning: one may wish one's audience to take an unfavorable attitude toward something as well as a favorable one, and may use this device to evoke the unfavorable attitude. Thus the word ' "bastard" once meant simply illegitimate offspring; but since the attitude toward people having such offspring was unfavorable, together with the legal consequences thereof, people took advantage of this unfavorable emotive meaning to give the term new and different cognitive meanings: for example, "He's a real bastard"—meaning now not that he is an illegitimate offspring but that he is a character to be disliked or despised, etc.

Many words—particularly in controversial subjects such as politics, religion, morals, and art—are constantly subjected to persuasive definition; it is wise to be on guard for such definitions. We need not conclude that persuasive definitions are necessarily and always a bad thing, nor are readers being advised never to use or countenance any persuasive definitions. The point is rather this: if you are subjected to one, be able to spot it for what it is. *Know what's going on.* And above all, don't be taken in by a persuasive definition and be led to wrong conclusions from it, such as the person (in our example) at the after-dinner speech at which the persuasive definition of "culture" was introduced who remarked, "Well, maybe that *is* what true culture is, really."

The definition of "philosophy."   Among the many words and phrases that have been infected by persuasive definition, the one of most interest to us is "philosophy" itself. Different people who all claim to be engaging in the philosophic enterprise have seized upon the aspects of the subject that have interested them most, or those that they considered the most important, and defined "philosophy" in terms of those only, thereby relegating the remainder of the group (including many professors of philosophy at universities and colleges) to the position of non-philosophers. (The group left in the cold by this definition would of course construct a persuasive definition of their own so as to exclude the first group.) The Romantic's statement, "Alexander Pope was no poet," and the statement made of the philosophical analyst, *"That* man is not doing philosophy," both capitalize on the favorable emotive meaning (or emotive effect) of the words "poet" and "philosophy" to give their own in-group exclusive possession of the field. A writer of analytical tendencies may identify philosophy with "conceptual analysis," and one who prefers to engage in flights of speculation without benefit of anchoring in clear concepts may say that "philosophy is the systematic interpretation of all experience"; the first leaves no room for the speculation so highly valued by the second, and the second will doubtless fail to state what he means by "interpretation" and "experience" in this context, for the two terms do require clarification, especially when placed in conjunction with one another. (We know what it is to interpret a cryptic saying or a difficult passage of poetry: we try to state the meaning in simpler words; but what is it to interpret experience? Such definitions usually lead to more confusion than they dispel.) Conflicts such as these have led to Bertrand Russell's facetious definitions of "philosophy": "Philosophy is that which is studied in philosophy departments in our universities and colleges," and "Philosophy is the systematic abuse of terms deliberately devised for that purpose."

Let us try, however, to suggest some of the principal defining characteristics of philosophy: (1) Philosophy is concerned with the clarification of our concepts or ideas, and, accordingly, with the clearer usage of our key terms. And since the concepts it deals with are highly abstract, questions of the "What do-you-mean?" type are constantly and characteristically asked by philosophers. This aspect of philosophy is emphasized by the "conceptual analysis" school of philosophy. (2) Philosophy deals with issues and problems of the *highest degree of generality:* not with "What is a chair?" but with "What is it to be a physical object?"; not with the contents of your or my mind but with "What is mind?"; not with your or my free acts as studied by psychologists but with "What is freedom?"; not with your or my right or wrong acts but with "What is it for an act to be right?" This generality is so great as to transcend the limits of any one of the special sciences; indeed, it has sometimes been said (though this is often questioned) to be "a synthesis of all the sciences." (3) Philosophy proceeds not by unsupported *obiter dicta* nor yet by experimentation (there are no philosophy laboratories) but by reasoning and argument. No matter how important its subject or how wide its scope, an oracular pronouncement ("Reality is basically spiritual") is hardly worthy of being called philosophical. It only becomes so when it is defended (or attacked) by reasoning, not by recourse to authority, intuition, or faith; in these latter cases, it is no longer employing philosophical method, however general or important its pronouncements may be. (4) Philosophy asks *ultimate* questions; it inquires into the foundations and presuppositions underlying every other subject-matter, by asking questions of the "How-do-you-know?" type, inquiring into our basis for asserting even the most apparently self-evident statements (such as "A is A"). It *probes,* investigating and questioning the underpinnings of all the special sciences, arts, theology. It asks not "What are people's religious beliefs and institutions?" (as sociologists and anthropologists do) but "How do we know they are true? Do they rest on a solid foundation?"

While attempting to be impartial, it may be that in listing these conditions we have ourselves given just one more persuasive definition of "philosophy." In any event, we shall be surveying a good deal of both "critical" (analytical) and "speculative" philosophy in this book. We shall be presenting and assessing various theories about human freedom, mind, God, the good life, and many other issues; but it would be idle to pursue these profound and highly abstract issues without a solid conceptual base. Accordingly, with each problem we discuss, we shall usually discuss meaning-questions first, as an indispensable means toward the clarification and solution of the knowledge-questions. This will be our procedure regardless of the subject-matter of the questions. The main subject-matters will be (1) Metaphysics, dealing with the nature of reality, or more simply, "what there is." For example, "Are matter and energy all that exists?" (is materialism true?) is a metaphysical question. (2) Epistemology, or theory of knowledge, dealing with our knowledge of what is. How do we know that a physical world exists? that other people are conscious? that electrons, magnetic fields, God, and other things that cannot be perceived by means of the senses, exist? (3) Theory of value, particularly questions of *ethics* (what is the good life? what kinds of actions should we perform?) and *aesthetics* (what is beauty? what makes a work of art valuable? what is aesthetic expression, meaning, symbolism, etc.?). But the method in each case is the same: once the tangled meaning-questions have been adequately analyzed, the philosophical enterprise with regard to each of these subject-matters will consist of a systematic and reasoned attempt to examine the ground or basis of belief in each of these areas.

Ostensive Definition

In the methods of defining discussed so far, the meaning of a word was conveyed by using *other words;* that is, they were *verbal* definitions. But not all definitions are verbal definitions.

Suppose for a moment that we have only verbal definitions. Each word is defined, and in doing so, other words are used. This will help us only if we already know what these other words mean. How will we find out what they mean? By having their meaning explained by the use of still other words. And so on. But how can this process go on forever? Must we not eventually come to the point where we directly connect words with things, and not with other words, lest we be caught up forever in the circle of our own words? If we do not sooner or later come to a point where we directly connect a word with a thing—sometimes by pointing, sometimes by more complicated non-verbal means—then the realm of words would be forever separated from the realm of things. The process of making clear the meaning of a word by non-verbal means, such as pointing, is called *ostensive definition*.

Ostensive definition need not employ any words other than the word to be defined. One might be tempted to suggest that in that case it should not be called definition. This, of course, is a verbal matter concerning how broadly we wish to use the word "definition." But whether or not we call it definition, it is a way of explaining to someone the meaning of a word. Ostensive definition, as the name implies, *shows* you, *confronts* you with an instance or instances of the word's denotation. Showing someone a beech tree would be giving him an ostensive definition of the phrase "beech tree." No words except "beech tree" (together with the act of pointing) need be used.

To connect words with the world, we need ostensive definition; it is the most fundamental kind of definition, in that without it no other kind of definition could even get started. Without ostensive definition, how could we have *begun* to learn the meanings of words? When we learned our first word, we could not learn its meaning by having other words thrown at us, for we would not have known what they meant. As a matter of fact, we probably learned most of the words of ordinary life ostensively, although now, being adults and having accumulated a considerable reservoir of *words,* we learn most of our new words by means of them.

How do we learn the meaning of a word ostensively? If Mother points to the table and says "table," how can we know from this what "table" means? We can know that *this particular thing* is called "table," but what about that thing over there? Is it a table too? Now Mother has to go through another act of pointing and says "chair." Then what about this thing here? It looks more like the first thing she pointed to than the second. Yes, here too she says "table." And that thing in the corner? It's sort of like the others. No, here she says "desk." Well, the two things she called "table" were more alike than either of them were to the thing she called "chair."

Or perhaps you thought that Desk and Table No. 1 were more alike than Table No. 1 was to Table No. 2. That puzzled you. Then you had to sit down to think what it was about Desk that was different from either of the others. After all, Desk was brown, Table No. 1 was brown, Table No. 2 was white. So it couldn't be the color. Desk was square, Table No. 1 was square, Table No. 2 was round. So it couldn't be the shape. Maybe it was that in Desk there were some funny-looking things that extended almost all the way to the floor and that you could pull out, but not so with Table No. 1 or Table No. 2. Or maybe it was that Mother sat down with pen and paper at Desk. Thus, by a gradual process of abstraction (sifting out the characteristics that all the things with one name had but none of the others did), you got a fair idea of what Mother meant when she used these words.

This is not intended to be an accurate description of a process through which you went in learning words; especially at an early age, it could hardly have been as explicit as that. Yet something of the kind must have gone on, otherwise you would never have grown up to use these words in the same way your parents did, even in the case of words standing for objects that you had never seen before. You certainly didn't learn them verbally; few adults have ever asked themselves, "What is the definition of 'table'?"

The business of giving ostensive definitions, and of learning them, is much more detailed than just pointing to something and pronouncing a word. At the least, it consists of a series of successive pointings and pronouncings, so that you can reflect on what the things given the same name had in common which weren't shared by those not given the same name. Indeed, with just one act of pointing to a table you couldn't be sure what was meant—the table itself, its color, its shape, its upright position, what it was made of, or some other characteristic.

Let us say that we are playing golf and that we have hit the ball in a certain way with certain unfortunate results, so that our companion says to us, "That's a bad *slice*." He repeats this remark every time our ball fails to go straight. If we are reasonably bright, we learn in a very short time to say, when it happens again, "That's a bad slice." On one occasion, however, our friend says to us, "That's not a *slice* this time; that's a *hook*." In this case we wonder what has happened, and we wonder what is different about the last stroke from those previous. As soon as we make the distinction, we have added still another word to our vocabulary. The result is that after nine holes of golf, we can use both these words accurately—and perhaps several others as well, such as "divot," "number-five iron," "approach shot," *without ever having been told what they mean*. Indeed, we may play golf for years without ever being able to give a dictionary definition of "to slice": "To strike (the ball) so that the face of the club draws inward across the face of the ball, causing it to curve toward the right in flight (with a right-handed player)."[18]

Nor is it always pointing that will do the trick. You certainly can't point to thoughts, emotions, or acts of willing. You can't point to fear or anxiety—you can only point to manifestations of them. You can't indicate the meaning of these terms directly at all—you can't enter your son's mind when he is afraid and say "That's fear"; but you can watch him when he gives every indication of being afraid and say "When you act that way, you're afraid." In doing this we rely on the assumption that when one person feels fear he behaves pretty much as another does when he feels fear, at least enough so that it is safe to use the same word for both persons' states. Because you cannot always tell, you sometimes label something "fear" which closer inspection or observation makes you label "anxiety."

Even the meanings of abstract words, like "change" and "again," can be

[18] S. I. Hayakawa, *Language in Thought and Action* (New York: Harcourt, Brace & World, Inc., 1941), p. 45.

indicated ostensively—we certainly never learned *them* verbally. (Try to define them verbally!) When you saw the neighbor's car parked every day in front of your house, and finally it parked next door; Mother said "Now it's in a different place," but she may also have said, "Well! that's a change." And lest you think that "change" just meant "cars parking in a different place," she used the same word the next day to label something quite different—the turning of the weather, or the sudden increase in the price of eggs. By a gradual process of abstraction you learned how to use the word "change." Or, when the car had a blowout in front of your house, and the next day it happened to another car there, Mother said, "Why, it's happened *again.*" But you learned that it had nothing to do with cars having blowouts when she used the word after you spilled soup on the table for the second time. And so on—by this gradual process of repetition and abstraction you came to know (though not in these words, of course) that the word "again" has to do not with any event or type of event, but with the general *repetitiveness* of the events. And in every case, you learned the meanings of the words ostensively—it was a long time before you could grasp the meaning of a word verbally, without being confronted with an instance of its application.

Are there words that can be defined only ostensively? It is clear that some words must be defined ostensively if language is to find an anchor in the world. But this does not yet settle the question whether the meaning of any *particular* word, such as "cat," has to be learned ostensively.

"Are there indefinable words?" it is sometimes asked. If this question employs a broad definition of the word "define," so that to define a word is to indicate *in some way or other* what it means, the answer is clearly no. If there were no way of indicating to another person what you meant by it, its meaning could not be communicated, and it could never become a word in a language. It might be an item in your private vocabulary, to be used in communing with yourself, but it could never become a part of a public language.

But if, in asking the question, one means to ask whether there are words whose defining characteristic cannot be explained (by using other words)—that is, whether there are words whose meaning cannot be indicated verbally, but only ostensively—then the question is a controversial one. The issue might be argued this way:

A. Some words, principally those standing for elementary sense-experiences such as "red," "color," "shrill," "pungent," "bitter," fear," "anger," "love," "thought," and so on, simply cannot be defined verbally. Who can say in words what the word "fear" means? Fear is something with which everyone is acquainted through personal experience, but who can define the word "fear" verbally? You may be able to state scientifically the conditions under which people have this feeling, or what the state of the nervous system is when fear is experienced, or what things fear is a response to, or to give a psychoanalytic explanation of it, but all these after all are not definitions of the *word* "fear" but facts about the *thing,* fear, and an acquaintance with the meaning of the "word" fear is *presupposed* in all these descriptions. The same is true of many other words: how, for example, would one define the word "red"? It may seem that here the case for definability is much easier, because we can give a definition in terms of wave-lengths of light. But this again is a confusion. What we want defined is the word naming the color that we see—and it is not the wave-lengths that we see. Waves of light (within the span 4000–7500 Angstrom units) are only *correlated* with the colors that we see, but are not themselves the colors. We can say that *when* I see red, light-waves of this kind are emanating from the object to my eye; when I see orange, . . . and so on. But the presence of light-waves of this length is only an *accompanying* characteristic. I want to know what the word "red" means, not what the color red is correlated with. And this is just what no words can give me; only direct first-person experience of red can give that to me. If you have been born blind, I can never, by any number of words, tell you what "red" means; I could only talk about accompanying characteristics like the waves of light. If you have seen red, words are unnecessary; and if you haven't, they are useless. In short, here is one of those ultimate words in terms of which other words can be defined, but which cannot itself be defined by means of other words. Here language comes into direct contact with the world, and using more language won't help; for terms like "red" are the rock-bottom of language. Like the ultimate particles of physics which are the building-blocks of the physical universe, they cannot be broken down into further constituents.

B. But *are* words like "red" indefinable verbally? Granted, we can't define "red" in terms of wave-lengths. But can't we define "red" verbally as *the one and only color invariably associated with this range of wave-lengths?* or perhaps as the color occurring at a given place on the spectrum? This is not a crude identification of red with a wave-length, but a definition of "red" as that which alone is associated with that wave-length. Why isn't this satisfactory?

A. But please keep in mind the distinction between defining and ac-companying characteristics. Your attempted definition makes the same mistake as the one we both reject, though not as crudely. We see the color red; very well. Now suppose that in the course of events we came to see this color even in the total absence of wave-lengths—as indeed we now do when we see red spots before our eyes or see red in our dreams. Even if we never did in fact see red under these unusual conditions, it is always conceivable that the conditions under which we regularly see various colors might change. Then we couldn't say that red was associated with this wave-length; after all, if red became associated with a different wave-length, it would still be red, so the wave-length can't be a part of the definition. Just as steel which is no longer used for purposes of construction would still be steel, so red which is no longer correlated with a certain wave-length would still be red, if it looks the way red now does. The same would hold if we no longer saw the colors in their present order on the spectrum. The fact is this: regardless of where we see it, or with what concomitants or correlations, or in what order or arrangement, it's still red we see!

B. Couldn't we say that the word "red" names the color which to the normal eye, or to the normal eye under normal conditions, is accompanied by light-waves of length 4000–7500 Angstrom units? Then we'd get around these exceptional cases.

A. But suppose that the structure of the eye changed or optical laws changed, and nobody any longer saw red when light-waves of this length impinged on the retina? Just as it is possible that people now and then see red in the absence of these physical conditions, so it is possible that people regularly would come to see red in the absence of them.

B. But all these changed laws and changed conditions are hypothetical—the fact is that we *do* see red regularly when light within a definite span of wave-length is present.

A. True, but—so what? *If* we saw red without these physical conditions being present, it would still be red we saw. As long as that is the case, the physical conditions cannot constitute a defining characteristic. *If* steel were no longer used in construction, it would still be steel. Steel doesn't have to stop being used in construction in order for that statement to be true. Remember Venn's motto: "The practical test in fact, when we wish to know whether any proposed definition is a true one or not, is to try whether by conceivable variation of circumstances we can cause it to break down, by its exclusion of what we are resolved to retain or its inclusion of what we are resolved to reject." In the present case all the conditions suggested break down—by easily conceivable variation of circumstances. Which shows again that these are merely *accompanying* characteristics—the mere external trappings of the red, as it were, not the red itself.

B. Perhaps. But here is a consideration that may not have occurred to you. You say that the man born blind can never know what the word "red" means, since the word names a color and he can't see colors. But he may be able to use the word as correctly and as accurately as any of the rest of us. He may be infallible in his use of the word. He can always tell when something is red—perhaps by feeling with his fingers the indicator on a machine that records wave-lengths of light. How could he use the word "red" correctly so systematically if he didn't know the meaning of the word?

A. Here again we get involved in accompanying characteristics. Remember the red-round example? Let's suppose that the man who is supposed to find out what things are red is blind. But he has been told reliably that everything that's red is round, and everything that's round is red. Each always accompanies the other. He can easily tell whether to say "That's red" or "That's not red" by feeling the thing's shape. One could accept his word on which things are red just as well as the word of a man who can see. An outsider might not even know that he couldn't see red but was just taking the presence of roundness as a sure sign that there was redness too. Yes, he would use the word "red" correctly—*as long as redness and roundness continued happily to go together*. The minute this perfect correlation stopped, he would be lost. Don't you see? The man doesn't know what "red" means; he doesn't know what a thing has to look like in order to be red. Surely not that it be round—and yet *that is all he has to go by!*

The word "red," then, designates a color-quality which is the very thing the blind man can have no experience of. The blind man can never know *what* it is that the man with sight means by the term. All he can know is that the word "red" stands for an X which is distinguished from Y's and Z's. He can make the distinction too if redness always goes along with *other* characteristics which he *can* detect; but he can never make the distinction on the basis of a thing's *redness*.

B. What about the man who can see? Can *he* state a criterion for the use of the term "red"?

A. He has a criterion, of course—otherwise he would not know when to use the word "red" and when not to. But the criterion is simply whether this particular shade of color is present to his consciousness. *He* knows how to distinguish it from other colors, but there is no way of stating in *words* how to do this, and therefore he cannot communicate the criterion to those who do not also see red. In short, he has a criterion for the use of the word "red," but he cannot state it in words; all that can be stated in words turn out to be accompanying characteristics. The defining characteristic of "red" cannot be stated so as to distinguish it from other colors. Thus, you see, "red" is *verbally* indefinable.

This by no means puts an end to the controversy, but it will perforce put an end to this section.

Exercises

1. Defining and accompanying characteristics. Which of the following (as the word is most commonly used today) state defining characteristics (and thus are statements about what the word means) and which state accompanying characteristics (and thus are statements about the things named by the word)? Explain, in each case.
   a. Triangles have three sides.
   b. Tigers are native to India.
   c. Dogs are carnivorous.
   d. Books contain paper.
   e. A good player seldom loses a game.
   f. Ladies don't use vulgar words.
   g. An axe is an instrument used for cutting.
   h. Uranium is used in atomic bombs.
   i. Human beings are less than 25 feet tall.
   j. Eggs have yolks.

2. Assume that A is a defining characteristic of class X, and that B is an accompanying characteristic. Which of the following statements is/are true?

a. This wouldn't be an X if it didn't have A.

b. This wouldn't be an X if it didn't have B.

c. If it weren't an X, it wouldn't have A.

d. If it weren't an X, it wouldn't have B.

3. Show by examples how the denotation of two words or phrases can be the same while the designation of the words is different.

4. "What a word means is what it refers to." What is wrong with this statement?

5. Consider the following verbal issues, using your knowledge of defining and accompanying characteristics to clarify the controversy in each case:

a. Is this a table if I cut off its legs? if I cut it up for firewood?

b. Is it still water even if it's not liquid now?

c. Is it still wood after I've burned it?

d. Is he an adult before he is 21 years old?

e. Is this still the same train, even though it's a different set of cars?

f. Is this still the same train, even though it leaves the station at a different time each day?

g. Is this iron even though it's not magnetic?

h. Is this a zebra even though it has no stripes?

i. Am I the same person as ten years ago, though all the cells that were then in my body have been replaced by others?

j. Is this a watch even though it has no dial?

k. Is this a hill or a mountain?

l. Is it still grass after the cow has eaten it?

6. Are the following disputes verbal? How would you proceed to settle them?

a. You have an old car. One part is defective and you get a new part to replace it. The next day you do the same with another part, and so on for each part until you have replaced every part in the entire car. Is what you have left at the end of this process the same car as when you began the replacements?

b. Jack said to his brother Dick, "When I die I'll leave you my money." Next day he changed his mind and decided to leave it to his wife instead, so he wrote in his will, "All my money I leave to my next of kin" (his wife). But unknown to Jack, his wife had died. Next day Jack himself died, and his money went to his next of kin, his brother Dick. The question is: Did Jack keep his promise to Dick or didn't he?

7. People *found* that whales are mammals (contrary to what was originally thought). Moreover, being mammalian is a defining characteristic of "whale." Thus, don't we *find* defining characteristics rather than give them?

8. To discover what characteristics a word designates, it is a common practice to list as many instances as possible of what the word denotes and then discover what characteristics all these particular things have in common. These common characteristics are then called the defining ones, and the list of all of them constitutes the definition. Why is this method not a safe one? Can you think of any word in which using this method would lead to inaccurate results?

9. Does it make any difference as far as the denotation of the word "man" is concerned whether "man" is defined as a rational animal, a featherless biped, or a laughing animal? Try to state as accurately as you can a reportive definition of "man" (in the generic sense of "mankind"), the way the word is actually employed in common usage—that is, what are the characteristics which a

creature could not do without and still be called "man"? (If someone suggested another definition, would you call it the wrong definition? a false definition?)

10. Evaluate the following definitions, with reasons.

    a. Bird: feathered vertebrate.

    b. Fanatic: one who redoubles his efforts after he has forgotten his aim.

    c. Sage: a spice used in turkey stuffing.

    d. Tree: the largest of all plants.

    e. Liberal: one who values liberty.

    f. House: a building designed for human habitation.

    g. Twilight: the period between day and night.

    h. Motion: change of position with respect to the earth's surface.

    i. Wastebasket: a basket used for containing discarded trash.

    j. Book: anything containing paper, covers, and print.

    k. Equator: an imaginary line extending around the earth, midway between the poles.

    l. Marriage: legalized prostitution.

    m. Left: opposite of right.

    n. Religion: what you do with your leisure time.

    o. Wednesday: the day that follows Tuesday.

    p. Pump: an instrument used for drawing water from under the earth's surface.

    q. Eat: ingest through the mouth.

    r. Heart: the organ that pumps blood through the body.

11. "The reason we take property A as being defining of X (for example, not having legs as defining of snakes) is that all X's do have this characteristic." What is mistaken about this?

12. "What is an apple?" "An apple is a fruit that grows on a tree." "I didn't ask you what classification it falls under; I only asked you what it *is.*" "Well, an apple grows. . . ." "I didn't ask you what it *does;* I asked you what it *is.*" "Well, an apple is something composed of the following chemical elements. . . ." "I didn't ask you what it is made of, or what I'd see if I looked at it under a microscope. I asked you, quite simply, what it *is.*" What is wrong in this interchange?

13. Fifty years ago it was considered so certain that schizophrenia was incurable that if any case of mental disease was cured, it was automatically concluded that the diagnosis of schizophrenia had been mistaken. Today incurability is no longer taken as a defining characteristic of schizophrenia. Does this show that the definition of fifty years ago was false?

14. A: Those characteristics which all X's have in common must be defining characteristics of X.

B: No. All tables are solid objects, yet that isn't a satisfactory definition of "table." The definition is too broad, for it doesn't distinguish tables from all the non-tables that are also solid objects. You have to know not only what is common to all tables, but what is *peculiar to* them.

A: Very well; suppose you know something peculiar to X's, something that nothing else has. For instance, only elephants have trunks used to draw up water. This tells us what is peculiar to elephants. Is this then a satisfactory definition?

B: No, for it may not tell us what is common to all elephants, but only what is peculiar to them. A satisfactory definition must include both.

A: Very well, but now suppose that all elephants have trunks: all elephants have them, and only elephants have them. Now, at last, we have a satisfactory definition of "elephant."

B: No, not necessarily, because. . . .

You fill in the rest. Why may the definition fulfilling both requirements still be inadequate?

15. Try to formulate a satisfactory definition of the word "act" in the light of the following considerations and questions.

"In law, there must be an act." Attempted murder is considered an act; but intended murder is not. However, what is involved in being an act? If you shoot someone and the victim dies, what was your act: the crooking of your finger around the trigger? the crooking of the finger around the trigger plus the bullet leaving the gun? these two plus the bullet entering the victim's body? these three plus the bullet entering the victim's heart? these four plus the death of the victim? Which count as part of your act, and which as consequences of your act?

Which of the following would count as acts, and why? (1) You kill someone while sleepwalking. (2) You stab a person to death but have no knowledge of doing so and no recollection of it afterwards. (3) You do something unthinkingly, from sheer force of habit, without any reflection or premeditation. (4) You do nothing at all, but let someone die of starvation when you could have fed him, or let him drown when you could have rescued him. (5) You omit to take care of your car, so when the brakes fail to function your car hits a pedestrian and he dies as a result.

16. Try to define the words "vegetable" and "fruit" in such a way that you could tell, from knowing the definition, which things are fruit and which vegetables. Keep in mind that both terms are ambiguous: something can be a fruit in a biological sense (being part of the plant that bears the seeds) without being a fruit in the culinary sense (being typically served in a sweetened form). Name some things that are fruit in both senses, and some that are vegetables in both senses; then some things that are fruit in one sense and vegetables in the other. Use your analysis to answer the question "Is a tomato a fruit or a vegetable?" (What about pumpkins? beans? rhubarb? See William P. Alston, *Philosophy of Language,* p. 87.)

17. Can a person know anything about X's without knowing what X's are? More precisely, can a person know any facts about X's without knowing what the word "X" means? (Construe "what X means" as synonymous with "what the definition of X is." Then construe it in some wider sense.)

18. What a dog gives birth to must be a puppy, whatever it looks like, for the word "puppy" is defined as "the young offspring of a dog." What's wrong with this? If a dog gave birth to a kitten, would the kitten be a puppy?

19. "Is music a language?" "That's merely a verbal question—a question of whether you want to extend the use of the word 'language' to cover the case of music, or whether you want to restrict it to conventional signs. And as a verbal question, it is comparatively uninteresting." Explain what is involved in deciding whether music is a language. First of all, what do you take the defining characteristics of a language to be?

20. "If you're so sure you know the meaning of this word, give me a definition of it." Why is this request not always fair? not always possible to fulfill?

21. "Nobody knows what electricity is; we only know what it does." "Nobody knows what a cold is; we know only what its symptoms are." Evaluate these statements.

22. "Is this a fox or a wolf?" Is this question verbal or factual, (a) when

you see the creature in the forest at some distance in the early morning mists and cannot make it out distinctly? (b) when you have the creature before you, examine it in detail, make chemical tests, and so on, and after doing all these things, still ask the question?

23. Evaluate each of the following assertions. Clear up whatever confusions they may contain.

a. Controversies about the nature of beauty or the nature of justice are silly and futile. People can define the words "beauty" and "justice" any way they want to, can't they? They have freedom of stipulation, so what are they arguing about?

b. "This author defines one's religion as whatever values one holds highest in life. This of course is a *false* definition; this isn't what religion really is at all." "But a person can use the word 'religion' to mean that if he wants to. Nor is his statement false; for he is stating a definition, and definitions can't be true or false."

c. For generations scientists tried to discover what pneumonia really is. At last they discovered it. It is a special kind of virus disease. So now at least we have the true definition of "pneumonia."

d. No one has yet found an answer to the question: How can a human being change and yet remain the same human being that he was before?

e. You can't step into the same river twice; for the water that was there the previous time has already flowed downstream.

f. This egg before me would not be the egg that it is if it had not been laid by this hen, at this time, at this place, if it were not being seen by me now, and about to be eaten by me. (Everything is what it is because of *everything* that ever happened to it and *all* the conditions under which it exists.)

24. List ten words which have a strong emotive meaning; then state what you think some of their persuasive definitions might be.

25. "The only *true* criminal is the one who commits crimes, not in the heat of passion, but calculatingly, cold-bloodedly." Show how persuasive definition enters here, as into the use of "insane," "neurotic," "man." (Can you think of a case in which the use of a persuasive definition caused a human life to be lost?)

26. Does the example of the man and the squirrel (pp. 37–38) contain any ambiguities other than the one described in the text? Is there any way the word "around" could be construed in the example other than the ones given?

27. What connotations do these animal-words have, as ordinarily used in English? Weasel; wolf; cat; owl; cockroach; beaver; hippopotamus; vulture; duck; snake; reptile; eagle; cow; wolf; rat; mouse.

28. Considering connotation as well as designation, would you consider any of the following pairs of words to be exact synonyms, and why? Conquer, subdue; vex, annoy; scream, yell; lighted, lit; father, dad; asteroid, planetoid; accidentally, inadvertently; supine, recumbent; sophisticated, refined; perceptive, discerning; naked, nude; spatter, splatter; rich, wealthy; potable, drinkable; small, tiny; delete, omit.

29. We have considered some cases of "Is it the same X or isn't it?" (pp. 31, 38). Now consider the question, "Is it the same *word* or isn't it?" Are the following examples cases of two words, or of one word with two different meanings? State what your criterion is for calling it the same word (must they be spelled the same? pronounced the same? must the meanings be related? in present meaning, or in etymology?). Know, no; leek, leak; desert

(sand), desert (justice); seal (animal), seal (on an envelope); slide (verb), slide (noun); excuse (verb), excuse (noun); tap (faucet), tap (on the shoulder); lark (bird), lark (adventure); wind (the wind), wind (to wind); saw (to cut), saw (past tense of "see"); mouth (of organism), mouth (of river); even (adjective, opposite of "odd"), even ("even a pauper can become president").

30. List twenty words which, in your opinion, can be defined only ostensively. Why can't they be defined verbally, in each case?

3. Vagueness

Why is it often so difficult to define a word? The ambiguity of a word is not what makes it difficult to define: we need only list a different definition for each of the senses of the ambiguous word. A much greater difficulty is a pervasive feature of language called *vagueness*. "Vague" is the opposite of "precise," and words and phrases that are vague are accordingly lacking in precision. But there are various ways in which words can fail to be precise.

1. The simplest form of vagueness occurs when there is *no precise cutoff point* between the applicability and non-applicability of the word; in some situations the word is clearly applicable, in other situations it is clearly not applicable, but between these there is a no-man's-land of meaning in which one cannot say whether the word is applicable or not. Red shades into orange, and orange into yellow. A task that was easy becomes progressively less easy until it is no longer easy but difficult. You may drive ever so slowly, but if you drive one mile per hour faster each day, the time will come when you are driving fast; but there is no clear boundary line between the two. If a person is driving at 60 mph in a residential zone, he is clearly going fast, and at 15 mph he is going slowly; but what if he is going 30? One could, of course, arbitrarily define "fast" (in this context) as "in excess of the posted speed limit in that area"; if that speed limit is 25, he is going fast, but if he continues the same speed into a 35 mph area, he is not. But as the word "fast" is used in ordinary discourse, it is not precise but vague: there is no one point of increasing speed at which one stops going slowly and starts going fast. There is a considerable "area of indeterminacy" in which one would not be able to say whether he is driving fast or not. (Note that the application of the word also depends on the context: a speed that is fast for a bicycle is slow for an automobile; one that is fast for an automobile is slow for an airplane; and one that is fast for an automobile in a business district is slow for the same automobile on the open highway. The term, then, is relative to context—but it is still vague in *each one* of these contexts.)

Vagueness is not always an unfortunate feature of language; in fact, vague words are quite indispensable. If you know exactly at what speed someone was driving, you do not need to use the words "fast" or "slow"; you simply state the speed. But if you don't know exactly, you might say, somewhat vaguely, "around 65," or, more vaguely still, "pretty fast." We have indeed a whole series of vague words, such as "slow," "medium," "pretty fast," "fast," "very fast," which we need to use when our information is not precise; but imprecise information is often better than no information at all.

Countless words are vague in this way. The "polar words" are obvious examples: fast, slow; easy, difficult; hard, soft; light, dark; hot, cold; large, small; and so on indefinitely. Each of them shades gradually into the other, and there is no one point where you can draw the line and say, "At this point the object stops being small and starts being large." Or consider the word "between."

```
A                            C                            B
._____._____.
                             . D
                             . E
                             . F
```

Going from A to B in a straight line, you would cross C; C without doubt would be said to be *between* A and B. But would D be between A and B? We might feel more hesitation here. "Well, not *directly* between. But close enough. Let's say it is between." Ordinarily, for example, we would say that Cleveland is between New York and Chicago, even though it is not on a straight line connecting them. (In that strict sense, *no* city would be between New York and Chicago, for a straight line between them would pass through the interior of the earth. Even if you choose some other strict sense of "between," such as "on the arc of a great circle connecting them," probably there is no city right on the line traced by this arc.)

Suppose our answer then is yes; now what of E? Is it between A and B? Well, if D is, you can hardly say that E is not—after all it is so close to D, it would be a bit arbitrary to say that D is but E is not. Then what of F? The same principle would apply again: E is between A and B, and F is right next to E, so F must be too . . . and so on until we have a point ten thousand miles away still between A and B!

Well, *that* point—call it X—isn't between A and B, surely. Yet E is, by our own admission. What can we make of this? Drawing the line between E and F seems unjustified: E would be between and F wouldn't, and they are so close together. But so is the line between F and G, between G and H, and so forth. There is *no* place where it is satisfactory to draw a boundary line. This is the "difficulty of the slippery slope": you want to go down from the top (you want to admit more than just C as being between A and B); but once you start down the slope, you can't seem to stop short of the bottom; yet you don't want to land *there* either. Set the boundary line anywhere you like, but you will fly in the face of common usage of the word.

You might say that this particular source of difficulty is nature's fault and not ours. We cannot draw a boundary line, except very arbitrarily, for the area of application of a word, simply because nature has presented us with a continuum which makes it impossible to do it satisfactorily.

Sometimes, for one special purpose or another, we have to do it, even though we feel uncomfortable about it. We have to draw the line between passing grades and failing grades, say, at 60, even though there is not much difference between a grade of 59 and a grade of 61—certainly far less than there is between the two passing grades of 61 and 100! But we are forced to draw it somewhere. Ordinarily we do not distinguish sharply between the area of application of the word "city" and that of the word "town," but for statistical purposes the Bureau of the Census has to draw it somewhere, so it draws the line at 2,500. In a town of 2,499 a child is born, and lo, we have a city. In common usage, however, we do not draw such a sharp line, for we can see no justification for it. Thus in common usage these terms remain vague.

The kind of vagueness we have been considering is quite simple: there is one line or axis, at one end of which the word in question definitely is applicable, at the other end of which the word is definitely not applicable, but in the middle of which we can't say (unless we set up a new and arbitrary usage) whether it is applicable or not. But what if there is not one line, but many lines, all intersecting?

2. There may be *multiple criteria* for the use of the word. By this phrase we do not mean multiplicity of senses: a word may have many senses and yet each sense may have a precise criterion for its application; this is not vagueness. Nor do we mean that in order for a word to be applicable, a multiplicity of conditions must be fulfilled, as in the case of "triangle." Several conditions have to be fulfilled in order for something to be a triangle, and yet this word is not vague. What we mean here is that there is *not any one definite set of conditions* governing the application of the word. The word lacks precision because there is no set of conditions (as there is in the case of "triangle") to enable us to decide exactly when the word is to be used. There is no set of conditions each of which is necessary and which are together sufficient, for the application of the word to the world.

Consider for example the proceedings that we call "games". I mean board-games, card-games, ball-games, Olympic games, and so on. What is common to them all?—Don't say, "There *must* be something common, or they would not be called 'games',"—but *look and see* whether there is anything common to all. —For if you look at them, you will not see something that is common to *all*, but similarities, relationships, and a whole series of them at that. To repeat: don't think, but look!—Look for example at board-games, with their multifarious relationships. Now pass to card-games; here you find many correspondences with the first group, but many common features drop out, and others appear. When we pass next to ball-games, much that is common is retained, but much is lost.—Are they all "amusing"? Compare chess with noughts and crosses. Or is there always winning and losing, or competition between players? Think of patience. In ball games there is winning and losing; but when a child throws his ball at the wall and catches it again, this feature has disappeared. Look at the parts played by skill and luck; and at the difference between skill in chess and skill in tennis. Think now of games like ring-a-ring-a-roses; here is the element of amusement, but how many other characteristic features have disappeared! And we can go through the many, many other groups of games in the same way; we can see how similarities crop out and disappear.[19]

There is a group of characteristics C_1, C_2, C_3 . . . C_n that games typically have. Among these characteristics are the following: C_1, there are rules that govern the activity; C_2, there is the possibility of winning; C_3, it is pleasant diversion; C_4, the players need to exercise certain skills; and so on. If *all* games had all of these characteristics, and *only* games did, then the word "game" would have a unitary meaning; the statement of its meaning would consist of a statement of the characteristics C_1 to C_n. One game may have only C_1, C_2, and C_7; another may have only C_1, C_3, C_6, and C_7; another only C_2, C_5, C_6; and so on. All that is required in order for something to be a game is that it have *some* of the cluster of game-characteristics C_1 to C_n, not that it have *all* of them. Not every combination of game-characteristics will do, of course: for example, it is not enough that something have only characteristic C_2 (the possibility of winning) in order to qualify for gamehood. In wars and duels and debates, there is the possibility of winning, but none is a game. There is no way of specifying ahead of time and in the abstract just how much *is* enough; it would be absurd to suggest, for instance, that in order for an activity to be properly counted as a game, it is a necessary and sufficient condition that the activity have some combination of four or more of the C_n game-characteristics. It might well be that some activities that have only three game-characteristics are without doubt games, and that others which have five are not.[20]

Try for a moment to define the word "dog." What are some typical dog-characteristics? Dogs have four legs and fur; they typically have long (or longish) noses in relation to other mammals; they are able to bark, and sometimes do so; they wag their tails when pleased or excited; and so on. Clearly one or more of these characteristics could be absent: a three-legged dog would still be a dog as long as it had the *other* dog-characteristics (all of them? not necessarily); a dog that couldn't bark would still be a dog—there are whole species of "barkless dogs"; and so on. There is clearly one defining characteristic: being a mammal; doubtless the creature would immediately be disqualified from being called a dog if it were not mammalian. But this doesn't get us far, for there are countless mammals that aren't dogs. When we go on to the other "doggish" characteristics, we may find one or two that we could consider defining, but for the most part we find a *cluster* of characteristics associated with the word "dog," not all of which have to be

[19] Ludwig Wittgenstein, *Philosophical Investigations,* trans. G.E.M. Anscombe (New York: The Macmillan Company, 1953), §66.
[20] George Pitcher, *The Philosophy of Wittgenstein* (Englewood Cliffs, N.J.: Prentice-Hall, Inc., 1964), p. 220.

present; in fact, each of them can be absent (and therefore the characteristic is not defining) and the creature be still a dog as long as all, most, or some (this varies too) of the *other* characteristics are there.

Let us see now how our picture of language has changed. We began with the picture of a word designating all of a definite number of characteristics, let's say A, B, C, and D; unless a thing had all four of these, it would not be an X. But now we find that in the case of many words (most words?), it can be an X and have only A, B, and C, or A, B, and D, or A, C, and D, or B, C, and D; thus none of the four is defining. Indeed, it might be an X and have only A and B, or A and C, or A and D, or B and D, etc. In other words:

a. Among a definite set of characteristics, *no one* characteristic has to be present as long as all or even some of the others are present; but it cannot do without all of them. This might well be called the *quorum feature of language*. A quorum of senators must be present before the senate is officially in session, but no particular senator has to be there; there isn't one senator who cannot be dispensed with, as long as a minimum number of *other* senators is there. This is the quorum requirement.

b. But what constitutes a quorum varies from one group to another, and from one word to another. It isn't necessarily "all the X-ish characteristics but one"; nor need it be "the majority of the characteristics—anything over 50 per cent." The more of the X-ish characteristics there are, the more confidently we apply the term; but we can't say that any given percentage of the entire set has to be there. One can't say it's a game if four or more game-characteristics are present, and not if there are fewer than that. The word is *vague* with respect to the percentage that must be present in order for the word to be applicable.

c. Thus far we have assumed that there is at least a definite number of X-ish characteristics in the set, and that the only difficulty was in settling on the percentage. But this is not so: often there is no definite number of X-ish characteristics constituting the set—at least we can't be sure that there are. It's not only that we can't settle the matter (of applying the word) by finding the percentage of the X-characteristics that constitutes a quorum, but also that we can't settle on any definite number of characteristics as being *the* set of X-characteristics. Consider the word "neurotic": is there any definite set of X-characteristics here? Perhaps a person is extremely nervous and irritable; perhaps he bursts into a temper at the slightest provocation; perhaps he always has guilt feelings in very strange circumstances (such as when touching glass) or lacks them when others have them; perhaps he is unstable and can't be depended on even in the most ordinary non-conflict situations; perhaps he can never make up his mind about anything and always vacillates; and so on. None of these things is defining of being neurotic; he could do without one or more—even most—of them and be neurotic in spite of it. But is there a definite set of characteristics to choose from? Who could make such a list, and if one did, could he be quite sure that it was complete, that nothing could ever be added to it as part of the X-cluster for "neurotic"?

d. Not all the characteristics carry the same *weight*. Some may count more heavily than others: thus A alone may count more heavily toward something being an X than B and C do together. Inventiveness counts more heavily in estimating one's intelligence than does sheer memory.

e. Some characteristics are not merely absent or present but present in *varying degrees,* and the higher the degree to which the characteristic is present, the more it gives weight to calling the thing in question an X. Everyone has *some* degree of memory, but the greater the degree, the greater the intelligence (other things being equal). In most cases one cannot state in mathematical terms how much weight is added by how much greater the degree of the characteristic; one can only say, vaguely, "the greater the degree to which characteristic A is present, the more confidently we can say that this is an X."

We begin to see now the multiplicity of respects in which a word can be vague. This is such a pervasive feature of language that it infects even the most technical scientific terms. You may have thought that "mammal" meant any animal that suckles its young; but if you look in the *American Dictionary of Biology,* you will note *eight* characteristics associated with this word, together constituting the X-set for it, of which an indefinite quorum must be present, and each one carrying a different (but not precisely specified) weight. Or consider the word "gold." A number of characteristics are associated with this word: gold produces certain spectral lines, has a certain atomic number (79), a certain atomic weight, a characteristic color, a certain degree of malleability, a certain melting-point, and enters into certain chemical combinations and not others. Many chemists would say that the atomic number alone is enough to define the term—that this is its defining characteristic, and the only one needed. Yet chemists themselves would be quite nonplussed if something with that atomic number occurred that was *not* yellow but purple, not malleable, and had a different melting-point and produced a different series of spectral lines. Would they call it gold? Some doubtless would; others would not. Some would doubtless consider *all* of these characteristics to be defining—"it wouldn't be gold if it lacked even one of them"—but this is a dubious position in view of the fact that an isotope has a different weight from that normally characterizing the element, and yet chemists call it X ("X, but an isotope of X") as long as it has the *other* characteristics of X. Indeed, it is far from clear *what* chemists themselves would say if something like this occurred; they are so accustomed to seeing all the characteristics occur together that they have not given thought to the question of what they would call a thing that turned up which lacked one or two of them.

We simply have not anticipated what we would say if various kinds of new and unexpected developments were to arise. Would we still call something an

X if unforeseen events E, F, G occurred? We may have made no provision for this possibility one way or the other. Consider, for example, when we do, and when we do not, use the word "cat." This word is certainly subject to what we have called the quorum feature of language: there are a number (not a very definite number) of characteristics associated with this word, such as being four-legged, bearing fur, having whiskers, stalking its prey and eating it, purring, meowing, and so on. No *one* of these characteristics seems to be necessary: there could be a cat that never meowed, a cat that never purred, a cat that was a vegetarian, etc. A quorum of features must be present, for it couldn't be a cat and have *none* of them; and doubtless some features count more heavily than others. The more of them there are (particularly the ones that count most heavily), the more we are inclined to call something a cat. But now suppose that, in the presence of numerous witnesses as well as recording machines, the creature uttered a few lines of English poetry. What would we do then? Would we still call it a cat, or would we say it was a human being that *looked* like a cat? Or what if, before our eyes, it suddenly expanded to a hundred times its normal size?

. . . Or if it showed some queer behavior usually not to be found with cats, say, if, under certain conditions, it could be revived from death whereas normal cats could not? Shall I, in such a case, say that a new species has come into being? Or that it was a cat with extraordinary properties?

Again, suppose I say "There is my friend over there." What if on drawing closer in order to shake hands with him he suddenly disappeared? "Therefore it was not my friend but some delusion or other." But suppose a few seconds later I saw him again, could grasp his hand, etc. What then? "Therefore my friend was nevertheless there and his disappearance was some delusion or other." But imagine after a while he disappeared again, or seemed to disappear —what shall I say now? Have we rules ready for all imaginable possibilities? . . .

Suppose I come across a being that looks like a man, speaks like a man, behaves like a man, and is only one span tall—shall I say it *is* a man? Or what about the case of a person who is so old as to remember King Darius? Would you say he is an immortal? Is there anything like an exhaustive definition that finally and once for all sets our mind at rest? "But are there not exact definitions at least in science?" Let's see. The notion of gold seems to be defined with absolute precision, say by the spectrum of gold with its characteristic lines. Now what would you say if a substance was discovered that looked like gold, satisfied all the chemical tests for gold, whilst it emitted a new sort of radiation? "But such things do not happen." Quite so; but they *might* happen, and that is enough to show that we can never exclude altogether the possibility of some unforeseen situation arising in which we shall have to modify our definition.[21]

---

[21] Friedrich Waismann, "Verifiability," in *Logic and Language,* First Series, ed. Antony Flew (Oxford: Blackwell, 1953), pp. 119–20.

The point is that we cannot foresee all the possible circumstances which, *if* they arose, would lead us to doubt whether or not the word should be applied to the thing in question. No matter how clear we may think we are in our use of the word, situations could be imagined in which we simply would not know what to say. We can try to block off doubt in certain directions by saying, "Well, if it did *that,* it wouldn't be a cat," but then what of countless other directions that we have never thought of?

Try as we may, no concept is limited in such a way that there is no room for any doubt. We introduce a concept and limit it in *some* directions; for instance, we define gold in contrast to some other metals such as alloys. This suffices for our present needs, and we do not probe any farther. We tend to *overlook* the fact that there are always other directions in which the concept has not been defined. And if we did, we could easily imagine conditions which would necessitate new limitations. In short, it is not possible to define a concept like gold with absolute precision—i.e. in such a way that every nook and cranny is blocked against entry of doubt.[22]

Are all words imprecise in this way? No, but probably most of them are. Many words in mathematics (including geometry) are defined with absolute precision, such as "triangle," "plus," and "cosine." We know exactly when to apply these terms and when not to, without any penumbrae of doubt arising from unexpected or unthought-of situations. It is a triangle if it fulfills all the three conditions, and if it doesn't it isn't, and that's that. But virtually all the words we use in daily life, at least those we use to talk about things and processes and activities in the world, lack this precision.

3. *Vagueness in the words by which we define.* One final aspect of the subject of vagueness must still be drawn to our attention. Let us examine a word that is vague on one or more counts already discussed, and then show how it is vague in still another way. Consider the term "inhabitant."

Under what conditions is a person to be counted an inhabitant of a community? It is clear that a person who resides and works within the boundaries of a community is an inhabitant; and it is clear that one who has never set foot within it is not an inhabitant. But what if he owns a residence in the community that he occupies only in the summer, renting it out and living elsewhere the rest of the year? What if he attends college in the community, living in a dormitory while the college is in session but living outside the community while the college is not in session? What if he is living and working in the community for a fixed two-year period, but owns a home in another community which contains most of his belongings and to which he plans to return after this assignment is complete? Is he an inhabitant of the community during this two-year period?[23]

[22] *Ibid.,* p. 120.
[23] William P. Alston, *Philosophy of Language,* p. 90.

But now suppose that we have settled all these problems by stipulation of new and more precise meanings. Even after this is done, another problem arises:

Even if we could decide just which combination of conditions was necessary and sufficient for the application of the term "inhabitant," the *terms in which these conditions are stated are themselves more or less vague.* For example, we made use of the term "works in the community." No doubt, there are many cases in which the applicability or inapplicability of this term is unproblematic, but there are problematic cases as well. What of a salesman, the home office of whose company is in the community, but who, by the nature of his work, spends most of his working hours elsewhere? Or, conversely, what of a man whose employer is elsewhere but who spends most of his working hours in the community in question, as a consultant or lobbyist? And what of a writer who happens to do most of his writing within the boundaries of the community? Does he "work in the community"? The term "occupies a home" is also subject to vagueness. If a person owns several houses, does not rent any of them to others, and spends part of his time in each, does he occupy all of them or one or more of them? And so it goes.[24]

The point is this: When we define words by using other words—as we do in all except ostensive definition—these other words are usually vague themselves. We can define "X" in terms of characteristics A, B, and C, but it may not be clear what exactly constitutes the possession of characteristics A, B, and C. A dog is a mammal of a certain kind—but what exactly is a mammal? A mammal has four legs—but what exactly is a leg? (Is it a leg if it is microscopically small? if the creature can't walk on it? if it looks like the things we call legs but protrudes from the top or side of the body? if its circumference is more than twenty times its length? and so on.) A dragon is a fire-breathing serpent—but when exactly is something on fire (what of possible cases in which some of the characteristics of fire are present but not others?), when can it be said to breathe (many borderline possibilities here), and when is it a serpent? Killing is taking a life—but when exactly is a life being taken? When you leave a person to die of exposure, not shooting or poisoning him but just letting him lie there as you found him, can you be said to have killed him? If you drive your wife to suicide, is that killing? If a pedestrian dies because you didn't stop your car in time, and you didn't stop in time because the brakes unexpectedly didn't work, is that killing? And so on. The same vagueness that we find in the original term is likely to crop up again in the terms we use in defining it. Every time you think you have an airtight rule for applying word "X," it may turn out that the very constituents of the rule are not airtight themselves; the plugs that have been put in to fill the gaps have to be filled themselves.

[24] *Ibid.*, p. 91. Italics mine. The word "community" itself is similarly vague; see p. 90.

All these aspects of vagueness characterize the way in which any living language is built. As long as words are defined by means of other (previous) imprecise words, and those in turn by others, there is no alternative. These words rest in turn on ostensive definitions, but ostensive definitions are also imprecise: they point out *instances* of the application of a word, but no amount of ostensive definition will tell us what the exact boundary-lines are, particularly when the vagueness occurs in many directions at once. Mathematical terms are the least subject to vagueness; and second, perhaps, the words devised for special purposes in the various sciences. But even here, as we have seen, considerable vagueness appears. The only way to avoid this difficulty would be to invent an artificial language and not use a "natural language" like English at all. In an artificial language we would start with a few words left undefined ("primitive terms"), and then would define others entirely in terms of these, and so on, being sure at each stage not to use any words that had not been explicitly defined before by means of the primitive terms. But however amusing a game such an artificial language might be, it would be of little help in the analyses of meanings in a living language—and it is precisely the words in a living language that give rise to the problems we discuss in philosophy, as well as in most other disciplines.

Exercises

1. Do you consider the following words to be vague? If so, in what respect(s)? Happy; above; 3; east; salary; run; impatient; and; solid; shout; plus; drink.

2. Try to analyze the vagueness of the word "hat" along lines similar to those in "dog," pp. 70–71. Can you think of any characteristics that have to be present in order for something to count as a hat? Is anything worn on the head (or designed to be worn on the head) a hat? If not, what distinguishes hats from other things such as caps and turbans? Is there a cluster of hat-like characteristics? Can you define "hat" in such a way as to include those things we call hats but exclude other headgear to which we do not apply the word "hat"?

3. Are there multiple criteria for the use of the following words? Which of the five features described on pp. 71–72 holds true of them? Cat; chair; living organism; inhabitant; leg; nervous; box; boat; curtain; poem.

4. The following characteristics are all associated with the word "religion." Which of them, if any, do you consider essential (defining)? Which can be dispensed with as long as the others are present? Which ones have greater weight than others in counting toward being a religion? Which combination(s) would, in your view, constitute a quorum sufficient to entitle one to use the word? (The list is taken from William P. Alston, *Philosophy of Language*, p. 88.)

    a. Beliefs in supernatural beings (gods).
    b. A distinction between sacred and profane objects.
    c. Ritual acts focused around sacred objects.
    d. A moral code believed to be sanctioned by the gods.

e. Characteristically religious feelings (awe, sense of mystery, sense of guilt, adoration, etc.), which tend to be aroused in the presence of sacred objects and during the practice of ritual, and which are associated with the gods.

f. Prayer and other forms of communication with gods.

g. A world view, that is, a general picture of the world as a whole and of the place of the individual in it, including a specification of its over-all significance.

h. A more or less total organization of one's life based on the world view.

i. A social organization bound together by the preceding characteristics.

5. "When we are trying to bring out the meaning of an expression as it actually is rather than polish it up, what we need is another expression that matches as exactly as possible the vagueness of the former. Thus, in defining "adolescence" as *the period of life between childhood and adulthood,* we presumably have a good match. For the indeterminancy of the boundaries of adolescence is just the same as that which attaches to the upper boundary of childhood and the lower boundary of adulthood." Can you think of other examples of definitions of vague words being satisfactory because of the use of words in the definition which are equally vague? (See Alston, *Philosophy of Language,* p. 95.)

4. Sentence-meaning

Up to this point we have been considering the meaning of words and phrases. But ordinarily we do not utter isolated words or phrases—we utter whole sentences. Every sentence must be composed of words (which have, by definition, a meaning, else they would not be words); but not every string of words is a sentence. Word-meaning does not guarantee sentence-meaning. The meaning of a sentence has to do with the use to which certain strings of words are put. One of the main uses of expressions which are composed of words is to make *assertions;* but there are also other ways in which sentences are used. A number of new considerations will now concern us as we discuss sentence-meaning.

We shall leave to grammarians the difficult task of giving an exact definition of "sentence," except to say that a sentence must contain at least a subject and a verb. Thus "The sun rose" is a sentence, but "Because thoroughly run" is not (of course it may be an elliptical way of expressing a complete sentence). A string of nonsense-syllables lacks both word-meaning and sentence-meaning: "Reth mambol selehu"; and a string of words may have word-meaning but lack sentence-meaning: "Run very eat and." ("Pirots carulize elatically" sounds like a sentence, for "-ize" is a verb-suffix and "-ly" an adverbial suffix; but until these three noises are given a meaning, we must still consider them nonsense-syllables.) We shall not have to concern ourselves with these; our main concern will be to discover the conditions of sentence-meaning, so as to distinguish meaningful sentences from meaningless ones—but they must first *be* sentences, and this requires that they be composed of words, not mere noises.

Propositions.   We shall have to make one distinction at the outset—between sentences and propositions. A sentence, like a word, has a meaning: a sentence is not merely a string of marks on paper or a series of noises but is either or both of these things *with* a meaning. But when we talk about a proposition, we are talking not about the sentence itself but about what the sentence means. Two or more sentences can be used to express the same proposition—that is, the same meaning. "New York is larger than San Francisco" and "San Francisco is smaller than New York" are two different sentences, and they are quite different from one another: for example, the first sentence contains the word "larger" but the second one does not; the first sentence begins with the letter 'n', but the second does not, and so on. Yet they state, or express, the same proposition. They both give the same information; they both assert the existence of the same state-of-affairs. If you believe that the first sentence expresses a truth, you are committed to believing that the second one does so also; and if someone said, "I'll give you two bits of information: New York is larger than San Francisco, and San Francisco is smaller than New York," we would say that he was giving us not two pieces of information but one. The reverse also occurs: the same sentence can be used to express different propositions, when the sentence is ambiguous. "He rents the house" could mean that he rents it *to* someone or that he rents it *from* someone—two different meanings, but one sentence.

It is the proposition that is true or false, but the sentence that has meaning or fails to have it. A sentence is only a vehicle of meaning, and only when we know what that meaning is can we know whether the proposition it expresses is true or false. A proposition has, indeed, often been defined as "anything that is true or false."

The word "proposition" is used in philosophy in a special sense, not the popular sense in which we say "I have a proposition to put to you." Many pages could be spent—and largely wasted—in discussing propositions: we could ask questions such as "Are propositions temporal or non-temporal entities?" and "Do propositions exist before anyone states them in a sentence?" and "What are propositions apart from their expression in sentences?" So many questions arise here that many students of the subject have been led to abandon the use of the term "proposition" entirely and speak only of sentences and classes of sentences. Yet the distinction is useful, for it marks an important difference: between the sentence itself (as it would be studied by grammarians) and the meaning that it conveys. Philosophers are concerned with sentences only insofar as they are carriers of meaning; the analysis of sentences (and the words they contain), together with their history, origin, and relations, is the concern of linguists, philologists, etymologists. Our only concern with sentences in philosophy is simply that in order to state propositions we must use sentences. There are non-linguistic substitutes for sentences, as, for instance, when I tell a friend that I am going to pull a handkerchief out of my coat-pocket during a party to indicate that I'm going to leave within the next ten minutes. But such a signal has to be arranged in advance, and I have to use language in order to explain what proposition the signal is to express.

We shall have to use the technical term "proposition" quite often in our inquiry. Sometimes we shall employ the more usual word, "statement," which can mean either the proposition expressed or the sentence expressing it. In many cases it is clear from the context which of these is meant. But in many cases the distinction is important to avoid confusion, and then we shall employ the more precise language of "sentences" and "propositions."

Nonassertive sentences.   Propositions, we have said, are true or false. But not every sentence states a proposition. Only sentences that we use to *assert* something express propositions.[25] But there are many other things we do with sentences: we command, we suggest, we ask questions, we exclaim. If you said "Shut the door!" and I said "Yes, that's true," or if you said "What time is it?" and I replied, "No," it would be obvious that I was not understanding the meaning of your utterance. Here, then, are the principal non-assertive functions of sentences: (1) *Questions.* "What time is it?" asserts nothing, and hence is neither true nor false; yet we all know what it means well enough to know how to answer it. (2) *Imperatives.* "Shut the door!" is not true or false; it asserts nothing; rather it commands. ("I have just shut the door," however, is an assertion, and it must be either true or false.) Milder imperatives which are not commands but rather suggestions, such as "Let's leave the room," assert nothing and thus are neither true nor false. They may, however, imply (in the sense of "presuppose") propositions. If I say, "Stop talking!" you may reply, "But I wasn't talking!" (3) *Exclamations.* "Oh!" and "What a day!" are not usually considered sentences at all; at any rate, they express no propositions. Some exclamatory sentences, however, in addition to exclaiming, *imply* propositions. When you exclaim, "What a sunny day it is!" you are implying a proposition, namely that it is a sunny day, and this, of course, is either true or false. Someone might reply, "Why, that's not true, it's not a sunny day at all," thus showing that he interpreted your sentence to assert something. In every case the test to apply is "Is the answer 'That's true' or 'That's false' appropriate?" One and the same sentence uttering an exclamation might be intended to assert, when uttered by one speaker, and intended merely to

[25] Not every writer on the subject slices the distinctions in the same way. For example, according to Professor C. I. Lewis, a proposition is a real or alleged state-of-affairs, such as Mary-baking-pies; next, there are various things we can *do* with this proposition: we can assert it ("Mary is baking pies"), deny it ("Mary isn't baking pies"), question it ("Is Mary baking pies?"), suggest ("Please bake some pies, Mary"), command ("Mary, bake pies!"), and so on. All of these are meaningful as long as the core-proposition is: Mary-baking-pies is meaningful; Saturday-being-in-bed is not. See C. I. Lewis, *Analysis of Knowledge and Evaluation*, pp. 48–55.

exclaim and not assert at all, when uttered by another speaker. "What a horse!" may be intended merely to let off steam, but more probably it is intended not only to do this but to assert that this creature is, in the opinion of the speaker, a fine horse.

We shall be primarily concerned with the meaning of sentences that are assertive, such as "There is a mouse in the closet." But our inquiry into the conditions in which sentences are meaningful could easily be extended to cover nonassertive sentences. Thus if the assertion "There is a mouse in the closet" is meaningful (as it is), the corresponding question "Is there a mouse in the closet?" would also be meaningful; and if the assertion is meaningless, such as "Saturday is in bed," the corresponding question "Is Saturday in bed?" is also meaningless.

Word-meaning and sentence-meaning.   Many of the points about word-meaning that we have already discussed are applicable also to sentence-meaning. Just as words can be ambiguous, so sentences too can be ambiguous. A sentence may be ambiguous because it contains an ambiguous word (for that single word, such as "rent," makes the sentence liable to being taken in more than one way); but it can also be ambiguous even if the words it contains are not: not only the individual words, but the *order* in which they occur in the sentence, can make the sentence capable of carrying more than one meaning. "Mary wanted to hear the famous soprano sing very badly" could mean that she wanted badly to hear the soprano sing, or that she wanted the soprano to sing poorly. "Two minutes after Mrs. Smith christened the ship, she was afloat on the river" does not make clear whether it is Mrs. Smith or the ship that is afloat. The kind of ambiguity that depends on word order and can be corrected by changing that order is called *syntactical* ambiguity, as opposed to *semantic* ambiguity (which we have already discussed), in which a single word or phrase has more than one meaning.

Sentences, like words, can also be *vague*. Again, a single vague word is enough to render vague the entire sentence in which it occurs ("bald" is vague, having no clear cutoff point, and consequently "Jones is bald" is vague). But sentences also have a vagueness of their own that is not merely a function of word-vagueness.

If someone says, "We must take steps to meet this emergency," or if an advertisement reads, "It's the hidden quality that spells true value," people are likely to respond with, "That's a very vague statement" or "Can't you be less vague?" . . . It is not that the word "steps" is vague in that there are cases when it is not clear whether something should or should not be called a step; and it is not that there are cases where it can't be decided whether something is or is not a quality or is or is not hidden. (I am not denying that the words "steps," "hidden," and "quality" are vague to some extent. I am saying that it is not the vagueness that attaches to these words that is primarily responsible for the insufficient determinateness of these statements.) The trouble lies in lack of specificity, in simply using the very general term "steps" instead of spelling out some specific steps, and in using the very general term "quality" instead of saying specifically which quality.[26]

Sentences, as well as words and phrases, have what we have called "secondary meaning." Sentences have indeed far more suggestive and associative power than individual words and phrases do. If you say, "They had children and got married," this *suggests* (but does not state) that they had the children before they were married; but since this is only suggested by the way in which the sentence is phrased, it is doubtful whether a libel suit based on this allegedly insulting remark would be successful.

The suggestion is part of the full meaning of the sentence, but its presence is not felt to be as central or as basic as the primary meaning, on which it nevertheless depends. That is why I call it "secondary meaning." It is usually less emphatic, less obtrusive, less definitely and precisely fixed than the primary meaning, but it may be no less important, even from a practical point of view. What a sentence suggests it says implicitly, rather than explicitly, in the form of insinuation, innuendo, hint, or implication. The difference between "Mrs. Smith is prettier than Mrs. Jones" and "Mrs. Jones is uglier than Mrs. Smith" is a difference of suggestion. If either is precisely correct, the other is misleading. But, "On a scale of beauty, Mrs. Smith would rank somewhat higher than Mrs. Jones, and both would rank very high" approaches scientific language. It may be false, but it cannot be misleading, and therefore suggests nothing.[27]

Criteria for sentence-meaning.   When does a sentence have meaning? If a sentence is meaningless, it cannot express any proposition at all, true *or* false; if there is no meaning, there is not anything that could be true or false. The distinction between the false and the meaningless is important (falsity presupposes meaningfulness), and people often confuse the one with the other. If one philosopher condemns the theories of another philosopher as false, he is paying him one considerable compliment, that they have meaning and that he knows what they mean (otherwise how could he say they are false?). A far more serious condemnation of them would be that they are meaningless—a charge that is often made in philosophy—and if they are really meaningless, the question of truth or falsity does not even arise. "There are intelligent beings on other galaxies" may be false, but it is certainly meaningful, whereas "Saturday is in bed" is neither true nor false but meaningless.

This leads us to our final problem in this chapter: Under what conditions can a sentence be said to be meaningful (or have meaning)? There are clear cases of meaningful sentences that we utter every day, whose meaning we know well enough, such as

[26] William P. Alston, *Philosophy of Language,* p. 85.
[27] Monroe C. Beardsley, *Aesthetics,* pp. 123–124.

He is sitting on a chair.
Mars has two moons.
Some dogs are white.
Isosceles triangles have two equal sides.
Reptiles can't hear.
Los Angeles covers a larger area than New York City.
The curtains in your room are dirty.

But there are other ones, which are sentences in the grammatical sense at least (they all use words, and they seem to say something about something—they obey the rules of grammar), but to which, if they were uttered, we would respond by saying "That's meaningless!"

Green ideas sleep furiously.
Seven is blue.
He stood between the post.
Quadruplicity drinks procrastination.
Books drink kittens.
Your watch is above the universe.
Refrigerators respond adverbially.
The square root of -1 is blue.

What is it about these that inclines us to say that these sentences are meaningless? If we said merely, "It's false that green ideas sleep furiously," we would be doing the sentence too much honor—if it is false it must at least be meaningful, and what does a sentence like this mean? If you said it was false, you would invite the reply, "You mean they sleep calmly? Or perhaps it is red ideas that sleep furiously?" We don't know what it would be for red ideas to sleep furiously any more than for green ideas to do so, or for either to sleep furiously rather than in any other way—indeed for them to sleep at all; what would *any* of these sentences mean? "None of them make any sense," we would be inclined to say.

But why don't they? This is not an easy question to answer, and a full discussion of this question alone could take hundreds of pages. Many philosophers sharply disagree about what makes a sentence meaningful. Not only do they disagree about the designation of "meaningless" (the characteristics a sentence must have to be meaningless) but about the denotation as well (there are examples that some philosophers would say are meaningless that others would say are meaningful but false). For example, with regard to theological statements like "God exists," "God created the world," "God influences the course of our lives," and "God is three in one," there are some who would say they are all meaningless, others who would say they are meaningful but false, and still others who would say they are meaningful and true—and often for very different reasons. In what remains of this chapter we can give only a few preliminary remarks, and shall treat the subject anew as it arises in different contexts.

1. Imaginability. How do we tell whether a sentence is meaningful? One possible answer is that we must be able to imagine what the situation is that the sentence is being used to describe: "I know that snow isn't pink, but I can easily *imagine* pink snow, so talking about pink snow is meaningful even though it's not true that there is such a thing"; "There are no unicorns, but we can easily imagine horses with horns in the middle of their foreheads, so it is certainly meaningful to talk about them." But what if we are unable to imagine it? Is it then meaningless? We seem to understand very well what is meant by the phrase "a million-sided polygon," but it is doubtful whether any human being can form an image of a polygon with a million sides. If you say you can, how is your image of a million-sided polygon different from your image of a million-and-one-sided polygon? Again, we understand what is meant by "The United States national debt is almost $400 billion" (at any rate, economists claim to do so), but can we imagine a debt of this magnitude? Imagining a large number of million-dollar bills would not be enough, for it would not convey the idea of a debt. There are many sentences of whose meaning we can form no images at all, because what is being talked about is not sensory items like sights, smells, and sounds but abstractions. If someone says, "Honesty is a desirable trait," what are we imagining? And whatever we do imagine (such as an honest person we know), is *this* the meaning of the sentence? Each of us may imagine many things, and some of us nothing at all; does this make any difference to knowing the meaning? We have already noted (pp. 49–50) that what we imagine has to do with the effects of an utterance upon its hearers, not with what the utterance means. Besides, this criterion if accepted would be extremely subjective, for some people have better powers of imagination than others.

2. Describability. "The sentence is meaningful if one can describe a situation (or situations) that will exemplify it—that is, count as an example of it." For example, if I say "Ectomorphs are mendacious," I can explain to you in other words, by using synonyms and definitions of the key terms, what I mean by this sentence. Description in other words is helpful when you do not know the meanings of the words in the original sentence but do know the meanings of the words in my explanation or translation.

But this is not always possible. Suppose I say, "I am in a state of intellectual excitement," and my hearer does not understand because he has never been in a state of intellectual excitement. Now what can I do to describe the situation I am talking about? When I have reached certain key terms that are only ostensively definable, if my hearer has never had the experience to which these terms refer, there is nothing I can do unless perchance I can induce the experience (as I normally can in the case of simple color-words like "green"). Sometimes I cannot describe the situation in any other words, since there are no other words, not even roughly synonymous ones, by means of which to do so—and even if there were, my hearer would not know the meanings of these synonymous terms either.

More serious still, it is difficult to see how the criterion could be kept from being so permissive as to include all sentences, even meaningless ones. If you say to me, "Describe to me the situation you have in mind when you say, 'Water flows uphill,' " I might simply reply, "Water flowing uphill would be that situation." In this case the sentence is meaningful enough; the proposition it expresses just happens to be false, since water does not flow uphill. But now what if you say, "Saturday is in bed," and I say "That's meaningless! Please describe to me the situation you are talking about when you say that," you may reply, "Well, Saturday being in bed would be the best description I can think of."

It is impossible to specify the meaning of an assertion otherwise than by describing the state-of-affairs that must obtain if the assertion is to be true." To take only one example, . . . "Caesar crossed the Rubicon." In the instance of this sentence we can all doubtless describe the state-of-affairs that must be obtained if the sentence is true. Presumably what is here wanted as a description of the state-of-affairs is not the sentence "Caesar crossed the Rubicon," though this sentence describes the state-of-affairs in question adequately, but rather some other sentence which uses a different set of words but describes the same state-of-affairs. We may offer the sentence "Caesar went from one bank of the Rubicon to the other" as a description of the state-of-affairs that must have obtained if and only if Caesar crossed the Rubicon. . . . The criterion of significance amounts to the assertion that a sentence is significant (meaningful) if it is possible to formulate another sentence which is synonymous with the given sentence.[28]

Moreover, this second sentence itself would have to be meaningful—and by what criterion? If you said, "Saturday is in bed," and I said, "I don't understand you; describe it in other words, please," what would I say if you answered, "The day after Friday is in bed"?

3. *Truth-conditions.*   "You know what it means if you can tell me *under what conditions* the statement would be true. It needn't be true, of course; it may be false. But if you can tell me what the conditions are under which the statement *would* be true, then I will grant that it is meaningful." But one might reply: "Well, you know what the conditions are which would make 'Water flows uphill' true, don't you? If you saw water flowing uphill, you would say that the statement is true; and even if you never saw it, you know what the conditions *are* which, *if* they existed, would make the statement true (its truth-conditions). Very well; you ask what I mean by 'Saturday is in bed.' I can't describe it to you in *other* words, but I can say that Saturday being in bed would be the condition under which one can say that the statement 'Saturday is in bed' is true."

"State the conditions under which you would call the statement true (even

---

[28] Paul Marhenke, "The Criterion of Significance," in Leonard Linsky (ed.), *Semantics and the Philosophy of Language*, p. 150.

if it isn't true)"—this sounds promising indeed as a candidate for the criterion of a sentence's meaningfulness. But the same difficulty vitiates it that destroyed the previous one: no matter what the sentence is, the person could utter the same sentence over again and say that the occurrence of *that* alleged situation would be what makes the statement true. (Saturday being in bed would be the condition under which "Saturday is in bed" is true.) And then what could we do? This criterion would admit everything whatever, and hence would be useless as a means of distinguishing the meaningful from the meaningless.

4. *"Knowing what it's like."*   "I may not know what you mean when you say 'Saturday is in bed' or 'The square root of −1 died yesterday,' but I'm willing to admit that these sentences are meaningful, even if I can't *imagine* the situations you refer to, if you can tell me *what it would be like* for them to be true. They needn't be true, of course; you yourself say they are false; but even if they are false, I want to know what it would be like for them to be true. 'Snow is pink' is false, but I know what it would be like for it to be true, and if I saw pink snow I would say that it *is* true. 'Elephants fly' is false, yet I know perfectly well what it would be like for it to be true—not just because I can imagine it (though in this case I can), but because I know what would have to happen in order for the statement to be true. But when you say 'Saturday is in bed,' I don't even know what it's like—what situation would have to occur or exist in the world which, if it occurred or existed, would make the statement true. Tell me what it would be like, and I'll admit that it's meaningful."

Now, "tell me what it's like" is perilously close to "describe it." What if you have no other words for it at all? And what if there *are* no other words even roughly synonymous in our language? How then can you tell me what it's like?

Besides, what if it's like nothing else whatever? What if it is so different from everything else that nothing I can tell you would give you an idea of it? True, everything in the world is like everything else in *some* way or other: a fly, a table, running, fortitude, and being above—all are alike in that they characterize some feature of the world. But this isn't much help; if you tell me what a situation is *like,* it must be like enough to something I already am acquainted with to give me some conception of what you mean. "The taste of a lemon? Well, it's like that of a *very* sour orange." But now what of "Saturday being in bed? Well, it's rather like Friday being in bed, although of course it is somewhat different too, since it's a different day"?

These candidates for the position of criterion-of-meaningfulness have not gotten us very far. Let us now discuss some which, though they do not attempt to take care of *all* cases of meaninglessness, are extremely useful in attempting to eliminate some.

5. *Meaninglessness outside a given context.*   Words are usually learned within the context in which they are properly used, and they have meaning

only within that context. Consequently it (and with it the sentence in which it occurs) is meaningless if the word is used outside that context. For example, the word "above"—taken in its literal sense, not in some figurative sense such as "I'm above such paltry considerations"—ordinarily means "higher than." The chandelier is above the table; that is, it is higher than the table is. And "higher than"—again, in its literal sense, not in a figurative sense such as "Today's speech reached higher levels of eloquence than yesterday's"—means farther from the center (more accurately: center of gravity) of some gravitational body, which in the case of earth-dwellers means the center of the earth. The satellite is higher than the balloon, because it is farther from the center of the earth than the balloon is. Now, *in this context,* "above" and "higher than" have a clear meaning, having to do with the spatial relations of objects to one another. Of course, if we lived on Mars, then "up" and "down," "above" and "below," "higher than" and "lower than" would have reference to the center of Mars and not to that of the earth. We can still speak of the moon as above the earth, because the moon revolves around the earth; and because it revolves at an average distance of 240,000 miles, we can say it is considerably higher above the earth than are most of the objects we talk about. But what would it mean to say that Mars is above the earth? (When we see Mars in the night sky, we do sometimes say that it and the stars are all above the earth, but this is far from accurate: Mars isn't above the *whole* earth, including our antipodes. What we should say in this situation is that Mars *appears to be* above the *portion of the earth's surface* on which we are standing.)

But now suppose that we are in the midst of outer space, midway between Mars and the earth: are we above the earth or above Mars? Even here one might say, "We're above them both; we are 18 million miles from the center of the earth, and an equal distance from the center of Mars." We might even say, "We're very *high up.*" But in reference to what? We are now losing the context in which the words were defined (given meaning) in the first place: an astronaut who was nearing Mars would do better to say "I'm now 200,000 miles above Mars" than to say "I'm 35½ million miles above the earth." Mars has now become his center of reference, not the earth.

And now if we imagine ourselves in a space-ship many light-years away from the solar system, and not near any other star or solar system, "above" and "below" have lost their meaning entirely. These terms have meaning only with reference to some body, usually a body, such as the earth, large enough to exert a considerable gravitational attraction; apart from reference to such a body, they have no meaning at all. Half a million light-years away from our galaxy, it would be meaningless to say that we were above the earth or below it.

Now suppose someone said, "This object is above the universe" (still taking the word "above" literally). This would be meaningless: "above" is a spatial term, and has meaning only when we are talking about the relation of bodies in space; and if the universe includes all space, how could anything be above it? Even more obvious would be these examples: "This object is above time": how could a spatial relation, such as being above, characterize something that is not spatial at all? "This object is above the number 2": but numbers are abstract entities that do not exist in space at all (what would it mean to say, "You'll find the number 2 on Jupiter"?)—but of course it could be above the *numeral* 2, which I might write on the blackboard; the numeral exists in space and time, and I can write many numerals at many different places and then erase them all, thus destroying these numerals but not the mathematical entity 2. The same with "above steadfastness," "above triangularity," "above aboveness." In these examples the word "above" is used outside the only context in which it has a meaning, which is a spatial context and a reference to some body considered as a reference-point. In short, the word "above" is here used meaninglessly, in that the sentence containing it is meaningless. Don't say, "Maybe it has some meaning, but a meaning we can't understand; perhaps it's too profound for us." If we say this, we forget the fundamental point that meanings are *given* to words, not *inherent* in words; "above" has a meaning—it has been given one—in the context of spatial relations, and apart from that context it has no meaning (in its literal sense). A sentence containing the word in which that context is not present, either explicitly or implicitly, is meaningless.

Or suppose we say of a certain object, O, that it is large. Now, "large" is a relative term: it means that it is *larger than* something else. A large cat is a cat that is larger than most cats; and a small elephant (though it may be larger than a large cat) is an elephant that is smaller than most elephants. Usually this reference is implicit: by "a large O" we mean an O that is larger than most objects of its kind or class. But now suppose we say of something that it is large, *without* any such reference. "That's large," I say. "Larger than what?" you ask. "Oh, nothing at all," I reply, "just large." "You mean, larger than most things? larger than most things of its type?" "No, just large, period." What could I possibly mean by this? If there were only two objects in the universe, we could say that one of them was large (larger than the other), but if there were only one object, what would it mean to say that it was large, or, for that matter, small? How could it be large if there were nothing else to compare it with? "Large" is a comparative term; its whole meaning is embedded in that context, and it becomes meaningless when used in a sentence in which that basis for comparison is lost. ("Large" is also a spatial term, and hence it is meaningless when used in non-spatial contexts, such as "This is larger than brevity," "larger than precociousness"—unless, of course, we use the word in some figurative sense, as in "Let's get a larger look at the problem.")

Suppose someone says, "He stood between the post." We say, "Don't you mean between the *posts?*" "No," he says, "between the post." "Between the post and what?" "Not between it and anything else—just between the post, period." Now we can attack him in a similar way: "between" is a preposition that has meaning (in its literal sense) only as a term of spatial relation—something is between A and B when it is on the path from A to B (though this is somewhat vague, as we shall see on pp. 174–75). But it must always be between A and *something else*. It has meaning only in that kind of context, and apart from that context it is used meaninglessly.

Finally, consider "motion." Motion, we say, is change of position. But change of position is always *with respect to* something. The train is moving—that is, it is changing its position with respect to the point on the surface of the earth from which it started (or for that matter any point on the earth's surface). But the table in this room is not moving: that is, it is not changing its position with respect to the floor on which it rests; nor is the floor, with respect to the house of which it is a part, unless we're in the midst of an earthquake; nor is the house, with respect to the earth on which it stands. In this context, it is not only meaningful but true to say that the table is not moving; and this is the context that is usually implicit in our daily discourse. But at the same time, the table, the floor, the house, and the portion of the earth on which it rests are all moving with respect to the sun, for the earth and everything on it revolve around the sun at approximately 18 miles per second. "But how can it be moving and standing still at the same time?" It is standing still with respect to the earth below it, but moving with respect to the sun. Motion is change of position with respect to something, and to know whether something is moving you have to know the reference-point implicit in the assertion. The sun itself is moving with respect to other things, carrying the solar system with it—it is revolving around the center of our galaxy (many thousands of light-years distant from the sun) at a speed of over 200 miles per second; and the same may be true of our galaxy itself, with respect to a system of galaxies or something else of which we are so far ignorant. Once a reference-point (to provide a "with respect to") is supplied, talk about motion has meaning, though of course many statements about it may be false; but without such a reference, any talk about motion is meaningless, even though the sentence in question may have a subject and a verb and be in impeccable grammatical form.

But why does a word have no meaning outside a certain context? Why does "above" have no meaning apart from reference to space, or "between" apart from reference to two other places? Is it because we haven't bothered to give it one? If this were so, we could easily remedy the deficiency by a stipulative definition simply extending the meaning of the word to cover the new cases. But this is not the source of the trouble in the examples we have considered. Of course we could always stipulate some new and entirely different meaning for the old word: we could use the word "between" so as (in its new meaning) to mean the same as "against," and then "He stood between the post" would be meaningful because it would mean the same as "He stood against the post." All this is true, but trivial. What we cannot do, however, is mean the same thing as we always have by "above" and "between," or even anything similar to it that merely extends the usage somewhat, and yet meaningfully say, "He stood above the universe" or "He stood between the post."

Similarly, "Saturday is in bed" is meaningless. We could make it meaningful by saying that "Saturday" is the name of a human being; but as long as it *is* the name of a day of the week, it would seem that "Saturday is in bed" is meaningless. But why is this? Because, it may be said, we are *mixing categories:* we are ascribing to a span of time, a day, a characteristic that does not apply to time but only to space. This leads us directly into another suggested criterion of meaningfulness.

6. Category-mistakes.   Everything we can talk about, it is said, falls into certain broad classes, or categories. Thus we can say that books are used for reading, that they contain pages and print, that they have certain sizes and weights, but not that they are numbers (for numbers are non-temporal entities, while books exist in time), or that they themselves read books (for books are inanimate objects, and reading is something applicable only to conscious beings), or that they are days of the week. It is meaningful (it is suggested) to ascribe a characteristic to something in a given category only if the characteristic also belongs in that category. Let us take a few examples of category-mistakes to see how they operate.

a. If someone claimed that he had tasted a smell or smelled a taste, he would be guilty of a category-mistake. Whatever you smell, whether it is acrid or pungent or stale, it is always a smell and not a taste. Smell-words apply to smells and taste-words to taste. True, we smell things—such as roses and ammonia—but it is the smell of it we are aware of through our sense of smell and not the taste or sight or touch. Each of our senses, according to this account, constitutes a special category, and the rule for every category in relation to every other is "no trespassing." One may think there are exceptions to this: for example, people say they see sounds when they look through an oscilloscope and see waves of various kinds when certain sounds are heard and simultaneously fed into the machine. But of course we don't see sounds in this case or in any other: we can ask about any sound, "What did it sound like?" but we cannot meaningfully ask this of the waves that we *see*. What happens is that *when* we hear a certain sound we simultaneously see a set of visual curves on the machine. But this goes no distance whatever toward saying that we see the sound itself; the sound is something we hear, and we see the sight that accompanies the sound.

b. "The number 7 is blue." This again would be a category-mistake. Numbers are not physical objects and do not have the characteristics of physical objects. Numbers are timeless entities; they have no history, no before and after; it would be meaningless to say that the number 7 came into existence yesterday or had a heart-attack today. Temporal characteristics —those that characterize things existing in time—cannot be attributed to timeless entities, or vice versa. Here are two very general and very important categories that should not be intermixed. Mixing them accounts for many cases of meaninglessness. Thus "Quadruplicity drinks procrastination" would be neither true nor false but meaningless. Quadruplicity is a characteristic, or, as philosophers often say, a property, and a property of something cannot *do* anything, such as drink. For that matter, neither can procrastination, which is a property of individuals, do anything or have anything (such as drinking) done to it; that would be another category-mistake.

c. "Quadratic equations go to horse-races." Is this true, false, or meaningless? There is a category-mistake involved here: equations are not the kind of thing that can do things in time, such as go to horse-races; quadratic equations are mathematical entities, which have no histories. You might think: "I can write a quadratic equation on a piece of paper, put the paper into my pocket, and go to the horse-race; thus the equation has had the trip along with me." But it is not the equation that you put into your pocket but a piece of paper with certain marks on it, marks that stand for the equation. Other persons may have written on other pieces of paper certain marks that also stand for the same equation. By destroying the piece of paper you would not destroy the equation but only one representation of it. Even if all such representations were destroyed, a certain portion of mathematics would not thereby be destroyed—to the great disappointment of some students. You would destroy certain marks (numerals, equals signs, etc.) but not what they stand for.

But perhaps "Quadratic equations go to horse-races" is simply false. In that case, "Quadratic equations do not go to horse-races" is true. Well, isn't it true? They don't go, do they? Haven't we just proved this? But here we should be most careful to distinguish the false from the meaningless. "I went to London yesterday" is false but surely meaningful. But is "Quadratic equations go to horse-races" meaningful? What would it be like for a quadratic equation (not marks on a piece of paper) to go to a horse-race? "What would it be like" is a criterion we have already considered, along with "Can you imagine it?" and "Under what circumstances would you say it was true?" All these criteria were found wanting in some respect, but it is well to remind ourselves that "Quadratic equations go to horse races" would not fulfill any of them, whereas "I went to London yesterday" would fulfil all of them. There is surely some difference between them. Quadratic equations just aren't the kind of things that can go to horse-races—*or fail to go,* for that matter. If "Quadratic equations go to horse-races" is meaningless, then its negative, "Quadratic equations do not go to horse-races," is meaningless also. And isn't it? If a category-mistake is made in the affirmative form of the statement, it is equally made in the negative form.

But now we come to a difficulty: what exactly is a category-mistake? How do we know when we are making one? Suppose I said, "He sprained his ankle." That will pass, whether true or false. Now "He sprained his brain." At first you will not understand me, but then you may perhaps smile and construe my statement as a strange way of saying something else, that he had overworked his brain and was tired of thinking, or something of that sort. But now suppose I said, "He sprained his liver." What would this mean? What state-of-affairs would I be reporting? Is the liver the kind of thing you can sprain? What would be the meaning of "sprain" in this context? Perhaps it will suffice to say that there is a category-mistake here. But now we close in on ever smaller categories. "He smoked a cigarette," "He drank some lemonade," "He ate a sandwich." Now suppose we change these around to read, "He smoked a sandwich," "He ate some lemonade," "He drank a cigarette." What would these mean? Are they meaningless? What is being asserted in each case? Is it a category-mistake? Do cigarettes, sandwiches, and lemonade belong to different categories? If so, they are very different from the broad categories with which we began. What two things will *not* constitute two different categories? Is "She lay on the sofa" meaningful but "She lay on the candlestick" meaningless by virtue of a category-mistake? It does not seem that we have a clear criterion for deciding when something is a category-mistake.

"Well, a category-mistake is one in which the statement is meaningless whether you affirm it or deny it." Perhaps, but let us notice that (a) here we are using the term "meaningless" to define the term "category-mistake," whereas what we began attempting was to use the idea of a category-mistake to define "meaningless"; besides, (b) if category-mistakes result in meaninglessness, it does not seem that they are the *only causes* of meaninglessness. "Pirots carulize elatically" is meaningless, but not because a category-mistake is committed.

7. *Self-contradictoriness.*   Suppose we said, "He drew a square circle," "She was naked but wore a red dress," "She lay in her bed, striding indignantly out of the room," "The room was empty but full of books." If we were speaking literally and not using the words in some new and different sense, we would be guilty of contradicting ourselves, for we would be saying of something, X, that it had one characteristic, A, and in the same breath that it had another characteristic, not-A, which was inconsistent with it. To be a cube is *not* to be a sphere; to be naked is *not* to be clothed, in a red dress or anything else; and so on. A thing could not have both of these characteristics at the same time. It is not merely that we could not *imagine* anything having these incompatible properties. This is true enough: you cannot imagine a square circle. (If you think you can, you are probably imagining a square, then a circle, then a square again, and so on, oscillating rapidly between the two images; but what you cannot imagine is a circle that is also square—a figure that is round but not round, four-sided but not four-sided. If you think you can, try to draw one.) But, as we have already seen, your failure to imagine such a thing would not by itself prove that it was meaningless. If it is

meaningless, it is so for a different reason: that the sentence describing this alleged state-of-affairs is self-contradictory.

Are self-contradictory statements meaningless? Some might say that they are not: "I do know," one might suggest, "what is meant by 'That's a square circle,' and it's because I know what it means to say this that I know it's self-contradictory. I grant you that there are no square circles—the statement is false; and even that it *has* to be false, for there couldn't be any square circles; but it isn't meaningless. Don't you know what it means? I do, and it's just because I know what it means that I can assert with confidence that it is self-contradictory."

We might reply, however, "You know what the *word* 'square' means, and also what the word 'circle' means; but I submit that you do not know what the phrase 'square circle' means, or any sentence containing this phrase. What could its meaning possibly be? It's true that the words taken *individually* have a meaning, but it doesn't follow that the words *taken in conjunction* (together) have a meaning." We know what "fall" means (it means at least going downward, though doubtless another defining characteristic should be added about the manner of going downward, since you can jump or plunge or dive, and these cases of going downward are not falling); you also know what "upward" means. But do you know what "falling upward" means? "Falling upward" is a contradiction in terms; one can fall, and one can go upward, but one can't *fall* upward. "Certainly it's self-contradictory, but it does have a meaning, else I wouldn't even be able to say that it's self-contradictory." But has it? Have the two words in conjunction a meaning? What possible state-of-affairs could be referred to by "I fell upward"? None, for there is no such possible state-of-affairs. "But," one might still contend, "this doesn't prevent the sentence from having a meaning; a sentence can mean without referring to any possible situation, just as the word 'unicorn' means without referring to any creature. 'Falling upwards' doesn't refer to anything, for it has no instances; let's even add that it could have no possible instances—and yet it has defining characteristics, doesn't it? The defining characteristics are that (a) one goes downward (b) in a certain way (not jumping or diving), and (c) one goes upwards." "But these defining characteristics are incompatible with one another." "True, but that's just the point: the sentence is self-contradictory, but it has meaning just the same."

Admittedly, self-contradictory expressions are peculiar; they are not like the cases of meaninglessness we find in "Walking very eat aha" or "The watch was above the universe." Still, one could make a case for saying that the sentences "There is a square circle" and "I fell upwards" are meaningless: their individual words have meaning, but the sentence as a whole does not. But how is one to establish this? Why insist that it's meaningless? Isn't it quite enough to say that it is self-contradictory—isn't that condemnation enough?

We shall have a great deal to say about self-contradictoriness in the coming pages, and most of it will have to wait until we have made some important other distinctions. But several points already can be clearly stated. If self-contradictory statements are meaningless, they are not the *only* meaningless ones, for many other sentences, like "Quadruplicity drinks procrastination," seem to be utterly meaningless for reasons having nothing to do with self-contradictoriness. We might say that such sentences are not even clear enough to enable us to say whether they are self-contradictory or not—we have no idea what they could possibly mean. Moreover, in the case of most meaningless sentences, they are equally meaningless *whether you assert them or deny them:* if "Saturday is in bed" is meaningless, so is "Saturday is not in bed." If you don't know what is being asserted in the first, you don't know what is being denied in the second. But if you say "Squares are four-sided," this is obviously true, whereas the denial of it—"Squares are *not* four-sided"—is self-contradictory.[29] It is a peculiar kind of sentence that is meaningful in its affirmative form but meaningless in its negative form! Self-contradictoriness, it would seem, is different from the other cases. When we come across such statements, we shall call them simply "self-contradictory," and not go on to call them "meaningless," for to do so would be to run the risk of confusing them with sentences that *are* meaningless, or are meaningless for different reasons.

   8. Untranslatable metaphors. Another sticky issue involving the distinction between meaningful and meaningless arises when we consider *metaphorical* use of language. To define "metaphor" precisely would take many pages, and many writers on the subject have given radically different accounts of what it is for a linguistic expression to be a metaphor.[30] Let us rather begin with an example of what everyone would agree to be a metaphor (for here again, people agree on the denotations of the term more than on the designation), and see what problems arise about meaning. The poet Dylan Thomas wrote

> The force that through the green fuse drives the flower
> Drives my green age.

"That's meaningless!" a literalist might say. "How can flowers be driven? How can fuses do it? How can ages be driven? And how can they be green?" Much poetry will turn out to be meaningless if we respond in this way to it. But such passages do have meaning, or so at least every teacher of literature

---

[29] To put the issue more clearly, in terms that will be developed in Chapter 3: "Squares are four-sided" is analytic, and its negation, "Squares are not four-sided," is self-contradictory. But "Saturday is in bed" is neither analytic nor self-contradictory.

[30] For example: Paul Henle, "Metaphor," in *Language, Thought, and Culture* (Ann Arbor, Mich.: University of Michigan Press, 1958); Max Black, "Metaphor," in *Proceedings of the Aristotelian Society,* 1954–55; Monroe C. Beardsley, *Aesthetics,* pp. 134–44; William Alston, *Philosophy of Language,* pp. 96–106; Isabel Hungerland, *Poetic Discourse* (Berkeley: University of California Press, 1958), Chapter 4.

would insist, and they can be translated into literal sentences (paraphrased), such as "The same forces that operate in the development of a flower are operating in my own growth." Well, if this is its meaning, why not just state it? Because

> . . . the literal sentence appears to be nothing more than a slightly silly version of what is for the twentieth-century reader a familiar and obvious fact, namely, that the laws of physics and chemistry apply to men as well as to non-human things. The statement in Thomas' poem blocks the kind of routine and inactive reading we give to the platitudinous, and starts in us complicated processes of thought and appraisal which are skillfully shaped, and controlled by the rest of the poem.[31]

To call a stem a "fuse" is to call attention to the explosive quality of plants growing in the springtime; and to call an age "green" is to point up the relation of greenness to immaturity and youth: green things are still growing, not yet ripe. The "secondary meanings" of these terms are skillfully and forcefully used to shock us into a kind of awareness we would not have if we used the literal sentences.

Notice that the metaphor operates by *similarity:* if we could discern no connection between greenness and immaturity, we would not know what to make of the phrase "green age" and would be likely to dismiss it as meaningless. But it is a similarity that may not have occurred to us before, and a poet who uses metaphor extensively is one who enables us to discern likeness or similarity in apparently unlike or dissimilar things; and by doing so he heightens our perception of the world around us. Metaphor is far from being a mere "emotive adornment" of language; it can, in just a few words, point up a surprising similarity between apparently unlike things.

Let us observe also that a metaphor goes beyond any established usage of a word. "Viewless winds" is not an established usage, and one would be at a loss to discover its meaning by looking up "viewless" or "winds" in a dictionary. We see the meaning of a metaphorical expression when we see the similarity of the meaning in the metaphorical usage to the meaning in the literal usage, but metaphors are *extensions* of this usage, and the point of the extension is often very difficult to discern. Metaphorical usage of language is thus included in, but narrower than, figurative usage (which we discussed on pp. 15–16) such as "leg of a table," "in the back of his mind," "going to pieces" (said of a person), and "passing the buck." All these are figurative (non-literal) usages, but they are well established in our language and can be found in any unabridged dictionary. Some of them are what we call "dead metaphors": they once were not established usages but became so.

[31] Isabel Hungerland, *Poetic Discourse,* p. 127.

Consider such phrases as "fork in the road," "leg of a table," "leaf of a book," "stem of a glass," and "eyelids." In the present state of the language, the word "fork" has as established a sense in this phrase as it does in the phrase "knife and fork." But we can well imagine that at an earlier time, when the word was regularly applied only to the eating and cooking implement, people would use the word metaphorically in speaking of a place in which a road divided into two parts, each of which continues in roughly the same direction but making an acute angle with the line of direction of the original road. This use then "caught on," and because new generations could learn to apply the term directly to situations of this sort without needing to go through the older use, the sense in which the word is applied to roads came to be one of the established senses of the term. This example illustrates the very important role of metaphor in initiating uses of words that can eventually grow into new senses.[32]

Consider the sentence "He is a fox." Taken literally, this statement is self-contradictory if the "he" referred to is a human being—for one would be saying that a human being (two-legged) is a fox (four-legged), which is a contradiction in terms. Nevertheless, the statement is not self-contradictory, for one is saying something about him, that he has the characteristics (or some of the characteristics) of foxes—or at any rate traditionally imputed to foxes—such as craftiness, cleverness, untrustworthiness. (Note that this is not emotive use of language: characteristics are being imputed to him, and it is either true or false that he has them. The sentence has a clear meaning, though admittedly it is somewhat vague, since it does not say *which* characteristics of foxes are intended; but the sentence achieves by means of this one word, "fox," a characterization of a person that it might take many sentences to paraphrase.) But, like "fork in the road" and "leg of a table," this use of "fox" has come to be an established one, and can be discovered in a dictionary as a sense of the word "fox" in addition to the literal zoological sense. It is still a figurative use, for "he is a fox" is figurative with respect to the literal zoological sense ("I saw a fox in the forest"). But, although figurative, it is an established use, and hence does not count as a metaphor.

Much more could be said about metaphors, but the point that concerns us here is the issue of the meaningful against the meaningless. Can the extension of meaning that we find in a metaphor become so tenuous as to be not discernible at all, in fact nonexistent? And if this happens, don't we have a meaningless expression? Consider the poet E. E. Cummings' phrase "rubber questions"; this is meaningful enough: rubber questions are questions that bounce back at you when you ask them ("questions bouncing back" would in turn have to be paraphrased, of course). But now what about "rubber cube

---

[32] William P. Alston, *Philosophy of Language*, p. 99. In common usage of language, the distinction between "figurative" and "metaphorical" is not this sharp. The definitions given here are, to that extent, stipulative. The line between being established and not being established is not very sharp either. Is "green age" established usage because "green" sometimes means immature?

roots," "rubber melody," "rubber joy," "rubber hopes"?[33] Have these phrases, and the sentences containing them, any meaning at all? What can we make of them? Surely not just any combination of words can be passed off as a metaphor and hence meaningful. Where are we to draw the line? Where do we pass over from a meaningful expression to a meaningless one? True, none of the phrases here has any established usage, but then neither do "rubber questions" and "green age," and yet they are meaningful. Where then lies the difference?

Perhaps we can answer this question if we impose one requirement on metaphor: the alleged metaphor must be *translatable*. We have already seen how the Dylan Thomas line can be translated, and also "rubber questions," and similarly with most passages of poetry that are metaphorical. The translation (paraphrase) will not be as rich in suggestion (secondary meaning) as the original passage, and hence it will lose some of its effect upon the reader (and meaning, too, if one counts "secondary meaning" as meaning), but a translation can be given nevertheless. To a reader who does not understand a certain metaphor, the paraphrase will help him at least to focus his attention in the right area, to grasp the direction of the poet's thought, and thus, hopefully, to understand the meaning of the metaphor. When *no* translation can be given at all, the expression must be considered not a metaphor (since metaphors are meaningful) but a meaningless collocation of words.

Translatable—but translatable into what? Suppose someone translated an apparently meaningless line of poetry into "Saturday is in bed"—what then? Would we say it was meaningful because it was capable of being paraphrased? Doesn't it matter *into what* it is translated? Surely it must be translated into something that we already know to be meaningful. A criterion of meaning, then, is already presupposed.

9. *Translatability into the ordinary idiom.* It has been suggested that what distinguishes meaningless expressions is that they are "not in the ordinary idiom" of our language, and seem to defy any attempts to be translated into this idiom. Every day we utter sentences like "I am going downtown to do some shopping," "Most dogs are more affectionate than most cats," "What interests you may not interest me," "The American bald eagle is gradually becoming extinct," and countless other sentences that, though they may be vague, are perfectly meaningful and whose meaning we can explain to others who fail to understand them. Why not say, then, that

. . . if a sentence is significant (meaningful), we require that it be translatable into the ordinary idiom. The ordinary idiom may be characterized, somewhat vaguely it must be admitted, as the idiom we use in communicating with one another. It is the idiom in which most conversations are conducted and in which almost all books are written. Translatability into this idiom is a

[33] See Monroe C. Beardsley, *Aesthetics,* pp. 143–44.

necessary condition of significance, because we have but one recourse when we are asked to clarify the meaning of a sentence that is not in this idiom. It would not be to the purpose to answer the question by translating the sentence into another sentence of the same idiom, for its meaning, if it has one, would not thereby become any clearer. The problem can be met only, if at all, by translating the sentence into the ordinary idiom.[34]

Metaphorical expressions would fulfill the criterion, for they can be paraphrased—that is, translated (though with some loss of secondary meaning) into the ordinary idiom. But there are many sentences that are not so translatable. Let us examine a couple of examples.

Hegel's famous statement "Being and Nothing are one and the same" is undeniably in need of clarification, as Hegel himself admitted. But his own explanation is not in the ordinary idiom, since Hegel uses the terms "the being" and "the nothing" as designative expressions, while the ordinary idiom does not countenance the use of these expressions as designative. It would be unreasonable to conclude, on this ground alone, that the statement is nonsense. But if it is not, its cognitive content cannot be appraised until it is translated into the ordinary idiom.[35]

Now consider a second example, from the work of the German philosopher Heidegger:

Why are we concerned about the nothing? The nothing is rejected by science and sacrificed as the unreal. Science wants to have nothing to do with the nothing. What is the nothing? Does the nothing exist only because the not, i.e. negation, exists? Or do negation and the not exist only because the nothing exists? We maintain: The nothing is more primitive than the not and negation. We know the nothing. The nothing is the simple negation of the totality of being. Anxiety reveals the nothing. The nothing itself nots.[36]

Few, if any, whole sentences in this quotation can be translated into the ordinary idiom. To show this, each sentence would have to be analyzed separately, but perhaps the following considerations will suffice: In the ordinary idiom the word "nothing" is not used as a name. We do use the word "nothing" as the subject of sentences, as in "Nothing is greater than integrity," but here we do not use the word "nothing" as the name of anything; we could easily say the same thing without using the word "nothing" at all, by saying instead "Integrity is the greatest thing there is." Accordingly we are left without any clue to the meaning of the phrase "the nothing," so presumably it has none unless some translation is provided, which it is not.

[34] Paul Marhenke, "The Criterion of Significance," in Leonard Linsky (ed.), *Semantics and the Philosophy of Language*, p. 142.
[35] *Ibid.*, pp. 143–44.
[36] Quoted in Paul Marhenke, *op. cit.*, p. 158.

(Even here we should not be too hasty: we might be able to fathom the meaning of this curious phrase by examining the total context—that is, reading the whole book of which this is a small part. Sometimes we can do this, but sometimes not; commentators notoriously translate into more sentences in the same idiom as the original sentences, which does not help us.) Again, the word "not" is used as a verb (in the last sentence of the quotation); now we know the meanings of such verbs as "to run," "to eat," "to doubt," but what is the meaning of "to not"? Whatever the ordinary idiom contains, it does not contain *this,* and we are provided with no key for translating it into anything we can understand; and consequently, until such translation is provided, we must consider it to be meaningless.

But even if we agree that the sentences criticized are indeed meaningless, we may be disturbed by the suggested criterion, translatability into the ordinary idiom. For what exactly *is* the ordinary idiom? How are we to tell, in doubtful cases, whether a given sentence is to be construed as being in the ordinary idiom or not? "Dogs drink water" is certainly in the ordinary idiom; but what about "Quadruplicity drinks procrastination"? We are surely inclined to call the second sentence meaningless, but it is like the first sentence in at least two respects: it is composed entirely of words (there are no nonsense-syllables in it), and it fulfills the requirements of a grammatically correct sentence. Indeed, it could easily be translated into French, German, and other languages. Yet it seems to be meaningless. Is it in the ordinary idiom or not?[37] If it isn't, why not? It certainly is not subject to the kind of criticism given of the two quotations above. But if it *is* in the ordinary idiom and is nevertheless meaningless, what then becomes of translatability into the ordinary idiom as a criterion of the meaningfulness of sentences?

In this rather chaotic state we shall have to leave the matter until some further distinctions have been drawn, hoping that a discussion of these later issues will shed some light on this vexed subject.

Exercises

1. Which of the following pairs of sentences express the same proposition?
   a. Johnny is taller than Billy.
      Billy is shorter than Johnny.
   b. Mary is prettier than Jane.
      Jane is uglier than Mary.
   c. I like custard pudding.
      I do not dislike custard pudding.
   d. They got married and had children.
      They had children and got married.

[37] Marhenke says that it is (*op. cit.,* p. 142); but, he adds, translatability into the ordinary idiom is a *necessary* condition of meaningfulness, not a *sufficient* condition. No satisfactory sufficient condition (or set of conditions together constituting a sufficient condition), he says, has ever been provided.

  e. A is larger than B, and B is larger than C.
     A is larger than C.
  f. I went to the movies last night.
     I did not fail to go to the movies last night.
  g. I was surprised by what I saw.
     I was shocked by what I saw.
  h. Either you go or I go.
     Either I go or you go.
  i. The man whom they saw at the bazaar wore a pin-striped suit.
     The man, whom they saw at the bazaar, wore a pin-striped suit.
  j. I made him retract his statement.
     I made him eat his words.

  2. Do you consider the following to be self-contradictory? Justify your
answer.
  a. Quadratic equations go to horse-races.
  b. The king was the slave of his slaves.
  c. He ate and drank persistency.
  d. This polygon has an infinite number of sides.
  e. She wore a red dress which was green.
  f. She wore a red dress which was made of marble.

  3. Do you consider the following suggestions (or apparent suggestions)
meaningful? Why?
  a. "How do you know there isn't a big hole in space?" "In space? Don't
you mean in some *bodies* in space? Planets might have holes." "No, I mean
not a hole in any body of matter, but a hole in space itself."
  b. "I might be able to jump in one second from the earth to a star a
million light-years away, by traveling through the fourth dimension."
  c. "Perhaps the chair on which you're sitting and the floor on which your
feet rest have thoughts and feelings and pains just as you do."
  d. "Perhaps there was nothing at all for twenty billion years, and then
all of a sudden there was something—matter."

  4. Try to give a satisfactory paraphrase of the following brief passages of
poetry:
  a. To be imprisoned in the viewless winds . . .
     To lie in cold obstruction and to rot. . . . (Shakespeare, *Measure for
     Measure*)
  b. [Life] is a tale told by an idiot, full of sound and fury,
       Signifying nothing. (Shakespeare, *Macbeth*)
  c. Life, like a dome of many-colored glass,
     Stains the white radiance of eternity. (Shelley)
  d. To prepare a face to meet the faces that you meet. (T. S. Eliot)
  e. We are the eyelids of defeated caves. (Allen Tate)

  5. Can you attribute any meaning at all to the following expressions? If so,
what? Defend your answer.
  a. mathematical bathrooms   f. man-eating quadrilaterals
  b. four-sided lassitude   g. sleeping temples
  c. participial biped   h. supine idioms
  d. fatuous integers   i. aggressive vases
  e. salacious tables   j. stipulated refraction

  6. Do you consider the following to be meaningful sentences? Can you
translate them or paraphrase them? If meaningless, what requirement(s) do
they violate?

a. Chicago is between Detroit.
b. He drew a line that was −2 inches long.
c. Pirots carulize elatically.
d. He believes that pirots carulize elatically.
e. The color tastes bitter.
f. The number 3 died yesterday.
g. This problem is red.
h. His thoughts are heavy. (taken literally)
i. Books are probably.
j. He sleeps more slowly than other people.
k. Antelopes introduce salivation.

Selected Readings for Chapter 1

Anthologies of readings:

Anderson, Wallace and Norman Stageberg (eds.), *Introductory Readings on Language*. New York: Holt, Rinehart & Winston, Inc., 1962. Paperback.

Caton, Charles E. (ed.), *Philosophy and Ordinary Language*. Urbana: University of Illinois Press, 1965. Paperback.

Chappell, V. C. (ed.), *Ordinary Language*. Englewood Cliffs, N. J.: Prentice-Hall, Inc., 1964. Paperback.

Linsky, Leonard (ed.), *Semantics and the Philosophy of Language*. Urbana: University of Illinois Press, 1952.

Primary sources:

Alston, William P., *Philosophy of Language*. Englewood Cliffs, N. J.: Prentice-Hall, Inc., 1964. Paperback.

Austin, John L., *How to Do Things with Words*. New York: Oxford University Press, Inc., 1965. Paperback.

Beardsley, Monroe C., *Thinking Straight* (3rd ed.). Englewood Cliffs, N. J.: Prentice-Hall, Inc., 1966.

Black, Max, *Language and Philosophy*. Ithaca, N. Y.: Cornell University Press, 1949.

———, *Models and Metaphors*. Ithaca, N. Y.: Cornell University Press, 1964.

Brown, Roger, *Words and Things*. New York: Free Press of Glencoe, Inc., 1958. Especially Chapter 3.

Drange, Theodore, *Type Crossings*. The Hague: Mouton & Co., 1966.

Johnson, Alexander B., *A Treatise on Language*, ed. David Rynin. Berkeley: University of California Press, 1947. Originally published 1836.

Katz, Jerrold J., *The Philosophy of Language*. New York: Harper & Row, Publishers, Inc., 1966.

Mill, John Stuart, *A System of Logic*. London: Longmans, Green & Company, Ltd., 1843. Book 1.

Plato, *Laches; Euthyphro; Meno; Cratylus*. Many editions.

Quine, Willard V., *Word and Object*. New York: John Wiley & Sons, Inc., 1960.

Robinson, Richard, *Definition*. New York: Oxford University Press, Inc., 1950.

NOTE: Most of the items in the reading lists are books rather than essays or articles. Since articles in philosophical periodicals are usually less available to the reader, they have been listed only when they are of special interest or when they contain ideas not contained, or not expressed as clearly, in available books.

2

Knowledge

5. Concepts

Our primary purpose in this chapter is to examine human knowledge—its sources, its nature, and the various kinds of it that there may be. This is the principal task of the branch of philosophy called "epistemology" (from the Greek *episteme*, "knowledge"), or "theory of knowledge." But before we come to this task, we must briefly examine another matter which is preliminary to it: the nature of *concepts*.

Knowledge is expressed in propositions: "I know that I am now reading a book," "I know that 2 plus 2 equals 4," and so on. But before we can understand any propositions at all, even false ones, we must first have concepts. I cannot understand what is meant by the sentence "Ice melts" before I have the concept of ice and melting. We might well express this otherwise by saying that in order to understand what is meant by "Ice melts" we must understand the meanings of the *words* "ice" and "melt." But to understand the meanings of words, we must have concepts: to understand the meaning of a word already involves having a concept.

How do we acquire the concepts that we have? It was once thought that at least some of our concepts are *innate*—that they are, so to speak, "wired into us." Suppose that the concept of redness (or being red) were innate: then we would have it without having to experience any instances of it—that is, without ever having to see anything red. A person born blind could have the concept just as well as a man who could see. It seems so obvious that a person born blind does not possess the concept of redness, or of any other color, that no one has held that this concept, or the concept of any other sensory property, is innate. *Some* concepts, however, have been believed to be innate: for example, the concept of cause and the concept of God. If the concept of cause is innate, then we could know what the word means, and be in full possession of the concept, without ever having seen causes operating.

This too seems implausible to us, but we shall examine the concept of cause in detail in Chapter 5. Perhaps the God example seems more plausible, since God, if one exists, is not seen or otherwise perceived, and yet we do seem to possess the concept (though this too has been denied). If we cannot perceive God and we nevertheless have the concept, how, it might be asked, do we come by it? May it not be innate? We shall try to answer this question when we consider the alternative theory, that concepts are derived from experience. Meanwhile, it is worth noting that the theory of innate concepts is no longer held. The rise of modern psychology has dealt it a death-blow. No evidence has ever arisen to show that any concept that people have is innate; perhaps they don't have certain concepts that they claim to have, but when they do have a concept, it is derived in some way from experience—that is to say, they would not be able to have the concept unless they first had certain experiences.

The obvious next step, then, is to say that all concepts are acquired through *experience*. (This view is sometimes called "concept empiricism," and the view that some concepts are innate is called "concept rationalism," but these names are liable to be misleading because they become confused with the far more important sense of "rationalism" and "empiricism" to be discussed in Chapter 3, which has to do with propositions and not with concepts.) This view was defended and made famous by three British philosophers: John Locke (1632–1704), George Berkeley (1685–1753), and David Hume (1711–1776).

Instead of the word "concepts," these philosophers all used the word "ideas," and the problem they undertook to answer was: "How do we come by the ideas we have?" All the ideas we have or ever shall have, they said, come from *experience:* (1) some through the "outer" senses, such as sight, hearing, and touch, and from these all our concepts involving the physical world are drawn; and (2) some from the "inner" senses, such as experiences of pain and pleasure, feelings of love and hate, pride and remorse, experiences of thinking and willing—from these we get all the ideas about our inner life. All our concepts are derived from these two kinds of experience. (Locke called the first "ideas of sensation" and the second "ideas of reflection.")

The use of the word "idea" was so general in the 17th and 18th centuries as to include all experiences, of whatever kind; but Hume made a clear distinction among experiences, between "impressions" and "ideas." Neither word was used in the 20th century sense, in which we say "I have the impression that someone is watching me" and "The idea of human progress is a delusion." Hume's use of these words can be illustrated as follows: If I see a green tree, I have a green *impression* (sense-impression), and then if I close my eyes and imagine something green, I have an *idea* of green—an idea being a kind of weak copy of an impression. You have the impression when your eyes are open, but you can have the idea of something whenever you care to imagine it. Hume's main thesis in connection with these terms was *"No ideas without impressions."* If you have never seen anything green—that is, if you have never had a green sense-impression—it is impossible for you ever to have any *idea* of green. You must first have the impression in order to have the idea, and a man born blind could never have any idea of green or any other color, because he has never had any sense-impressions of colors. Similarly, a man born deaf could have no idea of tones, nor would a man born without a sense of smell have any idea of odors, and so on. For every idea X', there is a corresponding sense-impression X; and without first having the sense-impression X, we cannot have the corresponding idea X'. The same considerations apply to the ideas gleaned from the "inner" senses: a man who has never experienced pain can have no idea of pain; a man who has never experienced fear can have no idea of fear; and so on. And a child who has not yet experienced sexual love can have no idea of love: he can observe how people having this experience *behave,* but he does not yet have any idea of what the feeling is like that impels them to behave in this way.

So much for the outlines of the theory. But as it stands it will not do, as Locke and Hume were well aware. For can't we have ideas of lots of things of which we have never had any impressions? We can imagine a golden mountain even though we have never seen one; and we can imagine a creature that is half man and half horse. True, we have seen pictures of centaurs, mythical creatures that are half man and half horse, but we could imagine these without ever having seen the pictures, and the persons who first drew such pictures must have been able to imagine them before they drew the pictures. And we can imagine (have an idea of) black roses even though the only roses we have ever seen are red, yellow, pink, and white. We can have ideas of all these things before we have ever had sense-experiences of them, and even if we never experience them at all.

Thus Locke was led to distinguish between *simple* ideas and *complex* ideas. We can imagine golden mountains and black roses without ever seeing them because, after all, we have seen the colors gold and black in other things. The idea of golden mountains and black roses are complex ideas: we simply take ideas we have *already* acquired through other experiences and put them together in our imagination in new combinations. The human mind can create all sorts of complex ideas from simple ideas already gleaned from experience; but the human mind cannot create a single simple idea. If we have never seen red, we cannot imagine red; and if we have never felt a pain, we cannot imagine pain. Red and pain are simple ideas. It is true that we might well be able to imagine a mountain or a rose without ever having seen one, but that is only because the ideas of mountain and rose are themselves complex ideas. If we have seen a hill and also have the idea of height from having seen some things higher than others, we can then form the idea of something higher and steeper than a hill, namely a mountain, even if we have never seen one. Similarly, we can have an idea of God, because we can

combine certain ideas we derive from our experience of human beings, such
as power, intelligence, kindness, and so on, and imagine these as being
present to a greater degree than in any person we have ever encountered.
There are problems here that we shall consider in detail in Chapter 7, but it is
sufficient to note here that the idea of God, whatever it is, is a *complex* idea.
(Having the idea of God, of course, does not prove that anything exists corresponding to the idea, any more than in the case of the golden mountain or
the unicorn.)

The relation of simple to complex ideas is somewhat like the relation of
atoms to molecules. Without atoms, you cannot have molecules; and atoms
can be combined in different ways to form different molecules. Without
simple ideas, you cannot form complex ideas; but once you have a number of
simple ideas, you can combine them in your imagination in all sorts of
different ways to form the ideas of countless things that never existed on land
or sea.

Nothing, at first view, may seem more unbounded than the thought of man,
which not only escapes all human power and authority but is not even re-
strained within the limits of nature and reality. To form monsters, and join
incongruous shapes and appearances, costs the imagination no more trouble
than to conceive the most natural and familiar objects. And while the body is
confined to one planet, along which it creeps with pain and difficulty, the
thought can in an instant transport us into the most distant regions of the
universe. . . .

But though our thought seems to possess this unbounded liberty, we shall
find, upon a nearer examination, that it is really confined within very narrow
limits, and that all this creative power of the mind amounts to no more than
the faculty of compounding, transposing, augmenting, or diminishing the materials afforded us by the senses and experience. When we think of a golden
mountain, we only join two consistent ideas, gold and mountain, with which
we were formerly acquainted. . . . In short, all the materials of thinking are
derived either from our outward or inward sentiment; the mixture and composition of these belongs alone to the mind and will.[1]

It has never been made quite clear *which* of the ideas we have are simple
ideas and which are complex; no complete list of them has ever been offered,
but only scattered examples. In general, the ideas of senory qualities have
been the stock examples of simple ideas: red, sweet, hard, pungent; pain,
pleasure, fear, anger; thinking, wondering, doubting, believing. It may not be
of great importance to decide in every case which ideas are simple ideas, but
there is a problem about them nevertheless. "Simple ideas are those that cannot be broken down, or analyzed, into other ideas"—so runs the suggested

[1] David Hume, *An Enquiry Concerning Human Understanding*, Section II, paragraphs 4 and 5.

criterion. But this does not always help us in trying to determine which ideas can, and which cannot, be further analyzed.

There is even a problem in the case of color-ideas, such as red, which are usually taken as the standard case of simple ideas: it is doubtless true that if you have never seen *any* shade of red, you cannot imagine any; but what if you have seen two or three shades of red? Can you then imagine only those shades but not the others? Or can you imagine (have an idea of) *any* shade of red after you have experienced (had an impression of) a few samples? Hume discussed such a case: Suppose that you have seen all the shades of blue there are except one, but you are told where that missing shade of blue lies in relation to the other shades on a scale ranging from the lightest to the darkest. Is it really impossible for you to imagine that shade without ever having seen it? Many persons would say that you *can* imagine it; or at least—what is not the same thing—that whether you can imagine it prior to seeing it or not, that you can *recognize* it as the missing shade after you *have* seen it. But if you *can* have an idea of it before you have had an impression of it, what happens to the view that "for every (simple) idea there must be a corresponding impression?" Is the idea of it then not a simple idea? Or if it is a simple idea, must there be perhaps a million simple ideas of blue corresponding to each of the million or more specific shades of blue? If the idea of each of these million shades is a simple idea, then it should be impossible to imagine the missing shade without having first seen it. On the other hand, if the simple idea is only blue-in-general (not any specific shade of blue), then presumably you *could* imagine the missing shade; but then you would have to say that the idea of this missing shade is a complex idea, composed of (1) the idea of blue-in-general and (2) the idea of being darker than, or lighter than, some other shade.

Here problems multiply: If you have seen only primary red, can you imagine scarlet, crimson, magenta? Are the ideas of these simple or complex ideas? If you have seen many shades of yellow and many shades of red, but no orange, can you imagine orange without ever having seen it? (Might some people be able to, but not others? Could an idea then be simple for some people but complex for others?) And if you answer "Yes" to the previous question, try this one: If you have seen blue and yellow, but no green, can you imagine green? (It is most important not to confuse the physical and the psychological here. Orange, we say, is a mixture of red and yellow, and green is a mixture of yellow and blue. But green doesn't *look* like a mixture of yellow and blue the way orange looks like a mixture of red and yellow. What color you get when you mix different paints, or combine different lights, has nothing to do with the question of what colors you can imagine [without having seen them] on the basis of other ones.)

Whatever the outcome of these speculations, it seems to be quite clear that without some impressions we cannot have certain ideas. A man born blind can have no idea of colors. And if we had never experienced shapes of *any* kind, we could have no idea of shape—not of triangular, rectangular, circular, or any other—though it may well be that if we had experiences (impressions) of *some* shapes, say a triangle and a pentagon, we could form the idea of other shapes, such as a rectangle and a hexagon, without having seen them. Clearly *some* impressions are indispensable before we can form *some* ideas, though it may be a matter for legitimate dispute just which ones these are.[2]

In general, the Lockean simple ideas are those whose names can be defined only ostensively. The reason we can define "red," "sweet," "pain," and many other sensory words *only* ostensively—by confronting the learner with the kind of experience of which these words are the labels—is that there is *no other way* of communicating to others what these words mean. These ideas are simple—that is, unanalyzable into other ones—so there is no way of acquainting people with what these words mean than to confront them with the relevant sense-experiences (impressions). By contrast, it *is* possible to provide someone with a set of instructions so that he will recognize a horse, a chair, or a tablecloth even though he has never experienced them, provided that he already has certain *other* ideas (of shape, size, solidity, and so on) derived from sense-experience. That is to say, the ideas of horse, chair, and tablecloth are complex ideas.[3] But there is no set of instructions we could give for shape, color, or solidity (or, for that matter, certain types of color such as red, or types of shape such as round) such that he would be able to form an idea of them without first having experienced them through his senses. This, then, is the connection between verbally indefinable *words* and simple *ideas*.

Concept v. image.   At this point, however, it is most important to expose an ambiguity in the word "idea" of which the philosophers we have just been discussing seem to have been unaware: In using the word "idea" one can be talking about either a *concept* or an *image*. Most of the time, they appear to have been talking about images, but sometimes the discussion of "ideas" shifted in such a way that it would be more appropriate to a discussion of concepts. Without having seen red we cannot form in our minds red *images;* but from this we cannot conclude that we can have no *concept* of red. To illustrate this point, let us take the example of ultraviolet. No human being

[2] Ideas of shape are different from those of color, in that shape is accessible to us through both sight and touch, whereas colors can be experienced through sight only. Thus, one may say, a man born blind can have an idea of shape—gleaned from the sense of touch—but no idea of color.

But we must be careful about this. Ideas of visual shape are not the same as ideas of tactual shape. (We use the word "shape" to cover both of them, forgetting that two very different kinds of ideas are involved here.) A man born blind can have, through the sense of touch, ideas of tactual shape, but he could have no more idea of visual shape than he could have of color.

[3] We probably *did* learn the meanings of all these words ostensively, by being confronted with instances of their application; but we didn't *have* to. A set of careful instructions about what a horse looks like could enable us to imagine a horse before we ever saw one, as well as to recognize one after we did see it.

can have ultraviolet images, since the human eye is not sensitive to that part of the spectrum; bees and certain other creatures can see it, but we cannot. Since we have no ultraviolet impressions, we can have no ultraviolet images. But we do appear to have a *concept* of ultraviolet. Physicists speak of ultraviolet light, and can identify it and relate it to other parts of the spectrum; indeed, they can talk about ultraviolet just as easily as they talk about red. Similarly, human beings do not have any sense that acquaints them with the presence of radioactivity the way they have senses like sight and hearing and touch that acquaint them with the sensible properties of physical objects. ("Sensible" in philosophy means "capable of being sensed.") We can't see, hear, smell, or touch radioactivity; we have to rely on instruments like Geiger counters to detect its presence. If any creature did have a sense acquainting him directly with the presence of radioactivity, we would have not the faintest conception of what it would be like; we simply have no "image" of radioactivity. (Remember that images need not be visual: there are auditory images, tactile images, olfactory images, and so on. When you imagine the smell of ammonia or the taste of scalloped potatoes, you are having olfactory images and gustatory images respectively.) Yet we do, it seems, have the concepts—at any rate physicists do—and physicists work as easily and familiarly with this concept as they do with concepts of which they *do* have sense-impressions (and consequently images). Hume's dictum "If no impressions, then no ideas" applies to images; it does not seem to apply to concepts.

Indeed, we can go further: A man born blind might become a physicist and specialize in the physics of color; this would be a somewhat peculiar choice, no doubt, but it would be a possible one. Such a man would never have seen any colors, and therefore he would have no color-images. But he might well know more *facts* about colors than you or I: he could tell us more about the light-waves and other physical properties of colored objects, and more about the physical conditions under which colors are seen, than most people can. He would in fact be able to tell us what the color of every object is; not by looking at it as we do, but by reading in Braille the pointer readings on instruments that record the wave-lengths of light emanating from the objects. He would be able to impart to us a great deal of knowledge about color and colored objects; and how could he do this if he did not have the concept of color? If he did not possess this, how could he know what he was talking about? Of course, he could correctly identify colors only as long as the correlation held between the seen color and the wave-lengths of light; if this correlation were no longer to hold, he would start making mistakes in color identification because he could not see the colors but had only the indirect evidence of the instruments recording light-waves. Still, must we not admit that he has the concept of color, even though he is unable to experience any color-images? How could he use the word, and even impart to us new knowledge that presupposes knowledge of what the word means, unless he had the concept?

What is a concept? We are thus led to the all-important question: What *is* a concept? It is clear enough that there is something different from images, something that we have called concepts. But what is a concept? How do we tell when we have one?

Let us try one possible answer to these questions: (1) We have a concept of X when we know the definition of the word "X." But this answer is far too narrow: we do know the meanings of countless words—"cat," "run," "above"—and use them every day without being able to state a definition for them. We observed on pp. 67–76 why this is so. Whatever having a concept involves, it does not require being able to state a definition—something that even the compilers of dictionaries often have a hard time doing. And in the case of words like "red" that are not verbally definable at all, we can never state a definition—from which we would have to conclude, according to this view, that we can never have a concept of red.[4]

So let us try again: (2) We have a concept of X when we can apply the word "X" correctly; we have a concept of redness and orangeness when we can correctly apply the words "red" and "orange" in all cases. This criterion does not require us to give a definition but only to use the word with uniform correctness It is also much more in line with our actual use of the term "concept": we do say, for example, "He must have some concept of what a cat is, for he always uses the word 'cat' in the right situations—he never applies the word 'cats' to dogs or anything else."

There is, however, one way in which this criterion is still too restrictive: it assumes that in order to have a concept we must first be acquainted with a *word*. Doubtless this is usually the case, but it is not *always* the case. A person may have something in mind for which no word yet exists, and he may then *invent* a word for it; or he may use an old word in a new sense, giving it a meaning it never had before. In either case, it seems plausible to say that he had the concept *prior* to the existence (or new usage) of the word. When the first physicists adapted the use of the common word "energy" for their own special purposes, they had in mind a highly abstract concept, and they presumably had this concept in mind before they had a word for it. Doubtless there are many concepts that one cannot have without much prior acquaintance with language, but this cannot be the case for all concepts, else how would language have got started? Using a word correctly seems to be a *consequence* of having the concept, but not a precondition of having it: that is, if you have a concept, *and* know the word for it, you will then be able to

---

[4] Strictly speaking, we should say a concept of red*ness*. Redness is a property—the property that all red things have in common—and the property is not red but red*ness*. By contrast, we have red images; a red image is a particular instance of the property redness.

use the word correctly; but having the concept is not the same thing as being able to use the word.

Let us, then, try once more, so as not to involve the acquaintance with a word in the having of a concept. (3) We have a concept of X (of X-ness) when we are able to distinguish X's from Y's and Z's and indeed from everything that is not an X. We might well do this whether we had a word for X or not, though of course it would be most convenient if we did have a word, and normally we would have. Thus if a child can distinguish cats from dogs and pigs and all other things, he has a concept of what is a cat, even though he cannot state a definition and even though he has never heard the word "cat" and connected the word with the thing by way of ostensive definition.

We have now specified what a concept is in such a way as to make it possible to have a concept without knowing any words. A dog that can distinguish cats from birds can be said to have these concepts, although it knows no words. Even this definition might be objected to, however, on the ground that being able to distinguish X's from Y's is, once again, a *consequence* of having the concept of X, but not what having the concept consists in. One is tempted to say that if you have a concept of X, you can, *as a result,* distinguish X's from other things; but you have to have the concept first. But what then would having the concept be? Moreover, we can devise machines that can effectively differentiate some things from others; do we wish to say that these machines have concepts?

In reply to such objections, we might say (4) that to have a concept of X is simply to have some *criterion-in-mind*. It would consist in some kind of "mental content" quite independent of words and quite independent of distinguishing X's from Y's and Z's. But it is not easy to state what such a criterion-in-mind would be like, or how one would know, through introspection alone, whether one possessed such a criterion. Surely the way one would know whether one had a criterion for X would be whether it would enable one to distinguish X's from Y's and Z's. A criterion for identifying X's would (it would seem) automatically be a criterion for distinguishing X's from non-X's. And so we would be back with our third criterion after all.

I can, of course, have a concept of X even though there are no X's in the world at all. I may have a concept of a sort of thing that is a reptile, larger than an elephant, and flies through the air. I could easily identify such a creature if it existed, and the fact that it does not exist does not prevent me from having the concept of such a creature. I have such a concept, then, although no such creature exists and there is no word to designate this peculiar combination of characteristics. (Let us take care to note that I can have the concept even if I cannot state any characteristics at all; for in the case of verbally indefinable words, no characteristics can be stated. I cannot state in words what distinguishes red from orange, though I know how to make the distinction in practice, and therefore I have a concept of these two colors.)

It is clear, then, that we can have a concept without having an image. If scientists can have a concept of ultraviolet without being able to visualize ultraviolet, surely a blind man can have a concept of red without being able to visualize red. True, for both the scientist and the blind man have a criterion for distinguishing X (ultraviolet, red) from non-X. But, we can now say, the blind man, though he has *a* criterion for distinguishing X from non-X, does not have *the same concept* as seeing men do, for he does not have the same criterion for distinguishing red from non-red that seeing men have. The blind man must use wave-lengths as his criterion, whereas we use (as men from time immemorial have used) the easily distinguishable (but not verbally describable) difference in the way red *looks*. Both have a concept, and there is a high degree of correlation between the concepts; but they are not *the same* concept, for there is not the same means of distinguishing red from non-red. (We, of course, *can* use both ways of distinguishing red from non-red, whereas the blind man can use only one.) Similarly, a person who could see ultraviolet would have a concept of it over and above the one we have, for he would be able to distinguish that color from others by means of direct inspection, without having to resort (as we do) to instruments for distinguishing it.

Are all concepts based on experience?   Let us return, finally, to our main question: what are we to say of the view that all concepts are based on experience—which means that in the case of simple "ideas" a concept of X is impossible without a prior experience of X, and in the case of "complex ideas" that the concept of X is impossible without a prior experience of the simple ideas of which it is constituted? The view seems not only plausible but inevitable, for what is the alternative? We are not born with concepts, nor do we (as Plato thought) remember them from a state of existence prior to our birth; so how else could we acquire them except through experience?

The difficulty lies in showing in each case how the concept was actually derived from experience. With sensory concepts like redness, the case is relatively easy: as small children we had various red things pointed out to us, and by acts of successive abstraction (such as were described on pp. 57–58) we came to recognize the characteristic, redness, that all the cases pointed to had in common. But how did we derive through experience the concept of liberty, of honesty, of marginal utility, of four, of logical implication? We do have these concepts, and, let us quickly note, we have them *without* any corresponding images. When we think of liberty, we may imagine the Statue of Liberty, and when we think of slavery, we may imagine African slaves being whipped; but neither of these images constitutes the meaning of the words "liberty" and "slavery"—others may imagine something very different when they think of liberty or slavery, and still others may have no images at all. There is no image *of* liberty or slavery the way there is an image of red or sweet. These are abstract concepts, to which there are no corresponding images. If we have images, they are not *of* liberty but of particular things or situations that may or may not exemplify liberty. We can all understand the same concept, liberty, even though we all have different images (or none at all) when we think about it. What we *think* of when we think of liberty is very different from what we *imagine* when we think of it; what we imagine, if anything, is only an incidental accompaniment.

This is not to say that we could have the concept of liberty if we had never had any sense-experiences at all: our having the concept is in some way or other dependent on experience; but it is far from easy to say how. Perhaps if we had always lived under a tyranny and never seen or heard of people who could express their opinions without fear of punishment, we would not be able to form the concept of liberty—though even this is doubtful, for as long as we were aware of restraints upon our behavior, we could conceive of a state-of-affairs in which these restraints were absent. It is, indeed, very difficult to know upon *what* experiences our concept of liberty is dependent. At any rate, the relation between the concept and sense-experience is very indirect: there is no particular sense-experience, or even any single kind of sense-experience, that we must have had before we can have this concept. Whatever the connection is between the concept and experience, it is sufficiently indirect that no one has given a clear account of exactly what this connection is in every case.

Let us consider another type of concept, those of arithmetic. Since we can distinguish between two things and three things, were did we get our concepts of two and three? "From experience," Hume would say. But exactly how? Arithmetic, we might say, studies the *quantitative* aspects of things; when we consider the sum of two and three, we don't care whether it's three apples, three boats, or three bales of hay. The concept of three (or three-ness) is formed through abstraction from many cases. What three apples, three boats, and three bales of hay have in common is their numerical *quantity;* that there are three *of* them is relevant to mathematics, not what it is that they are three *of*. The concepts of arithmetic are all quantitative—that is what defines them as arithmetical; and they are abstracted from experience, from our experience of things in the world. Without any experience of quantities of things, we would have no arithmetical concepts. So far so good. The problem comes when we realize that we have a concept of 12,038,468 just as much as we have of 3. Yet we have probably never observed exactly that number of things, and did not know it even if we did. What, we can then ask, is the relation between that number and our sense-experiences?

Or consider the meanings of such terms as "equality," "infinity," "implication," "deduction." We have concepts of all of these, for we can distinguish cases of the application of these words from cases of their non-application. Yet they do not seem to correspond to anything that confronts us in experience. If they are derived from experience in some remote way, it is not clear how, or what exactly the steps are.

Perhaps the experience we must have gone through in order to derive our concepts of numerical equality and of 12,038,468 is simply our experience of learning mathematics, or the experience of learning to use these words. But if so, this is a broader sense of the word "experience" than we have thus far been using, namely sense-experience (or sense-impressions).

More puzzling still, there are words that we can use with systematic accuracy that do not seem to be connected with experience, even by way of abstraction: consider connective words like "and" and "about," which have a function in a sentence but do not correspond to any distinguishable items in the world:

One must not only know the meanings of nouns, verbs, and adjectives, one must also understand the significance of the syntactical form of the sentence; and for many sentences, one must understand various kinds of words that serve to connect nouns, adjectives, and verbs into sentences so as to affect the meaning of the sentence as a whole. One must be able to distinguish semantically between "John hit Jim," "Jim hit John," "Did John hit Jim?," "John, hit Jim!," and "John, please don't hit Jim." This means that before one can engage in conversation one must be able to handle and understand such factors as word order; "auxiliaries" like "do," "shall," and "is"; and connectives like "is," "that," and "and." These elements can neither get their meaning by association with distinguishable items in experience nor be defined in terms of items that can. Where could we look in our sense-perception for the object of word-order patterns, pauses, or words like "is" and "that"? And as for defining these elements in terms of words like "blue" and "table," the prospect has seemed so remote that no one has so much as attempted it.[5]

The acquiring of such concepts as these seems to require experiences of a different kind: learning a language, understanding sentences and sets of sentences, and the operations or performances with such symbols that are governed by linguistic rules.

In the light of such difficulties as these, Hume's requirement "If no impressions, then no ideas" seems thus far to be little more than a promissory note.

Traceability to impressions as a criterion of meaning.   At any rate, this discussion has confronted us with yet another criterion of meaning (though it has more to do with the meanings of individual words and phrases than with the meaning of sentences). According to this criterion, every word or phrase that we use must be traceable back to sense-experience in some way, whether the route be short (as with "red") or long (as with "liberty"). Or to put it in a different way, every word, to have meaning, must be either capable of ostensive definition itself or defined by means of other words, and these perhaps by still others, which are ultimately definable by ostensive definition. If this cannot be done, then the word or phrase is meaningless. If anyone claims, says Hume, that he has some idea (concept), we need only ask him,

[5] William Alston, *Philosophy of Language*, p. 68.

"From what impression is that supposed idea derived? And if it be impossible to assign any, this will serve to confirm our suspicion. . . . Commit it then to the flames: for it can contain nothing but sophistry and illusion."[6]

Is this criterion satisfactory? That depends on whether Hume's thesis "If no impressions, then no ideas" is acceptable. And is it acceptable? We must wait a while before judging it. If we cannot trace a concept back to a sense-impression, this may be because we have not tried hard enough; it may be that the relation is very tenuous and difficult to trace. But, on the other hand, it may be because there is no such connection, and in that case it will be fatal to Hume's criterion. We shall, in the coming chapters, encounter some concepts—or at any rate alleged concepts—that seem impossible to trace back to any sense experiences whatever. If we can nevertheless satisfy ourselves that they are genuine concepts, and not meaningless strings of words, we shall then, and only then, have satisfied ourselves that Hume's criterion is inadequate.

Exercises

1. Could you imagine what a sweet taste was like if you had experienced only sour and bitter tastes? Could you imagine the taste of a tangerine if you had tasted only lemons and oranges? or the taste of a nectarine if you had tasted only plums and peaches? Could you tell in advance what the experience of sadness at the death of a loved one would be like, if you had experienced only sadness in other contexts, such as sadness at the cessation of enjoyment and sadness at the theft of a prized possession? Could you tell in advance what the sadness of a Mahler andante would be like if you had experienced (in music) only andantes by Mozart? Can you know what it is to be greedy if you have never yourself experienced greed? (Would the word "greed" be meaningless to you unless you had experienced greed? If Mr. X was described to you as greedy, would you have no idea what his feeling-states were like? what to expect from him?)

2. Can you have any idea of the following without having experienced them at first hand? Would you consider the ideas of them simple or complex in Locke's sense? State whether you are using "idea" in the sense of image or of concept. (a) space; (b) book-ends; (c) nothing; (d) motion; (e) swimming; (f) life; (g) novelty; (h) regret.

3. Can you state in what way(s) the following concepts are based on experience? What experiences or kind of experiences must a person have in order to have each of these concepts? (a) door-knob; (b) racial integration; (c) morally deserving; (d) welcome; (e) probability; (f) soap; (g) economic opportunity; (h) infinity.

4. What is a concept? Attempt a definition of your own.

[6] David Hume, *An Enquiry Concerning Human Understanding*. Concluding sentences of Sections 2 and 11.

6. Truth

We are now well on our way to considering our main topic, knowledge; but we must make yet another brief stop along the way to consider truth. One characteristic of any proposition we know is that it must be true; isn't "knowing the proposition *p*" the same as "knowing the proposition *p* to be true"? If it isn't true, we can't be said to know it. Hence truth is involved in knowing. And so we come to the question, what is truth? Or more accurately, what is it for a proposition to be true? (A proposition can be true without being *known* to be true; but it cannot be known to be true without being true.)

The problem may well seem to be an unreal one. We may ask, with an air of mystery, "What is truth?" yet in daily life we never seem to have any trouble in dealing with this concept. If someone says that snow is white, we will say "That's true"; if he says that snow is green, we will say "That's false"; but the fact that we have never thought of such a thing as the definition of "truth" is no barrier to us. We seem already to know what truth is, since we are able in countless cases to distinguish true propositions from false ones.

Yet it is imperative for us as students of philosophy to consider this question. Much of philosophy consists of making the implicit explicit. We have used the words "cat" and "dog" all our lives, although we may not be able to give a word definition of either term; so we may have used the word "truth" all our lives without being able to give a definition of it. But "truth," unlike "cat" and "dog," is a general term of great interest to philosophy.

The word "true" is used in many senses. "That's a true emerald" may mean the same as "It's a genuine emerald, not an imitation." Or we may use the word as an intensive, to add emphasis to our assertion. "He is a true friend" means only that he really is a friend. But we are concerned here only with the sense of "true" in which truth is a property (characteristic) of *propositions*.

What, then, is a true proposition? How is a true proposition different from a false one? (Let us remember that there is no such thing as a meaningless proposition; if a sentence is meaningless, it expresses no proposition at all, true *or* false. See p. 81.) We are able to make the distinction a thousand times a day, but how shall we put the distinction into words?

Let us first introduce the concept of *states-of-affairs*. There are numerous states-of-affairs in the world. For example, if snow covered all the New England states last January, that is a state-of-affairs; if your cat is black, that is another state-of-affairs; if you have five brothers and six sisters, that is still another state-of-affairs. These states-of-affairs occur or exist in the world even if no one reports their occurrence in language. Their existence is independent of language, but we can describe them by means of language.

It would seem that we can now define "truth" quite easily. A true proposition describes a state-of-affairs that occurs; or, in the case of a proposition about the past, a state-of-affairs that did occur; or in the case of the future, that will occur. If "There are five chairs in this room" reports a state-of-affairs that actually exists—that is, if the state-of-affairs is one of five chairs actually being in the room—then the proposition is true; otherwise it is not. By contrast, a false proposition reports a state-of-affairs that does *not* occur (or did not, in the case of the past, or will not, in the case of the future). "I am eight feet tall" is a false proposition, because if I assert it I am asserting the existence of a state-of-affairs that does not actually exist. A true proposition describes a state-of-affairs which is actual—that is, which actually exists—and a false proposition reports a state-of-affairs which does not (or did not, etc.) actually exist. It describes a possible state-of-affairs that is not actual.[7] When a sentence is used to report a state-of-affairs, and the state-of-affairs the sentence is used to report is actual, then the proposition that the sentence expresses is true—and, we may add, any other sentence that is used to express the same state-of-affairs will also express a true proposition.

It may be that there are different kinds of truth, and that we can discover the truths of different propositions in many different ways; of this we shall have much more to say shortly. But by whatever means we may discover them to be true, they are true if they report an actual state-of-affairs. With this consideration out of the way, what more is there to say about truth? Have we not defined it satisfactorily, and can't we now breathe more easily and turn at once to something else? Perhaps.

Truth as correspondence.   But let us stop to consider some traditional accounts of "the nature of truth." The most popular of these consists in saying that the truth is *correspondence*. "A proposition is true if it corresponds with a fact"; for instance, if it is a fact that you have a pet leopard, and if you say that you have a pet leopard, your statement is true because it *corresponds* with the fact. Truth is correspondence with fact.

But what is fact? (1) The word "fact" is sometimes used to mean the same as "true proposition": thus we say, "It's a fact that I was gone last week"—that is, "The sentence 'I was gone last week' expresses a true proposition." But this definition of "fact" will be of no use here: A proposition is true if it corresponds with a true proposition. This gets us not one step ahead. (2) But the word "fact" is also used to mean the same as "actual state-of-affairs," referring to the state-of-affairs rather than to the proposition. But if we use "fact" in this way, then we are back again with the definition we gave above: A proposition is true if it describes a state-of-

___

[7] We should add, a *logically* possible state-of-affairs (see below, pp. 169–72). "Cinderella turned into a pumpkin at midnight" is false, but the state-of-affairs is logically possible (in a rough sense, conceivable). But the sentence "Quadruplicity drinks procrastination," while it does not describe an actual state-of-affairs, does not describe a possible one either: it is a meaningless sentence.

affairs that is actual—that is, a *fact*. This may be unobjectionable, but it only repeats what was already said.

"Except for one thing," one might reply. "In this last definition there is a reference to correspondence: a true proposition is one that *corresponds* to a fact—that is, to an actual state-of-affairs. In the earlier definition, the word 'correspond' did not appear." This is true, but it is precisely the word "correspond" that may cause much unnecessary mischief. For *how* does a true proposition correspond to a fact? The word "correspond" is here being ripped out of its usual context. Does a true proposition correspond to a fact in the way that the color sample on the color-chart corresponds to the color of the paint on my wall? No, there is certainly no *resemblance* between a proposition and a state-of-affairs (or even between a sentence and a state-of-affairs). Does it correspond in the way the names of books on library cards correspond to the books themselves—that is, is there a one-to-one correspondence between them?—for every card a book, and for every book a card? There may well be a correspondence in this sense. If we wish to say there is a correspondence between a proposition and a fact in this sense, no harm is done. But what is gained by this? It is at least as clear to say that a true proposition is one that describes an actual state-of-affairs—which was our original definition. And this way of putting the matter is not misleading, as the use of the word "correspondence" may be.

The word "correspondence" suggests that, when we make a true judgment, we have a sort of picture of the real in our minds and that our judgment is true because this picture is like the reality it represents. But our judgments are not *like* the physical things to which they refer. The images we use in judging may indeed in certain respects copy or resemble physical things, but we can make a judgment without using any imagery except words, and words are not in the least similar to the things which they represent. We must not understand "correspondence" as meaning copying or even resemblance.[8]

Truth as coherence.   Sometimes the correspondence view of truth is denied and the view that truth consists in *coherence* substituted for it. It is not the correspondence of propositions with facts that constitutes truth, according to this view, but rather the coherence of propositions *with one another.* Coherence is a relation *among propositions,* not a relation between a proposition and something else (a state-of-affairs) which is not a proposition.

But what kind of a relation among propositions is coherence? Are a group of propositions coherent with one another when they are consistent with one another? No, for this relation is too weak: the propositions "2 plus 2 equals 4," "Caesar crossed the Rubicon," and "Minks are fur-bearing animals" are all consistent with one another: that is, not one of them contradicts any of the

[8] A. C. Ewing, *The Fundamental Questions of Philosophy*, pp. 54–55.

others. But a group of propositions is not coherent unless each of them supports the other ones—they are *mutually supporting*. If five witnesses who do not know one another each testify (independently of one another) to seeing Mr. White in Pillsville last Thursday evening, their reports are mutually coherent in this sense. If nothing is known about the veracity of the witnesses, the testimony of each witness taken alone would easily be discounted; but if they all say the same thing without having been in conspiracy with one another, the testimony of each one of them tends to support the testimony of the others; each lends strength to the other. But let us notice a few things about this:

1. The testimony of one or even all of the witnesses taken together is not what makes the proposition (that Mr. White was in Pillsville last Thursday evening) true. Does not its truth consist in the fact that the proposition describes an actual state-of-affairs, namely that White *was* in Pillsville on Thursday evening? The testimony of the witnesses is only *evidence* that the statement is true; it does not *make* it true; it *points* to the truth of the statement without being what the truth of the proposition consists in. Indeed, the combined testimony of the witnesses is quite compatible with the falsity of the statement about Mr. White: all the witnesses may have been victims of mistaken identification.

2. Even if what made the statement about Mr. White true were the testimony of the witnesses, what made *their* statements true? Again, the fact that they saw Mr. White. But this is correspondence; it is not the coherence of their statements with *other* statements that made them true. If proposition p is true because it is coherent with propositions $q, r,$ and s (which, as we have seen, does not seem to be the case), what is it that makes $q, r,$ and s true? Their coherence with still other propositions? And what makes these in turn true? Somewhere in this chain we have to leave coherence and come to correspondence—that is, to a relation between the proposition and a state-of-affairs in the world *outside* this proposition or any body of propositions.

3. A body of propositions may be coherent and yet not true. There are numerous systems of geometry, each of which consists of a body of coherent propositions, but not all of these systems of propositions can be true of the world. Whatever the relation of a group of propositions may be to *each other,* the question of truth does not arise until we consider whether any or all of these propositions reports an actual state-of-affairs in the world—or, if you prefer, corresponds to a state-of-affairs about the world.

Truth as what "works."   There is still another suggested definition of truth: that truth is what *works,* and a true proposition is one that works. Here, however, we must pay very careful attention to the meaning of the word "work." It, too, is being used far from its home base. What does it mean to say that a proposition (or, as would more usually be said in this context, a *belief*) works? We all know what is meant when we say that a car works: first it won't start at all; then you fix something in it, and it works—that is, it runs again. Even here, is your belief that the starter button was disengaged made *true* by the fact that when you made a certain repair the car then worked? Not at all: you might have done one thing, A, which unknown to you caused something else, B, to happen, and B was what caused the car to work again although you thought it was A. Your belief in A was not made true by the fact that the car subsequently worked. So even here it is false to say that "the true belief is the one that works."

The fact is that the word "working" has a meaning in only a rather limited context: that of *things* working—that is, functioning in a certain way that we consider normal or satisfactory, with respect to certain goals or objects the statement of which makes clear what we mean by "working" in the given context. But what is meant by a *belief* working? Suppose I believe that there are living organisms on Mars. In what sense does that belief work—or for that matter fail to work? If I go to Mars and find living organisms there, then indeed my belief has turned out to be true; but what made it true was that the proposition describes an actual state-of-affairs. If this is all that is meant by "working," then we are back with our original definition. But if something other than this is meant by "working," what is it, and how does the truth of a belief consist in its "working"? Even if true beliefs in some sense work, is this not because they are first *true*? It is, of course, possible that the word "works" in the sentence "The truth is what works" can be given some broader interpretation, so as to make the theory more plausible. But even if this is done, it does not appear promising to extend the word "work," which is defined in a quite different context, to perform a task in *this* quite different context, where other words will function much better.

Truth and belief.   It is quite clear that these two propositions have different meanings:

1. *p* is true.
2. I believe (or think) that *p* is true.

A person may believe that a proposition is true even though it is not true, and a proposition may be true though neither he nor anyone else believes it. "The earth is flat" was once universally believed to be true, although it is false. The truth or falsity of propositions is not influenced by our beliefs about them. To be true, our beliefs must accord with the facts of reality; the facts of reality do not accommodate themselves to our beliefs.

These points may seem obvious, but people occasionally make utterances that show that they are confused about them or have forgotten them:

1. "A proposition is false until it's proved true" and "A proposition is true until it's proved false" reveal equally obvious mistakes. It may be that some people will not *believe* a proposition until it has been proved to be true, or sometimes not even then; and that others will not disbelieve a proposition until it has been proved false (if then). But the degree of one's belief concerning it has nothing to do with its truth. A person who says, "It's false

till it's proved true," may mean thereby (and saying it in a very misleading way), "I'll *believe* it's false until it's proved true."

Assuming that this is what is meant, what are we to say of such belief? Believing it's false until it is proved true would seem to be just as irrational as believing it's true till it is proved false. If it has been shown to be false, then one should disbelieve it; if it has been shown to be true, one should believe it; and if it has not been shown to be either, one should not believe it or disbelieve it. One's belief should be proportioned to the evidence: if it is very likely true but not proved, the proper attitude is "I believe that it's very *probably* true." (When can we be *sure* that it's true? This question will occupy us during the remainder of this chapter.)

2. During an argument, when a proposition has been attacked, one sometimes hears, "Well, at least *as far as I'm concerned,* it's true." But what on earth does this mean? When you say it, are you saying that it *is* true, or that you *believe* that it is true? More likely it is the latter; but when you say you believe it is true, remember that your believing that it is true is quite compatible with its not *being* true—that is, your belief may be false. To say "As far as I'm concerned, it's true" is extremely misleading: it sounds as if you are saying *more* than that you believe it (rightly or wrongly) to be true—that not only do you believe it to be true, but that it *is* true. But if you are saying that it *is* true, then what does the "as far as I'm concerned" add? Is it said to let you off the hook in case the statement turns out not to be true? But you cannot eat your cake and have it: you cannot declare that it *is* true and, when it is shown to be false, claim as a defense that you said it was true only as far as you're concerned.

3. The most misleading of all the formulations of this kind is *"To me* it's true, *to you* it may not be." What does it mean to say "To me it's true?" Perhaps it just means "It's true *according to me"*—that is, "I *believe* it's true." But this, as we have seen, is quite compatible with the statement's actually being false. If all you mean is that you believe it's true, then why not say just that, instead of generating confusion by saying *"To me* it's true"? Perhaps the answer is that this last formulation makes it sound as if it *is* true and that your believing it guarantees it.

Discussions often end with one person saying "Well, to me it's true" while another one says "And to me it isn't." But what do these statements mean? If they mean simply that the first person believes it and the second person doesn't, then the statements only repeat what is already known to both disputants. And if they mean something more, what is it? This kind of conclusion to a discussion leaves entirely unanswered the question *"Is* it true or *isn't* it?" What does it mean to say "To you there is a God, to me there isn't?" Either there is or there isn't, and one of them is mistaken. The same proposition cannot be both true and not true. Either there is a cat in this room or there is not; either there is a God or there isn't. What is "To you there is, to me there isn't" except a confusing and perhaps dishonest way of saying "According to you there is, according to me there isn't"—that is, "You believe there is, I believe there isn't"? thus leaving it an open question which of the beliefs is true.

Truth is not relative to the individual, even though there are truths *about* individuals. Suppose that Smith has a toothache and Jones does not. Does this show that the statement "I have a toothache" is true for Smith but not true for Jones? Not at all: it means only that the proposition "Smith has a toothache" is true, and the proposition "Jones has a toothache" is false. We must remember that the word "I" refers to a different person every time it is used by a different speaker; when Smith says "I" he means Smith, and when Jones says "I" he means Jones. Once this is clear, we can see that the sentence "I have a toothache" expresses a different proposition when Smith utters it from when Jones utters it. And since it expresses two different propositions, it is no surprise that one of these propositions is true and the other false.

Assertions of belief, then, are different from assertions of truth. If White says *"p is true"* and Black says *"p is not true,"* they are contradicting one another, and one of them must be mistaken (*p* cannot be "true for you and not true for me"). But if White says, "I *believe p* is true" and Black says "I *believe p* is not true," their statements do not contradict one another, and both of them may well be true. It may be true that White believes *p* and also true that Black does not. Whether or not *p* is true, then, is an entirely different question from whether or not one *believes p* to be true.

Almost as misleading as saying that a proposition can be true for one person but false for another is saying that a proposition can be true at one time or place and false at another. Yet can we not say that "Chicago has over 3,000,000 people" is true today but was false 50 years ago? Not if we wish to be accurate. The sentence "Chicago has over 3,000,000 people" expresses a different proposition when uttered in 1875 from what it does in 1975. To be quite clear, the two propositions should be expressed in different sentences: "Chicago had over 3,000,000 people in 1875" (false) and "Chicago has over 3,000,000 people in the second half of the 20th century" (true). Just as the word "I" refers to different individuals when uttered by Smith and when uttered by Jones, so words like "this" and "now" refer to the aspects of the times and places at which they were uttered, and consequently the same sentence uttered in 1875 and 1975 refers to different states-of-affairs, or expresses different propositions. The failure here is one of incomplete specification of meaning: once the meaning is specified, by the substitution of nouns for pronouns, there is no longer any confusion.

The example about Chicago referred to two different times but the same place. The reverse, of course, also happens. If I say "My letter opener is here" when I am sitting at my desk where my letter opener is, what I say is true, but not if I say it when I am swimming in the ocean. But the guilty word in this situation is the word "here": "here" normally refers to the place or vicinity where I am, and thus it refers to a different vicinity after I change my location. This difficulty can be corrected in the same way as before, by removing the expression that changes its reference (not its meaning) when the speaker changes his location: "My letter opener is (specifying the time) on my desk" is true; "My letter opener is in the ocean" is false.

Once the meaning of the sentence is completely spelled out, it will be apparent that the truth of a proposition is not relative to time or place, although it may be *about* a time and place (just as we saw earlier that it is not relative to the speaker, although it may be about a speaker). If it was true that Caesar was assassinated in 44 B.C., then it was, is now, and ever will be true that Caesar was assassinated in 44 B.C.—it was not merely true in 44 B.C.; it is just as true now or at any other time. A true proposition does not cease to be true with the passage of time; but the time when the state-of-affairs occurred or existed must be specified in order to make the statement complete. When this is done, the truth is independent of changes in time and place. What is true always will be true: if people were burned as witches in the 17th century, it always will be true that people were burned as witches in the 17th century. But this is not to be confused with saying that a state-of-affairs that existed at one time must exist at all other times, or indeed at any other time. Caesar's assassination occurred at only one point in space and time; and the burning of people as witches, though it occurred at different places and times, did not on that account occur at *all* places and times. States-of-affairs come and go, but truths are eternal.

Exercises

1. Analyze the meaning of the word "true" or "truth" in each of the following:
   a. He is a true friend.
   b. He is true to his wife.
   c. This character (in a novel) is true to the way people of that kind behave in actual life.
   d. The equator is not a true physical place.
   e. The true way of solving this problem is . . .
   f. This line is not a true plumb.
   g. The true meaning of "democracy" is . . .
   h. It's the truth that hurts.
   i. This is certainly a true portrait of her.
   j. You can't draw a true circle.
2. Is it true now that the sun will rise tomorrow?
3. If truth is construed as being correspondence with reality, explain as best you can what are the facts of reality with which the following propositions correspond. If you do not consider them to be true, in what does their falsity consist?
   a. The cat is on the mat.
   b. I have the concept of redness.

    c. Man is a rational animal.

    d. The deliberate infliction of suffering is evil.

    e. This painting is beautiful.

    f. If you were in this room now, you would see me.

4. Can you think of any beliefs that, though true, do not "work"? or any which, though they "work," are not true? Before answering, specify as carefully as you can what you mean by the word "work."

5. Suppose that "work" means the same as "having satisfying consequences." Could one proposition then be both true and false, true for one person and false for another? Explain.

6. Critically evaluate the use of the following forms of speech. If you do not consider the expression meaningless, put it in other words.

    a. That's true for him, but not for me.

    b. That's true of him, but not of me.

    c. A proposition is neither true nor false until we have some evidence for it or against it.

    d. A proposition isn't true or false until someone is thinking about it.

    e. A proposition may be neither true nor false: (1) it may be meaningless, or (2) its truth or falsity may never be known.

    f. A proposition may be true at one time and not at another—for example, "The earth has a population of over three billion people."

    g. A proposition may be true in one place and not in another—for example, "This place has an annual rainfall of under 30 inches."

    h. A proposition may be true for one person and not for another—for example, "I frequently have migraine headaches."

7. Can a proposition be partly true and partly false? What about half-truths?

7. The Sources of Knowledge

We are now ready to consider some aspects of knowledge. A proposition may be true although one does not *know* it to be true. By what means, then, do we come by knowledge? What are the avenues by means of which we are enabled to know propositions to be true? Let us now consider some alleged roads to knowledge.

1. **Sense-experience.** Of all of them, sense-experience is the most obvious. If you were asked, "How do you know that there is a book in front of you?" you might well reply, "Because I can see it and touch it"—what could be more obvious? It would certainly seem that you can know many things about the world—that physical things exist, and what their characteristics are—by seeing, hearing, touching, smelling, tasting. It is primarily through seeing and touching that we know *that* physical things exist: we see the chair, and then we sit on it; but all our senses on various occasions inform us of *what* a thing's characteristics are: we can see that it is red, smell its pungent odor, taste its bitterness, feel its hardness, hear it being struck.

It is not all as simple as this, of course. Sometimes we have sense-experiences when there is nothing at all to be perceived: we may be having a hallucination, such as when we are thirsty and think we see water and trees in the desert and there are none there. Or sometimes what we see is really there, but we think it has one characteristic when it really has another; if we are color-blind, we think it is gray when it is green; or we may see one kind of thing, which is really there, but mistake it for another, as when in the darkness or fog we mistake a dog for a wolf, or a donkey for a horse.

These are all *perceptual errors,* and we shall discuss them in detail in Chapter 8. It is commonly believed that the existence of perceptual errors shows that our senses are fallible, but it would be more accurate to say that our *judgment* is fallible. Our senses haven't really deceived us: *we* have been led (on the basis of our sense-perceptions) to make judgments that we subsequently find to be untrue; had we withheld judgment—had we not *taken* the donkey to be a horse—there would have been no error. The error is always one of judgment, not of sensation. All the senses can do is present us with experiences, which we then classify, sometimes erroneoeusly.

It is worth noting also that when we make a perceptual error owing to incomplete or fragmentary sense-experiences, it is always further sense-experiences that lead us to discover our error. If you are not sure this is a real apple, bite into it or cut it open and see whether it is made of wax; if you are not sure that it's a man walking down the road in the distance, wait till he comes closer and then judge, or look through a pair of binoculars; if you are not sure you hear a clock ticking in the next room, go there, approach the source of the sound, and then judge. There is no cure for erroneous judgments based on sense-experiences but other judgments based on *further* sense-experiences. So the fact of error based on sense-experience does not show that we must appeal to something over and above sense-experience; it only shows that we need more sense-experience, and that if we had waited to have it, we would not have made the mistaken judgment in the first place.

Before it can become embodied in knowledge, all sense-experience requires *judgment.* The sense-experiences you are now having do not constitute knowledge; you must first *judge* that this is a chair, that this is a book, and so on. And it is the proposition that you judge to be true or false; the sense-experience itself is neither true nor false: it merely exists or occurs. It is there to form the basis of a perceptual judgment, but it alone is not enough to constitute that judgment. The role of judgment in perception is easily overlooked because in so many cases we only use concepts like "chair" and "tree" which are so familiar that it seems that when we make the judgment we are just making a report of sense-experience with no concepts involved. But that this is false can be shown easily when we take even slightly more complex cases: "I hear a Lincoln Continental coming up the hill," one may say; but another person who has the same (or very similar) sound-experiences may not recognize it as the sound of a Lincoln Continental at all: he is not able to interpret his auditory experience as being the experience *of* a Lincoln Continental. Thus, to make perceptual judgments, we must not only be able to perceive but must also know the meanings of words, and how to apply words to what we perceive.

Thus far we have been speaking only of the so-called "external senses," those through which we get information about the outside world. But there are also the "internal senses," acquainting us with our own internal states (feelings, attitudes, moods, pains, and pleasures), as well as our own mental operations such as thinking, believing, and wondering. In these cases we do not have sense-*organs* at all; nevertheless, on the basis of certain experiences we *are* entitled to state certain propositions. But the only propositions we are here entitled to assert are about our own internal states: for example, I am having a toothache, I feel drowsy, I feel ill this morning, I am thinking about next summer's vacation, and so on. In all these cases the fact that we are *having* the experience in question is the only guarantee we have or need for the truth of the proposition. If I have a headache, this is all that is required to make the proposition "I have a headache" true. The proposition "I have a toothache" is *about* nothing but my present experience, so having the experience is enough to make that proposition true.

It is important to be very careful about this kind of knowledge: we can easily use it to make unjustified claims. Two points in particular should be kept in mind:

1. The only kind of proposition that the having of these experiences entitles us to utter are propositions *about* those experiences themselves. If you have a headache you are entitled to say, "I have a headache"; and if you are asked how you know you have a headache, you can say, "Because I feel it, that's all." But do not extend this convenient formula, "I feel it," to other things: "Next winter will be a severe one." "How do you know?" "I *feel* it." This will not do. You cannot feel that next winter will be severe in the way you feel your present headache or drowsiness or pain or pleasure. In the latter case you simply feel the pain or whatever; in the former case you claim to feel that such-and-such is or will be the case. And feeling *that* so-and-so (as opposed to feeling so-and-so, the headache) is never a guarantee that the proposition which you "feel" to be the case is true. The word "feel" has in fact changed its meaning here. When you feel the headache, you have *immediate acquaintance* with a certain feeling-state you are having; but when you "feel" *that* next winter will be severe, whatever internal feelings you may have do not guarantee the truth of the proposition in question, for what you claim to know in this case is *not* just that you have a certain feeling but that a certain state-of-affairs in the world will exist or occur. The way to discover whether next winter will be severe is to wait for next winter to come and then discover whether it is severe. Your present state-of-feeling may or may not be a reliable indicator of next winter's weather; but even if it is, your present feeling is one thing and next winter's weather another, and the statement about your present feeling should be sharply distinguished from the

statement about next winter's weather: they are clearly not the same statement.

The word "feel" is, indeed, misleadingly ambiguous: (1) "I have a headache"; that is, "I feel it"—though here it would be much clearer simply to say that I have it and not talk about feeling. (2) "I feel the sharpness of this knife"; here the word "feel" refers to a *touch*-experience, and touch is one of the external senses. As if this ambiguity were not enough to cause confusion, we have still another: (3) "I feel *that* . . ." (followed by a proposition). Sometimes "I feel that this is true" means no more than "I *believe* that this is true" (perhaps not very strongly). And having a "feeling" that *p* is true is not enough to entitle me to say that I *know* that *p* is true. Believing is not knowing; whether one believes weakly or strongly, one may still believe many propositions that are false. However strongly you may "feel" (have the belief) that the President will be assassinated during the coming year, your "feeling" (belief) does not guarantee that it will be so. Belief does not guarantee knowledge, as we shall observe in greater detail in the coming section. Thus "feeling" in the sense of belief does not guarantee knowledge either. For the sake of semantic clarity, it would be preferable not to use the word "feeling" in this sense at all. Instead of saying "I feel that people are persecuting me," say "I believe that people are persecuting me," and then judge by the evidence as best you can whether this belief is true.

2. Not all cases in which we say "I feel X" are immediate experiences. We have just indicated the dangers in saying "I feel *that* . . ." (followed by a proposition); now we must point to a danger in saying "I feel X" and concluding that the statement "I am in state X" is true. To make this clear, we must make an important distinction, between occurrent states and dispositional states.

A stab of pain, an itch, a pang of regret, a feeling of drowsiness are all *occurrent states* in a person's consciousness. When a lump of sugar is dissolved in a cup of coffee, the dissolved state of the sugar is occurrent, for it is occurring at that moment, and doubtless it will continue to occur as long as the cup of coffee remains. However, if the lump of sugar is in the sugar bowl, it is not dissolved, but it is still *soluble*. To say that it is soluble is to say that it *will* dissolve *if* it is put into the coffee (or other liquids in which it will dissolve). Its state of solubility is dispositional: it has a disposition to dissolve—that is, it will dissolve given the right circumstances—but since it is not yet dissolved, the state of being dissolved is not yet occurrent. The state of the sugar in the bowl is, however, occurrent. Anything that *is* happening is occurrent: a flash of lightning, sitting down at your desk, eating your dinner; but most of the properties we ascribe to things are dispositional: we are describing what the thing *would* do or how it *would* behave if something were done to it which is not being done. Thus "Milk is nutritious"—that is, it *will* nourish you if you drink it; "Gold is malleable"—that is, it will change its shape if you try to mold it; "Gasoline is inflammable"—that is, it will burn if you light a match to it; and so on.

Now, if you have a toothache, or feel sleepy, or are wondering about what to do next, or are thinking about China, all these are states of consciousness of yours, and all of them are occurrent. (If you did them yesterday, they were occurrent then.) Throbs of pleasure, pangs of regret, itches, thinkings, wonderings are all occurrent. And when a state of consciousness is occurrent, then its occurrence entitles you to utter the appropriate statement, such as "I have a toothache," "I am wondering what to do next." If you feel a pain, that is all that is required for a pain to exist: for the pain to exist is for it to be felt, and the pain has no other existence than this. "I have a severe pain, but I can't feel it" would be a contradiction in terms. ("I *would* have a severe toothache except for the fact that my tooth is anesthetized" is different, of course, and may be true; what is self-contradictory is saying that the pain exists and yet that you don't feel it, since for pain to exist simply *is* for it to be felt.) In general, feelings are occurrent states, and their occurrence warrants your saying that you have them.

But there are other words that we use to describe people's "inner states," which are *disposition*-words: Our words for moods and emotions are disposition-words. "I am in an irritable mood" means that *if* someone were to cross me or in some other way annoy me, I would be irritated more quickly than usual. "I dislike chicken liver" doesn't mean that I am always in the occurrent state of feeling repelled by chicken liver, but that *if* I were to be served it, I would experience this state. When you say, "I love her," you are not stating merely that you are in a certain (verbally indefinable) state of consciousness at this moment; love involves many dispositions. If you love someone, you will want to do things for her, you will be happy when she is happy, and so on. If you claim to be in love but do not enjoy doing things for the loved one, and so on, then someone can quite rightly say to you, "You don't really love Miss X." You may say that you do love her, and you may not be lying (that is, deliberately telling a falsehood); but still what you say will not be true. You may experience all kinds of spasms of feeling (occurrent states), but if you are not disposed to *behave* in certain ways toward the other person, you are not in love. Love involves not only certain occurrent states (feelings) but, far more importantly, many dispositional states (a disposition to behave in certain ways *a, b, c, . . . n* toward the other person). And if you do not behave in those ways, even on the appropriate occasions, someone may well doubt that you feel love, no matter what your *occurrent* feelings are. It is, therefore, not enough to say "I know that I'm in love because I feel that I am." If an adolescent daughter says this, her mother may respond, "What you feel is not love but only infatuation. If you were really in love, you'd behave differently." The mother can watch the daughter's behavior, and probably does so with more care than the daughter does herself; and since tendencies to behavior (dispositions) are part of the meaning of "love," the mother may be a better judge of whether her daughter is in love than the daughter is. Not that the mother feels what the daughter is feeling (we shall discuss the possibility of this on pp. 382–85), but she can observe her behavior and make her inferences from that. No matter how many throbs or twinges a person may feel, he is not in love unless he tends to act in certain ways toward the beloved: thus if someone observes you *saying* you are in love but sees you conspicuously *not* acting in these ways, he can say with justification, "Whatever feelings or other inner episodes you are experiencing, you are not in love, for love involves the tendency to behave in certain ways—and I've watched you, and you just don't exhibit these tendencies."

Another example: To say that a person is vain is to attribute to him a disposition or tendency to consider his own interests above others, to be inconsiderate of other people, to act as if he alone existed, and so on. But the vain man does not *feel* vain; if he did, he might be disposed to change his behavior in the future. Calling someone vain attributes to him a set of dispositions but not any occurrent states. The person himself might be the last person to give a fair estimate of whether or not he was vain. Whether you are vain, or in love, or conscientious, or envious of someone, and so on cannot be discovered merely by introspection but only by an impartial examination of your behavior over an interval of time; and another person may be far better fitted to render an impartial examination than you are.

These, then, are the main precautions we must keep in mind in judging whether we are entitled to say we know something simply on the ground that we are in a certain occurrent state. There is a great deal of confusion about this: people constantly make claims on the basis of "feeling" something or having some other "inner experience," when the proposition that they claim to be true goes far beyond that experience and would require much more than the having of the experience to guarantee its truth.

Thus far we have not questioned that we are entitled to make reports of our experience on the basis of having the experience, plus a knowledge of the meanings of the words and sentences in the report. But even this has sometimes been questioned. If I say "Next winter will be severe," I may be mistaken—I shall have to wait to find out, and in any case my present feeling will not guarantee it, even though next winter *does* turn out to be severe. But "I feel drowsy" seems to be nothing more than a report of a presently experienced state. How could it possibly be mistaken? I have the experience, and I know the meaning of the sentence I am uttering. What more could be required to know that it is true? The statement is not a prediction of how I shall feel later, nor a dispositional statement about present or future tendencies toward behavior.

We cannot discuss this issue further until we have made some important distinctions, which we shall do in Chapter 8. Meanwhile, it is extremely important that we distinguish carefully between those statements that do not make any claims other than that I am having a certain experience and those that do. Often statements that *appear* to be of the first kind are actually of the second. Some of them, in fact, may be ambiguous, and can be taken either way. "I have a toothache" seems to be merely a statement about what I am feeling now; but if there is involved in it in any way a claim about the condition of my tooth (that it has a cavity, etc.), then it is not merely a statement about what I am feeling at this moment but a statement about the condition of my mouth, whose truth my dentist probably would be in a better position to discover than I am. Many statements may parade as pure experience when in fact they include further claims, hidden for the moment by the façade of an experience-statement. If we are taken in by these, we shall run the danger of admitting as true the claims of those who utter them, on the ground that they are merely reports of experiences, though they actually include considerably more.

2. **Reason.** But sense experience is not our only source of knowledge. If someone asks you, "How do you know that 74 plus 89 equals 163?" you don't reply "I looked and saw it" but "I've figured it out." You resort to calculation, not to seeing or hearing or touching. You have arrived at the answer by means of *reasoning*. Reasoning is one source of knowledge, although, as we shall see, "reasoning" is not the only sense of the term "reason."

People are engaged in reasoning when they take certain statements as the basis for making one or more other statements; or in other words, when they take one or more statements, called the *premises* of an argument, and use these to *infer* another statement, called the *conclusion* of the argument. Thus we use the statements "I have only a dime and a nickel in my pocket" as a basis for inferring the statement "I have less than 25¢ in my pocket."

a. Deductive reasoning. The most familiar kind of reasoning, which is often taken as the model for all reasoning, is deductive reasoning. In a deductive argument, the conclusion must *logically follow* from the premises; or, in other words, if the premises of the argument are true, the conclusion must be true. For example,

> 1. If it is raining, the streets will be wet.
>   It is raining.
> Therefore, The streets will be wet.

This is a *valid* deductive argument: if you accept the two premises, you must also accept the conclusion—the conclusion, as we say, *follows from* the premises. Or again,

> 2. All dogs are mammals.
>   All mammals are animals.
> Therefore, All dogs are animals.

is a valid deductive argument for the same reason. The following argument, however, though its proponent may claim it to be a deductive argument, is not valid:

3.   All dogs are mammals.
     All cats are mammals.
Therefore, All dogs are cats.

Unfortunately, we cannot pause here to examine the many kinds of deductive arguments to see why some are valid and some not. The above cases are doubtless simple enough to convince you that the first two are valid and the third invalid. The study of why some are and some not is reserved for a special branch of philosophy, *logic*. Logic is the study of valid reasoning, and it attempts to show why some types of argument are valid and others are not.

It is important at this point to distinguish *validity* from *truth*. In a valid argument, the premises need not be true: it is only required that the conclusion follows logically from the premises—that is, that *if* the premises are true, then the conclusion must be true. In argument 2 above, the premises are true. But in the following argument they are false:

4.   All cows are green.
     I am a cow.
Therefore, I am green.

—yet the argument is still valid. Though the premises are not true, the conclusion still follows logically from them. If the premises were true, the conclusion would have to be true; that is all that validity requires. On the other hand, the following statements are all true,

5.   Caesar crossed the Rubicon.
     2 plus 2 equals 4.
Therefore, I am now reading a book.

yet the argument is not valid; the conclusion does not follow from the premises, although it and they happen to be true.

It is important not to confuse validity with truth. Propositions are true or false; reasoning or argument is valid or invalid. The propositions in a valid argument may all be false, and the statements in an invalid argument may all be true. Deductive logic is the study of validity, not of truth.

In order to know, then, that a conclusion is true, (*a*) we have to know that the premises are true and (*b*) the argument must be valid—that is, that the conclusion follows logically from the premises. In argument 5, the premises were true although the argument was not valid, and in argument 4, the premises were false although the argument was valid. A course in logic will tell you which arguments are valid. But to know that the conclusion of an argument is not only validly arrived at but also true, you must know that the premises are true—something that logic alone will not tell you but that sense-experience (perhaps among other things) will; we have yet to examine other possibilities.

These two requirements are probably already familiar to us from other contexts. If you want to know whether or not your monthly bill from the department store is correct, it is necessary to add up the items to see whether the addition is correct. But this alone will not do, for you might have been charged for things that you never bought: it is also necessary that you examine whether each number entered corresponds to the price of an item that you bought. Until both requirements are met, you cannot be sure that your bill is accurate.

But now it may occur to us that we can never learn anything new from deductive reasoning, since everything that is contained in the conclusion of the argument is already contained in the premises. Consider:

> 6. All human beings have heads.
>   John Stewart is a human being.
> Therefore, John Stewart has a head.

This conclusion, one might remark, is already contained in the premises of the argument, and therefore the conclusion tells us nothing new. In fact, in order to know the major premise—that all men have heads—we already have to know that John Stewart has one! What, then is the use of deductive argument, and of rules of deductive inference?

When it is said that the conclusion is already contained in the premises, the word "contained" is ambiguous. The conclusion is not literally contained within the premises as a marble is contained in a bag. Nor is it contained in the sense that it *occurs* in the premises, for the statement "John Stewart has a head" does not occur in the premises. The conclusion is, however, contained in the premises in the sense that it is *deducible from* the premises. But to say this is only to repeat what we said at the start. The question, then, still faces us (and we shall phrase it now without using the word "contain"): When the conclusion is deducible from the premises, are we learning anything from the conclusion that we did not already know in stating the premises?

We can answer this quite simply: sometimes we do and sometimes we don't. It all depends on the complexity of the argument and the intelligence of the individual. The question "Do we learn through deductive reasoning what we did not know before?" is a psychological question, the answer to which varies from person to person. In the case of the syllogism given above, the conclusion probably does not give us any new information; before we get to the conclusion we already know what it is. Sometimes, however, even in simple arguments, we do not immediately draw the required conclusion,

> Everyone on board the ship was lost.
> Mabel was on board the ship.

and then it may come to us with a sudden shock that if these statements are both true, Mabel was lost. Here already we may be said to have learned something. We were told nothing about Mabel except that she was on board the ship; we also learned that everyone on board was lost; we are thus enabled to deduce validly that Mabel was lost, *without ever having been told this fact about Mabel.* In coming to know this fact about her, were we not acquiring new knowledge?

This becomes more apparent as the complexity of the argument increases. The conclusion to the following argument would probably constitute new knowledge to most people:

> 7. If the guard was not paying attention at the time, the car was not noticed when it came in.
> If the witness's account is correct, the guard was not paying attention at the time.
> Either the car was noticed or Jones is hiding something.
> Jones is not hiding anything.
> Therefore, The witness's account is not correct.

To a person with perfect reasoning powers, who could instantly see the implications of every statement or combination of statements that he uttered, doubtless no conclusion would come as new information; but since human beings are not thus gifted, there are many conclusions of valid deductive arguments which do come as new information, in spite of the fact that "the conclusion is contained in (deducible from) the premises."

b. Inductive reasoning. But not all reasoning is deductive. We also argue inductively: we may know the truth of the premises, but we still do not know that the conclusion is true—the premises provide *evidence* for the conclusion, but not *complete* evidence. Or, in other words, even if the premises are true, they do not render the conclusion *certain* but only *probable* to one degree or another. We may argue,

> 8. Crow #1 is black.
> Crow #2 is black.
> Crow #3 is black (and so on for 10,000 crows).
> Therefore, All crows are black.

Here, even if all our 10,000 premises are true, the conclusion is not thereby established. It does not follow even from such numerous premises. But it is rendered probable—to what degree is a matter of dispute. But at least you are more justified in saying that all crows are black after you have examined 10,000 of them and found them all to be black than you would be if you had observed only one. We all argue inductively whenever we take certain samples—whether of crows in nature or wheat from a carload (to see whether any of it is spoiled)—and conclude that all the things in the collection, or the whole thing, resemble the samples that we have examined. This kind of induction is called "induction by simple enumeration."

Suppose our conclusion had been not "All crows are black" but "The next crow we see will be black." Even this modest conclusion would not be established by the premises of the argument. But there is an interesting difference between the two conculsions: If the next crow were not black, the probability that all crows are black would drop to zero (we would have found it to be false since we would have found one crow that was not black); but the probability that the next crow after that would be black would still be very high. Unfortunately, the concept of probability is extremely complex, with many aspects that require considerable mathematical dexterity to pursue or even to present, and we shall have to omit consideration of them here.

But not all induction is of this kind. Inductive reasoning is not always from "one, two, three . . ." to "all." Sometimes the conclusion is not about all things of a certain kind but about one thing, or this thing. We may argue:

> 9.   Smith's blood was found on Jones's clothing.
>   Jones was seen entering Smith's house a few minutes before Smith's death.
>   Smith was found with a knife wound in his heart.
>   Jones's knife was later found with Smith's blood on it.
>   Jones was found an hour later trying to avoid the police. Etc.
> Therefore, Jones killed Smith.

This conclusion has some probability on the basis of the evidence presented in the premises. But of course it may not be true: the evidence is still circumstantial, and the clues may all have been planted by someone else. Even if Jones confessed to the crime, we could not say with certainty that he was guilty, for he might have made a false confession. Juries must usually reach their verdicts on the basis of probability; they only want the probability to be as great as possible (in criminal cases, "beyond reasonable doubt"). But probability is not yet certainty, and certainty in these matters is very difficult to come by. One might formulate the matter differently and say that there *is* certainty, but the proposition that is certain is not that Jones killed Smith but rather that it is *probable* on the basis of the evidence that p, q, r Jones killed Smith. Doubtless probability is preferable to no evidence at all, and in countless situations in daily life it is all that is available to us.

What is it that makes the propositions in the premises render the conclusion probable? If one of the premises had been "Jones was wearing a black suit," this would not have counted as evidence one way or the other, unless the person who was leaving Smith's house just after the murder had been seen wearing a black suit. We are relying, in inductive argument, on certain *laws of nature*. We shall discuss laws of nature in detail in Chapter 4. It will suffice to say now that laws of nature formulate certain *recurring uniformities* in the course of our experience. Heavier-than-air bodies fall; friction produces heat; water boils at 212° F. at sea level; and so on. These and countless other uniformities are quite familiar in our experience, and on the basis of them we construct inductive arguments. People who are stabbed shed blood; the same blood may appear on the clothing or body of those in contact with him; and so on. Such uniformities (most of them consequences of laws of nature) are appealed to in the above inductive argument. When we find no such uniformities, we do not take the statements in the premises of the argument as providing evidence for the conclusion.

Thus suppose that someone aged 20 argues that for 20 years now every time he has awakened in the morning he has been alive at nightfall, and therefore it is very probable that he will be alive at nightfall today. Now suppose that the same person at the age of 90 argues that he now has far more inductive evidence for the same conclusion that he did at the age of 20, since he now has been alive for 90 × 365 days instead of a mere 20 × 365 days. Yet we would not agree with this inductive argument. We would say that at the age of 90 it is far *less* probable that he will survive the day than it was at the age of 20. Why is this? It is because of *other* things we have learned about living organisms: (1) We know that many more people live past the age of 20 than live past the age of 90. At the age of 20, most of one's high-school classmates are still alive, but not so at the age of 90. (2) We also know some biological laws about organisms: that they live for only a limited span of time, that hearts wear out and tissues become diseased, and so on, and that (in the case of human beings) the age of 90 is already far beyond the average life-span.

"Reason."   Thus far, we have considered different types of *reasoning*. But, one may object, this does not exhaust the meaning of the word "reason," and it is reason that we are supposed to be considering as a source of knowledge. Let us consider this broader sense. Reason*ing* is something that you do; but reason is an *ability*. Briefly, reason is the ability to think, and the degree of your rational powers, or powers of reason, is the degree of your ability to engage in thinking. It is in this sense that man is a rational animal. If we could not think, we could not acquire any knowledge at all; having this ability is indispensable to having knowledge of any sort, including knowledge acquired through sense-perception. To formulate or to understand the proposition that this object before me is a book requires the ability to understand words and form concepts. It is true that you would not be justified in asserting it if you had no sense-experiences, but neither would you be able to assert it if you did not have the power of reason.

"But to identify something as a book you don't have to state the proposition that this is a book." This is true, but you must at least have the ability to recognize something in your experience as a book, on the basis of certain characteristics that it has. And this already requires a considerable power of abstraction: you must be able to recognize various characteristics as they recur in your experience (color, extension, rectangular shape, pages, etc.) and then be able to recognize as a book that which presents to your senses a certain combination of those characteristics. In order to isolate, out of the total welter of experience, this one thing and classify it as a book, you must be able to identify features of experience and abstract these features from all the others—and this requires something far more than the use of your senses: it requires the use of your mind, your intellect, your reason. Sense-experience provides the raw material for your judgment that this is a book, but without reason you could not formulate the judgment at all, even wordlessly. Certain of the "lower animals" have varying degrees of this power: a dog can identify a cat and distinguish it from all the other items in his environment; but the degree of abstraction of which the animal is capable is ever so much smaller than that of man. Reason in this sense, then, is a prerequisite for *all* knowledge.

There are, however, certain propositions, which are sometimes called "truths of reason," that we seem to know. We do not know them on the basis of sense-experience, and we do not know them through reaso*ning* either. For example:

A book is a book.
A thing can't be in two places at the same time.
A thing can't be black all over and white all over at the same time.
An object can't be both a book and not a book.
One can't smell a taste or taste a smell.

There are many statements of this kind, which we don't arrive at by means of reasoning, but which (it would seem) we don't know through sense-experience either. You can know through sense-experience that a book is green or blue, but how does sense experience tell you that a book is a book? You can see that the book is in this position or that position; but how can you "see" that it can't be both in this place and in that place at the same time? And so on. We shall be running into statements of this kind throughout our study of philosophy, but Chapter 3 will be devoted largely to a consideration of statements of this kind and how we know them. We shall defer any further consideration of them until that time.

Are there any other sources of knowledge? Here are some more disputed candidates for that position:

3. Authority.   "I know it's true because Mr. X says so, and Mr. X is an authority on the subject." By such statements as these we often invoke authority when we are asked how we know that a certain statement is true,

and we often claim this knowledge without bothering to check the statement for ourselves.

The statements we hear or read are nearly infinite in number, and many of them would require years of investigation before their truth could be ascertained. On the other hand, life is short, and it is impossible to check the truth of every assertion we encounter. Consequently, we either take on authority the vast majority of the claims to truth that come our way, or suspend our judgment about them. If we tried to discover for ourselves whether every statement in an elementary chemistry book is true—the chemical composition of organic molecules, what chemicals will dissolve granite, whether there is anything that the so-called inert gases will combine with, and an indefinite array of other things—it would take more years than we have in a lifetime. We might prefer to be able to investigate all these things for ourselves, but we cannot. So, as a practical expedient, we usually take the author's word for what he says, confident perhaps that if he made any false claims in the book, many of his colleagues and other readers would write in demanding that he correct the mistake. There are, however, several precautions to be observed:

1. The person whose word we take on authority must really be an authority, one who is a specialist in his field of knowledge. We cannot take just anybody's word for it. Nor does the fact that he is an authority in one field make him an authority in another. A man may be a specialist in nuclear physics, but this does not entitle us to take on authority his assertions about international relations.

2. In some areas "the doctors themselves disagree." When the authorities themselves are at variance with one another, we can only suspend judgment for the time being. Psychiatrists often disagree about a patient's diagnosis, but chemists do not disagree about the melting point of lead.

3. Whenever one accepts another person's statement on authority, he should be able to find out for himself whether the authority's statement is true, if he were to take the time and trouble. We could check the melting point of lead for ourselves, though usually we do not bother. We could even check the truth of Einstein's theory of relativity, though it would take years of special training and technical experimentation to do so. But if someone says "There is no God but Allah" and expects us to take his word for it because he is an authority on Mohammedanism, we must recognize that this statement is of an entirely different order. He may be an expert on the history and practices of Mohammedanism, and we can investigate the accuracy of his reports and historical scholarship; but the statement that there is no God but Allah is something that no one could check. If we do not know how he could verify such a claim, how could we possibly verify it for ourselves? And if we did accept the claim on the basis of his authority, how could we refrain from also accepting, for the very same reason, the claim of the specialist in Judaism who said "There is no God but Jehovah," although both of these

claims contradict each other, and both of them cannot be true (assuming that "Allah" and "Jehovah" are not two names for the same real or alleged being)?

There is one point about authority, however, that is fundamental: No matter how reliable an authority may be, and no matter how often his statements have turned out to be true when checked, authority cannot be a primary source of knowledge. If you believe a statement on the authority of Mr. X, Mr. X cannot know it on the basis of authority. He has to know *by some means other than authority* that what he claims is true. You might, of course, believe it on the basis of Mr. X's word, and Mr. X (himself not an authority) might believe on the authority of Mr. Y, who *is* an authority; but in that case it is Mr. Y who must know it, not on the authority of someone else, but because he has investigated the facts of the case and knows the statement to be true—perhaps by sense perception (which may include a series of investigations extending through years, as in the case of a zoologist investigating insect-behavior), perhaps by reasoning, and most likely by a combination of both. And if we accept Mr. X's or Mr. Y's word for what he says, we who are not authorities should do so only because we have reason to believe that what Mr. X or Mr. Y says is true. We have reason to believe this if we have checked *some* of the things he says and found them to be true, if his present claim is one that *can* be checked, if we know from previous experience that Mr. X is a reliable and trustworthy person, not given to making false claims, and if the claim does not conflict with another one that we already know to be true. Even if these conditions are met, however, they are no guarantee that what Mr. X says on this occasion is true. If we accept it, we do so at our own risk.

4. Intuition.   "I know by intuition"; "I had a flash of intuition, and suddenly it was all clear to me"; "I intuit that you're not feeling well"; "My intuition tells me that that's the direction we have to go to get back to civilization"; and so on. These are all familiar ways of speaking; claims to know something by intuition are very often made.

What is intuition? We need not stop to try to define this word precisely; we may even admit that it is verbally indefinable. At any rate, the word "intuition" in its most limited sense is merely the label for a certain kind of experience, one that (like so many) is not easily described. A conviction of certainty comes upon us quite suddenly, like "a light going on inside" and instantly we are convinced that what comes to us in this "flash" is true. The experiences commonly spoken of as intuitions typically come all at once, as if in a blinding flash; if the conviction grew upon us over a period of months or years, we would be less likely to call it an intuition. The existence of intuition *as an experience* can hardly be doubted; we have doubtless all had experiences that we could call intuitions.

The only question we are concerned with, however, is the acceptability of intuition when it is made to underwrite a claim to knowledge. If a composer has a "sudden intuition" for his next symphony, no doubts need be raised as long as he is not claiming to *know* anything by means of this intuition; a bit of inspiration has simply come to him in a flash. But if someone claims to know by intuition *that a proposition is true,* then we would do well to ask a few questions concerning it. It is not the occurrence of his experience that we question but *that which he claims to know* by means of the experience. (The intuition must be *propositional* before we are concerned with it in a discussion of knowledge.)

Let us point out first that much of what we claim to know by intuition is actually not this. A person enters the room and is asked to locate an object that the members of a group have hidden (as in the game of hide the thimble); the person notices at once what part of the room the guests carefully avoid looking at, and concludes correctly that the object is there. When asked how he knew, he may reply, "My intuition," which is far more likely to impress the assembled guests than a less mysterious account of how he arrived at this conclusion. Many people are quick to notice "minimal cues" in the behavior of other persons and are able to "gather the sense of a meeting" or conclude correctly that the audience is becoming tired or bored; they arrive at this estimate on the basis of rapid but precise observation (sense-experience) and not by intuition, as they claim. Let us be careful, then, that we do not confuse claims to know by intuition with knowledge by other means.

1. It is a well-known fact that different people's intuitions conflict. If I assert one proposition, claiming that I know it by intuition, you can assert just the opposite, claiming to know *that* on the basis of intuition. And where do we go from there? It would seem that "here ends the argument and begins the fight." It is true that such conflicts can sometimes be settled. If you intuit that it will rain tomorrow and I intuit that it won't, we can wait for tomorrow to come to discover which of our claims is true. But when we do discover it tomorrow, we discover it by sense-experience (seeing it rain, etc.), not by intuition. Intuition itself provides no way of deciding which of two conflicting intuitions is correct.

Suppose you claimed to know by intuition which of two conflicting intuitions was right; you have a superintuition that decides the issue between the two. Then how would you know that your superintuition was right? What could you say to another person who claimed to have a superintuition opposite to yours? Within intuition itself there would be no answer: you would have to go outside the realm of intuition to settle the matter. In short: not all intuitions can be true, since they sometimes contradict one another; and there is no criterion to be found in intuition itself that will distinguish between true claims and false ones.

2. But even if intuitions never conflicted, the claim to know something by means of intuition would still not be warranted. Everyone might agree that a

certain proposition, *p,* was true, and claim to know it by intuition, and this still would not prove that *p* was true.

If you say "I know by intuition," this really doesn't explain *how* you know. You may arrive at a correct conclusion and not know *how* you came by it. But to say "I know by intuition"—how does that help? Does this really explain how you came to know it, if you did know it? The word "intuition," when employed to justify a claim to *knowledge,* really leaves us as much in the dark as before. We still do not know *how,* if at all, a person came to know what he says he knows. All the reference to "intuition" enables us to conclude is "He doesn't know *how* he knows (if he knows)." As an explanation it is quite empty. I know, of course, that I have the intuition (I have the *experience* that I call "having an intuition"), but I do not thereby know that what I claim on the basis of this experience is true.

"But what if a person made a prediction a day for a year, and claimed to know its truth by intuition, and his prediction turned out to be right every time? Wouldn't that justify his claim?" Suppose, for example, that D. H. Lawrence's story "The Rocking Horse Winner" were fact and not fiction; suppose that every time the little boy rocks very hard he has a vision of which horse will win the race the next day, and that the horse he predicts always does win the next day's race. In that case, we would doubtless be justified in laying odds on the truth of the boy's predictions. But we would still not know *how* the boy was enabled to make the right predictions. The answer "By intuition," as we have seen, would tell us nothing about the "validating procedure." The word "intuition" is simply a cover-up term for our ignorance, revealing only that we do not know how he was able to do this. If asked to explain his successful predictions, we would be at a loss. In fact, of course, this phenomenon does not occur; people's intuitions are notoriously fallible, and only when they turn out to be right do their authors proudly claim that they "knew it by intuition" (when the intuitions don't turn out right, their authors do not advertise this fact).

But if the intuitions did always turn out to be right, what would we say? Should we still say that he *didn't* know which horse would win the race, or that he *did* know but we don't know *how* he knew?

This is a difficult question, and its answer depends on how we define "knowledge," which we shall attempt to do in the next section of this chapter. But we can point out here that whether or not he can be said to know (assuming this astounding run of successes to occur), he does not know *by* intuition, since the formula "by intuition" tells us nothing at all about how he knows, if he knows.

Thus far, we have mentioned only intuitions about what can later be verified in sense-experience. What about intuitions where no such check is possible? "Reality is one," "There is a God in heaven," "I saw eternity the other night," "There is a witch inside her"—these and many other statements have been claimed to be true, solely on the basis of intuition. What shall we say of such claims? We have already observed that intuition itself cannot suffice as a means of adjudicating between conflicting claims, so we must look beyond intuition to discover whether or not the intuitions were mistaken. In cases we previously considered, we could look to sense-experience. But when this does not suffice, where shall we turn? It would seem that we are forever prevented from knowing whether such claims are true or not. But even this conclusion would be premature: perhaps some of them are meaningless; perhaps some, though meaningful, are untestable; and perhaps some, though they may not seem at first to be testable, will turn out to be so when their meaning has been more clearly set forth. It is clear that a meaningless utterance does not become meaningful when it is clad in the mantle of "intuition," and that no reference to intuition will tell us whether it is meaningful and, if so, what its meaning is. Meanwhile, let us examine one more alleged source of knowledge.

5. Revelation.   Sometimes one claims to know something by means of revelation; but what this claim comes to depends on how one came by the revelation.

"It was revealed to me in a dream" (or a vision). In this case we run into the same problems as we did in intuition. What if one person had a vision that told him one thing, and another person had a vision that told him the opposite? The fact that the person had a dream or a vision, of course, does not show that its message is true or can be trusted. If what it says is true, its truth can be discovered only by other means.

"It was revealed to me by Mr. Jones that. . . ." This ordinarily means that Mr. Jones told you, and that you are accepting what he says. Since you are accepting it on his authority, this takes us back to authority as an alleged source of knowledge.

"It was revealed to me by God that. . . ." But by what means did the person identify the source of the revelation? How did it come to him—in a vision, as voices, or a clap of thunder? And what is the evidence that these experiences, whatever they are, are manifestations of God? And what, again, if two persons claim to have revelations that contradict one another? Each person will doubtless declare the other's revelation to be false, but this does not help the situation: we want some criterion that will enable us to distinguish the false ones from the true ones. Moreover, assuming that one person has had some experience or other that he calls "a revelation from God," what entitles other people to believe it? What comes to you as revelation comes to me (from you) as mere hearsay.

"It was revealed to me in a sacred book. . . ." Here the alleged revelation is still from God, but God is revealed not through visions or voices but through a book. But the same questions recur: how does one know that *this* book is a sacred book? (Being sacred would imply at least that it speaks the truth.) That the author of the book claims that it is true, or even infallible, does not substantiate the claim that it is so. I too can claim that everything I say is true, but this does not make it so. Moreover, there are competing candidates for the position of true revelation: the Bible, the Koran, and numerous other works each make this claim. How then are we to know which if any of these various claimants to accept? If the claims made are such that sense-experience or reason could substantiate them, then it is because of this, and not because the book says so, that we believe that the claims are true. But if, as often happens, the claims made are of such a nature that we could never verify them, how can we ever be in a position to select one of them as "the true revelation"?

6. **Faith.** Another type of claim to knowledge, which somewhat overlaps the previous one, is faith. "I know this through faith"; "I have faith in it, so it must be true"; "I believe it through faith, and this faith gives me knowledge."

The same difficulty that plagued the claims to knowledge by intuition and revelation occurs here. People have faith in different things, and the things they claim to know by means of faith often conflict with one another. One person claims to know by faith that Jesus was the Son of God, and another claims to know by faith that Jesus was but a man and that the true Messiah is still to come. If faith is the sole basis for the claim, the same thing (having faith that it's true) that validates the first claim to knowledge also validates the second. In this respect they are equal. And yet they cannot both be true, since they contradict each other. It doesn't follow, of course, that neither of them is true, but only that neither of them can be known by faith: for if the one were known by faith, so would the other, which conflicts with it.

In daily life we do often say things like "I have faith in him," which means approximately the same as "I have confidence in him"—that is, I believe he will be reliable, trustworthy, and so on. One may indeed be perfectly justified in having such confidence, and thus, in this sense, in "having faith in him." But the question is, what justifies this confidence? If one simply has faith in a vacuum, so to speak, without knowing anything about the person in whom one has faith, then one has no justification whatever; there would be no reason at all for picking the name of a total stranger out of a telephone directory and saying "I have faith in him." But faith (confidence) in a person may often be justified on the basis of his past record: one may have good evidence that he is honest and reliable. But one acquires this evidence not by "having faith" but by observing his behavior, particularly in trying situations, and noting what he does in a variety of these circumstances. One learns through sense-experience over a period of time how he behaves, and then one concludes that he will be reliable in the next situation as the result of an inductive inference. Thus sense-experience and reasoning, not faith, are the basis for the claim of reliability.

Indeed, it seems too obvious to mention that when people appeal *solely* to faith as a way of knowing, they do so because there is no evidence that what they say is true, and yet they very much want others to believe it. What they often do not realize is that the very thing—faith—that they invoke to establish their claim would, if accepted, establish the conflicting claims of their opponents as well. The appeal to faith is a double-edged knife. That is why it is usually appealed to only as a last resort. "Faith" has been defined as "a firm belief in something for which there is no evidence. We do not speak of faith that 2 plus 2 equals 4 or that the earth is round. We only speak of faith when we wish to substitute emotion for evidence."[9] But if faith is an attitude —an attitude of belief in something in the absence of evidence—then faith cannot be a source of knowledge. What feeling or attitude you have toward a belief, and whether that belief is true, are two very different things. It is folly to confuse one with the other.

Exercises

1. In which of the following cases does the "feeling" guarantee the truth of the statement about what is felt? Give your reasons.
   a. I feel anxious.
   b. I feel sick.
   c. I feel as if I'm about to be sick.
   d. I feel that I am about to be sick.
   e. I feel able to do anything.
   f. I feel as if I have a frog in my throat.
   g. I feel that she has been unjustly treated.
   h. I feel that God exists.

2. Do you require anything other than your present experience, plus knowledge of what the words mean, to know that the following propositions are true?
   a. I have a toothache.
   b. I ate breakfast this morning.
   c. I exist.
   d. I hope it rains tomorrow.
   e. I think it will rain tomorrow.
   f. It will rain tomorrow.

3. Do you consider the following to be occurrent states, or dispositional, or both?
   a. He is angry.
   b. He is quick-tempered.
   c. He is religious.
   d. He is boiling over with rage.
   e. He is fat.
   f. He is restless.
   g. The fruit is rotten.
   h. Her face is ashen.
   i. The coffers are empty.
   j. Her tastes are expensive.

4. Describe the kinds of sense-experiences which would be relevant to ascertaining the truth or falsity of the following propositions:
   a. She is frugal.
   b. The valence of oxygen is 2.

[9] Bertrand Russell, *Human Society in Ethics and Politics*, p. 215.

c. The earth's axis is inclined 23½° to the pole of the ecliptic.

d. The present north star was not the north star in ancient times, owing to precession of the equinoxes.

e. The ratio of the circumference of a circle to its radius is π.

f. Chemical, electrical, and other forms of energy are transformable into heat-energy, but not the other way round.

g. The universe, though it is many millions of light-years across, is yet finite in extent.

h. For every molecule of matter there exists a molecule of anti-matter.

i. The force of gravitation is decreasing with time.

5. In a valid deductive argument, (a) can the premises be false and the conclusion false? (b) can the premises be false and the conclusion true? (c) can the premises be true and the conclusion false? Explain and illustrate.

6. Assess the value of each of the following inductive arguments, with reasons.

a. If every fifth president of the United States had been assassinated while in office, would you consider it probable that the fifth president after the last one to be assassinated would also be assassinated?

b. Monday I got drunk on whiskey and soda, Tuesday on gin and soda, Wednesday on vodka and soda, Thursday on rum and soda. I don't want to get drunk any more, so no more soda for me!

c. Every time I bowed before the sun at sunset, the sun rose the next morning. I have done this every day for years. So (1) if I bow to the sun at sunset tonight, the sun will rise tomorrow morning; and (2) if I do not bow to the sun at sunset tonight, the sun will not rise tomorrow morning.

d. When I was hungry, I ate a pound of steak and felt better; so if I am hungry again and eat five pounds of steak, I shall feel five times better.

7. Assess the following claims to knowledge by intuition, and indicate whether some other basis for the claim could be made which would strengthen it.

a. I have a woman's intuition and I *know* he's lying.

b. I know he is lying because I have always been right about him in the past.

c. I know intuitively that it can't be true that a self-contradictory proposition implies any and every other proposition.

d. My intuition tells me that *this* is the way to get out of the forest.

e. Don't eat that mushroom; my intuition tells me that it's poisonous.

f. My intuition tells me that being absolutely frank with all your friends is not a good thing to do.

8. Which of the following statements would you be justified in taking on authority from some expert in the field? Which would you have no reason to take on authority at all, and why?

a. Gold is malleable.

b. According to this ancient manuscript, the world was created in six days.

c. The world was created in six days.

d. Every even number is the sum of two prime numbers.

e. Some day there will be no more war.

f. The value of π is 3.1416 . . . but the exact value cannot be ascertained in any finite series of decimal points.

g. Some cats can talk.

9. Assume that you claim to know each of the following propositions. How

would you back up your claim if someone challenged you by asking *"How do you know that proposition is true?"*

    a. The earth is approximately spherical.
    b. The sun is between 90 and 95 million miles from the earth.
    c. I feel depressed for about an hour after I wake up each morning.
    e. When his mind is made up, there is absolutely no changing it.
    d. She feels depressed for an hour after she wakes up every morning.
    f. She has many repressed guilt-feelings.
    g. The hydrogen atom has one electron.
    h. Allah and Jehovah are two manifestations of the same god.
    i. Eating green apples isn't good for you.
    j. Flattering a person to gain his confidence isn't good.

8. What Is Knowledge?

Having examined some candidates for the position of *sources* of knowledge, let us turn now to the question, what *is* knowledge? or, in other words, what is it to know something?

The word "know" is slippery. It is not always used in the same way. Here are some of its principal uses:

1. Sometimes when we talk about knowing, we are referring to *acquaintance* of some kind. For example, "Do you know Richard Smith?" means approximately the same as "Are you acquainted with Richard Smith?" (have you met him? etc.). You might know him, in the sense of acquaintance, without knowing much *about* him; and you might know a great deal *about* someone but not know him because you have never met him. Or, we might ask, "Do you know that quaint old country lane seven miles west of town?" and here, though we can hardly speak of knowing it in quite the same way (we haven't been introduced), we are still talking about acquaintance: have you been there, have you seen it for yourself? You might know *that* it exists without knowing *it,* being acquainted with it. You know (are acquainted with) Yosemite Falls if you have been there, though you may not know it in this sense yet know many facts *about* it from reading in an encyclopedia.

2. Sometimes we speak of knowing *how:* Do you know how to ride a horse, do you know how to use a soldering iron? We even use a colloquial noun, "know-how," in talking about this. Knowing how is an *ability*—we know how to ride a horse if we have the ability to ride a horse, and the test of whether we have the ability is whether in the appropriate situation we can perform the activity in question. If you place me on a horse, you will soon discover the merits of the claim that I know how to ride a horse.

3. But by far the most frequent use of the word "know"—and the one with which we shall be primarily concerned—is the *propositional* sense: "I know that . . ." where the word "that" is followed by a proposition: "I know that I

am now reading a book," "I know that I am an American citizen," and so on. There is some relation between this last sense of "know" and the earlier ones. We cannot be acquainted with Smith without knowing some things about him (without knowing *that* certain propositions about him are true), and it is difficult to see how one can know *how* to swim without knowing some true propositions about swimming, concerning what you must do with your arms and legs when in the water. (But the dog knows how to swim, though presumably he knows no propositions about swimming.) Nevertheless, a person may have considerable acquaintance with a countryside without knowing as many facts about it as a person who has never been there but gleaned the information from other sources; a person who knows how to swim well may not be able to write a manual on swimming; nor need a good rider of horses know as many facts about horses as the animal psychologist who writes books about horses without being able to ride them.

Now, what is required for us to know in this third and most important sense? Taking the letter *"p"* to stand for any proposition, what requirements must be met in order for one to assert truly that he knows *p?* There are, after all, many people who claim to know something when they don't; so how can one separate the rightful claims to know from the mistaken ones?

a. *p must be true.* The moment you have some reason to believe that a proposition is not true, this immediately negates a person's claim to know it: you can't know *p* if *p* isn't true. If I say, "I know *p,* but *p* is not true," my statement is self-contradictory, for part of what is involved in knowing *p* is that *p* is true. Similarly, if I say, "He knows *p,* but *p* is not true," this too is self-contradictory. It may be that I *thought* I knew *p;* but if *p* is false, I didn't really know it. I only thought I did. If I nevertheless claim to know *p,* while admitting that *p* is false, my hearers may rightly conclude that I have not yet learned how to use the word "know." This is already implicit in our previous discussion, for what is it that you know about *p* when you know *p?* You know *that p is true,* of course; the very formulation gives away the case: knowing *p* is knowing that *p* is true.

In this respect, "know" is different from other verbs like "believe," "wonder," "hope," and so on. I can wonder whether *p* is true, and yet *p* may be false; I can believe that *p* is true, although in fact *p* may be false; I can wish that *p* were true, though *p* is false; and so on. Believing, wishing, wondering, hoping, and so on are all psychological states (occurrent and dispositional); if you tell me that you believe something, I know that you are in a certain psychological state—one of belief—but am not entitled to conclude anything about whether *what* you believe is true. But I am not entitled to say that you *know p* unless *p* is true. Unlike wondering, believing, and doubting, knowing is not merely a mental state: it requires that the proposition you claim to know is true. Thus, when you read in a novel, "She was convinced that she was incurably ill," you are not yet entitled to conclude that she *was* incurably ill, but when you read, "She knew that she was incurably ill," you *are* entitled to draw this conclusion, and to accuse the author of inconsistency if it subsequently turns out that her illness is not incurable after all.

But the truth-requirement, though necessary, is not sufficient. There are plenty of true propositions, for example in nuclear physics, that you and I do not know to be true unless we happen to be specialists in that area. But the fact that they are true does not imply that we know them to be true. And there are plenty of true statements we could make about the flora and fauna on the ocean floor if we were in a position to go there and observe for ourselves; but at the moment, though many statements we might make about them could well be true, we are not in a position to *know* that they are true. What more, then, is required?

b. *Not only must p be true: we must believe that p is true*. This may be called the "subjective requirement": we must have a certain attitude toward *p*—not merely that of wondering or speculating about *p*, but positively *believing* that *p* is true. "I know that *p* is true, but I don't believe that it is" would not only be a very peculiar thing to say, it would entitle our hearers to conclude that we had not learned in what circumstances to use the word "know." There may be numerous statements that you believe but do not know to be true, but there can be none which you know to be true but don't believe, since believing is a part (a defining characteristic) of knowing.

"I know *p*" implies "I believe *p*," and "He knows *p*" implies "He believes *p*," for believing is a defining characteristic of knowing. But believing *p* is *not* a defining characteristic of *p's being true: p* can be true even though neither he nor I nor anyone else believes it. (The earth was round even before anyone believed that it was.) There is no contradiction whatever in saying "He believed *p* (that is, believed it to be true), but *p* is not true." Indeed, we say things of this kind all the time: "He believes that people are persecuting him, but of course it isn't true." Now at this point we must be very careful, for whereas there is no contradiction involved in "He believes it, but it isn't true," or in "It's true, but he doesn't believe it," there *is*, if not a contradiction, at least a great oddity, about saying, "It's true, but *I* don't believe it." Of course one might say this in jest, or as a deliberate lie. But what if I say it sincerely? That *would* be not only odd but self-contradictory; for then my statement would come to this: that I say it and believe it, yet I don't believe it—and this last part, "I believe it yet I don't believe it," would involve me in a contradiction.

1. It's true, but I don't believe it.
2. I say it's true, but I don't believe it.
3. I say sincerely that it's true, but I don't believe it.
4. I say and believe it, but I don't believe it.

There is no problem about 1: there are no doubt countless true propositions that I don't believe, even if for no other reason than that I have never heard of them. Nor is there a problem about 2: I may be lying or joking. The problem begins with 3, because saying it *sincerely* means that I *do* believe what I say. This is brought out further in 4, where we spell out what is meant by "sincerely," and here we come upon the contradiction: believing it but not believing it.

We may, however, have some doubts about this second condition. Believing seems to be a matter of degree; we can believe with various degrees of conviction, which shade off into doubt and finally disbelief. "I believe this," we may say, "but not very strongly." How strongly must we believe it in order to fulfill the condition? Need we, in fact, believe it at all? As long as the proposition is true, can't we know it without really believing it? "I know I've just won the million-dollar prize, but I still can't believe it." But this last utterance is usually rhetorical: we do believe it (otherwise we wouldn't be so surprised), but it is still very *hard* for us to believe it; or we believe it ("with our minds"—we know that it's true), but we still can't digest it, can't *feel* toward it as we normally do when we believe something (our feelings are not yet attuned to the belief). "I know that the world isn't flat, but I still *can't believe* it"—but now "believe" has shifted its meaning to "respond emotionally to it as I do to my other beliefs." Or: I may know the answers to all the questions on the examination, but I may not *believe* I know them—that is, I may have no great *confidence* that I know them. But this case is tricky: when I have no great confidence that I know them, it's not that I don't believe *them* (the answers) but that I don't know *that I can give them*. Knowing them involves being able to give them, and believing that I know them involves believing that I can give them; but knowing them does not involve believing that I can give them. Let us not confuse these two; knowing or believing the answers and knowing or believing that I can give the answers are two different things.

In spite of varying degrees of conviction with which one may believe, it would be extremely odd to say, in any but a rhetorical sense, "I know p, but I don't believe p"—so odd, indeed, that a person who went around saying things like "I know that dogs have four legs, but I don't believe it" and "I know that 2 plus 2 equals 4, but don't believe it" could well be accused of not having learned what the word "know" means in our language, just as he could be accused of this if he kept claiming to know propositions that he admitted to be false. With these qualifications, then, our second requirement may stand.

We have now discussed two requirements for knowing, an "objective" one (p must be true) and a "subjective" one (one must believe p). Are these sufficient? Can you be said to know something if you believe it and if what you believe is true? If so, we can simply define knowledge as true belief, and that will be the end of the matter.

Unfortunately, however, the situation is not so simple. True belief is not yet knowledge. A proposition may be true, and you may believe it to be true, and yet you may not *know* it to be true. Suppose you believe that there are sentient beings on Mars, and suppose that in the course of time, after space-travelers from the earth have landed there, your belief turns out to be true. The statement was true at the time you uttered it, and you also believed it at the time you uttered it—but did you *know* it to be true at the time you uttered it? Certainly not, we would be inclined to say; you were not in a position to know. It was a lucky guess. Even if you had *some* evidence that it was true, you didn't *know* that it was true at the time you said it. Some further condition, therefore, is required to prevent a lucky guess from passing as knowledge.

We would have suspected in any case that "knowledge is true belief" is not enough. Consider some matter that no one yet knows anything about, such as whether there are planets circling around some distant star; consider, in fact, a thousand such stars. Or consider whether the next hundred tosses of a coin will turn up heads or tails. You might guess "heads" for them all, and let us suppose that 50 per cent of the time you guess correctly. Now, if you are the kind of person who quickly believes everything he says, you might actually believe you will be right all those times. But surely you did not *know* whether it would be heads or tails during that 50 per cent of the time you were right, no matter how strongly you believed it. One's knowledge is not greater merely because one has a greater confidence in one's own beliefs than other people do. It depends not on how firmly you believe but on what *grounds,* what *reason,* you have, for believing it. This brings us to our third condition:

c. *You must have evidence for p (reason to believe p).* When you guessed which tosses of the coin would be heads, you had no reason to believe that your guesses would be correct, so you did not *know.* But after you watched all the tosses and carefully observed which way the coin tossed each time, then you knew. You had the evidence of your senses—as well as of people around you, and photographs if you wished to take them—that this throw was heads, that one tails, and so on. Similarly, when you predict on the basis of tonight's red sunset that tomorrow's weather will be fair, you don't yet *know* that your prediction will be borne out by the facts; you have some reason (perhaps) to believe it, but you cannot be sure. But tomorrow when you go outdoors and see for yourself what the weather is like, you do know for sure; when tomorrow comes you have the full evidence before you, which you do not yet have tonight. Tomorrow "the evidence is in"; tonight, it is not knowledge but only an "educated guess."

This, then, is our third requirement—evidence. But at this point our troubles begin. How much evidence must there be? "Some evidence" won't suffice as an answer: there may be *some* evidence that tomorrow will be sunny, but you don't yet know it. How about "all the evidence that is available"? But this won't do either; all the evidence that is now available may not be enough. All the evidence that is now available is far from sufficient to enable us to know whether there are conscious beings on other planets. We just don't know, even after we have examined all the evidence at our disposal.

How about "enough evidence to give us *good reason* to believe it"? But how much evidence is this? I may have known someone for years and found him to be scrupulously honest during all that time; by virtually any criterion, this would constitute good evidence that he will be honest the next time—and yet he may not be; suppose that the next time he steals someone's wallet. I had good reason to believe that he would remain honest, but nevertheless I didn't *know* that he would remain honest, for it was not true. We are all familiar with cases in which someone had good reason to believe a proposition that nevertheless turned out to be false.

What then *is* sufficient? We are now tempted to say "Complete evidence —all the evidence there could ever be—the works, everything." But if we say this, let us notice at once that there are very few propositions whose truth we can claim to know. Most of those propositions that in daily life we claim to know without the slightest hesitation we would *not* know according to this criterion. For example, we say "I know that if I were to let go of this pencil, it would fall," and we don't have the slightest hesitation about it; but although we may have excellent evidence (pencils and other objects have always fallen when let go), we don't have *complete* evidence, for we have not yet observed the outcome of letting go of it *this* time. To take an even more obvious case, we say "I know that there is a book before me now," but we have not engaged in every possible observation that would be relevant to determining the truth of this statement: we have not examined the object (the one we take to be a book) from *all* angles (and since there are an infinite number of angles, who could?), and even if we have looked at it steadily for half an hour, we have not done so for a hundred hours, or a million; and yet it would *seem* (though some have disputed this, as we shall see) that if one observation provides evidence, a thousand observations should provide more evidence—and when could the accumulation of evidence end? Or again, we say "I know that Mr. Jones's house is on the corner—I've lived in that block all my life, I've seen the house a hundred thousand times, so I ought to know," although we certainly don't have "all the evidence there could ever be." How could we, since the accumulation of evidence never seems to come to an end? However much we have, we always *could* get more—it's just that in daily life we don't believe we need more; beyond a certain point we don't consider it necessary, but we always could get more if we wanted to.

We might, nevertheless, stick to our definition and say that we really do *not* know most of the propositions that in daily life we claim to know: perhaps I don't *know* that this is a book before me, that I am now indoors and not outdoors, that I am now reading sentences written in the English language, or that there are any other people in the world. But this is a rather astounding claim and needs to be justified. We are all convinced that we know these things: we act on them every day of our lives, and if we were asked outside a philosophy classroom whether we knew them, we would say "yes" without hesitation. Surely we cannot accept a definition of "know" that would practically define knowledge out of existence? But if not, what alternative have we?

"Perhaps we don't have to go so far as to say 'all the evidence,' 'complete evidence,' and so on. All we have to say is that we must have adequate evidence." But when is the evidence adequate? Is anything less than "all the evidence there could ever be" adequate? "Well, adequate for enabling us to know." But this little addition to our definition lands us in a circle. We are trying to define "know," and we cannot in doing so employ the convenient phrase "enough to enable us to know"—for the last word in this definition is the very one we are trying to define. But once we have dropped the phrase "to know," we are left with our problem once more: how much evidence is adequate evidence? Is it adequate when anything less than all the evidence is in? If not all the evidence is in, but only 99.99 per cent of it, couldn't that .01 per cent go contrary to the rest of it and require us to conclude that the proposition might not be true after all, and that therefore we didn't know it? Surely it has happened often enough that a statement that we thought we knew, perhaps even would have staked our lives on, turned out in the end to be false, or just doubtful. But in that case, we didn't really know it after all: the evidence was good, even overwhelming, but yet not good enough, not really adequate, for it was not enough to guarantee the truth of the proposition. Can we know p with anything less than all the evidence there ever could be for p?

Strong and weak senses of "know."   In daily life we say we know— not just believe or surmise, but know—that heavier-than-air objects fall, that snow is white, that we can read and write, and countless other things. If someone denies this, and no fact cited by the one disputant suffices to convince the other, we may well suspect that there is a verbal issue involved: in this case, that they are operating on two different meanings of "know," because they construe the third requirement—the evidence requirement— differently.

Suppose I say, "There is a bookcase in my office," and someone challenges this assertion. I reply, "I know that there is a bookcase in my office. I put it there myself, and I've seen it there for years. In fact, I saw it there just two minutes ago when I took a book out of it and left the office to go into the classroom." Now suppose we both go to my office, take a look, and there is the bookcase, exactly as before. "See, I knew it was there," I say. "Oh no," he replies, "you believed with good reason that it was still there, because you had seen it there often before and you didn't see or hear anyone removing it. But you didn't know it was there when you said it, for at that moment you were in the classroom and not in your office."

At this point, I may reply, "But I did know it was there, even when I said it. I knew it because (1) I believed it, (2) I had good grounds on which to base the belief, and (3) the belief was true. And I would call it knowledge whenever these three conditions are fulfilled. This is the way we use the word 'know' every day of our lives. One knows those true propositions that one believes with good reason. And when I said the bookcase was still in my office, I was uttering one of those propositions."

But now my opponent may reply, "But you still didn't know it. You had good reason to say it, I admit, for you had not seen or heard anyone removing it. You had good reason, but not *sufficient* reason. The evidence you gave was still compatible with your statement being false—and if it was false, you of course did not *know* that it was true. Suppose that you had made your claim to knowledge, and I had denied your claim, and we had both gone into your office, and to your great surprise (and mine too) the bookcase was no longer there. Could you *then* have claimed to know that it was still there?"

"Of course not. The falsity of a statement always invalidates the claim to know it. If the bookcase had not been there, I would not have been entitled to say that I knew it was there; my claim would have been mistaken."

"Right—it would have been mistaken. But now please note that the only difference between the two cases is that in the first case the bookcase was there and in the second case it wasn't. *The evidence in the two cases was exactly the same.* You had exactly the same reason for saying that the bookcase was still there in the *second* case (when we found it missing) that you did in the *first* case (when we found it still there). And since you—as you yourself admit—didn't know it in the second case, you couldn't have known it in the first case either. You believed it with good reason, but you didn't *know* it."

Here my opponent may have scored an important point; he may have convinced me that since I admittedly didn't know in the second case I couldn't have known in the first case either. But here I may make an important point in return: "My belief was the same in the two cases; the evidence was the same in the two cases (I had seen the bookcase two minutes before, had heard or seen no one removing it). The only difference was that in the first case the bookcase was there and in the second case it wasn't (*p* was true in the first case, false in the second). But *this doesn't show that I didn't know* in the first case. What it does show is that *although I might have been mistaken, I wasn't mistaken.* Had the bookcase not been there, I couldn't have claimed to know that it was; but since the bookcase in fact *was* still there, I *did* know, although (on the basis of the evidence I had) I *might* have been mistaken."

"Yes, it turned out to be true—you were lucky. But as we both agree, a lucky guess isn't the same as knowledge."

"But this wasn't just a lucky guess. I had excellent reasons for believing that the bookcase was still there. So the evidence requirement was fulfilled."

"No, it wasn't. You had good reason, excellent reason, but not *sufficient* reason—both times—for believing that the bookcase was still there. But in the second case it wasn't there, so you didn't know; therefore, in the first case, where your evidence was *exactly the same,* you didn't know either; you just believed it with good reason, but that wasn't enough: your reason wasn't sufficient, and so you didn't *know*."

Now the difference in the criterion of knowing between the two disputants begins to emerge. According to me, I did know *p* in the first case because my belief was based on excellent evidence and was also true. According to my opponent, I did not know *p* in the first case because my evidence was still less than complete—I wasn't in the room seeing or touching the bookcase when I made the statement. It seems, then, that I am operating with a less demanding definition of "know" than he is. I am using "know" in the *weak* sense, in which I know a proposition when I believe it, have good reason for believing it, and it is true. But he is using "know" in a more demanding sense: he is using it in the *strong* sense, which requires that in order to know a proposition, it must be true, I must believe it, and I must have absolutely *conclusive* evidence in favor of it.

Let us contrast these two cases:

Suppose that after a routine medical examination the excited doctor reports to me that the X-ray photographs show that I have no heart. I should tell him to get a new machine. I should be inclined to say that the fact that I have a heart is one of the few things that I can count on as absolutely certain. I can feel it beat. I know it's there. Furthermore, how could my blood circulate if I didn't have one? Suppose that later on I suffer a chest injury and undergo a surgical operation. Afterwards the astonished surgeons solemnly declare that they searched my chest cavity and found no heart, and that they made incisions and looked about in other likely places but found it not. They are convinced that I am without a heart. They are unable to understand how circulation can occur or what accounts for the thumping in my chest. But they are in agreement and obviously sincere, and they have clear photographs of my interior spaces. What would be my attitude? Would it be to insist that they were all mistaken? I think not. I believe that I should eventually accept their testimony and the evidence of the photographs. I should consider to be false what I now regard as an absolute certainty. [When I say I know I have a heart, I know it in the weak sense.]

Suppose that as I write this paper someone in the next room were to call out to me, "I can't find an ink-bottle; is there one in the house?" I should reply, "Here is an ink-bottle." If he said in a doubtful tone, "Are you sure? I looked there before," I should reply, "Yes, I know there is; come and get it."

Now could it turn out to be false that there is an ink-bottle directly in front of me on this desk? Many philosophers have thought so. They would say that many things could happen of such a nature that if they did happen it would be proved that I am deceived. I agree that many extraordinary things could happen, in the sense that there is no logical absurdity in the supposition. It could happen that when I next reach for this ink-bottle my hand should seem to pass *through* it and I should not feel the contact of any object. It could happen that in the next moment the ink-bottle will suddenly vanish from sight; or that I should find myself under a tree in the garden with no ink-bottle about; or that one or more persons should enter this room and declare with apparent sincerity that they see no ink-bottle on this desk; or that a photograph taken now of the top of the desk should clearly show all of the objects on it except the ink-bottle. Having admitted that these things *could happen,* am I compelled to admit that if they did happen, then it would be proved that there is no ink-bottle here *now?* Not at all. I could say that when my hand seemed to pass through the ink-bottle I should *then* be suffering from hallucination; that if the ink-bottle suddenly vanished, it would have miraculously ceased to exist; that the other persons were conspiring to drive me mad, or were themselves victims of remarkable concurrent hallucinations; that the camera possessed some strange flaw or that there was trickery in developing the negative: . . . Not only do I not *have* to admit that those extraordinary occurrences would be evidence that there is no ink-bottle here; the fact is that I *do not* admit it. There is nothing whatever that could happen in the next moment or the next year that would by me be called *evidence* that there is not an ink-bottle here now. No future experience or investigation could prove to me that I am mistaken. Therefore, if I were to say, "I know that there is an ink-bottle here," I should be using "know" in the strong sense.[10]

It is in the weak sense that we use the word "know" in daily life, as when I say I know that I have a heart, that if I let go this piece of chalk it will fall, that the sun will rise tomorrow, and so on. I have excellent reason (evidence) to believe all these things, evidence so strong that (so we say) it amounts to certainty. And yet there are events that could conceivably occur which, if they did occur, would cast doubt on the beliefs or even show them to be false. (If you claim to know many of the propositions in Exercise 3, it is, in most cases, in the weak sense of "know.")

But the philosopher is apt to be more concerned with "know" in the strong sense. He wants to inquire whether there are any propositions that we can know without the shadow of a doubt will never be proved false, or even rendered dubious to the smallest degree. "You can say," he will argue, "and I admit that it would be good English usage to say, that you know that you have a heart and that the sun is more than 90 million miles from the earth. But you don't know it until you have absolutely conclusive evidence, and you must admit that the evidence you have, while very strong, is not conclusive. So I shall say, using 'know' in the strong sense, that you do not know these propositions. I want then to ask what propositions can be known in the strong sense, the sense that puts the proposition forever past the possibility of doubt?"

And on this point many philosophers have been quite skeptical; they have granted few if any propositions whose truth we could know in the strong sense. Many of them would not even have agreed with the illustration about the ink-bottle: they would have said that our evidence for the ink-bottle was not conclusive, and that if we had suddenly found ourselves transported into

[10] Norman Malcolm, "Knowledge and Belief," in *Knowledge and Certainty,* pp. 66–68.

a garden with no ink-bottle around, this would have entitled us to doubt that we were right in the first place in saying that there was an ink-bottle there. Many of them would add that even if there were no mysterious sudden change of location, we could still not know (in the strong sense) that there was an ink-bottle there. They would say that even for the presence of an ink-bottle there is an infinite number of tests, that they can never all be made, that we cannot look forever, but that every added observation adds further evidence in favor of the proposition without ever rendering it certain. Such a person is a *skeptic*. We claim (he says) to know many things about the world, but in fact none of these propositions can be known for certain. What are we to say of the skeptic's position?

Let us first note that in the phrase "know for certain," the "for certain" is redundant—how can we know except for certain? If it is less than certain, how can it be knowledge? We do, however, use the word "certain" ambiguously: (1) Sometimes we say "I am certain," which just means that I have a feeling of certainty about it—"I feel certain that I locked the door of the apartment"—and of course the feeling of certainty is no guarantee that the statement is true. People have very strong feelings of certainty about many propositions that they have no evidence for at all, particularly if they want to believe them or are consoled by believing them. The phrase "feeling certain," then, refers simply to a psychological state, whose existence in no way guarantees that what the person feels certain about is true. But (2) sometimes when we say "I am certain," we mean that it *is* certain—in other words, that we *do* know the proposition in question to be true. This, of course, is the sense of "certain" that is of interest to philosophers (the first sense is of more interest to psychiatrists in dealing with patients). Thus we could reformulate our question, "Is anything certain?" or "Are any propositions certain?"

"I can well understand," one might argue, "how you could question some statements, even most statements. But if you carry on this merry game until you have covered *all* statements, you are simply mistaken, and I think I can show you why. You may see someone in a fog or in a bad light and not know (not be certain) whether he has a right hand. But don't you know that *you* have a right hand? There it is! Suppose I now raise my hand and say, 'Here is a hand.' Now you say to me, 'I doubt that there's a hand.' But what evidence do you want? What does your doubt consist of? You don't believe your eyes, perhaps? Very well, then come up and touch the hand. You still aren't satisfied? Then keep on looking at it steadily and touching it, photograph it, call in other people for testimony if you like. If after all this you still say it isn't certain, what more do you want? Under what conditions would you admit that it *is* certain, that you *do* know it? I can understand your doubt when there is some condition left unfulfilled, some test left uncompleted. At the beginning, perhaps you doubted that *if* you tried to touch my hand you would find anything there to touch; but then you did touch, and so you resolved *that* doubt. You resolved further doubts by calling in other people and so on. You performed all the relevant tests, and they turned out favorably. So now, at the end of the process, what is it that you doubt? Oh, I know what you *say:* 'I still doubt that that's a hand.' But isn't this saying 'I doubt' now an empty formula? I can no longer attach any content to that so-called doubt, for there is nothing left to doubt; you yourself *cannot specify any further test that, if performed, would resolve your doubt.* 'Doubt' now becomes an empty word. You're not doubting now that *if* you raised your hand to touch mine, you would touch it, or that *if* Smith and others were brought in, they would also testify that this is a hand—we've already gone through all that. So what is it specifically that you doubt? What possible test is there the negative result of which you fear? I submit that there isn't any. You are confusing a situation in which doubt is understandable (*before* you made the tests) with the later situation in which it isn't, for it has all been dispelled. Suppose you doubt that this substance on the table is cheese. You agree that if it is cheese it has certain defining properties A, B, C, and D. I show you that it has A, then B, then C, then D. And yet you doubt that it's cheese. What more can I say? You agree that *if* it has A, B, C, D it's cheese, and you agree that it has A, B, C, D; so logically you can't escape the conclusion that it *is* cheese."

"You have misunderstood me," says the skeptic. "I grant that *if* it has A, B, C, D then it's cheese, if cheese is defined in terms of those very characteristics. I agree, that is, only to the definition. But I do not agree that what I see before me conforms to that definition. Just as I doubt that it's cheese, so I doubt that it really has A, that it really has B, and so on. It may *appear* to have, but we may be mistaken in thinking that it really has. I don't *know* that it has A any more than I know that it's cheese."

"But your so-called doubt becomes meaningless when there is nothing left to doubt—when the tests have been carried out and their results are all favorable. Suppose a physician examines a patient and says, 'It's probable that you have an inflamed appendix.' Here one can still doubt, for the signs may be misleading. So the physician operates on the patient, finds an inflamed appendix and removes it, and the patient recovers. *Now* what would be the sense of the physician's saying 'It's *probable* that he had an inflamed appendix'? If seeing it and removing it made it only *probable,* what would make it certain? Or you are driving along and you hear a rapid regular thumping sound and you say, 'It's probable that I have a flat tire.' So far you're right; it's only probable—the thumping might be caused by something else. So you go out and have a look, and there is the tire, flat. You find a nail embedded in it, change the tire, and then resume your ride with no more thumping. Are you *now* going to say 'It's merely *probable* that the car had a flat tire'? But if given all those conditions it would be merely probable, what in the world would make it certain? Can you describe to me the circumstances in which you would say it's certain? If you can't, then the phrase 'being certain' has no meaning as you are using it. You are simply using it in such a special way that it has no application at all, and there is no reason at all why anyone else should follow your usage. In daily life we have a very convenient and useful distinction between the application of the words 'probable' and 'certain.' We say appendicitis is probable *before* the operation, but when the physician has the patient's appendix visible before him on the operating table, now it's certain—that's just the kind of situation in which we apply the word 'certain,' as opposed to 'probable.' Now you, for some reason, are so fond of the word 'probable' that you want to use it for everything—you use it to describe *both* the preoperative and postoperative situations, and the word 'certain' is left without any application at all. But this is nothing but a verbal manipulation on your part. You have changed nothing; you have only taken, as it were, two bottles with different contents, and instead of labeling them differently ('probable' and 'certain'), as the rest of us do, you put the same label ('probable') on both of them! What possible advantage is there in this? It's just verbal contrariness. And since you have pre-empted the word 'probable' to cover *both* the situations, we now have to devise a *different* pair of words to mark the perfectly obvious distinction between the situation *before* the surgery and the situation *during* the surgery—the same difference we previously marked by the words 'probable' and 'certain' until you used the word 'probable' to apply to both of them. What gain is there in this verbal manipulation of yours?"

"It is not just verbal manipulation," the skeptic replies. "The issue between us is not one of words but of fact. I do not call a proposition certain, or claim that I know it to be true, until *all the evidence for it is in*. Now the reason I decline to say that it's certain that this is cheese, or that the patient had appendicitis, or that the tire was flat is that the evidence for these propositions is not all in: there always could be more, and that more could turn out negatively. Your examples sounded plausible because in describing them you assumed without proof that certain *other* statements were certain: that there really was a car, that you weren't dreaming it all, that the physician really was looking at the patient's appendix, that there really was an operating table, and so on. Now all *these* statements, I contend, are subject to the same uncertainty as the original statements about the patient having appendicitis and the tire being flat. You had no right to smuggle them in as if *they* were certain. I would want to question each of these in turn, and for the very same reasons. They are not certain because the evidence for them is never in: there always could be more, and that more could have a negative result. That's why I even have to object to your example of the hand. If I admit that I'm really seeing and touching the hand, I can't very well turn around and doubt that it exists, for the statement 'I am *really* seeing it' already entails 'It exists.' But how do I know that I am really seeing and touching a hand; or, to put it differently, that I am seeing and touching a real hand? If I admit that I am, then of course you have me. But this initial admission, which you take for granted in your example, is precisely what I will not grant."

It would seem that the opponents are deadlocked. The fundamental issues that are raised in this imaginary dialogue are extremely complex: How do I know that my sense-perceptions can be trusted? How can I know whether I am having hallucinations or dreaming? Is every statement about the world subject to an infinite number of tests, which of course can never be performed? And if so, does it follow that we can never know any of these statements to be true? Having taken the controversy up to this point, we must unfortunately postpone a discussion of these deeper issues until Chapter 8. The reason for this, though it may not be obvious just now, is that the discussion of these problems becomes quite technical, and we cannot fruitfully raise them until a number of other problems have been discussed first. Chapter 8 will be devoted to a discussion of these and other issues having to do with perceptual knowledge. At present, our concern is merely to *define* "knowledge," and the case of perceptual knowledge was used only for purposes of illustration. Until we raise the issue again in Chapter 8, we shall not question the assertion that there is a physical world, that we can gain knowledge of it by means of our senses, and that sometimes, at any rate, our judgments about it are true. Since we have believed these things all our lives anyway, there may be no harm in believing them uncritically for a while longer.

Meanwhile, it is well to point out that there are two other classes of propositions that are not chopped down by the skeptic's axe:

1. I may utter propositions about my own existence and my own states of consciousness, which, as we saw earlier in the chapter, are self-authenticating: that I feel the pain or the drowsiness is itself sufficient to entitle me to say "I feel a pain" or "I feel drowsy." It is very peculiar to speak of evidence at all in such cases. I don't need *evidence* for saying I feel drowsy, as I do for saying that the sun is more than 90 million miles away. That I feel the pain is sufficient to make the statement "I feel pain" true. Knowing these propositions is not well covered by the definition of knowing that requires evidence. Shall we say that I *have* no evidence that I have a pain? No, the fact that I *have* the pain is my sole and sufficient evidence that the statement is true. Shall we say then that I *need* no evidence? True, I do not need evidence in the way I need evidence for the distance of the sun, for the experience itself constitutes all the evidence I need. Perhaps it is preferable to say that I do need evidence, but that the experience *itself* constitutes all the evidence I need. Whichever way we put it, the same fact remains: I can *know* the statement to be true, simply on the basis of having the experience. (And this, we cannot emphasize too strongly, holds only of propositions reporting the occurrence of sense-experiences. Almost all the statements we make in daily life, including all those used as examples in this section, go beyond this.)

2. There are also statements that make no claim about ourselves or about the world at all, such as "Cats are cats" and "Red roses are red." These statements are called "analytic," and we shall begin the next chapter with a discussion of them. An analysis of these statements is an indispensible condition for considering an entire class of statements, called "truths of reason," for which we need either no evidence or, if we do, not evidence in the sense we have been discussing in this chapter. These are truths in "the realm of necessity."

Exercises

1. In which of these cases is the "knowing" in question propositional? Explain in each case, stating the propositions where there are any involved.
    a. Do you know what the solution is to this problem?
    b. Do you know her intimately?
    c. Can the human mind know reality?
    d. Do you know how to perform an appendectomy?
    e. Do you know why he walked out on his family like that?
    f. Do you know which of the suitors she accepted?
    g. A person doesn't know war until he's seen war.
    h. Do you know what the feeling of *déjà vu* is like?
    i. I wouldn't know what to do in such a situation.
    j. Do you know the meaning of that word?
2. Can you know (as opposed to having good reason to believe) any proposition about the future? Give your reasons.
3. In each of the following examples, do you *know* (not merely believe, or even have some reason to believe) that the proposition is true? Defend your answer.
    a. The road continues on the other side of the hill.
    b. If I let go of this piece of chalk it will fall.
    c. The first floor of this building is not now submerged in water.
    d. The table has a back side and an inside even though I'm not now perceiving them.
    e. This crow before me is black.
    f. All crows are black.
    g. You have an optic nerve.
    h. You are not now a multimillionaire.
    i. Julius Caesar once lived.
    j. You had breakfast this morning.
    k. The sun will rise tomorrow.
    l. You are not the reincarnation of Bach.
    m. I have blood and bones and vital organs and am not made of straw.
    n. This table won't turn into an elevator and carry us all downstairs.
    o. A dog will never give birth to kittens.
    p. You will not some day be father (or mother) to an orange.
    q. You are not now asleep (or dead).
    r. You did not eat mothballs for dinner yesterday.
    s. This table is the same one that was in this room yesterday.
    t. Some motion-picture theaters now exist in the world.
    u. You were born (not hatched or spontaneously generated).

    v. All human beings are mortal.

    w. The earth is (approximately) spherical.

    x. You are not having a hallucination now and only think you see a table.

    y. The earth did not come into existence five minutes ago.

    z. 2 plus 2 equals 4.

    aa. You are not dreaming at this moment.

    bb. You are now seeing several colors.

    cc. You are younger than your parents.

    dd. You are not a nightingale.

    ee. Electric wiring in a house is something that should be done well or not at all.

4. Which of the above propositions would you claim to know in the strong sense, and why?

5. Would you agree with the following statements? Why, or why not?

    a. A person can know only that which he has perceived with his senses.

    b. Seeing is believing.

    c. Believe nothing of what you hear, and only half of what you see.

    d. Any verdict based on circumstantial evidence falls short of certainty.

    e. You can't know anything until you've proved it.

    f. By faith, you can know what you could never know via sense-experience or reason.

    g. To believe something implies that you are prepared to act on the assumption that it is true.

    h. The great present range of our knowledge would be impossible if authority were not accepted as a means of knowing.

    i. If something was revealed to me, it must be true; if it isn't true, then it only *seemed* to be revealed to me.

6. To know something, you must have evidence in its favor. Must you also know *that* it is evidence, or is it enough that you *have* the evidence?

7. Evaluate the following definition of "knowing": Knowing is the ability to be regularly right. If I can always tell you what your thoughts are, I know what they are—even though I don't know how I know (I can't state any evidence), and I may not even believe what I say (I may just say whatever pops into my mind, without giving it any particular credence). So belief and evidence both should be deleted from any definition of knowledge: all that knowing requires is the ability to be regularly right.

8. Evaluate this assertion: "Some propositions must be certain, for if none were certain, none could be probable. Probability is a concept derived from that of certainty. If we didn't know what it was for something to be certain, we would have no standard of reference for estimating probability. We wouldn't even be able to know what the word 'probable' would mean."

Selected Readings for Chapter 2

Ambrose, Alice, "Moore's Proof of an External World," in *The Philosophy of G. E. Moore,* ed. P. A. Schlipp. Evanston, Ill.: Northwestern University Press, 1942.

Ayer, Alfred J., *The Problem of Knowledge.* New York: St. Martin's Press, Inc., 1956.

Bouwsma, O. K., "Descartes' Evil Genius," *Philosophical Review,* 1949.

————, "Descartes' Skepticism of the Senses," *Mind*, 1945.

Descartes, René, *Meditations*, 1621. Many editions.

Edwards, Paul and Arthur Pap (eds.), *A Modern Introduction to Philosophy* (2nd ed.). New York: Free Press of Glencoe, Inc., 1965. Chapter 2

Hume, David, *An Enquiry Concerning Human Understanding*, 1751. Section 2. Many editions.

————, *Treatise of Human Nature*, 1739. Book I, Part 1. Many editions.

Lewis, Clarence I., *An Analysis of Knowledge and Valuation*. LaSalle, Ill.: Open Court Publishing Co., 1947. Chapters 7–9.

————, *Mind and the World Order*. New York: Charles Scribner's Sons, 1929.

Locke, John, *Essay Concerning Human Understanding*. Books 2 and 4. Many editions.

Malcolm, Norman, "Knowledge and Belief" and "The Verification Argument," in *Knowledge and Certainty*. Englewood Cliffs, N. J.: Prentice-Hall, Inc., 1963.

————, "Moore and Ordinary Language," in *The Philosophy of G. E. Moore*, ed. P. A. Schlipp. Evanston, Ill.: Northwestern University Press, 1942.

Moore, G. E., "Proof of an External World" and "Certainty," in *Philosophical Papers*. London: George Allen & Unwin, Ltd., 1959. Also Collier Books paperback, 1962.

————, *Some Main Problems of Philosophy*. London: George Allen & Unwin, Ltd., 1952. Especially chapters 4, 15, and 16.

Nagel, Ernest and Richard Brandt (eds.) *Meaning and Knowledge*. New York: Harcourt, Brace & World, Inc., 1965. Chapter 2.

Pap, Arthur, "Indubitable Existential Statements," *Mind*, 1946.

————, "Ostensive Definition and Empirical Certainty," *Mind*, 1950.

Price, H. H., *Thinking and Experience*. London: Hutchinson & Co. (Publishers), Ltd., 1953.

Rollins, Calvin D., "Are There Indubitable Existential Statements?" *Mind*, 1949.

Scriven, Michael, *Primary Philosophy*. New York: McGraw-Hill Book Company, 1966. Chapter 2.

Stace, Walter T., "Are All Empirical Statements Merely Hypotheses?" *Journal of Philosophy*, 1947.

Yolton, John, *John Locke and The Way Of Ideas*. London: Oxford University Press, 1956.

3

Necessary Truth

9. Analytic Truth and Logical Possibility

Analytic propositions. If someone said, "Black cats are fierce," or "Black cats bring bad luck," one might question whether his statement was true; but probably no one would question that, whether true or false, it is a genuine proposition. However, if someone said, "Black cats are black," we might be tempted to say that he was saying nothing, or that he was saying something true but so utterly trivial as to be not worth saying.

"Black cats are black" is an example of an *analytic* proposition. The term is perhaps unfortunate, because the word "analytic" means other things as well. Nevertheless, it is now well established in common usage among philosophers, and it runs constantly through the literature of the subject. The use of this word originates in the fact that you have only to *analyze* a statement of this kind in order to know whether or not it is true. For example, you can analyze "All black cats are black" into the general form "All AB is A"—and you find that the term "black," what is called the "logical predicate" of the sentence, merely repeats what is already contained in the subject of the sentence. You would not even have to know what the word "black" means: it would be enough to know that, whatever it means in the subject, it has the same meaning in the predicate. "Black is black" would also be analytic, although it is slightly different in form: "A is A" instead of "AB is A."

Analytic propositions are of considerable interest to philosophers, since once you know that a certain proposition is analytic, you know it to be true without any further investigation—specifically, without any observation of the world, which is required before we can know the truth of most of the propositions we believe. It might seem, however, that whether or not a proposition is analytic is so obvious that there would never be any problems about it: certainly this is true of "Black is black," which is so obvious that it would not even occur to us to utter the sentence that expresses it. But the analytic quality, or analyticity, of some propositions is by no means obvious.

160

"All brothers are brothers" is *explicitly* analytic: the repetition is right there before us in the words themselves. But "All brothers are males" is, as it stands, not analytic at all: one must define "brother" and substitute a specific definition for the word in order to make it so. After all, the noise "brother" could have been used to mean anything, and it is only when used to mean what we mean by it in common usage—male sibling—that is, male offspring of the same parent—that we get an analytic proposition out of it, by substituting the definition for the defined term: thus we get "All male siblings are male," which is explicitly analytic. Similarly, "A yard is three feet" becomes analytic when we substitute for the word "yard" its definition, "three feet," and thus get "Three feet is three feet." In the latter case we have a complete definition, which results in "A is A"; in the former case we have a statement of a defining characteristic, which results in "AB is A"; but in both cases the proposition is analytic.

If these examples too seem obvious, it is only because the definitions of the words are so simple and clear to us. "Bachelors are unmarried" is similarly simple and clear, for being unmarried is a defining characteristic of being a bachelor. "All matter occupies space" will doubtless not bother us very long, for we soon reflect that we wouldn't call anything matter unless it occupied space—that is, occupancy of space is a defining characteristic of matter. But in other cases it is not so simple: "The best players are the ones who win the most games" is more troublesome: whether we call it analytic or not depends on what characteristics must be possessed by those whom we call "the best players." If we define "best players" as those with the highest winning record, the resulting proposition is analytic; but if we do not—for example, if a player does not win as often as another but is counted better because of his superior skill or style—then it is not analytic. Whether it is analytic or not depends on the definitions of the terms it contains; and if we are not clear about the definitions (as often happens, for most words often have no clear-cut definition in common usage), then we cannot be clear about whether the proposition is analytic either.

Nor should we always go by the way a sentence looks. "Blackbirds are black birds" appears to be analytic but is not; it is not a defining characteristic of the class of birds we call blackbirds that they must be black: an albino blackbird would still be a blackbird. Most of the members of the species are black, hence the name "blackbird," but this should not lead us into assuming that the characteristic that gives the species its name is always a defining characteristic. Again, "Business is business" looks like a simple "A is A"; but, as used on most occasions, its meaning is something like "In business, anything goes," and the proposition expressed by *that* sentence is not at all analytic. On the other hand, "If you study this chapter long enough, you'll understand it" doesn't appear to be analytic at all, but let us look again: How long is long *enough*? Suppose you read the chapter 50 times and still don't understand it, and someone says to you, "That only shows that you haven't read it long *enough*." We now begin to suspect that he is using "long enough" to mean "till you understand it." And if this is its meaning, it *is* analytic: "If you read it till you understand it, you'll understand it." (If, after you read it 50 times, he said, "I guess I was wrong—you've read it long enough and you still don't understand it," then he would *not* be using the sentence to express an analytic proposition.)

Precisely what makes a proposition analytic? Numerous definitions of "analytic" have been advanced, of which we shall mention the two principal ones. (Each of them has variations.) The designation of the term "analytic" is different in these two definitions, though the denotation of the term is very nearly the same—that is to say, a proposition that is analytic by one definition will also be by the other, with certain exceptions, which we shall notice in due course.

1. An analytic statement is a statement whose negation is self-contradictory. If someone said, "Black is not black," he would be contradicting himself; he would be saying in effect that A is not A. If you deny a true analytic proposition, you always get a self-contradictory proposition. (A *false* analytic proposition would be a *self-contradictory* proposition. But it is usual to describe such propositions simply as "self-contradictory," leaving falsehood to characterize nonanalytic propositions, and to describe *true* analytic propositions simply as "analytic.") Similarly, "A yard is not three feet" becomes, by substitution, "Three feet is not three feet," which is self-contradictory. But if you negate "Snow is white"—assuming that whiteness is not a defining characteristic of snow—you get "Snow is not white," which, though false, is not self-contradictory.

Synthetic propositions are propositions that are not analytic. Thus we get:

Analytic propositions ("Snow is snow")	True synthetic propositions ("Snow is white")
Negative: self-contradictory propositions ("Snow is not snow")	Negative: false synthetic propositions ("Snow is not white")

2. An analytic proposition is one whose truth can be determined solely by an analysis of the meaning of the words in the sentence expressing it. You do not have to investigate anything in the world apart from language to discover whether or not the proposition is true. If you analyze the meaning of "father" (male parent), you know that "Fathers are male" is true; you know it from analyzing the sentence itself, not from observation of the way the world is. Knowing the meanings of the words is all that you need in order to determine the truth of the proposition.

The first definition describes a property of propositions themselves, and the second definition tells us how we discover them to be true. But for most purposes it will not matter which definition we choose.

Several precautions are required if we are to identify certain propositions as analytic:

1. When a sentence is ambiguous, it may express an analytic proposition when used in one sense but not when used in another. "All bars serve alcoholic beverages" is analytic if "bar" means the same as "place where alcoholic beverages are sold"; but if "bar" means what it does in the phrase "chocolate bar" or in "bar examination," of course the proposition is not analytic in these senses; indeed, it is not the same proposition.

2. Sometimes usages differ from person to person; and when they do, a sentence may express an analytic proposition when used by one person but not when used by another. If you take being supported from below (for example, by legs) as defining of "table," then "Tables are supported from below" is analytic as you are using it. But if another person uses the word differently—if, for example, he would accept a table-top hung by a wire from the ceiling as being a table—then, as he is using the sentence, the proposition it expresses is not analytic. When you are in doubt whether a sentence someone is using expresses an analytic proposition as he is using it, you must ask him to define his terms.

3. A proposition may be analytic at one time but not at another. Strictly speaking, the sentence used to express an analytic proposition at one time may no longer express an analytic proposition at another time. The proposition always remains analytic, but a sentence may at a later time be used to express a different proposition. The sentence "Whales are mammals" was formerly not used to express an analytic proposition—indeed, the sentence would have been thought to express a false proposition. But now that the mammalian characteristic of whales has been incorporated into the definition of "whale" (see pp. 26–27), "Whales are mammals" as used today would be analytic, since being a mammal is part of the definition of "whale."

Immanuel Kant (1724–1804) first introduced the term "analytic," but he defined it in a narrower way than we have done here. According to Kant, an analytic statement is one in which the predicate repeats the subject in whole or in part: in "A is A" (birds are birds) the predicate repeats the whole of the subject, and in "AB is A" (birds—that is, feathered vertebrates—are feathered) the predicate repeats a part of the subject. All the examples of analytic propositions we have considered thus far fall into one of these two patterns. But later philosophers were quick to point out that if Kant's definition is accepted, many other propositions that fulfill our definition of "analytic" do not turn out to be analytic at all, because they are not cast in this traditional subject-predicate form. Thus, "Not both A and not A" (not both a chair and not a chair) is analytic, for if you denied it you would get "Both A and not A," which is self-contradictory. Again, "If A, then A" is analytic, for if one denied it one would get "It is not the case that if it's A, it's A" (it's not true that if this is a horse, then it's a horse), which again is self-contradictory. Such propositions also fulfill the second definition: one can know that this is not both a chair and not a chair, and that if it's a chair then it's a chair, without knowing anything about what the world is like. It would be very strange indeed to say that "All cats are cats" is analytic whereas "If it's a cat, then it's a cat" is *not* analytic, simply because the first statement is in subject-predicate form whereas the second one is not. If "analytic" is defined as we defined it earlier, then Kant's definition, which restricts analytic propositions to those expressed in the form of subject-predicate sentences, must be considered too narrow.

Tautologies. But not all sentences are cast in that form. The following sentences are all in subject-predicate form,

List 1: All lions $<$ are fierce.
Some men $<$ are cowards.
People $<$ are funny.
Cats $<$ have kittens.
Cats $<$ are cats.
No cats $<$ are dogs.
Most cats $<$ are deaf.

though they differ considerably in other ways: some are analytic, some not; some are true, some false; some make assertions about all the members of a class, some do not. But all of them have this feature in common: when they are broken down into subject and predicate (separated by the $<$ mark), the constituent parts are *terms,* not *sentences.* Now let us contrast them with the following:

List 2: If you are a person, then you are a person.
If you are a horse, then you are a horse.
If he waits much longer, he'll starve.
Either this creature is male or this creature is not male.
Either this creature is male or this creature is female.
Either the water is hot or it is not hot.
Either the water is hot or it is cold.
The water is not both hot and not hot.
This is not both a table and not a table.
This is not both a table and a chair.
This is not both a table and a piece of furniture.
Either you are in this room or you are not in this room.
Either you are in this room or you are in that room.
If this creature is a dog, then it is carnivorous .
If no dogs are cats, and this is a dog, then it is not a cat.
If all cats are mammals and all mammals are animals, then all cats are animals.
This is a cat and this is a mammal.
This is a cat and this is not a cat.

The members of List 2 also differ widely from one another: some are true and some are not; some are self-contradictory to deny and others are not; some are hypothetical (if . . . then . . .), some are alternatives (either . . . or . . .), some are disjunctive (not both . . . and . . .), and some conjunctive (. . . and . . .). But in each one of them, the sentence can be broken down further, and the constituents into which they can be broken down *are themselves sentences.* "Either the water is hot or it is cold" consists of *two complete sentences,* "The water is hot" and "It is cold." "If this is a cat, then it is a mammal" consists of two complete sentences, "This is a cat" and "This is a mammal." In each case the relation between the parts is different: in "Either . . . or . . ." we are told that one of the two constituent propositions must be true, that they cannot both be false; in ". . . and . . ." we are told that both of the constituent propositions are true; in "if . . . then . . ." we are told that if the first one is true, then the second one is true also (the first cannot be true while the second is false). The meaning of "He will go *and* she will go" is very different from that of "He will go *or* she will go," and different again from *"If* he will go, *then* she will go." But every one of these is a *compound* sentence: it can be broken down into two or more parts, each of which is itself a sentence, and expresses a proposition.

Now let us use the letter p to stand for any proposition whatever; then let us use the letter q to stand for some *other* proposition; and r to stand for still another proposition, and so on. In List 1, the letter p could stand for the entire sentence "All lions are fierce," since it cannot be broken down into constituents that are themselves sentences; and q could stand for the entire second sentence, "Some men are cowards," and so on. But List 2 consists of compound sentences, so the first example, "If you are a person, then you are a person," could be symbolized "If p, then p." The second sentence could be symbolized in exactly the same way, only if we are viewing it in relation to the first one we will have to give it a different letter, and symbolize it "If q, then q." But the third one is of the form "If p, then q," for the constituent sentences are different.

All of the sentences in List 2 express propositions. But if we substitute the symbols p, q, r, etc. for the propositions, retaining in words only the relation between the sentencees, we get not propositions but what are called *propositional forms:*

List 3: If p, then p (that is, p implies p).
    If p, then q.
    If p, then not-p.
    If p, and p implies q, then q.
    Either p or not-p.
    Either p or q.
    Not both p and not-p.
    Not both p and q.

p and p.
p and q.
p and not-p.

We cannot describe these compound propositions as either true or false, since we have not been told what proposition, in each case, the symbols "p" and "q" stand for. For example, is "p implies q" true or not? That depends on what propositions the letters "p" and "q" are being used to stand for. If "p" is "This is a square," and "q" is "This is a rectangle," then "p" *does* imply "q" (that is, "If p then q" is true). But if "q" is "Athens is in Greece," then "p" does not imply "q." We can convert a propositional form into a proposition only if we substitute actual sentences for each of the letters, just as we cannot answer the question in algebra "Is x larger than 10?" until we know what quantity the symbol "x" stands for.

A *tautology* (from the Greek *tautos*, "the same") is a propositional form in which *all* the statements we get by substituting sentences for the symbols are true. In other words, the resulting statements are all true, *no matter what propositions* the letters "p," "q," etc. stand for. "Either p or not-p" is a tautology, for no matter what propositions we substitute for p, the resulting compound proposition is always true: "Either it is true that snow is white or it is not true that snow is white," "Either it is true that grass is purple or it is not true that grass is purple," and so on indefinitely. No matter what propositions one thinks of, as long as they are of the form "Either p or not-p" they are all true. "Either p or not-p" is a tautology, since this propositional form does not depend on *what* particular propositions we use to fill the form. Similarly, "Not both p and not-p" is a tautology: "Not both 'Water is a liquid' and 'Water is not a liquid' are true," "Not both 'Snow is white' and 'Snow is not white' are true," and so on. By contrast, "Either p or q" is *not* a tautology: if "p" stands for "You are in this room" and "q" for "You are in that room," the resulting proposition, "Either you are in this room or you are in that room," need not be true at all; you might be in another room, or walking outdoors, or in an airplane. Sometimes "p or q" is true ("Either he is alive or he is dead") and sometimes it need not be ("Either you are in this room or you are in that room"); but whichever it is depends on the particular propositions we substitute for the propositional forms p and q. Thus "Either p or q" is not a tautology, for a tautology is true no matter *what* propositions we put in the place of p and q; but "Either p or not-p" *is* a tautology, for no matter what proposition I write in, the resulting compound proposition is always true.

Some compound sentences can be very complicated indeed, being composed of a vast array of constituent sentences. In such cases, it would require a course in logic, which provides ways of figuring out which compound sentences express tautologies and why, to determine the answer in each case to the question "Is this a tautology?" But some tautologies, such as those we have used thus far in our examples, are not at all complicated, and only a minimal amount of reflection is required in order to determine whether or not a given proposition is a tautology.[1] Whether or not a given propositional form is tautological can be determined in logic by employing what is called the "truth-table" method.

In logic, the difference between analytic propositions in the Kantian sense and tautologies is extremely important: the validity of arguments using compound sentences is tested very differently from that of those employing sentences of the traditional subject-predicate form. But for purposes other than those of logic, the distinction is far less important. Thus, following the common usage of philosophical writers, we shall refer to *all* propositions whose negation yields a self-contradiction (first definition), and whose truth can be ascertained by an analysis of the meanings of the words in the sentence (second definition), as *analytic,* whether they are in the subject-predicate form or are tautologies. If the context requires the distinction between the two types of analytic propositions to be drawn, we can always recall the distinction.

Objections to the analytic-synthetic distinction.   Clear though the distinction between analytic and synthetic appears to be, it has sometimes come under attack. Two main lines of criticism should now be mentioned:

1. "The analytic-synthetic distinction does not mark a real difference, since on closer examination it turns out that all propositions are analytic."

What could possibly be the reason for holding such a bizarre view? The reasoning goes as follows: Everything we know about X is embodied in the concept of X; the more we know, the richer the concept of X becomes; and we would have a complete concept of X only if we knew everything there is to be known about X. To use the example given by the philosopher Gottfried von Leibniz (1646–1716): Our concept of Adam is limited, for we know only a small number of things about him—that he was the first man, that he ate the apple that Eve offered him, and so on. The more we know about Adam, the richer becomes our concept of Adam. "Adam was the first man," according to Leibniz, is analytic. But there are presumably many propositions about Adam with which we are not acquainted; once we do know them, they too are analytic, for they all constitute part of our total concept of Adam—a concept that is not exhausted until we know everything about Adam that there is to know. Or to take a more everyday example (since it is questionable in any case whether we can be said to have a concept of an individual—of Adam—as opposed to man): We know a great many things about hydrogen—that it is the lightest element, that it is combustible, that it combines with oxygen to form water, and so on. Each of these facts constitutes part of our concept of hydrogen, and we would not have a

---

[1] The word "tautology" is commonly used *both* for the propositional forms (If *p* then *p*; either *p* or not-*p*) *and* for the propositions themselves (If it's snow, then it's snow; either it's snow or it's not snow). We shall conform to this dual usage here.

complete concept of hydrogen until we knew all the facts there are to be known about hydrogen. All the facts there are to be known about hydrogen constitute the complete concept of hydrogen, and to explicate this concept we would have to state every one of these facts, $a, b, c \ldots n$. But since every one of these is a part of the concept of hydrogen, every one of them—every proposition we can utter truly about hydrogen—must be analytic.

We *can* use the phrase "the concept of X" in such a way that every fact about X is a part of the concept of X. But the phrase is never so used in daily life or in science. We distinguish clearly what constitutes the concept of X from facts about X that do *not* form part of the concept; or, to put it otherwise, we distinguish between those features of X that it must have in order to be called X (defining characteristics) and those features of X without which it would still be X (accompanying characteristics). Surely we do not have to know every fact about X to have a concept of X (or X-ness). Do we lack the concept of gold before we know that gold dissolves in aqua regia? Or if one prefers to say that every fact about X forms a part of the concept of X, and that the concept of X becomes "richer" the more we know about X (thus using the phrase "the concept of X" in a way very different from our ordinary one), we must still distinguish—and we all do in practice—between those characteristics by means of which we recognize and identify something as *being* an X and those characteristics we subsequently discover *about* X but that are not involved in our identification of it as an X.

Thus not all of the facts about X are embodied in the concept of X. The concept of a brother is only that of a male offspring of the same parents. That is what we mean by "brother," and that is how we distinguish brothers from nonbrothers. That your brother is a male offspring of your parents is an analytic proposition, for it only states what it is to be a brother. But that your brother is tall and red-haired is a fact *about* him and not a part of the meaning of "brother": he would still be your brother if he did not have these characteristics. "My brother is male" is analytic, and "My brother is tall" is synthetic. It is true, of course, that if you know *everything* about your brother, you would also know whether he is tall and red-haired (this statement itself is analytic, for "everything" includes *all* his characteristics). But this does not keep the statement about his height and hair-color from being synthetic: if your brother is tall, then to say that he isn't is false, not self-contradictory. But your brother must be a male to be a brother at all—so "He is my brother but is not male" is self-contradictory, whereas "He is my brother but is not tall" is not.

2. "There is no clear difference between analytic and synthetic, so the distinction is useless."

But there *are* clear cases of analytic statements, as we have tried to show, such as "All bachelors are unmarried," and also clear cases of synthetic statements, such as "There are two books on this table" (who would say that *that* is a defining characteristic of "table"?). It must be admitted, however, that there are cases that are by no means clear. Usually this is because we at-tach no definite meaning to a crucial word in the sentence we are uttering, and until its meaning is specified, we are not in a position to say whether the sentence is being used to express an analytic proposition or not, just as when we see an object through a fog we cannot tell what its exact shape and color are. We have already used the example of "The best players are those who win the most games" (p. 161). Another example would be "An intelligent person wouldn't have made that mistake." With a little ingenuity, such examples could be multiplied indefinitely. As they stand, such propositions are more like propositional forms than like propositions: an important ingredient of their meaning must still be specified, and as long as it is not, it is no wonder that we can't say whether they are to be classified as analytic or synthetic.

3. It sometimes happens that a proposition is a part of a large body or system of propositions, and whether the individual proposition is considered analytic or not depends on its place in the entire *system* of propositions. This is often the case with laws of nature (which we shall consider in detail in Chapter 4), particularly in well-developed sciences such as physics, in which we have entire systems of laws. It is not easy to give examples without going into a fairly long discussion of the science itself. But perhaps the following will suffice as an example: Newton's three laws of motion were important discoveries, yet each of the laws, taken alone, could be construed as analytic (as definitions); but if they are analytic, how can they be regarded as discoveries about the universe? Each of Newton's laws *could* be construed as a definition relating several terms used in physics. Newton's second law of motion may be construed as a definition of "force," and the third law as a definition of "mass"; but if they are so construed, then *other* laws in the system are synthetic and not analytic. There is a variety of ways of construing these laws, each way imposing somewhat different definitional content upon the axioms. But in no case does such definitional content exhaust the entire meaning of the laws taken together systematically as a theory of motion. Even when the over-all system governed by these laws is so interpreted that some of the statements in it come out to be definitions (and therefore analytic), others remain non-definitional or synthetic statements having the character of empirical laws. Whether a statement in the context of a systematic body of statements is definitional (and therefore analytic) or non-definitional (and therefore synthetic) depends on this context and on the manner in which the entire system is construed for possible application to the world of things.

Possibility

We have just been considering kinds of propositions; we shall now consider situations or *states-of-affairs*. But there is a close connection between them. A state-of-affairs is said to be *logically possible* whenever the *proposition* that this state-of-affairs exists is not self-contradictory, and logically *im*possible when the proposition *is* self-contradictory.

It is logically impossible for there to be a square circle. If we mean what is conventionally meant in English by the words "square" and "circle," the definitions of the two words contradict each other. A circle is, by definition, something which (among other things) is not four-sided; hence, saying that a circle is square would be saying that something not four-sided is four-sided, which of course is self-contradictory. It is logically impossible for there ever to be a square circle: if it's a circle it can't be square, and if it's square it can't be a circle. The "can't" here is a *logical* "can't," meaning that it is *logically* impossible for it to be so.

On the other hand, it is logically possible for you to jump 10,000 feet into the air by your own unaided muscular power. If you said that you had done so, you would be stating a false synthetic proposition, but not a self-contradictory one. There is nothing self-contradictory about "I jumped ten thousand feet into the air." The state of affairs described by the proposition is *logically* possible.

If this seems strange, it is because we seldom use this sense of "possibility" but another, the *empirical*. A state of affairs is empirically possible when it is not contrary to laws of nature. Thus, it is empirically, not logically, impossible for you to jump 10,000 feet in the air, or to jump out of a tenth-story window and not go downward.

As far as we know, the states-of-affairs expressed by laws of nature do not change; hence what is empirically possible at one time is empirically possible at any other time. What we *thought* a hundred years ago to be empirically impossible may have turned out to be empirically possible after all; but in that case we were simply mistaken about the laws of nature. At one time no one suspected that phenomena such as radioactivity and atomic fission were empirically possible, but they were wrong. Nature works in ways with which even now we are far from completely acquainted, which only means that more things are empirically possible than we now know.

What does change from one age to another is *technical* possibility. Technical possibility involves not merely the laws of nature but our ability to make use of these laws to produce conditions which we were unable to produce before. A hundred years ago the making of jet aircraft was not technically possible, but now it is. A spaceship landing on Mars is today not a technical possibility, but a few years hence it may be. The laws of nature themselves have not changed; what has changed is our knowledge of them, which renders technically possible many things that were not technically possible, or even imagined, a few years ago.

Relation among the types of possibility. If a state of affairs is logically impossible, then it is impossible in the other senses too. For example: it is logically impossible to fall upwards, because "fall" means to go downwards;

so falling upwards would be going downwards upwards, which is a self-contradiction. It is, then, logically impossible to fall upwards, and of course empirically impossible and technically impossible as well. (The definition of "fall" may, of course, change in outer-space contexts.)

But this does not work the other way around: what is technically impossible (at any given time) need not be empirically impossible at all—for example, photographing a galaxy 500 million light-years away; and what is empirically impossible need not be logically impossible—for example, light becoming stronger with increasing distance from its source. Traveling from New York to California in three minutes is not now technically possible, but who can say that there is anything empirically impossible about it? A body not subject to gravitation is (as far as we know) empirically impossible, but it is not logically impossible because there is no contradiction in asserting it. Thus we have:

Logically possible _____   _____ Logically impossible
Empirically possible _____   _____ Empirically impossible
Technically possible _____   _____ Technically impossible

It is for the empirical sciences, such as physics, to tell us what is empirically possible. It is for the *applied,* or practical, sciences, such as engineering, to tell us what is technically possible. Our chief concern here is what is logically possible. The others are introduced here only to distinguish them from logical possibility. The question that will confront us many times in the coming pages is, "Is or is not this or that state-of-affairs logically possible?" In doing this, we must be careful not to give a premature answer of "No" by confusing logical with other types of possibility. For example, it is *logically* possible for objects to fall faster or slower depending on their color; for you to chin yourself six million times in quick succession; for a man to live to the age of a million years; for cats to give birth to pups, and dogs to give birth to kittens. As far as we now know, none of these things is empirically possible. When we say that they are logically possible, we do *not* mean that we expect them to happen, or that we think there is the remotest *empirical* possibility that they will happen; we only mean that if we asserted that they did happen, or would happen, our assertion would *not* be self-contradictory, even though it would be false.

Another way of expressing the same idea is this: what is logically impossible could not be the case in any universe; what is only empirically impossible might be the case in *some* universe, but does not happen to be the case in ours. For example, it seems to be empirically impossible for living things to exist without oxygen, nitrogen, carbon, and hydrogen. But it is logically possible that life in some form could exist without one or more of these. It is logically possible that Newton's law of gravitation might not apply to such a universe: that whereas actually "every particle of matter attracts every other particle with a force varying inversely as the square of the distance . . ." it might vary inversely as the cube of the distance, for example. Such a law would not describe the universe we live in, but the situation it describes is just as *logically* possible as the one in our present universe. A universe in which the attraction varied inversely as the cube of the distance is logically possible; it does not happen to be actual. On the other hand, a square circle, or a male aunt, or *falling* upwards, could not occur in any universe; the states-of-affairs asserted are logically impossible, since they involve contradictions; there can be nothing for such expressions as "square circle" to refer to. We shall have abundant occasion in the coming pages to refer to states-of-affairs in (logically) possible universes which are not actual.

Conceivability. If some state-of-affairs is logically possible, is this the same as its being conceivable? It might easily seem so: "It's logically possible for you to jump out of a tenth-story window and not go downward" would then be equivalent to "It's *conceivable* that you might jump out of a tenth-story window and not go downward" (even though of course we don't expect it to happen). Of course we *can* define "conceivable" so that it means the same as "logically possible"; this is indeed one of the most common usages the word "conceivable" has in philosophy.

"Conceivable" is ambiguous, however. It may also mean "imaginable," and in this sense it is *not* equivalent to "logically possible." A thousand-sided polygon is surely logically possible; I cannot imagine one (form the image of one); what I am tempted to call my mental image of a polygon with 1,000 sides is no different from that of a polygon with 999 sides, but I would not want to deny categorically that somebody, somewhere, can form the image of a thousand-sided polygon. People's powers of imagination vary. What is imaginable depends on who is doing the imagining. You may be able to imagine things that I cannot. What is logically possible does not have this variability. Whether I can imagine it or not, a thousand-sided polygon, an animal that's a cross between a walrus and a wasp, and a color different from any we have ever seen, are *all logically possible;* we need not stop to ask whether we can *imagine* them. Something can be logically possible and yet unimaginable (by you or by me, or even by everybody) because of the limitation of our powers of imagination.

On the other hand, if a state-of-affairs is really logically *im*possible, it is not imaginable by anybody: no one can imagine a tower that is both 100 and 150 feet high, or a circle that is square. If someone says he *can* form the image of a square circle, he is probably forming the image of a square, then of a circle, then of a square in rapid succession. But he can hardly imagine a figure that is both circular and not circular. (If he still says he can, let him draw one on the blackboard.)

"Conceivable" is used in other senses as well. Whether or not a certain state-of-affairs is conceivable will then depend on the sense of "conceivable" which is being employed at the time. But until the sense is clearly stated, one should not be satisfied with the simple equation "The logically possible = the conceivable."

Examples.   Let us now run through a few examples of logical possibility and impossibility. There is an almost ineradicable tendency at the start to confuse logical impossibility with empirical impossibility, which only time and numerous examples can dispel; yet it is essential that it be dispelled.

1. Is it logically possible for a solid iron bar to float on water? Of course it is. There is no contradiction at all in it. It is a law of physics that objects with a greater specific gravity than water (i.e., weighing more than an equal volume of water) do not float on water (with certain exceptions such as the phenomenon of "surface tension"). There is no *logical necessity* about this—that is to say, it is logically possible for it to be otherwise. You can even imagine it now (remember, if you *can* really imagine it, it is logically possible, but if you can't, it may only mean that your powers of imagination are limited): you take a piece of iron (a chemist has verified that it really is iron), you weigh it, then you plunge it into a vessel of water, and behold, it floats. You have also verified that it is a solid iron bar, not hollow inside with large air-filled spaces like a battleship; indeed, you have weighed it and measured it so as to make sure that its weight is really greater than that of an equal volume of water. This is a logically possible state-of-affairs; it does not actually occur, but there is nothing *logically* impossible about it.

2. Is it logically possible to remember something that never happened? As in so many cases, the answer is "Yes" in one sense and "No" in another, depending on the sense of the word "remember" that is employed. It may be used in a "weak" sense, so that you remember something whenever you have "that recollective feeling" about it, regardless of whether it really happened or not. In this sense, clearly, people often remember many events which, as it turns out, never really happened at all.

Here someone might object, "Then you didn't *really* remember it, you only thought you did!" This person is using "remember" in the "strong" sense, in which remembering involves not only "having a feeling of recollection" but also that the event about which you have this feeling really did occur. If it didn't really occur, then "you don't really remember it, you only *think* you did." In this sense, it is a defining characteristic of "(really) remembering" that the event actually occurred; therefore, in this sense it is logically impossible to remember something that never happened.

3. Is it logically possible for a cat to give birth to pups? Biologically impossible, doubtless (and hence empirically impossible), but logically possible. It is a fact of nature that like produces like, but there is no logical necessity about this.

"But isn't anything that a cat gives birth to, by definition, a cat?" You need only think this through for a moment to see that it is false. Suppose that what the cat gave birth to barked, wagged its tail, had all the contours of a dog, exhibited typical dog-behavior, and was unhesitatingly identified by everybody as a dog. Would you still call it a cat? In such a situation no one would say that the offspring was a cat—rather, they would be astounded by the unusual phenomenon that a cat had produced, not another cat, but a dog.

"But if a pup was the offspring, the mother must not have been a cat!" Not even if it looked like one, meowed, purred, and had all the other characteristics which cause us to call it a cat? Would you have hesitated to call it a cat *before* the strange birth took place? Must you wait to see what the creature's offspring look like (if it has any) before being able to identify it as a cat? Once again, cats are distinguished from dogs and other creatures (somewhat vaguely, as we saw in Chapter 1) by their general appearance, and it is logically possible for something with all the feline appearances to give birth to something with all the canine appearances. That nature does not operate in this way, that like produces like, is a fact of nature, not a logical necessity.

4. Is it logically possible to go from Chicago to New York without traversing the distance in between? Unless some unusual sense of the word is being employed, it is logically impossible to go from Chicago to New York (or anywhere else)without traversing distance, for to *go* from one place to another *is* to traverse distance; this is what "going" means. To assert that you went from one place to another place, and yet deny that you traversed distance, would be self-contradictory.

The word "between," however, may cause difficulty; it all depends on what it is taken to mean. One may take the word strictly, so that you are not going *between* A and B unless you are taking the shortest possible route from A to B. In this sense, you can surely go from Chicago to New York without traveling the distance *between* them. Indeed, no one has probably ever gone the distance between them in this sense, for the shortest route would be through the interior of the earth. At the other extreme, you might use "between" so loosely that *any* route you would take to get from A to B would be called "between" A and B—so that if you went from Chicago to New York by way of New Orleans or San Francisco, or by way of Shanghai, or by way of Mars, these places would be said to be *between* Chicago and New York. In this sense, of course, it would be logically impossible to go from Chicago to New York without traversing the distance in between, for any route you would take to get from the one place to the other would *ipso facto* be said to be between them.

Common usage of the word "between" seems to lie somewhere between(!) these two extremes. In common usage, any route that is within certain vague limits of the shortest distance, and especially any route that is on a standard air or railroad route from the one place to the other, is said to be between the two places. But as we have already seen (pp. 68–69), the distinction is a vague one, and one could easily be pushed down the slippery slope of vagueness: "Cleveland is between New York and Chicago? Very well—then what of Cincinnati? Is it too? What about Memphis? New

Orleans? Mexico City?" Here the familiar pattern is exhibited: probably most people would say that Cleveland is between Chicago and New York, and no one would wish to say that Mexico City is, but they would not know where to draw the line, nor would they probably wish to draw it at any specific point. In any *common* usage of "between," then, it *is* logically possible to go from one place to another without traversing the distance *between*.

5. "Is it logically possible to go back in time—say, to 3000 B.C., and help the Egyptians build the pyramids?"

We must be very careful about this one. We can speak quite easily and literally about going backward and forward in space, and it is tempting to use the same language about time as we do about space, and assume that time-language is meaningful in all the same contexts as is space-language. But, as we shall see, this is a dangerous assumption. Let us also be clear that when we talk about "going back to 3000 B.C." we mean it *literally;* taken in a figurative sense, there is no problem, for we certainly can and do *imagine* ourselves being at far distant places in space and at various eras in time. We can *imagine* ourselves being there as the pyramids were being built. "But if we can *imagine* it, then surely it's logically possible. If we can't imagine it, that doesn't show that it isn't logically possible (our powers of imagination may be limited), but if we *can* imagine it, then it is logically possible, and we can imagine this as clearly as we can imagine anything. In fact, H. G. Wells did imagine it in *The Time Machine,* and every reader imagines it with him." But let us be quite clear about what we are imagining. We can imagine ourselves as having been born in a different era[2] and being with the Egyptians building the pyramids. But can we imagine ourselves *now,* in the 20th century A.D., *being* (not merely in our imagination) in 3000 B.C.? How can we be in the 20th century A.D. and the 30th century B.C. *at the same time?* Here already is one contradiction. We cannot *be* in the 20th century A.D. and *not* in the 20th century A.D. (for example, in some other century, like the 30th century B.C.) at the same time. It is logically possible that you might live a very long time, and have lived during the construction of the pyramids and still be alive to tell the tale in the 20th century A.D. But it is *not* logically possible to be in one century of time and in another century of time at the same time.

"But," one may object, "this is not the situation we are imagining. What we are imagining is being one day in the 20th century and then moving backward in time so that the next day we are in the year 3000 B.C.—and on that day we are no longer in the 20th century A.D." But let us be careful: suppose the day you are talking about is January 1, 1969, and that on January 2, 1969, you use the time machine and go back to some day in 3000

---

[2] Even here there is a question: Would it still be *you* if you were born in 3000 B.C.? Our discussion of personal identity in Chapter 6 may cast some light on this question.

B.C. Isn't there a contradiction here again? For the next day after January 1, 1969, is January 2, 1969. The day after Tuesday is Wednesday (this is analytic—"Wednesday" is defined as the day that follows Tuesday), and the day after January 1 is January 2 (this also is analytic). So it is logically impossible to go from January 1 *to any other day* except January 2 of the same year. You may not live past January 1, but whether you do or don't, the next day (by definition) will be January 2. But to be living on January 2, 1969, *and* (at the same time) January 2, 3000 B.C., is a contradiction in terms, and hence logically impossible.

"That's true, but you still miss the point. The point is that we go *backward* in time, *not to the next day,* but to a day almost 5,000 years earlier. (It doesn't matter whether this is by means of a time machine, a magic wand, touching a crystal ball, or some means unknown to us.) So we don't go to the *next* day (if we did, it *would* be January 2), but to a *previous* day."

This argument presents a more difficult challenge, but there is still a confusion in it. Here is something we all *can* imagine easily: On January 1, 1969, you wake up and find that you are surrounded, not by modern streets and houses and automobiles, but by the environment of the 19th century (say Victorian England—horses and carriages, London streets as depicted by Dickens, women wearing hobble-skirts, and so on). This would be very strange, and you would probably not be able to explain the sudden change of environment, but you can easily imagine it happening. Then when you wake up on January 2, 1969, you find yourself surrounded by the environment of the 18th century, such as depicted in Fielding's *Tom Jones.* On the morning of January 3, the environment changes again—now it is the 17th century; and so on. On each successive day, you find yourself in a different environment, which fulfills the description of the historical period of a century earlier. While it would be most bizarre and unaccountable, this *is* logically possible —there is no contradiction in it, for the days would still be January 1, January 2, January 3, and so on. You could still mark them off on the calendar, and write in your diary for January 3, "Today I lived in the environment of the 17th century; I wonder what tomorrow will bring." Time would still be *going forward,* only the environment would be changing in unexplained ways; but each day you would still be getting *one day older.*

And here is the point: isn't "Time goes forward" analytic? "What else can it do but go forward?" we are tempted to ask. People can walk backward in space, but what would "going backward in time" literally mean? And if you continue to live, what can you do but get one day older every day? Isn't "getting younger every day" a contradiction in terms—unless, of course, it is meant figuratively, as in "My dear, you're getting younger every day," where it is still taken for granted that the person, while *looking* younger every day, is still *getting older* every day? In the description we have just given, you are still going from January 2 to January 3 (and so on) and getting a day older every day (analytic); so we have not been guilty of any contradiction. We have not said that you ever become younger or literally *go* backward in time. By definition we assign *numerically* later time to *successively* later events, no matter what characteristics these later events have.

"I'm still not convinced. The situation I am speaking of is that of going from January 1, 1969, *not* to January 2 but to 3000 B.C. And I still don't see how this is *logically* impossible, though it may be empirically impossible."

Let us try once again. Many centuries B.C., the pyramids were built, and when all this happened you were not there—you weren't even born. It all happened long before you were born, and it all happened without your assistance or even your observation. This is an unchangeable fact: *you can't change the past*. That is the crucial point: the past is what has happened, and you can't make what has happened not have happened. Not all the king's horses or all the king's men could make what *has* happened *not* have happened, for this is a logical impossibility. When you say that it is logically possible for you (literally) to go back to 3000 B.C. and help build the pyramids, you are faced with the question: did you help them build the pyramids or did you not? The first time it happened, you did *not:* you weren't there, you weren't yet born, it was all over before you came on the scene. All you could say, then, would be that the *second* time it happened, you *were* there—and there was at least a difference between the first time and the second time: the first time you weren't there, and the second time you were. But now we are speaking of *two* times, the first time being 3000 B.C. and the second time being A.D. 1969.

Now it *is* logically possible that history might suddenly start repeating itself: that on January 1, 1969, all of our modern buildings and machinery would disappear and we would find ourselves among sand and pyramids and the world of 3000 B.C. This repetition *is* logically possible (though not empirically, to the best of our present knowledge), but it would be a repetition with a difference: the first time you were there (3000 B.C.), you weren't there; and the second time (A.D. 1969), you were. This would not be a case of literally *going back* in time to 3000 B.C.: it would be a case of history repeating itself (with a slight difference), with the world of 1969 suddenly vanishing and the world of 3000 B.C. suddenly replacing it. But time would still be going forward (if you want to use that expression), and the day *after* the sudden transformation would *not* be a day in 3000 B.C. (*that* day is long past and gone, and irrecoverable like everything else in the past), but January 2, 1969.

Once you are convinced of the logical impossibility of changing the past (or making what has happened un-happen), you will doubtless see the logical impossibility of literally "going back in time" to 3000 B.C. We are inclined to be misled into thinking that it is logically possible because we see movies like *The Time Machine* in which a person in 1900 pulls a lever on a machine and suddenly is surrounded by the world of many centuries earlier. What doesn't occur to the viewer is that he is in the world of many centuries earlier *after* he has pressed the lever. The inventors of these tales are involved in other logical difficulties as well: for example, our hero in 1900 pulls the lever in the other direction and finds himself in an unrecognizable world of many centuries in the future. There he meets a girl, marries her, and takes her back with him in the time machine to the year 1900. The girl wasn't born until A.D. 40,000, yet she gave birth to his child in 1900, long before she was born. One is tempted to speculate: What if he had decided, in the year 40,000, *not* to marry her and bring her back after all? Then her child (born in 1900, though the mother wasn't born until 40,000) wouldn't have been born either; and yet after 1900 he had already been born. Indeed, that child might have become the prime minister of Britain, and affected the course of the world in such a way that no human beings would have existed on the earth in the year 40,000. What if there had been a nuclear explosion in 1990 that obliterated life forever from the earth? What then would have happened to the charming hypothesis that he "went into the year 40,000" and brought the girl "back into 1900"—an event that the events of 1990 would have rendered impossible? The whole alleged situation is riddled with contradictions. When we say we can imagine it, we are only uttering the words, but there is nothing in fact even logically possible for the words to describe.

Exercises

1. Which of the following propositions are analytic? State why.
   a. All swans are white.
   b. All swans are birds.
   c. All aunts are female.
   d. All aunts are blood-relatives.
   e. All human beings are mortal.
   f. All human beings are selfish.
   g. Normal persons behave like the majority.
   h. Circles never contain straight lines.
   i. All minks are fur-bearing.
   j. Water at sea level boils at 212° F.
   k. All fish live in water.
   l. People are funny.
   m. When large numbers of people are out of work, unemployment results. (Calvin Coolidge.)
2. Which of the propositional forms on List 3 stand for tautologies (which would yield true propositions for all values of p and q? Justify your answer.
3. Which of the propositions on List 2 are tautologies (substitution-instances of propositional forms that yield tautologies in all cases)? Justify your answer.
4. Are there any items on Lists 1, 2, or 3 that are, in your opinion, self-contradictory? Justify your answer.
5. Could anything refute the following statements? If not, are they therefore analytic? Explain.
   a. If you study this book long enough, you'll understand it.
   b. Unless I'm mistaken, I'm now in Baghdad.

    c. Some day there will no longer be conflict among nations.

    d. Time cannot go backwards.

    e. Everyone acts from the motive which (at the time of acting) is the strongest.

    f. The best runner in this race is the one who will win.

  6. Are the following logically possible? Justify your answer in each case.

    a. To jump 10,000 feet into the air.

    b. To see a sound.

    c. To have an unconscious desire.

    d. To see something that doesn't exist.

    e. To read tomorrow's newspaper today.

    f. To cross a river and be on the same side you started from.

    g. To see without eyes.

    h. To be knocked into the middle of next week.

    i. For a solid iron bar to float on water.

    j. For a sound to exist that no creature in the world can hear.

    k. For a table to eat the book that's on it.

    l. For a box to be pure red and pure green all over its surface at the same time.

    m. For Thursday to follow Tuesday without Wednesday in between. (Assume that you remain in the same spot, not crossing the International Date Line.)

    n. For no world to exist at all.

    o. For a part of space to move to some other part of space.

    p. For a thought to occur without someone to think it.

    q. For a straight line not to be the shortest distance between two points.

    r. For time to reverse itself. (Try to clear up the statement first, before saying yes or no.)

    s. For someone to have experiences after he no longer has a physical body. (More on this in Chapter 6.)

    t. There was a young lady named Bright
      Who could travel faster than light.
          She eloped one day
          In a relative way
      And returned on the previous night.

10. The A Priori

We have distinguished two kinds of propositions, analytic and synthetic. We must now turn to another important way of classifying propositions, which may seem at first to be the analytic-synthetic distinction over again, but is not. Let us try to forget the distinction between analytic and synthetic, for these first few pages, and start afresh with a different way of classifying propositions, which may turn out to be even more important. There are some propositions that, when we reflect on them, seem to be *necessarily* true—they could not possibly be false—and others that seem to be *necessarily* false, and could not possibly be true. For example, "One can't be in two different places at the same time," "Whatever has shape has size," and "If one event precedes a second event and the second precedes the third, then the first precedes the third," we are tempted to say, *must* be true—we need not even bother to examine whether they are, for they are necessarily true (they would be true in all possible worlds). These we call *necessary* truths, and their negations would be necessarily false. By contrast, there are other propositions which are true, but "just happen to be true"—there is no necessity about them: "There are six people in this room," "Some dogs are white," "People can't run as fast as jackrabbits." These are only *contingently* true—their truth is contingent on what the universe happens to be like. Their negations would be contingently false. All these we call *contingent* propositions.

What is it that makes necessary truths necessary? It is that they are knowable *a priori;* indeed, the terms "necessary truth" and "truth knowable a priori" are interchangeable expressions. They are knowable a priori because they necessarily hold true for all cases—today, tomorrow, or a million years from now. If someone is in New York, we do not need to investigate further to discover whether he is also in California. If we know that something is red, we do not have to investigate further to discover whether it is colored. Any statement that we do have to test to see whether it holds for future cases is a contingent statement, knowable only *a posteriori*. (Any true statement whose truth cannot be known a priori is knowable, if at all, only a posteriori.) What makes a statement a priori—and hence necessary—is how we come to know it, not the structure of the statement itself, as with analytic statements. An a priori statement—that is, one whose truth is knowable a priori—needs no verification by further experience: we can know that it holds true, everywhere and always, without investigating all the various cases to which it applies.

What of statements such as "Water boils at 212° F. (at sea-level pressure)," "Water flows downhill," "All white tomcats with blue eyes are deaf," "All solid objects whose weight per unit of volume exceeds that of a liquid will sink in that liquid," and so on? These express uniformities of nature, which we shall examine more closely in Chapter 4 when we consider laws of nature. Our present question is: Are these statements necessarily true? At first, we may be inclined to think that they are: we have become so familiar with these uniformities that we have come to take them for granted. But let us reflect: they are all statements of uniformities to be found in nature; have we any guarantee that a uniformity that held yesterday and today will continue to hold tomorrow and forever after? Don't we have to observe nature again tomorrow to see whether it behaves as it did today? Many statements have been made expressing what were thought to be uniformities of nature that on subsequent investigation turned out not to be so: the alleged uniformity had exceptions, or was true only with qualifications, etc. The test of further experience showed that it did not hold true as it was originally stated. May the same not be true of some of those we now believe to state genuine uniformities? But if we have to observe nature further to discover whether the uniformity continues to hold, then the statement in question is contingent, not necessary.

There are several common misunderstandings of the a priori against which we should guard ourselves at the outset.

1. If a man undermined the foundations of his house, wouldn't he know a priori that the house would collapse? No, not in the sense philosophers employ when they speak of a priori knowledge. At best it can be called *relatively* a priori knowledge, or knowledge *relative to* a certain body of statements *which are not themselves knowable* a priori. Relative to certain general gravitational and architectural principles—that is, assuming them to hold in all cases—a man would know that his house would collapse if he uprooted its foundations. Relative to the principle that all stones fall, he would know a priori that the stone he now holds in his hand will fall if he lets go of it. But the principles on which he rests this knowledge are not themselves knowable a priori: only by means of observation of the world around us do we know that stones fall when we let go of them, and that houses depend on what is below them for support. We are concerned here not with relatively but with absolutely a priori knowledge: that which we can know a priori, not on the basis of other pieces of knowledge which are a posteriori, but on the basis of no a posteriori knowledge whatever—prior to all experience of the world.

2. This last phrase leads us to a second distinction. It is clear that *chronologically* nobody knows anything prior to all experience. Your experience began even before you were born—a time when you can hardly be said to have *known* anything. Surely all knowledge comes posterior to experience, in the sense that if you had experienced nothing there would be nothing you could know. So how could anyone seriously suggest that anything can be known absolutely a priori?

But in calling it a priori we do not mean that a person's knowledge of it occurred prior in time to all his experiences. In calling it a priori we are not referring to the time of origin at all. We are referring not to the way of coming by the piece of knowledge in question but to the way in which it must be *verified*. For example, you can know a priori that thunder is thunder, but not that thunder follows lightning. Even in the case of "Thunder is thunder" you can hardly be said to have known this before you had any experiences, before you knew what thunder was and knew what word was used to refer to it. It was not a priori in *that* sense; but what *is* true is that in the case of "Thunder is thunder" *you do not have to await the verdict of experience to find out whether the statement always holds true.* You do not have to investigate any instance of thunder to see whether it is really thunder. (Indeed, what would it be like to do this?) On the other hand, you cannot safely say that thunder follows lightning without experiencing instances of this relationship. There lies the difference: not in the amount of experience required prior to uttering the statement but in the process required to ascertain whether it is true. When a statement is known to be true a priori, one does not need to experience any further instances of the classes of things in question in order to know that the statement always holds.

Are there synthetic necessary statements?　At this point one might remark: "Of course there are necessary statements, knowable a priori—plenty of them. But they are all analytic statements or tautologies; the denial of any of them would result in a self-contradiction. In other words, none of them is *synthetic*. A is A, cats are cats, you can't be both here and not here at the same time, cats are mammals (since being a mammal is one of the defining characteristics of being a cat), and so on. I don't deny that all these statements are necessary, and it would be foolish indeed to feel that you had to verify them by observing the world. The reason that we don't have to test them by observation of the world is simply that they are empty of any factual content: they are all analytic. This is quite obvious in the examples just given, but it holds also of not-so-obvious cases like 'Everything that has shape has size.' This statement, of course, is necessarily true, and we don't have to go around testing things of various shapes to see whether they all have size. But the reason for this is that the statement is really analytic: just analyze the concepts of shape and size. Whether something is two-dimensional like a square or three-dimensional like a cube, its shape is only the total configuration of the *boundary* of its spatial extension, and its size is only the *amount* of this spatial extension. You can't have an amount of something (at least if it's of finite size) without its coming to an end somewhere, and wherever it comes to an end is its boundary. The two concepts are logically interconnected. A mathematical point, of course, has no shape, but then, it has no size either—although the little dot we write on paper to represent a point has both shape and size. So I agree that the statement is necessarily true, but only because it's analytic."

It does, indeed, seem to be true, thus far, that all the cases of necessary statements (knowable a priori) are analytic. They are, at any rate, the most obvious instances of a priori statements. But are they the only ones? Are there any a priori statements that are also synthetic—necessarily true yet not analytic?

This is one of the most controversial problems in the history of modern philosophy. Let us pause for a moment to grasp its full impact. Early in this chapter, we distinguished between analytic and synthetic statements, and later we distinguished truths knowable a priori from those knowable only a posteriori. What is the relation between these two distinctions?

A priori (necessary)	A posteriori (contingent)
Analytic	Synthetic

Most, at any rate, of the synthetic statements we hear and utter are contingent: "The desk is brown," "There are six cars in the driveway," "I feel drowsy," "1964 was a presidential election year in the United States,"

"Water boils at 212° F.," and so on endlessly—all of these are synthetic statements, none of them knowable a priori. Such are the vast majority of statements uttered in daily discourse. On the other hand, we have statements that we seldom have occasion to utter but that are nevertheless true, and necessarily true, such as "If you're here, you're here," "Squares are rectangles," "Quadrupeds have four legs," "Either grass is green or grass is not green," and so on—but they are all analytic. The tantalizing question is: Can we break these pairs? Are there some statements that are *not* analytic, that convey genuine information about reality, that are yet knowable a priori, so that we can know them to hold true of the world for all cases without awaiting the verdict of experience to assure us that they always hold true?

It will seem to many persons that this is like trying to eat one's cake and have it too. If a statement gives genuine information *about* the world, how can one know that it is true except by observation *of* the world? And if one doesn't have to do this, but can know a priori that it always holds true, how can it be anything other than analytic? How can one have the advantages of both sides at once? Wouldn't one be trying to run with the hare and hunt with the hounds?

Those who declare that there are no synthetic a priori truths are called *empiricists*. For every alleged instance of a synthetic a priori truth, they contend that the statement is either (1) synthetic but not a priori or (2) a priori but not synthetic: there are no truths that are both synthetic *and* a priori. On the other hand, those who declare that there are synthetic a priori truths are called *rationalists*. Rationalists may not all agree on which truths are synthetic and a priori, but anyone who holds there is even *one* synthetic a priori truth is a rationalist, for he denies the empiricist claim that there are none.

Here are some propositions that rationalists have held to be synthetic a priori truths:

2 plus 2 equals 4.
Every event has a cause.
Everything that is colored is extended. (Extended = spread out in space.)
Everything that has volume has shape.
All cubes have 12 edges.
Parallel lines never meet.
A straight line is the shortest distance between two points.
If A precedes B and B precedes C, then A precedes C.
A whole is the sum of its parts.
All sounds have pitch, volume, and timbre.
An object cannot be in two different places at the same time.
An object cannot have two different colors at the same place at the same time.
Time proceeds forward, never backward.
Space is three-dimensional.

The empiricist holds that none of these propositions, nor any other alleged synthetic a priori truths, are synthetic a priori: if a priori, they turn out to be analytic, and if synthetic, they turn out not to be a priori. But the rationalist holds (in one form of rationalism—we shall come across another form shortly) that some of them—or at any rate some propositions, even if not those above—are both synthetic and a priori.

How is synthetic a priori knowledge possible?   The usual rationalist position on this is quite simple: it has been called the "rational insight theory." The rationalist simply holds that we derive certain concepts from experience, but that after we have thus derived them (for example, the concept of color and the concept of extension), we see that they necessarily go together. Once we understand through sense-experience what it is to be colored and to be extended, we see (have rational insight) that what has the first property must also have the second. The mind simply has the power to grasp certain necessary features of reality. That reason enables us to know these things seems to the rationalist no more surprising than that sense-experience enables us to know that the grass is green.

Another, and far more involved, account of the matter was suggested by Immanuel Kant. He explained the possibility of synthetic a priori truths by the nature of the human mind. It is because the human mind is structured the way it is that certain truths are both synthetic and a priori. Let us consider a simple analogy. Suppose that you always wore red glasses; then it would be no accident that everything always appeared to you as some shade of red—some lighter and some darker, but everything tainted with red. You might think that every object in the world was red, but in fact it would only be a statement about the-world-as-seen-through-red-glasses. But as long as you kept on the glasses, everything you saw would appear some shade of red. In actual fact, of course, we can take off the glasses and see the world without the red tinge; moreover, if everything always appeared red, we would probably have no words for any other colors, only for different shades of red. But the mind is like the eyes and unlike the glasses—we cannot remove it and think (or see) with a new one. Or suppose that you are fishing in the sea with nets, and that the interstices of the net are all one inch apart. Every time you take in the net to discover what fish you may have caught, any fish that are less than an inch long slip through the net back into the sea. If you knew nothing about the nature of the net, or if it did not occur to you that the nature of the net had something to do with what you caught, you might after a time put it down as a fact about fish in the sea: "There are no fish in the sea less than one inch long." But we who do know about the net would realize that your statement would reflect a fact not about fish but about the net.

According to Kant, our synthetic a priori knowledge has its source in a similar condition. There is a "real world"—a noumenal world, as he called it—that has many features that we cannot even imagine. They are kept from us by the structure of our minds, just as fish less than one inch long are never caught in these nets. Our minds are constituted in such a way that only certain kinds of material are presented to it. Anything other than these slip through the net, as it were. Concerning the noumenal world as it exists apart from the mind we have no knowledge at all: we can know only what comes to us in the net, and nothing of what slips through. What reality is like apart from what we catch in the net is forever beyond us: we cannot even imagine it, and we are in no position to utter statements about it. But the knowledge we have of what comes to us by way of the net (the structure of the mind) is synthetic and a priori. As long as the fisherman sticks to his net and knows only what the net yields him, it is an a priori truth that he will never catch any fish less than an inch long. In the same way, the mind is so constituted that every datum it presents to us is always seen through certain "forms of the intuition" (space and time) and "form of the understanding" (such as substance and causality). Since everything non-spatial and non-temporal will slip through the net, certain fundamental truths about space and time can be known a priori—for example, that time moves in one direction only; that if A precedes B and B precedes C, then A precedes C; that if A is north of B and B is north of C, then A is north of C; that if A is larger than B and B is larger than C, then A is larger than C; and so on. These hold true only of the world-as-known-by-the-mind—that is, the *phenomenal* world—not the noumenal world, or world-as-it-is-in-itself. But of the phenomenal world the statements about space and time are synthetic and a priori. Similarly, we cannot know a priori what causes what, but we can know that everything that happens has a cause, for events are presented to our minds only within the net of causality.

Space does not permit here a critique of this Kantian thesis. It appears to introduce more problems than it solves. For example:

1. We seem to be left with total skepticism as to the nature of the real (noumenal) world: if time is not real but only a "form of the intuition," it seems that we are committed to saying that there is "really" no before-and-after, and that the real world contains no events and processes, since these occur in time; and the same with regard to space: in the real world nothing can be to the left of anything else, since in the real world no spatial categories apply. Since we speak, conceive, and experience entirely in temporal and spatial terms, it seems that we are left with nothing to say about the real world. Must we go so far to show how synthetic a priori knowledge is possible? Is not the cure (total skepticism) worse than the disease?

2. How can we know that there is a real world and that it is unknowable?

3. If the phenomenal world is a function of the structure of the human mind, how do we know that the structure of the mind won't change? Can we know this a priori? If we cannot, then we do not have synthetic a priori knowledge even of the phenomenal world.

From this point on, we shall discuss the rationalists' claim in a non-Kantian context: we shall consider the rationalists' view as one about our knowledge of a reality that exists independently of human minds. Rationalists themselves (except for Kant) have so considered it: in believing in certain synthetic a priori truths, they have believed that these were truths about reality, about the world as it exists apart from human minds and would presumably exist even if no human minds existed at all.

A priori assumptions. It is, of course, a priori *knowledge* that we are here concerned with, propositions whose *truth* can be known without further recourse to experience. This is to be distinguished sharply from a priori *assumptions,* which are propositions that a person assumes to be true so staunchly that he will not admit that they can be refuted or even doubted, even though such a refutation, or grounds for doubt, may be at hand. A patient said to his physician, "Doctor, I'm dead." The doctor tried in vain to convince him otherwise and finally said, "Well, dead men don't bleed, do they?" "No." "I am now going to prick you with a pin." The doctor did so, and the patient bled. The patient said, "Doctor, I was wrong—dead men *do* bleed." The patient was so convinced that he was dead that he would accept no contrary evidence, not even the fact that he bled. That he was dead was in the case of this patient an a priori assumption.

Most people entertain many a priori assumptions. They are usually of more interest to the person's psychiatrist than to a philosopher: philosophers are concerned with the rational grounds of belief, not with whether a certain person believes this or that and why. The list of propositions that various people assume a priori to be true would be as long as the list of groundless prejudices.

An a priori assumption may, of course, be true; but it is not knowledge, because the person does not hold it on the basis of sufficient evidence. Those who refused to look through Galileo's telescope at the moons of Jupiter were assuming a priori that no such thing existed, and would accept no evidence to the contrary. In this case their assumption was false, as was the assumption of most people in ancient times that the earth was flat. But a person who today assumes that the earth is round without having evidence for it, but would refuse to accept any evidence against it even if such evidence did turn up, would be assuming "The earth is round" a priori, although in this case the assumption would be true.

Arithmetic

If we want to discover truths that are necessary yet not analytic, the most obvious candidates for this position would seem to lie in the realm of mathematics. Are not mathematical truths eternal and unchangeable? And are they not true necessarily? And do they not give us genuine information about reality? Consider a simple statement in arithmetic, such as $2 + 2 = 4$. Aren't we quite certain that this is true, that it always will be true, and that it always *must* be true? How could it be false on Mars or on the farthest star in the universe? We may not know anything about what conditions exist in these far places, but can't we be sure at any rate that if there are two things and then two more things there, then there are four things? And can't we be just as sure that this was true a million years ago or will be true a million years from now as that it is true today? Surely such a proposition is not like "All crows are black," which you couldn't really know to be true until you had examined all the crows there are. Isn't it a necessary truth, knowable a priori, and at the same time one that gives genuine information about the world, unlike "Black cats are black"?

It has sometimes been held that such statements as "2 + 2 = 4" are non-analytic (synthetic) but also non-necessary (contingent)—in short, that they are really no different from "All crows are black" or "Water boils at 212° under standard conditions." No exceptions to these last two statements have ever been found, and similarly no exceptions to the statements of arithmetic have ever been found: we have never come across any case in which two things plus two things did not equal four things. The mathematical laws are more general than are the laws of physics and chemistry and biology, for they apply to everything—not only to physical things but to thoughts, images, feelings, and to everything one could possibly think of: it is true of absolutely everything that two of it and two more of it make four of it. The mathematical laws are also better established than even the laws of the physical sciences. For thousands of years before anything was known of the laws of physical science, people had found that statements such as "2 and 2 makes 4" always hold true; it had been found to be true countless times, without one single negative instance. Nevertheless, according to this view, the laws of the physical sciences and those of arithmetic are of the same fundamental kind: they are both synthetic and contingent. Both can be known to be true only by observation of the world, and both can be falsified by observation of the world. Just as it is logically possible that we might find exceptions to well-established laws of physical science (it is logically possible that we might find water when heated turning into ice instead of boiling), so it is also logically possible that we might find exceptions to the laws of arithmetic (2 plus 2 equaling 5, for example). We never have, of course, in spite of countless observed cases throughout human history, and that is why we are so sure that these laws always hold true. But if we are more certain of "2 plus 2 equals 4" than we are of the proposition about water and crows, it is only because human beings have had evidence to support the arithmetical propositions many times a day for thousands of years, while our experience of crows is more limited and intermittent.

Virtually no one today holds this interpretation of arithmetical statements. In whatever ways people may differ about arithmetical statements, they all agree that they are necessary (necessarily true) and knowable a priori, unlike the statements in the physical sciences. There might be white crows on Mars, or even on the earth; there might be vast reaches of the universe in which physical laws we believe in now do not hold; but always and everywhere and forever, 2 plus 2 equals 4. There may somewhere exist creatures so different from ourselves that we cannot even imagine them; the biological laws that would describe their function and operation might be far different from those in our biology textbooks; but this much is sure, if there are two of such organisms, and then two more, then there are four. Could anything be more certain than this? And do we not know it a priori? Do we really have to wait for further observation to decide the matter for future instances? Is there any danger whatsoever that the next time we have two and then two more we may *not* have four? As we shall see in the coming pages, there is no such danger, since there is no way this arithmetical proposition can be refuted.

But whether or not such propositions are necessary, let us ask whether they are analytic or synthetic. They seem at first glance to be synthetic: "2 plus 2 equals 4" does not seem to be at all like "Black cats are black" or "Tigers are tigers" or even like "Either snow is white or snow is not white." Arithmetical statements seem to give us knowledge of things in a way that these other statements do not. We can figure out sums in arithmetic, for example: we add, subtract, multiply, and divide large numbers, and the outcome gives us new information; we know something we didn't know before. And we can certainly think of the numbers involved in an addition without knowing what their sum is: if we did know, we wouldn't have to figure it out.

In spite of all this, it is customary today to hold that arithmetical propositions are analytic. What does "4" mean, we might ask, but "2 + 2"? And what does "2" mean but "1 and 1"? When we say "2 + 2 = 4," we are saying merely that "1 + 1 + 1 + 1" equals "1 + 1 + 1 + 1," which is just as analytic as "Black is black." The reason we can be so sure—and are *entitled* to be so sure—that these propositions necessarily hold true and always will, is simply that they are analytic.

But how can this possibly be true, in virtue of the fact that we do get new information from these propositions? Let us consider several objections to the view that arithmetical propositions are synthetic, and then see how the proponents of the objections would try to answer them:

1. "I can think of 2 and 2 without thinking of 4." Probably I can, or at any rate I could in childhood before I learned that 2 and 2 makes 4. So can I think of the sum of 7 and 5 without thinking of 12, as Kant pointed out. But the statement that 7 and 5 makes 12 is not a law of psychology: it does not state that when I think of this I also think of that; it states that this *is* that, whether I think of the two together or not. I can think "He is my brother" without thinking "He is my male sibling," but the two have the same meaning anyway, and "He is my brother but not my male sibling" is self-contradictory whether I know it or not. It is the equivalence of one number with another set of numbers that we are talking about, not what our psychological processes are like.

2. "But even if I grant that '2 + 2 = 4' is analytic, what about more complex calculations like '40694 plus 27593 equals 68287'? Surely the principle of the two is the same, and if the first is analytic, so is the second.

Yet how can the second be analytic, when it requires us to figure out whether it is even true, and when we can make mistakes in addition besides?"

The principle of the two *is* the same (it would be replied): they are both analytic. It would take a long time to write out the second into a series of $1 + 1 + 1$'s, but if we did so we would find that it is the "$2 + 2 = 4$" story all over again, only with more 1's. And if we made a mistake in addition, our statement that the two figures added together equals that sum would be self-contradictory: we would be stating that $1 + 1 + 1 \ldots$ does not equal $1 + 1 + 1 \ldots$.

The sum in the second case is, of course, not so obvious as it is in the case of 2 plus 2. But again, this makes no difference. To be analytic it is not required that it be obvious. What is obvious to one person is not obvious to another, and what is obvious to a person at one time may not be at another time. What may not be obvious to you and me may well be obvious to a mathematical genius. Obviousness is a psychological characteristic that is in no way involved in the conception of being analytic. Propositions of arithmetic are analytic because their denial is self-contradictory, whether the self-contradictoriness is immediately obvious or not. To a being with very great mathematical powers the sum of very large numbers would be as obvious as "$2 + 2 = 4$" is to us.

3. "But the *meaning* of the two is not the same: 40694 and 27593 are not a part of the meaning of '68287.' When you ask me what I mean by this number, I don't give the other two—or any of the other sets of numbers that when added together would yield it. So how can the statement be analytic if the one is not all or even a part of the meaning of the other?"

But it doesn't need to be a part of the meaning, in the sense of *what we mean* when we say it. A may be B although "B" may not be what we mean when we say "A." 68287 may not be what we mean by 40694 and 27493, but it is the sum of those two numbers just the same. It is still a necessary truth, and the denial of it would still be self-contradictory.

4. "But isn't even such a simple statement as '2 plus 2 equals 4' a generalization from experience? Don't we *learn* its truth from experience? And isn't it based on instances? I first learn about 2 and 2 houses, then about 2 and 2 apples, and so on. How is its being learned from experience compatible with its being analytic?"

Of course I learn that 2 and 2 makes 4, and probably we all learned it as children, using examples such as houses and apples. But what is it that we learned? Is it anything about apples and houses? No, it is simply that 2 and 2 when added together makes 4; all the business about houses and apples was just window-dressing. What we learned was that the symbol "4" is equivalent in meaning to the symbol "2 and 2"—that *these two expressions can be used interchangeably*.

We do indeed learn the meanings of words through experience—how else? But this does not have anything to do with whether the propositions in which they occur are analytic. What makes them analytic is whether or not their negation is self-contradictory. To say that 2 and 2 does *not* make 4 would be to say that 1 and 1 and 1 and 1 does not make 1 and 1 and 1 and 1, which is self-contradictory.

When we put two pennies into our new piggy bank, and later two more pennies, we learned to say that we had put in four pennies, simply because "putting 4 pennies in" means the same as "putting 2 pennies and 2 pennies in." We learned to say it as a result of our experience—our experience of learning language—but *what* we said was a necessary truth, and analytic. But we *also* learned to predict that if we should open the bank later we would find four pennies in it. In this case what we learned was not an arithmetical truth but a truth about the world that we might call the *conservation of pennies;* and, unlike "2 plus 2 equals 4," this proposition might have turned out to be false without contradiction. If it had turned out to be false, we could still agree that "2 and 2 makes 4" is an analytic truth following from the definition of what we mean by "2," "4," "plus," and "equals."

This leads us directly into the next, and very important, objection.

5. "Far from being analytic, the propositions of arithmetic are not even true—at least not in all cases. Two and two doesn't always make four. For example, if you add two quarts of water to two quarts of alcohol, you ought (if the arithmetical proposition is true) to get four quarts—but you don't; you get a little less, owing to the interpenetration of molecules of the two substances. If you put together two lions and two lambs, and turn your back for a moment, you will have not four things, but only two—two lions. When two amoebas subdivide, they become four—what was two is now four! How can arithmetical propositions be necessary at all, much less analytic, if they aren't even true in all cases—when reality often shows them to be false?"

But this objection is the result of a total misunderstanding. When we say that 2 plus 2 equals 4, we do not deny for a moment that what *was* two can *become* four (the amoebas), or that you can have four things at one time and have only two things at a later time (the lions and the lambs). It says only that *if* you have two and two, then at that moment you have four. Arithmetic does not tell you anything about natural processes—how two things can become four things, or how four things can be reduced to two things. Arithmetic doesn't even tell you that there are four of anything in the world at all, or even that there *is* a world in which such distinctions can be made. It says only that *if* there are two, and then two more, *then* there must be four: that *to say there are two plus two and to say that there are four is to say the same thing.* When there are two lions and two lambs, then there are four things; when there are only two lions, then there are only two—that is, one plus one—things. If two things gave rise to a million things, this would not violate "2 and 2 equals 4" or any other proposition of arithmetic. Two rabbits soon become a million rabbits; and if two things exploded into a million things, or into nothing at all, this would not refute any law of arithmetic.

What turns into what, what becomes what, how one thing changes into another—all these are matters for the physical sciences to investigate; these are all a part of what happens in the world, and propositions about these things are all synthetic and contingent. But the propositions of arithmetic say nothing whatever about the changes that go on in nature; they say nothing at all about the kind of a world we live in, nor would they be changed in the slightest if the world were quite different from what it is, for the laws of arithmetic do not describe what the world is like. Arithmetic doesn't even tell you that the number 4 applies to anything in the world, but only that *if* it applies, then "2 plus 2" also applies, because the two symbols mean the same thing.

Now consider the example of the water and the alcohol. It is a proposition in chemistry, not in arithmetic: it tells you what happens when you do something to something else. The formulation of the example, in fact, is quite misleading: we speak of "adding" water to alcohol. But adding is an arithmetical process: it is an operation we perform with numbers, not with physical things. Strictly speaking, we do not *add* water to alcohol; we *pour* some water into a vessel of alcohol. (Or if you do want to call it adding, it is adding in a very different sense from the one we use in arithmetic.) You have to discover what happens when you pour something into something else by observation of the world. If you pour water into gasoline, you get no mixture at all. If you pour water onto pure sodium, you get an explosion, with neither water nor sodium left at the end of it. What happens when you do something to something else is a matter for the physical sciences to investigate, but nothing thus discovered can refute any law of arithmetic, since they have nothing whatever to do with arithmetic.

"But arithmetical laws are not just about combinations of symbols: they are very general statements about reality. How else could the laws of arithmetic *apply to the world?* Yet they do. It is not merely true that 2 and 2 is 4; it is also true that 2 trees and 2 trees makes 4 trees. Laws of arithmetic have to do with quantities, but quantities of anything—trees and everything else. It is because they are so general that they seem to be about nothing—but they are about things, only *all* things."

Suppose you are counting trees: 2 trees to your left, 2 trees to your right, but every time you tried to count them all together you got 5 as your result instead of 4. What would we say if this kept on happening? Would it refute any of the laws of arithmetic? Would textbooks of arithmetic have to be revised, saying "Sometimes 2 and 2 makes 5"? Not at all; "2 and 2 makes 4" would remain true *no matter what happened in the counting process*. If you kept on getting 5 trees as a result, you might decide that you were systematically miscounting; more probably you would decide that in the very act of counting, another tree was created, or just popped into existence. But the one thing you would *not* say is that 2 and 2 sometimes makes 5. If you found an additional tree every time you tried to count them all together, you would say that 2 trees plus 2 trees plus the 1 tree that seems to pop into existence when you count, together makes 5 trees. So the arithmetical law would not be refuted after all.

"Granted that it wouldn't, I still insist that it's a necessary truth. Not merely '2 plus 2 equals 4'—that is only a generalization of '2 trees and 2 trees makes 4 trees,' '2 apples and 2 apples makes 4 apples,' etc. The arithmetical law says that two *of anything* and two more *of anything* makes four, and this is a law about reality, not about the manipulation of symbols. The law that 2 and 2 makes 4 *does* hold true of apples, as of everything else; it holds true *of reality*."

"I think you are confusing two different things. It's easy to see that '2 plus 2 equals 4' as a proposition of pure arithmetic simply entitles you to use '4' equivalently with '2 plus 2.' It's easy to see that 'If you add 2 quarts to 2 quarts (pour into, that is), you get almost 4 quarts' is not a proposition of arithmetic at all. But if you say '2 apples and 2 apples makes 4 apples,' it isn't clear which side of the fence this statement is on. It sounds *both* like a statement of pure mathematics *and* like a statement about physical objects, apples. But no wonder, for the statement is ambiguous, and that is what I now must expose: '2 apples and 2 apples makes 4 apples' is a 'straddling' statement. To find out how the speaker means it, one has to ask, 'Is it of importance whether it's *apples* that are being talked about?' Suppose it were 2 cc.'s of sodium being poured into 2 cc.'s of water, would that make a difference? (1) If it's a statement of pure (unapplied) arithmetic, then it doesn't matter whether it's apples, elephants, grains of sand, thoughts about Thursday—what the statement is about is numerical quantities, and the rest is merely illustrative. Such statements are all a priori and analytic. (2) But if it *does* matter that it's apples that you're talking about, then the statement is not about arithmetic at all, and may not even be true. We are easily misled about this, because apples, unlike water and sodium, normally sit quietly side by side and don't interact with each other. So if that's what it means—that apples when put together remain apples as they were before—then it is true, but a synthetic truth about physical reality, not a truth of mathematics. It is logically possible that when they are placed together the four apples would all coalesce into one huge apple, or spawn a thousand little apples, or explode in one another's presence. What happens when you put apples together is a matter for observation of nature, not for a priori pronouncements. Any statement that is about apples in which it matters that it's apples *and not something else* is a synthetic statement, but it is also contingent. It all depends on which of these you mean. But if you just say '2 apples and 2 apples makes 4 apples' and squint a bit, forgetting about these distinctions, you may think that you have achieved the necessity of the first statement together with the synthetic character of the second, and that then, presto, you have a synthetic a priori statement on your hands. But you haven't. You have the same sentence expressing two different propositions—the one necessary and analytic, the other synthetic and contingent."

There is still another point, which would require a long and technical discussion once it was introduced, without substantially changing the outcome. Speaking of pure (not applied) mathematics, one might say:

6. "Arithmetical propositions are not analytic by themselves: they are analytic only in the context of an arithmetical *system*. If you accept Peano's postulates, you can generate all of arithmetic as a logical consequence of these postulates; but you must first accept the postulates."

Peano's postulates are as follows:

1. 0 is a number.
2. The successor of any number is a number.
3. No two numbers have the same successor.
4. 0 is not the successor of any number.
5. If P is a property such that (a) 0 has the property P, and (b) if a number *n* has P, then the successor of *n* has P, then every number has P.

Using three undefined terms—"number," "0," and "successor"—he was able to generate an infinite series of numbers from these axioms. The axioms yield the entire system of integers. Are the axioms themselves analytic? If they are taken as definitions and statements of defining characteristics, they are; and since any propositions deduced from analytic propositions are also analytic, the propositions of arithmetic are as analytic as before.

For the sake of accuracy, however, we must remind ourselves that the postulates can be construed (and were intended to be construed) not as propositions but as propositional forms, like the *p, q,* and *r* of our tautologies (pp. 164–65). Peano left the terms "number," "0," and "successor" un-interpreted. We might then give the postulates an entirely non-arithmetical interpretation: for example, we could take "successor" to mean offspring, and "number" to mean chicken, and then by Axiom 2 we could derive the conclusion that the offspring of a chicken is a chicken—which is a synthetic statement about the world, and although it happens to be true, it is a contingent truth, not a necessary truth. The axioms become arithmetical only when the terms "number," "0," and "successor" are interpreted in accordance with customary arithmetical usage (as is done for example in Bertrand Russell and Alfred Whitehead's *Principia Mathematica* and Gottlob Frege's *Foundations of Arithmetic*). The only point that concerns us here is that when this is done, the axioms become analytic, and in consequence all arithmetical propositions deducible from these axioms are also analytic.

Geometry

But now what of geometry? When we study geometry, we find numerous propositions that strike us as being necessarily true and also synthetic. "The sum of the angles of a triangle is equal to 180°." "Two parallel lines cannot be drawn through a given point." "A straight line is the shortest distance between two points." "A cube has twelve edges." "A circle encloses the largest possible area for a given perimeter." And so on.

Not all these propositions have the same status, and we shall be able to discuss only a few of them, and only very briefly. Consider, for example, the statement about the sum of the angles of a triangle. One might well ask: "Don't you *know* that this statement is true? It may not seem obvious, but any high-school geometry student who has just studied the proof can prove it for you. And once you have the proof before you, you can no longer deny that it holds true for all cases—in other words, you can know it a priori, and you don't have to go through a separate process of measurement or observation for every triangle, the way you do for every crow that comes along to see whether it is black. But the statement is also synthetic: there is nothing in the definition of 'triangle' about 180°. So here we have a statement that is both necessary (a priori) and synthetic. Thus the rationalist is right: there is at least one synthetic necessary proposition."

What shall we say of this contention? In dealing with it we must first make some distinctions.

The statement about the sum of the angles is a *theorem* in geometry. You doubtless remember from high-school geometry that you begin with certain *axioms,* or unproved statements, together with certain *definitions* of important terms to be used in the study, and from these you begin proving various theorems by showing that they can be deduced from certain of the axioms and definitions. Once you have proved the first theorem, you can get the second by means of it plus previous axioms and definitions. We do not use all of them all of the time: we may get Theorem 50 from Axioms 1 and 3 plus Theorems 3, 13, and 42, for example.

Though you may not have known it when you studied geometry, one thing more is needed: *rules of inference.* You need some way of getting from the axioms and earlier theorems to later ones, to be sure that your deductions are valid. These are rules of logical inference, of which simple examples are "If p is true and p implies q, then q is true"; "If p implies q and q implies r, then p implies r"; "If p implies q and r implies s, and either q or s is false, then either p or r is false," and so on. These rules are used and analyzed in courses in logic, and we shall have more to say about them later in this chapter. Without rules of inference we could not get from the axioms even to the first theorem.

The theorems, including the one about the sum of the angles of a triangle, do follow logically from the other propositions prior to it in the geometrical system; that is, they are logically deducible from those earlier propositions. The actual deductions often become quite complex, but in principle they are no different from simple ones we are accustomed to making every day; for example, given "All members of the crew were drowned," and "Smith was a member of the crew," we are entitled to assert that "Smith was drowned" (if p then q, and p, therefore q). In both cases, if the premises are true then the conclusion must be true. Thus if the premises from which the theorem about the angles is deduced are true, then (assuming the deduction is valid) the theorem is true.

But are the premises true? Here, as in the case of arithmetic, we must make an important distinction, between *pure* and *applied* geometry. The geometrical system of Euclid (fl. ca. 300 B.C.), which is the one you learned in high school, does not make this distinction: the tacit assumption is that the premises are true, and if this is so and the deductions are valid, the theorems of the Euclidean system must be true. But how does one know that the axioms are true? The pure geometer does not care. He is concerned only in making sure that the complex deductions are correct, the reasoning valid. He does not care what kind of meat goes into the grinder, but only that it is thoroughly ground. He is like the accountant who checks the addition on all your bills but does not check into the correctness of the entries (p. 130). Like the logician, the geometer is concerned with valid reasoning, not with the truth of propositions. It does not even matter to him whether the axioms are interpreted as statements about space, which is what they seem to be. Instead of talking about points, lines, and planes, he would just as soon talk about x, y, and z, leaving it open what the terms "x," "y," and "z" mean, so long as the system of relations between the terms remains the same. In short, he is interested in *uninterpreted* geometry, not in *interpreted* or applied geometry.

For many centuries, Euclid's was the only geometrical system that had been developed. But other geometrical systems were developed during the nineteenth century, notably those of Lobachevski and Riemann. One of the axioms of Euclid's system is that given a straight line and any point outside the line, there is only one straight line that can be drawn through that point (in the same plane as the line) that does not intersect the line; that line will be parallel to the other line, and the axiom is known as the "axiom of parallels." Once we understand this axiom, it seems to be obviously true. But no attempt to prove this axiom by means of the other ones has succeeded. (Indeed, geometers have proved it is *not* derivable from them.) In a system of geometry designed by Lobachevski, it is assumed that *more than one* straight line can be drawn through a given point yet fail to intersect the other line. And in the geometry of Riemann, it is assumed that *no* such lines can be drawn. Each of these three systems of geometry is perfectly consistent. As deductive systems, there is nothing to choose among them. The difference among them is that each begins with a somewhat different set of axioms, and for that reason they each yield somewhat different conclusions. If you start with a different set of premises, you will naturally get different conclusions, all reached by perfectly valid reasoning.

"But they can't all be true!" This objection takes us out of the realm of pure or uninterpreted geometry into that of applied or interpreted geometry. You could doubtless build a whole deductive system with such propositions as "All people are over ten feet tall" and "No one over ten feet tall is green," and arrive at utterly false conclusions by means of valid reasoning. But aren't we interested in whether the initial premises are true? Certainly the person who wants to apply geometry to the world is interested in truth—for example, surveyors, whether in America in the 20th century A.D. or in Egypt in the 20th century B.C. They were attempting, surely, to begin with true propositions, and by means of these to arrive deductively at other ones.

For example, isn't it true that the angles of a triangle equal 180°, quite apart from the fact that this proposition can be deduced from other ones in the Euclidean geometry? Isn't it true that on measuring the angles you always get 180°? So isn't the proposition, regardless of its place in a deductive system, true of the world?

"I hold that it is a necessary synthetic statement about the world. Everything that is a triangle necessarily has this property."

"As a part of a deductive system (if . . . [premises], then . . . [theorem]) it is a priori, but only because it is analytic. As a description of the world, it is synthetic all right, but not a priori."

"What? You mean we don't know a priori that the angles of a triangle will be 180°? that we have to measure it for every separate case?"

"I agree that we seem to know it in a way we don't know that all crows are black, which is always in danger of being refuted by the next case. Still, are you quite sure that we do? What would you say if you were measuring a triangular field and found that the angles always added up to 181°?"

"I would say either that there was an observational error or that the field was not really triangular."

"If you and others always got the same results, you would finally have to discount the possibility that it was an observational error. So you would say the field was not really triangular. You would not admit even the logical possibility that a triangular field could be other than 180°. So it's analytic after all, isn't it? You won't call it triangular unless it does add up to 180°."

"Well, how could it be triangular if it didn't add up to 180°?"

"It couldn't, by the Euclidean definition of 'triangle.' Adding up to 180° is not a part of the explicit *definition* of 'triangle' in Euclid's system, but it *is* logically deducible from that definition, together with other propositions in the system. We are justified, then, in saying 'if not 180°, then not triangle'; this is analytic *within the Euclidean system*. But what about the actual field out there? Suppose you kept getting this peculiar result that you could no longer put down to observational error. Then you would have to say, puzzling as it might seem at first, that Euclidean geometry does not describe our actual space—that actual space is *not Euclidean*. The deductive system is one thing, actual physical space another. Whether physical space is obliging enough to follow the simple Euclidean system, only careful observation can tell."

"But if the premises are true, and the deduction valid, the conclusion must be true. Now if the conclusion is false, and yet the deduction is valid, then . . . ."

"Then one or more of the Euclidean *premises* is false, if interpreted as description of physical reality."

Let us turn, then, to the premises of the system.

Are the premises true? We cannot answer in general, for not all of them are of the same nature. Some are definitions; for example, "A circle is a plane closed figure all the points on whose circumference are equidistant from the center" is not a true proposition about the world but a definition of "circle": it tells us under what conditions a given figure is to be called a circle. But others *seem,* at any rate, to make statements about the world. Consider, for example, "A straight line is the shortest distance between two points."

It seems intuitively obvious that a straight line must be the shortest distance between two points. Surely we know it a priori, and don't have to measure every straight line to see whether it really is the shortest distance between the two points it connects. "Obviously it's true," someone may say, "but equally obviously, it's analytic. What do we mean by the phrase 'straight line' *except* 'the shortest distance between two points'? That's what a straight line is, by definition."

But this is too easy a way with the problem. As Kant remarked, straightness is a qualitative concept and shortness a quantitative concept, and they are not identical. To have the idea of a straight line is one thing, to have the idea of the shortest distance is another; indeed, one might have the one concept without having the other. One *learns* that a straight line is the shortest distance between two points; this fact isn't already contained in the concept of what it is to be the shortest distance. The definition of "straight" contains no reference to its being the shortest distance between two points that it connects.

What, then, *is* the definition of "straight"? That is the crux of the whole problem. As with "colored," we seem to know what it means yet are unable to define it. "A straight line is a line no part of which is curved" will not help us, for, asking what a curved line is, we are told, "A curved line is a line not all of which is straight." Nor will it do to identify the quality of straightness with some physical entity, such as "A straight line is the path of a ray of light." Is this really what is meant by "straight"? Don't we understand what a straight line is before we know anything about rays of light? If rays of light travel in straight lines, isn't that a synthetic proposition rather than a definition? Isn't it logically possible that rays of light might travel in curved or jagged lines, so that one might see around corners, for example? If the world were like this, the statement would be false. In this case, however, it can hardly be a definition. It would seem that straightness is a quality we can recognize but not define; and in that case, all the statements we make about it will be synthetic, not analytic.

What alternatives, then, are open to us? We can hold that the statement is a synthetic a priori truth, with all the discomforts involved in attempting to justify it. Or we can hold that it is a contingent truth: that all straight lines are the shortest distance between two points, but that there is no logical necessity about this—that it would be logically possible for it to be otherwise. Or we can hold—and this may be somewhat surprising—that not only is it not a necessary truth, it is not even a truth at all. It is an axiom in Euclid's geometry, but it has been questioned whether space is Euclidean, the point being that Euclidean geometry gives us only an *approximate* description of actual space, which suffices for terrestrial distances but will not suffice in our measurements of the millions of light-years in vast interstellar spaces. The shortest distance on the surface of a sphere is the arc of a great circle; and perhaps owing to the "curvature" of space, the shortest distance from one place to another in space is not a straight line at all. The physics of the matter would be far too complex to enter into here, but the moral of the tale should be clear enough: applied geometry has to do with the structure and properties of actual space, and one cannot know a priori what they will be. For this, one requires empirical investigation (observation and measurement). As the starting point of a deductive system, Euclid's axiom is unexceptionable; but as a true description of the universe, it is subject to all the qualifications and all the uncertainty that attends any proposition purporting to describe the universe: it can always be upset by discoveries (embodied in a posteriori propositions) about the way the universe actually is.

Thus far, it would seem, geometry presents no satisfactory recruiting-ground for synthetic a priori propositions. A given proposition within a deductive system (including a system of geometry) is analytic in relation to the premises $p, q, r \ldots$ from which it is deduced: that is, "If $p, q, r \ldots$ then x" is analytic, and it would be self-contradictory to deny it if the reasoning is valid. But as propositions *about reality* (applied geometry), they are synthetic all right, but thus far, at any rate, they do not seem to be knowable a priori. The statements of applied Euclidean geometry, which seemed a priori, turn out to be a posteriori, and many of them not even true.

The distinction between pure and applied geometry appears to have put an end to the search for synthetic a priori propositions in geometry: the sense in which such a proposition is a priori is not the sense in which it is synthetic, and in the sense in which it is synthetic it is not a priori.

This, however, is not the end of the matter. The rationalist may still have a case, for there may be certain propositions about space that are necessarily true. If so, and if they are also synthetic, then we may still be able to arrive at some synthetic a priori propositions. To this we now turn.

Other A Priori Propositions

Any attempt to extract a synthetic a priori from mathematics has, it seems, been doomed to failure: a confusion between pure and applied mathematics. There are those who say that the whole search for a synthetic a priori is bound to be fruitless, for there is no such thing: not that by definition there *could* not be (for the terms "analytic" and "a priori" do not mean the same, as we have seen), but that in fact there is none, and that the belief in such a thing, though not self-contradictory, is highly implausible. How could there be, it is argued, a statement that is necessarily true, holds for all reality at all times, and yet is not subject to the test of experience like the admittedly synthetic statements we utter by the hundreds every day ("It's going to rain this afternoon," "There are six people in this room," and so on ad infinitum)? If a statement is synthetic—that is, if its negation is not self-contradictory—then how could we possibly know that it is true except by recourse to experience, in which case the statement is not a priori? "By reflection," we may say; but two people may reflect and arrive at opposite conclusions.

I have no clear notion of what it would be like to justify by reflection alone the truth of *p* when not-*p* is consistent [not self-contradictory] . . . . But this *may* be only a fact about *me*. I cannot see how, of two equally consistent alternative propositions (*p* and not-*p*), reflection alone will determine which one describes the facts. But to say this does not *prove* that there cannot be synthetic a priori propositions.[3]

Where, then, shall we continue our search? Apart from mathematics, there are certain *recurrent features of experience* that are, according to some rationalists, the basis for belief in synthetic a priori propositions: when we state what the connections are between these features, we find that the statements in question are true a priori yet not analytic. Let us take some examples:

1. *"All red things are colored."* At first glance this may seem to be as obviously analytic as "All squares are rectangles." A square, we say, is *defined* as a rectangle whose sides are equal; to say that all squares are rectangles is merely to say that rectangles of a specific kind are rectangles—which is obviously analytic. Why can't we do the same with red? "Red" is *defined* as a color of a certain kind . . . . But here is the trouble: "red" can't be defined at all, except ostensively. And if we cannot state in words a definition of "red," how can we show that the negation of a statement about red is self-contradictory?

One avenue might be suggested: " 'Colored' just *means* red or blue or yellow and so on. Thus if you say that red things are colored, you are just saying that red belongs to a class including red—and this is analytic." But this will not do, for this is not what "colored" means. It is true, of course, that red, blue, etc. are all colors, but the word "color" is not the name for any specific class of colors: being colored is a certain kind of (indefinable) property, and the meaning of the word "colored" does not contain any reference to the particular items that have that property—any more than the meaning of

[3] N. R. Hanson, "The Very Idea of a Synthetic A Priori," *Mind,* 1962, p. 523.

"triangle" is given by listing the kinds of triangles that there are. In fact, "colored" is just as indefinable as "red." Being colored is a quality that a person born blind could no more conceive than he could a specific color.

"But we wouldn't *call* anything red if it weren't colored. If I am told about something that it is red, I can conclude without observing it for myself that it *must* be colored. To say that it is red but not colored is self-contradictory."

"No, all you've shown is that if it's red it must be colored; to only this much I agree. But you have not shown me that 'It's red but not colored' is *self-contradictory*. 'It's a square but not a rectangle' *is* self-contradictory, for it means that a rectangle with equal sides and all of whose angles are right angles isn't a rectangle. But 'It's red but not colored' is not. At least, you haven't shown me that it is, and I don't see how you can, since you will admit yourself that neither 'red' nor 'colored' can be defined, so you can't deduce the contradiction from the definitions."

"What, then, is your view on the status of 'All red things are colored'?"

"It is a priori, since we know it to hold for all cases. But it is not analytic. So it's a synthetic a priori proposition."

"I'm sorry, but I can't buy that. I know that everything that's red is colored; but this is not a fact about the world. It's more like a rule of language, isn't it? I admit that I cannot show its negation to be self-contradictory, so I can't show that it's analytic—at least, not by *that* definition of analytic. But, you will remember, there is *another* definition of 'analytic' (p. 162), according to which a statement is analytic if you can know it to be true solely in virtue of the meanings of the words. I believe that the statement is analytic in *that* sense. If you tell me that something is red, I can infer without the slightest doubt that it is colored—*not* because I have observed it for myself but because of a *rule of language* that entitles me to go from 'X is red' to 'X is colored.' I know this because of the very meanings of the words—meanings, not definitions (since I can't define the crucial words). But the rule of language explicates a *relation* between being red and being colored, and for this I don't need a definition of the words at all. It is, however, because I understand the meanings of the words that I can make the inference to 'X is colored.' So the statement is analytic in the *second* sense, though I haven't shown it to be so in the first sense."

"Well now, you have switched meanings on me. I said that the statement is not analytic, meaning 'analytic' in its traditional sense, having to do with the structure of the proposition: it's analytic if its negation is self-contradictory. You don't deny this, so you haven't shown that the statement isn't synthetic and a priori in that important sense. Very well; if that is clear, let's turn to the second sense of 'analytic.' I grant that you can pass from 'X is red' to 'X is colored' by a linguistic rule, and that you don't have to look to see if something is colored if you already know that it's red. But now let me ask you an important question: What is the basis of this linguistic rule? Why do we have *this* linguistic rule rather than another one—for example, one that would enable us to pass from 'X is red' to 'X is round'? Isn't it because there is a *necessary connection between the properties* in question: a red thing must be colored but need not be round? If there were no necessary connection in nature between the properties of redness and coloredness, we would have no 'rule of language' justifying the inference from 'X is red' to 'X is colored.' You have tried to justify the statement by reference to a verbal convention, and I agree that there is such a verbal convention; but I also assert that there is something 'lying behind' this verbal convention, and that is a necessary connection in reality. Our verbal conventions reflect the way reality goes."

With this new turn of the argument, we now have a second way of distinguishing rationalism from empiricism, depending on the definition of "analytic." (1) According to the first, a rationalist says that there are synthetic a priori truths, and the empiricist denies that there are any, holding that all a priori truths are analytic. "Analytic" here means in our first sense, any proposition whose negation is self-contradictory. This sense of the rationalist-empiricist distinction we have already discussed. (2) According to the second, an empiricist holds that analytic statements in the second sense of "analytic" (a statement whose truth can be known solely by an analysis of the meanings of the words) owe their analyticity to rules or conventions of language, and the rationalist believes in necessary connections in reality that are antecedent to these linguistic rules. It is rationalism against empiricism in this second sense that has increasingly become an arena of controversy. It will turn up again in the following examples.

2. *"All colors are extended."* In other words, all colors are spread-out-in-space; they need not be the colors of physical objects but may be the colors you see in dreams and after-images and hallucinations, and the space need not be physical space but may be the imaginary space of dreams. But wherever and whenever a color occurs, it is spread-out-in-space. In fact this seems too obvious to be worth mentioning. Our question, however, is: What kind of a statement is it? Is it contingent? Could the next color we come across *not* be extended? Apparently not: we are sure that every color we shall ever experience is extended. But what is the justification for our certainty?

Perhaps the statement is analytic. But here we run into the same problem: neither "color" nor "extension" seems to be definable. Hence the contradiction, if there is one, cannot be shown.

"But we wouldn't say that anything was colored unless it was extended." Doubtless this is true, but what makes it true? "It's a rule of language: color implies extension." So speaks the empiricist. But now replies the rationalist: "What underlies this rule of language? Granted that we know the statement is true 'from the meanings of the words alone'; but do not the meanings reflect the fact that color implies extension, that the two properties are necessarily related in nature? Isn't it because everything colored must be extended that we can infer 'X is extended' from 'X is colored'?"

3. *"A thing can't be red and green all over at the same time."* A thing can be all red at one time and all green at another. It can *appear* green to one person and red to another at the same time. It can be partly green and partly red: it can be striped, checkered, mottled. It can be covered with paint that's half green and half red, mixed. It can be covered with green paint, which in turn is covered with red paint. All these things can and do happen: what cannot happen is for it to be all red and all green over its entire surface at the same time. But why can't it be both red and green? The same object can be both red and square, both red and hard, or both red and heavy. Why can't it be both red and green? That it cannot seems to be a necessary truth. But whence arises the necessity?

"There is a time-worn principle in philosophy, the Principle of Determinables. Color, shape, size, weight are all determinables—that is, there are different ways of being colored, and so on. Red and green are determinates under color; weighing six pounds and weighing ten pounds are determinates under weight; being square and being triangular are determinates under shape; and so on. The principle says that you can't simultaneously have two different determinates under the same determinable. Something can't weigh six pounds and also ten pounds. Something can be both red and hard, because these determinates belong under different determinables (color and degree-of-hardness). But it can't be both red and green, since these determinates both come under the same determinable, color."

"Very interesting, and doubtless true. Now what is the status of this Principle of Determinables? Is it synthetic and a priori? How do you know that *it* will always hold true? Indeed, how do you know that something that's colored will always have some specific color, or that something that has weight will always have some specific weight? Why can't it just be colored-in-general without being any specific color, or heavy without having any specific degree of heaviness? I grant that it seems impossible, and I can't imagine anything colored that isn't some specific color. But how do you know that it can't be so? I think it's an a priori truth, but can you show me that it's analytic? If not, then we have at least one synthetic a priori truth, and rationalism (in the traditional sense) is right after all."

"I can't show you that it's analytic: it does seem to be a necessary feature of reality that it must be so. But let's go back to our specific example about red and green. Why can't a thing have both these determinate qualities all over its surface at the same time? Let me appeal to the meaning of the word 'red.' If you understand the word 'red,' you understand that it means not-green."

"In a sense, that's true; but then 'red' also means 'not-blue,' 'not-yellow,' and so on; in fact, it also means 'not-hard,' 'not-square'—in fact, 'red' means *only* red and nothing else."

"But there's a difference. Being red is *compatible* with being hard; it is not compatible with being green."

"True, but why not? That's the question. Why are red and green incompatible and red and hard not? Being red is admittedly *different* from being green; but being red is also different from being hard."

"Well, being hard is just *different* from being red; but being green is not only different from being red, it is *incompatible* with being red."

"Incompatible—there we go again. And why is it incompatible? What is the meaning of 'incompatible' here?"

"Being red contradicts being green; but being red does not contradict being hard, it is only *different from* being hard."

"Contradicts? Only propositions contradict one another. Things in nature don't contradict one another. Things in nature just *are*—the contradiction occurs only in propositions."

"Very well then. Definitions are propositions; the definition of 'red' is only *different* from that of 'hard,' but it *contradicts* the definition of 'green.' "

"But you know that this won't do. You can't define either 'red' or 'green.' And since you can't state definitions of them, the definitions can't contradict one another."

"I grant you that I can't display a formal contradiction here. The proposition is not analytic in *that* sense. If I know that something is all red, I do have to examine it to see if it is also hard or heavy, but I do *not* have to examine it to see if it is (at the same moment) green, for I already know that it is not. That is, I can pass from 'it's red' to 'it's not green' as a verbal rule. It's analytic in the *second* sense of analytic, that 'If it's red, it's not green' is true by virtue of the meanings of the words alone. If I told you that something was entirely red, and you then asked me if it wasn't also entirely green, I would doubt that you had learned the meaning of these words. But 'It's red, but is it also hard?' would not be an absurd question. To know that 'If it's red, it isn't green' is true, I only need to be acquainted with the rule of language that entitles me to infer 'not-green' from 'red.' So you see, I can know that if it's red it's not green solely by virtue of the meanings of the words in the language—which is the second definition of 'analytic.' "

" 'Rule of language'; there we are again. It isn't just because of the words, but because you understand the *meanings* of the words, that you can make this inference. And the meanings of the words are such that being red *excludes* being green. And why does the one exclude the other? Because it is a necessary fact about reality that a thing can't simultaneously be both red and green, whereas it is not a necessary feature of reality that it can't be both red and hard. *That* is the fact about reality that underlies our verbal conventions. If verbal conventions were arbitrary, why should we have just this one? Why have one that enables us to say 'red, therefore not-green?' Is this an accident? Again, our verbal rules reflect the way reality goes: the reason we have the verbal rule in the red-green case but not in the red-hard case is that there is *in reality* a relation of necessity between red and not-green, but not between red and not-hard. We have come once again to our usual impasse."

4. *"If A precedes B and B precedes C, then A precedes C."* What, one might ask, could be more plainly true than this? Every child knows it. How could A precede B and B precede C and yet A *not* precede C? The statement surely seems to be necessarily true.

Suppose one believes that it is not a necessary truth but only contingent, like "All crows are black." It would be a generalization from experience, tested many millions of times, but still not absolutely certain: it *might* not hold true the next time. The cars were approaching each other before the collision; the collision occurred before the occupants were taken to the hospital; and, of course, the cars approached each other before the occupants were taken to the hospital. Queen Elizabeth reigned before James I, and James I reigned before George III; and, of course, Queen Elizabeth reigned before George III. This sort of thing has been verified so many times in our experience that it never even occurs to us that it might not always hold. If the statement is only contingent, however, it might not hold in some future case; no matter how regularly some sequence of events may have occurred in the past, it might be different in the future. The proposition would then only be an unusually well-founded generalization, not a necessary truth.

Surely, however, such an account is most implausible. We may not know anything about future events; but don't we know a priori that *if* there are three of them, such that A precedes B and B precedes C, then A precedes C? Could anything be more absurd than to believe that nine o'clock comes before ten o'clock and ten o'clock before eleven o'clock, but that nine o'clock does *not* necessarily come before eleven o'clock? The statement, then, is necessarily true. But is it analytic or synthetic?

"It is analytic," says the empiricist. "It is necessarily true only because it's analytic. If you said that A was prior to B and B to C, and yet said that A was not prior to C, you'd be guilty of a contradiction."

"Why?" asks the rationalist. "Show me the contradiction. I grant that if anyone said that, it would not be *true,* but that's a very different matter from saying that he'd be guilty of a *contradiction.* Absurd though his statement would be, I can see no contradiction. A has a certain relation to B, and B to C; what is the contradiction in saying that A does *not* have this relation to C? Indeed, in many other situations it's often true. If team A wins over team B, and team B wins over team C, it doesn't necessarily follow that A will win over C; in fact team C may turn around and best team A. If Mr. A likes Mr. B, and Mr. B likes Mr. C, it doesn't follow that Mr. A likes Mr. C. So you see, it is not in general true that if A has a relation to B and B to C, A has that same relation to C. When it *is* true, the relation is said to be *transitive;* but not all relations are transitive."

"But it *is* necessarily true in this case—the case of temporal precedence."

"Indeed it is; it is necessary, not contingent, and knowable a priori. This I have not denied; I only deny that it is analytic. I contend that it is a synthetic a priori truth."

"I hold that it is a priori but not synthetic. That the time-relation is transitive, unlike the relation of winning or liking, is built into our very language. When you say that A precedes B and B precedes C, you implicitly mean that A precedes C. If you go on and say explicitly that A precedes C, you are adding nothing to the content of the statement. Suppose you said to the police inspector, 'Here's a piece of information: she struck him before he shot her; and here's another piece of information: he shot her before the neighbors ran in.' And then the inspector said, 'Is that all you know about it? Is this all the information you have?' and you replied, 'Oh yes, I do have one more bit of information: she struck him before the neighbors ran in.' The inspector would consider this at best a bad joke. 'But I knew that already' he might reply. 'You already implied that in what you said before.' This alleged 'added bit of information' was not an added one at all but a part of what he had already said."

"The police inspector was right in that he was justified in making the inference for himself; he knew that the time-relation is transitive, and that this is a necessary truth. He didn't have to wait for the man to tell him *that*. Nevertheless, saying 'A precedes C' is not saying *the same thing as* 'A precedes B and B precedes C.' It is not the same bit of information. 'A precedes C' is indeed an added bit of information, but one that the inspector was entitled to infer from what the citizen had already told him."

"That's the point: he *was* entitled to infer it, and he would not have been entitled to infer it if the truth had not been analytic. The time-relation is transitive, and its transitivity is *part of the very meaning* of time-words. And if someone said that A is before B and B before C, yet A is not before C, we would conclude that he had not learned the meaning of these time-words; he had not yet learned the verbal conventions governing our use of these words."

"You mean he would not have learned a necessary fact about reality, that the time-relation is transitive. Once he knows that the time-relation, unlike many other relations, is transitive, he is entitled to make the inference. But the basic fact in the situation is that the time-relation is transitive; the secondary, and consequential, fact is that we order our verbal conventions in such a way that the transitivity is 'part of the very meaning' of the time-words. But the reason we have established our verbal conventions in this manner is that reality is this way, and our linguistic conventions must reflect the way reality is. Can you conceive of a relation exactly like the time-relation but *not* transitive? Of course you can't: the time-relation is *necessarily* transitive. You see, it's no accident that the transitivity has come to be 'part of the very meaning' of time-words; a word that meant the same as 'precede' except that it was *not* transitive would have nothing to apply to. Again, our verbal conventions reflect the way reality goes. The time-stream runs one way and is irreversible in its direction; this is the feature of reality that you dismiss as a 'verbal convention.' "

5. *"Two things can't be at the same place at the same time."* "As you stand watching traffic, you may observe that two cars can be at the same place at two different times (perhaps just a split second apart), and that they can be in two different places at the same time (right next to each other), but that two cars can't occupy the same place at the same time. When they try to, there's a collision."

"True; now what kind of a statement is it, that the two cars can't be in the same place at the same time? Isn't it true a priori? Do you have to observe its truth in each new instance? Don't you know a priori that if there are two objects, they can't both occupy the same place at the same time?"

"Well, it depends. Cars are relatively impenetrable, but what if they sort of melted together into one when brought into contact, as they might well do under enormous heat or pressure? What if they coalesced like two pats of melting butter when squeezed together?"

"But when the two pieces of butter did this, they would no longer be two pieces but one. Moreover, they wouldn't occupy the same place: they would still be beside each other, only they would be indistinguishable from one another, and so would be considered one piece. There would still be two things if they were there side by side, but once they had made contact to form one object, there would be one and not two."

"Suppose you have two one-quart containers of a gas, and you release both quarts of gas into one one-quart space. Don't you then have two things—the two quarts of gas—now occupying the same space?"

"But now they are no longer two quarts. Gases are mostly empty space; so of course it is possible for the particles of gas that formerly occupied two quarts of space to occupy one quart. You could, I suppose, *call* this two things at the same place at the same time. But if you did, it would be very misleading, for there is *another* sense in which they would still *not* be occupying the same place: take any of the millions of molecules of gas in the container, and no two of these molecules can occupy the same place at the same time."

"And why can't they? Because you wouldn't call it *the same place;* our criterion for *calling* it the 'same place' is that there is no more than one thing (particle, molecule) there."

"Perhaps; but let's turn back from single particles to whole objects. Can't you imagine two objects getting stuck together, not just on their surfaces as with glue, but interpenetrating to a considerable extent? The particles in the one come to occupy a considerable amount of the space in the other, but they still retain their identity as two objects: they might even be pulled apart and be as they were before. Couldn't these objects, when interpenetrating, be said to occupy the same place at the same time?"

"In a loose sense you could say this, but be careful what you mean by it You would mean only that a given region of space, say two cubic inches, would be occupied by particles from both objects; that is surely possible. But what is *not* possible is for a molecule of one of the objects and a molecule of the other object (or of the same object, for that matter) to occupy the same bit of space at the same time. *That* is what cannot be. And that it cannot be is a necessary truth."

"Why is it a necessary truth?"

"Because you are entitled to say it a priori. If I know that there are two molecules of matter, I know a priori that they occupy two different places."

"Now show me that the statement is analytic."

"I can't show it to be analytic in the first sense. I can't exhibit a contradiction in denying it. The word 'place' can be defined ostensively, but I don't see how it can be defined verbally any more than 'red.' So I can't exhibit a contradiction. But I believe that the statement is analytic in the second sense of 'analytic'; one knows it to be true if one knows the meaning of the words. We can never give a case of 'two objects in the same place' because the very admission that there are *two* objects is sufficient for us to describe their location as two places, not one."

"Once again, what you describe as a verbal convention I describe as a necessary feature of reality. Reality is such that certain things necessarily hold true of it—and this is one of them."

"But if you take it to be a feature of reality, I don't see how you can know that the proposition will *continue* to hold true for all cases in the future—that reality will *keep on* being like that. After all, we derived the concepts of place, body, and so on from experience."

"Of course we did. But having acquired the *concepts* from experience, we learned to use them in asserting *propositions,* and soon we realized that the propositions (such as the one we are now considering) are necessarily true."

Exercises

1. In each of the following examples, is the proposition a necessary truth? Is it a truth at all? Justify your answer.
    a. "Everything that has color has shape." But what about the sky?
    b. "Everything that has shape has color." But what about an ice cube?
    c. "Everything that has shape has size." What about a rainbow or the round spots in front of your eyes?
    d. "Everything that has shape has volume." What about a triangle? (Is the statement true if three-dimensional shape is meant?)
    e. "Everything that has volume has shape." What about the water in a glass or gases released into a chamber?
    f. "All matter is either solid, liquid, or gaseous." What about a single molecule?
2. Classify each of the following propositions as
    (1) necessary but not synthetic,

(2) synthetic but not necessary, or

(3) both necessary and synthetic.

Give your reasons in each case.

a. Everything that has shape has size.

b. Everything that has volume has shape.

c. Everything that has shape has color. (Note: does "colored" include transparent?)

d. Every sound has pitch, volume, and timbre.

e. Every color has hue, brightness, and saturation.

f. Everything that has shape has extension.

g. Everything that has extension has shape.

h. 40694 + 27593 = 68287.

i. No mammals grow feathers.

j. Every particle of matter in the universe attracts every other particle with a force varying inversely with the square of the distance and directly with the product of the masses. (Newton's Law of Universal Gravitation.)

k. A straight line is the shortest distance between two points.

l. Given any line L and any point P not on that line, only one line can be drawn through P parallel to L.

m. If p is true, p is not also false.

n. Either p is true or p is false.

o. It is right to do your duty.

p. If A is north of B and B is north of C, then A is north of C.

q. If A is east of B and B is east of C, then A is east of C.

r. If San Francisco is east of Tokyo and Tokyo is east of London, then San Francisco is east of London.

s. A person cannot be born three months after the death of his mother.

t. A person cannot be born three months after the death of his father.

u. All cubes have twelve edges. (See C. H. Langford, "A Proof that Synthetic A Priori Propositions Exist," *Journal of Philosophy,* 1949.)

v. If A eats B, and B has eaten C, then A has eaten C.

w. If A occurs before B and B occurs before C, then A occurs before C.

x. If A hires B and B hires C, then A hires C.

y. There cannot be, at the same place and time, two different determinates (such as red and green) under the same determinable (such as color).

z. Every even number is the sum of two prime numbers. (Goldbach's theorem.)

aa. If A is indistinguishable from B, and B from C, A is indistinguishable from C.

3. Comment on the following assertions:

a. An amoeba splits into two and we have two amoebas. So $1 = 2$.

b. Try to divide a 5-pound sack of flour into five 1-pound sacks, and you can't do it—each sack will contain slightly less than 1 pound. So $1 + 1 + 1 + 1 + 1$ doesn't necessarily equal 5.

c. Two apples and two more apples necessarily make four apples.

d. Truth is irrelevant to the science of geometry.

e. The propositions of arithmetic are empty of factual content.

f. To infer one proposition from another, we need only devise the appropriate verbal convention.

g. One geometry is no more true than another, as the existence of alternative geometries proves.

h. We learned as children that $2 + 2 = 4$, so it can't be a priori.

11. The Principles of Logic

We come now to an even more fundamental subject: the principles presupposed in all human thought and discourse. The propositions of arithmetic, we have seen, are necessary; so are those of geometry (in the context of a geometrical system); so are many others, which we have considered in the preceding section. But now let us turn to certain principles of logic, which appear also to be necessarily true. Let us begin with the three Laws of Thought laid down by Aristotle (384–322 B.C.).

1. The Law of Identity: A is A.[4]
2. The Law of Non-contradiction: Nothing can be both A and not-A.
3. The Law of Excluded Middle: Everything is either A or not-A.

Why are these fundamental? Because if they were not true, none of the other truths could be formulated, or even thought of. Everything you say presupposes that A is A: if you speak of a table, you are presupposing that the table is a table; if the table were *not* a table, what could you even be talking about? A table or not a table?[5] Or again: we defined analytic statements, in one sense at least, with reference to the Law of Non-contradiction. If you say that a square is a circle, you are in effect saying that the figure is both four-sided and not four-sided, which is to contradict yourself. That is, you are violating the Law of Non-contradiction, which says that nothing can be both A and not-A (both four-sided and not four-sided). It is the Law of Non-contradiction on which the first definition of "analytic" itself is based.

To one seeking specific information, these three "laws" may well be disappointing. They don't tell us much. "A is A" does not tell you what the properties of A are, whether the A in question is round or heavy or soft; it just tells you that A is A, that the thing is itself. It doesn't tell you whether A lasts a long time or, like a flash of lightning, exists for an instant and is gone forever. If the universe consisted of an unending series of evanescent events like lightning-flashes, "A is A" would still hold true. It tells you nothing about the particular character of the world: it holds true for "all possible words."[6]

[4] Here "A" stands for anything (any entity) whatever, not only (as in earlier chapters) for a property.

[5] "A table is a table" is a necessary truth, but "This object before me is a table" is not. The latter statement may be false: you may mis-identify the object before you, or believe there is one when there isn't.

[6] We mean here *logically* possible worlds, since the Law of Non-contradiction is used to define what is meant by logical possibility. To say that something is logically possible is to say that there is *no contradiction* involved in denying it. See pp. 170–71.

Nor does the Law of Non-contradiction say anything specific about anything in the world: it says that if this is a table, it isn't also *not* a table; and that if snow is white, it isn't also *not* white. The Law of Non-contradiction tells us that it can't be *both;* but lest we countenance the possibility that it can be *neither,* the Law of Excluded Middle comes in to exclude a middle ground between A and not-A: it says that everything is either A or not-A—that is, it must be one or the other, it can't be neither. This is either a table or not a table, either a unicorn or not a unicorn; and either snow is white or snow is not-white—it cannot be *neither* white nor not-white.

It is inaccurate to call these "the Laws of Thought," as if they were laws of human psychology describing how people actually think. If this were what they are, they would be untrue, for people do not always think in accordance with them: people do, for example, contradict themselves, thus violating the Law of Non-contradiction. They are not laws of thought in the way that the traditional "laws of association" were considered laws of thought. They are, rather, presuppositions (*sine qua non*) of all consistent (non-self-contradictory) thinking.

They are, moreover, the most general statements that can be made; even the laws of arithmetic come in only when you are talking about numerical quantities. But the Laws of Thought are involved every time you talk about *anything at all:* no matter what it is you are talking about, the thing you are talking about is itself, namely, the thing you are talking about (A is A). It is not both itself and not-itself, nor does it have a property and not have it (not both A and not-A); and either it has the property or it does not (either A or not-A). Not only can you not speak, you cannot *think,* even to the extent of identifying something as an A, without presupposing at least the Law of Identity: for the moment that, out of the sum total of all the things there are, you pick one thing or one feature, A, you presuppose that it is A you are talking or thinking of rather than something else.

As we have stated the three laws, they have to do with things, relations, properties, etc. in the world. Sometimes, however, they are formulated as truths about propositions, in which case they are all tautologies:

Law of Identity: If *p*, then *p*. $p \supset p$
Law of Non-contradiction: Not both *p* and not-*p*. $\sim(p \cdot \sim p)$
Law of Excluded Middle: Either *p* or not-*p*. $p \lor \sim p$

In other words: if a proposition is true, then it is true; no proposition is both true and not-true; and every proposition is either true or not-true. There is an advantage in this formulation in that the three laws can now be used as rules of inference in the logical deduction of propositions. But these are nevertheless only special cases of our first formulation: unless it were true that A is A, one could have no basis for asserting that *p* is *p* (or that *p* implies *p*). A proposition, *p,* is just another A, another distinguishable item to which the law applies.

Suppose someone were to deny the Law of Identity. What would result? "I deny that A is A." "I see. And do you think your denial is a denial?" "Of course." "Then A is A—you presupposed it in what you just said. If you didn't presuppose it, you couldn't even state the proposition that you just did." Without presupposing the law, he could not assert anything, even a denial of the law itself; for the moment he opens his mouth to speak (or begins even to think) about anything at all, call it A, then it is that A he is talking about and not something else. How could it be A and also not-A that we were talking about? What would it be that we were talking about then—A or something other than A, say B? But in either case, A is A, and B is B.

Or suppose that someone were to deny the Law of Non-contradiction. "This is a table and also not a table," he says, thus saying that it can be both (whereas the Law of Non-contradiction says that it can't). What could we say to him? Could we even understand what he meant? What situation is he trying to describe?

"This is a table, and it also isn't a table? But you already said in the first part of your statement that it *is* a table—so now what do you mean in the latter part of the same statement by saying that it is *not* a table? Is it a table that you're talking about, or isn't it?"

"I'm saying simply that it is, and is not, a table."

"But in calling it a table, and then denying it in the same breath, you are contradicting yourself."

"O. K., so I'm contradicting myself. What's wrong with that?"

"What's wrong with it is that what you say is *unintelligible:* if it's a table you're talking about, then it isn't also *not* a table. If you say it's both, what *are* you talking about?"

"I'm sorry if you can't understand it; it may be unintelligible to you, but it isn't to me."

"But please explain to me *what you mean* by saying it's both a table and not a table; first you say it is, then you say it isn't, so what *is* it you are talking about? A or not-A?"

"Both. The thing I am talking about is A and not-A."

What has happened here? Why has he passed beyond the pale of significant discourse? Out of all the infinite array of things in the universe (the large circle), he picks out one (small circle), which we call A. Everything other than this is called not-A. If he claims to be talking about A, then it is something in the small circle; if he is talking about something other than A, it is something in the large circle (exclusive of A). When he says that the thing he is talking about is both A and not-A, he is in effect saying that it is in the small circle and also not in it (outside it). Thus he is contradicting himself. What more can we say? He may admit, even boast, that he is contradicting himself, but he goes on talking anyway. But about what? About A? Or about other-than-A (not-A)? There we are again—A or not-A.

We may not have stopped him from talking further, but we are sure that if he talks about anything, A, that excludes not-A (everything other than A), and that to the extent that he himself is able to talk about anything, he too must obey the Law of Non-contradiction—whether he knows it or not, whether he denies it or not. When he says A, he implicitly denies not-A; and when he thinks A, he cannot think it also as not-A. Otherwise, once again, what is it that he is thinking about?

Or suppose that someone said to you, "I accept your invitation to dinner this evening," and a few minutes later he says, "By the way, I can't accept your invitation to dinner this evening." "You mean you've changed your mind?" "No, I'm just not coming." "But you said before that you *are* coming." "I know; that's true too—I'm coming and I'm not coming." "But which do you mean?" "Both." What are you now to expect? What is he asserting? Surely what he says is unintelligible—not only to you, but to him. He has violated the Law of Non-contradiction.

Justification of the principles.   "You've shown me that the Laws of Thought are presupposed in all discourse, and indeed in all thought; but still you haven't *proved* to me that they are true. How would you prove them?"

Let us consider the concept of proof. To prove something is to establish it beyond doubt. But there is more than one way to do this. (1) We prove a theorem of geometry by deriving it, deductively, from previous theorems and other statements in the system. We prove a conclusion by showing that it is deduced validly from premises, provided we already know the premises to be true. But (2) we can also prove by giving evidence for it that does not employ reasoning at all. Someone says, "Prove to me that you're now reading a book." There are no other *propositions* from which you can deduce this one as a conclusion (or, if there are, they are less obvious than this one); you prove it by showing him, by confronting him with the situation, by telling him to see, touch, and so on. When the judge says, "Prove to me that you were in Atlanta the night of the murder," he is not asking the defendant to deduce that proposition from other ones but to give evidence supporting his claim; this evidence can be gleaned from the testimony of people who saw him, from a motion-picture record of his activities, and so on.

In most cases the demand for proof is a demand of this second kind. But in the case of these principles of logic it is not: how could you prove that A is A by saying "Look and see"? Whom would this convince who had not been convinced before? Here the request for proof seems to be the request that one *deduce* the proposition from other ones. But in the present case, what other ones are there? How can you prove that A is A by deducing it from other propositions, when in fact all other propositions depend upon *it?* We have to start somewhere, and this is where we start. You cannot prove something except by means of something *else:* there is the proposition to be proved, and there are *other* propositions by means of which it is proved. But in this case no such deduction can be performed; in fact, every attempted deduction would presuppose the truth of the very proposition to be proved. You cannot prove the laws of logic by means of other propositions, for the other ones presuppose them. Nor can you prove them by means of themselves: this would be begging the question (assuming the very thing to be proved). But how, *other than* by the principles of logic, can we establish the principles of logic?

It cannot be done, of course; and even if it could, it would not help us. For suppose we could deduce the principles of logic, L, from a body of other statements, K. Then how would we prove K? By something else, J? And how prove J? The question here is infinitely self-repeating: we are caught in an *infinite regress*. Besides, how could we prove anything except by means of principles of logic? These are themselves (along with several other principles) the very principles of proof. If another set of principles, K, could be used to establish the principles of logic, then K would be the principles of proof and not L.

We cannot establish them by means of themselves; we cannot establish them by means other than themselves; therefore, we cannot establish them at all. (Even in saying this we are using a principle of logic, though a slightly more complex one: "If p, then q or r; not q, not r, therefore not p.")

Is this result unsettling? It should not be; if proof is not to go on infinitely, it must stop somewhere. But we are so accustomed to being barraged by the request "Prove it" that we tend to think that this is required also of the very bases of proof themselves. "If you can't prove it, you can't know it." But the principles of proof themselves make proof possible. We cannot prove *them* in turn; we can only show, as we have done, the results one would get by trying to deny them.

Still, the uneasiness may persist. We want every statement to rest on another one. We are in the position of the lady and the rock: The earth rests on an elephant; what does the elephant rest on? A rock. What does the rock rest on? Another rock. What does that rock rest on? Another rock . . ., and so on, ad infinitum. A lady in the audience keeps asking this question over and over again; finally in exasperation the speaker says to her, "Lady, it's rock *all the way down!*" All the way down—to what? The speaker can stop her endlessly repeated question only by teaching her a little astronomy and curing her of naïve notions of up and down—though perhaps she will never quite overcome a feeling of dissatisfaction with the explanation. You too may remain dissatisfied with our conclusions about logic unless you get over the idea that the ultimate principles of proof must themselves be proved. They can be *justified,* as we have tried to do, but they cannot be proved in the sense of deduced from other propositions by means of principles of logic.

Objections to the principles of logic.   There have, however, been objections raised even to the three simple laws we are considering. Some are based on obvious misunderstandings, but not all.

1. " 'A is A' does not always hold true. Sometimes A is not A, for what was A becomes B. Tadpoles become frogs and are no longer tadpoles." But the answer to this is quite easy. Just as in the case of arithmetic, "A is A" does not say anything about what A may become or turn into: it tells you nothing about what the processes of the universe are like. It only tells you that when you have an A, then it is an A that you have and not something other than A. The next moment the A may turn into a B, and then it is a B and not an A.

"But it may be an A in one sense and not in another. The man in relation to the squirrel (pp. 37–38) may be a case of going around in one sense but not in the other sense." This of course is true, but it in no way touches the Law of Identity. A word may have different senses. But in saying that A is A, the Law of Identity says only that this thing, A, by whatever name we call it, is A and not something else. Cats are cats, eating is eating, and going around is going around. "Going around" has at least two senses; very well, this only shows that "going around$_1$" is not to be confused with "going around$_2$." The Law of Identity doesn't say that A$_1$ is A$_2$ but only that A$_1$ is A$_1$ and A$_2$ is A$_2$.

2. "The Law of Excluded Middle doesn't always hold true. Suppose I say, "This unicorn is either white or it's not-white. But neither of these alternatives is true, for there is no unicorn at all."

But to use the phrase "this unicorn" presupposes that there is a unicorn here; if you say that this unicorn is white, your statement consists of two separate propositions: (1) there is a unicorn here, and (2) it is white. The second proposition presupposes that the first is true. But it is not true. So let us re-state the matter: Either there is a white unicorn here or there is not. And that statement is true: there is not a white unicorn here. Similarly it is true that either there is a black unicorn here or there is not. State the matter so as to avoid the tricky formulation, in which there are two statements posing as one, and the difficulty is overcome.

3. "Something need not be either hot or cold, nor need a car go either fast or slow. The liquid may be lukewarm, the car may travel at a medium speed."

But this objection is a confusion of *negatives* with *opposites*. The Law of Excluded Middle does not say that the car is going either fast or slow. Nor does it say that a given temperature is either hot or cold, or that an examination must be either easy or difficult. Each of these is a pair of opposites, and there may be a middle ground between them. The temperature of a liquid may be neither hot nor cold but lukewarm; an examination may be "middling" neither easy nor difficult; a car may go at a medium speed that is neither fast nor slow. The Law of Excluded Middle does not say that there is no middle ground between *opposites* (hot and cold), for of course there is. It only says that there is no middle ground between a term and its *negative* (hot and not-hot). Wherever you draw the boundary-line between hot and not-hot, there is no middle ground between them—the law, true to its name, excludes any such middle ground: any temperature that isn't hot is not-hot, but of course the not-hot includes *both* lukewarm and cold.

4. What about category mistakes? "Do you mean that my mental state must be either hot or not-hot? And that the number 2 is either fast or not-fast? And that smells must be either white or not-white? But that's absurd!"

But the law does not say this either: it does not say that *every* adjective must meaningfully apply to every subject. It only says that *either* a predicate A applies or it does *not* apply. For example, the number 2 is either fast or not-fast. That is true enough; it is not-fast. But that doesn't mean that it must be slow, for the concept of speed doesn't apply to it at all (to apply it would be a category mistake). Remember that not-fast includes *every predicate other than fast:* it includes slow but also triangular, edible, shopworn, lovesick, and anything else you could say. Thus construed, it remains true that the number 2 either falls into the category of fast or it doesn't. In this case, it doesn't; but don't assume therefore that it falls into the category of slow or medium speed: it only falls under the huge category that includes everything *but* fast.

5. "I still think there are exceptions. For example, you might say that either Jones is at home or Jones is not at home. But suppose that Jones is dead: then he is neither at home nor not at home."

Not at all, we may reply. One could get around this by considering double-barreled propositions. Here we have the proposition (1) that there exists a man, Jones (presumably alive), and (2) that he is at home or not at home. The second cannot be true unless the first is. "Jones is either . . . or . . ." presupposes that Jones exists. So we can say: either there exists a man, Jones, or there does not; and if there is such a man, either he is home or he is not. In both cases the Law of Excluded Middle holds.

We could state the point another way: *Either* there exists a man Jones who is at home *or* there does not. Now if there *was* a man Jones, but he is now dead, then the second alternative is true. His corpse may be at home, or at what was his home when he was alive; but if the corpse is not Jones, then it is not true that Jones is home. In that case, however, the second half of the statement (what follows the "or") is true: it is *not* the case that there exists a man Jones who is at home. But we must be careful not to confuse this with "Jones is not at home," for this last statement is only *one* of the alternatives possible under the second half of the statement. "Jones is no longer alive" is another one. A person who consents to saying "Jones is either at home or not at home" and then is told that Jones is dead, and that therefore neither *p* nor not-*p* is true, is falling into a trap. He has not guarded himself carefully against this trap, for he has not distinguished between these two propositions: "It is not the case that there is a man Jones who is at home" (which is true) and "Jones is not at home" (which is false, since Jones no longer exists).

6. "But the Law of Excluded Middle doesn't apply in cases of vagueness. Concerning a speed one may say, 'It's either fast or not-fast.' "

If the person was going 60 miles per hour on the turnpike, it isn't clear whether this should be called fast or not; there is no clear rule here to decide either way; like countless other words, "fast" is vague. (See p. 67.) Still, the fact remains that the principle holds *wherever* we decide to draw the line. If we draw the line at 60 miles per hour, then it is true that either there is a car going at least 60 miles per hour or there is not. And the same for any other speed one chooses to mention. It is equally true that either it is going fast or it is not; it's just that the word "fast" is vague, so that one doesn't know (until someone chooses to specify it) where the boundary is to be drawn between fast and not-fast.

7. "The Law of Non-contradiction becomes so ridden with qualifiers as to be made to come out true no matter what the conditions. For example: "A man may love his wife and also hate her."

"Yes, but not in the same respect: he may love her for her attractiveness yet hate her for her character. So, though he both loves and hates her, he loves her in one respect and hates her in another. The law, properly formulated, only says that he cannot love her and not-love her at the same time *in the same respect.*"

"But he may hate her and love her *both* in respect of her character: he may love her for her patience and hate her for her irritability—both character-traits."

"Well, that only means that he loves her for her character in one respect and hates her for her character in another respect."

"But may he not love and hate her for the very same trait, in the very same respect? He loves her for her quick temper and also hates her for it."

"Surely then he loves her for it in one way and hates her for it in another."

"Why must we conclude this? Every time I show you that the love and hate co-exist with respect to the very same trait, you assume that it *must* be in a different respect, even if you can't name it. Every time I show you a contrary case, you manufacture a new 'respect.' But you have not told me what you mean by the phrase 'in the same respect.' What is needed is an *independent* definition of that phrase. What constitutes 'the same respect' and 'a different respect'? Once we have an example that is troublesome you say 'Oh, then it's a different respect'—but this doesn't satisfy me: it smacks of a priori assumption. You are hiding behind the covering phrase 'the same respect.' How do you know that when there is an apparent counterexample to the principle, there is always a different respect? I believe that this business about a different respect is thrown in in order to rescue the Law of Non-contradiction."

"I believe the love-hate problem can be solved without it. Love and hate aren't necessarily opposites. Push them far enough, and, like the sequence of sharps and flats in music, they come together again, full circle. If this is so, love and hate may exist together, but this *isn't* love and *not*-love existing together (and only *this* would violate the principle). It is not even love and a *part* of not-love existing together (taking hate as a part of not-love). In emotional states of great intensity, hate may become a form of love and love of hate, or perhaps neither: perhaps the names aren't even applicable any more."

"I think this is just an evasion. Love and hate are opposites; love and not-love are negatives. If you don't love, you don't necessarily hate (you might be indifferent, for example); but if you do love, surely you don't hate. 'I hate spinach' would usually be taken as incompatible with 'I love spinach'—and it *is* incompatible with it, isn't it? So it is here. Thus my original charge remains: that you manufacture a new respect every time there is an incompatibility, so as to make the Law of Non-contradiction come out unscathed."

"The logic of 'love' and 'hate' is tricky. In one sense they *are* opposites, and in that sense they cannot both occur at the same time in the same person. But there may well be another sense in which they are not opposites, and hence not incompatible at all. And in that sense there is no violation of the law of Non-contradiction in saying that they both do occur."

Verbal rules, or facts of reality?   Finally, what is the status of these principles? Are they analytic or synthetic, a priori or a posteriori? Here we enter an area of considerable controversy.

Rationalist: We may assume, I take it, that they are a priori. What would it be like to find out through investigation or observation that a table is a table, or that an object isn't both a table and not a table? If they are true (and we have considered some objections to saying that they are), they are necessarily true, not contingently. They would be "true in all possible worlds."

Empiricist: Granted; the question is, are they analytic? And surely they are. They are the very paradigm of cases of analytic statements. A is A—deny it and you get the statement that A is not-A, and what could be more clearly self-contradictory than that? Nothing can be both A and not-A—deny it, and you get the statement that something *can* be both A and not-A, and what could be more obviously self-contradictory? Surely these principles are the clearest cases of statement whose necessity can be attributed to being analytic.

R: But this won't do. Of course the denial of the Law of Non-contradiction is itself self-contradictory. Every time you deny an analytic statement, you are violating the Law of Non-contradiction. But notice that "analytic" is defined with reference to the Law of Non-contradiction itself. The principle is the criterion for the self-contradictoriness of other statements. What of the Law of Non-contradiction itself? Certainly its denial yields a contradiction ("both A and not-A"). Any proposition that contradicts the Law of Non-contradiction is self-contradictory, and this includes a denial of the Law of Non-contradiction itself; it itself provides the test criterion for the analyticity of all *other* statements. So, rather than say that the law is analytic, I would prefer to say that it stands *outside* the system of statements, providing a touchstone whereby *they* can be tested as analytic.

E:　Perhaps. But now let us look at the other sense of "analytic"; you can tell from the meaning of the words that the statement is true. And so you can with the principles of logic. The principles themselves supply the verbal convention that makes *other* statements analytic. For example, "Cats are cats" is simply a special case of "A is A," and "This is not both a cat and not a cat" is a special case of "Not both A and not-A." The principles of logic state explicitly the verbal conventions that make the special cases analytic. In other words, if we know the verbal convention "Not both A and not-A," we know the principle that makes all special statements—"Cats are cats," "This is not both a chair and not a chair"—analytic. Are we still agreed?

R:　I'm not so sure. If you say that "Not both A and not-A" is *merely* a verbal convention, I would disagree violently. I hold that the so-called principles of thought are fundamental *laws of reality,* as Aristotle believed. They don't merely tell us to use words a certain way: they tell us something about *the nature of things.* They inform us of certain general facts about reality, and these facts are not of our making as verbal conventions are.

E:　We do disagree here. I don't think that the principles of thought state any facts about reality at all. To say "a table is a table" doesn't tell us anything at all about tables: when I know this, I know nothing more about the table than I did before.

R:　No specific information, I grant you: you know nothing about its color or size or weight. But it is a *fact* that the table is the table, and it is a *fact* that it's not both a table and not a table. Not a specific fact, not a fact you ask about when you want information about furniture, but a fact nonetheless.

. . . That the desk I am writing on is either a desk or not may be admitted to be a most unhelpful truth and one in which nobody but a philosopher would take the slightest interest. Does it say something true, however? Try to deny it and see. Does it say something about this particular desk? Yes, and this is not controverted by pointing out that what it says holds equally of all desks, clouds, and lamp-posts. We must repeat that a statement does not say nothing simply because it applies to everything.[7]

E:　I still say that it's empty of content. It says nothing about anything in this world or any other world. It *seems* to say something about the world because we use words like "desk" and "cloud," which denote things in the actual world; but this delusion is dispelled once we realize that desks and clouds aren't ingredients in the statements at all—the principles of thought aren't *about* those things. We saw that in "$2 + 2 = 4$" the reference to apples

[7] Brand Blanshard, *Reason and Analysis,* p. 427.

and amoebae was so much window dressing. So here: the assertions about desks and clouds are all merely cases of "A is A," "Not both A and not-A," and so on.

R: No, the statement *is* about these things—desks, clouds, etc.—and it *does* make true statements about them. But these are highly *general* truths: that is to say, they are true of desks and clouds and *everything else*. Please don't confuse *generality* with *emptiness*. They strike you as empty because they apply to everything; but they are no less true because of this. "A is A" applies to everything in this world, indeed to everything in any possible world; that is how general it is. But it is still true. (Similarly, I would contend, truths of arithmetic are truths about all possible quantities, and are no less true for holding equally of all of them.)

E: The point that you don't see is that we have in the principles of logic only a series of *verbal conventions*. Here is something, call it X. What is not-X? Everything other than X. What makes this proposition true? The use of the word "not." That's how we use the word "not": the whole statement is a kind of implicit definition of "not." It tells us that in our use of language, we are not to use the term "not-X" where we use "X." We might not have the word "not" or its equivalent in a certain language, and then we wouldn't be able to formulate any such law. But it is extremely convenient to have the word, for we want to be able to talk about the absence of something as well as its presence, and the word "not" is the one we use for doing this.

R: In such a language we wouldn't be able to *formulate* the Law of Non-contradiction, but the principle would still be true. It holds true of *all* reality—of everything that can be named, everything that can be thought of, everything that anyone ever will be able to think of. Even if a certain language doesn't have the equipment for stating it, this doesn't interfere with its truth.

E: Its truth is due entirely to the fact that the word "not" has a certain meaning. If someone said, "This can be both a table and not a table," I would conclude that he hasn't learned the meaning of the word "not." Once he *has* learned what "not" means, he has learned (as we all have) not to say that. Once you understand what "not" means, you understand why "It isn't both a table and not a table" is true. Its truth is entirely dependent on that verbal convention.

R: Here I believe you are mistaken: it isn't a verbal convention. A verbal convention can be changed, but the truth of the Law of Non-contradiction can't. When you play bridge or chess, there is a set of conventions or rules that govern the game; and if the game is uninteresting when played one way, some of its rules can be changed so that the game is improved. Defining words is also a matter of convention: a meaning is assigned to a noise, and to define a word is to state what meaning you have given it (stipulative definition) or what meaning others have given it (reportive definition). But the principles of logic cannot be conventions in this sense. There is *no alternative* to them. For example: you say that the principles of logic are conventions; I say they are not. Surely we cannot both be right; one of us must be mistaken. That this is so is a necessary fact about reality, not a verbal convention that we arbitrarily set up. Even you, a conventionalist, will agree that if I say they are facts of reality, and you say they aren't, we are contradicting one another, and we can't both be right. This is simply a fact about reality. But if the principles of logic are merely conventions, then we can simply change the conventions and get around the contradiction. But you can't escape contradictions that way!

We are offered as true the statement that all logic is conventional, and expected to accept without question that the contradictory proposition, "Some logic is not conventional," is false. But if the law of contradiction is really only a convention with alternatives, why should we be expected so firmly to take this contradictory as false? If there really is an alternative to the law, *both* sides of a contradiction may be true, and to insist on either to the exclusion of the other is dogmatism. But in spite of their view that logic is conventional, positivists do not think it dogmatic to insist that if their view is true, its contradictory must be rejected.[8]

E: I would remind you, however, that alternative logics have been devised. According to the two-valued logic of Aristotle, every proposition is either true or false (not merely true or not-true). (If the sentence is meaningless, of course it states no proposition at all.) But suppose one constructs a three-valued logic (this has been done), in which every proposition is either true, false, or indeterminate. Then what happens to your assertion that there is no alternative?

R: (1) It doesn't deny that a proposition is either true or not-true (which is all the Law of Excluded Middle requires). It only denies that every proposition is either true or *false.* But (2) I contend that as a matter of fact "Either true or false" is tantamount to "Either true or not-true"—that is, there is no third possibility. If a proposition is not true, it must be false. We may not *know* which it is, and then we call it "indeterminate," but the indeterminateness is the result of our lack of knowledge; the proposition is not indeterminate in reality. The proposition *is* either true or false, though we may not *know* which it is. "True, false, or indeterminate" may be the proper categories as far as our *knowledge* of things goes (just as "Yes," "No," or "I don't know" may be proper alternatives on an objective examination); but I am speaking of the way things *are.* In reality, the proposition is either true or false—there is no middle ground—even though we don't know which of the two it is. "True, false, or indeterminate" as the alternatives in *reality* (not our knowledge of reality) is a simple category-mistake.

[8] *Ibid.,* p. 275.

In a realm where no proposition excludes its contradictory, nothing could be asserted as true rather than its opposite; assertion and negation would vanish . . . . To us the source of this constraint seems clear. If it came from our own will, as conventions do, we could change it, whereas we cannot. If it came from experience, the law would be only probable, and positivists agree that it is more. To say with Kant that it comes from some uncontrollable region of our own minds compels us to say that though the contradictoriness of the real world may be unthinkable, it may nevertheless be true. Our own view of the source of constraint is presumably that of the "plain man." We accept the law and must accept it, because "nature has said it." If we hold that a thing cannot at once have a property and not have it, it is because we *see* that it cannot. The law of contradiction is at once the statement of a logical requirement and the statement of an ontological truth.[9]

E: It's true that there is no alternative to "Not both A and not-A" *as long as we mean what we now mean by "not."* For you will remember what I said before: Here is reality, or as much of it as you care to investigate. Here is some item in it that you want to talk about; you call it "A." Now, we use the term "not-A" to cover all the territory that isn't covered by A. So now when you say "Nothing can be both A and not-A," *of course* that's true, and *of course* there are no alternatives, *as long as you stick to that convention* about the meaning of the word "not." But there *could* be alternative conventions, though none perhaps as useful as this, for to be able to say "This is a cat" and "That and that and that are not cats" is very useful indeed: it enables you to say that something is not an A even though you do not know positively what it *is*.

R: Of course it is useful—but you are putting the cart before the horse; it is useful because it is *true*. It's true that nothing can be both A and not-A; and since this is true, and since we want our picture of reality to be true, we must not say that something is both A and not-A. As a consequence, it's useful because we are interested in seeking truth and avoiding error.

E: It is you who are putting the cart before the horse. The Law of Non-contradiction holds because of the convention we have governing the use of the word "not." To deny it is to exhibit one's ignorance of the verbal convention governing "not." Once you understand the meaning of "not," you understand why something can't be A and not-A. If someone said, "I saw a table that was not a table," and he wasn't joking, I would say that he didn't know how the word "not" was used in our language: "not-A" is used to cover all cases except those already covered by A.

R: You try to make the verbal convention the fundamental thing; I say that the convention is employed because it follows "the way reality goes." You say the truth is a consequence of convention; I say the convention is a

[9] *Ibid.*, p. 276.

consequence of the truth. If the principles of logic weren't already true *before* you established any verbal conventions, you couldn't even establish any conventions. If a convention could also be a non-convention, what would it mean to say that it was a convention after all? Don't you see how the truth of the principle is presupposed in the very attempt *to say anything at all*—whether about conventions or about anything else? Reality lays down these First Principles: "A is A" and "Nothing is both A and not-A." If we don't follow them, we talk nonsense.

E: We couldn't even formulate these principles unless we understood the linguistic conventions, such as the one I was just describing about the use of the word "not."

R: It's true that we couldn't *formulate* them, for to formulate them is to use words. But they would be *true* even if unformulated. It would still be true that this isn't both a table and not a table even though we had no language at all and no word "not." The truth of these propositions is presupposed in the conventions we adopt; and if they weren't true, neither you nor anyone else could adopt any conventions at all (for then they could be non-conventions at the same time). If the Law of Non-contradiction is a convention, why not, as I said before, adopt a different convention? The point is we can't: there *is* no alternative.

E: Once you have assigned a meaning to the word "not" (the one I gave you earlier), then *of course* there is no alternative. "Not both A and not-A" is true, and necessarily true, only *if* you adopt the convention about "not" (not-A including everything except what's in A). *With respect to* that convention, "Not both A and not-A" is necessarily true: to deny it would be to go back on the convention we introduced about "not."

R: "To go back on" means "to be inconsistent with," and it is the Principle of Non-contradiction itself that prohibits inconsistencies: it tells us that if we say "This is both A and not-A" we are contradicting ourselves. The truth is still prior to the convention.

E: No, the principle is true only if the convention is presupposed. Let's start from scratch. Let's make up a language. There will be one word for each situation, and the negative of the word for the absence of that situation. Give any situation a name, such as "A," and give a second situation a different name, such as "B," and so on indefinitely. Just be careful to keep the names separate, so we know what situation we are identifying with each name. And since we want a name for the *absence* of situations as well as their presence, we will use "not-A," "not-B," etc. for the absence of each situation. These are the basic rules of our language-game. If someone were to say, "This thing is both A and not-A," we would say to him that he has violated the rules of the game, since we have used "not-A" as the name for the *absence* of the very situation we had used "A" for the presence of. There now, do you see what a simple move in the language-game this is?

R: An inevitable move, I would say. We must adopt these rules because "A is A" and "not both A and not-A" are true antecedently to the adoption of the rules.

E: No, we need not have *these* rules. The rule about "not" is useful as long as we want to refer to the absence of situations as well as their presence. If we had the same word for A as for B, or for A as for the absence of A, communication would be impossible, for nobody would know, when we used the word "A," *what* we were talking about: A, or something else, B, or the absence of A (not-A), etc. Let me use an analogy: When you get a claim-check in the baggage room, you have a number on the claim-check and that same number on your suitcase. The person next to you will have a different number, but his number will be the same as the one on *his* suitcase; and so on. It is more useful to have it that way, so that each of us can retrieve and identify his own baggage without confusion. We *could* have a different convention: everyone might have the same number on his claim-check. But then there would be no point in having claim-checks at all, for their utility lies in each person being able to retrieve his own baggage, without confusion in identification. The same consideration applies to the principles of logic. They are the prerequisites for useful communication.

R: They are the prerequisites of all communication, because their truth is presupposed in every assertion we make. Again, our verbal conventions are rooted in the facts of reality.

E: Here we go again. If you mean what we now mean by "not," then there is no alternative to the Law of Non-contradiction. We mean to exclude all alternatives by saying that "not-A" will cover all the territory other than what is covered by "A." But this very fact helps to make it clear, doesn't it, that it is *not a fact about reality* that is being stated by the law? It doesn't tell you anything about "how reality is" or "the way reality goes." It doesn't tell you "Reality is *this* way," for there is no specifiable other way. Why not? How do we know there isn't? Is it that you know exactly what other way is meant, but know that it will never come about? No. You aren't told what the other way is. And if you were told, how could you possibly be sure that it will never occur? But if the principle doesn't tell you which way reality is (from among other possible ways), how are you to be taught what is meant by the expressions "A is A" or "not both A and not-A?" What else is it to teach the meaning of an expression that purports to represent a state-of-affairs than to show *when* we are to use it and when we are not? For example, we use the word "snow" under certain circumstances, and not under all other circumstances. We are always taught the meaning of a sentence by being shown cases of its truth ("This is snow") as distinguished from other cases when it is not true, when the expression does not apply. You can't be taught the meaning of "This is snow" by being told when it is *not* true but never when it *is;* and in the same way you can't be taught the meaning of an expression only by being shown when it *is* true or *does* apply to reality, but never when it is false or does *not* apply. Now, "A is A" and "Not both A and not-A," I'm sure you would say, cannot ever be false. So how can you say they refer to some fact of reality? "This is snow" *does* refer to a fact of reality, for I know when the expression should be used in reference to reality—and when it should not. But you can't show me what "fact of reality" "A is A" refers to because there is *no possible case* of its falsity—there is no conceivable case to which it *does not* apply. But if I know when to apply an expression, I must also know when to refrain from applying it. And when am I to refrain from applying this one?

R: Never. It always applies, necessarily, to everything. That is how it's different.

E: But since you can't tell me what would ever count as a case of the falsity of "A is A," you have not described any situations in which I could use the expression "A and not-A," and hence it is meaningless. A strange proposition, whose negation is not false but meaningless. Is it a proposition at all?

R: Indeed it is, but a proposition of a different kind. I agree that "This is an A and not an A" is meaningless, *if* you include self-contradictory statements as meaningless. But this merely confirms my thesis. It is meaningless because there is *no* alternative to "A is A." To contingent propositions, there is an alternative: there could be and might be white crows even though there aren't any in fact; but with necessary propositions like "A is A," this is not the case. Your analysis applies only to contingent propositions; we can distinguish, at least in thought, cases to which they apply from cases to which they don't apply. But the principles of logic are things of a different kind: they are true, and necessarily true, because they necessarily apply to everything; hence in their case there is no consistent negative, no other way, no consistently thinkable alternative.

E: And I contend that the reason there is no alternative is that we have framed a convention about "not" that excludes any such alternatives in its very formulation. There are alternative systems of conventions, but only when you have a convention like ours about the use of the negative term is there no alternative to "not both A and not-A." The necessary truth of the proposition is only *with respect to* the prior adoption of a convention.

R: With respect to a prior fact of reality, you mean.

E: No, that is *not* what I mean. But we seem to have reached an impasse. Let me now introduce another consideration. We have been speaking thus far only of Aristotle's three Laws of Thought. But these principles do not suffice for carrying out *proofs*. We need others; and among these some must be rules that permit us to pass safely from a true proposition (or set of true propositions) to another true proposition—that is, to make valid inferences. By "safely" we mean without any logical possibility of inferring a false proposition. Some such rules are:

From "*p* and *q*" we can infer "*p*."
From "If *p*, then *q*" and "*p*" we can infer "*q*".
From "If *p*, then *q*" and "If *q*, then *r*" we can infer "If *p*, then *r*."

Without rules of inference we could advance not one step toward constructing a proof. Now, rules are neither true nor false: they are more like recommendations or suggestions for carrying out a procedure. Rules are pragmatic devices, defensible or not depending on whether they do or do not serve certain ends. They may be useful or useless, helpful or not helpful, simple or cumbersome; but they are neither true nor false. The rules of logic are no exception. They are justified by their utility, and their utility lies in the fact that they enable us to pass from true propositions (premises) to other propositions (conclusions) whose *truth* requires no further investigation because the rules were designed to guarantee it.

But it is an elementary fact about logic that we have a wide latitude of choice about which principles we wish to regard as the laws and which as the rules. Our system of logic comes out essentially the same for each choice. In other words, any principle of logic, even our three Laws of Thought, can be formulated as an inference rule. Thus it is easily shown that any of the three laws can be expressed as the following rule of inference: "From '*p*' we can infer '*p*'." Our rules of logic are required to take us from true propositions to other true ones, and they can be conclusively tested for their ability to do this—that is, for their validity. If they are valid in this sense, they qualify; if not, they are banished from our system of logic. Our basis for doing it this way is to enable us to make inferences. And if this ultimately means "to enable us to make intelligible discourse," then this too is an end on which to base our justification of the procedure and of the rules that govern it. In short, our final justification is pragmatic.

R: I grant that the end is pragmatic if you include as "pragmatic" the attempt to find truth. (This is not the usual meaning when we call a procedure or justification pragmatic.) Framing rules of inference so as to enable us to get from true propositions to other true propositions is surely done in the interest of finding truth, isn't it? And truth, I insist, is the fundamental thing here; utility is only a *consequence* of truth. The principles of logic, I hold, are very general truths. They can also be formulated, as you say, as inference-rules, and as rules they are not true or false but useful, in that they enable us to go from true propositions to other true propositions. But though they can be *stated* as inference-rules, I would remind you that any inference-rule still *presupposes* certain general truths, which Aristotle called "laws of thought." A is A—for example, an inference-rule is an inference-rule and not something else. Not both A and not-A—for example, a proposition can't be both true and not true. If these general principles didn't hold, we could not speak of inference-rules or, indeed, of anything else. Facts of reality still underlie verbal conventions.

Exercises

1. Comment on the following assertions:

a. "He's in the room or he's not in the room"—an instance of the Law of Excluded Middle; but suppose he's half in and half out? or suppose he is dead? or suppose we were mistaken in thinking that he ever existed? For such cases the Law of Excluded Middle doesn't hold true.

b. A man may love his wife and hate her at the same time, even with respect to the same characteristic. So the Law of Non-contradiction doesn't hold true in such a case. Similarly for "I'm with it yet not with it," and so on.

c. A isn't always A—a boy becomes a man, a tadpole becomes a frog. The universe is dynamic, not static—and Aristotle's Law of Identity cannot take account of the dynamic character of the universe.

d. In deducing conclusions from premises, we may learn in the conclusion things we did not know when we stated the premises. So we have drawn new knowledge out of the situation. Accordingly, they cannot be analytic.

e. It is impossible to prove that A is A, or that something that's a table isn't also not a table. It can't be proved by means of something other than itself, and to prove it by means of itself would be arguing in a circle. So it can't be proved at all. Therefore, there is no basis for believing it.

f. "Either A or not-A." For example, either ideas are green or they are not-green. But that's ridiculous. They are neither green nor not-green: the concept of color simply does not apply to ideas at all. To do so is to be guilty of a category-mistake.

g. "This can't be both a table and not a table" is a statement absolutely empty of content. It tells us nothing whatever about the table; it conveys no information, has "no factual content."

h. The so-called laws of logic are nothing but rules of inference—and rules, of course aren't true or false, though they can be useful or not useful.

i. When a parent teaches a child the meaning of a word, "A," he teaches him when "A" is applicable to reality and also *when it is not*. The same holds for teaching the meaning of a sentence, such as "Snow is falling." In that way, the child can learn what situations in reality the sentence refers to. But how can the child learn the meaning of "Not both A and not-A," since it can never be false? Since there is no possible situation to which it does *not* apply, how can he learn its meaning?

2. Summarize as clearly as you can all the arguments you can think of for the empiricist position on the principles of logic, and then all the arguments for the rationalist position. Which do you find the more convincing, and why?

Selected Readings for Chapter 3

Ayer, Alfred J., *Language, Truth, and Logic*. London: Victor Gollancz, Ltd., 1936. Chapter 4.

Barker, S. F., *Philosophy of Mathematics*. Englewood Cliffs, N. J.: Prentice-Hall, Inc., 1964. Paperback.

Benacerraf, Paul and Hilary Putnam (eds.), *Philosophy of Mathematics*. Englewood Cliffs, N. J.: Prentice-Hall, Inc., 1964.

Black, Max, "Necessary Statements and Rules," *Philosophical Review,* 1958.

Blanshard, Brand, *The Nature of Thought.* London: George Allen & Unwin, Ltd., 1939. Vol. 2, chapters 28–30.

———, *Reason and Analysis.* La Salle, Ill.: Open Court Publishing Co., 1963. Chapter 6.

Campbell, C. A., "Contradiction: Law or Convention?" *Analysis,* 1958.

Castaneda, Hector N., "Arithmetic and Reality," *Australasian Journal of Philosophy,* 37 (1959).

Cohen, Morris R., *Reason and Nature.* New York: Harcourt, Brace & World, Inc., 1931. Especially Book 2, Chapter 1.

Ewing, Alfred C., "The Linguistic Theory of A Priori Propositions," in *Clarity Is Not Enough,* ed. H. D. Lewis. London: George Allen & Unwin, Ltd., 1963.

Frank, Philipp, *Philosophy of Science.* Englewood Cliffs, N. J.: Prentice-Hall, Inc., 1962. Chapter 3.

Frege, Gottlob, *The Foundations of Arithmetic.* Oxford: Blackwell, 1953.

Gasking, Douglas, "Mathematics and the World," in *Logic and Language,* First Series, ed. Antony Flew. Oxford: Blackwell, 1953.

Grice, H. P., and P. F. Strawson, "In Defense of a Dogma," *Philosophical Review,* 1956.

Hempel, Carl G., "Geometry and Empirical Science," *American Mathematical Monthly,* 52 (1945). Reprinted in H. Feigl and W. Sellars, *Readings in Philosophical Analysis.* New York: Appleton-Century-Crofts, 1949.

———, "On the Nature of Mathematical Truth," *American Mathematical Monthly,* 52, 1945. Reprinted in Feigl and Sellars, *Readings in Philosophical Analysis.* New York: Appleton-Century-Crofts, 1949.

Hume, David, *Enquiry Concerning Human Understanding,* 1751. Section II. *Treatise of Human Nature,* 1739. Book I, Part 1. Many editions.

Kemeny, John G., *A Philosopher Looks at Science.* Princeton, N. J.: D. Van Nostrand Co., Inc., 1959. Chapter 2.

Kneale, William, "Are Necessary Truths True by Convention?" *Proceedings of the Aristotelian Society,* Supplementary Volume, 1947. Reprinted in H. D. Lewis (ed.), *Clarity Is Not Enough.* London: George Allen & Unwin, Ltd., 1965.

Körner, Stephen, *The Philosophy of Mathematics.* London: Hutchinson & Co. (Publishers), Ltd., 1960.

Lewis, Clarence I., *Analysis of Knowledge and Valuation.* LaSalle, Ill.: Open Court Publishing Co., 1947. Chapters 3–6.

———, *Mind and the World Order.* New York: Charles Scribner's Sons, 1929. Chapters 7 and 8.

Locke, John. *Essay Concerning Human Understanding.* Especially books II and IV. Many editions.

Malcolm, Norman. "Are Necessary Propositions Really Verbal?" *Mind,* 49, 1940.

———, "The Nature of Entailment," *Mind,* 1940.

Nagel, Ernest, *Logic without Metaphysics.* New York: Free Press of Glencoe, Inc., 1956.

Pap, Arthur, "Are All Necessary Propositions Analytic?" *Philosophical Review,* 58 (1949).

————, *Introduction to the Philosophy of Science*. New York: Free Press of Glencoe, Inc., 1962. Chapters 5–7.

————, *Semantics and Necessary Truth*, New Haven, Conn.: Yale University Press, 1958. Also in paperback.

Pears, David, "Incompatibilities of Colors," in *Logic and Language*, Second Series, ed. Antony Flew. Oxford: B. H. Blackwell, Ltd., 1953.

Putnam, Hilary, "The Analytic and the Synthetic," in *Minnesota Studies in the Philosophy of Science*, Vol. 3, ed. H. Feigl and G. Maxwell. Minneapolis: University of Minnesota Press, 1962.

Reichenbach, Hans, *The Rise of Scientific Philosophy*. Berkeley: University of California Press, 1951. Especially chapters 3 and 8.

Robinson, Richard, "Necessary Propositions," *Mind*, 1958.

Russell, Bertrand, *Introduction to Mathematical Philosophy*. London: George Allen & Unwin, Ltd., 1919.

————, *The Problems of Philosophy*. New York: Oxford University Press, Inc., 1912. Chapters 7, 8, 11.

Ryle, Gilbert, Karl Popper and Casimir Lewy, "Why Are the Calculuses of Logic and Mathematics Applicable to Reality?" *Proceedings of the Aristotelian Society*, Supplementary Volume 1946.

Waismann, Friedrich, "Analytic-Synthetic," *Analysis*, 1949-1952.

————, "Are There Alternative Logics?" *Proceedings of the Aristotelian Society*, 1945–1946.

————, *The Principles of Linguistic Philosophy*. London: Macmillan & Co., Ltd., 1965.

Wittgenstein, Ludwig, *Remarks on the Foundations of Mathematics*. Oxford: B. H. Blackwell, Ltd., 1958.

4
Empirical Knowledge

12. Law, Theory, and Explanation

By means of sense-experience we learn many things about the physical world—we perceive countless physical things, processes, and events, as well as the interaction of our own bodies with these things in nature. But if our knowledge ended there, we would have no means of dealing effectively with the world. The kind of knowledge we acquire through the sciences begins only when we notice *regularities* in the course of events. Many events and processes in nature occur the same way over and over again. Iron rusts, but gold does not. Chickens lay eggs, but dogs do not. Lightning is followed by thunder. Cats catch mice, but cows don't. (Even to speak of a cat or a cow is to have noted some regularity—that some characteristics regularly recur, or go together.) Amidst the constant diversity in our daily experience of nature, we try to find regularities: we trace "the thin red vein of order through the flux of experience."

If we were as interested in discovering *ir*regularities in our experience as we are in regularities, the task would be much easier. Some rocks are hard and some soft, some heavy and some light. Some rains are helpful, some ruinous. Some people are tall, some short. If *all* experiences were like this, we would not know what to expect next: each new situation would confront us as if no past situations had ever occurred, and years of experience would give us no hint about the way future events would occur. But nature is not like this; nature does contain regularities, difficult though they sometimes are to find.

Why are we interested in tracking down these regularities? Not, as a rule, because we enjoy contemplating them for their own sake but because we are interested in *prediction*. If we can rely on it that when we see a twister in the sky a tornado is approaching, then if we see one we may be able to take precautions by finding shelter before it strikes. If people who are in proximity to others who have colds get colds themselves, we may keep Johnny from getting a cold by keeping him temporarily away from Billy, who has a cold. We want some basis for prediction, so that we will not always be taken by surprise at the next series of events with which nature confronts us. And often when we can predict, we can also *control* the course of events; at least we are in a better position to control if we can first make a reliable prediction. We can reliably predict eclipses, but we cannot control their occurrence; but in many cases we can control as a result of our prediction: if we can predict reliably that after heavy rains the river will flood, we can get out of the way of the flood, or even (if it happens repeatedly) build a dam.

Most of the regularities that we find have many exceptions: they are not *invariants*. There is a certain regularity to children getting colds when they play with other children who already have colds, but it doesn't always happen that way. Chickens lay eggs and never cans of sardines, but how many eggs they do lay and at what intervals is extremely variable. Trees are more likely to fall during a severe storm, but they don't always: some do and some don't. The scientific enterprise could be described as the search for genuine invariants in nature, for regularities without exception, so that we are enabled to say, "Whenever such-and-such conditions are fulfilled, this kind of thing *always* happens." Many times we think we have found a genuine invariance, but we have not. We may have been sure that water always boils at 212° F., since we have tried it many times and it has always happened. But if we try it on a mountain top, we discover that the water there boils at a slightly lower temperature, so our hope that we had found a true invariance is upset. We try some more, however, and find that the temperature of water boiling depends not on the moisture in the air, not on the time of day, not on anything except the pressure of the surrounding air. We are thus able to say, "Water at the pressure found at sea level boils at 212°." Here at last we have a statement of genuine invariance; and behold, we have a *law of nature*.

Prescriptive v. descriptive laws.   The word "law" is ambiguous, and the ambiguity can be extremely misleading if we are not aware of it.

(1) In daily life we most often use the word "law" in the context of "passing a law," "the law prohibits you from . . .," and so on. Law in this sense is *prescriptive:* it is a rule of behavior imposed by a monarch or passed by a legislative body, and enforced by the legal machinery of the state. Laws in this sense are not propositions, because they cannot be false (it is, however, true or false *that* certain laws have been passed); they are, rather, imperatives, in effect "Do this," "Don't do that." The law does not state that anything *is* the case; rather, it issues a command, a *pre*scription, usually with penalties attached for failure to obey. But this is not the sense of "law" that is involved in speaking of laws of nature.

(2) Laws of nature are *descriptive:* they describe the way nature works. They do not prescribe anything: Kepler's laws of planetary motion do not prescribe to the planets that they should move in such-and-such orbits, with penalties invoked if they fail; rather, Kepler's laws *de*scribe how planets

actually *do* move. Laws in this sense describe certain uniformities that exist in the universe. Sometimes, for the sake of simplicity, they describe only what would happen under certain ideal conditions: Galileo's Law of Falling Bodies describes only the velocities at which bodies fall in a vacuum. But such a law is still descriptive: it describes our universe (not any logically possible universe), and it prescribes nothing. Only conscious beings can prescribe, since only they are capable of giving orders. But the uniformities of nature would still occur even if there were no human beings to describe them.

Several confusions can be avoided if we keep this distinction in mind. (1) "Laws should be obeyed." Whether or not you should obey all the laws of the land is a problem in ethics. But a law of nature is not the sort of thing you can obey or disobey, since it is not an order or command anyone has given. What could you do if someone said to you, "Obey the Law of Gravitation?" Your motions, along with those of stones and every particle of matter in the universe, are *instances* of this law; but since the law only tells us how matter *does* behave, and cannot prescribe how things *should* behave, you cannot be said either to obey or disobey it. A prescriptive law, moreover, could still be said to exist even if it were universally disobeyed. (2) "Where there's a law, there's a lawmaker." Again this applies clearly to prescriptive law: if a course of action is prescribed, someone must have prescribed it. But the same consideration does not apply to laws of nature. Did someone make the planets move in a certain way? The belief that someone designed the entire course of nature will be discussed on pp. 455–78; meanwhile, it is sufficient to observe that "law implies lawmaker" is not a necessary proposition in regard to descriptive law as it is with prescriptive law. (3) "Laws are discovered, not made." This applies only to descriptive laws: we *discover* how nature works, we do not make it work that way. But statute laws are made, devised, passed by human beings in positions of authority. Such laws do not exist but for human beings, but laws of nature would—that is, the uniformities of nature would exist whether men were there to observe them or not, although the *formulation* of these uniformities is the work of men.

Laws of nature constitute a smaller class of propositions than empirical statements in general. Any statement whose truth can be tested by observation of the world is an empirical proposition. "Some chickens lay eggs," "World War I lasted from 1914 to 1918," "She fell ill with pneumonia yesterday," and "New York City contains approximately 8 million residents" are all empirical statements. Indeed, most of the statements we utter in daily life are empirical statements. But none of these is a law of nature: laws of nature are a special class of empirical statements. Since laws of nature are the very basis of the empirical sciences—physics, chemistry, astronomy, geology, biology, psychology, sociology, economics —it is important that we be clear about the principal defining characteristics of laws of nature.

The meaning of "law of nature."   What, then, is a law of nature? What requirements must an empirical proposition fulfill in order to be a member of that select class of propositions which we call laws of nature?

1. It must be a true *universal* empirical proposition. To say that a proposition is universal is to say that it applies to *all* members of a given class without exception. That all iron rusts when exposed to oxygen is a universal proposition, but that *this* piece of iron rusts, or even that *some* iron rusts, is not a universal proposition.

a. A proposition about a single thing—"This piece of rock is metamorphic"—may be *material* for a law of nature, but it is not a law. Science does not consist of such singular propositions. Books on physics, the most developed of the empirical sciences, make no reference (except by way of example) to the motions of particular bodies, nor do chemistry books tell us about this piece of lead or that vessel of chlorine. But one does find many such references in psychology books (psychiatry division), for example in case-histories of patients. In this area few genuine laws have yet been discovered, so the psychologist must rely on individual case-histories as a means toward finding laws of human behavior. In this sense, psychology is still very much in a pre-scientific stage, a stage physics had already passed out of three centuries ago. But physics is in an advantageous position in that its laws are *simpler*—not in the sense of "easier to understand," for physics is more difficult for most students than any of the other empirical sciences, but in the sense that a law of physics can be stated in terms of the smallest number of conditions. In stating the velocity at which objects fall, one can ignore most of the universe: one can ignore the color of the object, its smell or taste, the temperature of the environment, the number of people watching the event, and so on for thousands of factors. By contrast, in dealing with human behavior it would be difficult to say what might *not* turn out to be relevant. A trivial event that occurred in your childhood, which neither you nor anyone else may remember, may still influence your behavior today and cause you to react differently to a given stimulus. The best we can do, usually, is to state certain general tendencies of human behavior, allowing for many exceptions. In psychology we hardly have laws at all, only tentative blueprints for laws; laws about human behavior that are both true and exceptionless have seldom been found.

The obvious examples of "laws of human nature" that come to mind all turn out on examination to be analytic. "People always act from the strongest motive" sounds like a plausible candidate for a law of human nature: people do a tremendous variety of things, but whatever they do, don't they always do what their strongest motive impels them to do? Waiving the fact that people don't always act from motives (they sometimes act from habit), the uncomfortable fact is that there seems to be no way of specifying what is meant by "strongest motive" except as the motive from which one acts. Thus: one acts from the motives from which one acts—true, but analytic.

Similarly, "People always do what they most want to do" is either synthetic but false or true but analytic, depending on what one means by the sentence: in a familiar sense, we all do things (like coming to class) that we don't want to do; we often perform unpleasant chores even though we hate them. If one says even in these cases that we always do what we want to do, we must mean "want" in some unusual sense—and indeed this sense is not far to seek: for the only criterion for knowing what we "really want" to do turns out to be what we actually do. So once again we have "We do what we do," which is true but analytic.

The universal proposition constituting the law must, then, be an empirical truth: it must not be analytic. "All A is B" is true in the case of "All triangles have three sides," but this statement, being analytic, is not a law of nature. Nor is "All gold is yellow," if being yellow is considered a defining characteristic of gold; in that case it would have to be yellow in order to be called gold in the first place, and the statement would be analytic. But if gold is defined by other means (such as atomic number), then it is a law of nature that everything having this property is also yellow. The B in "All A is B" must be connected with the A as a matter of contingent fact, not a priori or of necessity, if "All A is B" is to count as a law of nature.

b. Even true propositions about *some* members of a class are not usually considered laws of nature, though sometimes they are given the honorary title of "statistical laws." If 90 per cent of the A's there are are B's, there is a considerable regularity between the two, and the statement is far from useless as a basis for prediction. But, we are led to ask, if only 90 per cent of A's are B's and the remaining 10 per cent are not, why are the 90 per cent B's and not the others? What we want to find is some uniformity of a universal character underlying the statistical one. In daily life, however, we are constantly confronted by such regularities that are not universal: People with a cold usually have the sniffles, but not always; if one person hits another in the nose, the second person often gets a nosebleed, but not always. We have not yet formulated any universal statement about the precise conditions under which people get nosebleeds when struck on the nose, though we have a fairly adequate idea on what factors it depends. There is some regularity here (the harder you hit him, the more likely he is to get a nosebleed, and so on), but no invariant relationship.

2. These universal propositions are hypothetical in form. Now, universal propositions, both in logic and in science, are usually interpreted *hypothetically*—that is, as propositions of the "if . . . then . . ." form. "All iron rusts when exposed to oxygen" would thus be translated as *"If there is iron, it will rust when exposed to oxygen."* Thus formulated, the proposition does not tell us that there *is* any iron (it makes no existential claim), but only what happens under certain circumstances *if* there is. "All bodies freely falling in a vacuum accelerate at the rate of 16 feet per second per second" does not imply that there actually were or are any bodies falling in a vacuum. "At 99.9

per cent of the velocity of light, organisms grow old far more slowly than do those traveling at slower velocities" is a universal proposition that scientists believe to be true, but no one would declare that any organism is now traveling at that velocity.

The hypothetical interpretation of laws, however, can get us into trouble. The hypothetical "If p is true, then q is true" in logic is equivalent to "It is not the case that p is true, but q is false." For example, "If there is friction, then there is heat" (a law of nature) would be translated "It is not the case that there is friction but no heat." But now let us take the proposition "All unicorns are white." This is translatable into "It is not the case that there is a unicorn that is not white." And since there are no unicorns, the proposition is true: there are no nonwhite unicorns, for the excellent reason that there are no unicorns at all. Moreover, by the same reasoning, "All unicorns are green" would also be true, since there are no nongreen unicorns. When p is false, then anything whatever follows, so we can put what we like into q.

Of course, "All unicorns are white" would never be counted as a law of nature; yet it is a universal proposition, construed as a hypothetical. Why would the proposition about unicorns not be considered a law, whereas the propositions about friction and organisms at almost the velocity of light are so considered? The difference lies in the fact that there is evidence from *other* laws that these laws are true. Indeed, the proposition about aging more slowly as one approaches the velocity of light is a logical consequence of (deducible from) Einstein's relativistic laws of time, whereas the proposition about unicorns is connected with no laws at all.

But even this is not sufficient to characterize laws of nature.

3. There are many true, universal propositions of hypothetical form that do not pass as laws of nature. Suppose I were to say, "All the dogs in this kennel are black," and that my statement were true: it would still not qualify as a law of nature. It is limited to a definite area in space and time—this kennel today. Even if its scope were broader ("All the dogs I've ever had in my kennels are black"), it still would say nothing about *all* dogs, or even all dogs of a certain breed. But if I say that all crows are black, I mean that all crows, *wherever* they may be, and *whenever* they may exist or have existed or have yet to exist, are, were, and will be black. (Blackness is not here considered defining of crows, else the proposition would be analytic.) The law is "open-ended": it has an infinite range, both in time and in space. This does not mean that there is an infinite number of crows—nor indeed that there are any crows at all—but that it is an *open class,* with *no strictures of time and space* operating to limit the scope of the law. There is no time or place at which the law will not hold true: considerations of when and where are irrelevant to the application of the proposition. By contrast, the proposition about the dogs in my kennel will not pass as a law because (1) though universal in form, the universality is restricted to a specifically delimited time and space; (2) the number of things covered by the proposition is not only finite, but this

finiteness may be inferred from the terms in the proposition itself; this is not so for Kepler's laws of planetary motion, for example: though there are a finite number of planets, this fact cannot be deduced from the law; and (3) the evidence for the proposition exhausts its domain of application—the proposition is simply a summative report of what *has been* observed to be the case.

Since laws of nature apply to all places and all times, their claim extends into the future. This is perhaps the most important single feature of laws, for it enables them to be made the basis for prediction. If the proposition merely read "All crows thus far have turned out to be black," one might say "So what?"—we could not deduce any predictions from it; but if we say that *all* A's, no matter when or where, are B's, we can deduce from it, plus the proposition that this is an A, that it will also be a B. (There are problems about this that we shall consider in the next section, on the problem of induction.)

4. But even when all these conditions are met, a proposition may not be classified as a law of nature. "All crows are black" is unrestricted in time, place, and number of individuals in its domain of application. Yet it would generally not be counted as a law, because the only evidence for it is direct evidence, and a proposition is not usually accorded the status of a law unless there is some indirect evidence for it. This requires a word of explanation.

The laws of any science are not viewed in independence of one another. Together they form a vast body or system of laws, with each law fitting into a system including many other laws, each mutually reinforcing the others. The laws that scientists are most loath to abandon are those that form such an integral part of a system of laws that the abandonment of the one law would require the abandonment or alteration of a large number of other laws in the system. Thus an observation that directly confirms one law indirectly confirms a group of other laws, because of the interconnection of the laws in a system. (Physics is, again, the most systematized science. Biology was not very highly systematic until the present century: until then, it was for the most part a classificatory science, recording the properties of various species of creatures but discerning no interconnectedness among them. It was in much the state of chemistry before the rise of atomic theory. We shall have more to say about theory very shortly.)

"All crows are mortal" is supported by much indirect evidence: the mortality of organisms in general, the biochemical deterioration of tissue, increase in auto-allergenic response, and so on. But "All crows are black" seems to relate to no other significant regularities, of either greater or lesser generality. A crow that was not black would change no other laws known to us; but a crow that was immortal (or even one that lived a thousand years) would excite considerable scientific surprise, because it might force us to reconsider the many other laws (about deterioration of tissue, etc.) with which it is interlocked. Whether or not something is called a law, then, depends to a large extent on how deeply embedded it is in a wider system of laws. A true universal proposition for which there was no indirect evidence would have little fundamentality in science: it could easily be abandoned without effect on the rest of the system. But "All metals are good conductors" is so fundamentally tied to other laws (of atomic structure) that a counter-instance would have far-reaching consequences.

5. Even when all this has been said, many propositions that satisfy all these criteria are often denied the status of laws. The difference seems to lie in the proposition's degree of *generality*. "All metals are good thermal conductors" and "Silver is a good thermal conductor" are both universal propositions, since both apply to all members of the given class; but the first statement is more general than the second, for it covers a wider scope. Universal propositions whose degree of generality is greater are more likely to pass as laws; thus the statement about metals is considered a law, but the statement about silver is not. While "All rare-earth metals have higher melting points than the halogens" may pass as a law, one would not likely hear the fact that tungsten melts at 3,370° C. referred to as a law but only as a fact.

Sometimes one of these conditions works against another, and the outcome is not certain. Einstein refers to the constancy of the velocity of light in a vacuum as a law of nature, and this is referred to as a law, in spite of its limited generality, because of the fundamentality of this item in the system of physical laws. On the other hand, while the mass of the electron is an elemental fact of physical science, its precise value remains largely independent of the main body of scientific theory, and therefore it is not accorded the status of a law.

Laws v. theories.   Not long after we have observed certain invariant relations in nature, we are led to construct theories to explain them. The distinction between a theory and a law is somewhat vague, but it is very important: in general, we *construct* or devise theories, but we *discover* laws of nature. A scientific theory always contains some term that does not denote anything that we can directly observe. If we can observe something only through a telescope or microscope, we are still said to observe it. But if there are no conditions under which we can observe it, it is a theoretical entity; and when the theory-word is a part of a statement, that statement is said to be a theory. Thus the proposition that there are protons and electrons is a theory. These entities cannot be observed, though we do observe many things that are presumed to be effects of them. Statements about protons and electrons (together with their progeny, such as neutrons and neutrinos) are theory, not law. This belief in the "ultimate constituents of matter" is perhaps the most comprehensive and thoroughly worked-out theory to be found in the empirical sciences.

How did such a theory arise? It began in ancient times with some rather obvious observations. From time immemorial, certain empirical truths had been observed that seemed to call for an explanation in terms of what could not be observed. The stone steps wear away bit by bit, year after year. Put a few drops of berry-juice into a glass of water, and in a moment the entire liquid has become red. Or put some sugar into it, and immediately the sweet taste pervades the entire liquid. How can these and countless other things be explained unless by the existence of very small particles, invisible to the unaided eye? The stone steps are composed of these particles, which wear away gradually one by one until after years of wear we can finally notice the difference. The berry juice is composed of very small particles that spread throughout the entire liquid and color it red. The same with the sugar we dissolve in water, which makes the entire liquid taste sweet. Besides, the things we observe must be composed of something. I can cut this piece of chalk in half and rub against it with my fingers, with the result that pieces of it color my fingers white. But these small bits (it was reasoned) must in turn be composed of smaller ones, and these in turn of still smaller ones. At the end of this process, however, there must be particles that cannot be split any further, the ultimate constituents of matter (atoms, from the Greek *"atomos,"* meaning "unsplittable"). All the things we see and touch are composed of these very small particles that can no longer be subdivided. We cannot observe them with our eyes; but if we assume that they exist, we can account for an enormous number of different things that we do observe.

So went the reasoning of Democritus (born about 460 B.C.) and Lucretius (ca. 96–55 B.C.). Their atomic theory was primitive, but the principle involved was no different from modern theories: the unobserved was invoked to explain the observed. More refined atomic theories today have explained countless phenomena undreamed of by the ancients: why element A combines with elements B and C but not with D and E (and some with none at all), why certain elements and compounds have the properties that they do, why they evaporate or ignite at the temperatures they do, freeze at other temperatures, and so on. Virtually all the facts of modern chemistry have been explained in terms of atomic theory. But it is theory, not observed fact. (Certain complex molecules have now been seen through electron microscopes, and thus they no longer belong to theory. But atoms and electrons, together with the other and more minute "particles" that physics now deals in, remain unobservable.)

Do these tiny "particles" exist? Are they particles at all, like tiny marbles, or should they be called something else? There is scarcely a physicist who would deny that these entities exist, and that it is only the hypothesis that they exist that explains why certain observed facts are as they are. It has sometimes been suggested that they do not really exist but are simply "convenient fictions" by means of which we explain a diverse range of phenomena. But if they are only convenient fictions, how is it that the tremendous variety of occurrences they explain regularly happen as they do? Would it not be one vast coincidence if there are not really atoms and electrons that have the explanatory properties we attribute to them? Why should things behave just *as if* they are composed of very tiny particles if no such particles actually exist?

Some scientific theories, however, do involve concepts that are merely convenient fictions. Freudian psychology has as its first premise that there is a vast reservoir of *unconscious* mental events consisting of three departments: id, superego, and ego. These are theory, since no such inhabitants of the human psyche can be observed. Yet in postulating these entities, Freudian psychology endeavors to explain a vast number of psychological phenomena (mental conflicts, neuroses and psychoses, dreams, slips of the tongue, moods, depression) on the basis of a comprehensive theory involving these concepts. The id is the vast reservoir of human desires, most of them prohibited, so that they are repressed from the conscious into the unconscious; the superego is the prohibitor or nay-sayer, which refuses the granting of many of these desires; the ego is the adjudicator of the conflicting claims of these two parties, providing a defense for one or the other party in response to its claims. When one becomes acquainted with the literature of psychoanalysis, one is struck by the enormous variety of explanations of human behavior that are provided by this conceptual framework. Yet no one believes that there are really three people inside one's head; it is just as if there were, but of course there are not. Here the theory is an elaborate "as if," yet the theory has very great explanatory power (though it is not the only theory that attempts to explain human behavior, as the existence of numerous and conflicting schools of psychiatry indicates). Similarly, when one speaks of valence in chemistry, it is just "as if" the atoms had little hooks on them, one on hydrogen (for example) and two on oxygen, so that the two hooks on an atom of oxygen latch into the one hook on each of two atoms of hydrogen to form H_2O, or water. Yet no one believes that the atoms really have little hooks (but perhaps they have something like them?).

In either case, however, it is important to remember that the theory contains more (has more content) than the observed facts that are explained by means of it. A theory is not just a summary of facts already observed; it is not merely a shorthand way of referring to a diverse collection of facts: it involves concepts from which new and hitherto unknown facts can be inferred. This is as true of the "as-if" theory in psychoanalysis as it is of the "really-exists" theory of atomic structure. A theory that was merely a *summary* of the observed facts already known would have no explanatory power whatever.

Some statements we make *are* merely "summary-statements." When we say that there is a current in the wire, it is plausible to analyze this statement (though some have contested this) as a statement about a diverse group of observable phenomena: the wire affects voltmeters, gives us a shock when we touch it, throws off sparks, runs batteries, and so on. Saying that there is a current in the wire *is* just saying that the wire does these various things. But theories in science are not of this kind: a theory must always explain more facts than it was invoked to explain; the scientific potency of a theory is in direct proportion to the quantity and (more important) the *range* of facts it explains, particularly those that had not been known when the theory was devised. In this respect, both the atomic theory and the theory of the unconscious have remarkable explanatory power.

Hypotheses.   It is important in this connection to distinguish theories from hypotheses. In daily life these two words are used interchangeably, but in science they are distinguished. Theories are continuous with laws: they both involve general statements about some aspect of the world, differing only in whether their key terms refer to what is observable in the world. But a hypothesis is not a universal proposition at all; it is a particular statement that *in conjunction with* laws or theories can be used to explain certain occurrences. Thus we speak of atomic *theory,* but we speak of various *hypotheses* to explain the origin of the solar system. We devise hypotheses every day of our lives: we arise in the morning and notice that the street is wet, so we devise the hypothesis that rain has fallen during the night; we press the starter of the car and hear that ominous growling sound, followed by silence, and we devise the hypothesis that the battery is dead; we see the dog hovering around his dish and showing signs of restlessness, and immediately we devise the hypothesis that he is hungry and hasn't been fed; we see that Johnny is doubled up with stomach pains, and that the entire mincemeat pie is gone, and we devise the hypothesis that he has the stomach-ache from eating the entire pie. A hypothesis is a particular fact (or presumed fact) that, if true, explains, *together with certain laws or theories,* why something is as it is. A hypothesis may be improbable or even outlandish (such as the astrological hypothesis that you are due for bad luck today because the planets are in a certain conjunction), or it may be so probable that you take it as virtually certain (such as the hypothesis that the streets are wet because it has rained during the night). The degree of probability has nothing to do with whether it is a hypothesis, only with whether it is an acceptable or satisfactory hypothesis.

Moreover, a hypothesis is not concerned with something you have observed: if you have seen the rain falling, you would not call "Rain has fallen" a hypothesis but an observed fact. Normally, however, a hypothesis is about something observ*able:* rainfall, the dog not having nourishment for 24 hours, Johnny eating the pie—all these could have been observed, even if they were not. But some hypotheses do involve the unobservable, such as "The ominous feeling I have is a warning from God that I shouldn't do this."

Both law-theories and hypotheses have their part to play in the main function of the scientific enterprise, *explanation.*

Explanation

Scientific explanation.   The great advantage of scientific theories is that they possess enormous explanatory power. Without them, biology would still be in the classificatory stage, modern advances in genetics would be impossible, and physics would still be very nearly where it was three centuries ago. Let us now try to clarify just what a scientific explanation is. This topic is of special importance since we shall be employing the concept of explanation in the coming chapters.

Why-questions.   "Why" normally introduces a request for an explanation. But "Why?" is an ambiguous question: it may be the request for a *reason* or the request for an *explanation*. When you ask me why I believe a proposition is true, you are asking me to give reasons in support of my belief. Reasons for *p* are propositions that, if true, make belief in *p* more plausible. Reasons are propositions that are given in support of other propositions, and if they are good reasons they do make *p* more probable (that is what is meant in calling them good reasons). One gives reasons for holding beliefs, or believing something to be true. On the other hand, explanation is of events, processes, happenings in the course of nature: one explains why iron rusts, why rivers flood, why carbon monoxide kills, and so on. (This is true of explaining *why* certain things happen; we also speak of explaining in other contexts, however: we explain in the sense of making something clearer—"explain what that passage in the poem means"—and we explain where, when, how, how much. Explanation of why events occur, which is what is involved in scientific explanation, is only one of several kinds of explanation.) If a person is rational, the reason he holds a certain belief also explains why he holds it: he wants to believe what is true, so the explanation and the reason coincide. It is not always so, however: the reasons a person may give for belief in a benevolent God (the propositions he may give to support it) may be various arguments for God's existence, such as we shall describe in Chapter 7; but the explanation of his having such belief may have nothing to do with the arguments—the explanation may be that he wants a father-substitute or a protector in a cold, harsh world. The giving of reasons, then, is not the same thing as the giving of explanations, though the two are often confused with one another because they are both answers, though in different senses, to the ambiguous question "Why?"

We shall be concerned here only with the sense of "why" in which why-questions are requests for explanations—specifically, explanations of occurrences in nature. In this area we can ask why a specific event occurred (why did the pipes in the basement burst last night? why did the window break?) or why a certain *kind* of event always occurs as it does (why do balloons rise? why does iron rust?). The pattern of explanation is somewhat different in the two cases.

When we ask for the explanation of a particular event, such as "Why did the pipes burst?" the explanation includes (1) certain *laws* of nature (such as that water expands when it freezes) and (2) certain particular facts (such as that the temperature dropped below the freezing point in the basement last night). We have to have both of these in order to explain the event. The laws and particular facts involved may be numerous: we need to know not only that water expands when it freezes (law) but that the pipes were filled with water (particular fact), that the strength of the expanding ice was greater than that of the resisting pipes (particular fact), and that when this happens the retaining vessel breaks since its contents must have someplace to go (law). The particular facts may be known from direct *observation* or may be a *hypothesis:* if we were in the basement and watched the thermometer and felt the cold, we can be said to have observed the particular condition for ourselves; but if we were sleeping soundly upstairs all the while but noticed how cold it was when we got up in the morning, the below-freezing temperature of the basement during the night was a hypothesis. The hypothesis alone (it was freezing in the basement) does not explain the event (pipes bursting) without the law (water expands on freezing), nor does the law alone explain the event without the particular fact (observed, or inferred by hypothesis) that the temperature in the basement dropped to below freezing during the night. In the same way, the breaking of the window requires reference to a particular fact or condition (someone threw a rock at it) and a law (about the fragility of glass and the mass and velocity of the object striking it).

But sometimes it is not particular events that we wish to explain, but laws of nature themselves. Why do balloons rise? Why does iron rust? Why does sugar dissolve in water? Why does water expand when it freezes? We explain these laws by means of other laws and theories. Why do balloons rise in air if they contain hydrogen or helium? Because hydrogen and helium are lighter than the mixture of oxygen, nitrogen, etc., constituting our atmosphere (law), and a gas that is lighter per unit of volume than another gas will go upward (law). Why does water, unlike most liquids, expand when it freezes? Because of the crystalline structure of the water molecule (theory). Why does iron rust? Because molecules of iron combine with the oxygen in the air (theory), and the resultant compound iron oxide forms (law). Both theories and laws are normally involved in explaining laws; certainly we cannot go far in explaining laws without reference to theory.

Sometimes we telescope the process—explaining events and then explaining laws—by mentioning a law and nothing else, thus obscuring the pattern of explanation. "Why does this wire conduct electricity?" "All copper conducts electricity." But the full explanation would be "This wire is made of copper (particular fact) and copper is a conductor of electricity (law)." The next question would then be, "Why does copper (unlike some other things) conduct electricity?" and the answer to this would take us into physical theory, of both electricity and the crystal structure of metals.

Whether we explain particular occurrences or laws, reference to laws or theories is always involved in their explanation; and the law or theory must be one we already accept, else we will not accept the explanation. "Why doesn't the red liquid mix with the transparent liquid?" "Because the red liquid is colored water, and the transparent liquid is gasoline." The law involved here is that water and gasoline do not mix, and our acceptance of the explanation depends on our acceptance of this law. If the answer "Because it's red" had been given instead, we would not have accepted it as an explanation, because we know of no law of nature according to which transparent liquids will not mix with red ones.

Sometimes an explanation that we accept involves laws only in a very loose sense—a rough-and-ready generalization that is true much of the time but does not hold true for all cases. "Why does Billy have a cold?" "He's been playing with Bobby, and Bobby has a cold." It is not a law that those in contact with others who have colds always get colds themselves; but there is some degree of uniformity here, sufficient to make us accept the explanation. We could, of course, go on to say, "But Johnny also played with Bobby, and Johnny didn't get a cold," and then we would have to try to find some statement of the conditions under which people always get colds. Meanwhile, we tend to accept the generalization as an explanation of the facts. Similarly, if we ask, "Why were so many of the members absent from the meeting tonight?" and are told, "There was a conflict with a meeting of another organization to which most of our members also belong," we accept this as an explanation, although there is no law here, merely the necessary truth that people can't be in two places at the same time and the generalization that people who preferred meeting B to meeting A, or felt a stronger obligation to go to B, would tend to go to meeting B.

Explanation and prediction.   The explanation of an event or of a law must explain why this event occurred rather than some other one. "That which explains everything explains nothing." Suppose that someone asked why water expands when it freezes, and the answer was given, "God wills everything that happens, and God has willed that water has this property, and so it does." No scientist would accept this as an explanation, nor would we in daily life. The scientist might indeed believe that God wills everything that happens, as well as all the laws involved, and yet as a scientist he would want to know why water expands on freezing whereas most liquids do not. We would want, in other words, an explanation that goes beyond the immediate event to be explained, one that explains other events or laws as well, including some whose existence was not suspected when the explanation was given. The expansion of water on freezing explains not only the water pipes' bursting but also the cracking of the pitcher of water left on the window sill on a cold night and the formation of ice on the top of lakes and ponds rather than on the bottom. If we know that water expands on freezing, we know why all these various things occur, and why they would not happen if the pitcher or the pipes had been filled with kerosene instead.

It is sometimes said that the test of an explanatory principle (law or theory) is that it should have *predictive* power, enabling us to make accurate predictions on the basis of it. Since laws explain many other things besides the events they were invoked to explain, and since many of these other occurrences will quite naturally be in the future, the laws would consequently explain these also. Knowing that water expands on freezing, we can predict the conditions under which water pipes will burst in the future, and many other things. But some laws known to us are very well established and yet have virtually no predictive power. Geologists know quite well the laws involved in the occurrence of earthquakes, yet attempts to predict when and where the next earthquake will occur have not been particularly successful. This is not because the laws are not known but because the specific facts (initial conditions) are not known: we do not know enough about what is going on far below the earth's surface, what stresses and strains, rock faults, inequality of weight distribution, and so on exist at what places in the earth's core. The laws have explanatory power, but they must be combined with a statement about particular conditions if they are to yield a prediction.

On the other hand, Newton's Law of Universal Gravitation is a law with remarkable explanatory power. It brings the fall of an apple to the ground together with the motions of the planets in the solar system and the furthest star in the heavens under one mighty generalization. On the basis of it (together with other laws and statements about particular states of affairs, or initial conditions) one is enabled to predict such diverse phenomena as eclipses of the sun and the evolution of galaxies into a spiral structure. Similarly, the reason why laws about electrons and similar unobservables are so universally accepted among scientists is that, as explanations, they have such remarkable predictive power. On the basis of certain laws of atomic structure, one can predict what many of the chemical properties of substances will be, such as density and ability to combine with other substances, even before they are discovered.

Unsatisfactory explanations.   In daily life, however, we are often presented with so-called explanations that explain nothing. "Why do these pills put people to sleep?" "Because of their soporific power." This may sound impressive until we realize that "soporific power" means nothing more or less than the power of putting people to sleep. The so-called explanation does not tell us what we presumably wanted to know: what there is in this pill that causes it to put people to sleep. "Why does hydrogen combine with oxygen to form water?" "Because hydrogen has an affinity for water." But an affinity for X is only a tendency to combine with X, and the explanation does not tell us why hydrogen has this tendency: it has only repeated the question in other words. "Why does the mother cat take care of her kittens?" "Because she has a maternal instinct." This one is not entirely empty, for it tells us something, that the behavior is not learned; but apart from that it tells us nothing. No matter what an animal does, we can say that the creature has an instinct for that type of behavior. But the important question remains unanswered: what is there in the physiological constitution of the cat that causes it to exhibit this maternal behavior? Something about its genes and chromosomes, perhaps? This is an extremely difficult question, but at any rate we should be clear that the reference to instinct tells us virtually nothing. Maybe robins have a "migratory instinct"—that is, they do migrate—but this does not tell us why robins do and not sparrows. Instead of information, we are given merely words: "instinct," "affinity," "power," "faculty," and so on.

Suppose your watch does not work, and someone says, "There's a gremlin in it." If such a creature could be seen inside the watch every time it does not work, this would indeed be an interesting fact about nature. Perhaps then the little creature has been doing the mischief every time the radio doesn't work. But since no such creature can be seen, touched, etc., how does its existence count as an explanation? How is an undetectable gremlin different from no gremlin at all? Between an undetectable gremlin and no gremlin at all, which would you choose? Is there anything to choose between? Belief in a gremlin has no explanatory value whatever. It seems to be a matter of what label you want to paste on the back of the watch to remind you of exactly the same characteristics of the watch.[1] You may say, every time the watch doesn't work, "That gremlin is at it again," but since the gremlin cannot be detected in any way, what is this but a picturesque way of saying that the watch doesn't work?

The gremlin is unobservable; but it is not only the unobservability of the gremlin that keeps it from having explanatory value. Electrons too are unobservable, but they have remarkable explanatory power; from the belief in electrons we can deduce many consequences, and the occurrence of these consequences (which we *can* observe) serves to confirm the theory. But in the case of the gremlin-theory this condition is not fulfilled. If we assume such a gremlin, we cannot explain by means of it anything other than the fact to be explained (the watch not working). We cannot deduce from it any *further* consequences. The theory is impotent as an explanation. Even the simple statement that the radio doesn't work because the plug has been pulled out has some predictive value: that if we put the plug back in, the radio will work again. But there is nothing *beyond the watch not working* that we can talk about in the case of the gremlin-theory. There are no creatures we can chase out of the watch to make it work again. All we can do is what we would have done without the gremlin-theory: take the watch apart and attempt to repair it. The watch-not-working does make a difference to our experience, but the gremlin-theory makes no difference to our experience beyond the fact that the watch doesn't work.

Teleological, or purposive, explanations.   Nothing has been said thus far about explanation in terms of purpose, yet this is the oldest type of explanation. Storms and other natural catastrophes were thought to be explained by the wrath of gods or other beings who controlled these events,

[1] John Wisdom, *Other Minds* (Oxford: Blackwell, 1949), Chapter 1.

and the gods were believed to do these things *in order* to wreak vengeance on human beings, or bring them back into line, or display their power, and so on. We no longer use such explanations for natural events, but we do explain events in the human realm by bringing in purpose: "Why did he eat a whole pie in five minutes?" "Someone bet him $100 that he couldn't do it."

The word "purpose" is somewhat tricky, and we shall do well to track down its most important senses.

1. The most common use of "purpose" is in the sense of conscious intention by living beings, particularly human beings. "Why did you go downtown today?" "I wanted to do some shopping." That was your purpose in going, that is why you went. And, assuming that you are able to do the act in question, the fact that this was your purpose (conscious intent) explains why you did what you did.

2. We also explain some human behavior by invoking *unconscious* purposes. The man did not consciously desire unhappiness in his marriage, but he unconsciously selected a partner in such a way as to provide the maximum irritation and friction for himself, which, psychiatrists would say, is exactly what he wanted—not consciously but unconsciously. Many otherwise baffling bits of behavior can be explained in terms of unconscious drives.

3. "What's the purpose of that machine?" "To stamp labels on cans." "What is the purpose of the hammer?" "To pound nails." And so on. Here the machine, not being a conscious being, has no conscious purpose—and no unconscious ones either, since the unconscious is present only in beings who have consciousness (in general, the unconscious material is what has been repressed from the conscious mind). The machine has a purpose only in a derived sense: it has not consciousness itself, but it has been devised in such a way as to serve the purposes of conscious beings. Instead of asking "What is the purpose of the machine?" we should ask, "What was the purpose of the person who constructed the machine?" Whatever that purpose was we call the purpose of the machine itself.

4. Thus far, every time there was a purpose there was a conscious being to have it. But there is a much-diluted sense of "purpose" in which no consciousness is involved at all. "What is the purpose of the heart?" one might ask, and receive the answer, "To pump blood through the body." How is the word "purpose" being used here? The heart is not a conscious being, and it has no purpose in the sense of intention, conscious or unconscious. Nor was it an object of human making or manufacture: it does not reflect our purpose in making it since we did not make it. Perhaps then the statement is a disguised theological statement about God's purpose in making the heart? It might be so used by some, but the question can equally well be asked by someone who does not believe in God or does not believe that God designed the human organism. When medical researchers ask questions of this kind, they are not asking theological questions. They are asking, simply, what the

function of the organ is. What is the function of the heart in relation to the rest of the organism? What does it do? Strictly speaking, this is not a question about purpose at all, and it is misleading to use the word "purpose" in referring to it.

Purposive explanations are acceptable only when there are conscious beings who can conceive purposes and carry them out. Since most explanations in the physical sciences do not involve the presence of conscious beings, there can be no answer to "why" questions in these areas in terms of purpose. Why do balloons rise? Why does iron rust? Why do pipes burst? These questions are answered in terms of physical laws, and these laws involve no reference to purposes. Only when there are laws about human purposes can we give explanations of events in terms of such purposes; and such laws are very rough-and-ready ones indeed, such as that people ordinarily do what they intend to do unless they are unable to do so.

Sometimes people (particularly children) are not satisfied with explanations unless they receive some answer in terms of purpose. Since this is the type of explanation most familiar to everyone in his own consciousness, one tends to assume that all explanation must be of this form. "Why did he die?" "Well, the car hit him as he was crossing the street and. . . ." "No, I mean *why* did he die, not *how* did he die." If a complete account of what happened and the laws involved does not satisfy the questioner, what he is probably seeking (perhaps without being clearly aware of it himself) is some explanation in terms of purpose: in this case, perhaps, a divine purpose or intent in bringing about the person's death. Whether such explanations—in terms of divine purposes—are ever true is a question we cannot pursue here but shall touch on in Chapter 7. Here we can only remark that *if* there are such divine purposes, and we can know this, then the events in question can be explained in terms of purpose; otherwise not. It remains true in either case that whenever there is a purpose, there must be someone to have that purpose.

Description v. explanation.   "Science only tells us *how* things happen; it cannot tell us *why* things happen." This popular notion has very little to recommend it. Science tells us why iron rusts, why balloons rise, why the pipes burst, and so on; it gives us an explanation of these occurrences in terms of laws and theories, and that is what is meant in science by an explanation. If this isn't an explanation, what is? True, it describes how things happen; but in showing how things happen, it tells us why they happen: it brings the events under laws. If someone says that science does not explain why this event occurs, what would count as an explanation? Perhaps the critic has in mind the fact that the question "Why?" cannot always be answered in teleological or purposive terms, and he is using the question as a request for purposive explanation. In that case, science cannot tell us why the lighter gases rise, but neither can anything else—indeed, he would fall into self-contradiction if he granted that a purpose implies a purposer and that no purposer is involved here.

Ultimate laws.   We can explain an event by means of laws, and we can often explain the law by means of other laws or theories, and sometimes these in turn by other laws and theories. But sooner or later, our knowledge comes to a stop: we cannot explain the law or theory by means of anything else.

We explain the bursting of the pipes by the law that water expands on freezing; let us assume that we can explain the expansion of water on freezing by some theory about the structure of the water molecule. Why does the water molecule have this structure? Is this an instance of some more basic law or theory? Let us suppose that it is; then what about *that* law or theory—how is it to be explained? We cannot explain it. We say, "That's the way things are—this is just an ultimate law (theory) about the universe. We can explain other things in terms of it, but *it* we cannot explain. It's just a 'brute fact' things are this way." When we have traced explanations down to certain elementary structures or elementary processes, we do not seem able to go any further; the fact is that the thing has this structure, or that processes of this or that type govern change, and this explains why things have the properties they do, singly and in combination; but we cannot explain why they have them. Another example: When light of one wave-length impinges on the retina of my eye, I see yellow; when the light is of slightly longer wave-length, I see orange; and so on. But I cannot give any explanation why the light of these wave-lengths should cause me to have the specific visual experience that I do when I see yellow. The correlation between the light and the visual experience seems to be sheer "brute fact."

It would seem, then, that there are certain basic or ultimate laws of the universe, basic invariants in nature that cannot be explained by means of anything else. We can never be sure, however, that any law that actually confronts us is basic; tomorrow it may be explained by means of another. It was long thought that Newton's Law of Universal Gravitation, though it had remarkable explanatory power, could not itself be explained, and was therefore an ultimate law of nature; but Einstein's theory of relativity makes Newton's law a special case of a much wider theory. We cannot be sure at any given time whether the laws thus far considered ultimate really are so.

If a certain law (or theory) is really an ultimate one, then to request an explanation of it is self-contradictory. To explain a law is to place it in a context or network of wider and more inclusive laws and theories; a basic or ultimate law is by definition one of which this cannot be done; therefore to ask of an admittedly basic law that it be explained is to deny in effect that it is a basic law. It is a request for explanation in a situation where by one's own premise no more explaining can be done. One always explains in terms of *something else;* it is logically impossible to explain when there is no something else in terms of which to do the explaining.

Exercises

1. Mathematics is sometimes called a science, but it is not an empirical science. Why not?

2. Why are astrology, alchemy, and phrenology not considered sciences? Should geography be considered a science? (Does it have laws?) What about engineering and medicine?

3. Which of the following are theoretical concepts, and which refer only to things that can be observed? (a) gravitation (in physics); (b) mass (in physics); (c) light-waves (in physics); (d) convection currents (in physics); (e) quasars (in astronomy); (f) cosmic rays (in physics and astronomy); (g) magnetic fields (in physics); (h) isotopes (in chemistry); (i) gene (in biology); (j) the average American voter (in sociology); (k) I. Q. (in psychology); (l) pent-up aggression (in psychology).

4. Keeping in mind the distinction between descriptive laws and prescriptive laws, evaluate the following comments:
   a. We shouldn't disobey laws of nature.
   b. Laws of nature have pre-ordained what I shall do tomorrow.
   c. When there's a law, there must be a lawgiver.
   d. We don't make laws, we find them.
   e. Laws of nature control the universe.
   f. Our behavior must conform to psychological laws.

5. Which of the following propositions would you consider to be laws of nature? Why?
   a. Iron rusts when exposed to oxygen.
   b. Gold is malleable.
   c. All human beings are mortal. (They die at some time or other.)
   d. All white tomcats with blue eyes are deaf.
   e. When organisms reproduce, the offspring is always of the same species.
   f. All the crows in the United States are black.
   g. All oceans contain water.
   h. One-third of American voters belong to the Republican Party.

6. Which of the following why-questions are requests for a reason, and which are requests for an explanation? Can any of them be construed in both ways?
   a. Why did the water boil? Because I lighted a burner under it.
   b. Why did you flatter the boss? Because I wanted to get a raise.
   c. Why do you think it will rain this afternoon? Because dark clouds are gathering.
   d. Why do you think there won't be another world war in our century? Because with present nuclear weapons no nation would dare to risk it.

7. Evaluate the following as explanations. In the case of unsatisfactory explanations, show what makes them unsatisfactory.
   a. Why do birds build nests? Because they want to have a place to lay their eggs and bring up their young.
   b. Why do birds build nests? Because it's their instinct to do so.
   c. Why do most creatures lay more eggs than can possibly develop into full-grown offspring? Because they want to protect the species from extermination by competing organisms, cold, storms, and other destructive agencies.

d. Why did the Allies win World War II? Because they wanted to, and people generally do what they want to do.

e. Why does this substance become lighter (per unit of volume) as it becomes hotter? Because it contains an invisible substance, phlogiston, and the more of this it contains, the hotter it becomes; phlogiston is so light that an object is heavier for losing it.

f. Why did he arrive last night? Because God willed it so, and whatever God wills happens.

g. Why did that object sink in water? Because it is made of iron.

h. Why did you and I happen to meet downtown today? Because we both wanted to be at the same store when it opened this morning.

i. Why does this watch stop several times every day? Because there is a devil in it.

j. Why did you win the thousand dollar prize in the lottery? Because some people have all the luck.

k. Why did that door open just now? Because some door-opening force caused it to do so.

8. "Why did she stab him?" Answer #1: "Because she hated him intensely and wanted more than anything else to see him dead." Answer #2: "Because, as a result of the motion of certain particles of matter in her brain, electro-chemical impulses were discharged along certain neuronic pathways, stimulating certain efferent nerves, activating the muscles in her hand and arm, causing them to move in a certain way . . ." Do these two explanations conflict with each other? Does purposive explanation necessarily conflict with such "mechanical" explanations as given in Answer #2? How do you conceive the relation between them? Are they both parts of the whole explanation?

9. Examine the following dialogue, noting what you consider to be its good points as well as its bad points.

A. Did Newton discover any hitherto undiscovered empirical facts?

B. Yes, he discovered gravitation.

A. But we didn't need Newton to tell us that apples fall.

B. He explained *why* apples fall. They fall because of gravitation.

A. But gravitation isn't an explanation of *why* they fall. It is simply a fancy word stating a familiar fact, namely that things *do* fall. It is not an explanation, but simply a re-description in more general terms of the familiar fact that they do fall. (Compare the physician's statement that you are in this physical condition because you are run down.) What *is* gravitation but the fall of apples and the like?

B. Ah, you have admitted my point: gravitation is, indeed, much more than the fall of apples—it is the fall of apples *and the like*. Newton connected apples in orchards with stars in heaven. He brought seemingly disconnected events together under a general law, and to do this is to have explained them. Of course, if you think animistically of gravitation as a pull exerted as if by some super-giant, you are mistaken. Gravitation is not a pull; the word is simply a name for the fact that matter behaves in a certain definite and specifiable way. But the law that it does behave in this way is a genuine explanation, and it explains a vast number of phenomena, including the revolution of planets and the fall of apples.

10. We can explain some laws by deriving them from other laws; the uniformities referred to in the laws in the first group are as they are because of the uniformities described in the laws in the second group. But what about the laws in the second group—the basic, or underived, laws? Does it make sense

to ask why the uniformities described in these are as they are? What would you do with the question "Why are the ultimate laws of nature as they are?"

11. Which of the following alternatives would you prefer, and why?

a. We can't explain why the basic uniformities of the universe are as they are. This is a mystery we cannot solve.

b. To explain a law is to place it into a context of a wider law or laws. If a law is a basic or underived law, then by definition this can't be done—it is logically impossible. The request to explain is, therefore, illegitimate: to explain (subsume under a more basic law) a basic law is self-contradictory.

12. Should the fact or law to be explained always be logically deducible from the explanation? First read an account of the view that this deducibility relation must always hold if an explanation is to be considered satisfactory: for example, Carl G. Hempel, *Aspects of Scientific Explanation,* Part 4, and the same author's "Deductive-Nomological vs. Statistical Explanation" in *Minnesota Studies in the Philosophy of Science,* Vol. 3; also May Brodbeck, "Explanation, Prediction, and 'Imperfect' Knowledge," in the same volume. Then read an account of the view that the deducibility relation is not required, for example, Michael Scriven, "Definitions, Explanations, and Theories," in *Minnesota Studies in the Philosophy of Science,* Vol. 2, and the same author's "Explanations, Predictions, and Laws," in Vol. 3. Then state the pros and cons of the issue as you see them.

13. The Problem of Induction

A law of nature, as we have seen, is more than a description of an invariance observed in the past. It says "All A's are B's"—not only here but everywhere else, not only now but always. Yet our basis for believing in the law is that all A's have been B's *in the cases we have thus far observed.* And if the cases we have thus far observed are not all the cases there are, all we have done is to discover that *some* A's are B's.

How, then, do we get from the some to the all? Not *deductively:* if we are in a position only to say that some A's are B's, we cannot validly deduce from it that all A's are B's. Yet the law of nature tells us that all A's are B's. Since we cannot arrive at this conclusion by deduction, what entitles us to assert it?

It seems clear enough that the leap from "some" to "all" is *inductive.* This, indeed, is how we characterized induction when we introduced the concept of inductive reasoning in Chapter 2. We are not entitled to say, because some A's are B's, that it is *certain* that all A's are B's, but only that it is *probable* to a certain degree that all A's are B's, the degree of probability increasing with every added case of an A that is B without any A's turning up that are not B's. How strong one believes the probability becomes depends on one's view of probability, on which there are many conflicting views. At any rate, if all the millions of A's that have been observed are B's, and no A's have ever been observed that are not B's, it surely seems to some degree probable that all A's are B's—certainly more probable than that some A's are *not* B's, for which we have no evidence whatever.

It would seem, then, that we do have some *evidence* that the sun will rise tomorrow and that the Law of Gravitation will continue to hold true. But if we were asked, "Do you *know* (in the strong sense) that they will?" we would have to reply in the negative, for the evidence is not yet all in, and tomorrow's observations may go in a direction contrary to the way today's evidence points. We should, however, notice a difference between the two examples just given. In spite of the millions of times the sun has risen, we have less evidence in the case of the sun rising tomorrow than we have in the case of the Law of Gravitation. Many uniformities have occurred in the past and then ceased to occur. For many centuries, animals (such as horses and donkeys) were man's primary mode of transportation other than walking; but with the advent of the automobile, this ceased to be the case, in spite of many centuries in which it had regularly been so. Many centuries passed in which no man ascended beyond the earth's atmosphere, but that uniformity too has been broken in the last decade. The hand that feeds the chicken throughout its life finally beheads it. And so on. In the case of the sun rising, it is not difficult to discover what conditions would have to be met for the sun to fail to rise on some day in the future: an object from outside the solar system, or even an unusually solid comet from within it, could hit the earth head-on and disturb its regular axial rotation; and we do not *know* that this will not happen one day in the future. Indeed, it might well happen *without in any way being an exception to a law of nature;* it would, in fact, be a further example of laws of nature we are acquainted with already. Once we see this, we would not stake our lives, careers, or reputations on the sun rising every day in the future, the way we would (or might) in the case of the Law of Gravitation. Any particular event, such as the earth being struck by another object, is not only logically possible but empirically possible; but the Law of Gravitation ceasing to operate (that is, ceasing to be a description of the actual motion of objects in the universe) would be logically but not empirically possible, since "empirical possibility" is defined in terms of the laws of nature themselves. Scientists are far more confident of the continued operation of laws of nature than they are about the occurrence or non-occurrence of any particular event, as long as that event is not incompatible with those laws. Accordingly, our questions about induction will be centered around the continued operation of *laws* rather than around the occurrence of particular events, such as the sun's rising.

But now we come to a much more fundamental and far-reaching question about the continued operation of laws of nature. We have been content to say, common-sensically, that though we do not *know* that laws of nature will continue to operate in the future as they have thus far, we have every *evidence* that they will. Now, however, comes a question that at first sounds so incredible that even to raise it may seem bordering on insanity: do we really have *any evidence at all* that the laws of nature will continue to operate as they have thus far? At first the answer will seem obvious: "Of course we do! Doesn't the fact that the law has operated all these many years without a single exception constitute very good evidence that will continue to operate tomorrow? What better evidence could there be? Indeed, what other evidence could there be?" And perhaps this answer is the right one. But many thoughtful persons have denied it, or at least questioned it, and it is worth stopping to consider what the questioning is all about.

A person who asks such a question would argue as follows: "It's happened a certain way regularly in the past—so what? You project the past uniformity into the future, but what right have you to do this? You show me the record of the past, and I agree: the correlation between A and B is uniform; but what has that to do with the future? Why are you so convinced that the operation of the universe in the past gives us any clue to its future operations? I see no reason at all to believe that the past record of uniformities, however often repeated, is any guide at all to the future. Have you any reason to believe that it is? If so, will you kindly give me this reason?"

Let us note that the skeptic's question is *not* "How do you *know* that the past uniformities will continue into the future?" for here we can answer simply, "We don't, but we have considerable evidence." The skeptic is far more radical than that. He is asking, "How do you know that the existence of past uniformities provides *any evidence at all* that the future will be similar to the past?" and he continues, "Not only do you not *know* that the Law of Gravitation, for example, will continue to operate tomorrow, but you have *no evidence* that it will. You cite the so-called evidence from the past, but I don't grant that this is evidence. I say that this has nothing to do with the matter at all. You are presupposing, when you say this, that the past *is* a reliable guide to the future. And this is precisely what I am questioning. At any rate you have not shown me that it is. Thus, no matter what past observations you cite, I can still regard the future with one fundamental query: So what?"

What are we to answer to the skeptic's question? Is there any way at all of answering it? A great deal of ingenuity on the part of philosophers has gone into various attempts to provide an answer and many of the attempts are so technical that we cannot explore them here. Let us first attempt to forestall certain objections by giving several facile replies to the skeptic that do *not* answer him.

1. "The laws of nature must hold in the future; they wouldn't be laws of nature if they didn't. It's a defining characteristic of laws of nature that they hold true regardless of time and space."

This last statement is true; this was one of the defining characteristics of laws we listed on p. 235. This is one way a law is distinguished from a description of past performance. But the argument is nevertheless unsuccessful. You cannot define anything into existence (p. 30). You can say that this wouldn't be an X if it didn't have characteristic A, but all that follows is that if this doesn't have characteristic A, then it isn't an X. The question is only shifted to "Is there then an X?" Perhaps the uniformities thus far observed, which have led us to believe they are genuine laws of nature, will *not* continue, and thus what we thought was a law of nature really is not. The skeptic's question could simply be re-formulated: "How do we know that there are laws?"

2. "There may be something about A that shows that it *must* be a B, and in that case we know that A must always be B, in the future as well as in the past. For example, if we discovered something about the atomic structure of gold that showed us that anything with just that structure would necessarily emit certain spectral lines, then we would know that gold will always continue to emit these lines; and we would thus have established that uniformity ("if gold, then these spectral lines") for the future as well as for the present and the past. Or if we discovered something about the genes of crows that showed that all crows have to be black. . . . And so on."

But this will not suffice either. The suspicious words here are "necessarily," "have to," "must be." Nature only shows us what properties things have, and which ones go along with which other ones. Everything that has the defining properties of gold *also* has had, thus far, certain spectral lines. Assume this as a law of nature. Our skeptic now asks how we know that this correlation, or this law of nature, will continue into the future. "But it has to! Anything with this atomic structure must. . . ." And how do we know this, since it is not a matter of logical necessity? Since *all* laws of nature are now in question, we cannot support one by means of another; the skeptic will only ask us what is our basis for this last one.

The principle of uniformity of nature. Let us then try to find some general principle about the workings of nature, presupposed perhaps in our everyday thinking, that will enable us to *deduce* from it that the laws of nature (or what we think are laws of nature) will continue into the future. We may try this simple one: "The way things have happened in the past is the way they will continue to happen in the future."

We should, however, be extremely careful in the formulation of such a principle. As stated above, it will not suffice. Clearly the fact that meteorites have fallen to the earth frequently in the past does not entitle us to infer that they will continue to do so in the future (the number already seems to be decreasing, and perhaps most meteoric objects have already been swept up in the planetary orbits). No matter how uniformly passenger pigeons crossed the skies of America in past centuries, we do not expect them to do so in the future, since early in our century they became extinct. In many respects we do not expect the future to be like the past, or even very much like it. We do not expect the world in the atomic era to be very much (in many respects) like the world in the preatomic era. We anticipate that only certain uniformities will continue. But which ones? Only those, perhaps, that we believe to constitute genuine laws of nature. It is only of these, at any rate, that scientists would wish to say that "as they have occurred in the past, so will they occur in the future." Propositions about the continued fall of meteorites or the migration of passenger pigeons are not counted as laws of nature. Let us put the matter, then, as follows: "As certain uniformities—those we believe to constitute genuine laws of nature—have occurred in the past, so they will continue in the future." Let us call this the Principle of Uniformity of Nature.

Armed with this principle, we can now arrive at our desired conclusion against the skeptic by means of a valid deduction:

Those uniformities (that we believe to constitute laws of nature) that have occurred regularly in the past will continue to occur regularly in the future.
This uniformity has occurred regularly in the past.
Therefore, this uniformity will occur regularly in the future.

Now we have deduced the desired conclusion. But by means of what? The major premise (first statement in the argument) is required for us to do this, but how do we know that this major premise is true? Is the Principle of Uniformity of Nature just something we *postulate*? But how do we know that what we postulate is true? Is it simply a matter of faith, or hope, or wishful thinking? Just to postulate something will not satisfy the skeptic. We can postulate anything we like in order to bail ourselves out of a difficult situation, as long as we do not care whether the postulate is true.

Yet how can we do without it? If you want to deduce a conclusion about the future, there must be something about the future in at least one of the premises from which the conclusion is deduced. But once we introduce such a premise, the skeptic can ask the same question about *it* that he did about the conclusion itself. The problem has only been shifted, not resolved.

"Well, perhaps we can't prove that the Principle of Uniformity of Nature is true. Still, it is more than wishful thinking or an article of faith. There is considerable *evidence* that it is true. For example, every time in the past that you predicted that the pencil in your hand would fall if you let go of it, it did so; never once did it fail. If anyone had bet against it, you would have won all the bets. Like a tried and true friend, we could always depend on it. When the then-future became present, it turned out that the law held. This of course doesn't prove that it will hold true for any time after the present—but surely it lends it some probability, doesn't it? Don't you trust a friend who has proved trustworthy in the past, rather than someone unknown to you or someone who has double-crossed you? Don't even dogs behave differently toward people who have been kind to them than toward strangers or enemies? That things have acted or behaved in certain ways in the past doesn't of course *prove* that they will continue to (that is, you can't deduce this as a conclusion), but it surely lends it some probability. It's not as if the situation were entirely new to us, as if we were approaching it from scratch. It's not as if we had never placed our bets on it in the past, or done so and lost. It's held true so often in the past—indeed, every single time that we made a prediction on the basis of it—that surely we are justified in holding that (at least probably) it will continue so in the future."

But the skeptic, of course, will not buy this at all. "Certainly," he will say, "men as well as animals are inductive creatures. But what *justifies* being so? The argument just given will not do it. I grant that in the past when you predicted that the pencil would fall, it always did. But that doesn't show that *now,* when you predict that it will, it will—or even that it's probable that it will. You predicted it in the past, and you turned out to be right. What you predicted was *then* in the future. But now it has all happened, it's past; and what evidence have you that *future* futures will be like *past* futures? Prove to me that as past futures were, so future futures will be—even probably be! The fact that the prediction of the future was fulfilled in the past—what has this to do with what is *now* future?"

Let us consider another point. We can make particular predictions if we assume the Principle of Uniformity of Nature; but how can we prove, or even render probable, the principle itself? Future continuations of past uniformities can be guaranteed only if we assume that the principle is true, and they can be rendered probable only to the degree to which the principle itself is probable. But how can we show that the principle is even probably true? The principle, it would seem, states the standard of probability in terms of which we frame all *particular* judgments of probabilities. All belief in the continuation of uniform sequence into the future *presupposes* the Principle of Uniformity of Nature. When we say that the continuation of sequence X from past to future will occur, we use the principle to make this inference. But we cannot use the principle to prove itself. This, of course, would be circular. We cannot even use the principle to show that it is even probable, for all estimates of probability (of future events) presuppose the principle itself.

The situation seems to be this: we cannot prove the principle deductively from anything more fundamental than itself. Nor can we do so inductively: we cannot even render it more probable by inductive argument, since the principle is presupposed in all inductive arguments.

We seem to be in an utterly hopeless situation. How can we possibly say anything to support the Principle of Uniformity of Nature? Is it utterly without defense? Yet we do not wish to abandon it. We may, indeed, be somewhat suspicious about the skeptic's maneuvers—for what *would* satisfy him? Nothing that has been observed in the past, will satisfy him; nor will any predictions made in the past that later were fulfilled. He would say of all these, "What has this to do with the future?" It appears that nothing whatever would satisfy him. Indeed, it is *logically* impossible to fulfill his demand. The only thing that would fulfill his demand would be to point *now* to events that are still future, and this is logically impossible. Pointing to events that have already occurred will not satisfy him, for he will simply say they have nothing to do with the future, and predictions fulfilled in the past will not impress him, for he will say that they are now irrelevant to his claim, which was that we have no evidence about the now future, not about past futures. Thus we have from the skeptic a demand that is logically impossible to satisfy. In that case, of course, no one can ever satisfy it. So why should we make the attempt?

Yet hasn't the skeptic a case? How *do* we know that the Principle of Uniformity of Nature is true, or even that there is any evidence for it?

Attempted solutions.   Is there any way out of these difficulties? Several have been suggested, but we can only give a brief résumé of some of the lines of argument. Much of the controversy on this issue that fills the philosophical journals is far too technical to explore here, and even the outlines of many solutions can be presented only by means of elaborate mathematical formulas.

Some "solutions" to the problem consist in attempts to show that there is really no problem to be resolved. The attempt to show this consists largely in calling our attention to the uncritical use of certain crucial terms in the argument. For example:

"There is no *evidence*," says the skeptic, "that as the uniformities of nature have been in the past, so they will be in the future." No evidence, we may say? A thousand times in the past I let go my pencil and it has fallen; never once has it flown into the air. This, and all the things I know about the behavior of physical objects, lead me to believe that the pencil will fall when I let go of it this time. Is this *no* evidence at all? If not, then what *could* count as evidence? Surely we have here the very paradigm of "good evidence"; if the facts just mentioned are not evidence, what is? What could be? We may ask the skeptic, "What is it you are saying does not exist when you say that good evidence does not exist in this case? What is it that we lack? What are you waiting to have supplied?" And the answer seems obvious: there is nothing that the skeptic would count as evidence, nothing that is now missing that he would consider evidence, other than the occurrence of the future event itself—and when it has occurred the event is no longer future, and he repeats the same story with regard to the events that are still future. There is nothing available *now* that he would count as evidence one way or the other for the future, whereas the rest of us *do* count the past behavior of the pencil as evidence that it will fall this time. It is not as if the skeptic were awaiting some magical rabbit to be pulled out of the hat, some momentous empirical discovery that, if we only had it, would allay his skepticism; there is *nothing* that would allay it, nothing that we could confront him with *now* that would convince him, for the simple reason that anything we can show him now is *now* and not the future, and he won't consider anything that happens now as in any way evidence for the future. What he demands it is logically impossible to supply. But doesn't the logical impossibility of the skeptic's demand defeat his cause? If he raises a logically impossible demand, can we be expected to fulfill it? He says we have no evidence, but whatever we adduce he refuses to count as evidence. At least *we* know what we would count as evidence, and we show him what it is. But he only shakes his head and says it isn't evidence. But then surely he is using the word "evidence" in a very peculiar way (a meaningless way?), so that nothing whatever would count as a case of it. Is he then using it in some new and special sense, like a new stipulative definition? Apparently not, for he has not supplied us with any such sense; he simply reiterates, no matter what facts we adduce, that he doesn't count these as evidence. As what? As evidence. And what is evidence, as he uses the term? He doesn't say. Isn't he then using it meaninglessly? "There is no evidence." Might he not just as well say "There is no glubglub"? What are we to say of someone who repeatedly tells us that there are no X's, but refuses to tell us what would count as an X?

The skeptic's situation is no different if we substitute related words for "evidence." "There is no *reason* to believe that the pencil will drop if I let it go." But there is, we reply, every reason to believe it—the very reasons we have given. What more reason could there be other than the pencil actually dropping, in which case we could speak of an observed fact and not of a reason to believe something that hasn't yet happened? If the skeptic says that there is no reason to believe it, what *would* he count as a reason? Let him describe something that in his opinion there *would* be a reason for believing. If there is none, is it not because he refuses to attach any meaning to the word "reason" in this context? He says there is no reason. No what? Reason. And what does it mean to say so, since nothing would count as being a reason? Again, his claim seems to reduce to meaninglessness, since he has not told us what he means by one of the crucial terms ("reason to believe") in it. But surely we need not respond to a meaningless charge.

Let us make another observation in this connection: Induction isn't deduction. We can't logically deduce valid conclusions about the future from premises that say nothing about the future; granted. But what does this show? Only that induction isn't deduction. The two are different, and we should not expect from the one what we expect of the other. Induction isn't a bad or unsuccessful version of deduction: it isn't deduction at all, and one shouldn't expect from inductive procedure the same certainty one gets from deduction. If induction *did* yield such results, it would be deduction and no longer induction. Why blame a dog for not being a cat?

It has, indeed, cogently been argued that there is, can be, and need be no such thing as a general justification of induction—that the whole enterprise is a mistake. We can justify certain procedures, such as random sampling, as instances of induction (by seeing which ones yield reliable results), but we cannot and need not justify induction in general.

It is generally proper to inquire *of a particular belief,* whether its adoption is justified; and, in asking this, we are asking whether there is good, bad, or any evidence for it. In applying or withholding the epithets "justified," "well founded," etc., in the case of specific beliefs, we are appealing to, and applying, inductive standards. But to what standards are we appealing when we ask whether the application of inductive standards is justified or well grounded? If we cannot answer, then no sense has been given to the question. Compare it with the question: Is the law legal? It makes perfectly good sense to inquire of a particular action, of an administrative regulation, or even, in the case of some states, a particular enactment of the legislature, whether or not it is legal. The question is answered by an appeal to a legal system, by the application of a set of legal (or constitutional) rules and standards. But it makes no sense to inquire in general whether the law of the land, the legal system as a whole, is or is not legal. For to what legal standards are we appealing?

The only way in which a sense might be given to the question, whether induction is in general a justified or justifiable procedure, is a trivial one . . . . We might interpret it to mean "Are all conclusions, arrived at inductively, justified?" i.e., "Do people always have adequate evidence for the conclusions they draw?" The answer to this question is easy, but uninteresting; it is that sometimes people have adequate evidence, and sometimes they do not.[2]

Many persons will consider these arguments decisive in resolving—or dissolving—the problem. Others, however, may be left unsatisfied. Is there nothing more we can say? they may ask. And indeed more—much more—has been suggested. We shall conclude our account with one such suggestion.

We cannot prove the Principle of Uniformity of Nature (or any other principle that could be considered the basis, or basic premise, of induction) by deducing it from a more fundamental principle, at least from one known to be true. Nor can we render it probable inductively, since the principle itself is presupposed in all inductive reasoning. (There is a strong similarity here to the basis of deductive reasoning, pp. 212–13.) But what we *can* do is give a *pragmatic justification* of it—not of the principle itself, but of our *adoption* of it. Our adoption of it is an act, something we *do;* and we can justify an act by showing what ends or goals are served in performing this act. We can give a pragmatic justification for adopting certain rules of baseball or chess or tennis: by adopting certain rules rather than others we make the game more challenging, a better test of ingenuity, more amusing, interesting, or exciting and so on. Perhaps we can do the same with the Principle of Induction. We cannot defend *it* (deductively or inductively), but we can justify our *adoption* of it, as a kind of rule-of-the-scientific-game, in terms of the ends to be achieved by this adoption: the discovery of further laws, which gives us greater success in predicting the course of events. Specifically, we wish to discover nature's secrets, so that we can understand, predict, and control. We cannot do this by crystal-gazing, intuiting, or tossing coins; we can do this, if at all, only by the slow and patient method of carefully observing the way nature works, noting apparent uniformities, noting exceptions to the uniformities, trying again for genuine uniformities, devising explanatory hypotheses, testing these hypotheses, and so on without end. This is the only

[2] P. F. Strawson, *Introduction to Logical Theory*, p. 257.

way we can unlock nature's secrets; *if* we wish to gain knowledge, and through knowledge predictive power, this is the only way it can be done. Thus, *if* there is an order of nature, the method of induction can discover it.

Of course we do not *know* that there *is* an order of nature—at least not one extending from the past into the future; it is possible that the universe tomorrow will behave in such a way as to refute all our well-attested generalizations of today. But if there is a continuing order of nature, the procedures described can enable us to discover its nature in detail. We are rather in the position of a patient who is suffering from a serious disease:

The physician tells us: "I do not know whether an operation will save the man, but if there *is* any remedy, it is an operation." In such a case, the operation would be justified. Of course, it would be better to know that the operation will save the man; but, if we do not know this, the knowledge formulated in the statement of the physician is a sufficient justification. If we cannot realize the sufficient conditions of success, we shall at least realize the necessary conditions. If we were able to show that the inductive inference is a necessary condition of success, it would be justified; such a proof would satisfy any demands which may be raised about the justification of induction.[3]

There may, of course, be no continuing order of nature, just as the man may not live even if he has an operation. In that case, all our efforts to unlock the secrets of nature by inductive procedures would be in vain. But, if there *is* an order of nature, whose laws continue through all time and space, as the inductive principle assures us, then we *may* be able to discover it—we cannot say we *will,* for that depends on our ingenuity. If we wager that there is no such order, we shall not even bother to look—we shall throw in the towel at the outset. But if we wager that there *is,* we shall go to work and attempt to discover it; and if we try hard enough, we may succeed. This, then, is our pragmatic justification for adopting the Principle of Uniformity of Nature. Without it, we cannot but fail; with it, we may succeed.

Exercises

1. Assess the claim that it is meaningful to request a justification for individual inductive procedures but meaningless to request a justification for induction in general.

2. Assess the following attempts to solve (or help to solve) the problem of induction.

    a. The Law of Gravitation has always held true in the past, to the best of our knowledge; there are no known exceptions to it. Therefore, it is probable that it will hold true in the future.

    b. In the past, when we predicted that a given law of nature would hold true the next day, our prediction turned out to be right. This makes it probable

[3] Hans Reichenbach, *Experience and Prediction,* p. 349.

that if we predict the same thing today, our prediction will turn out right this time also.

c. We can't deduce the Principle of Uniformity of Nature from any other principle we believe to be true, but we can present inductive evidence in its favor.

d. The whole so-called problem can be solved definitionally. We wouldn't call anything a law of nature unless it did hold true in the future. Isn't that part of what we mean by the phrase "law of nature"?

e. Induction is similar to deduction in that there are unprovable basic principles in both. We can't prove the Law of Identity or the Law of Non-contradiction, yet we accept them. Why can't we do the same with the Principle of Uniformity of Nature?

f. How can we know the future? Well, we just can't, that's all. So much for the problem of induction.

3. Show how proving a principle is different from justifying our adoption of it. Then show exactly how this latter concept is involved in one attempt to justify induction.

14. Testability and Meaning

In empirical science, whether we are uttering singular statements (This is a piece of metamorphic rock), laws (Water boils at 212° F), or theories (The helium atom has two electrons), every assertion we make must be in some way *testable*. Its truth or falsity must make some difference to our sense-experiences. Thus we are led into still another criterion of meaningfulness, the *testability* criterion.

If someone utters a sentence that you do not understand, such as "All of reality is an illusion" or "Altarwise by owl-light in the half-way house / The gentleman lay graveward with his furies . . ." (Dylan Thomas), your first reply might be, "What does it mean?" or "I don't understand, please explain." But you might also say, "Please tell me how one would proceed to discover whether what you say is true or false," hoping that if he can tell you that, you might discover what he means by his assertion. At this point appears the *testability criterion* of meaningfulness: If no way can be indicated by which a sentence (more precisely, the proposition that it expresses) could be tested, then the sentence is meaningless. To know the meaning is to know how it could be tested.

Verifiability.   The view that meaning involves testability has two principal versions: *verifiability* and *confirmability*. To verify a proposition is to make such observations as would entitle us to conclude definitely that the proposition is true or false. (Sometimes we make a further distinction, saying that to verify it is to determine that it is true and to falsify it is to determine that it is false.) To confirm it is to make one or more observations that would increase or decrease the *probability* of its truth or falsity, without definitely establishing it either way. If I have examined 50 of the 100 marbles in the bag and found all 50 to be black, I have confirmed but not verified the proposition that all the marbles in the bag are black. I would not have verified it until I had examined the entire 100.

Verifying and confirming are both things we do, operations we perform. We verify that this is sugar or salt by performing certain chemical tests. Do not say that the *proposition* that this liquid turns red litmus paper blue verifies or confirms the proposition that this liquid is a base; propositions do not verifiy one another: *people* verifiy propositions.

The verifiability criterion does not say that a statement is meaningful only if it is verified, or the confirmability criterion that it is meaningful only if it is confirmed. We have not found how many mountains are on the other side of the moon, but the statement that there are 2,000 mountains there is surely meaningful. Indeed, we cannot verify or confirm it until we know the meaning of the statement to be verified or confirmed. What the testability criterion prescribes is that we know the meaning only when we know *how it would* be verified or confirmed, whether anyone has actually done so or not. Meaning depends not on actual verification but on verifi*ability*—in other words, *possibility* of verification (or of confirmation).

In what sense of "possibility" is possibility of verification required? Not *technical* possibility: it is not technically possible at present to travel in a spaceship to the star Sirius, but statements about what we might find if we could take such a trip are not therefore meaningless. Not *empirical* possibility: if a star is 1,000 light-years away, it is empirically impossible for us to discover what is occurring on the surface of that star today, since at the rate of 186,000 miles per second the light leaving the star today will not reach the earth for a thousand years; yet if we say that there are spots on the surface of that star today, we are not saying something meaningless. What is required is *logical* possibility of verification. And logical possibility, once again, means only that there is no contradiction in the proposition. "I discovered today what is occurring at the surface of the star today" is not self-contradictory, but to discover it today is empirically impossible in view of the velocity of light. Thus it is logically possible to verify the statement, but not empirically possible (and consequently, of course, not technically possible either) to do so.

What the testability criterion prescribes seems very plausible indeed: Whenever you can't make out what someone means by a sentence, ask him "How would you find out if it's true?" By this criterion, "Seven is blue," "Saturday is in bed," and a host of other sentences would immediately be thrown out as meaningless; whereas most statements made in daily life and in science—such as "I am now reading a book," "There is life on other planets," "Gold is malleable," "At constant temperature, the volume of a gas varies inversely with its pressure"—are all meaningful because we know how one would find out whether or not they are true (even if one is not always in a position to find out now). Perhaps at last we have a satisfactory criterion for distinguishing meaningful from meaningless sentences.

But whatever virtues the criterion may have, lack of ambiguity is not one of them. We shall try to bring out some of the most important of these ambiguities, and then make some general comments on the criterion.

Let us anticipate one objection at the outset. "If every statement must be testable to be meaningful, what about this very statement? Is *it* testable? If not, then your statement itself is meaningless."

"We must distinguish between statements and meta-statements—that is, statements about statements. My statement that every meaningful statement must be testable is not a statement about the world but a statement about statements. What I say about meaningfulness is intended to apply only to statements about the world."

"I still don't understand the status of your testability-criterion. Is it a generalization about meaningful statements? Are you saying that all statements that are meaningful are also verifiable? If so, I could offer you some counterexamples, but most important I would remind you that if this is what you are doing, you are not giving me a criterion of meaning but are *presupposing* the existence of such a criterion. You are saying that what is meaningful (apparently by some other criterion, which you haven't given) is *also* verifiable."

"But that is not what I am doing. I am giving a definition of 'meaning,' not a generalization about meaningful sentences."

"Are you giving a stipulative definition? In that case, I see no reason to go along with your stipulation: I am free to reject your stipulation and construct another. But if you are reporting how people actually use the word 'meaning,' I can only say that it is a false report: I don't use 'meaning' in this way, and neither, I suspect, do most people."

"I do think, as a matter of fact, that most people *do* use 'meaning' this way—that if there is no conceivable way to test a statement, they don't know what it means. To know what a statement means, we must know how it could be tested. We do use this criterion in daily life. But I don't want to stake my case on that: some people do talk nonsense and think they are talking sense. Yes, it is a stipulative definition. But the stipulation is not just arbitrary or idle. By stipulating this meaning for the word 'meaning,' I am setting forth a clear and definite criterion, which I urge you to examine before you reject it. A statement, I submit, has meaning if and only if it's testable in some way. If you present me with a statement and can think of no way it could be tested, if no observation you can think of would have any bearing on its truth or falsity, would you know what it means? And if two statements could be verified by exactly the same series of observations, wouldn't they have the same meaning? I put it to you that if this is not the criterion you have used so far (and on the whole I think it is), then it *should* be, for only by using this criterion can you clearly separate sense from nonsense (the meaningful from the meaningless)."

"Nonsense according to your criterion, you mean. But I don't accept it."

"There's no way I can make you accept it. I can only attempt to show you that the statements you and all of us make every day, which we obviously understand, *do* fulfill the criterion, and that statements that we can't understand (even though we mouth the words) do not fulfill it."

Let us see, then, whether the criterion does what its proponent claims for it. Is meaningfulness always a function of testability? We shall begin with some observations about specific kinds of statements, and then proceed to some more general comments on the testability criterion in general.

1. *When* must the verification take place? Must the statement be verifiable *now?* This is an important consideration, for no statement about the past or the future can be verified now. "Julius Caesar was assassinated in 44 B.C." describes a past event that can never be recaptured; we have considerable evidence that it is true, but we are not in a position to verify it, since that would require our being present at the Roman Senate in 44 B.C., which is logically impossible for us to do *now.* (See pp. 175–78.) The sentence is about a past event, but any evidences we may find of the statement are *present* evidences, because nothing will bring us back to the past. The most we can do in the present is *confirm* it (find *some evidence* as to whether it is true), but it is logically impossible now to verify it.

On the other hand, it was possible to verify it on a certain morning in 44 B.C.; indeed, it would appear that it *was* verified then. Since we do not want to dismiss all statements about the past as meaningless, we shall have to state explicitly that all that is required is that the statement be verifiable *at some time or other.* With this proviso, then, we can assert that the statement is meaningful (that is, the *sentence* is meaningful, expresses a genuine proposition) since it was verifiable at the time the event occurred.

The same proviso will help us with regard to statements about the future. "There will be a severe economic depression in the United States within the next five years" can certainly not be verified *now,* but it certainly has a meaning, and we know what that meaning is (though like many statements it is somewhat vague). But it can be verified in the future, and this is sufficient to make it meaningful according to the criterion. In general, with statements about the future we simply wait and observe what happens at the time predicted.

2. *By whom* must the verification be performed? Some have held that the statement must be verifiable by anyone. I am not in London now, so I cannot verify that the Houses of Parliament are still standing; but I can go there and verify it if I choose, and moreover *anyone* who is in the proper position in space and time (in the borough of Westminster, London, now), and has functioning sense-organs and brain, can verify it for himself. The nature of the rock strata in the Grand Canyon could be verified by anyone who took the trouble to go there and observe it for himself; of course he would have to familiarize himself with geology sufficiently to be able to identify different types of rock and remember their names, but presumably he could do this

also by taking the trouble. He *could* verify the statement, then, even if he has not actually bothered to do so. So much, then, for the contention that the statement must be publicly (inter-subjectively) verifiable—verifiable by anyone with sufficient intellectual and perceptual equipment who is at the requisite place and time.

But there is a hitch. Aren't there statements that only *one* person can verify? If I have a toothache, only I can verify that I have it. You may open my mouth, see the cavity, and *infer* that I am probably having a toothache; you can watch me grimacing and crying "Ouch!"; and so on. But this is only indirect evidence that I am in pain. Only I can verify that I am in pain, for only I can feel the pain, and feeling the pain is the only *sure* way to know that one has it. At least, I am in a better position to say it than anyone else is. Others observing me have to *infer* that I am in pain by watching my behavior; but I do not have to infer it, I know it non-inferentially: I do not have to look in a mirror, examine my tooth, and so on, to be able to say with perfect certainty that I have a toothache. It appears then that statements about your feeling-state can be verified only by you, statements about my feeling-state can be verified only by me, and so on; thus such statements are not publicly (inter-subjectively) verifiable. (Much more will be said about such statements on pp. 382–85.)

"But you are assuming that the only way to verify that I have a pain is to *feel* it, when all that is required is that someone *knows* that I am in pain. Surely my doctor, who sees me lying in bed with gaping wounds, knows that I am in pain as well as I do." This depends on whether one uses "know" in the strong or weak sense (pp. 149–52). In the ordinary use of "know" as we employ it in daily life, the physician does know that I am in pain; he knows it through inference, but he still knows it. But has he verified it? Not in the way that *only I* can verify it, since I alone can feel the pain. There is an avenue of verification open to me that is not open to the physician, one so decisive that, unlike the physician, I do not *need* any of the other evidences that I am in pain. Thus, if verification involves finding out decisively whether I am in pain, I am the only one who is in a position to do that when it is my own pain that is involved—just as only the physician can decisively verify that *he* is in pain. Verfication has usually been taken to involve having the *best* method of finding out whether a statement is true: the best method of finding out whether Caesar was assassinated would be to be there on that day; the best method of finding out whether someone is in pain would be to be that person, since he has a kind of evidence that no one else has. If this is so (and it is in this way that verifiability has usually been conceived), then there remains a class of statements that are not verifiable publicly but by one person only.

One might preserve the public-verifiability requirement by saying that the meaning of statements about your pain is different from the meaning of statements about my pain. "What is verifiable is different," one might argue, "therefore the meaning is different." What I can verify in my own case is that

I feel the pain, therefore that is what the statement means when it is about me; but what I can verify in your case is only that you behave in a certain way, therefore that is what the statement means when it is about you. But this way out is most bizarre, and seems to be an obvious dodge. For surely when I say that you are in pain, I am attributing to you exactly the same kind of feeling-state that I attribute to myself when I say that I am in pain. The two statements—"You are in pain" and "I am in pain"—differ in meaning only because of the personal pronoun: the first statement is about you, the second about me, but that is the only difference. It would be a gross distortion of facts to fit a theory to say that the one statement is about a feeling-state and the other is about behavior, simply because the latter is all we can verify in this case. It may be that "You grimace and scream, etc." is all I can *verify* in your case, but what I *mean* by saying that you have a pain is that you have a feeling-state of which this behavior is only the manifestation, which is exactly what I am saying in my own case—in spite of the fact that what I can verify in my own case is more than I can verify in yours.

A way round this difficulty is easily suggested: the statement is meaningful as long as it is verifiable *by someone or other*. I can verify that I have a pain, though I cannot verify that you have; but the fact that I *can* verify it is enough to make it meaningful. I have privileged access to my own pains, and perhaps no one else can tell for sure whether I have a pain or not, but that doesn't matter: since I *can* verify the proposition, the statement is meaningful. And the same of course for statements about your pain, since they are verifiable by you, although by no one else.

This conclusion may be somewhat discomfiting, but we shall have to settle for it if we are to retain verifiability as a criterion and yet say that statements about other people's experiences are meaningful. (Would the experience of pain by cats and dogs be counted as verification by them?) The idea of verifiability-by-only-one has been considered somewhat suspect, in the fear that it would permit many statements as meaningful which should not be so permitted: for example, "I verified the proposition that infinity is like glass, because I experienced it today." But if we keep clearly in mind that any such statement must be *about* one's feeling-states only, and make no claims to an objective reality apart from that which *could* be tested by someone else, we need not fear this condition.

Another fear—that the concept of verification and verifiability may not even be *applicable* to statements about one's experiences—has a better foundation. *Do* I verify the statement that I am in pain? If so, *how* do I verify it? Verification is a procedure; what procedure do I go through to verify that I feel a pain? What do I *do* to discover whether the statement is true? "Well, you verify it by just feeling the pain. The very existence or occurrence of the pain itself constitutes the verification." But something is wrong here: granted that I know that I am in pain, do I know it by *verifying* it? Verifying is something one does to find out whether a statement is true, and here there appears to be nothing that one *does*. There is nothing that one *has* to do. (Does one introspect, and ask oneself "Do I really feel a pain or not?") One has the pain, and one doesn't *have* to verify it. Concerning one's own experiences, it would seem preferable to say that one doesn't *need* to verify them rather than that one verifies them by introspecting, reassuring oneself that one feels pain, and so on. In daily life we never speak of "finding out that it's true" when talking about our own experiences: we talk about verification when we are confronted with a statement about something other than our own experiences, when we have to find out through some procedure whether the statement is true. There is no such procedure in the case of "I have a pain" or "I feel drowsy." Thus it would seem that the term "verification" (and hence "possibility of verification") should not be used in this context—that the proponents of the verifiability criterion, by extending the criterion to cover such cases as these statements about one's own experiences, are trying to make a square peg fit into a round hole. But if the peg doesn't fit, all such statements should (according to the verifiability theory) be consigned to the limbo of meaninglessness. Yet don't they have meaning, and don't we know what they mean?

3. How can statements with an infinite or indefinitely large range ever be verified? Consider laws of nature. "Every particle of matter in the universe attracts every other particle . . ." begins Newton's Law of Universal Gravitation. The statement of the law makes no limitations on its application: it applies to all places and all times. This is an enormous claim, and how would one verify it? How could any collection of persons acting together ever verify it? Even a more modest universal statement like "All crows are black" is in the same fix. There are not an infinite number of crows, but the class is open-ended; and even if one had examined all the members, one would not know it (the last crow wouldn't have a tag on it saying "I'm the last one"). Besides, one could not examine future crows, nor all the crows that lived and died for centuries before one's birth. (Even if crows became extinct, could we be sure that no such species would evolve again, perhaps long after human beings had disappeared from the earth to verify it?)

"But an omnisentient God could verify it, even if no human being or group of human beings could do so. Such a being could simultaneously see all time and all space, and he would *know* whether there were any non-black crows." Perhaps; if one builds into the definition of "God" the capacity to do this, it follows that he can do it. But if the meaning of the statement about crows is in doubt, surely the translation statement about such a being is more so. Do we really know what is meant by saying that such a being could scan past and future simultaneously? Isn't its meaning far more dubious than that of the original statement?

Perhaps we can get by without resorting to this desperate maneuver. We might say, "No human being lives forever, but it is logically possible that one might; and if he did—that is, if a person's life span were coextensive with the entire history of the universe, and if he could scan the entire universe so that no event escaped his attention—he could verify laws of nature. It is only that he couldn't verify them under *present* conditions; but under different conditions, which are logically possible, he might. Thus we have supplied the logical possibility of verification, which is all that is required." Perhaps. But the meaning of the statement about crows seems to be so simple and straightforward that it is difficult to believe that a statement so easy to understand requires us to go through such imaginative gymnastics to clarify its meaning—if, indeed, its meaning is rendered at all by specifying the method of its verification.

4. There is a small but peculiar class of statements whose verifiability has a different status in the affirmative than in the negative. Suppose I say, "I shall survive my bodily death." How do I verify this? One might reply, "As with all other statements about the future, that's easy—just wait and see. If after dying, you wake up again and remember your bodily life, then you have verified that you have survived your bodily death. True, you can't verify it *now,* but you can *then.* And maybe no one but you can verify it even then. (You could verify that you survive, and Jones that Jones survives, but it might not be possible for you and Jones to communicate, or even to know that the other exists.) But we have already admitted verification that can be performed only at a particular time and by a particular person." Let us assume that "I shall survive my bodily death" can be verified. But now take the statement "I shall *not* survive my bodily death." How do I verify that? If the statement is true, I shall never be able to discover it; I just won't wake up again, and thus I won't be able to verify the statement. There is not even a *logical* possibility of verifying it, if I don't survive my death. There is just *no* logical possibility of saying truly, "I see now that I did not survive my bodily death."

But now we have a strange situation: it is logically possible to verify that one has survived his bodily death, but logically impossible to verify that he has not survived. If meaning depends on verifiability, the first statement is meaningful and the second is not. But it is a strange statement whose denial is meaningless but whose assertion is meaningful. Does it not seem plain that the one is as meaningful as the other, and that we know what both statements mean? (Or perhaps neither, but not the one without the other.) We do seem to know what "I shall survive my death" means, and no less clearly "I shall not survive," even though there is no logically possible means of verifying the latter.

Or consider the statement "The earth will continue to exist even after living things no longer exist on it." No human being could verify this statement, since no one would be there to do the verifying. Still, we do know what the statement means, and can speculate about its truth; we can even draw a picture of the earth, rocks, oceans, etc., without people in it, just as easily as we can draw the same picture *with* people in it. There is no meaning-difficulty in the statement; but the problem for the verifiability criterion is that it is logically impossible to verify it, since there would be no one to do the verifying, the sole means of the verification (sentient beings to make observations) having been removed. We certainly know what *state-of-affairs* would have to exist in order to make the statement true, but that is a different criterion (pp. 84–85)—it is not verifiability. Verifying is something we do, and it requires someone present to do the verifying. It would appear that the verifiability criterion is in serious trouble.

Confirmability.   In view of such difficulties as these, the verifiability criterion has been relaxed somewhat; instead of verifiability, we now speak of confirmability. I cannot verify that you have a pain, but I can confirm it by watching your gestures and facial expressions. I cannot verify that all crows are black, but I can confirm it by examining thousands of crows and finding all of them to be black. I cannot verify that some day there will be no life on earth, but I can confirm it *now* by noting that inanimate objects constantly go on existing even after living things die, that intense cold kills living things but leaves mountains and valleys in existence, and so on; and I infer that when the heat and light of the sun have been spent, the earth will become too cold to support life.

It seems, then, that the substitution of confirmability for verifiability has eased many of our troubles. But the difficulties they have eased appear to be difficulties about *verification,* not about *meaning.* It is easy to see how we can confirm laws of nature (this is all we can do in the case of laws), not how we could verify them. But their meaning seems to be perfectly clear all the time. Don't we all know the meaning of "All living things die," "Water boils at 212° F.," and countless other laws, in spite of the difficulty about verification? We know what is meant by speaking of other people's experiences, even though we cannot verify their existence—whether we talk about verifiability or confirmability, there is no lack of meaning in talking about other people's experiences. And we know what it means to say "I shall not survive my bodily death" even though we can neither verify it nor confirm it.

Indeed, confirmability involves some special problems of its own. How can I know that observing that this crow is black is a confirmation of "All crows are black" *unless I already know* what "All crows are black" means? How can I know that seeing blood on Smith's sleeve is confirmation of "Smith killed Jones" unless I already know the meaning of the assertion? It would seem that to know what confirms what, I must first know the statement's meaning—so the meaning cannot lie in the confirmability.

If one does not already know what the statement to be confirmed means, how can one exclude *any* observation that is put forth as confirmation of it? Suppose someone said, "Mice eat ducks," and claimed that he had confirmed this statement by observing that the sky is blue. We would ask, "What's the connection? How does observing the color of the sky confirm or disconfirm the statement about mice?" But in order to know what does or does *not* count as confirming a statement, we must first know what that statement means. And if we already know what it means, we need not make its meaning dependent upon its confirmability. (Another example: Perhaps the fact that the baby recovered does not confirm the proposition that a benevolent God exists, since many babies do not recover. But if we did not already know what was meant by "God exists," how could we know that the recovery of the baby confirms it? Perhaps we do not know what "God exists" means—we shall discuss these matters in Chapter 7—but in that case neither do we know that the recovery of the baby confirms it. If a sentence is meaningless, how could anything confirm it?)

There are many other difficulties about the testability criterion, which are present whether it is the verifiability or confirmability version that we are attempting to defend. The verifiability version says, "Logical possibility of verification is required"; the confirmability version says, "Logical possibility of confirmation is required." But in either case, does not *the logical possibility of p* come before the *logical possibility of testing (verifying or confirming) p?* For example, "Water flows uphill," though false, is meaningful. This has been defended by showing that it is logically possible for water to flow uphill. But the logical possibility of water flowing uphill is not the same as the logical possibility of *verifying* or *confirming* that water flows uphill—and it is the latter that the testability criterion asserts. If you said merely, "It is logically possible for water to flow uphill; therefore 'Water flows uphill' is meaningful," you would not be using the testability criterion at all. You would be using the *absence of self-contradictoriness* as your criterion of meaningfulness, for "logical possibility" is defined as the absence of self-contradictoriness (pp. 170–73). It may be that lack of self-contradictoriness is a better criterion of meaningfulness than testability is, but at any rate it is different, and the two should not be confused with one another.[4]

One has to know whether "*p*" describes a logically possible situation before one can know whether it is logically possible to test it.[5] Whether *p* is logically possible is a *prior* consideration to whether it is logically possible to test it. One has to know what a sentence means before one knows what observations would verify or confirm it; otherwise, how would one know

[4] For examples of the confusion between "*p* is logically possible" and "It is logically possible to verify *p*," see Moritz Schlick, "Meaning and Verification," in H. Feigl and W. Sellars, *Readings in Philosophical Analysis;* and for criticism, see Paul Marhenke, "The Criterion of Significance," in L. Linsky (ed.), *Semantics and Philosophy of Language.*

[5] One might go further and ask, What does "It is logically possible to verify *p*" mean? A state-of-affairs, such as water flowing uphill, is logically possible or impossible; but how can an operation or procedure be logically possible?

what to verify, or that one's observation was a verification of it? Knowing what the sentence means is primary, and knowing how to verify it is a consequence of knowing its meaning.

"It rained yesterday." . . . Surely this sentence seems to have a clear meaning straight away. However, if I were asked how it could be verified, I should perhaps in the first moment be at a loss and then make various suggestions: I could ask other persons, or look up the meteorological report of the previous day, I could examine the traces of moisture on the ground, or resort to my own memory. There is a vast number of possibilities which can hardly be exhausted. It is even possible that some discovery might be made by which the time of the last rain could be exactly ascertained. But do I *mean* by the statement the existence of any one of these facts? What I mean is surely that yesterday a definite occurrence took place of which the traces of moisture, etc., are only "indications." Now it seems that the meaning of a sentence has nothing whatsoever to do with its verification. One is inclined to say: "I just do understand the sentence, I understand it because I know the English language." . . . Usually, when considering such statements of daily life, I do not think of the verification, but could, if necessary, propose this or that procedure. By doing this, however, the meaning is, of course, not changed, nor does it become *clearer* to me what I originally meant by the statement. On the contrary: the method of verification is irregular, loose, fluctuating, while the sentence always remains the same.

Obviously I know what it means that it is now raining; I also know what the word "yesterday" means; and now I understand the sentence "It rained yesterday," and I understand it only because I understand the single words and know the usage of English syntax. This, however, does not mean that I know how the proposition is to be verified. If, subsequently, I learn to know one or the other method of verification, nothing is added to the meaning. . . .

If a child does not understand a sentence, then what we explain to him is the meaning of the words, but not the method of its verification. In the normal use of language the questions "What does this sentence mean?" and "How do I find out whether this sentence is true?" are two entirely different questions, and everyone will refuse to regard them as alike.[6]

Thus we seem to have clinched the case against testability as a criterion of meaning. And as a general criterion for sentence meaning, testability will not suffice. But not all sentences are alike: it seems that there *are* sentences that lack meaning until a method of verification is supplied. Consider the statement "The universe has expanded to twice its original size while you slept." We tend to think at once that we know exactly what this means—everything is twice the size it was yesterday, what could be simpler? But let us notice that there is no way in which such a difference could ever be discovered. We would measure the length of this table to see whether it had doubled in size, but the result of this measurement would be exactly the same

---

[6] Friedrich Waismann, *Principles of Linguistic Philosophy*, pp. 329–30.

as it was yesterday: if it was 3 feet long then, it is 3 feet long now, since everything, including the measuring stick, has doubled in size. If the table was as long as the yardstick yesterday, it is still so today. The ends of the table are still coincident with the ends of the yardstick. And so on with every other object. There would be no measurable difference whatever, no difference detectable by any means.

At this point we might begin to be suspicious: there seems to be something phony about the case presented. "Everything has doubled in size" sounds like a straightforward empirical proposition, yet there is no empirical observation that could show it to be either true or false—there is no "difference that makes a difference." There is no *detectable* difference; *is* there a difference at all? *Is* there a meaning to the assertion that every object has doubled in size? We know what it means in the *usual* situation to say that something has doubled in size. We mean, for example, that if we measure the length of this table, it will measure 72 inches today if it was 36 inches yesterday. But that is not what we mean in this case, since the measurement of the table today has the same result as before. What then *is* meant by saying that the table, along with everything else, has doubled in size? If we measure the length of the table, and find its ends to be coincident with the edges of the yardstick, as they were yesterday, we take this observation as sufficient reason for saying that the table has *not* changed in size. Yet on this occasion we are asked to believe that it is compatible with the table and everything else having doubled in size.

"Well, if you can imagine the table alone doubling in size, there should be no difficulty in imagining the table *and everything else* doubling in size." But is this so? We can easily imagine the table doubling in length in relation to all other things, but if everything doubles, how would "everything doubling in size" be different from "everything remaining the same"? It would seem that when we say "the table has doubled in size," we can only mean that it has doubled *in relation to other things,* at least some of which have *not* undergone the change. (If half the objects had doubled in size but the other half remained the same, how would this be different from the first half remaining the same but the second half having shrunk in size?) The concept of length seems to be relational: length is a property a thing has *in relation* to other things. If there is no change in the relation, there is no change in the length.

We see now what "length" ordinarily means: it is the outcome of a measurement made in relation to other things. But in the doubling-hypothesis, this is *not* what it means, for there is no relational change. Therefore either the phrase "doubled its length" is being used meaninglessly in the new case or it is being used in accordance with rules that have not been specified. The concept of length is *tied to a verification-procedure.*

Many statements in science are of this character. "Electrons exist," the physicist says. And we think we know what is meant (tiny marbles) even though we have no idea what the verification procedure would be. But the physicist would tell us, "Whatever *you* mean in talking about electrons, what I mean is nothing more or less than the outcome of certain complex physical operations—just as in the case of 'length.' That is how we introduce the concept of 'electron' in physics, regardless of what mental pictures you may have. So I can tell you what I mean by 'electron' only by informing you of those observations by means of which I would introduce the term. It is only in these observational terms that the term 'electron' is introduced into the scientific language. When this occurs, the meaning is supplied only by specifying the verification-procedure."

How is it that sometimes the meaning of a sentence is absolutely certain while the method of verification is loose and variable—while in other cases the blurred meaning becomes clear and definite only when the method of verification is given? . . . One could formulate the difference thus: When I say "If it rained yesterday, the earth is moist today," then this is not a rule of inference, but an empirical statement. Empirical statements of this kind help us to find out the truth of the assertion, but they do not determine its meaning. The meaning was already established before a method of checking was even mentioned. Therefore the method of testing conforms to the meaning. On the other hand, when I say "If the ball is [electrically] charged, the leaves of the electroscope diverge," I am giving a rule of inference which explains the meaning of the first sentence. The meaning of the sentence is now dependent upon the method of verification. If I specify other rules for the expression, then I thereby change its meaning.[7]

It is probably not quite accurate even in the latter case to say that "the meaning is the method of verification," or even that "to know the meaning is to know the method of verification." It would seem more accurate to say that the sentence is not provided with a meaning until it is *translated into some other sentence or sentences that already have a meaning.* When this translation is supplied, and I know what it means, I thereby know what the original statement means. Only then can I verify the original statement, simply by verifying the second one. I verify the original statement, "The ball is electrically charged," by verifying the second statement, "The leaves of the electroscope diverge." Even here, then, meaning is not verifiability: meaning is supplied by a translation, which then lets me know *what* to verify.

What shall we say, in conclusion, about the testability criterion? As a *general* criterion of meaning, it will not suffice. (1) It will not cover analytic statements, since these are not verified by observation of the world at all. (2) It will not cover nonassertive sentences, such as questions, imperatives, and exclamations; since these assert nothing, there is nothing that could be true or false. (The criterion was never intended to cover these first two types.) (3) It seems that it will not cover statements about one's own experiences, since these are not verified in any easily intelligible sense of

[7] Ibid., p. 332.

"verified." (4) It will not cover value-statements such as "This is good" or "This is praiseworthy" (which we shall consider in Chapter 9), which seem to be statements of an entirely different order. (5) It will not cover metaphysical statements, such as those we are going to discuss in the next three chapters. In general, such statements are defended or attacked by argument, and not by pointing to empirical facts with which one's opponent is unacquainted. Argument is to philosophy what empirical evidence is to science. (One could, to be sure, make a desperate move by saying that all metaphysical controversies are meaningless; but this is to throw out a whole series of problems by means of an arbitrary criterion of meaning. Anti-metaphysicians themselves have admitted that the elimination of meta-physics will have to proceed piecemeal, that each metaphysical problem will have to be dispelled and disposed of separately; they cannot all be eliminated a priori.)

The only area in which the testability criterion is at all plausible is in reference to *empirical* statements, such as are made in daily life and in science. If you make some assertion about the world, you should be able to indicate what observations of the world would count for or against it. But even here, as we have just noticed, we must make a distinction: we already know the meaning of most empirical statements before we know how we could verify them, and knowledge of how to verify them adds nothing to the meaning. Testability as a criterion of *meaning* is plausible only in that rather narrow range of empirical statements the meaning of whose crucial terms is introduced by a translation rule that tells us under what observational conditions the original statement is to be considered true or false.

Meaning-criteria in general. We have now concluded our survey of criteria of sentence-meaning. Is there any one acceptable criterion of sentence-meaning? There is no single one that will cover all cases; there are only separate errors, such as using words outside a given context, mixing up categories, contradicting oneself, etc., which may have no elements in com-mon. We can group all these sentences together and call them all "meaningless" if we like, but the word itself is of no great importance. "Meaningless" is an expendable term. There need be no one criterion for meaninglessness, any more than there is one test for all diseases. To greet someone's sentence by saying "It's meaningless!" is like the physician diagnosing the patient by saying "You're ill." His diagnosis is of no value until he tells the patient what the illness is; and the philosopher who repeatedly says "It's meaningless" without diagnosing the source of the error is being no more helpful than the physician. There is no short and easy way with it; the philosopher must track each specific source of error to its lair, and when he has done so, and his hearer sees for each individual case what has gone wrong, he will no longer need to use the pejorative word "meaningless." Indeed, the use of this term without further explanation will incline others to lump together a large number of errors that should be carefully separated from one another.

Exercises

1. Comment on the following: "I know what it means to say that the star Betelgeuse has a diameter of 200,000 miles and is 650 light-years away, although I haven't the faintest idea how to verify it. I know that astronomers have ways of verifying these statements, or at least confirming them, although I haven't any idea how they do so; but I still know what such statements mean."

"No, you don't know what they mean unless you know how they might be verified. But that needn't be the same as how astronomers actually verify them. For example, by saying that the diameter is 200,000 miles, you would be saying that if you had a foot rule, you would have to use it 5,280 (the number of feet in a mile) × 200,000 times in order to get from one surface of the star to the other, passing through its center. That is what you mean, and it is specified in terms of a logically possible verification, although of course this is not how astronomers actually verify it."

2. Is the concept of "empirical verification" itself clear? How would you verify "George looks more like his younger brother than like his older brother"? Suppose we enumerate contrasts and resemblances, and can list more resemblances to the older brother than to the younger, but someone disagrees with us, saying, "I agree about the points you list, but still I say George looks more like his younger brother." Or consider John Wisdom's example of the lady who was trying on her new hat, was pleased with it, and asked her friend what she thought of it. The friend replied, "My dear, the Taj Mahal!" The first lady could never again bring herself to wear the hat. She now saw it in a new light: it did have something of a dome-like quality. Had she verified the statement "My new hat looks like the Taj Mahal"?

3. "All crows are black" is not verifiable, but it is *falsifiable*. Seeing just one nonblack crow could falsify the statement. Would it be more satisfactory therefore to substitute falsifiability for verifiability in the criterion? Consider such statements as "All swans are white," "Somewhere in the world there is a lavender duck," "There is a solution to this problem, could we but find it." What would be required to verify them? What would be required to falsify them?

4. Which of the following statements would pass the testability criterion, and which would not? In either case, do you consider them meaningful, and why?

   a. There is a deposit of coal 500 feet below where I am now standing.

   b. The temperature at the center of the sun is 40,000,000° C.

   c. The earth is 3,000,000,000 years old.

   d. In the middle of a wilderness 500 miles from the nearest other human being, a hermit has just sneezed.

   e. The hydrogen atom has one electron.

   f. Ghosts exist.

   g. There are cosmic rays even in the enormous interstellar spaces that contain no matter.

   h. The universe had a beginning in time.

   i. Some day there will be no war.

   j. No man is immortal.

   k. The world came into existence (including human beings and their memories) five minutes ago.

   l. God created the world in 4004 B.C., complete with fossils, strata of rock, etc., that would make it look as if it were much older.

5. In each of the following pairs of statements, is there a difference in their meaning? Is there a difference in what you would do to verify them (would anything count as verification of the first but not of the second, and vice versa)?

    a. A is larger than B, and B is larger than C.
      A is larger than C.
    b. This is a mammal.
      This is an animal.
    c. I like custard pudding.
      I do not dislike custard pudding.
    d. Little green elves live in the forest.
      Little blue elves live in the forest.
    e. Invisible elves live in the forest.
      Invisible brownies live in the forest.
    f. Perceivable chairs are in this room.
      Unperceivable chairs are in this room.
    g. Ghosts exist.
      Ghosts do not exist.
    h. The wire gives off sparks, gives electric shocks if one touches it, and affects the voltmeter.
      There is a current in the wire.
    i. Water comes in at one end of the pipe and goes out the other.
      Water flows through the pipe.
    j. Oxygen has a valence of 1.
      Oxygen has a valence of 2.
    k. She has strong, unconscious, guilt-feelings, which demand punishment.
      She acts (without consciously intending it) in such a way that she regularly brings upon herself unfortunate accidents, disapproval of her friends, loss of her job, and other misfortunes.

6. In which of the examples in question 5 is it self-contradictory to assert the first statement and deny the second?

7. Discuss in relation to the testability criterion:

    a. Is it meaningful to talk about other people, perhaps conscious beings on Mars, having senses that enable them to perceive in ways of which we human beings have no conception?

    b. "Imagine a community of men living on a cell in the blood stream of one of us, but so small that we have no evidence, direct or indirect, of their existence. Imagine further that they themselves are provided with scientific instruments of the type we use, and possess a method of science and a body of scientific knowledge comparable to ours. One of the bolder of these thinkers proposes that the universe they inhabit is a Great Man. Is this hypothesis admissible on scientific grounds or is it to be laughed down . . . on the ground that it is 'metaphysical'? . . . Why at our own level cannot a similar hypothesis be raised: namely, that *we* are parts of a Great Man, the whole of our known universe being perhaps but a portion of the Great Blood Stream?" (Charles W. Morris, "Empiricism, Religion, and Democracy," *Conference on Science, Philosophy, and Religion,* p. 219.)

8. What would you say of the following criterion of meaning? "Any statement is meaningful to me if it makes (or can make) some difference in my subsequent experience."

9. "If this is a base, it turns red litmus paper blue." Is "This is a base" a statement that has meaning independent of the other statement? Or is the second statement, "It turns red litmus paper blue," introduced to give meaning to the first one?

10. Read the historic essay by Moritz Schlick, "Meaning and Verification," in *Philosophical Review*, 1936 (reprinted in H. Feigl and W. Sellars, *Readings in Philosophical Analysis*), and Chapter 1 of A. J. Ayer's *Language, Truth, and Logic* for early defenses of the verifiability criterion. Then read a late presentation, for example Carl Hempel's "Problems and Changes in the Empirical Criterion of Meaning," in *Revue Internationale de Philosophie*, 1950 (reprinted in E. Nagel and R. Brandt, *Meaning and Knowledge*). Follow this with an attack on the testability criterion in all its forms, Chapter 5 of Brand Blanshard, *Reason and Analysis*.

11. Professor W. T. Stace has amended the verifiability criterion into the "principle of observable kinds": the existence of some things, such as future sunsets and other people's pains, need not be verifiable, but they must belong to the *kind* of things that can be verified (sunsets, pains). Summarize and comment on this view as set forth in two articles, "Metaphysics and Meaning" in *Mind*, 1935 (reprinted in P. Edwards and A. Pap, *A Modern Introduction to Philosophy*, 2nd ed.), and "Positivism" in *Mind*, 1944.

12. Now consider the following criterion: "A sentence is meaningful if it has a use; we know its meaning if we know its use." (G. J. Warnock, "Verification and the Use of Language," *Revue Internationale de Philosophie*, 1951.) Consider various possible meanings of the word "use." Read further, in this connection, essays by Gilbert Ryle, "Ordinary Language" and "The Theory of Meaning," and P. F. Strawson, "On Referring," all reprinted in C. E. Caton (ed.), *Philosophy and Ordinary Language* (Urbana: University of Illinois Press, 1963), paperback; also W. P. Alston, "Meaning and Use," *Philosophical Quarterly*, 1963.

Selected Readings for Chapter 4

Law, hypothesis, explanation:

Broad, C. D. *Scientific Thought*. London: Routledge & Kegan Paul, Ltd.; 1923.

Campbell, Norman, *What Is Science?* London: Methuen & Co., Ltd., 1920.

Danto, Arthur and Sidney Morgenbesser, *Philosophy of Science*. Cleveland, Ohio: World Publishing Company, 1961. Meridian Books.

Frank, Philipp, *Philosophy of Science*. Englewood Cliffs, N. J.: Prentice-Hall, Inc., 1962.

Hanson, Norwood R., *Patterns of Discovery*. London: Cambridge University Press, 1958.

Hempel, Carl G., *Aspects of Scientific Explanation*. New York: Free Press of Glencoe, Inc., 1966.

————, *Philosophy of Natural Science*. Englewood Cliffs, N. J. Prentice-Hall, Inc., 1966. Paperback.

Hospers, John, "What Is Explanation?" in *Essays in Conceptual Analysis,* ed. Antony Flew. London: Macmillan & Co., Ltd., 1956.

Mill, John Stuart, *A System of Logic*. London: Longmans, Green & Company, Ltd., 1843. Part 3.

Nagel, Ernest, *The Structure of Science*. New York: Harcourt, Brace & World, Inc., 1961.

Pap, Arthur, *Introduction to the Philosophy of Science*. New York: Free Press of Glencoe, Inc., 1962.

The problem of induction:

Black, Max, "Can Induction Be Vindicated?" *Philosophical Studies,* 1959. Reprinted in M. Black, *Models and Metaphors.* Ithaca, N. Y.: Cornell University Press, 1962.

————, "Pragmatic Justifications of Induction," in *Problems of Analysis.* Ithaca, N. Y.: Cornell University Press, 1954.

————, "Induction and Probability," in *Philosophy in the Mid-Century,* Vol. I, ed. R. Klibansky. Florence: La Nuova Italia Editrice, 1958.

Edwards, Paul, "Bertrand Russell's Doubts about Induction," in *Logic and Language,* First Series, ed. Antony Flew. Oxford: B. H. Blackwell, Ltd., 1951.

Harre, R., *An Introduction to the Logic of the Sciences.* London: Macmillan & Co., Ltd., 1960.

Katz, Jerrold J., *The Problem of Induction and Its Solution.* Chicago: University of Chicago Press, 1962.

Kneale, William, *Probability and Induction.* Oxford: Clarendon Press, 1949. Part II.

Madden, E. H. "The Riddle of Induction," in *The Structure of Scientific Thought.* Boston: Houghton Mifflin Company, 1960.

Nagel, Ernest and Richard Brandt (eds.), *Meaning and Knowledge.* New York: Harcourt, Brace & World, Inc., 1965. Chapter 5.

Popper, Karl. *The Logic of Scientific Discovery.* London: Hutchinson & Co. (Publishers), Ltd., 1959.

Russell, Bertrand, *Human Knowledge.* London: George Allen & Unwin, Ltd., 1948.

Salmon, Wesley, "Should We Attempt to Justify Induction?" *Philosophical Studies,* 1957.

————, "Vindication of Induction," in *Current Issues in the Philosophy of Science,* ed. H. Feigl and G. Maxwell. New York: Holt, Rinehart & Winston, Inc., 1961.

Strawson, P. F., *Introduction to Logical Theory.* London: Methuen & Co., Ltd., 1952.

Will, Frederick, "Will the Future Be Like the Past?" *Mind,* 1948.

Williams, Donald, *The Ground of Induction.* Cambridge, Mass.: Harvard University Press, 1947.

Testability and meaning:

Alston, William P., *Philosophy of Language.* Englewood Cliffs, N. J.: Prentice-Hall, Inc., 1964. Paperback. Chapter 4.

Ayer, Alfred J., *Language, Truth and Logic.* London: Victor Gollancz, Ltd., 1936.

————, (ed.), *Logical Positivism.* New York: Free Press of Glencoe, Inc., 1959.

Berlin, Isaiah, "Verification," *Proceedings of the Aristotelian Society,* 1938-1939.

Blanshard, Brand, *Reason and Analysis.* LaSalle, Ill.: Open Court Publishing Co., 1962. Chapter 5.

Carnap, Rudolf, *Philosophy and Logical Syntax*. London: Routledge & Kegan Paul, Ltd., 1935. Reprinted in William Alston and George Nakhnikian (eds.), *Twentieth Century Philosophy*. New York: Free Press of Glencoe, Inc., 1963.

————, "Testability and Meaning," *Philosophy of Science*, 1936-1937.

————, "The Criterion of Cognitive Significance: A Reconsideration," *Proceedings of the American Academy of Arts and Sciences*, 1951.

Hempel, Carl G., "Problems and Changes in the Empiricist Criterion of Meaning," *Revue Internationale de Philosophie*, 1950. Reprinted in Carl G. Hempel, *Aspects of Scientific Explanation*. New York: Free Press of Glencoe, Inc., 1966.

Lazerowitz, Morris, *The Structure of Metaphysics*. London: Routledge & Kegan Paul, Ltd., 1955.

Marhenke, Paul, "The Criterion of Significance," in *Semantics and the Philosophy of Language*, ed. Leonard Linsky. Urbana: University of Illinois Press, 1952.

Passmore, J., *Philosophical Reasoning*. London: Gerald Duckworth & Co., Ltd., 1961. Chapter 5.

Schlick, Moritz, "Meaning and Verification," *Philosophical Review*, 1936. Also in H. Feigl and W. Sellars, *Readings in Philosophical Analysis*. New York: Appleton-Century-Crofts, 1948.

Stace, Walter T., "Positivism," *Mind*, 1944, and "Metaphysics and Meaning," *Mind*, 1936.

Watkins, J. W. N., "Confirmable and Influential Metaphysics," *Mind*, 1958.

5

Cause, Determinism, and Freedom

In this chapter we shall be concerned with one aspect of empirical knowledge, our knowledge of causes. Not only will this issue provide a good testing ground for our remarks about theories of meaning, it is also of considerable interest for other reasons. We use causal language constantly, and the attempt to track down the meaning of "cause" will be an interesting exercise in philosophical analysis; people often think they know what is meant by the word—at any rate, until they are asked. Moreover, the issue leads directly into two of the most discussed problems of philosophy: whether everything that happens has a cause (universal causation), and the relation of cause to human freedom.

15. What Is a Cause?

When we say that drafts cause colds, or that striking a match causes it to light, or that taking arsenic causes death, what do we mean by the word "cause"? What, precisely, are we saying about the relation of the cause, C, to the effect, E, when we say that C causes E?

Our first reaction may be to say, "That's easy. To cause something is to *produce* something, to *bring about* something." Doubtless this is true, but it hardly answers the question: it only shifts it: what does "produce" mean? It is roughly synonymous with the word "cause" itself, and thus we are back where we started. Instead of defining "produce" and "cause" in terms of each other, we should state what they both mean. We want to know what characteristics a C must have in order to cause an E.

Temporal precedence. The simplest empirical statements are those that can be verified by direct observation: "I am sitting down," "Three books are on my desk." We can also observe that some events occur before or after other events: for example, smoke issues from my pipe after I have lighted it but not before, and intoxication follows the consumption of liquor but does not precede it. But do we also observe that one event *causes* another? And if so, what is it that we are observing when we observe this? We observe that someone scratches a match, and that the match lights; but what do we observe when we observe (if we do) that scratching the match *causes* the match to light?

To say that C causes E is not merely to say that C precedes E. Many events occur before others without causing them. Perhaps a moment ago the President of the United States sneezed; but this is in no way a cause of the fact that I am now entering my car. If I ate breakfast at 7:30 this morning and you ate breakfast at 7:31, my eating did not cause yours.

To say that C precedes E, then, is not enough. One might even question whether it is true that whenever C causes E, C precedes E.[1] Your standing in front of a mirror is the cause of your reflection in the mirror; aren't the two simultaneous? Not quite. Light travels at 186,000 miles per second, so the cause of your reflection appearing in the mirror at time t_2, would be your standing in front of the mirror at time t_1, a very small fraction of a second earlier. In most cases, at any rate, the cause precedes (though ever so slightly) the effect. Does it always? If you jump on one side of the seesaw, the other end of the seesaw flies up. Does the other end fly up at the same moment or slightly *after* you have jumped on the first side? Even here it could be argued that it takes time for the effect to occur, since the motion must be imparted all along the board, from one end to the other. But this contention is more dubious than the one about light. There is no known time-lapse in the case of gravitation as there is in the case of light and other forms of radiation. If you throw a ball into the air, it takes time for it to fall back to the earth, but it does not (as far as we know) take time for gravitation to be exerted upon it. If we want to be quite safe, we do not say that the cause always precedes the effect but that the cause *never comes after* the effect.

Even this has sometimes been denied, but this denial seems to be due to a misunderstanding. Suppose I have a goal, such as passing an examination; will this future goal cause me to do certain things in the present, such as study in order to pass it? No, the future event (passing the examination) has not yet occurred and is not yet there to do any causing; indeed, it may never occur at all. What causes you to study, or do anything else in the area of goal-oriented behavior, is your *present* thought of that future goal and your *present* desire to attain it. These states exist now, though the goal itself does not; if it existed now, you would not have to strive to attain it. In general, only something that is already present can do any causing. Rain falling today cannot revive the crops yesterday. Swallowing poison on Tuesday cannot cause a person to die on Monday of the same week.

---

[1] Strictly, that events belonging to a certain class, C, always precede events of a class E. This distinction will become important later in the chapter. Until then we shall not burden our discussion with the rather technical way of speaking that the distinction will require.

A cause, then, never occurs after its effect; but this simple reflection has not taken us very far. We need to know much more than this. Not just anything that precedes something else is its cause. What distinguishes C causing E from C simply preceding E but not causing it? At this point we enter a major arena of controversy.

Necessary connection. Deeply embedded in our ways of talking and thinking is the idea that when the cause, C, brings about the effect, E, there is some "necessary connection" between C and E—that when C occurs, E in some sense *must* occur. Perhaps this will provide us a lead in our attempt to find an answer to our question, "What is a cause?" But what is meant by saying that a given effect *must* occur? What is the meaning of the word "must" in this locution? Let us try some main senses of this word.

1. "You *must* be in by midnight or else . . . ." This is the *imperative* sense of "must," the sense appropriate to commands and laws. A person is told that if he does not do a certain thing, certain punishments will be forthcoming. But this cannot be the sense of "must" appropriate to events in nature. When we say that wood must burn or water must flow downhill, the wood and the water are not being commanded.

A close variant of the first sense occurs when we say "I *must* return the money, since I borrowed it," even though no penalty is attached to failure to do so. Here we mean merely that we believe we are morally obliged to return the money.

Or when someone says, "You *must* come to my party tonight," he is not implying that the person is morally obliged or that there will be penalties if he does not. His statement comes to something like this: "This (x, y, z) is what you'll be missing if you don't come. You must come; that is, if you don't come, you'll be missing x, y, z."

Another variant is still weaker: "It simply *must* be nice weather for tomorrow's picnic." Nature is not being commanded. About all that is expressed by this form of words is wishful thinking: "I wish very much that it would be nice weather tomorrow."

2. Often "must" is used in the context of *inference*. "If p is true, and p implies q, then q *must* be true." Here we mean that q is logically *deducible* from the premises given. We are not saying that q by itself must be true: we are saying that q must be true *if p* is true and p implies q. The "must" here is not contained *in* any one of the statements, not even in the conclusion; the relation of "mustness" (logical necessity) lies in the *relation* between the premises and the conclusion. The conclusion should not be stated as "Therefore q must be true" but rather "Therefore it must be the case that q is true."

In the case above, the inference is deductive, and the "must" is one of logical necessity. But sometimes we use "must" even if the inference is inductive: "He must have been the killer," we say, somewhat loosely, meaning only that we inductively infer it, that the evidence points to it.

3. Often "must" is used to indicate a *necessary condition*. A is a necessary condition for B when, in the absence of A, B never occurs. Oxygen is a necessary condition for human life—that is, in the absence of oxygen human life would be impossible. The heat and light of the sun are necessary conditions for life on the earth—that is, if the earth did not receive heat and light from the sun, there would be no life on the earth. We often use "must" to express this empirical relation: for life to exist, there must be oxygen, there must be heat and light from the sun. We shall have much more to say about necessary conditions shortly.

What is the relevance of these senses of "must" to our discussion of causality? There are several confusions involved in our use of "must" in talking about the processes of nature. We would do well to dwell on these confusions before proceeding, for if we are not thoroughly acquainted with them our discussion of causality may be riddled with these confusions.

1. Confusion of causality with logical necessity. If the premises are true, and the argument is valid, then the conclusion *must* be true. This, as we have seen, is the "logical necessity" sense, or more simply the logical sense, of "must." This relation holds between propositions. There are also statements that by themselves are necessary: the necessary (necessarily true) propositions we considered in Chapter 3, such as "A is A," "Whatever is red is colored," and "Nothing can be red and green all over at the same time." But statements about causality are not logically necessary. "Friction causes heat" is not a logically necessary statement: it is logically possible that friction might have produced magnetic disturbances instead. It is only by empirical observation that we discover what causes what. "Moisture, warmth, and soil cause crops to grow," "Getting one's feet wet causes colds," "Pneumonia is caused by a virus," "The cause of the car's breakdown was a faulty generator"—these and countless other statements about what causes what are empirical statements, which we can know to be true only a posteriori, often after years of investigation. Detailed answers to the questions "What causes cancer?" "What causes the aurora borealis?" "What causes quasars?" and so on are to be found only after prolonged empirical investigation. We cannot get the answers by sitting in an armchair and figuring it out, as we do in mathematics.[2]

This fact is obvious once pointed out, yet people are extremely likely to become confused about it—the logical "must" will still be smuggled in. Let us see how this can happen: Consider the statement "Johnny is taller than Billy." It is, of course, an empirical statement, not a necessary statement. The same is true of the statement "Billy is shorter than Johnny." We have to see Billy and Johnny to discover whether these statements are true. But the statement *"If* Johnny is taller than Billy, then Billy is shorter than Johnny" is

---

[2] The statement "C causes E, but C is not always followed by E" is, of course, self-contradictory *if* "C causes E" means the same as "C is always followed by E." But this, of course, does not make it logically impossible for C *not* to be followed by E; if this happened it would only mean that this C was not the cause of this E.

a logically necessary statement, and we need not know anything about Johnny and Billy to know whether it is true. The same holds true for the uniformities of nature. "Whenever friction occurs, heat occurs" is an empirical law of nature. "Friction occurs" (at some particular place or time) is an empirical statement, and so is the conclusion, "Heat occurs," that is logically deduced from these two statements. But "If whenever friction occurs heat occurs, and friction occurs, then heat occurs" is a logically necessary statement. That heat is produced in any specific instance when friction occurs *can be deduced from a general law of nature* asserting the constant conjunction of friction and heat. The statement *by itself* is not necessary, but when it is the "then" part of an "if-then" statement of which the "if" part asserts a law of nature plus some particular circumstance, *the whole proposition,* the hypothetical or if-then statement, is logically necessary.

Now, how is this apt to confuse us if we are not careful? In the following way: We can say "When there is friction there is always heat, and here there is friction, so it *must* be that there is heat." This is the *logical* sense of the word "must," which only means that the conclusion in question can be logically *deduced* from the premises. The same would apply even if the premises were false: "If all reptiles are green and my dog is a reptile, then it *must* be that my dog is green." The conclusion of a deductive argument can always be prefaced with the word "must," to indicate that the conclusion logically follows from the premises. The danger is that we are apt to put in the "must" *and then forget about the empirical premises from which the conclusion is deduced.* Thus we say, "Stones *must* fall," "Water *must* go downhill," "Organisms *must* die," and so on, forgetting that these are not necessary statements at all but that they can be deduced from general laws of nature. These general laws of nature, however, are empirical; and the conclusions can be called necessary *only with respect to* these non-necessary empirical laws.

But isn't it true that water must flow downhill, that organisms must die? If we still ask this question, we have not grasped the above analysis. What we can observe at best is that water always *does* flow downhill and that all organisms *do* die, and that the statements stating these facts can be deduced from general laws of nature and must (*in the logical sense*) be true *if* the laws are true. Only in this derived sense, then, can we speak of events in nature as if they *must* occur: they, or rather the statements asserting that they occur, can be deduced from general empirical laws, and are necessary only in relation to them, just as "Billy is shorter than Johnny" is necessary only in relation to the premise "Johnny is taller than Billy."

"But once you know the *nature* of the cause that is acting, you know that the effect *must* occur. For example, if you know that this is water, you know that it *must* boil at 212° F. It is of the nature of water to do this, and what is a part of its nature it *must* do." Here we have "must" with us once more; let us see what the confusion is. Probably the speaker means to say "If this is water, it *must* be that it will boil at 212°." (The "must" belongs in the *relation* between premise and conclusion, not in the conclusion itself: "therefore it must be—logically follows—that it boils at 212°," *not* "therefore it must boil at 212°.") Is this proposition true? It all depends on whether boiling at 212° is to be considered a defining characteristic of water. If it *is* a defining characteristic, then of course the statement that it boils at 212° is analytic: "Water boils at 212° F" becomes "Anything that has properties A, B, C (A being the property of boiling at 212°) has A," which is clearly analytic. In that case, if it doesn't boil at 212°, then it is not water. But if it is *not* taken as a defining characteristic—if it is water as long as it is H_2O, for example, regardless of what other properties it has—then the proposition is not analytic: it is synthetic and a posteriori (contingent) and provides no justification at all for saying that water *must* boil at 212°.

2. **Confusion of laws of nature with prescriptive laws.**   As we have seen, we often use the word "must" in the *imperative* sense. "You must be home by eleven o'clock or else . . ." means in effect that if you are not home by eleven o'clock, certain penalties will be imposed. The command imposes upon you a certain *compulsion*. You are not strictly compelled as you are when you are bound and gagged and have no control over your movements; it is always open to you to disobey the command and receive the penalty; nevertheless you are compelled in the sense that you have no choice but to obey the command or accept the penalty; and to this extent, compulsion is being exerted.

Prescriptive laws (see pp. 230–31) are of this same general sort. The law commands you not to drive over 25 miles per hour in a certain zone, and in doing so it compels. Here again we say, "You must obey the law or risk the penalty." The word "must" in the imperative sense usually carries a strong emotive meaning, in this case evocative (see pp. 51–53); it is intended to act as an influence upon the person being commanded, in the direction of obeying the command.

People who do not clearly distinguish descriptive from prescriptive law are all too inclined to talk about the laws of nature and the laws of a statute body as if they were the same. In doing so, they may use words like "must," which are legitimate enough when one is talking about prescriptive law, to apply to descriptive laws as well. But if we take such assertions literally, they make no cognitive sense. "Water must flow downhill," we say; but the water is not being commanded. The law simply describes a uniformity that occurs in the order of nature. It prescribes nothing, commands nothing.

The laws of celestial mechanics do not prescribe to the planets how they have to move, as though the planets would actually like to move otherwise, and are only forced by these burdensome laws of Kepler to move in ordinary paths; no, these laws do not in any way "compel" the planets, but express only what in fact planets actually do.[3]

[3] Moritz Schlick, *The Problems of Ethics* (Englewood Cliffs, N.J.: Prentice-Hall, Inc.), p. 147.

Historically, the two senses of the word "law" were not distinguished. The uniformities of nature were conceived as the expression of the will of the gods, or of God. God *commands* the forces of nature to operate in certain ways, *compelling* every event to occur. Since he is far more powerful than any government, his laws are inviolable. Moreover, since God is good, his laws are so also: the laws of nature are the expression of a *moral order* supernaturally imposed upon the universe. The workings of this order *must* be as they are because they are the expression of divine will. Effects follow causes much as punishment follows forbidden acts and reward follows approved acts; they follow necessarily, because the laws are enforced by an all-powerful Deity. With this conception of the universe, it is no wonder that words such as "must" and "necessary" came to be attached to statements about causes and effects.

It is not relevant at this point to discuss whether this view of the universe is true; the question is whether the truth of this view is presupposed in every statement we make about causes or effects. When we say "Friction causes heat" or "The appearance of the lion caused the antelope to flee," do we really mean to imply this view of nature, so that if this view of nature were not true, we would not be entitled to make any statements at all about causality? Surely this is not the case. Whether we view nature as a manifestation of divine will or not, this is *no part of what we mean* when we make causal statements in everyday life. We would wish to argue this view of nature *separately:* we would first utter the causal statements (about friction, the antelope, or about anything else) in any case, and then go on, *in addition,* to assess this view of nature.

The question which must be put to those who speak as if there were necessity in nature is whether they really mean to imply that the laws of nature are normative rules, enforced by a divine will. If they do not mean to imply this, their talk of necessity is at best an unfortunate metaphor.[4]

3. Confusion resulting from animistic use of language. One may object that the view of nature just described does not literally make sense: do not words like "command" and "compel" and "necessitate" have meaning only within the context of human beings, beings who have wills and can thus be made to do things against their will? Stones and waterfalls have no wills, and therefore they can hardly be said to be *commanded* or *compelled*.

This, of course, is true, *unless* stones and waterfalls *are* conceived as having wills. In the primitive view of things called "animism," this is precisely the case. Animism is the tendency to confer upon inanimate objects characteristics which belong only to animate beings.

Today people are no longer animistic in any literal sense: we do not believe that the mountains and trees are spirits, nor even that they contain

[4] A. J. Ayer, *Foundations of Empirical Knowledge,* p. 198.

spirits; we do not believe that the tree feels pain when it is cut down or that the stone is animated by a desire to get to the center of the earth; we do not believe that water is compelled to do anything, because only animate beings can have compulsion exerted upon them and water is inanimate. Nevertheless, we often talk *as if* we believed these things. We "read our feelings into nature." We speak of the sky as gloomy, though it is we who feel gloom and not the sky; we speak of the chasm as yawning, of the earth as smiling, of the train as "steaming away impatiently." Poetry is filled with animistic language, and the poetic quality is often enhanced by it. But in philosophy, it is important that we be careful about this way of using language. Animistic language can be misleading, as a few examples will show:

Originally the word "resistance" stood for a certain kind of feeling people had, for example when trying to move a boulder or hold a heavy door open. Now we speak of resistance even when no animate beings are involved: we say that the object resists pressure, resists our attempts to move it, and so on, although we do not mean that it *feels* resistance. The word "resistance" has become transferred from the feeling to the thing which occasioned the feeling. We impute resistance to the doorstop that holds the door open because if *we* were in the position of the doorstop we would feel resistance. "Resistance," "force," "energy" and other animistically tinged words are constantly used in the physical sciences. Here, however, they are comparatively harmless, for they are given special and precise meanings within these fields.

You push a large ball and start it rolling toward the place where you want it. On another occasion you see another ball strike it, thereby imparting the motion to it. The work done is approximately the same. But since on the first occasion you pushed to get the ball where you wanted it, you incline to say, when you see the other ball doing the same work, that the first ball *pushed* the second, or *forced* it to go in the path it took, or even *compelled* it to go. This language is, of course, somewhat misleading. If these expressions refer simply to what you observe, namely that one ball makes contact with another and the other starts moving in a certain direction (what a motion-picture camera would record), then you have not gone beyond the empirically observable facts. But the words you use to describe the situation *seem* to import into the situation something that is not there at all; they seem to imply that the first ball had a feeling of effort or strain in "pushing" the second one, and that the second felt "resistance" to the motion of the first. We do not really believe this, but our language leaves the impression that we do.

The same is true even when we say that the first ball *makes* the second one move. If this means merely that when the first ball hits the second the second moves, and that this regularly occurs, then we are merely describing what we observe. But there is an animistic ring about the word "makes," which seems to hint at some kind of compulsion. In using all these words, let us remember that what we observe is simply that when the first ball strikes the second the second moves, and that this regularly happens. There is no more. We probably do not seriously demand more; but our linguistic habits, a carry-over from primitive times when animism was literally interpreted, do not render this instantly evident, and they are apt to confuse us. Probably there is no objection to using this kind of language, provided that we are clear about what we are doing; but our language is so full of animism that *unconsciously our thought becomes so,* and we are left with verbal expressions which we have the impulse to defend even though we cannot seriously take them literally. That is why we often resist the tendency to describe causal relations exclusively in terms of what we can observe. We want to say, "The first billiard ball *compels* the second one to move," and "When the first hits the second, the second *must* move," or even "When the first hits the second, the second *can't help* moving" (as if it were a conscious being that could avoid doing things if it wished to) or "The first ball *forces* the second to move" (note the implicit comparison with a quite different kind of situation, such as a robber forcing you to give up your money). These are the ghosts of animism which haunt our everyday language. We have been so accustomed since childhood to talking in these ways that we come to feel we have lost something when we have translated "The first ball caused the second one to move" into "When the first ball contacts the second, the second regularly moves." We do not feel quite so much at home with this straightforward, nakedly empirical, studiedly non-animistic language; and so we feel that we mean more than this, even though we cannot discover what the more is. When we have reached this stage, we are ready to begin using such terms as "necessary connection," whether they stand for anything or not: they "have the right kind of sound," they fill the vacuum created by the removal of the animistic overtones from our everyday causal language.

Cause as "constant conjunction." If we are not entitled to say that the cause "must" be followed by the effect, if "necessary connection" (as applied to the processes of nature) is a myth or even a meaningless phrase, what then shall we give as a positive account of the causal relation? David Hume (1711–1776), the philosopher who more than any other attacked the necessary-connection theory, also set forth a novel analysis of the causal relation. Causality, he said in effect, is merely "constant conjunction"—or, in other words, "C causes E" means the same as "C is constantly conjoined with E"; or, in still other words (assuming the effect is later than the cause), "C is regularly followed by E." What is it, Hume asked, that entitles us to say that C causes E, that friction causes heat, that lightning causes thunder, that windstorms cause trees to blow down? Empirical observation, he replied. And what is it that we observe? We observe that C precedes E, but that of course is not enough. What observation is it then that entitles us to say that C causes E? Is it observation of a necessary connection among events in nature? No, said Hume, for we never observe any such thing. What we observe is always that things *do* occur in a certain way, never that they *must* occur in that way. Try as we will, we never find a "must" in the workings of nature. Empirical observation gives us no justification at all for using expressions such as "C is *necessarily connected* with E," "E *must* occur," "E *has to* occur."

But if causality is not necessary connection, what is it? What is it that we observe when we observe that C causes E? Let us see: When we observe the world around us, at any given moment we find many events occurring; some happen simultaneously with others, some earlier, some later. As we observe this shifting panorama of events around us, we begin, however, to notice certain *repeating sequences* of events—some C's which are *regularly* followed by certain E's. C is followed by E once, twice, ten times, a thousand times—and when we find that C is *regularly* followed by E, we say that C *causes* E. In other words, causality is *constant conjunction* among events. Observing a causal relation between C and E is merely observing that C and E regularly go together—that they are *constantly conjoined*. One observation, of course, is not sufficient to entitle us to say that C causes E; before we can say that we must have observed many conjunctions of C with E, the more the better. The difference between C being followed by E on one occasion and C causing E is that in the second case the conjunction between C and E is *regular,* or *constant.* In other words, "Always, if C, then E." As two modern Humeans put it,

To say that the electric current causes a deflection of the magnetic needle means that whenever there is an electric current there is always a deflection of the magnetic needle. The addition in terms of *always* distinguishes the causal law from a chance coincidence. It once happened that while the screen of a motion picture theater showed the blasting of lumber, a slight earthquake shook the theater. The spectators had a momentary feeling that the explosion on the screen caused the shaking of the theater. When we refuse to accept this interpretation, we refer to the fact that the observed coincidence was not repeatable.

Since repetition is all that distinguishes the causal law from a mere coincidence, the meaning of causal relation consists in the statement of an exceptionless repetition—it is unnecessary to assume that it means more. The idea that a cause is connected with its effect by a sort of hidden string, that the effect is forced to follow the cause, is anthropomorphic in its origin and is dispensable; *if-then-always* is all that is meant by a causal relation. If the theater would always shake when an explosion is visible on the screen, then there would be a causal relationship.[5]

The difference between a mere temporal sequence and a causal sequence is the regularity, the uniformity of the latter. If C is *regularly* followed by E, then C is the cause of E; if E only "happens" to follow C now and then, the

[5] Hans Reichenbach, *The Rise of Scientific Philosophy,* pp. 157–58.

sequence is called mere chance. And since (as we just saw) the observation of the regularity was the *only* thing that was done, it was necessarily the *only* reason for speaking of cause and effect, it was the *sufficient* reason. The word "cause," as used in everyday life, implies *nothing but* regularity of sequence, because *nothing else* is used to verify the propositions in which it occurs.[6]

To know whether C causes E, then, is to know whether C is regularly followed by E. If C is followed by E only sometimes, then the relation is not causal. Causation is nothing more or less than regularity of sequence. What entitles us to say that C causes E is the relation of *regularity* between C and E. This, together with temporal precedence, gives us a definition of "cause." C is the cause of E only if (1) C precedes E and (2) C and E *regularly* occur together.

It will be obvious that on Hume's account there is no such thing as a priori knowledge of causes. We cannot know in advance of experience what causes what, because we cannot know in advance of experience which events will be regularly followed by which other events. "There are no objects," wrote Hume, "which by the mere survey, without consulting experience, we can determine to be the causes of any other; and no objects, which we can certainly determine in the same manner not to be the causes."

When we see two trains rapidly approaching each other a hundred feet apart on the same track, can we not say a priori that they will have a collision? Even here the answer is no. Prior to experience of how solid objects behave, we could have no idea what would happen when they approached each other. It is always *previous experience* that enables us to predict what will happen. Since long before the time we began remembering events we have been acquainted with the behavior of moving bodies; but if we were opening our eyes on the world for the first time and saw the trains approach each other, we would have no more evidence that they would collide than that they would swerve apart, explode, turn to gas, dissolve, be annihilated, or fly to the moon. Experience and experience alone can tell us what causes what. A priori, any conjunction of events is equally probable; we have to learn through experience which are the ones that actually occur.

Volitions as causes. Yet one may object: "What you say may be true enough of events in external nature; but there *are* some events in which we are aware of a necessary connection, namely those involving our own will, or volition. I am not aware of any necessary connection between lighting the fuse and the explosion, only of constant conjunctions between these two events; but I *am* aware of it in the case of willing something and then doing it. Here there is real necessary connection between the cause and the effect."

[6] Moritz Schlick, "Causality in Everyday Life and in Science," in *Knowledge and Value* (1st ed.), ed. E. Sprague and P. Taylor (New York: Harcourt, Brace & World, Inc), p. 195. First printed in *University of California Publications in Philosophy*, XV (1932).

Hume replies that an act of will causing a motion of your body is no different from any of the other examples. The only difference here is that there is included in the cause (the volition) an *idea* of the effect to be produced. But we still have to know what causes what by observing constant conjunctions. I know from experience that willing to move my arm is followed by moving my arm, but that moving my liver, or my car, or the moon does not occur upon my willing to do these things. The new-born baby may assume that everything is under the control of his will, but many *failures* of constant conjunctions to occur teach him the bitter lesson that it is not so. What things he *can* do he finds out by noting what acts are constantly conjoined with their volitions: for example, bending his lower legs backwards, but not forwards.

Moreover, another condition is required, namely that one's limbs be in good working order, for if one is spastic or has suffered a paralytic stroke, no amount of willing will enable one's limbs to move in the desired manner. The real constant conjunction, then, is between C-1 (willing to raise the arm) *plus* C-2 (limbs in good working order) and E (raising the arm). How then can there be a necessary connection between the volition and the event, when in some cases the event does not even follow upon the volition?

A man, suddenly struck with palsy in the leg or arm, or who had newly lost these members, frequently endeavours, at first to move them and employ them in their usual offices. Here he is as much conscious of power to command such limbs, as a man in perfect health is conscious of power to actuate any member which remains in its natural state and condition. . . . Neither in the one case nor in the other, are we ever conscious of any . . . necessary connexion. We learn the influence of our will from experience alone. And experience only teaches us, how one event constantly follows another.[7]

Objections to Hume's account. This, then, is Hume's account of causality; but tempting as it is, this will not do as it stands. (1) There seem to be many cases of constant conjunction that are not cases of causality. The green lights at the traffic intersection go on, then the red lights, then the green, and so on in constant conjunction, yet the green ones do not cause the red ones to go on. Night and day regularly follow one another yet do not cause one another. The growth of hair in babies is regularly followed by the growth of teeth, yet the first does not cause the second. (2) There seem to be many cases of causality that are not cases of constant conjunction. Scratching the match, we say, causes it to light; but the scratched match doesn't always light. Eating spicy foods causes a man to have an attack of ulcers, yet eating spicy foods doesn't always lead to ulcers. Seeing you at a prizefight may cause me to be surprised, but if I see you there a second time I may not be surprised. I decide to raise my arm and my arm goes up, but if I suddenly thereafter have

[7] David Hume, *An Enquiry Concerning Human Understanding,* Part VII.

a paralytic stroke and cannot raise my arm, it remains true that my deciding to lift it is what caused it to go up the first time. And so on. A Humean kind of analysis may still suffice, but not Hume's analysis.

Let us analyze more carefully what is meant by "constant conjunction." Does it mean that every time C occurs, E occurs? Does it mean that if E occurs, we can infer that C has occurred? Does it mean that if C does not occur, E will not occur? Here we come to a distinction that is of great importance in talking about causality: the distinction between necessary and sufficient condition; for the phrase "constant conjunction" does not make clear whether it refers to necessary condition, sufficient condition, or both.

1. Necessary condition.   When we say that C is a necessary condition for the occurrence of E, we do not mean that there is a "necessary connection" between C and E, although we sometimes say "In order for E to occur, C *must* occur." What we mean (or should mean) is simply the empirical fact that in the absence of C, E never occurs. Thus, in the absence of oxygen, we never have fire. The presence of oxygen is in no sense a *logically* necessary condition for the occurrence of fire; indeed, it is conceivable that something quite different from oxygen, say the presence of an elephant, would be a necessary condition of fire. Only by experience can we know what the conditions are, the absence of which is followed by the absence of the event. "Oxygen is necessary for fire" is thus a simple empirical statement, testable in experience.

If oxygen (C) is necessary to fire (E), we can also say that if there is fire there is oxygen present. Thus we can say that when C is a necessary condition for E

If not C, then not E,

or, what is the same thing,

If E, then C.

But we cannot say either of these things:

If C, then E.
If not E, then not C.

2. Sufficient condition.   C is said to be sufficient for the occurrence of E if, invariably, whenever C occurs, E occurs. "If rain is falling on the street, the street is wet." The occurrence of the rain is sufficient for the street's being wet. It is not necessary, however: the street might be wet even if it had not rained at all, for example if a water sprinkler had just passed. To say that C is sufficient for E is to say

If C, then E,

or what is the same thing,

> If not E, then not C.

But we cannot say either of these things:

> If not C, then not E.
> If E, then C.

Thus, necessary condition and sufficient condition are the reverse of each other.

Cause as sufficient condition.   In the light of this distinction, is it plausible to define "cause" as necessary condition? Quite clearly it is not: there are hosts of necessary conditions that we would not call causes. For example, if someone asks you, "Why have you registered for this course?" and you reply, "Well, I was born, you know," your answer would not be considered satisfactory. Yet being born is a necessary condition for your being here or anywhere else at this moment. For any event at all to occur, it is a necessary condition that there be a universe; but if you are asked for the cause of a given event, it will not do to answer that there is a universe. Cause, then, is not the same as necessary condition. Necessary condition does have something to do with causality: we often speak of a necessary condition as *a* causal factor (not as *the* cause): for example, before something can burn there must be oxygen: oxygen is a necessary condition for combustion. It can be said to be *a* causal factor in combustion (unlike the color of the combustible object, which is not a causal factor at all), but it is certainly not *the* cause.

What, then, of sufficient condition? Attempting to remedy the defects in Hume's account of causality, John Stuart Mill (1806–1873) defined "cause" as sufficient condition. What conditions are sufficient for combustion? (1) There must be a combustible material. (2) There is a temperature requirement: when the substance is heated to a certain temperature, it will burn. (What the temperature is differs from one substance to another.) (3) There must be oxygen. When all these conditions are present, the substance burns; these conditions are together *sufficient*. Let us note that each of the conditions *alone* is necessary but that no one of them alone is sufficient. All three of them must be present before we have a sufficient condition. The combination of conditions that together constitute the sufficient condition is the cause of the event.

The case of combustion is unusually simple: only three conditions are sufficient for combustion. What is sufficient for the car to function properly? The conditions here are far more numerous: the wheels must be attached, the axles must not be broken, the motor and generator and countless other parts must be functioning properly and be connected in a certain way, and so on.

The list of necessary conditions would run into the thousands. And each one of these thousands would have to be listed as *part* of the sufficient condition, for anything less than *all* of them is not sufficient for the car to run. Yet this example is simple indeed compared with examples in the biological realm, and even simpler compared with examples in the human realm: what set of conditions must be fulfilled in order for a person to enjoy a philosophical discussion, for example? The conditions here are staggeringly complex, and even if we list many items, we probably do not yet have a sufficient condition. In general, it is much easier to list necessary conditions (conditions in the absence of which the event never occurs) than sufficient conditions (conditions in the presence of which the event always occurs).

Sufficient conditions, then, are far from simple. The only ones that can be easily stated are those that cause "negative events"—the *failure* of something to occur. For your electric radio not to work, it is sufficient to pull out the plug. It is also sufficient to remove one of the tubes. Here there are many conditions, each of which *alone* is sufficient. But for the positive event to occur—for the radio to function properly—there is no simple set of sufficient conditions; the list is long, but at least in this case the radio repairman knows the whole set of conditions on which the radio's working depends, for he *can* (usually) get a radio to work, and of course it would not work unless a set of conditions sufficient for its working had been fulfilled. In the case of preserving bodily health to the age of 100, no complete set of conditions is known.

"The cause, then, philosophically speaking," writes Mill, "is the sum total of the conditions, positive and negative taken together; the whole of the contingencies of every description, which being realized, the consequent [event] invariably follows." According to Mill, this is the correct scientific definition of "cause." *The* cause (the *whole* cause) is the set of conditions sufficient to produce the event—that is, the set of conditions upon the fulfillment of which the event invariably occurs. To state what is the cause of an event is to enumerate this whole set of conditions.

It is not a single *event* that causes another event. What causes an event (the effect) is a whole set of *conditions,* of which some are events (like lighting the fuse) but others are states of a substance (the powder is dry) and still others are states of the environment (there is oxygen in the air). Causation normally occurs in the history of enduring entities, which we call substances or, more popularly, things. (This may not be true in every case, however: lightning may cause a man's death; but is a bolt of lightning a substance?) Thus does Mill attempt to circumvent the objection often made against Hume's view, that events do not by themselves cause other events. Hume never said that they did, but his constant reference to constant conjunctions between cause and effect, as if the cause were one event and the effect another, led many critics to conclude that Hume thought that the cause of an event was always another event.

Does Mill's account square with our use of the word "cause" in daily life? Not entirely. Mill attempted to give the "scientific account," which required the listing of *all* the conditions upon which the event depends. But in daily life we say that scratching the match caused it to light, eating arsenic caused the man's death, lighting the fuse caused the gunpowder to explode, falling from a ladder caused the man to break his leg. Not one of these conditions is sufficient for the occurrence of the event in question: they all require the presence of countless other conditions, which are *assumed* to be present. Out of the vast variety of conditions that together constitute the sufficient condition, we select one and call it the cause, though they are *all* equally indispensable to the event in question, and all equally parts or components of the sufficient condition. We select the one that we do because (1) it is the last condition to be fulfilled before the effect takes place, or (2) it is the condition we believe our hearer does not already know about, or (3) it is the condition whose share in the matter is the most conspicuous. Thus the gunpowder is in place, there is oxygen in the air, etc., and lighting the fuse is the last thing you have to do in order to make the powder explode. Or we say that eating arsenic caused his death, although he could have eaten ten times as much arsenic with impunity if his stomach walls had been made of iron; but we assume that our hearer already knows that the stomach walls are not so constituted, so we do not mention this as a cause, though it is just as much a causal factor as eating the arsenic. Or we say that he broke his leg because he fell from a ladder, though we do not mention that he landed on solid ground rather than in a mud puddle, or that his body was heavier than air (without which he would not have fallen to earth after slipping off the ladder). In our daily causal talk, then, we talk as if one event by itself caused another event, but this is in fact not so: for various practical reasons we isolate one condition and talk as if this were the cause, though in fact there may be many causal conditions all of which would be required before we had a condition that is sufficient.

When the causal factors are extremely numerous, as they are in the realm of human behavior, we are more than ever inclined to speak in this way. What is the cause of this burglary? "The lock was easy to break open," says one person. "Everyone living in the house was out," says another. "The house was set fairly far back from the street." "It was a dark moonless night, in which detection and identification would have been difficult." "The burglar had just escaped in the prison break." "Consider his family background—there lies the *real* cause." All of these are causal factors; all of them may have had something to do with the effect in this case, but we single out one of them and talk as if it were *the* cause.

Often we call that one factor the "cause" and all the others the "conditions." But Mill concluded that there is no basis for such a distinction: all of the factors are causally relevant to the occurrence of the effect.

Not much remains of the original account of cause as event-C-followed-by-event-E. Often an event that is regularly followed by another event is not even a causal factor. The constant conjunction between C and E may be the result of something that causes them both. The red light goes on with monotonous regularity after the green light, and the green in turn after the red, but there is no causal relation: there is a mechanism that controls the patterns of succession of the lights, and if that mechanism were not working, neither the red nor the green would go on. For a similar reason, day is not the cause of night or night the cause of day, although there is a constant conjunction between them. There is a regular alternation of day and night, and the cause of this alternation is that (1) the earth rotates on its axis; (2) the sun continues to shine (if it didn't, the turning of the earth would be in vain as far as the coming of day is concerned); and (3) there is no opaque material between the earth and the sun, shutting off the sun's light. These are the conditions that are together sufficient for the alternation of day and night to occur, and each of them is a necessary condition.

Plurality of causes. Several conditions together make up a sufficient condition; but is each of these always a necessary condition? Perhaps conditions 1, 2, and 3 are together sufficient to produce E; but perhaps conditions 4, 5, and 6 are also together sufficient to produce E, even though 1, 2, and 3 do not occur. Then we have *two* sufficient conditions for E. Or perhaps there is an overlapping: 1, 2, and 3 may be sufficient for E, and 1, 2, and 4 are also sufficient for E. In that case, conditions 1 and 2 are necessary, for E does not occur without them, but conditions 3 and 4 are not, since sometimes E does occur without them.

It certainly *seems* as if plurality of causes often occurs. The same effect may occur from a different set of conditions. If we want to remove a stain from a garment, we can do so by using gasoline or carbon tetrachloride or any of a number of other chemical reagents. We can produce certain organic compounds either by inducing chemical reactions in living organisms or by synthesizing them out of their elements or simpler compounds. You can get expelled from school by writing inflammatory material in the college newspaper, by planting a bomb under the president's desk, and so on.

On the other hand, it often happens that the plurality of causes is only apparent. (1) Sometimes *too much* is included in the statement of the sufficient condition. If pulling the plug is sufficient for the radio not to play, then pulling the plug *plus* the moon being full is also sufficient: every time you pull the plug and the moon is full the radio stops playing. But we do not consider the moon a causal factor because the radio stops playing when you pull the plug whether the moon is full or not. In this example the irrelevance of the moon is easy to see, but other examples are not quite so obvious. Thus we may say that billiard ball B is caused to move in a certain direction not merely by being struck by billiard ball A but by being struck with your elbow, or by jiggling the table, or by a slight earth-tremor. But this can hardly be considered a genuine case of plurality of causes: what is necessary and sufficient for the movement of the ball in this direction is that a certain degree of force be applied upon it in that direction; it does not matter who or what wields the force, and therefore no mention of these particulars need be made in a list of the conditions on which the event depends. Thus, in the numbered conditions we considered two paragraphs earlier, to include 3 and 4 as conditions may be including too much: what really does the causing is a component, C, that 3 and 4 have in common. If this is so, plurality has been eliminated, because the total set of conditions is in both cases 1, 2, and C. (2) Sometimes the same *general type* of effect can be brought about by different means: a house may burn down as a result of lightning, an overheated furnace, arson, and so on. If "house burning down" is the effect, then it can certainly be brought about by different sets of conditions. But the insurance inspector who examines the ruins after the fire can often detect the difference between fire-from-lightning and fire-from-overheated-furnace through a careful examination of the ruins. The effect *is* somewhat different in the two cases, and "destruction by fire" is a blanket term that covers many *different* specific effects. Perhaps if we broke down the effects as carefully as we do the causes, we would end up with no plurality of causes at all.

We shall not try to decide the issue of plurality of causes: this is a matter for scientists to decide empirically; our only concern is to be quite clear what the term means. We shall talk about causality in such a way as to leave open the question of plurality of causes. When we say that C, the cause, is sufficient for E, the effect, we shall not be committing ourselves about whether it is the *only* set of conditions that is invariably followed by E.

Our knowledge of causes.   Since we have no a priori knowledge of what causes what, the answer to the question "How, then, do we know what causes what?" may seem simple indeed: empirical observation. But this is not a specific enough answer. What kind of observation will tell us what causes what? We can tell from observation that one event precedes another—that lightning precedes thunder; can we tell from one observation what causes what?

Suppose you have observed on innumerable occasions that a piece of paper burns when you put it into a fire. You assumed that heating a combustible substance to a certain temperature is sufficient for its combustion. Then you tried the experiment in a chamber containing no oxygen and found that it did not burn. You may never have thought of the presence of oxygen as a condition, since in our experience oxygen is normally present; but once it is absent, try to start a fire without it and you see that it is a necessary condition. You could not know a priori that it was oxygen rather than something else: you only know by repeated experiments. Similarly, if you want to know whether a vaccine is sufficient to keep guinea pigs from having a disease, inject them with the vaccine and see whether they get the disease when they are exposed to it. (If only some of them do, there are other conditions operating that you have not yet tracked down.) You can, indeed, know from one experiment that one condition, C, is the cause of E *only* if you know that everything else has remained the same. If I push a button and a light goes on, I can infer a causal relation between these two *only* if I know that everything else in the situation has remained the same; and how can I know this after only one trial? Something else might have happened just at the moment I pushed the button that was the cause (or at least a *part* of the sufficient condition). If I push it again and again, and every time I do the light goes on, then it becomes more and more likely that it was *a* causal factor (together with other standing conditions, such as the circuit not being broken and the power plant continuing to operate). If you want to know whether C is necessary for E, vary the conditions and see whether you *ever* get E without C. If you want to know whether C is sufficient for E, try the conditions C and observe whether E always occurs.

What is the force of the "always"? Presumably "always" is to be taken literally, meaning in all cases, past, present, and future. But if this is so, you cannot know now that C causes E, because you haven't observed any future cases (nor countless past and present cases). Nevertheless, as in any law of nature, all this is involved: when you say that a combustible material heated in the presence of oxygen causes combustion, you imply that if the conditions are fulfilled, it will occur tomorrow, not merely today and yesterday. And this, of course, you cannot strictly *know:* you can only get varying degrees of probability. All our past experience leads us to believe that paper will burn in the fire tomorrow if oxygen is present: it has always happened under these conditions, and we can think of no other conditions that are also necessary. This is all we need for practical purposes, and in any case it is all that is attainable. We need merely say, "All our experience thus far has shown that C causes E, and nothing in our entire experience has cast a shadow of a doubt upon it." Whether C will be followed by E tomorrow we do not know for sure till tomorrow comes.

Other anályses of causality. Thus far we have not questioned the definition of "cause" as "sufficient condition." Many, however, would disagree with this definition. They might not question Mill's right to use the word "cause" in this way, but they would point out that this is not the way we use the word in daily life, and that we ordinarily mean something quite different. Mill was attempting to give a scientific definition—that is, a definition that would reflect the way the word "cause" is used in scientific endeavor; and perhaps his use of the word does approximate the scientific usage. But, it is contended, in our everyday discourse we do not mean by "cause" what Mill means. What, then, is its meaning in daily life?

Person-to-person causality. According to R. G. Collingwood (1889–1943), the original, the fundamental, the primordial sense of "cause" occurs in the actions of human beings in relation to other human beings. Whenever I induce, persuade, urge, force, or compel you to do something, I am causing you to act in a certain way. The influence may range all the way from causing you voluntarily to act differently from what you otherwise would to my forcing you to do so. Clearly if I force you at the point of a gun, I am causing you to do something (something you would not otherwise have done). But when the headline reads "Churchill's speech causes adjournment of House of Commons," it does not mean that the speech compelled the Speaker to adjourn the House; it meant that on hearing Churchill's speech, the Speaker freely made up his mind to adjourn. In the same way we say that a solicitor's letter causes a man to pay a debt. It is to the influence of human agents on other human agents that we must trace the origin of the idea of causality:

From what impression, as Hume pertinently asks, is this idea derived? I answer, from impressions received in our social life, in the practical relations of man to man; specifically, from the impression of "compelling" or "causing" some other man to do something when, by argument or command or threat or the like, we place him in a situation in which he can only carry out his intentions by doing that thing; and conversely, from the impression of being compelled or caused to do something.[8]

It is this primitive sense of "cause" as directly influencing or even compelling another human agent that is responsible for our tendency to use the language of "necessary connection" in speaking of causality: we feel the influence or compulsion exerted by ourselves, or by others upon us, and when we tend to think of objects in the physical world whose course we change by our actions as if they too were other agents whom we could compel, then we have animism—which explains why our daily talk about causality is shot through with animism.

Though this is the most basic or primitive sense of "cause," it is not the only sense, or even the principal sense, in which we use the word today. But even so, says Collingwood, Mill is wrong; for our principal daily sense is an *extension* of this primitive sense, but not as far away from it as is Mill's. What, then, is this principal sense?

Person-to-thing causality.   By our actions we not only influence other human beings but change the course of events in nature.

In sense 2, no less than in sense 1, the word "cause" expresses an idea relative to human action; but the action in this case is an action intended to control, not other human beings, but things in "nature", or "physical" things. In this sense, the "cause" of an event in nature is *the handle, so to speak, by which we can manipulate it.* If we want to produce or to prevent such a thing, and

[8] R. G. Collingwood, "On the So-called Idea of Causation," quoted in *Freedom and Responsibility,* ed. Herbert Morris (Stanford, Calif.: Stanford University Press, 1961), p. 307. The article was first published in *Proceedings of the Aristotelian Society,* 1938, pp. 85–108.

cannot produce or prevent it immediately (as we can produce or prevent certain movements of our own bodies), we set about looking for its "cause." The question "What is the cause of an event y?" means in this case "How can we produce or prevent y at will?" . . .

This is an extremely common sense in modern everyday usage. The cause of a bruise is the kick which a man received on his ankle; the cause of malaria is the bite of a mosquito; the cause of a boat's sinking is her being overloaded; the cause of books going mouldy is their being kept in a damp room; the cause of a person's sweating is that he has taken aspirin; the cause of a furnace going out in the night is that the draught door was insufficiently open; the cause of seedlings dying is that nobody watered them; and so forth.[9]

In every one of these cases, the event is something we can either produce or prevent. The cause is the manipulatory handle by means of which we can do the producing or preventing. Just as we can alter the actions of other human beings, so we can alter the course of certain events in nature; and the cause is what we do to alter them.

When the pencil drops from your hand to the ground, nobody would say that the cause of its fall during the second movement of its downward journey is its fall during the first movement, or that the cause of the third was the second, and so on. Yet as long as the Law of Gravitation continues to operate, and no object is in the way to interrupt its fall, its being at one point at time t_1 is a sufficient condition for its being at a point 1 millimeter below it at time t_2, a small fraction of a second later. But we do not speak of causality in this way; rather, we say that my letting go of the pencil was the cause of its hitting the floor. Or if we heat a piece of iron by putting it into a flame, it will glow; but we do not normally say that we can cause the iron to glow: we cause it to heat (by putting it into the fire), and when it is sufficiently heated, it glows by itself without further activity on our part. In both cases, the condition mentioned is a necessary condition for the effect, as well as a component of the sufficient condition; yet we do not speak of it as a cause. Why is this?

According to the view we are now considering, the answer is that we do not call any condition a cause unless it involves something we can *do* to bring about the effect. We correctly say that our letting go of the stone is the cause of its falling: this is what we *do* to get the stone to fall. We don't do something to get the stone to fall the second moment of its fall that we didn't already do the first moment. After we let it go, there is no more we need to do for it to hit the ground. Letting go of the stone is a *manipulatory technique* we use to get the stone to fall. Similarly, in the case of the iron, we don't do something to get the iron to glow that we didn't already do to get it hot. There is no manipulatory technique for getting it to glow other than what we use for getting it hot. Hence we do not normally say that we cause it to glow, but only

---

[9] *Ibid.*, pp. 304–5. Italics mine.

that we cause it to become heated. After we put it into the fire, the rest occurs *by itself,* apart from our intervention.

From time immemorial, people have talked about causation in those situations in which they *do* something in order to get something else to happen—they move their bodies in a certain way in order to achieve a certain effect: you move your fist forward (cause) in order to hit someone in the jaw (effect); you lift the fork to your mouth (cause) in order to get the food in (effect); and so on. The condition we call the cause is the one we can manipulate, but it is not a sufficient condition; many other conditions are required for the effect to occur—for example, your arm must be in good working order. But though this is a condition for the event, it is not a cause. In daily life we distinguish sharply (Mill to the contrary notwithstanding) between causes and conditions. No matter how many conditions have to be realized before an effect occurs, we do not call it a cause unless it involves a manipulatory technique (a manipulation handle) by means of which we can get the effect to occur.[10]

Other philosophers, such as H.L.A. Hart and A.M. Honore,[11] also make a sharp distinction between cause and conditions, but in a somewhat different way. In daily life we often say that C caused E even though we are not at all sure that C would regularly be followed by E and do not wish to commit ourselves to the generalization that it will. We may believe, and rightly so, that A's hitting B on the nose caused B's nosebleed without believing that one person striking the other on the nose is always followed by nosebleed, and without knowing anything about how powerful the blow must be, or how weak the membranes in the nose, for the striking to be regularly followed by a nosebleed. It is true that we require *some* generalizations, though they are rough-and-ready ones. If someone said that A's death was caused by sunspots, we would want some generalization to explain the connection, since there is nothing in our experience to connect death with sunspots. But we do say, and truly, that throwing the lighted match in the wastebasket full of paper is the cause of the fire, even though we would not wish to say that every time someone throws a lighted match into a wastebasket full of paper there will be a fire. That there was oxygen in the air and paper in the wastebasket are conditions of the fire (the first surely a necessary one, the second not), but we do not call them the cause of the fire—we say the cause is that you threw the lighted match in. Gasking would say that we call this the cause because it involves a manipulation technique: throwing the match is something we *do* that results in the fire starting. But Hart and Honore give a somewhat different account. They say that we speak of the cause of the event (as opposed to mere conditions) as that factor which constitutes a *departure from the norm*—the normal procedure or normal working—of nature.

[10] Douglas Gasking, "Causation and Recipes," *Mind,* 1957. Gasking's view of causality is the same as Collingwood's second sense of "cause" in the article referred to above.

[11] H. L. A. Hart and A. M. Honore, *Causation in the Law,* especially Chapter 2.

Common experience teaches us that, left to themselves, the things we manipulate, since they have a "nature" or characteristic way of behaving, would persist in states or exhibit changes different from those which we have learnt to bring about in them by our manipulation. The notion, that *a cause is essentially something which interferes with or intervenes in the course of events which would normally take place,* is central to the common-sense concept of cause, and at least as essential as the notions of invariable or constant sequence so much stressed by Mill and Hume. Analogies with the interference by human beings with the natural course of events in part control, even in cases where there is literally no human intervention, what is to be identified as the cause of some occurrence; the cause, though not a literal intervention, is a *difference* to the normal course which accounts for the difference in the outcome.[12]

Thus we say that throwing a lighted cigarette into the inflammable material caused the fire in the building, the dryness of the building and the presence of the combustible material being only conditions.

In a railway accident there will be such factors as the normal speed and load and weight of the train and the routine stopping or acceleration. These factors are, of course, just those which are present alike *both* in the case where such accidents occur and in the normal cases where they do not; and it is this consideration that leads us to reject them as the cause of the accident, even though it is true that without them the accident would not have occurred. It is plain, of course, that to cite factors which are present both in the case of disaster and of normal functioning would explain nothing: such factors do not "make the difference" between disaster and normal functioning, as the bent rail or the dropping of a lighted cigarette do. . . .

Normal conditions . . . are those conditions which are present as part of the usual state or mode of operations of the thing under inquiry: some of such usual conditions will also be familiar, pervasive features of the environment: and very many of them will not only be present alike in the case of disaster and of normal functioning, but will be very generally known to be present by those who make causal inquiries . . . . What is abnormal in this way "makes the difference" between the accident and things going on as usual.[13]

Thus, if Mr. Smith ate poison or was stabbed, we give this as the cause of his death. If there is an inquiry into his death and an attorney says that the cause of his death is deprivation of oxygen to his blood-cells, the court would not be interested. The condition given is indeed sufficient for all human deaths; but the court wants to know not what is the sufficient condition for human deaths in general but what was the cause of *this* man's death at *this* time. Science is interested in the question "Under what conditions do events of this type always occur?" but in daily life, as in law, we are interested in asking, "What was the cause of *this* event?" which on the present account can be translated into "Why did this happen when it normally would not?"

---

[12] *Ibid.,* p. 27. Italics mine.

[13] *Ibid.,* pp. 32–33.

We distinguish, then, *standing* conditions (those that are necessary to the event but that occur whether the event occurs or not) from the *differential* conditions (those that "make the difference" between what happened and "normal functioning"). But the feature of the situation that we call the cause will vary somewhat, depending on what we take the standing conditions to be. For example: A man who has ulcers eats spicy foods one day and has an acute attack. The man's wife may give as the cause of the attack the fact that he ate the spicy food; the doctor who is called in may give ulcers as the cause. Both are right, but the standing conditions are somewhat different in each case. The wife is asking "Given that he has ulcers, why did he have the attack today when he usually gets by without one?" and to this the answer is that he ate the spicy food. The doctor, however, is asking "What gave *this* man the attack after eating spicy food when other men don't get it?" and to this the answer is that he has ulcers. (Others would not get an attack even if they ate spicy foods.) What one takes the standing conditions to be is relative to the context, and the wife's context is somewhat different from the doctor's. Another example:

A car skids while cornering at a certain point, turns turtle, and bursts into flame. From the car-driver's point of view, the cause of the accident was cornering too fast, and the lesson is that one must drive more carefully. From the county surveyor's point of view, the cause was a defective road-surface, and the lesson is that one must make skid-proof roads. From the motor-manufacturer's point of view, the cause was defective design, and the lesson is that one must place the center of gravity lower.[14]

But it is not true, according to the Hart–Honore view, that the cause is always something we *do*. When what we do is the "deviation from the norm," as it often is, then it is the cause; but often these deviations occur in nature apart from man, as when we say that lightning caused the fire or the clap of thunder caused the cattle to stampede.

Possible criticisms of these views. 1. These accounts of causality are themselves filled with causal language. Hume and Mill at least attempted to define "cause" by using terms that were not themselves causal. But to manipulate is to cause in a certain way, and the term "manipulation technique" or "manipulation handle" is thus itself a causal term, which cannot be used to *define* "cause" without circularity. Again, in Collingwood's volitional sense of "cause," causing is identified with inducing, persuading, urging, etc., which are all modes of causing. We would do well to stop to reflect in how many of the words we employ every day the concept of cause is already embedded: "to cut" means to cause a cut to exist; "to change" means to cause a change to occur; "to break" is to cause a break; "to release" means

[14] R. G. Collingwood, "On the So-called Idea of Causation," in Morris, *op. cit.*, p. 306.

to engage in actions that result in the person or thing's release; and so on through many cases. "Cause" is the general word, but for particular types or ways of causing we have other words, and these cannot be introduced as definitions of "cause" without circularity.

2. On the manipulability account, to cause is to *do* something that results in the effect. ("Results in" is a causal phrase: if C causes E, C results in E.) But we do often talk about causing and causes when there is nothing we can *do* to bring about the effect. We not only talk about the cause of the explosion in the munitions factory, we talk about the cause of the explosion of a supernova hundreds of millions of light-years away. In this latter spectacle we are entirely passive observers, with no manipulation handle for effecting any state-of-affairs related to it. We talk about causing the water level in a vessel to rise by placing it at a higher temperature so that the ice in it melts; but we also talk about the possibility of the melting ice in the Arctic seas causing a rise in the water level of the earth's oceans, and consequent flooding of coastal cities. It does not seem to matter whether there is a manipulation handle or not. One might say, of course, that "manipulatory technique" is the basic sense of which the others like the Arctic sea and super-nova examples are extensions—that the extended sense derives its meaning from its analogy to the original sense in which there *is* a manipulatory technique. But if so, this analysis of "cause" seems to lose much of its distinctive character, for now "cause" is no longer limited to what we can do or manipulate.

3. Similar questions could be raised about the deviation-from-the-norm account of causality. It is true that in daily life we usually ask causal questions about deviations from the norm: when the building burns down, we ask what caused the fire; but when it continues to stand without incident, we do not ask why it continues to do so. But we *could* ask it just the same. The scientist is one who asks causal questions about the most usual and familiar empirical facts: What causes bread to rise? What causes iron to rust? What causes the earth to go round the sun? What causes the moon to rise later each night and the stars earlier? And so on through countless questions about matters that, far from being deviations from the norm, are the normal and usual pattern of events, often operating without any exceptions whatever.

There is a possible reply to this contention: one can always phrase the question in such a way that the event in question is a deviation from another norm. Suppose a child who has seen bread rise asks why the dough expands. The answer is that there is yeast in the dough. This cause is normal, not abnormal; but of course the question *could* be taken to be "What causes this lump of stuff to get bigger *when other things don't?*" and the answer would be "Because it has yeast in it, and other things don't." If the norm is not-containing-yeast, then the answer in the case of something containing yeast is an answer involving deviation from this norm. Or if a child who has seen a ball break a window asks what the cause is (a ball breaking a window is a most usual type of occurrence), we might interpret his question as "Why did the ball go through the window whereas it doesn't go through a brick wall and most other solid objects?" and then we could answer it by explaining that the window is of glass and glass is fragile, while most other solid things aren't. We can always find *some* basis for contrast between this thing's occurrence, or type of occurrence, and other ones.

But what have we gained by this procedure of always rewording the question so as to make it a request for the cause of a *difference* between this kind of event and other kinds? It may rescue the theory, but only by extending it so that it loses the distinctive character it had at the beginning. The cases previously cited in support of the theory were genuine cases of deviation from a norm; but the cases cited just now can be turned into deviation-from-a-norm cases only by considerable effort and strain, since they are all cases that in any *ordinary* sense are cases of normal procedure or normal functioning. And the fact remains that we can ask for causes of these too. To say that they are all cases of deviation-from-a-norm in the sense of contrast-with-other-phenomena is to save a theory by violating the intent of these questions. When we ask what causes ice to melt or iron to rust, we are asking questions about perfectly normal procedure, "nature's usual way of doing things," without any implied contrast between this and other things—though such contrasts can, of course, always be pointed out.

4. It is a valuable feature of these theories that they show how inadequate any crude constant-conjunction theory is. In daily life, "C causes E" is not equivalent to "C is always followed by E." We can truly say "Diphtheria rarely causes death these days," but this statement is incompatible with "When we say that diphtheria causes death, we mean that diphtheria is always followed by death."

Still, is this really a criticism of Mill's view of causality? Mill would not deny that sometimes diphtheria causes death and sometimes not. Whether it does or doesn't depends on many things, such as the degree of infection and the state of health of the person before he became infected. But neither would Mill say that diphtheria is *the* cause of death. There are many causal factors involved, and if death occurs to one patient and not to another, it is because the causal conditions (other than just the fact that he was infected) were different. Mill would say that if *all* the causal conditions were the same, then the effect will always occur. That is the *only* sense in which "If C causes E, then C is always followed by E" is true. In daily life we often speak (as we saw earlier) of one of the causal factors as if it were the entire cause; but if we do so, the statement "If this factor is present, the effect always occurs" does not hold, for the uniformity (same cause, then always same effect) holds only between the effect and *all* the causal factors.

Indeed, the question "Does every event have a cause?"—which is the subject of the next section—arises only in the context of a Mill-type view of causality. (1) If a cause is always a deviation from a norm, then not every event can have a cause, because not every event can be a deviation from a norm. If every occurrence were a deviation, what would be the norm? (2) If we ask "Does every event that occurs have a manipulatory technique for bringing it about?" the answer is clearly in the negative, unless we extend the meaning of "manipulatory technique" to cover much more than it was originally designed to cover. There is no manipulatory technique in the case of solar eclipses, super-nova explosions, precession of the equinoxes, or virtually any other astronomical events, besides many terrestrial ones.

Exercises

1. How is the word "must" being used in the following examples?

    a. You must do as you're told or you'll be punished.

    b. It simply must be nice weather tomorrow or our picnic will be ruined.

    c. If I had $10 yesterday and haven't lost or spent any or received any since, I must still have $10.

    d. In order to catch a walrus, there must first be a walrus.

    e. If we want to understand Topic B, we must first discuss Topic A.

    f. If you want this cake to turn out well, you must have three large well-greased cake-pans.

    g. Why must you say such things?

    h. He must have been pretty thoroughly intoxicated or he never would have done it.

    i. You must be a mind-reader.

    j. You must have your yard looking quite beautiful by this time.

    k. Everything is disarranged—there must have been someone in the house while we were gone.

2. In each of these examples the relation of A to B is that of necessary condition. State whether it is a *causally* necessary condition, such as we have been examining in this chapter, or a *logically* necessary condition, such as we discussed in Chapter 3.

A	B
a. Presence of oxygen	Occurrence of combustion
b. Having three angles	Being a triangle
c. Having extension	Having shape
d. Existence of sodium	Existence of salt
e. Presence of moisture	Growth of crops
f. Presence of non-opaque object	Looking through that object
g. Presence of heat	Occurrence of flame

3. In the following examples, is the relation of A to B that of necessary condition, sufficient condition, both, or neither?

A	B
a. Overeating	Illness
b. Deciding to raise your hand	Raising your hand
c. Writing an essay	Reading that essay
d. Running	Feeling fatigue
e. Plug pulled out of socket	Radio not working
f. Plug inserted in socket	Radio working
g. Rock hitting window	Window breaking
h. Occurrence of friction	Occurrence of heat
i. Rain falling on the street	Street being wet

4. In what way is *too much* being included in the statement of the cause in these examples? In what way *too little?* (Assume the correctness of Mill's account.)

    a. Scratching the match caused it to light.

    b. Eating the poison caused him to die.

    c. Throwing the lighted match into the pile of paper caused it to ignite.

    d. The cause of the dart hitting its target was its being wielded by a man in a blue suit.

    e. The flood in the river was caused by heavy rainfall upstream.

5. Do you think there is genuine plurality of causes in the following cases?

    a. Headaches can be caused by many things: eyestrain, emotional tension, etc.

    b. The same message can be communicated by telephone, telegram, letter, etc.

    c. The stone can be moved by your lifting it, by my lifting it, by a pulley, etc.

    d. A woman can bear a child by sexual contact or by artificial insemination.

    e. There are many causes of death: heart disease, cancer, pneumonia, automobile accident, drowning, poisoning, stabbing. . . .

    f. Many different chemicals will take a stain out of a garment.

    g. There are various possible causes of erosion: wind, rapid drainage of water, failure to adopt contour plowing. . . .

6. Analyze critically the following expressions; if you find them faulty, indicate how they could be amended.

    a. The first billiard ball *compelled* the second billiard ball to move.

    b. When the first ball hits the second, the second one *can't help* moving.

    c. The motion of the second ball is *inevitable* when the first one hits it.

    d. The first ball hitting the second *made* the second one move.

    e. The first ball hitting the second *produced* the motion of the second one.

7. According to the regularity ("constant conjunction") view of cause (for example, that of Hume, Reichenbach, Schlick), "there would be no more special connection between the striking of a match and the flame which followed it than between the striking of a match and an earthquake which might also occur just afterwards. It would merely be that the striking of a match is usually followed by a flame and not usually followed by earthquakes, and that would be all. We could not say that the striking *made* the flame follow. . . . On this view to give a cause . . . does not in the least help to explain why the effect happened, it only tells us that it preceded the effect." (Alfred C. Ewing, *The Fundamental Questions of Philosophy,* p. 160.) Evaluate this passage sentence by sentence. (For example: Does the regularity interpretation of "C caused E" render it impossible to explain why C caused E?)

8. Which of the following causal statements appear to confirm Gasking's view of causality? Which, if any, appear to conflict with it?

    a. The fire was caused by an explosion in the engine room.

    b. His death occurred from natural causes.

    c. The stone continued to stay right there because nothing pushed it.

    d. The cause of the cut in his foot was that he stepped on a nail.

    e. The puddles were caused by the rainfall.

9. According to the Hart–Honore analysis, what would you say is the cause in these cases?

a. The fire would not have spread to the neighboring house without a normal breeze, yet we say that lightning and not the breeze was the cause of the disaster. Would it be different if someone deliberately fanned the embers, or if just as the fire was dying out a leaking gasoline can fell from the back of a jeep?

b. We say that the flowers died because the gardner neglected to water them. But couldn't we just as well say that they died because you or I or the President of the United States neglected to water them?

c. A pushes B off a skyscraper; during his fall, C shoots him from a window halfway down. What is the cause of B's death?

d. A ship engaged in convoy duty in wartime is insured against marine perils other than war. Under orders, the ship pursues a zigzag course and dims her lights, meets unexpected high waves, is driven off course and onto rocks in a fog. Should insurance be collectible?

10. "Suppose someone claimed to have discovered the cause of cancer, but added that his discovery though genuine would not in practice be of any use because the cause he had discovered was not a thing that could be produced or prevented at will. . . . No one would admit that he had done what he claimed to do. It would be pointed out that he did not know what the word 'cause' (in the context of medicine) meant. For in such a context a proposition of the form 'x causes y' implies the proposition 'x is something that can be produced or prevented at will' as part of the definition of 'cause'." (Collingwood.) Do you agree or disagree? Give your reasons.

11. "In person-to-person causality, I do not need to examine more than one case to know that C caused E. If someone bribes me into doing something, I know from this one case alone that the bribe caused my action; I do not need any further examples, nor is any prediction implied that I would ever respond to a bribe again. If you persuade me to attend a concert, I know that your persuading has caused me to go to the concert; I may never respond to your persuasions again, but from this one instance alone I know that your persuasion caused me to go to the concert this time. I know that it was the unannounced arrival of my sister from India (whom I hadn't seen in 30 years) that caused me to be surprised—although if she were to appear again, I wouldn't be surprised at all." Assess this view. (Hint: Beware of causal words introduced in premises of arguments whose conclusion states a causal relation.)

12. Do you agree or disagree with the following reasoning: "The cause and the effect must be simultaneous, for the effect occurs at the very moment that the last condition (of a sufficient condition) is fulfilled. If there is even the slightest waiting period between it and the effect, there must be something *else* that has yet to occur before the effect can occur; otherwise, why wouldn't the effect occur immediately?"

13. Evaluate this statement: "That C is regularly followed by E is our means of knowing that C causes E. But this is not what the causal relationship consists in; it is the mark but not the essence of the causal relationship."

14. "I said that because it's true." Can the truth of a statement be the cause (or a causal factor) of your uttering it? (Remember that the truth of a statement is a non-temporal fact, while a cause is always a temporal event or condition.) What change of formulation would make the statement more accurate?

16. The Causal Principle

Does everything that happens have a cause?

Let us continue to take "cause" to mean sufficient condition. Our question then becomes: Is there, for every event in the universe, a set of conditions such that if the conditions, C, are all fulfilled, the event, E, invariably occurs? The sets of conditions may be ever so complex and ever so difficult to discover, and perhaps we shall never discover them all, but the question remains all the same: is there, for every event, such a set of conditions? To answer yes to this question is to assert the Principle of Universal Causation, or, more simply, the Causal Principle.

When we try to answer this question, there is a difficulty right at the start. "Every time all the conditions in C are fulfilled, E occurs." But E is a particular, individual event, and *particular events never recur.* Events *like* them may occur, but the particular event E, once it has occurred, is gone forever. How, then, are we going to interpret the specification that E recurs?

If E does not occur a second time, an event *like* E may do so. The same, of course, applies to the C's. The principle is usually formulated approximately as follows (formulations vary somewhat): "For every class of events E in the universe, there is a class of conditions C, such that whenever an instance of each member of class C occurs, an instance of E occurs." For example: whenever an instance of the first class of conditions (combustible material) occurs, plus an instance of the second class (temperature), plus an instance of the third class (oxygen), all of which together constitute C, then an instance of class E (combustion) occurs.

Let us then restate our question: Is it true of every event that occurs in the universe (past, present, and future) that is is a member of a *class* of events which is related to a class (or classes) of conditions in such a way that every time a member of this class (or these classes) of conditions is fulfilled, a member of the class of events occurs? (The question is now far more complex, but complexity is often the price we have to pay for accuracy.) If the answer is yes, the Causal Principle is true; if the answer is no, it is false.

1. **The empirical interpretation.** We can observe only an infinitesimally small fraction of the events now taking place in the universe, and even if we could observe them all, there is an infinite reach of past events forever beyond recall, and of future events that have not yet taken place. It would seem, in fact, that we can be far less sure of the principle than we can of any ordinary empirical law, such as those of physics and chemistry, for it is more inclusive than any of them. Both the person who asserts the principle and the person who denies it are going far beyond what is empirically observable.

It would seem, indeed, that about all we can say is that as we examine nature we find some uniformities in it, some classes of events uniformly related to certain classes of conditions, and that the more carefully we look, the more of these uniformities we find. There are many investigations, of course, from which no discovery of uniformities results at all, and in which even the most exhaustive attempts to find them have failed. Sometimes we make tentative formulations of such conditions—such as the conditions under which cancer develops in an organism—and sometimes our hopes of finding the causal conditions are confirmed by experience, and sometimes not. When they are not, we simply try again, and see whether, by introducing other factors into the situation or qualifying our statements about the old ones so as to make them more precise, we can arrive at statements which *will* assert an invariant relationship that really holds between the events and their conditions. Sometimes we succeed in this, and sometimes we do not.

At any rate, the search for genuinely invariant relationships between events and conditions is a most difficult one. Consider a class of events which is perfectly familiar: trees blowing down. Is it true that whenever a member of a class of conditions C (wind blowing against tree) is fulfilled, a member of class of events E (tree falling down) invariably occurs? No; we must add endless qualifications: the wind must blow hard enough (and how hard is that?); the tree must be fragile (at least more than *so* fragile—and how is fragility to be defined?); and so on. Whether or not the event occurs depends on a multitude of factors such as the velocity and direction of the wind, the shape of the tree, its position among other trees and buildings, and its relation to the surrounding terrain. It would be difficult indeed to lay down any set of conditions, no matter how numerous, upon the fulfillment of which a member of the class of events tree-falling-down *always* occurs.

It it is difficult to state the conditions in the case of a tree, how much more difficult it is in more complex cases! What are the conditions under which the hearing of the *Eroica* Symphony of Beethoven is always followed by a certain kind of feeling-state, for example? Even if we have succeeded in pinning down in words what kind of feeling-state we mean, our troubles have only begun; for what possible account can we give of the conditions under which such a feeling always occurs? We may ordinarily like the symphony but may not be in the mood for it now, perhaps through concentration on other things, or through having already heard it several times the same day; and those who have never heard it before respond quite differently from those who have. What we feel when we hear it depends on such a bewildering array of factors that it would seem that we never shall be able to relate this class of events to any finite set of conditions. (We may some day be able to relate this kind of feeling to a definite kind of neurological state in the brain, but the same question could then be asked about the relation of this kind of neurological state to the conditions under which *it* always occurs.)

Would it not seem, then, that the Causal Principle is more likely to be false than true? If we despair of ever finding such a set of conditions for every class of events, may we not suspect that *there isn't any?*

To this suggestion, however, many persons will object at once: "The fact that these conditions are very hard to find doesn't mean that there *aren't* any. Some of them we have tried for generations to find, and finally succeeded; some we shall find in due time; some we shall never find. But even if we never find such conditions for every class of events, they do exist. Nature is uniform through and through, even though her uniformity is a bewilderingly complex one. Every event in the universe is related to a set of conditions in the way the principle specifies. The fact that we may never find it testifies only to our ignorance."

What are we to say of such an assertion? We may ourselves be inclined to agree with it; and yet we shall be hard put to it to defend it on empirical grounds. After all, how can we possibly know that it is true? What justifies our certainty, or at least the certainty of many persons, that it always holds?

There is another curious circumstance about the whole matter. With any empirical generalization, there is a possibility of refuting it by empirical facts. Thousands of generalizations have been devised and then abandoned because they failed to pass this test. The discovery of one white crow would wreck the generalization that all crows are black. (As we saw on p. 235, we would probably not call this one a law.) But what would, or possibly could, wreck the generalization that every event is related to a set of conditions in the way stated by the Causal Principle? The more causes we find, the more we say we have confirmed the Causal Principle; but if in some cases we do not find any, do we say, "For these events there are no causes?" No; we say, "We haven't *found* any," or, "There is a cause, and some day we may find it; but even if we don't, we have not shown that no cause exists, but only that our powers of detection are limited." In other words, the Causal Principle *can never be disproved*. The discovery of more causes is taken as confirming it, but failure to find causes disturbs it not a whit. What kind of a principle is it that can be confirmed by empirical observations but not disconfirmed by them?

"But it *can* be disconfirmed by experience," one may object. "If finding causes tends to confirm the principle, then failing to find them tends to disconfirm it. It would take quite a bit of careful investigation to show us that the principle was probably false, since we *could* always say that the causal conditions were so complex that our failure to find them was the result of their extreme complexity rather than of their nonexistence. Still, there would come a point when failure to find causes *would* count against the truth of the principle. For example: Right now we believe that there are definite conditions in which that light bulb will go on. We press the button one way, and it goes on; we press it the other way, and it goes off. This doesn't happen without exceptions, of course. Sometimes we press the 'on' button and the light doesn't go on, but then we find that the bulb has burned out; we then replace it with another bulb, and it goes on. Or the 'on' button is pressed and the bulb is all right but it still doesn't light, but then there is some defect in the wiring. And so on. There is a finite set of conditions on which the going on of the bulb depends, and we can find what those conditions are; we do get the light to work again even after it has gone out. But now suppose the light went on and off capriciously, with no apparent relation to any condition that we could specify. Sometimes the bulb lights up and sometimes it goes off, and we can't find any conditions on which either event depends. It doesn't matter which way we press the button: that has nothing to do with the going on or off of the bulb. It doesn't matter whether the circuit is complete or not: sometimes when it is the light goes on and sometimes it doesn't, and when the circuit is broken the same thing happens—sometimes the light goes on and sometimes it doesn't. We try thousands of other things, such as the time of day, the amount of light, the temperature of the room, the amount of moisture in the air. But none of them make any difference: the light goes on and off in serene independence of any of these conditions. Of course its going on and off *may* depend on some condition or combination of conditions that we haven't yet thought of. But if this continued to happen, not only to the light bulb but to lots of other things, we would start to question the Causal Principle. We would question whether it was true that every event in the universe depends for its occurrence on a definite set of conditions."

A person who argued thus would be accepting the empirical interpretation of the Causal Principle: certain empirical facts would count in favor of it, and others would count against it. But, unlike the case of the white crows, which *would* refute the generalization that all crows are black, we *wouldn't have to* believe that our failure to find causes is evidence against the principle. We could adopt an a priori interpretation of it.

2. The a priori interpretation. Many persons have held that the Causal Principle is not open to empirical disproof at all but is a necessary truth. At first, when one states the principle, it sounds like any ordinary law of nature; but as one begins to consider it, he begins to see that it operates quite differently from empirical laws, since it is not open to empirical disproof. Let us see how we might develop this view.

Thus far we have talked about classes of conditions and classes of events; and within these classes, individual conditions and events need not be exactly alike, only similar enough to be placed in the same classes. Let us now, however, be more exacting, and talk about identical conditions and identical events.

Two things, conditions, processes, or events are identical when they are *exactly alike*—in other words, when they have all their properties in common; all the properties, that is, that are compatible with their being two events rather than one. Two events that took place at the same time and at the same location in space would be one event, not two; they could still be two events if they occurred at the same time, as long as they occurred at two different places, or at the same place, as long as they occurred at two different times. So we shall have to say that two events are identical if they have all their properties in common other than their spatio-temporal properties. Now let us suppose that two events are identical in this sense. Can two identical events have two *non*-identical causal conditions? No, the a priorist about the Causal Principle would say; this cannot possibly happen. If there is some difference in the events (if they are non-identical), there must be some difference in the conditions leading up to them to account for the difference in the events. Suppose we refer to two identical conditions as C_1 and C_1, identical events as E_1 and E_1, non-identical conditions as C_1 and C_2, and non-identical events as E_1 and E_2. There are then four possibilities:

1.	C_1	E_1		2.	C_1	E_1
	C_1	E_1			C_2	E_2
3.	C_1	E_1		4.	C_1	E_1
	C_2	E_1			C_1	E_2

The first offers no difficulty: identical conditions leading to identical events. Nor does the second: non-identical conditions leading to non-identical events. Even the third would probably be admitted: non-identical conditions leading to identical events; this would merely be plurality of causes. But the fourth would not be admitted: identical conditions leading to non-identical events. If there is a difference in the outcome, there is always (it would be said) some difference in the conditions leading to that outcome, whether we ever find it or not.

In practice, of course, we never find identical conditions or identical events (they always differ in some way or other), yet we are just as confident that the principle holds here as we would be if we formulated it more loosely to read, "If similar conditions, then similar events," where we *could* confirm it. Why is this? It is not because we have observed identical events, or observed identical conditions leading to them. We have only observed events and conditions of varying degrees of similarity. Yet we are sure that it is true: how *could* the events have turned out differently, we say, if the conditions were exactly the same?

Suppose we performed an experiment twice and found that the results were markedly different even though the conditions were, to the best of our knowledge, exactly the same. What would we say? Would we abandon the Causal Principle, even in its precise form (identical conditions, identical events), saying that here was an exception and hence the generalization did not hold? In all probability we would not. We would always find some way to get around it. Specifically, what would we say?

We could say that we had not observed all the relevant conditions. "*If* we could observe (or have observed) them all, then we could have detected a difference in the C's; if all the known causal factors were the same in the two cases, the difference must be due to other factors which we had not previously considered which *were* different in the two cases."

This sort of thing, of course, often happens. If you thought that two clocks, in the same room, in the same atmospheric conditions, of the same make and construction, were identical in every respect, and it developed that the one kept perfect time and the other started to run fast, you inferred that there was some difference in the causal conditions, and then you found it, perhaps in some detail of their construction which you had previously overlooked. After some experience with this we say, even without further evidence, that if there was a difference in the E's there must have been a difference in the C's. *We take the very fact of there being a difference in the E's as evidence that there was a difference in the C's.*

Nor need we admit any exceptions to this principle. If two E's turned out to be quite different and we could find no difference in the C's, and we looked again and again and then some more and still found no difference in the C's, would we abandon the Causal Principle and conclude that, after all, even when the conditions are identical, the events may sometimes be different? Probably not. We would still keep on saying, "There was a difference between the two E's. Now, something or other must have caused that difference," even though a million years of investigation had not revealed any such difference.

Similarly, although we never find identical C's, do we not believe that *if* identity in the C's were attainable, there would be identity in the E's too? A boy is bouncing a ball against a wall, catching it and bouncing it back again. The ball never lands at the same spot on the wall twice; nor does it ever bounce back to him in quite the same way on any two occasions; every time the direction, speed, and distance are slightly different. But do we not believe that *if* on any two occasions the conditions could be made exactly the same (identical)—speed, direction, point from which it is thrown, etc.—then it would bounce against exactly the same spot and rebound back to him in exactly the same way? If you could only throw the dice tonight in exactly the same way you did last night, with each die in the same position, then surely the same sevens you threw last night would turn up again. If something else turns up this time, is it not because the conditions are different? The conditions are so intricate that we cannot be sure that they are even approximately the same on any two successive throws; but *if* they were exactly the same, would not the same thing have happened?

How far would we go in defending this contention?

Let us return to the case in which the E's are different and the C's appear to be identical. Suppose now that we have sub-microscopic eyes which can peer into every atom of matter involved in C; there is not a single aspect of C which is not visible to us. This being done, we find that the C's are identical; yet the E's are different. Would we not have to abandon the Causal Principle?

No; we could say, "All *these* conditions are identical in the two cases, but the fact that the E's are different only shows that we haven't included enough in the conditions. Some hitherto unconsidered factor was different in the two cases, and this difference accounts for the difference in the E's. So we must look around, outside the circle of factors we examined so exhaustively before."

Suppose now that we do this; we look outside the factors we originally considered, and still find no difference. So we look outside this in turn, to still other factors, hoping to find a difference there. Still we find none. We continue this process indefinitely.

Where must we stop in investigating this ever-enlarging circle of conditions? Only with the whole universe. And you could never find the universe as a whole to be in an identical state on any two occasions; *you* at least would be different on the second occasion, since you would remember that the universe had been like this on the previous occasion.

But even waiving this, even assuming that the total state of the universe (you included) is identical on the two occasions, and two non-identical events nevertheless followed, would we take this to be an exception to the Causal Principle? You would not have to, even then. One thing would be different, namely that the events took place at *two different times*. This difference could never be overcome. We could always hold that the mere fact that time had elapsed, and nothing else, was responsible for the difference. (If the two events are imagined as occurring at the same time but at two different places, the same objection can be made about space: the fact of being in two different places, even if all the other conditions were the same, was what made the difference.)

This is not a sort of thing which has ever been held, because in formulating scientific laws it has never been found necessary to introduce such a factor. Always when events were different, some differences could be found (or assumed to exist) in the conditions themselves, *other* than the mere fact of the passing of time. Nevertheless, it is logically possible that the time-factor would have to be considered in formulating laws: it is conceivable, for example, that water boiled at 212° in 1968, at 213° in 1969, 214° in 1970, and so on, not because of any difference in the conditions other than the lapse of time. This would be a highly peculiar state of affairs, and would excite much surprise simply because as far as we now know nature does not work this way; scientists would cast about desperately in search of conditions to account for the difference in the boiling-point *other* than the time-factor. But if they were forced to the wall, if they had to abandon the one principle or the other, the Causal Principle or the time-makes-no-difference principle, they would very probably abandon the time-makes-no-difference principle. They would rather say that *the mere fact that time had elapsed* caused the difference between E_1 and E_2 than say that E_1 and E_2 were different although there was *no* cause for the difference.

So far, then, we would probably go in defending the Causal Principle. We would hold to it *a priori*. We do not put it to an empirical test: the minute we find that the E's were different, we say that the C's were, whether we observe it or not. Perhaps they were different in some way we do not know about; perhaps years of research will not unearth the difference; perhaps we never shall discover it; but still, we are convinced, there is some difference, whether or not it is ever discovered; otherwise the E's would not have been different.

What kind of a priori?   If we take the position that the Causal Principle is a priori, our next question is: What kind of a priori is it?

a. If we could show that the Causal Principle is analytic, we would have no difficulty persuading ourselves that we can know its truth a priori. But it seems quite clear that it is synthetic. The concept of an event in no way involves the concept of a cause. The idea of an event is simply that of something happening: someone running, a shot being fired, and so on. It does not involve the idea of what caused it or brought it about. In a highly chaotic universe in which no uniformities had ever been discovered, there would still be events occurring, but the concept of causality might not even have arisen. If the proposition were "Every *effect* has a cause," it would indeed be analytic, for "effect" and "cause" are correlative terms: and event would not be called an effect unless it had a cause. But the Causal Principle states that every event, in addition to being merely an event, is also an *effect* of something—in other words, was caused by something. And this assertion is clearly synthetic.

b. If it is synthetic and also a priori, perhaps here at long last we have a case of a synthetic a priori truth. According to this view, our knowledge of particular causes and effects (for example, that drafts cause colds) is not a priori knowledge; it is empirical. But the general proposition that every event that occurs has some cause or other (whether we ever discover it or not) is what is held to be both synthetic and known a priori.

We have already considered synthetic a priori knowledge at some length in Chapter 3. Any considerations that may have operated for or against it would apply here also, and we need not raise the question again. But, lest a person call the Causal Principle synthetic and a priori simply because he feels that it is not empirical and yet is not tautological either, he may be invited to consider yet other possibilities.

c. It may not be a case of knowledge at all, but merely an *assumption*. We have already considered a priori assumptions (see p. 186), and perhaps the Causal Principle is one of them. Rather than know it to hold true for all cases, past, present, and future, we simply *assume* that it does; we refuse to grant even the possibility of any contrary evidence. Without further investigation we take the very fact of the E's being different as proof that the C's are different too. This sounds very much indeed like an a priori assumption.

Yet this interpretation too should not be accepted without further reflection; for surely the situation is not one in which we stubbornly refuse to accept any exceptions to the principle in the way people stubbornly refuse to accept any statement which conflicts with their pet prejudices. After all, we might say, are there not good empirical grounds for accepting this principle rather than some other? Have we not some evidence for it? Did not empirical observation lead us to state it in the first place? And has not the principle proved its worth in so many cases that we have some justification in trusting it beyond the extent to which it has actually been confirmed?

Difficulties in all the preceding interpretations.   Thus we seem once again to be led back toward the empirical view of the Causal Principle. Yet before we go back, let us once again remind ourselves that it is different from the empirical generalizations of which science is chiefly composed. In any empirical generalization there is always the possibility of disproof by counter-instances; even if no counter-instances actually occur, the fact is that *if* an A turned up that was not a B, the generalization would be upset. And no matter how many favorable instances one had observed, there is always this possibility. But the Causal Principle is not like this: there seems to be no possibility of refuting it.

To be quite clear about this, let us contrast for a moment how the Causal Principle operates with how the generalizations of science operate. Suppose a student in freshman chemistry reports (and he is not deliberately lying) that when he tested for the melting-point of lead it turned out to be different from what the chemistry book said. His teacher without further ado would say that he was wrong; the teacher would not grant for a moment any alleged exception to this generalization. Is this not an a priori assumption on the teacher's part? No, for the teacher is resting his claim on empirical evidence: all things considered, it is more probable that the student made a mistake in his experiment than that the melting-point of lead is not what the chemistry book says it is. Students have been found wrong before, and the melting-point of lead is something that has been tested empirically thousands of times. We tend to dismiss all alleged exceptions as errors simply because we have already amassed so much empirical evidence supporting the law. Without doubt the law is empirical: if not only the freshman but trained chemists kept reporting that the melting-point of lead was different from the figure given in the textbooks, a thorough investigation would be conducted and, if further tests bore out the student's claim, the generalization about the melting-point of lead would be revised.

Now what of the Causal Principle? Is it empirical in the same way? Probably it is empirical observation that led us to formulate the principle in the first place; had we never observed any uniformities in nature, the principle would never have occurred to us. But the peculiarity is that *no empirical evidence would require us to abandon it:* we could keep on holding to it no matter what we found in nature. We know what observations of the universe would lead us to abandon ordinary empirical statements. But what observations of the universe would ever make us abandon the Causal Principle? Apparently, none at all. If the universe were far different from what it now is, if few or no uniformities were discoverable in it, we would not have to reject the principle as false. Instead of saying, "The generalization has now been refuted," we need only say, "Events still have causes; they are just so much harder to discover these days." We would not say that there were non-identical events occurring with identical conditions, but rather, "The conditions differ in mysterious ways that we just can't seem to locate." In other words, we would hold to the Causal Principle no matter what happened, no matter how chaotic the universe became, no matter how hopelessly our attempts at detecting causes failed.

This, then, is the strange situation in which we find ourselves. This case is not like that of empirical generalizations, yet we cannot dismiss it as a priori either. We have a statement that empirical evidence can confirm but that no empirical evidence can disprove. What kind of hybrid is this, anyway? The Causal Principle does not seem to fit into any pigeonhole we have prepared for it.

3.   The Causal Principle as a leading principle of scientific investigation. There is a view of it that at first may seem strange, but which nevertheless has won considerable acceptance. The Causal Principle is neither a posteriori (an empirical statement) nor a priori, because *it is not a proposition at all,* and, not being a proposition, it is *neither true nor false.*

Surely this requires an explanation. How can it be neither true nor false? Does it not state something, whether we know it empirically or a priori, or indeed whether we know it at all? According to the present interpretation, the Causal Principle is indeed *about* something, but it is not a proposition, and therefore it is neither true nor false. It is more like the *rule* of a game. The rule of baseball "The batter shall not have more than three strikes" is neither true nor false. It is true that there exists such a rule in baseball, but the rule itself is neither true nor false; it merely prescribes how the game of baseball is to be played. Similarly, "Don't use your table knife with your left hand" is a rule of etiquette that prescribes how one is not to use his knife; it does not describe how people actually use knives, for the rule might be more honored in the breach than in the observance. Likewise, the Causal Principle functions as a rule of the scientific game—a far more important game than baseball, and not in the literal sense a game at all, but nevertheless an enterprise that is governed by rules. According to the present interpretation, the Causal Principle is one of these rules. (Perhaps the Principle of Uniformity of Nature is another.) The Causal Principle is a kind of *leading principle* of scientific investigation: by employing it we are led to find more and more causal conditions. Though neither true nor false, its adoption (not the rule itself, but *the adoption of* the rule) can be justified pragmatically, by its effects. If we adopt it, we are spurred on to find causes; if we adopted the opposite rule, we would give up.

It may be that the Causal Principle does not function wholly as a rule of the scientific enterprise. There may be something in it of a *suggestion:* "Let's find more uniformities." There may be in it something of a *hope* that we will find more of the conditions upon which events depend. There may even be in it a bit of whistling to keep your courage up, as if to say, "Never fear, the causal conditions we seek will yet be found." But whatever admixture of these elements there may be, the principle is not (according to this interpretation) a *description* of any state-of-affairs in the universe. And since it is not a description of anything in the universe, it cannot be a *true* (or a false) description of anything in the universe. It is not a truth at all, not even an assumed truth. Something that we would not have to abandon, no matter what the universe was like (for example, even if we steadily and continuously failed to find causes), cannot be a truth about the universe.

We would not *have* to abandon it. But we *might* abandon it just the same *if* the uniformities now observed did not continue and if repeated and continuous investigation did not reveal any other ones. Suppose that one time you let go your pencil and it drops to the floor; the second time it flies into the air; the third time it changes into an elephant; the fourth time it disappears completely without a trace; the fifth time it hits you in the nose and rebukes you for letting it go; and so on. Suppose this happened not only to the pencil but to everything else as well, so that you could no longer discover *any* uniform conditions on which events depended. It would still be open to you to say, "There are still conditions for each one of these events, but they are so tremendously complex that I haven't found them. Causes still exist; they have just become hard to find." But we could also *abandon* the principle—not that we would now say it was false (since we had never held it to be true), but we might no longer consider this rule of the game to be worth adopting. If they existed, causes would no longer be worth tracking down. We would abandon the principle as we might abandon a mine—not because we were convinced that it contained no more gold but because of a conviction that, whether it did or not, the gold was so minute in amount or so thinly scattered or so hard to reach as to make it not worth the mining. Our abandonment would then express the resolve, "Let's give it up."

Comparison with other scientific principles.   If this is the correct interpretation of the Causal Principle, it is not unlike certain other principles to be found in empirical science. Consider, for example, the Law of Conservation of Energy. Like the Causal Principle, scientists arrived at it by means of observation of nature, and as initially formulated, it was believed to be a truth about nature. In instance after instance, the principle turned out to be right. Then, when an observation seemed to go against it, scientists held onto the principle nonetheless: they had confidence in it all the same, so that when the principle got into trouble, types and quantities of energy were postulated in order to make the principle come out all right. When this happened—when empirical observations of one kind were taken as counting in its favor, but empirical observations of an opposite kind were not taken as counting against it—it came to be taken as an a priori truth, or as not a truth at all but a rule, or leading principle, of the scientific enterprise. (Whether it has actually reached this stage is a matter for scientists, armed with detailed empirical observations, to decide.)

The principle of "no action at a distance" is another case in point. At one time, it was thought that whenever C causes E, there is some *physical contact* between C and E—that even if C and E are spatially separate, there is a continuous series of contiguous events that can be traced between them. You hold one end of the poker in the fire, and, three feet away, the handle in your fingers becomes hot. But of course this is because the rapid motion of the molecules of iron that are in the fire is transmitted along the poker until it reaches your hand. The same holds true of convection currents. Or a bell rings a mile away and produces a disturbance in your ear and, via your ear, in your brain, The bell is not contiguous to your ear, but the bell and your ear are connected by particles of air that transmit sound waves from the one to the other by immediate contact of the molecules. If between the two there were a vacuum, the sound waves would never reach your ear. Thus the ringing of the bell causes the events in your brain through a whole series of contiguous events. "All causation is by contact," or, in other words, "There is no action at a distance."

But now consider other examples: the sun transmits heat and light to the earth, and undoubtedly there is a causal relation between them; but where is the contact? There is nothing, not even air, between them. "But surely there is some medium to transmit the radiation from sun to earth!" How does the person who says this know that it is true? Well, there is a transparent weightless substance, the ether, whose sole function is to transmit such radiation through a vacuum. But what is the evidence that the ether exists? There is no such evidence: the Michelson–Morley experiment and others ingeniously devised to detect it were entirely negative in their results. In this situation, what was one to say? Scientists *could* have held to the ether, simply in order to defend the principle of "no action at a distance"; they could have said that since nature abhors a vacuum, there is really no vacuum at all but an undetectable ether whose function is to transmit radiation through interstellar space. But after the negative results of the experiments, scientists instead abandoned the ether, and with it the principle of "no action at a distance." It was simply not worth saving. It was easier on the whole to change the conceptual framework of science, to the extent of abandoning the ether and the accompanying principle. Like the gold mine, it was simply abandoned. The abandonment of the Causal Principle, which is much more general in its application, would be a much greater conceptual jolt; but if the circumstances described above were to occur, it might (but would not have to) be abandoned, as the principle of "no action at a distance" already has.

Whichever interpretation of the Causal Principle we may accept, it is important to be consistent in our application of it. We should not first refuse to abandon the Causal Principle under any circumstances, and then argue as if it were a true description of the universe among conceivable alternative descriptions. If we take it as an empirical statement like a law of nature, then the failure to discover uniformities will have to count against it just as the discovery of such uniformities was taken to count in its favor. But if we adopt the last interpretation, saying that it is not a true statement about the universe at all (nor for that matter a false one), we cannot then reverse our position and say that it always holds true and make this the basis for assertions of determinism or denials of freedom of the will—to which, at last, we now turn.

Exercises

1. Which of the following would you take as empirical statements, confirmable by experience but also disconfirmable by experience? Why? (Don't assume that they all *have* been disconfirmed by experience, but ask yourself, *"Could* they be?" Can you think of any experiences that *would* disconfirm [count against] them?)

    a. Cats are quadrupeds.
    b. Cats are cats.
    c. Cats have fur.
    d. A perfect being never makes a mistake.
    e. Water is wet.
    f. Friction causes heat.
    g. Every effect has a cause.
    h. Every event has a cause.
    i. All crows are black.
    j. Every particle of matter in the universe is subject to the law of Gravitation.
    k. There is no such thing as "action at a distance."
    l. The total amount of energy in the universe remains constant.
    m. Laws of nature will hold true in the future as well as they did in the past.
    n. The uniformities which we believe to be laws of nature will hold true in the future just as they have in the past.
    o. A thing cannot be both A and not-A.
    p. If p is true and p implies q, then q is true.
    q. All propositions must be testable (confirmable or disconfirmable).
    r. All empirical propositions must be testable (confirmable or disconfirmable).
    s. Let's leave the room.
    t. No batter may have four strikes.

2. Among the items on the above list which you do not consider to be empirical propositions, which do you consider to be a priori propositions, and why? (Are there any you would consider to be a priori but false? any that you would consider a priori assumptions?)

3. Among those which you believe to be a priori, which do you consider analytic? Why? Are there any that you believe to be a priori and also synthetic?

4. If there are any which you do not believe to be either empirical or a priori, what is their status? Are there any items on the list which are not propositions at all? Are there any which, not being propositions, are "leading principles" or "rules of the game"? Justify your answer.

5. If you believe that the Causal Principle is an empirical proposition, describe some states-of-affairs that, if they were to occur, would disconfirm the principle. (Do you think that any such states-of-affairs do occur or have occurred?)

17. Determinism and Freedom

Discussions of causality usually go hand in hand with discussions of determinism and freedom. If everything that happens has a cause, then we live in a deterministic universe, or in other words, *determinism* is true; and if determinism is true, then, it is believed, there is no room for human freedom. Consider the following argument:

With every day that passes, science is able to tell us more about the causes of things—the *determining* factors which *make* things happen the way they do. This includes human actions as well as events in the physical world: we know more than ever before about what makes people behave as they do.

Future events are becoming increasingly predictable. Once eclipses were not predictable; now we can predict their occurrence to within a tenth of a second 10,000 years in advance. Once the path of a projectile could not be predicted; now it can be mapped out with such precision that we know how to make it hit a certain distant target at just the right moment. Even when we don't know exactly what a thing will do—for instance, just how a stone will roll downhill— this isn't because its path is not completely determined by the forces acting upon it—but because we don't know what all those forces are: just where the stone will hit this crevice, whether the slippery side of the stone in rolling down the hill will be against the smooth part of the ground on this part of its journey downward, and so on. We know the laws, but not all the initial conditions. But nobody imagines—at least, no one who has the slightest acquaintance with science—that its path *couldn't* be calculated if we knew, or bothered to acquaint ourselves with, all the million and one factors that would have to be considered in computing its course down the slope.

Now, nobody ever pretended that stones have freedom or free-will. But it *has* been contended that human beings have, and science is gradually showing up this claim for what it is—a mere superstition. We know far more today than ever before about people's hereditary constitution and environmental conditions, the laws of how people behave, all the factors that make people act as they do. The person is becoming more and more like the stone. He may fancy that he is free, but this is a delusion: he is no more free than the stone is. The forces acting on him are more *complex*, and therefore far more difficult to discover, than those acting on the stone, but they are there just the same. Whether he knows what they are or not, they are there, and they inevitably make him what he is and make him do what he does. Anyone who had knowledge of the laws and of his total state at any given moment would be able to predict everything that he would do in response to every future situation; he would, in short, be able to show how every moment of the person's life is determined.

The above argument is an imaginary one, but it closely resembles many arguments that take place around us every day. If anything, it is probably more clearly outlined than most of them are. Yet it is full of confusions. (Before reading further, you will do well to spot as many errors in it as you can.) For example, three of the concepts used in it—causality, compulsion, and predictability—are treated as if they were the same.

Let us, then endeavor to become as clear as we can about determinism and human freedom in the light of what has already been said about causality.

Determinism.   Determinism is the view that everything that happens is determined. The word "determined," however, requires clarification. In everyday usage, "to be determined" is roughly synonymous with "to be resolved," as in the sentence "I was determined to arrive there on time." But in the context of the problem of human freedom, "to be determined" is synonymous with "to be caused." Determinism then becomes the view that everything that happens has a cause. The word "determinism" is rather unfortunate, since it has connotations that the word "caused" does not have. If someone says to you, "Everything you do is caused," the remark may excite no surprise; but if he says, "Everything you do is determined," you may feel much more inclined to disagree, for the use of the word "determined" makes it sound as if everything happens in spite of you, that you have nothing to do with it. But this is not what determinism says: determinism is the doctrine of universal causation: it says only that every event has a cause. It does not say whether the cause is mental or physical, whether it is inorganic nature or organisms or people or God. As far as determinism is concerned, the cause can be anything. It is not even necessary that we ever know what the causes of events are—determinism only says that every event has a cause of some kind, whether we ever find out what it is or not.

"But if every event is determined (caused)," the objection arises, "how is human freedom possible? Everything that happens is caused by previously existing conditions, and these in turn are caused by conditions prior to them, and so on indefinitely back in time. But if your every action is caused, how can it be free?"

At this point it becomes very easy to confuse determinism with another doctrine, fatalism.

Fatalism.   Fatalism does not deny that everything that happens has a cause. It only denies that human beings have the power to change the course of events. "What's going to happen is going to happen," "Whatever will be will be"—these slogans of fatalism are not intended as analytic statements; what they mean is that the future will be of a certain nature *regardless of what we do,* and that therefore there is no point in our trying to do anything about it. A standard fatalist argument during the 1940 bombing of London ran as follows:

Either you are going to be killed by a bomb or you are not going to be. If you are, then any precautions you take will be ineffective. If you are not, all precautions you take are superfluous. Therefore it is pointless to take precautions.[15]

But this view, attractive as it may be to people who are looking for an excuse to do nothing, flies directly in the face of obvious empirical facts. People *do* sometimes take precautions and thereby save their lives. People who went to underground shelters were often saved from bombs that would have taken their lives if they had remained in their homes. People do have a better chance of staying alive on the highways if they drive with care. And so on. The fallacy in the fatalist's argument is not difficult to detect. He argues, correctly, "Either you are going to be killed in this raid or you are not." (Either A or not-A.) But then he argues, incorrectly, "If you are going to be killed, you will be killed whatever precautions you take" and "If you are not going to be killed, you will not be killed whatever precautions you neglect." And these two hypothetical propositions are about as clearly false as any empirical propositions can be. It is a plain empirical fact, which any set of statistics will bear out, that those who neglect to take precautions stand a higher chance of being killed and those who do take precautions stand a higher chance of remaining alive. People's actions *do* play a part in the causal nexus of events. Some things happen because of what people do that would not have happened if they had not done them. The bombs would not have dropped on London if some people had not manufactured them and others had not dropped them from the air. "Whatever will be will be," but human beings do play a role in determining what things will be. Even so, your safety is not guaranteed, of course: you may be the best driver in the world, but if some maniac drives his car head-on into yours, you may be killed; and a bomb may make a direct hit on the underground shelter, killing you there, whereas if you had stayed home, you might have survived. To live at all involves risks. Still, the fatalistic conclusion, that human beings are impotent to change the course of events, is simply a false empirical proposition.

In daily life, everyone is perfectly aware of this. People may be fatalistic about far-off events, or things they believe they cannot control anyway, but they cannot consistently be fatalists about *every* event in their lives. The student who said, "If I'm fated to pass this course, I'll pass it whether I study or not; and if I'm fated to fail it, I'll fail it whether I study or not; therefore I won't bother to study," would soon flunk out of college. A person who said, "If I'm fated to have my lunch today, it will somehow come to me; and if I'm fated not to have it, I won't get it even if I do go to a restaurant and order it; therefore I'll just sit here and wait," would soon starve to death. We all know, in these practical situations that we encounter hundreds of times a day, that what happens depends on what we do. It is true that the next solar eclipse will occur regardless of what you do, but it is *not* true that you will receive your

---

[15] Quoted by Michael Dummett, "Bringing about the Past," *Philosophical Review*, 1964, pp. 338–59.

grade of A regardless of whether you do anything to get it. Any person who claims to be a fatalist should be asked whether he is a fatalist also about these everyday situations, and how he has succeeded in remaining alive if he is. People can be fatalists only in classrooms: once they get hungry, they are not fatalists any more. So obvious is it that what the future will be depends, in part at least, on what we do in the present.

Confronted by such considerations, however, the fatalist may shift his ground. "I don't deny," he may say, "that I will get an A in the course only if I study, or that I will get my lunch only if I go to a restaurant and order it or go home and prepare it. Acts of mine are often necessary conditions for these other things to occur. But what I contend is that *whether or not you do these acts* is fated. Whether you get the A or not isn't fated, but whether or not you choose to study is. And so, *indirectly*, whether you get the A or not is fated, since it depends on whether or not you study, which *is* fated. In general, what happens depends in large measure on our actions, but our actions themselves are fated to occur as they do."

This is a considerable change in the fatalistic doctrine—so great as to make one doubt whether it should still be called "fatalism" at all. In this version, the fatalist does not deny that human acts have consequences; he no longer says that human will is impotent in the world and makes no difference to the course of events. He now says, on the contrary, that it does; only now he adds that whatever decisions we make are themselves "fated." What does this mean? Fated by whom or by what? Fated by a God who decides what we shall do? In that case, his view is a theological doctrine, which we shall discuss in Chapter 7. By an impersonal Fate, as in ancient Greek tradition and mythology? But that doctrine is itself very unclear, and does he really wish to revive it? Perhaps he just means that our acts are caused by our decisions, but that our decisions themselves are caused. But in that case, his view is simply one type of determinism, and we shall more appropriately discuss it under that heading.

Indeterminism.   But before we do, let us examine indeterminism, a view that is opposed to determinism. Indeterminism denies that everything that happens has a cause. For many events—probably most, but not all—there are conditions such that if they were repeated the event would be repeated. The indeterminist is not likely to press his case in the area of inorganic nature; here he will be content to let universal causality reign. The motion of each planet is caused (determined) by a set of prior conditions; so is the path of every projectile and the history of every molecule of oxygen. This is even true for the most part in the organic realm, as our scientific successes in finding causes in biology will bear out. It is only in the human realm that the indeterminist wishes to press his case. Reflex actions are 100 per cent caused, since with regard to them we are not active but passive; the only area in which universal causality does not hold is in the realm of actions, the things we *do*. With regard to these actions—or at any rate some of them—no one will ever be able to predict them, no matter how much physiological and psychological knowledge we get about their antecedent conditions, because the Causal Principle does not apply to them. Every condition may predispose you toward doing act X, but you may do act Y instead; in this consists your freedom. This typically occurs in situations of moral conflict, in which we must choose between our inclinations and what we believe to be our duty.

In the situation of moral conflict, I (as agent) have before my mind a course of action X which I believe to be my duty; and also a course of action Y, incompatible with X, which I feel to be that which I most strongly desire. Y is, as it is sometimes expressed, "in the line of least resistance" for me— the course which I am aware I should take if I let my purely desiring nature operate without hindrance. It is the course towards which I am aware that my *character,* as so far formed, naturally inclines me. Now, as actually engaged in this situation, I find that I cannot help believing that I *can* rise to duty and choose X; the "rising to duty" being effected by what is commonly called "effort of will." And I further find, if I ask myself just what it is I am believing when I believe that I "can" rise to duty, that I cannot help believing that it lies with me here and now, quite absolutely, which of two genuinely open possibilities I adopt; whether, that is, I make the effort of will and choose X, or, on the other hand, let my desiring nature, my character as so far formed, "have its way," and choose Y, the course "in the line of least resistance."[16]

The determinist, however, has objections to this view:
1. In the first place, he will ask, is there any evidence at all that some events are not caused by antecedent conditions? It is true that we do not know empirically that every event is caused, but our knowledge of causes is increasing every day, and there is no reason *not* to believe that every event without exception is caused. Whether we take this as a truth about the world or as a leading principle, there are very strong grounds for believing it (or adopting it). On the other hand, there is *no* evidence whatever for indeterminism. There is no area of events *known not* to be caused: there is merely an area of events *not known* to be caused, and that area is constantly diminishing. It is true that as long as there remains an area of events not known to be caused, indeterminism cannot be disproved; but, says the determinist, there is not the slightest evidence for it, and therefore no reason why anyone should believe it.

One may, of course, *feel* that indeterminism is true, but feeling that something is true is no guarantee that it is. My feeling afraid does make "I feel afraid" true, but the Causal Principle is not *about* my feeling-state, and is not made true by any such state that I experience. (See pp. 124–28.) I may "feel" that the world will explode tomorrow, but this is no evidence that it will. The sole reason why the indeterminist wants to deny the Causal Principle is that he wants to make room for freedom: he has no evidence *for* his view, but

[16] C. A. Campbell, "Is 'Free-will' a Pseudo-Problem?" *Mind,* 1951, p. 463.

he is convinced that if he doesn't deny the Causal Principle, human freedom will not be possible. But what if freedom is not even possible in the indeterminist's view? That is the point of the next objection:

2. How is freedom possible if indeterminism is true? "It is not possible," says the determinist. "Freedom is possible only to the extent that determinism is true. Suppose that some act of yours were causeless; it would not be caused by your character, by your habits up to now, by anything that constitutes *you* as a person. Don't you want your acts to be caused—caused by *you?* Can you really call them free if they are uncaused? They would then *not* be acts that have their origin in you. How can they be *your* acts if they are not caused by you? If they are not caused at all, they are cut off from all roots. They just pop into existence from nowhere, and could not even be called acts *of* or *by* the person who did them; in fact, he wouldn't be *doing* them, since doing them means causing them to happen: they would just *happen to* him. Suppose you have a friend whom you have known for years and learned to trust completely; now suppose that his next act were cut off from all causal conditions—that he were seized with an attack of the indeterminist's freedom (lack of causality). There would be no reason to trust him anymore, for what happened next would not be *his* act, it would not be an outgrowth of his character, it wouldn't be caused by *him.* When we attempt to train, educate, reform, reward, advise, punish other human beings (all these are causal words), we assume that determinism is true; we assume that by our actions we can *cause* a change in the actions of the person we are trying to change. But if indeterminism were true, all such attempts would be useless. To the extent that it was true, our efforts could have no effect, for the actions of the person would have no cause."

The indeterminist will reply: "Don't make my position absurd. No indeterminist believes that all events are uncaused, or even that all human actions are uncaused. Indeterminism applies to perhaps only .01 per cent of all human actions (perhaps only those in which moral choices are involved). This small amount of indeterminism would not interfere with the regularity and uniformity of the universe to any appreciable degree. It would not even interfere with prediction, except for the things that are not now predictable anyway—and human actions are notoriously unpredictable as things are now. The introduction of a bit of indeterminism would be no more noticeable than a drop of water in the ocean. You need not fear that all is lost if the universe is not rigidly deterministic: there are still plenty of causes for the sciences to unearth."

"Nevertheless, *to the extent* that we admit indeterminism, we admit chaos and unpredictability. It is a mistake to admit it at all. If indeterminism applies to only .01 per cent of human actions, then that .01 per cent is infected by the disease I mentioned: that .01 per cent of his actions would not grow out of the character of the person. It wouldn't be *his* act, but something that happened to him, like being struck by lightning. I believe that your sole reason for believing in indeterminism—it would never occur to anyone to believe it otherwise—is that you fear that human freedom is impossible if determinism is true. You want to rescue freedom, so you cling desperately to your indeterminism. But I shall try to show you that this move is unnecessary. Not only do you *not* have freedom if I grant you indeterminism—as I've just shown you—but you *do* have it if you assume the truth of determinism, and this I shall try to show you now."

Chance. "Clearly some things occur by chance. Indeterminism must be true, since according to it some things occur by chance." The question is: What is meant by saying that something occurs "by chance"? The phrase is ambiguous. Here are the principal senses:

1. When we say that you and I met downtown this morning by chance, we mean that the meeting was unplanned, not pre-arranged. Doubtless your going downtown had causes, and so did mine. By calling the meeting a chance one, we mean only that it was not our *intention* to meet.

2. "Mutations occur by chance." Here we do not mean that mutations are causeless but that we do not know exactly what these causes are. We use the word "chance" to refer to our *ignorance* of the causes. We know what the relevant factors are in the toss of a coin, but we do not know precisely how great is the upthrust, what is the direction of the throw, how many times it will turn over before it hits the table, and so on. If we knew all these things, we could predict the outcome of the throw, but since we do not, we say that it is a matter of chance.

3. "The chances are that. . . ." Here we are giving an estimate of *probability*. But not all estimates of probability are of the same kind. Estimates of *mathematical* probability are entirely a priori: if we know that there are two alternatives, we assign to each alternative a probability of 50 per cent, without knowing anything about either of them. Since we know nothing yet about either alternative, we cannot use mathematical probability as a basis for actual predictions. We can do so, however, once we know the *statistical* probability—that is, the past record of the relative frequencies for each alternative. If we know that 50.2 per cent of human births have been male, we will say that the chances of your next child being a male are 50.2 per cent and not the 50 per cent you would get from mathematical probability alone. The two are apt to be confused because often their results coincide. The chance that the next toss of the coin will be heads is 50 per cent, but that is not because of mathematical probability but because of the past records of coin throwing. Once you suspect that the coin is loaded, you will no longer assess the probability at 50 per cent. Any empirical information you may have about the behavior of coins or the behavior of this coin will be relevant to the estimate of probability in the statistical but not in the mathematical sense.

Many pages could be spent in setting forth various usages of the word "chance" and their relationships to one another.[17]

But is there not a sense in which "chance" does imply lack of causation? Do we not find in subatomic physics a reference to electrons moving in a certain direction "by chance," meaning, in this case, "without any cause whatever"—pure chance, as it were?

This is highly disputable. Is it really meant that there is *no cause* for the electron going this way rather than that? We can't predict which way it will go since we don't know of any laws in this area. But in that case, the direction of movement is not really a matter of chance (causeless) but is again a function of our ignorance.[18]

Determinism as compatible with freedom.   So we come back again to determinism. Once again, determinism merely says that everything that happens has some cause or other. But the word "determine" is so loaded with animistic overtones that the word "determinism" is a most unfortunate name for the doctrine; "universal causality" would be preferable. If you are told that everything that happens is determined, you might object. "Determined" sounds as if it happened *in spite of us*, as if *we* had no part to play in it, but were merely passive spectators of the course of events. And this, of course, is false, as we saw in discussing fatalism. If we use the words "determine," "determined," and "determinism," we should keep in mind that "determined" means no more or less than "caused."

1. Sometimes determinism—universal causality—has been identified with universal *predictability*. But they are not the same. *If* determinism is true, and *if* we knew all the laws of nature, and all the "initial conditions," *then* we could predict everything that would happen. But determinism could be true without our being able to predict, owing to our lack of knowledge. Determinism (universal causality) is a metaphysical theory: it has to do with *what is*, with what exists in reality; but predictability is an epistemological matter: it has to do with our *knowledge* of what is. To predict accurately we would require not only that everything have a cause but that we *know* in detail what these causes are and what are the laws connecting causes with effects. Predictability would be a *consequence* of determinism plus our knowledge of the laws, but it is not what determinism consists in.

2. "But if determinism is true, every event that occurs, including every human action, is *necessitated* by conditions and events that occurred prior to it. How is human freedom possible if everything occurs by necessity?" But the term "necessitate" in the present context is a rat's nest of confusions. Let us separate the principal senses:

[17] For a more detailed account of the various meanings of "chance," see A. J. Ayer, "Chance," *Scientific American*, October 1965.

[18] The Heisenberg Principle of Indeterminancy is a theory in one specialized branch of physics and can be explained only in the highly technical language of mathematical physics. In any case, it has nothing to do with the free-will problem discussed in this section.

a. There is the logical sense, in which "This is a triangle" necessitates "This has three angles." Only propositions can necessitate (entail) one another in this sense. We may extend this sense by speaking of certain properties entailing other ones: being red entails being colored, being a cube entails having twelve edges, and so on. But cause does not necessitate effect in this sense. It is always logically possible that a given set of conditions will not produce a certain effect, no matter how often the one has been followed by the other in the past.

b. It is sometimes said that an event occurs *necessarily,* meaning that its occurrence is an instance of some law, and can be deduced from the law; that is, the *proposition* that this E occurs follows from the premises "If C, then E" and "C occurs." And so it does: the deduction is valid. But the conclusion is true only if both premises are also true. If E on a certain occasion failed to occur (which is logically possible), even after C did, this would show that the premise "If C, then E" was false. The law itself ("If C, then E") that constitutes the major premise of the argument is an empirical proposition, which is always liable to refutation or modification by subsequent experience.

c. "But the law itself *necessarily* holds." This again is a mistake, unless it is a misleading way of saying that the law *holds for all cases.* But this doesn't mean that it is a necessary truth, only that it has no exceptions. One of the defining characteristics of a law is that it is exceptionless: if it isn't exceptionless, it isn't a law.

d. Perhaps "necessitate" is being used to mean the same as "compel." But causes do not necessitate effects in this sense. Effects occur as the result of causes, otherwise they wouldn't be effects, but to cause is not the same thing as to compel. In inanimate nature, no such thing as compulsion can occur: compulsion can be exerted only by conscious beings on other conscious beings. The first billiard ball does not compel the second one to move, as if it were saying "Move, or else!" We tend to think of things and events as *forcing* each other instead of simply succeeding each other. We talk as if there were an unhappy effect trying in vain to extricate itself from the clutches of an overmastering cause. But this, of course, is a mistake. The first ball strikes the second one, and the second one moves, and this regularly happens; that is all. "To compel" has meaning only when speaking of beings who can exert their will over other beings, thus changing the course of their decisions and actions. Since "compel" has its meaning only in that context, to say that inanimate objects compel one another is neither true nor false but meaningless, because the word is being used outside the only context in which it has a meaning. Human beings, on the other hand, do compel one another, and sometimes an act occurs because of compulsion: one person can compel another to do what he would not otherwise have done by threats of death or torture if he does not. But compulsion, in the human realm, is only a special case of causation: most human actions are not compelled, though they may all be caused. Nobody is compelling me to write a book, but I am writing one, and my desire to write one is one of the causes of my writing it. Only *some* human actions are compelled, but this is not the same as saying that only some human actions are caused. Compelled actions are all caused, but not all caused actions are compelled. Saying "Everything is caused, therefore everything is compelled" is the same kind of mistake as saying "Every object is colored, therefore every object is red."

That all causes equally necessitate is indeed a tautology, if the word "necessitate" is taken merely as equivalent to "cause"; but if, as the objection requires, it is taken as equivalent to "constrain" or "compel," then I do not think that this proposition is true. For all that is needed for one event to be the cause of another is that . . . there is an invariable concomitance between the two classes of events; but there is no compulsion, in any but a metaphorical sense.[19]

3. "But if everything is caused, aren't our own actions caused?" Certainly, the determinist replies, they are; one may indeed be grateful that they are, else we would be stuck with the indeterminist's causeless actions. Indeed, the determinist says, our actions *are* caused—*by us.* "*I* caused my actions" (active voice) and "My acts are caused by *me*" (passive voice) say the same thing. "I caused my actions" is the motto of freedom; "My actions are caused by *me*" is that of determinism. Determinism is not only compatible with human freedom, but human freedom is possible only on the assumption that determinism is true.[20]

"Freedom" is a slippery word, with many overlapping meanings in common usage. To discuss it in detail would require many pages. (1) We use it in a *negative* sense, in which it means the *absence of constraint.* We are free in this sense if no one is forcing us to do something against our will. If you are living in a tyrannical dictatorship in which most of your acts are forced upon you under severe penalties for not complying, you are not free. You are not able in such a situation to act on your own judgment but are forced to do as others order you to do. In such situations, you are acting *under compulsion,* and compulsion is the opposite of freedom: you are free if your acts are uncompelled. (Freedom in this sense, especially in political contexts, is often referred to as "liberty.") (2) We also use it in a *positive* sense, to mean roughly the same as *ability.* In this sense you are free, not *from* restraints, but *to do* certain things. You are free to do those things that you can do if you choose to do them. You are free to lift ten pounds, since you can do this if you choose, but not free to lift a thousand pounds, since you cannot do this whether you choose to or not. You are free to walk (if you are not crippled) but not free to fly through the air like a bird.

---

[19] A. J. Ayer, "Freedom and Necessity," in *Philosophical Essays,* pp. 271–84.

[20] See R. E. Hobart, "Free-will as Involving Determinism and Inconceivable without It."

No one is completely free in either of these two senses. The degrees of freedom, and the respects in which we are free, vary from person to person and from place to place. Our question, however, concerns the relation of freedom to determinism. Is determinism incompatible with freedom? And the determinist contends that it clearly is not. There *are* often restrictions on our freedom, as every victim of a holdup man and every disarmed victim of an armed dictatorship will testify, but it is not determinism that brings about these restrictions. Determinism only says that whatever happens has some cause or other. And as long as that cause can be *you,* and it often is (at least in part), there is no restriction on your freedom as far as determinism is concerned. The actions of other people and environmental conditions, or even conditions within yourself, such as irresistible urges, may restrict your freedom, but your freedom is not restricted by any doctrine of Universal Causality.

Let us say, then, that your act is caused: it is caused by your decision to do it. (This is not a sufficient condition by itself, of course; your limbs must be in working order, the act must be one you are able to perform, and so on.) Decision 1 leads to Act 1; Decision 2 leads to Act 2. What more freedom could one ask? Would you be more free if you decided to do Act 1 and found yourself doing Act 2 instead? What greater freedom could you want than that your acts be caused by your decisions?

4. "But if every event is caused, our decisions are also caused. And if they are caused, how can we be free?"

"Our decisions," replies the determinist, "are caused (usually, at any rate) by what we desire or prefer. I prefer cake to ice cream, so I decide to order it for dessert, and I do order it. Where is the lack of freedom? I should think that this is a paradigm case of a free decision."

"But our desires are also caused, if determinism is true. They are caused by a vast variety of factors, no doubt—our hereditary predisposition, our early environment, our habit-patterns developed through the years, and so on. But how can I be free if my choices are caused by my desires, which I did not create and over which I have no control?"

"It is true that we are less free with respect to our desires than we are with respect to our actions. If you have a certain desire, say the desire for alcohol, you may not be able to do anything that would change it at that moment. But you can work on it: you can turn down the next drink and the next, and perhaps join the Alcoholics Anonymous, until finally you may be without the desire. People do have *some* control over their desires, and often do succeed in changing them, through the exertion of self-discipline and will power."

"But some people have the ability to exercise this power, and some don't, some people are incapable of disciplining themselves and changing their fundamental habits, no matter how hard they try. Some can, and some can't. The difference lies in the causes, which are beyond our control. Some people have within them the *ability* to exert the effort required to change their habit-patterns, and some do not. And none of us gave ourselves this ability. We either have it or we don't. We don't know till we try, of course. But if we try as hard as we can and then fail, we know that it really was outside our control, and that we are not free."

"But I never said that everyone is free with respect to everything. Every person's freedom is limited, and some people have more of it than others. If you had a very unfortunate early environment and consequently developed certain strong habit-patterns, it is quite possible that nothing you do in later life—even going to a psychiatrist—will enable you to overcome them. With respect to these, then, you are not free, any more than you were free to be born male or female. I am only insisting that you are free with respect to *some* things, and that this is perfectly compatible with determinism. I only say that freedom exists, not that it is present in every human action and tendency. I don't have to prove that *every* act, decision, desire, is free to prove that there *is* such a thing as freedom. Remember, you said that according to determinism there can be no such thing as freedom. To prove that, it is not enough to point out areas of behavior in which we are not free, for when you do I have merely to point to areas in which we are."

"Very well then; let me take this line: If determinism is true, you *could not* have done other than you did, on any particular occasion in your life, *given* the total set of circumstances that led to the action. Those circumstances being what they were, only one act was open to you: the one you actually performed. We only believe differently because we don't know what those circumstances are."

"Aha! Now we have a philosophical claim. Let us assess it. On any particular occasion, you say, I could not have done anything but what I did. Now, 'can' and 'could' are ability-words. To say that I *can* do something is to say that I am *able* to do it—not that I constantly *am* doing it, but that I am able to, which means that if I decide to do it I will. I *can* walk at four miles an hour but not at forty; that is, my walking at four miles per hour will occur if I decide to do it, but no amount of deciding or willing or wishing will enable me to walk at forty. So there are some things I *can* do and other things I can't."

"In general, yes. But what I am saying is that *at any specific moment in your life*—when faced with a certain choice, let's say—you *can* do only one thing, the thing that you actually do."

"Not true. At this moment I can do several things. I can walk to the left, I can walk to the right, or I can stay where I am. Whichever of these things I do, it will have causes. Normally I walk if I want to walk, and stand still if I want to stand still. What I do depends on what I want to do; and thus, I repeat, I am free, at least with respect to these alternatives."

"I don't deny that you can do these things if you want to. But given just the circumstances in which you find yourself, you couldn't have *wanted* anything different. You can do as you please, but you can't please as you please."

"But surely I might have been able to want something different. If I originally wanted whiskey but gradually developed a taste for Coca-Cola instead of whiskey, I could in the end want Coca-Cola instead of whiskey, couldn't I?"

"Doubtless you could; but you still miss my point. Given just the circumstances in which you are at the moment your total physiological and psychological state at the moment of desiring, willing, choosing, or acting, you *could not* have desired, willed, etc. anything other than what you did."

"I wonder how you claim to know this. Since you don't know what the factors are, you are not in a position to know that the choice could have no other outcome."

"I don't claim to know this. I only claim that that's the way it is *if* determinism is true. I am trying to show you on your own deterministic doctrine that freedom is impossible."

"But why can't I do differently, or desire differently? Did my background and habit patterns *compel* me? But only people can compel (force their wills on others). Causality is not the same as compulsion. Don't fall victim to *that* fallacy."

"I am not saying that your background compelled you. I am only saying that, given the *total* background, you *could not* have done other than what you did."

"And I repeat that 'could' is an ability word. I *could* have done other than I did, because I *would* have done other than I did *if* I had chosen to."

"But you couldn't have chosen differently, the conditions being just what they were."

"You forget that what I desire is itself one of the conditions on which my choice depends. Suppose that a thousand factors are the same in two situations, all predisposing me to do X. But the first time I want to do X, and the second time I don't. So the first time I do X, and the second time I don't. My wanting or not wanting to do X can make all the difference."

"Of course it can. But again you miss my point. Your wanting or not wanting X is itself determined by previous conditions. Being just what you are at the moment, with just the factors operating that were operating, your choice could have had no other outcome, even though (because you don't know in detail what those factors were) you may *think* that the outcome could have been different."

"And so it could; that is, it would have been different if I had wanted it to be. Surely this is a familiar fact of experience."

"Listen. I am saying that given just *this* set of conditions, you could have done only *this* particular act. If the set of conditions had been somewhat different (say, if you had desired Y rather than X), then you could have done only that *other* act. Either way, you *could* have done only what you *did* do."

"I see your point, but I think you are making one fundamental mistake.

You forget that 'could' is an ability word. This is very important. You ask, 'Could I have done differently if *all* the conditions leading up to my action had been the same?' and I want to point out to you that *your very question is self-contradictory*. 'I could have' is synonymous with 'I would have if I had chosen to.' Now you ask whether I could have done otherwise if all the conditions leading up to the act had been the same. What you want, then, is for me to show you that I *could* have done otherwise—that is, done otherwise if I had chosen to—even if *all* the conditions, including the choosing, had been the same! But *choosing is itself one of the conditions of action;* and if the choice had been different, the act would have been different. Your demand is self-contradictory: you want me to say that I could have acted differently (that is, would have acted differently if I had chosen differently) even if *all* the conditions (including the choosing) had been the same. But the conditions you impose are self-contradictory. If I had chosen differently, then one of the conditions of action, the choice, would have been different, and so not all the conditions *would* have been the same: Don't you see that your very demand contains a self-contradiction? You want all the conditions the second time to be the same, and yet you want one of the conditions, the choosing, to be different. And you can't have it both ways."

"I see what you mean. Let me, then, reformulate my question. Instead of asking, 'Could you have acted differently if *all* the conditions had been the same?'—which I now see is self-contradictory—let me put it this way: '*Would* you have acted differently if all the conditions had been the same?' "

"Well, if the circumstances were the same today as they were a year ago when Jones asked me to lend him $100, I would act differently: I wouldn't lend it to him, since he didn't return it to me the time before."

"Of course; but I mean by 'all the circumstances' *really all* the circumstances, not just the external ones: and you yourself and your state of mind must be included among the circumstances. You of course are different now; lots of things have happened in the meanwhile, especially the fact that you got burned when you lent Jones money before. But suppose for a moment that you *were* exactly the same the second time. This never happens, of course, but suppose it did: The external circumstances are identical with those a year ago, and there is no memory trace left of the former occasion. Then you'd just be repeating yourself, wouldn't you? You'd do just what you did then, since you were (by hypothesis) exactly the same as you were then. You couldn't do differently."

"Couldn't? You mean I wouldn't even if I wanted to?"

"O.K., you wouldn't."

"And suppose that to the very best of our knowledge, after thorough investigation, we concluded that the circumstances were all exactly the same as they were then. And now suppose that I acted differently after all. What would you say then? Would you say that your belief (that I wouldn't act differently this time) had been disproved?"

"No, I wouldn't. I would say that the conditions weren't exactly the same."

"Of course. And even if we never discovered any difference in the conditions, you'd still say they were different, wouldn't you? You'd say they *must* have been different, because the outcome was different. And what kind of 'must' is this? You are making your hypothesis a priori, aren't you? You take the *very fact* of the outcomes being different as proving, without further evidence, that the conditions were different. So either you are taking the Causal Principle as an a priori truth, in which case I wonder how you know it to be true, or as a rule of the game, in which case it isn't a truth about the universe at all."

"Well, you are a determinist. How do *you* take it?"

"As a determinist, I could take it in either of these ways. Each interpretation would have to be argued separately. But if I take it as a *truth* about the universe, I would take it as an empirical truth, like a law of nature. As such, I admit that the evidence for it is inconclusive. But assuming that it *is* true, I want only to make you see that it is not incompatible with human freedom. To demand that I *could* have done differently, even if *all* the causal factors had been the same, is to make a self-contradictory request. Naturally I'm not going to fall into that trap. All that is left, then, is to say that if all the conditions had been the same, I *would* have done the same. And this I believe to be true. But if it is true, it is still not incompatible with freedom, for it is still true that I *could* have done differently; that is, I would have if I'd wanted to. This is all the freedom I need or could reasonably ask for."

Determinism as incompatible with freedom.   But, even with his mistakes, our questioner has latched onto something. I *could* have done differently; that is true. I could have done differently if I had wanted to, which would have changed one of the conditions. But I would have done differently *only* if some of the conditions had been different—if certain circumstances had been different, or if I had been a different kind of person. But how does this help freedom? It is not enough to be told that if I had been different in some respect, then I would have acted differently. I want to know whether I, *this* person, with just *these* characteristics, being just as I am now, would have done differently. Nothing less than this is what freedom requires, and many writers have testified to this fact:

We can only retain the ideas of obligation and guilt as properly ethical ideas, if we can also believe in actions which could have been other than they were *although everything else in the universe had remained the same*.[21]

Moral responsibility requires that a man should be able to choose alternative actions, *everything in the universe prior to the act, including his self, being the same*. I do not see how anything clearer can be said than that we seriously mean "he could have done otherwise" categorically. If analysis fails to do justice to this, so much the worse for analysis.[22]

[21] H. D. Lewis, "Guilt and Freedom," in W. Sellars and J. Hospers (eds.), *Readings in Ethical Theory*, pp. 615–16. Italics mine.

[22] J. D. Mabbott, in *Contemporary British Philosophy*, Third Series, ed. H. D. Lewis (New York: Humanities Press), pp. 301–2.

And yet the determinist cannot grant this condition. He cannot, as long as he remains a determinist. Given just this set of circumstances, he is committed to saying, only this desire will ensue (the circumstances are a sufficient condition for the occurrence of the desire). And given just this desire plus all its accompanying conditions, just this choice will ensue. And given this choice, only this action will ensue. Each step is a sufficient condition for the next step. So aren't we still caught in a web of cause and effect, each step being a sufficient condition for the one that follows? And if C is sufficient for E, E *will* invariably follow upon C. That is what is meant by "sufficient condition."

Does this not play havoc with freedom? Haven't we perhaps defined "freedom" too superficially? I am free to do X if I can do it, and to say that I can do it is to say that I *will* do it if I choose. In *this* sense, admittedly, we are all free in many of our actions. But if we probe more deeply, don't we find that this freedom comes to no more than the freedom of the hands of the clock to move over the face of the clock? Every motion of the hands is determined. Suppose

. . . that while my behavior is entirely in accordance with my own volitions, and thus "free" in terms of the conception of freedom we are examining, my volitions themselves are caused. . . . We can suppose that an ingenious physiologist can induce in me any volition he pleases, simply by pushing various buttons on an instrument to which, let us suppose, I am attached by numerous wires. All the volitions I have in that situation are, accordingly, precisely the ones he gives me. By pushing one button, he evokes in me the volition to raise my hand; and my hand, being unimpeded, rises in response to that volition. By pushing another, he induces the volition in me to kick, and my foot, being unimpeded, kicks in response to that volition. We can even suppose that the physiologist puts a rifle in my hands, aims it at some passer-by, and then, by pushing the proper button, evokes in me the volition to squeeze my finger against the trigger, whereupon the passer-by falls dead of a bullet wound.

This is the description of a man who is acting in accordance with his inner volitions, a man whose body is unimpeded and unconstrained in its motions, these motions being the effects of those inner states. It is hardly the description of a free and responsible agent. It is the perfect description of a puppet. To render a man your puppet, it is not necessary forcibly to constrain the motions of his limbs, after the fashion that real puppets are moved. A subtler but no less effective means of making a man your puppet would be to gain complete control of his inner senses, and ensuring . . . that his body will move in accordance with them. . . .

Nor does it . . . matter whether the inner states which allegedly prompt all my "free" activity are evoked in me by another agent or by perfectly impersonal forces. Whether a desire which causes my body to behave in a certain way is inflicted upon me by another person, for instance, or derived from hereditary factors, or indeed from anything at all, matters not the least. In any case, if it is in fact the cause of my bodily behavior, I cannot but act in accordance with it. Wherever it came from, whether from personal or impersonal origins, it was entirely caused or determined, and not within my control. Indeed, if determinism is true . . . all those inner states which cause my body to behave in whatever ways it behaves must arise from circumstances that existed before I was born; for the chain of causes and effects is infinite, and none could [in view of the preceding argument, let us substitute "would" here] have been the least different, given those that preceded.[23]

If this argument is valid, the determinist is still faced with the problem of how human freedom is possible if his view is true. He has pointed out many pitfalls and fallacies in his opponent's arguments (such as the one about "could"), but he is still faced with the allegation that if his view is true, freedom is a delusion. We can have freedom in the sense of doing what we choose, of choosing what we desire or prefer, even sometimes of desiring what we want to desire. Perhaps it is only this kind of freedom that we have, and can reasonably demand. But on a deeper level, it would appear, we do not have freedom at all, for the conditions that are sufficient for the occurrence of our desires, choices, etc. are still not within our control, and are linked in a chain of sufficient conditions to circumstances that existed long before we were born. Yet if we turn back from determinism to indeterminism, there is no hope there either: the "freedom" of indeterminism, to the extent that it exists, is quite incompatible with our actions being *caused by* our choices. But if neither determinism nor indeterminism can give a satisfactory account of human freedom, where then can we turn? Are there any options open to us that we have not yet considered?

There are. Each of them has been so hotly argued, and has been developed with so many technical and tortuous involvements in the recent literature of the subject, that we can do little more than mention them here. We shall conclude this chapter by summarizing some of the main lines of argument.

Alternatives.   1. "The exact size of each iceberg in the Antarctic is exactly fixed [determined] by its size a moment ago and the wind and weather then prevailing; and these things are fixed in their turn by preceding conditions. Hence the exact size of each iceberg in the Antarctic is fixed by the icebergs and the weather of a million years ago."[24] In the same way the actions, the choices, the desires of human beings are all fixed by preceding conditions that, once these conditions exist, will yield but one result: that which actually occurs. This chain of causes goes back as far as the history of the universe goes. If the universe goes back infinitely, then the chain of causes will be infinite (we shall examine this possibility in Chapter 7, pp. 433–36); but if there was a first series of events, then that first series was not itself caused: there was nothing for it to be caused by.

[23] Richard Taylor, *Metaphysics*, pp. 45–46.

[24] John Wisdom, *Problems of Mind and Matter* (London: Cambridge University Press, 1934), pp. 112–13.

Thus far, this will not help freedom. The ultimate origin of our actions is to be found in events long since lost in the mists of history, long before the earth even existed. We were certainly not free to originate *those* events. We appeared on the scene long after those events occurred, and (according to determinism of the kind we are now considering) once we did come on the scene and made decisions to do this or that, our decisions were determined by what occurred before we had any decision-making powers.

But what if we did *not* originate comparatively recently in the history of the universe? What if, in some form or other, we have existed ever since those hypothetical first events? What if we pre-existed, and this pre-existence was "world-long," as long as the history of the universe itself? In that case, *if* the history of the universe is of finite length (otherwise there would be no first events) our choices were not the product of forces acting outside us: they were formed by ourselves.

This alternative may seem to be the counsel of despair. To say that we pre-existed from all eternity, or at any rate as long as anything at all existed, is to go contrary to every bit of empirical evidence we have. But suppose it were true: then at least what we do is not the ultimate product of forces acting on us from the outside. But of what, then, were they the product? Previous decisions. And these in turn? Still earlier decisions. The series of decisions must be world-long. What then of the first decision? According to the hypothesis, it was not caused by conditions existing prior to it. Apparently, then, it had no cause whatever. But if it had no cause, then we are stuck with indeterminism, at least for this first decision. If it had no causes, it is like a bolt from the blue (except that bolts from the blue do have causes), and is no more *our* decision than a bolt of lightning. (And how could we make decisions if we did not already have some formed character? And what previous conditions could have formed this character?)

2. Or we might argue in a different vein: There are facts of experience that are certain, whereas any metaphysical theories, such as determinism and indeterminism, are much less probably true than these facts of experience. If we have to choose between them, then, the facts of experience must take priority, and any theories that are incompatible with them must go. But what are these facts of experience?

(a) "I have the *feeling* of being free. It is certain that I have this feeling, and if having it is incompatible with determinism (or any other theory), then so much the worse for the theory." But what exactly is this "feeling of freedom"? We are all aware of making decisions, and we see that our decisions often make a difference to what happens afterward. But none of this is denied by determinism. Determinism only reminds us that the fact that we have this feeling proves nothing about the status of the Causal Principle. Introspection tells us only that we have certain experiences: it cannot inform us of any facts other than that the experiences themselves occur. We have the experiences of decision making, reflecting, etc., but the causes of these decisions, as well as of desires and preferences, are hidden from us; these we cannot introspect. Thus what determinism says about these hidden springs may still be true, in spite of our "experience of freedom."

One might appeal, in this argument, not to the "feeling of freedom" but to the universal and ineradicable *belief* in freedom. But of course the prevalence, even the universality, of a belief is no proof that the belief is true. If one person can be mistaken, so can many people, or all people. Besides, what is this "universal and ineradicable belief in freedom"? Is it the belief in "contra-causal" freedom that the indeterminists defend? But it is very doubtful whether this belief is universal, or even that very many people have thought the matter out to the point where they could either assert or deny freedom in this very special sense. The "belief in freedom" that most people have is simply that they can often do what they want to do, that their actions occur in accordance with their choices, and so on—all of which is, of course, fully granted by determinists.

(b) But we can be more specific. We *deliberate*, and deliberation is more than a feeling. We deliberate about our own behavior, not that of others; we can deliberate only about the future, not about the past: we cannot deliberate about what we shall do if we already know what we shall do—there would be nothing to deliberate about—and even though we do not know what we shall do, we cannot deliberate about it unless we believe that what we are going to do is *up to us:* if we are at the mercy of others, or of circumstances over which we have no control, we cannot deliberate about them.[25] Now, it may be contended, that we do deliberate is a *fact*. And if this fact is incompatible with the theory of determinism, which (in its last form) says that the future is not up to us but that it is already in the cards what we shall decide, then the theory must go.

In all this, what is a clear "fact of experience"? That we make decisions, and that these decisions sometimes make a difference to what happens later. This is a fact whether determinism is true or not; and thus far, it is not incompatible with determinism at all. What *is* incompatible with determinism is the belief that these choices themselves are not caused by previous conditions; but whether they are or not is not a part of any indubitable "fact of experience." Introspection cannot tell us whether or not our decisions are caused by previous conditions. If it claims to, it may be the verdict of introspection and not determinism that is mistaken.

(c) It can be claimed that it is simply a fact that often I *could have done otherwise* than I did. Introspection cannot guarantee it, for introspection tells us only of the experiences we have, not of what *would* have occurred if something had been different. But though not introspectable, it is plausible to claim that we often could have acted differently from the way we did.

[25] Richard Taylor, *op. cit.*, pp. 37–38.

Assuming, then, that this is a fact, it runs head-on into determinism, which says that we could (or would) never have done otherwise than we did, granted the exact set of conditions that preceded our action. But this assertion is incompatible with the fact. There cannot be two incompatible facts: if one is true, the other must be false. That we often could have done otherwise is true; therefore the determinist's denial of it must be false. So runs the argument.

But is it a fact that we could sometimes have acted differently? This is precisely the question at issue. And what is the alleged fact—that we sometimes could (or would—the difference is important) have acted differently if one or more of the conditions had been different (who would wish to deny this?) or that we would have acted differently even if all the conditions had been *the same*? But since we never have the same exact set of conditions twice in human behavior, how can we know that "we would have acted differently" is a fact?

Indeed, the only sense in which it *is* an indisputable fact that we could have acted differently is also a sense in which inanimate objects can do so.

Suppose that a car is tuned and checked so that it is in perfect operating condition and is then placed in circumstances that must favor good perform-ance. If someone tries to start the car, turns the key, sets the choke, etc., and the car fails to start, that is evidence that it cannot start. On the other hand, if no attempt is made to start the car, then the mere fact that the car does not start in no way supports the hypothesis that it cannot start.[26]

In other words, the car could have started—that is, it would have started if we had pressed the starting button. We have every evidence that this is true. What this shows is that the car would have started *if* one condition had been different (pressing the starter). But how can this be an argument for freedom, since inanimate objects like cars are not free? (Neither are they unfree, of course: the distinction between free and unfree simply does not apply to inanimate objects, any more than does the language of compulsion.)

3. Thus far we have spoken of causes and not at all of *reasons*. But in human affairs the distinction between them is of great importance. The introduction of this distinction carries with it a new way of viewing the vexed problems of determinism.

"Determinism" to a scientist conveys the general proposition that every event has a cause. Whether this general proposition is true is a very difficult question to decide, but it is certainly assumed to be true by most scientists. . . . For example, given that under the conditions x, y, z, iron expands when it is heated, and given that the conditions x, y, z prevail and that this is a case of iron being heated, we can make the prediction that iron will expand.

[26] Keith Lehrer, "Disproof of Determinism?" in *Freedom and Determinism*, pp. 182–83.

Here we have a typical causal relation. . . . And these conditions are regarded as being *sufficient* to explain the effect.

Have we such relations in human affairs? The initial difficulty about saying that we have is that it is difficult to maintain that there are any psychological or sociological laws which would enable us to make such definite predictions. . . ."[27]

The only areas of human behavior in which there are known laws stating sufficient conditions are areas in which man is passive. We can often list the conditions sufficient for something happening to you, such as your leg getting broken, but we cannot list any conditions sufficient for a single human *action*, such as writing a letter or thinking about philosophy. At best we can list *necessary* conditions: you couldn't write a letter without fingers, you couldn't think without a brain. But exactly what you will do, *having* fingers and a brain, we cannot predict. If I predict that you will do one thing, you may do just the opposite in order to refute my prediction.

Freud's brilliant discoveries, for instance, were not of the causes of *actions* like signing contracts or shooting pheasants; rather they were of things that *happen* to a man like dreams, hysteria, and slips of the tongue. These might be called "passions" more appropriately than "actions," and in this respect they are similar to what we call "fits of passion" or "gusts of emotion." . . . One class of laws in psychology, then, gives causal explanations which seem sufficient to account for what happens to a man, but not for what he *does*.[28]

Thus far, we might ask, "So what? How does this attack determinism?" The causes for what people *do* are far more complex than for what *happens* to them. The sufficient condition for my writing a letter is much more complex than the sufficient condition for your leg getting broken; and that is why our ignorance is greater, and the full cause (sufficient condition) cannot yet be stated. But this is not to say that it does not exist. Surely there is a set of conditions such that if they were to occur again you would perform the same act again, even though these conditions are so complex that thus far nobody has been able to list all of them.

But now comes the main point:

When a man is solving a geometrical problem and his thoughts are proceeding in accordance with certain logical canons, it is logically absurd to suggest that any causal explanation in terms of movements of his brain, his temperament, his bodily state, and so on, is sufficient *by itself* to explain the movement of his thought. For logical canons are *normative* and cannot be sufficiently explained in terms of states and processes which are not. Of course there are any number of *necessary* conditions which must be taken account of. A man

[27] Stanley I. Benn and Richard Peters, *Principles of Political Thought* (New York: Free Press of Glencoe, Inc., 1965), pp. 232–33. Also published in Great Britain under the title *Social Principles and the Democratic State.*

[28] *Ibid.,* p. 233.

cannot think *without* a brain, for instance. But any *sufficient* explanation would have to take account of the *reasons* for his actions. We would have to know the rules of chess, for instance, which gave some *point* to a chessplayer's move.[29]

It appears, then, that by stating causal antecedents alone we never could arrive at a sufficient condition; to account for what a person does in his goal-directed activities we must know his reasons, and *reasons are not causes.* They constitute an entirely different order of being from causes. Causes are always antecedent conditions (events, states of substances, etc.), but reasons are not. But doing something for a reason presupposes a norm, or standard, for one's actions:

> Remembering is not just a psychological process; for to remember is to be *correct* about what happened in the past. Knowing is not just a mental state; it is to be sure that we are *correct* and to have *good grounds* for our conviction. To perceive something is to be *right* in our claims about what is before our eyes; to learn something is to *improve* at something or to get something *right.* All such concepts have norms written into them. . . . A human action is typically something done in order to bring about a result or in accordance with a standard. Such actions can be said to be done more or less intelligently and more or less correctly only because of the norms defining what are ends and what are efficient and correct means to them. It follows that a psychologist who claims that such performances depend on antecedent physiological conditions or mental processes, can at the most be stating necessary conditions. For processes, of themselves, are not appropriately described as correct or incorrect, intelligent or stupid. They only become so in the context of standards laid down by men. As Protagoras taught, nature knows no norms. . . . It may well be true that a man cannot remember without part of his brain being stimulated, or that learning is a function, in part, of antecedent "tension." But the very meaning of "remembering" and "learning" precludes a sufficient explanation in these sorts of naturalistic terms.[30]

It is impossible, then, in the very nature of the case, to give a causal account (sufficient condition) for human actions: no amount of investigation of antecedent events and processes would achieve it, for the explanation of human actions is to be found in the reasons men have for what they do (and reasons imply norms or standards), and not in the causes. (We have already seen in Chapter 4 how the question "Why?" is ambiguous: it can be the request for a cause or the request for a reason.) The attempt to find causes (sufficient conditions) for human actions is a failure, then, not because we have not discovered enough antecedent conditions (though this may be true also) but because the whole attempt is misplaced: we should be looking not in the realm of causes but in the realm of reasons.

[29] *Ibid.,* pp. 235–36.
[30] *Ibid.,* p. 234.

We know why a parson is mounting the pulpit not because we know much about the causes of his behavior but because we know the conventions governing church services. We would only ask what were the causes of his behavior if he fainted when he peered out over the congregation or if something similar *happened* to him. Most of our explanations of human behavior are couched in terms of a purposive, rule-following model, not in causal terms.[31]

What shall we say of this development? It is true, of course, that giving a reason is not the same thing as giving a cause. It makes perfectly good sense to distinguish between those human actions or beliefs that are based on reasoning and those that are not, but it does not follow that the former are in any way uncaused or that a person's belief in a certain proposition cannot be among the antecedent causal conditions of his action or belief. If a person knows what his reason is for acting in a certain way, could one not list having it as a cause? His *reason* for taking the short cut (the proposition he would have given if asked to defend his act) was that he could save time that way, and the *cause* of his taking the short cut (one causal factor, at any rate) was that he had at that moment the *belief* that he could save time by going that way, and that he wanted to save time. The view that because one can give reasons one cannot assign causes would seem, in the light of this, to be extremely dubious.

But what of the argument that human actions conform to rules, that we are often more interested in judging whether and how far they are up to standard than in discovering how they came about? I cannot see that it is relevant. From the fact that we can estimate an action in terms of its conforming to a rule, it no more follows that the performance of the action is not causally explicable than it follows that the appearance of a rainbow is not causally explicable from the fact that it can be made the subject of an aesthetic judgment. To explain something causally does not preclude assessing it in other ways. But perhaps the suggestion is merely that to relate an action to a rule is one way of accounting for it, and, in the present state of our knowledge, a better way of accounting for it than trying to subsume it under dubious causal laws. I cannot even agree with this because I think that it presents us with a false antithesis. The only reason why it is possible to account for the performance of an action by relating it to a rule is that the recognition of the requirements of the rule is a factor in the agent's motivation. He may attach a value in itself to performing a certain sort of action correctly; he may see its correct performance as a means towards some further end; or it may be a combination of the two. In any event this is as much a causal explanation as any other explanation in terms of motive. The invocation of rules adds nothing to the general argument. . . .

If we grant this point, what follows? Certainly not, as the philosophers who lay stress upon it seem to think, that these actions cannot be explained in causal terms. For when it comes to accounting for an action, the only way in

[31] *Ibid.,* p. 236.

which the social context enters the reckoning is through its influence upon the agent. The significance of the action is the significance that it has for him. That is to say, his idea that this is the correct, or expedient, or desirable thing to do in these circumstances is part of his motivation; his awareness of the social context and the effects which this has on him are therefore to be included in the list of initial conditions from which we seek to derive his performance of the action by means of a causal law. Whether such laws are discoverable or not may be an open question; but the fact that these items figure among the data has no important bearing on it.[32]

As far as the parson is concerned, we can indeed explain his behavior because we know certain rules and conventions, but we can do this only because we also assume or know that he is concerned to abide by these rules and conventions.

There seems to be another error as well. The authors rightly point to the "normative" nature of actions, and they then invalidly conclude that a causal explanation referring to non-normative phenomena cannot be given. But this does not follow at all. What follows is that such a causal explanation will not also at the same time explain *what it is to be* an action or any kind of normative phenomenon.

There is a confusion here between predicting an action on the basis of causes and explaining what it is to be an action. Must a causal account provide an analysis of the concepts embodied in a description of the effect? Would we reject an account of psychotic depression in terms of chemical imbalance in the brain because the reference to chemical imbalance does not tell us what it means to lack interest in things? Peters may be right, then, when he says that predictions of actions on the basis of movements are not 'sufficient explanations'; but many deterministic accounts are not sufficient explanations in his sense.

The same mistake is involved in Peters' reference to actions as intelligent or unintelligent. Why must a deterministic account of action show that the action is intelligent or explain the meaning of "intelligent"? The same may be said of Peters' reference to the fact that actions involve standards or rules.[33]

4. Still another alternative can be suggested. We believe ourselves to be self-determining beings—beings who are sometimes the causes of their own behavior.

In the case of an action that is free, it must be such that it is caused by the agent who performs it, but such that no antecedent conditions were sufficient for his performing just that action. In the case of an action that is both free and rational, it must be such that the agent who performed it did so for some reason, but this reason cannot have been the cause of it.

[32] A. J. Ayer, *Man as a Subject for Science* (London: Oxford University Press, 1964), pp. 22–24.

[33] Bernard Berofsky, "Determinism and Concept of a Person," *The Journal of Philosophy,* September 3, 1964, p. 473.

Now this conception fits what men take themselves to be; namely, beings who act, or who are agents, rather than things that are merely acted upon, and whose behavior is simply the causal consequence of conditions which they have not wrought. When I believe that I have done something, I do believe that it was I who caused it to be done, I who made something happen, and not merely something within me, such as one of my own subjective states, which is not identical with myself.[34]

I believe that I am a person, a *self-moving being*, a genuine originator of actions. I myself am the cause of my own actions. These actions, while caused by me, are not the inevitable product of conditions antecedent to them; if they were, I would not be the agent (actor) but only the vehicle or instrumentality through which the causal chain proceeded. I am a genuine originator, a *first cause* of my own actions.

If this view—the "theory of agency"—is true, it enables us to escape both indeterminism, in which no act is genuinely *caused by me,* and determinism, in which (in its last version) every action, every desire, every impulse, every thought is the inevitable consequence of antecedent conditions. It would give an account of ourselves as agents, which corresponds with what we normally believe ourselves to be.

But is it true? That it may enable us to escape two unpalatable alternatives does not prove that it is true. That our acts are caused by our decisions is plausible enough. But can it be true that our decisions are *self-originating,* not caused by anything that went before? Of what precise fact is this the description? (Let us try to imagine it in fact, not merely in words.) If it means that our decisions have no causes, we are back with indeterminism. But if it means that our decisions are *self-caused,* what does this mean? Can anything be the cause of itself? And what is its relation to antecedent conditions? "They incline without necessitating," it is sometimes said; but what does this metaphor come to? If two people are inclined toward intoxication and one gives in to the inclination and the other resists it, can the difference between the two never be accounted for causally? Must we say simply that one decided to resist and the other to give in, and that no more can be said because both decisions are self-caused and self-originating?

Unless this strange concept can be further clarified, it would seem that this view is palatable but unintelligible, whereas the previous ones are intelligible but unpalatable. Not a pleasant choice—and what will determine *this* choice?

Exercises

1. Distinguish determinism from (a) indeterminism; (b) fatalism.
2. A student who had long been troubled by the problem of free-will and determinism reasoned as follows: "Science has pretty clearly shown that every-

[34] Richard Taylor, *op. cit.,* p. 50.

thing that happens is determined. If this is so, it includes everything that I do. In that case, I have no free-will. If I have no free-will, I'd rather not live." So he committed suicide. Of what errors in reasoning was he guilty?

3. Examine critically the following assertions:

a. Determinism can't be true because there is chance in the world. We all speak of this or that event as happening "by chance."

b. If everything we are going to do is determined, we may as well sit back and take things easy (or break loose and do whatever we please); our own efforts are useless if everything is determined anyway.

c. "What significance is there in my mental struggle tonight whether I shall or shall not give up smoking, if the laws which govern the matter of the physical universe already preordain for the morrow a configuration of matter consisting of pipe, tobacco, and smoke connected with my lips?" (Arthur E. Eddington, in *Philosophy*, January 1933, p. 41.)

d. Determinism can't be true because we don't know the causes of everything that happens.

e. Determinism must be true because it is essential to the very existence of science that every event have a cause.

f. Determinism can't be true, because people aren't just machines.

g. Determinism can't be true, because I *feel* that I'm free; I know this by introspection. This is a much better proof than any arguments.

h. Free-will is incompatible with determinism.

i. Free-will is incompatible with fatalism.

j. Free-will is incompatible with indeterminism.

k. Laws of nature make everything happen the way it does.

l. My background compels me to behave as I do.

m. If I had been under different influences I would have acted differently; and if the set of influences acting upon me on two occasions had been exactly the same I would have acted the same way the second time as the first—I couldn't help doing it. So I'm not free.

n. I couldn't have acted differently from the way I did act. No matter what the act was which I contemplated doing, there was only *one* road open to me (though I didn't know it at the time), only *one* thing that under those peculiar circumstances I *could* have done: namely, the one I did do.

o. It is true—at any rate, more obviously true than any theory about determinism—that human beings *deliberate*. Now, deliberation involves a genuine choice among alternatives, with the outcome in doubt at the time of the deliberation. But if the outcome is already "in the cards," it's not a case of genuine deliberation. Since there is deliberation, determinism must be false.

p. "According to determinism," it is said, "every desire, every impulse, every thought, is the inevitable consequence of antecedent conditions." But the word "inevitable" here is misused. "Inevitable" is synonymous with "unavoidable"; and it is not true that everything is unavoidable. Some things, like death, are unavoidable, but others, like being killed in a motorcycle accident, can be avoided by not riding on a motorcycle. The fallacy here is the usual one of taking a word that is applicable to some things and extending its meaning so that it becomes applicable to everything. But once we have done this, we are no longer using the word in the same sense.

q. Heisenberg's Principle of Indeterminacy is now fairly well accepted in physics. If indeterminism is operative in the realm of inorganic nature, why not in man also? In that case, we have free-will after all.

Selected Readings for Chapter 5

Anthologies of readings:

Adler, Mortimer J., *The Idea of Freedom*. 2 vols. Garden City, N. Y.: Doubleday & Company, Inc., 1958, 1961.

Berofsky, Bernard (ed.), *Free-will and Determinism*. New York: Harper & Row, Publishers, Inc., 1966. Paperback.

Edwards, Paul and Arthur Pap (eds.), *A Modern Introduction to Philosophy* (rev. ed.). New York: Free Press of Glencoe, Inc., 1965. Chapter 1.

Hook, Sidney (ed.), *Determinism and Freedom in the Age of Modern Science*. New York: New York University Press, 1957. Collier Books paperback.

Lehrer, Keith (ed.), *Freedom and Determinism*. New York: Random House, 1965. Paperback.

Morgenbesser, Sidney and J. Walsh (eds.), *Free Will*. Englewood Cliffs, N. J.: Prentice-Hall, Inc., 1962.

Morris, Herbert (ed.), *Freedom and Responsibility*. Stanford, Cal.: Stanford University Press, 1961. Chapter 10.

Pears, David F. (ed.), *Freedom and the Will*. London: Macmillan & Co., Ltd., 1963.

Sellars, Wilfrid and John Hospers, *Readings in Ethical Theory*. New York: Appleton-Century-Crofts, 1952. Section 7.

Primary sources:

Ayer, Alfred J., *The Foundations of Empirical Knowledge*. New York: The Macmillan Company, 1940. Chapter 4.

California Associates, "On the Freedom of the Will," in *Knowledge and Society*. New York: Appleton-Century-Crofts, 1938. Reprinted in H. Feigl and W. Sellars, *Readings in Philosophical Analysis*. New York: Appleton-Century-Crofts, 1949.

Campbell, C. A., *In Defense of Free-Will*. Glasgow: Jackson Son & Co., (Booksellers) Ltd., 1938.

Ducasse, Curt J., *Nature, Mind, and Death*. LaSalle, Ill.:Open Court Publishing Co., 1951. Part 2.

Ewing, Alfred C., *The Fundamental Questions of Philosophy*. New York: The Macmillan Company, 1951. Chapters 8 and 9.

Fullerton, G. S., *A System of Metaphysics*. New York: The Macmillan Company, 1904. Chapter 33.

Hart, H. L. A., and A. M. Honore, *Causation in the Law*. Oxford: Clarendon Press, 1959.

Hobart, R. E. (Dickinson Miller) "Free-will as Involving Determinism and Inconceivable without It," *Mind*, 1934. Reprinted in Berofsky, above.

Hume, David, *An Enquiry Concerning Human Understanding*. Sections 7 and 8. Many editions.

Melden, A. I., *Free Action*. London: Routledge & Kegan Paul, Ltd., 1961.

Mill, John Stuart, *A System of Logic*. London: Longmans, Green & Company, Ltd., 1843. Book 3, Chapter 5, and Book 6, Chapter 2. Contained also in Ernest

Nagel (ed.), *John Stuart Mill's Philosophy of Scientific Method*. New York: Hafner Publishing Co., Inc., 1950.

Moore, G. E., *Ethics*. London: Oxford University Press, 1912. Chapter 6.

Rashdall, Hastings, *Theory of Good and Evil*. 2 vols. London: Oxford University Press, 1924. Chapter 3 of Book 3.

Reichenbach, Hans, *The Rise of Scientific Philosophy*. Berkeley: University of California Press, 1951. Chapter 10.

Ross, W. D., *Foundations of Ethics*. Oxford: Clarendon Press, 1939. Chapter 10.

Schlick, Moritz, "Causality in Everyday Life and in Science," *University of California Publications in Philosophy*, XV (1932).

Stebbing, Susan L., *Philosophy and the Physicists*. London: Methuen & Co., Ltd., 1937. Part 3.

Stevenson, C. L., "Ethical Judgments and Avoidability," *Mind*, 47, 1938. Reprinted in W. Sellars and J. Hospers, *Readings in Ethical Theory*. New York: Appleton-Century-Crofts, 1952. Section 7.

Taylor, Richard, *Metaphysics*. Englewood Cliffs, N. J.: Prentice-Hall, Inc., 1963. Chapters 3–6.

6

Some Metaphysical Problems

The problems of metaphysics and epistemology are inextricably interwoven. Indeed, the distinction is not always easy to draw. Metaphysical
problems have to do with *what is,* whereas epistemological problems have to
do with *our knowledge of what is;* but in the discussion of the one the other is
bound to enter. Our discussion in the previous chapter of the question "Does
everything that happens have a cause?" at first appears to be entirely a
question of what is—about whether reality is or is not of a certain kind; yet we
have seen how this question is involved with questions of knowledge, such as
whether the Causal Principle is a synthetic a priori proposition or a leading
principle of scientific investigation. In discussing causality we were
constantly shifting from metaphysical to epistemological issues and vice
versa. We shall examine some more problems about "what is" in this chapter,
but these too will be interwoven with epistemological problems: for example,
in discussing the relation of body and mind, we shall be confronted by such
epistemological questions as "How do we know that other people have
minds?" and "How do we know we are seeing the same color?"

Not all problems about "what is" are metaphysical problems. "How many
books there are on my bookshelves?" is a question about what is, but it
would not be called a metaphysical question. There are many reasons for
this, but the principal one is doubtless that the question is not sufficiently
general: what time of day it is, how many people are invited for tonight's
party, and countless other questions about what is are strictly "local"
questions of no metaphysical interest. Science, to be sure, treats of very
general questions: it attempts to discover laws and devise theories for
explaining phenomena; but since these are so clearly in the empirical domain,
they are, in spite of their generality, considered scientific questions and not
metaphysical ones. Many persons have alleged that all such general questions
are scientific ones, and that when the scientific questions have been
answered, there are none left—there is nothing left for metaphysics to discuss.
Even highly general issues such as the relation of matter and energy are, it

would seem, scientific questions. What, then, does metaphysics treat? "The fundamental nature of reality" is the standard reply. But if matter and energy and their various manifestations are not fundamental features of reality, what is?

This distinction is usually drawn as follows: Those "what is" problems that could, in principle at least, be resolved by empirical means alone are scientific ones, and those that could be solved by mathematical means alone are mathematical ones; the remainder are metaphysical ones. Whether light consists of waves or particles, whether matter and energy are interchangeable, whether the "big-bang" or the "steady-state" theory of the origin of galactic systems is acceptable—are all scientific questions, to be resolved by the empirical evidence if and when it is forthcoming. But there are other problems which appear to resist such attempts at solution. Into what classes or categories, for example, reality is to be divided—temporal v. non-temporal, material v. non-material, mental v. non-mental—is an issue left to metaphysics. It is wider even than empirical science, which normally treats only of the physical. We shall discuss a few of these issues in this chapter. The problems of substance and universals, which we shall briefly consider in the first section, are both traditional metaphysical problems dating back to the ancient Greeks, and neither of these problems seems to be solvable by empirical means. The categories of inorganic matter v. life will concern us in the second section, and that of matter v. mind will concern us in greater detail in the third section.

"But if these issues can't be resolved empirically, aren't they verbal?" In Chapter 1, we distinguished verbal from factual issues. If metaphysical problems are not factual, aren't they then verbal? There are those who say that this is the case; the reader will be left to decide this for himself after he has considered the issues raised in this chapter. But one should not assume that the denotation of "factual issues" is the same as that of "empirical issues." Metaphysicians would insist that they are concerned with factual issues, but they would then divide factual issues into two kinds, empirical and non-empirical. Metaphysical issues would belong to the latter. They would then be issues of fact, but facts that cannot be settled by the usual empirical means but only by the systematic exercise of the understanding.

18. Substance and Universals

The problem of substance. The world contains many things, or substances. These substances are of many different kinds—wood, chalk, granite, and so on—but their constituents of these various kinds are relatively small in number: about a hundred basic or ultimate substances (elements) are known, from which all the others are composed in various mixtures and combinations. These substances undergo *changes*, in the form of *events* that occur during their history. Change can occur only to things (substances) that undergo the changes: *things* change—they now have one characteristic and now another—but *events* are simply followed by one another. The green leaf changes into a red one, but an event such as a thunderclap is followed by silence, or another thunderclap. Change presupposes an enduring thing in which the change occurs. (Though this may sound like an empirical observation, it is a partial implicit definition of the word "change," telling us to what kind of entity the word "change" is applicable.)

Each substance has many different properties, or characteristics. Gold has a certain color, melting-point, malleability, weight per unit of volume, and so on. In Chapter 1 (p. 72) we asked how many of these qualities could be removed while the thing in question still remained gold. This, of course, is a verbal question, a request for the defining characteristics of gold. We then saw that even in the case of a comparatively precise word like "gold" the answer is not entirely clear, because there is no clear set of defining characteristics: rather, the word is subject to the quorum feature (pp. 70–72). But however numerous the features constituting the quorum, and however many of these features a thing must have in order to be called gold, it is quite clear that if *all* the features in the quorum were removed, the thing in question would no longer be gold, and we could no longer use the word "gold" to apply to it.

In all this, however, we never doubted that if we removed one or more of the defining characteristics, we would have left *some substance or other*. If it were no longer yellow, it would still be something, whether or not we continued to use the word "gold" to refer to it. But now let us ask: suppose we removed *all* the properties—not just the combination of properties peculiar to gold, but *all* of them, including extension, mass, and shape? Wouldn't we then be left with *nothing at all?* We would be inclined to say that it would not only no longer be gold, it wouldn't be anything: there would be no properties left, and no "it" to have the properties.

But is this true? Surely, we are tempted to say, gold is one thing, and its properties are something else. "Gold isn't the same as the properties of gold. Doesn't gold have to exist for the properties-of-gold to exist? Isn't substance prior (logically, not chronologically) to its properties?"

"Of course, I admit," one may reply, "that gold exists. But gold is nothing more than the total of its properties. Substances are simply the sum of their properties."

"*Their* properties! Doesn't that give away the whole case? There is, then, an 'it' that has the properties."

"Of course there is, but what is the 'it' involved here? The 'it,' the gold, is simply the name we give to the group of properties coexisting at this place and time. The word 'gold' is simply the name we give to the coexisting collection of properties. There's nothing more than the total of the properties coexisting: that collection *is* the gold."

"No. There can be no properties unless there is first a thing, or substance, that has them. There must be a substance for the properties to belong to, or inhere in. Things are logically prior to their properties; no things, then no properties."

"On the contrary; no properties, then no things. Things are simply a combination of properties. Can you show me one thing without properties?"

"Of course I can't: every thing or substance there is has some properties or other. But that doesn't show that things aren't distinct from properties. I can't show you shape without size, or color without shape, but that doesn't mean that shape is the same as size or color the same as shape. They are distinguishable, but not separable. So it is with substances and properties. There can be no properties unless there are things or substances for them to be the properties *of*."

"No: if there were no properties, there would be no things. The idea of a propertyless thing is self-contradictory, since the thing is no more than the sum of its properties. If you think that the thing is more than the sum of its properties, kindly tell me what the more is. In addition to being yellow, malleable, etc., what is gold? No matter what you point to, it is simply another property. In addition to showing me that this is yellow, malleable, etc., could you *also* show me the gold to which these properties belong? Of course you couldn't. You doubtless have in your mind's eye the image of something like a pincushion, from which you remove one pin after another until they are all gone and you still have the empty pincushion left. But don't be misled by this bit of picture-thinking. When you have removed all the properties, you have no substance left—you have *nothing,* not even an empty pincushion."

"I attach no importance to such images as that of the pincushion. I realize that this is only accompanying imagery, which tells us nothing about the present issue. I am simply pointing to what I consider to be a metaphysical fact, that substances must exist in order for there to be properties. Properties don't just float around disembodied. The snow is white, but it is the *snow* that is white—there is no whiteness just by itself. Since whiteness is a property, it always belongs to something. That is just a fact of reality: properties presuppose substances of which they are the properties. There are substances, and there are properties-of-substances; and now that I have spelled out this latter term, you see how absurd it is to claim that there can be properties-of-substances but no substances."

"I think you are misled by the grammatical division in our language between nouns and adjectives. Adjectives normally designate properties and nouns substances. But substances are, on analysis, only bundles-of-properties. Let me illustrate:

It happens to be the case that we cannot, in our language, refer to the sensible properties of a thing without introducing a word or phrase which appears to stand for the thing itself as opposed to anything which may be said about it.

And, as a result of this, those who are infected by the primitive superstition that to every name a single real entity must correspond assume that it is necessary to distinguish logically between the thing itself and any, or all, of its sensible properties. And so they employ the term "substance" to refer to the thing itself. But from the fact that we happen to employ a single word to refer to a thing, and make that word the grammatical subject of the sentences in which we refer to the sensible appearances of the thing, it does not by any means follow that the thing itself is a "simple entity," or that it cannot be defined in terms of its appearances. It is true that in talking of "its" appearances we appear to distinguish the thing from the appearances, but that is simply an accident of linguistic usage. Logical analysis shows that what makes these "appearances" the "appearances of" the same thing is not their relationship to an entity other than themselves, but their relationship to one another.[1]

"I cannot agree. A thing is more than a bundle of qualities; there must be something to tie the bundle together, to make it one thing; and that is the substance. There is substance, and then there are qualities—and which qualities there are determines what kind of substance it is."

"You mean that there is a something—a pure qualityless substance—which exists in the absence of qualities, and when the qualities are added on we can say it is this kind of substance (gold) rather than others (silver, brass)? Absurd! There is substance, of course, but I am saying that the substance is nothing over and above the complex of qualities. An unknowable substance (substratum) existing apart from any qualities—waiting, as it were, to take on the qualities—is a philosophical myth. There are only co-existing qualities. When certain qualities co-exist we call the combination gold, when others co-exist we call it silver, and so on. That's all."

"You are mistaken. A substance cannot be merely a group of qualities. Suppose we have two identical gold spheres—the same size, same weight, same color, and so on. Now, what is it that distinguishes this piece of gold from that piece of gold? They have the same qualities, so you can't distinguish the one from the other on the basis of their qualities. You can distinguish them only by their spatial location; here is the one (pointing), and there is the other. These are not two groups of qualities, as you would have it; they are two things or substances having the very same combination of qualities. 'Matter is the principle of individuation.' It is substance, not qualities, that distinguishes one thing from another thing."

Since this issue is not one that confronts us in daily life, it is likely to evoke in the reader who first learns about it a feeling of strain and artificiality. "Who cares?" one may say. "Let the metaphysicians argue. Gold still looks the same and has the same properties it had before, regardless of whether we decide that it is a complex of properties or that the properties presuppose a substance. It's all a matter of how we talk, of what language we prefer to use. The whole thing is verbal." But let us not be prematurely dogmatic about

---

[1] A. J. Ayer, *Language, Truth, and Logic*, pp. 32–33.

this. This conclusion may be right; on the other hand, it does not follow that because the issue is not empirically resolvable, it is simply a verbal issue concerning how to classify our experiences. According to some metaphysicians, at any rate, the issue is factual, about the ultimate categories of which reality is composed, and it is the metaphysician's task to "slice reality at its joints."

Without spending more time on this issue, let us turn to a related one, also metaphysical, also irresoluble by empirical means, but one that is the arena of considerably more controversy, and on which much more depends in one's philosophical reasoning: the problem of universals.

The Problem of Universals

The problem of universals is a very complex one, which many philosophers believe to be the central problem of metaphysics. Since the word "universal" is not ordinarily used as a noun in our language, it is difficult to convey briefly a conception of what the problem is. It can be approached in various ways.

1. Here are a number of blue things—this shirt, that chair, the ocean, the sky. They are different in many ways, but they are all alike in being blue. They all have a common characteristic: blueness. Now, the blue things are *particulars* (individual things in the world, in space and time), but the property blueness, which they all share, is a universal. The particular things or particulars are blue, the blueness is not. The particulars (the shirt, the ocean) occur in time, the blueness does not. The particulars exist in space, the blueness does not. The blue things are all instances of the property blueness. A universal is anything that can have instances.

2. Different particulars share a common property, blueness. Now, if they are a common property, there must be such a common property; the property must exist, not merely the particulars that are instances of the property. Thus we have two kinds of entity in the world: the particulars that have the properties, and the properties that the things have. One cannot do without the particular things, for there must be something for the properties to belong to; but neither can one do without the properties, for there must be something for the particulars to have; putting it somewhat ungrammatically, one might ask: how could something be blue unless there was blueness for it to be?

3. Proper names refer to particular things: "George Washington" to a particular man; "Washington, D.C." to a particular city; "Pacific" to a particular ocean. But what do general words such as "blue," "dog," "man," "run" refer to? They are not the names of particular things; but they must then be the names of general properties—the property of being blue, of being a dog (that is, of the defining characteristics of dogs), and so on. But if general words are the names of properties, these properties must exist as well as the things having them. These general properties are universals.

Plato's theory of universals.   The problem of universals was first introduced into philosophy by Plato, and a concern with it is apparent throughout his writings. We shall first try to see how the problem presented itself to him, and then turn to criticisms and later views. The Platonic view is often called "realism" (in one of the many senses of that overworked word), because Plato held that universals in some sense really exist. Reality consists of particulars—particular chairs, particular instances of blue—and also of universals, which the particulars exemplify. There is this blue shade and that blue shade, but there is also the universal, blueness, of which the particular shades are instances. There is this cat and that cat, but there is also the universal, "being-a-cat," or "cathood," which particular cats exemplify. There is often no word for the universal that sounds natural or idiomatic, so the suffixes "-ness" and "-hood" are often added: thus manhood, cathood, blueness, straightness. ("Cattiness" is more idiomatic than "catness," and cattiness is also a universal, but not the same one: cattiness is a property possessed by many human beings, whereas cathood is simply the complex set of properties defining of cats.)

But Plato's chief concern with universals was in the context of (1) moral properties and (2) mathematical entities. Perfect virtue, perfect goodness, perfect justice do not exist in this world; that is, no particular situation perfectly exemplifies these qualities. Nor is there in this world any such thing as a straight line or a perfect circle. Yet we do have an idea of perfect goodness and perfect straightness and circularity (some would dispute this in the case of moral qualities). When we say that this drawing is not a perfect circle, we must have some idea of what a perfect circle must be, for if we did not know what a perfect circle was, we could not know that this figure was only an approximation of it. The conclusion that Plato drew from this was that somewhere, in some way, there must be perfect circularity, of which this particular figure is but an imperfect and inadequate instance. (Plato also believed, with regard to the origin of these concepts, that we recollect them from a previous existence, prior to our brith in this world, in which we perceived them directly; but this part of Plato's theory seems today so fanciful that we shall not consider it here.) Plato believed that there was such a thing as inadequate or imperfect exemplification of universals by particulars, and he thus was primarily concerned with universals that were not exemplified in particulars experienced by us.

But what is the relation, according to Plato, between universals and particulars? They are so different in nature that it would be difficult to see how there could be any relation between them. Particulars exist in space and time—this blue coat, that diagram on the blackboard, that just man—but universals do not: universals are neither in space nor in time. Even if there is no example of a perfect circle anywhere, perfect circularity exists, but only in the realm of universals, timeless and unchanging. In the world are many blue things, but blueness does not exist in this world; it belongs in the realm of universals, which particulars only to one degree or another exemplify. But this does not yet tell us exactly how particulars and universals are related. On this problem Plato does not have one single consistent view throughout his works, but there are two principal views that he presented.

1. *Archetype.*   On the view that pervades all of Plato's early dialogues, the relation is like that of an original to a copy or imitation, or like that of a model to the thing drawn or copied from the model. The horses in this world are all imperfect, but somewhere in reality there is the Perfect Horse, of which all horses in this world are imperfect copies. Somewhere there is also the Perfect Circle, the Perfect Goodness, and so on. A drawing of a bed is an imitation of a real physical bed; but the physical bed in turn is an imitation or copy of the Perfect Bed. And so on through many examples scattered through the dialogues.

But however appealing this two-world concept may be—the world of imitations v. the world of perfect entities—it will not suffice as a theory of universals. For a model or archetype, if it exists, is still a particular—a perfect particular, perhaps, but a particular existing in space and time. The relation of a copy to the thing of which it is a copy is still the relation between one particular and another particular. The degree of correspondence between the two may not be perfect, and for this reason one may speak of an inadequate imitation of a model or archetype; but how could the exemplification of a universal by a particular be either adequate or inadequate, perfect or imperfect? Either this shade of color is an instance of blueness or it is not. The relation of copy to model is not that of instancing or exemplification. Many people have found Plato's two-world conception poetic and ennobling, and the belief that there is a better world beyond this world of space and time has inspired many people; but whatever the merits of the perfect world v. the imperfect world, it is not a theory of universals, since perfect particulars are particulars still. As a theory of universals, the model-imitation concept is merely a metaphor.

2. *Participation.*   Plato also used in this connection another metaphor, that of participation: The particular "participates in" the universal. But here the word "participation" is strained past recognition. Do particulars participate in universals as particular people participate in a dinner? If there are too many people at the table there is not enough dinner to go round. Is there any danger that if there are too many particular blue things, there will not be enough blueness to go round? Will the blueness be spread thin if there are too many blue things participating in it? Plato uses the example of different people being covered by (and thus participating in) the same sail; but it is surely true of the sail that it may not be large enough to cover all the people who seek refuge under it.

But again, as a theory of universals this will not suffice. In every use of "participate," in these ordinary contexts, the thing participated in is as much a particular as the things doing the participating. The sail is as much a particular, albeit a larger particular, as the people who are covered by it. Plato, of course, used these examples only as analogies, not as exact accounts of the relation between particulars and universals. But in every analogy there must be some point of comparison, though the analogy, or basis of comparison, need not be complete; and it would seem that in both the case of model vs. copy and participation vs. thing participated in, the analogy breaks down at once, for these are all cases of the relation of some particulars to other particulars.

It may be that Plato was primarily concerned to do two things at once—erect a two-world theory and also a theory of universals; but whatever his intent, his view is inadequate insofar as it is taken to be a theory of universals. The relation cannot be literally, or even similar to, any of the situations that Plato presents. A more accurate statement of the relation, at which Plato hinted but never fully stated, would be: The relation between universals and particulars is like no other relation. It is the relation of *exemplification* of instancing, which is uniquely different from any other relation that there is (hence no analogies can be found to illustrate it). A blue particular instances or exemplifies blueness, this triangle instances triangularity, and so on. The relation between the individual thing and the property is always that of instancing.

One difficulty, however, Plato did realize and discuss: This triangle instances triangularity, the blue sky is an instance of blueness. Does this large object similarly instance largeness? Does A, which is north of B, instance north-ness? But this cannot be: Objects are not just large or small, they are large or small in relation to others. If there were just one thing in the universe, say an elephant, it would be neither large nor small, for "large" and "small" are *relational* terms—things are not large or small by themselves but only in relation to other things: an elephant is large in relation to a mouse but small in relation to a house. The particular does not have the property by itself (or *simpliciter*) but only in relation to other things; in other words, largeness is not a simple property but a relation—or, if you prefer, a relational property. Even more obviously, being-to-the-north-of is a relation, and many things can instance this relation: the relation of Edinburgh to London is one instance of it, the relation of Montreal to New York another, and so on. We might state this by saying that there are three types of entities in reality: particulars, universals, and relations. But it would be less misleading to say that there are only two, particulars and universals, but that universals can be divided into (1) properties (squareness, blueness, etc.) and (2) relations (being above, being to the north of, being more educated than, being alert to, etc.). Both properties and relations have instances, and thus both are universals.

It is important to notice at this point that relations cannot be relegated to the mind. We cannot say that whereas things are "out there" in reality, relations between things are not but are contributed by the mind. Plato was perfectly aware of this. Here is Athens and there is Sparta, and the relation between them (Athens being to the north of Sparta, Athens being larger than Sparta) are as objective, as much "out there," as the cities themselves. Universals, said Plato, are as objectively existent as the things exemplifying them. Nor will it do to say, as some later followers of Plato such as the Neo-Platonists said, that universals are nothing but thoughts in the mind. For thoughts in the mind are also particulars. If I think about Athens, that thought is a particular thought—not a physical particular but a mental one (of which we shall have much to say later in this chapter)—and if you also have a thought of Athens, your thought is another particular. Thoughts, dreams, hallucinations, and other mental phenomena are as much particulars as the physical things that the thoughts are about. Plato was particularly averse to the view that mathematical entities exist only in the mind. When someone discovers a theorem, that is a discovery, not an invention. And it is a discovery of something—something as real (though not in the same category of reality) as the Rock of Gibraltar. The theorem is one thing, and one's thought of it is another; a second person's thought of it is still another. Thoughts are particular events, never universals. Even thoughts in the mind of God (with which some Christian philosophers equated universals) are particulars occurring in a particular mind, albeit a super-mind; they are not universals. To identify particulars with universals would seem to be the supreme example of a category-mistake.

Universals must not be identified, even by analogy, with any things that are particulars, for to do this would be to make them no longer universals. The relation of universals to particulars is indeed not like any other relation. It is all too likely, however, to be confused with a quite different relation, that of *genus* to *species*. Scarlet is a species of the genus red, and red is a species of the genus color. A rectangle is a species of quadrilateral, and a quadrilateral is a species of plane figure. (Strictly speaking, the property rectangularity is a species of four-sidedness, and so on.) But the relation of genus to species is the relation of one universal to another in a hierarchy of universals. A broader or more inclusive universal (coloredness) includes a narrower or less inclusive universal (blueness), but blueness is a universal just the same: blueness is a property and is not to be identified with the blue thing that has the property. Even if we distinguished a million shades of blue, these would not be particulars (though we misleadingly call them "particular shades of blue"); blue 68495 is still a property that different particular things might have in common, even if they actually do not. A thing (particular) would still have the property of being just that shade of blue; the shade, being a property, would still be a universal, forever distinct from the particular thing that instances this property. Similarly, you cannot go from material thing to living thing to animal to mammal to dog to collie-dog to Lassie; every step except the last one is acceptable: each is a universal (for example, collie-dog-ness) falling under a more inclusive universal (dog-ness); but being a collie-dog (having the properties of collies) is still a property; however, "Lassie" is not the name of a property but of a particular dog. Being a collie, being a dog, being an animal, etc., are properties of this particular creature; Lassie is not a property of this particular creature but *is* this particular creature.

According to Plato, then, there are universals, and they have an existence distinct from the existence of particulars. Indeed, they would exist even if there were no particulars to exemplify them. We need not take this to mean, however, as Plato seems to have done in his earlier dialogues, that there would still be a perfect circle somewhere even if there are no perfect circles on earth; for, as we have seen, even if there were such a perfect circle it would still be a particular, and we would still need the universal, circularity, which it exemplifies. The perfect circle would still not *be* circularity; it would be an *instance* of circularity. But Plato was undoubtedly right in believing that we can conceive of and understand the meanings of words that stand for properties, even though nothing in the world exemplifies these properties. We can understand what "chiliagon" means (million-sided polygon) even though there are no million-sided polygons anywhere. We can understand what "unicorn" means (having the properties of horses, plus having a horn in the middle of the forehead) even though there are no unicorns; and the same with the concept of any other mythical creatures (centaurs, elves, brownies, leprechauns, etc.). Of all these combinations of properties we see no exemplifications in the world, but we can nevertheless have a concept of them. All these universals exist, Plato would say, waiting (as it were) to be exemplified, but they are just as real in the realm of universals even if there are no particulars to exemplify them.

How can we have a concept of them if we have never seen particulars exemplifying them? Plato devised a doctrine of pre-existence in order to answer this question, but we need not go so far: pre-existence or not, there is no problem (as we saw on pp. 103–4) about being able to combine simple ideas into complex ones of our own making. What about apparently simple ideas, such as straightness? We have never seen an absolutely straight line, yet we know what a straight line would be. But not even this example requires a doctrine of pre-existence: we get the idea of straightness from things we do see and touch. Undoubtedly the line you draw with pencil and ruler is not really straight; but it looks straight, and your idea of straightness is derived from such percepts. The same line (or, rather, mark on paper representing a line) may look jagged through a microscope, but seeing it through a microscope is after all a different percept from seeing it without a microscope; and your idea of straightness can be derived from seeing it without. Strictly speaking, the geometer's lines, points, and planes are not the kind of thing anyone can see; but one can see dots representing points, marks representing lines, and so on that are perfectly sufficient to give rise to our ideas of straightness, circularity, and so on.

So much for the origin of these concepts. But the concept is the concept of something, and that something, Plato would remind us, is a universal. The concept is in our minds, but the something *of which* it is a concept is not in our minds: that something is "out there" in reality. And there are two kinds of something in reality: the particulars that exemplify the universals, and the universals that they exemplify. Though the universals cannot be seen and otherwise perceived with the senses as particulars can, they are just as real, just as objective, just as genuinely a part of the "furniture of reality" as are particulars.

Aristotle's theory of universals.   Plato's pupil Aristotle was dissatisfied with Plato's "two-world" theory. There is, said Aristotle, no second realm apart from particulars inhabited wholly by universals: Plato's realism in that sense was mistaken; the "realm of universals" is a metaphysical fiction. Even if a second realm were granted, it would not be a realm of universals but only of super-particulars, more perfect (in some way) perhaps than the particulars we are acquainted with in sense-experience, but particulars nonetheless; and there is no evidence that any such realm of super-particulars exists. Nevertheless, Aristotle too was a realist about universals: he held that universals as well as particulars really exist, that they are "out there" and not in our minds, and that their existence is in no way dependent on minds or our own process of conceptualization: they would exist just as they do now even if there were no minds to apprehend them.

What kind of existence then do they have? A universal, according to Aristotle, is simply a property (simple or complex, intrinsic or relational) that is common to a number of instances. And we arrive at the concept of these properties by a process of abstraction from particulars (we see blue sky, blue water, blue cloth, etc., and by abstracting we arrive at the concept of blueness). There could be no universals without particulars (no common properties with nothing to have the properties), any more than there could be particulars without universals (no things without properties). The two are logically dependent on one another—not, as in Plato, particulars depending on universals but universals existing serenely independent of all particulars. Universals exist only *in re* (in things), not, as in Plato, *ante rem* (prior to things). And since universals require particulars as much as particulars require universals, there can be no universals apart from particulars—no universals apart from properties actually shared by existing particulars. In the case of unicorns, centaurs, and so on, then, there is such a thing as the *concept* unicornhood: we can play around with ideas (pp. 103–7) and combine them in various ways to form concepts of things that do not exist on land or sea; but though we can have these concepts in our minds, there is no universal corresponding to them in reality, because there are no things having this combination of properties.

So far, all this sounds so common-sensical that one might think it difficult to deny it. Universals are merely properties common to various particulars, and of course properties-of-things exist only if there are things (just as things cannot exist without having properties). But what gives Aristotle's doctrine its peculiar twist is his view of the nature of these common properties.

Aristotle's view was that a universal is something that is identical in each of the particulars in which it occurs. Blueness is something identically present in all blue things, by virtue of which they are blue (they all contain a piece, as it were, of the very same thing, blueness); and the blueness is as objectively present an existent as is the thing that has it. Similarly, doghood is a property that is identically present in all dogs, and it is so whether or not anyone forms the concept doghood (or what-it-is-to-be-a-dog). Universals belong in things, in external reality, but they belong to things as objectively existing properties of things, not as archetypes or anything else that can exist apart from the things in which they occur. It is rather like (though the analogy should not be pressed) the identity a cookie-cutter gives to the cookies: All the cookies, no matter how numerous they may be or how many different kinds of dough they may be composed of, possess the same form by virtue of the fact that the form is imposed on them by the same cookie-cutter. A universal is a property that is identically present in all the particulars that instantiate it and does not exist apart from such instantiation.

Nominalist theories.   What Aristotle's view asserts is most easily seen if we contrast it with other theories about universals and particulars. One may feel, on reading our account of the problem thus far, that a great amount of "mythology" is present—that somehow the issue is a "phony" one, that we get ensnared in it only because of certain difficulties of language. "Really," one may say, "there is nothing in the universe except particulars; particulars are all we can perceive, and particulars are all there are. True, things have properties, but the properties are a part of the things themselves and not a kind of entity distinct from the things—certainly not as in Plato, in some realm apart from particulars, but not even as in Aristotle, objectively existing features that are identically present in each of the particulars and thus distinguishable from them in thought (even though never occurring apart from them in reality). Let's get rid of the excess baggage and stick to what we can perceive, and that is particulars: green trees, but no special kind of thing called greenness."

Most favorable to this way of thinking is the theory called "nominalism"—which, however, can cover a variety of somewhat different views. Extreme nominalism is the view that only particulars exist, and that all that a class of things (blue things, things we call cats) has in common is the name we give to them all. A universal is only a name, and what it names is only a particular or a collection of particulars.

But extreme nominalism has only to be described to be virtually ruled out of court. (1) In the first place, when we call different things "blue," we are not talking about the things per se but about a certain property of the things, a property that is not identical with the thing (the blue dress is not the same as the blue) but something that the thing has and that other things can also have—the property can be shared by many things. But once we have said this, we are back with objectively existing properties: there are things, and there are properties-of-things, with many things having properties in common. (2) Moreover, it is surely not true that all that different dogs have in common is the name "dog." Different things belonging to the same class do so because they have some properties in common—those properties that we make defining of the class. As we saw in Chapter 1, all classification is based on the presence of common properties—properties that exist in reality, not merely in our minds. (The concept may exist in our minds, but the properties don't.) There may not be one set of properties that is both necessary and sufficient: there may be a quorum, or any of the other kinds of vagueness described on pp. 67–76; but even though there is sometimes a rather loose family-resemblance among the members of a class, there is some relation: there may not be one set of properties that characterizes all games, but there are overlapping sets of properties, and these properties just as objectively exist as any others, and they do determine the applicability of the word "game" to a given situation. In short, there is some basis for applying the same word to a number of different things, and what is this basis other than the possession of some common properties? We cannot get rid of properties by substituting names for properties, for we are then faced with the question: What is the basis for applying to many particular things the same name?

Another view could also be described that has also been called "nominalism": In reality there are only particulars; but in our minds there are only images, not concepts (this view has been called "imagism"). Berkeley said that when I conceive of a triangle, I have in my mind the image of some particular triangle. Now, the concept of a triangle (of triangularity) cannot include as one of its properties that it must be isosceles, or that it must be equilateral, or that it must be scalene, for many triangles are not isosceles, many are not equilateral, and many are not scalene. All there is in my mind is an *image* of a triangle, and this image must be of a *particular* triangle: the image of a triangle in my mind must be the image of a scalene triangle, an isosceles triangle, or an equilateral triangle. You cannot form the image of a triangle that is not scalene, isosceles, or equilateral. But when we talk about triangles in general, we use the image we have of a particular triangle to stand for, or represent, any triangle; though my image is an image of an isosceles triangle, I can use this image to stand for any triangle, including those that are not isosceles. But at this point Berkely gets into a difficulty: An image, he says, is made to represent all figures of the same sort (in this instance, triangles). But what is meant by "the same sort" (or kind)? In order to know what that is, we must have before our minds a concept of what it is to be a triangle, and this concept is not an image. Before we can use an image in this representative capacity, to stand for or represent all other particulars of the same sort, we must know what a sort or kind is—and to know what that is involves having a concept of a common property. So we are back with common properties. To have a concept, triangularity, is not the same as having an image (as we saw on pp. 106–8), though images may be present in our minds when we do have the concept; to have the concept is to have in mind the defining characteristics of triangles, and having this concept, which is abstract, is not the same as having an image, which is particular—indeed, it does not involve having any images at all, and many persons have concepts with no accompanying imagery. So if nominalism says that what occurs in our minds is only images, it is wrong again; there are far more than images in our minds when we use general words: there are concepts, over and above any images we may have.

Conceptualism.   A still further departure from extreme nominalism has customarily been given a distinct name, "conceptualism," and was set forth by John Locke. According to conceptualism, a universal is not merely a name, nor an image, but a concept. In reality there are only particulars, but in our minds there is something else—not images but concepts. General words (all words except proper names) are the names of concepts; but these occur in our minds, not in nature. In nature there are no concepts, but only particulars. But once again we run into difficulty. Granted that in our minds there are concepts—but what are the concepts concepts of? And here the obvious answer again is "Of common properties—of those properties a thing must have to be classified under the concept." Thus we are back with properties again. How can we have concepts if there are in reality no common properties in which our concepts are to be anchored? Without common properties, no concepts—whether of doghood or blueness or straightness—are possible. Every time we use a general word, we do so on the basis of certain properties that the particulars having them possess in common; and the moment we have admitted that, we have to admit more into our account than just the concepts—we must admit that which they are the concepts of: the property or properties that make this concept the concept of this kind of thing.

The similarity (or resemblance) theory.   Must we, then, go back to Aristotle's account and admit that his view is the correct one—that there are no universals apart from particulars, that universals are common properties, and that these common properties exist in reality? These three propositions we might easily accept, but we may boggle over the peculiar feature of Aristotle's view, that there are certain properties that are identically present in each particular. Why, we may ask, need the same property be identically present in all the instances? Let us say, instead, that in reality there are only similars—countless particulars with properties in common, but properties not in the sense of something identically present in all the particulars but of certain discernible *similarities,* similarities sufficent, however, for us to include them all under the same concept. Thus we have a concept, blueness. But blue things are not identical, not even in color: there are countless shades of blue; perhaps no two shades are alike; perhaps no two particular blue things even have exactly the same shade of blue—but yet all blue things are similar to one another in color, and because of this similarity we call them all "blue." We can distinguish blue things from things of all other colors (though there may be some borderline cases), but what makes them all blue is that they are similar to one another in color, not that they have the same universal, blueness, identically present in all of them.

This may well strike us as the most sensible theory we have come across thus far. But what, one might ask, does this do to the thesis that general words are the names of properties, just as proper names are the names of particulars? If there is not one property that is identically present in all particulars of a certain kind, what is "blue" the name of? Here an answer can be given that may enable us to escape many confusions. Philosophers have tended to assume—and Plato and Aristotle certainly believed—that just as proper names like "Fido" are the names of particular things in the world, so general words like "dog" and "blue" (which apply to many things) are the names of properties. But according to the present view, there is no single property that the general word names; nor is it true that because a general word applies to a number of particulars, each of these particulars in some way embodies this one thing or property.

To say "Abstract words stand for a common property" is to use a form of linguistic expression which stresses an analogy between proper names and general words. It is only too easy and natural to use this statement as equivalent to "Abstract words name common properties." There are certain similarities between the function of proper names and the function of general words. These similarities seem to the realists more important than the differences between the two kinds of word. Thus, by saying "Universals exist and are the *designata* of general words," the realists mean no more than might be less misleadingly and more properly expressed by saying, "Let us classify general words with proper names." . . . The realist way of talking is an attempt to assimilate the lingustic function of general words to that of names.[2]

But the fact is that general words are not names at all; one should not be caught in the trap of saying that proper names are the names of particulars (which is true) whereas general words are the names of properties (which is false, since they should not be considered as names at all). We do not have to say that "blue" is the name of a property, blueness, which is identically present in all blue things; we can say, instead, that all things we call "blue" resemble one another in color sufficiently so that we can use the same word for all of them, but not that there is one property that is the same in each of the instances.

But at this point another objection confronts us. "You said that we lump different shades of color together and call them all 'blue' because they *resemble* one another in their color. Very well: but *resemblance itself is a universal.* It is a relational universal, granted; but a relational universal is a

    [2] D. J. O'Connor, "Names and Universals," *Proceedings of the Aristotelian Society,* 1952–53, pp. 175–76.

universal still. Largeness and betweenness are universals, though relational ones, and so is resemblance: a particular, X, doesn't just resemble, it resembles something else, Y. And another particular, V, may resemble still another particular, W. The relation of X to Y is that of resemblance, and that of V to W is also resemblance; so we have two instances of the universal, resemblance (or similarity). Resemblance is, indeed, a universal of which there are countless instances. So we are back with universals after all. Even if all the particulars don't share one property that is identically present in all of them—in this case, blueness—they do share another property, resemblance (since they all resemble one another). So you are still stuck with one universal, that of resemblance." Or as Bertrand Russell puts it,

If we wish to avoid the universals whiteness and triangularity, we shall choose some particular patch of white or some particular triangle, and say that anything is white or a triangle if it has the right sort of resemblance to our chosen particular. But then the resemblance required will have to be a universal. Since there are many white things, the resemblance must hold between many pairs of particular white things; and this is the characteristic of a universal. It will be useless to say that there is a different resemblance for each pair, for then we shall have to say that these resemblances resemble each other, and thus at last we shall be forced to admit resemblance as a universal. The relation of resemblance, therefore, must be a true universal, and having been forced to admit this universal, we find that it is no longer worth-while to invent difficult and implausible theories to avoid the admission of such universals as whiteness and triangularity.[3]

But what exactly is the force of this objection? We are not "trying to get rid of universals": there will remain in reality particulars and the properties that these particulars have—this much has already been suggested in our remarks about nominalism. Our attempt is rather to suggest that there need not be a common property in the sense of something identically present in all instances, but rather that we can classify things not on the basis of one such property but on the basis of one or a number of *similarities* that these things have to one another. Blueness is a universal, in the sense that various things are similar enough to one another to be called "blue"; and similarity too is a universal, in the sense that different things are in various ways similar to one another. No analysis that is at all plausible enables us to get rid of these facts.

But there is more to the objection than this. We call different things "blue" on the basis of some similarity between the shades we call "blue." But what, it is asked, of similarity itself? We have a similarity-relation between particulars X and Y, and also between particulars V and W: X and Y are similar to one another, and so are V and W; both are instances of resemblance. But now, it is asked, what about the relation between these two

[3] *The Problems of Philosophy*, pp. 150–51.

cases of resemblance? Are these two similarities not also similar? And is not this second similarity something identically present in all the instances of it? Is not similarity a peculiar universal, of which all similarity-relations are equally instances? The similarity of X to Y may not be the same similarity that V has to W (the first may be similarity of color, the second of shape), but are not the similarities between the X–Y relation and the V–W relation themselves instances of the very same universal, similarity? And having granted an identical relation in one case by saying that this second similarity is a relation that is identically present in all similar pairs, why not say as well that blueness is a property that is identically present in all blue things?

But one may reply that this criticism conceals an ambiguity.

The criticism seems to assume the principle that if A is similar to B and B is similar to C, then both similarities must be the same, and consequently that both are instances of a universal similarity. But this is to take advantage of an ambiguity in "same." Suppose that A is a blue object, B is a blue object, and C is a blue object; and suppose that we are asked whether the similarity between A and B is the same as the similarity between B and C. The answer is that *according to one usage of "same" it is, according to another it may or may not be.* According to usage (1) we say of any blue objects that they are all the same color, and in saying that they are all the same color we are simply saying that they are all blue; and according to this usage we would say that the similarity between A and B was the same as the similarity between B and C. Usage (2) provides for the case where, say, A is indigo blue, B is navy blue, and C is azure blue; in this case, and following this usage, we do not say that the similarity between A and B is the same as the similarity between B and C.

In fact, the general question whether two similarities are the same cannot be understood, let alone answered, until the usage according to which "same" is being employed is made clear. If we are employing usage (1), then the similarity between A and B and the similarity between B and C must be the same; but all that is meant by saying that they are, is that A and B and C are like each other in being blue; and therefore that the similarities are the same does not entail that they are *instances* of universal similarity. If we are employing usage (2), the similarities are not the same; and that they are not the same also does not entail that they are instances of a universal similarity.

Certainly for *us* similarity is the arch-universal; and what is meant by that is that, if we were not clever enough to detect any of the similarities which we do detect, we would have no general words at all. That is, words such as "similarity," "resemblance," "identity," etc., are logically presupposed by words such as "table," "typewriter," "kangaroo," etc., but the former are as much general words as the latter. If the world were exactly as it is now, except that there were no minds in it, then it would consist of objects between which various relations of resemblance and dissimilarity would hold. What reason have we for saying that the presence of mind makes similarity a universal of a different type from what it would be in their absence?[4]

[4] A. D. Woozley, *Theory of Knowledge*, pp. 100–101. Italics mine.

We conclude our account of the problem of universals, then, with the similarity theory: that in reality there are particular things and their properties (in this sense we may talk about universals), but that when we speak of different things having a common property, we need not thereby imply that there is one property identically present in all the things to which we apply the same word. Rather, there are similarities between them sufficient to entitle us to use one word in describing them all. These similarities are really "out there"—they are not products of our minds. We do not, of course, devise a word to designate every set of properties we come across. Our classification of properties (as we saw on pp. 44–46) is a joint work of nature and ourselves: it rests upon the facts of nature, on what properties things have and how much similarity there is among things in the world that we classify under the same concept; but it also rests upon our interests, on whether we choose to group certain similarities together, and if we do, on where we choose to erect the boundary between one property and another (such as between blue and green). The similarities exist in nature, but what we do with them in erecting a conceptual structure is up to us.

Exercises

1. Interpret and evaluate the following statements about substance:

a. John Locke, *Essay Concerning Human Understanding,* Book II, Chapter 23, section 1: "If any one will examine himself concerning his notion of pure substance in general, he will find he has no other idea of it at all, but only a supposition of he knows not what support of such qualities, which are capable of producing simple ideas in us; which qualities are commonly called accidents. If anyone should be asked, what is the subject wherein color or weight inheres, he would have nothing to say, but the solid extended parts: and if he were demanded, what is it that solidity and extension adhere in, he would not be in a much better case than the Indian, who, saying that the world was supported by a great elephant, was asked what the elephant rested on: to which his answer was, a great tortoise. But being again pressed to know what gave support to the broad-backed tortoise, replied, something he knew not what. . . . The idea we have, to which we give the general name 'substance,' being nothing but the supposed, but unknown support of those qualities we find existing, which we imagine cannot subsist . . . without something to support them, we call that support *substantia;* which, according to the true import of the word, is in plain English, standing under or upholding."

b. George Berkeley, *Principles of Human Knowledge,* paragraph 16: "It is said extension is a *mode* or *accident* of Matter, and that Matter is the *substratum* that supports it. Now I desire that you would explain to me what is meant by Matter's *supporting* extension. Say you, I have no idea of Matter; and therefore cannot explain it. I answer, though you have no positive, yet, if you have any meaning at all, you must at least have a relative idea of Matter; though you know not what it is, yet you must be supposed to know what relation it bears to accidents, and what is meant by its supporting them. It is evident *support* cannot here be taken in its usual or literal sense, as when we say that pillars support a building. In what sense therefore must it be taken?"

2. Examine the following assertions about universals:

a. In the world there exists nothing except particulars. Hence, nominalism of some kind must be true.

b. A property (such as blueness) must exist in time in order to be exemplified in time. Properties are no more timeless than are particulars.

c. Far from there being nothing other than particulars, it's the other way around: there is nothing other than properties (universals). A particular thing, such as a lump of salt, is nothing but a group of properties coexisting.

d. A property (universal) is nothing but a class, and a particular is a member of the class. "Universals exist" then means the same as "Classes exist."

e. Plato was right: universals exist quite independently of particulars. We have the concept of unicornhood even though there are no unicorns, and when we have this concept we do conceive of something: unicornhood must in some sense exist, even though it has no exemplification (as far as we know) in space and time. How could the word "unicorn" mean anything if it didn't have something to refer to? But it doesn't refer to any particular unicorns, so it must refer to the universal.

f. Aristotle was clearly right: properties (universals) are what particular things have in common. That's what properties are—that's just what it is to be a property. The statement merely gives us a definition, but one which does reflect the way we use property-words.

3. Can we have concepts of particular things (Fido, this blue thing) as well as of properties (doghood, blueness)?

4. Explain carefully how extreme nominalism, imagism, conceptualism, and Aristotelian realism differ from one another with regard to (a) the status of universals and (b) the status of concepts (what our apprehension of univerals consists in).

5. Explain the difference between the genus-species relation and the universal-particular relation. Is either of them the same as the member-class relation?

19. Matter and Life

Among the vast multitude of inorganic objects that constitute the earth, the other planets, and the stars and galaxies, there are objects that are conspicuously different from the rest: they are *living organisms*. As far as we know, they exist only on the earth, and even there they are present only on or near its surface; they are not found more than a few miles below its surface or more than a few miles above it. In the total amount of space they occupy, they are about as small in relation to the entire volume of the earth as the earth is in relation to the entire solar system. Yet they are quite different from the objects that surround them in a number of remarkable ways: (1) The matter of which they are composed is constantly changing; new matter is assimilated and old matter is excreted. What persists throughout this continuous process of change is the *form* of the organism, until the organism dies and loses its characteristic form. (2) Even the form changes somewhat, though in a regular way: until it reaches its maturity, an organism *grows*. (3) Moreover, the organism *reproduces,* producing other organisms of the same kind or species as itself; this is something that does not happen in the realm of inorganic matter. (4) Organisms (animal organisms, not plants) display varying degrees of *impression-reaction* activities. They respond to stimuli, and not merely in the way in which certain chemicals respond to the presence of other chemicals; they do not always respond the same way each time, but they learn through experience. This phenomenon occurs to a far larger extent in the "higher" and more complex organisms, but it happens to some extent even on the humblest levels of animal life. A tiny organism is hit by a stream of water and it shrinks and curls up into its stalk; a minute later it expands to its normal size; when the stream of water strikes again, precisely as before, the creature pays no attention to it—the creature has already adapted itself to the harmless stimulus. Sticks and stones do not do this.

The boundary line between the living and the non-living is not in every case clear and sharp. (For example, some crystals duplicate part of the behavior of living organisms in that, in some sense at least, they *grow*.) Between the most complex phenomena of inorganic matter and the simplest phenomena of the organic realm, there is no clear-cut boundary. But this, of course, does not destroy the distinction between organic and inorganic, any more than the fact that red shades into orange shows that there is no distinction between red and orange (pp. 67–68).

Perhaps the most remarkable feature of the behavior of living things, something to which all the four characteristics listed above contribute, is the *teleological*, or purposive, behavior of living organisms as opposed to rocks and rivers. Their behavior seems to be directed to some *end*, to be animated by a *purpose*. Specifically, living things behave in such a way as to keep themselves alive, and if this is impossible, to keep their offspring alive and thus assure the perpetuation of the species. Most of their activities seem to be directed toward this end.

But if it is true, as we said in discussing explanation (see pp. 245–46), that "when there is a purpose, there must be someone to have the purpose," are we to assume here that even the least complex organisms have purposes, and act from a conscious intent to keep themselves and their species alive? Are we to assume that the hen has a conscious intent in sitting patiently on her eggs until they hatch? Is she animated by visions of motherhood and the chicks that will later hatch? Is the squirrel who stores nuts for the winter doing so with conscious purpose of eating them after the snow falls? Perhaps some will answer these questions with a Yes. But then what of examples such as that of the complex and intricate embryonic development of an organism, in which organs are developed for future use, though they have not yet been used?

In the case of the human eye, for example, 120 million rods, more than one million cones, and 400,000 ganglionic cells must be developed and brought into functional alignment prior to the functioning of the eye and in order that the normal functioning may be possible at all. These cells cannot be arranged under the influence of external stimuli which might facilitate the division of labor or determine the alignment, but must be produced, coordinated, and connected with the sensory centers of the brain entirely from within the growing embryo and prior to, yet for the sake of, their balanced functioning.[5]

Surely in this case the embryo has no conscious purpose in growing thus; yet it behaves exactly as if it had the conscious purpose of being able to see when once confronted by the outside world. Or consider the development of antitoxins in the human blood stream when toxins are introduced—a different specific antitoxin for each toxin, as if the organism *knew* that it needed just this antitoxin in order to survive and regain health. Digestion is another case in point. The highly complex carbohydrates which enter the stomach are broken down by complex organic compounds (the diastatic ferments) secreted by the pancreas, and are transformed by them into glucose. In this form the food enters the blood stream and is carried to the cells, particularly in the liver and muscles, which store it. The storage is an extremely complicated process requiring many different cells, each with a specific function. Special chemical agents produced in different regions of the body are then transported to the scene and build up the glucose into a more complex compound, glycogen, and store it. In case of need, however, the glycogen is transformed back into glucose and is liberated into the blood stream. "In case of need!"—it is as if each of the cells knew what it was doing, as if each had been assigned its specific task to perform, and all were working together to produce the desired end, like the people in a well-organized state.

Now, it is not the aim of a book in philosophy to regale the reader with facts of biology, however fascinating these facts may be. There are hundreds of books in which these facts are available to anyone who is interested. What we are concerned with here are questions about what to make of these facts, or how to interpret them. Is there, as some have argued, a special Life-force, or *élan vital,* present in living things which makes their behavior different from that of non-living things? Are living things merely complicated machines? Do living things exist somehow on a higher "level" of existence, and is there more to them than the physicist and chemist could ever possibly discover? Are biological phenomena reducible to those of physics and chemistry? These questions, though related, are not quite the same; indeed, some of them at least are by no means clear, and it is the question of what they mean which has first to be clarified.

On all of these questions there are two opposing points of view, known as *mechanism* and *vitalism,* mechanism emphasizing the continuity and likeness between living and non-living things and vitalism the discontinuity and difference. But since both these terms are used to tag now one doctrine and now another, and since many of the doctrines themselves are not very clear, the terms "mechanism" and "vitalism" are both vague and ambiguous.

[5] W. H. Werkmeister, *A Philosophy of Science* (New York: Harper & Row, Publishers, Inc., 1940), p. 332.

Let us consider several of the ways in which it is possible to state the issue between mechanism and vitalism.

1. A non-material Life-force.   A very common way of distinguishing between mechanism and vitalism is this: according to vitalism there is a special *non-material Life-force*, or *élan vital*, which is present in living things but not in non-living things. Its presence in living things explains the difference between the behavior of living things and that of the non-living.

If one asks *where* this force is, the answer is that it is no*where,* for it cannot be pinned down to any place in space, not even inside the organisms, for no observation has ever revealed such a thing there, nor is it expected ∴ ɔ. It is not located in space any more than numbers or thoughts are. It is something that can never be discovered by the methods of the empirical scientist, but nevertheless it exists, and its existence explains the remarkable differences that can be observed between living and non-living things. The mechanist is the one who denies these contentions.

Now, if the issue is put in this way, there are very strong arguments that can be brought to bear against the vitalistic position. If the non-material Life-force is set forth as an *explanation* of the observed behavior of living organisms, one can reply that it is surely not an explanation in any sense that a scientist would accept. One can, of course, argue as follows:

> Whenever a Life-force is present, things exhibit the properties of life.
> In this thing a Life-force is present.
>
> Therefore, This thing exhibits the properties of life.

But how does one know that the first premise is true? The Life-force cannot be observed. Nor does introducing it as a theoretical concept enable us to predict a single observable phenomenon; unlike atomic theory, in no way whatever does it extend our knowledge. "The behavior of living things, as opposed to non-living things, is explained by the presence of a non-material Life-force," we are told; but having been told this, we are confronted with the same questions as before. Consider some particular phenomenon, such as the ability of some pigeons to find their way back home after being released from an airplane in unfamiliar terrain hundreds of miles away. The scientist, being told that this is explained by the presence of a Life-force, still wants to know by exactly what means the pigeons are enabled to do what they do, while other birds cannot: is the pigeon sensitive to magnetic stimuli radiating from the earth's magnetic poles—is it equipped with "built-in compasses"? In short, even if a scientist assented to the vitalist's account, he would say that it was useless: the vitalist's claim, even if true, would be empty. Indeed, the vitalist could invoke the same "explanation" for every remarkable new bit of organic behavior that turned up; and each such "explanation" might be equally true, but equally useless. (Remember our previous examples of unsatisfactory explanations, pp. 243–44.)

The mechanist's objection to a Life-force, or *élan vital,* is not that it is unobservable—in fact, not even that it is logically impossible to observe it. (Whatever one observed, it would be more bits of matter and not a Life-force.) As we have already seen (pp. 236–39), there are many entities which the scientist accepts, such as electrons and magnetic fields, which are unobservable. But for each of these there is empirical evidence, for the hypotheses in question have *definite empirical consequences,* and if observation shows that the predicted consequences do not occur, the hypotheses must be abandoned or altered. A person who disagrees with the present electron-hypothesis and submits another in its stead can put the matter to the test of observation: are the consequences which he predicts actually forthcoming? Are there consequences of the present hypothesis which are *not* forthcoming? The vitalist, however, is able to submit nothing like this; the only things he can point to as evidence for his hypothesis are *the same facts of organic behavior* with which the mechanist is already familiar and readily admits to exist.

But the vitalist may take another line of defense. "Perhaps the *élan* does not give an explanation in the scientist's sense," he may say, "but still, it may exist. The *élan* is a reality, but not the kind of reality which the scientist's method permits him to discover. Not being the sort of thing which is available to empirical observation, it is no wonder that he cannot discover it by empirical observation. Why should you assume that all realities are realities that the scientist can discover?"

What can the mechanist say in reply to this charge? First, he can appeal to the Law of Parsimony, or the principle sometimes known as Occam's Razor: "Do not multiply entities beyond necessity." "If the behavior of living things, or some aspects of them, is a mystery," he may say, "then by accepting the *élan* we have two mysteries on our hands instead of one. Surely this does not help the situation!" But the vitalist may question this principle. "This may be a very convenient methodological procedure for you to use," he may reply. "But if there *are* two entities and not one, whether mysterious or not, there is no point in trying to talk the second one out of existence. And you still haven't proved to me that the second—the non-material Life-force—does *not* exist."

The mechanist will then reply along the following lines. "Pray tell me *what* precisely it is that you believe exists when you say that a Life-force exists. I first objected that the concept had no explanatory power, and that accordingly there was no evidence in favor of the view that any such mysterious entity exists. But this objection did not go deep enough. Indeed, it was misleading: it assumed that we do have a concept of an *élan vital,* and that the only difficulty was that we had no evidence that anything of the kind actually existed. My real objection is that '*élan vital*' is a mere phrase, standing for nothing whatever. All you have given me is a phrase, not a thing for which the phrase stands. What I am now saying, therefore, is not that no *élan* exists; it is that you haven't told me what it means even to say that it exists, or for that matter that it doesn't. Indeed, what *does* the phrase mean? If it stands for merely the observed facts of organic behavior which we all agree upon, and is simply a convenient shorthand way of lumping these bits of behavior together and talking about them, then there is no disagreement among us: we all agree that organisms behave in these ways. But if it stands for something *more,* as you vitalists say, then please tell me what the something more is. What would you say to someone who agrees that this organic behavior occurs but denies that there is an *élan vital?* What are you asserting to exist over and above the organic behavior which your opponents too are asserting to exist?

"The fact is," the mechanist concludes, "that the vitalistic argument is an argument from ignorance. You say, 'Here is all this behavior of living things which you cannot explain!' I reply that some of it we *can* explain, and the amount being explained is increasing all the time. But let that pass; even where I cannot yet explain, you are in no better position; *all you offer is a mere word.* But the addition of a word can no more assure that a reality corresponding to it exists than you can furnish your house with the *names* of various items of furniture." As one writer puts it, vitalism "simply fills up the gaps in mechanistic descriptions after the fashion of Columbus' map-maker, 'Where unknown, there place Terrors.' "[6]

The mechanism-vitalism controversy, however, can take other forms than the one we have just considered.

2. Emergence. It is said that vitalism asserts that the characteristics of living things are *emergent,* while mechanism denies it.

Before we can argue this position we must be clear about what is meant by calling a characteristic emergent. An example may give the best preliminary indication—an example, moreover, drawn not from the biological sciences at all but from chemistry: Water is composed of hydrogen and oxygen. Hydrogen is gaseous at ordinary temperatures and is highly combustible; oxygen is also gaseous at ordinary temperatures but is incombustible; instead, it is a necessary condition of combustion. The two together form water, which is not gaseous but liquid at ordinary temperatures, and is neither combustible nor a necessary condition for combustion; on the contrary, it is used to stop combustion. Is it not strange that two elements should combine to form something with such utterly different chemical properties? Examples of this in chemistry could be multiplied: for instance, the combination of sodium, which is highly corrosive when exposed to air or water, with chlorine, a semipoisonous greenish gas, to form ordinary table salt. The question arises: If we had never had any experience of water or salt, *would we be able to predict* what properties they would have just from knowing the properties possessed by hydrogen and oxygen alone, or sodium

[6] J. Needham, *Science, Religion, and Reality* (New York: The Macmillan Company, 1925), p. 245.

and chlorine alone? If we would *not* be able to predict the existence of these properties, then they are emergent; but if we would be able to predict them, they are not emergent. (The word "emergent" here is metaphorical, but it seems to arise from the fact that the properties of a compound seem to *emerge* from the elements without having been apparent in the elements themselves.)

At this point it may appear that whether the answer is yes or no is simply a question for empirical observation to decide. If this were so, philosophy would have no business with it and it would be left to the natural sciences, which handle such questions on the basis of empirical evidence. However, this is not the case, at least on the level of clarification we have reached thus far. Let us ask: *On the basis of exactly what* are the qualities of water and salt predictable or nonpredictable? On the basis of a knowledge of the properties of the elements of which they are composed. But on the basis of *how much* knowledge of these properties? Presumably on the basis of complete knowledge. But what would a complete knowledge be? Would we not say our knowledge was incomplete *until it did enable us* to predict the properties of water or salt? In this case, however, the statement is analytic, "A complete knowledge (i.e., a knowledge that will enable us to predict X) will enable us to predict X." Anyone, vitalist or not, who denied this would be foolish indeed!

Clearly, then, if we include among the properties of hydrogen the property of combining with oxygen to form water (and this *is* undeniably one of its properties), then we can predict that it will combine with hydrogen to form water, for the very simple reason that the statement is analytic. But surely this is not what the mechanist is concerned to assert or the vitalist to deny. Let us amend the statement, then, to read: "A complete knowledge of the properties of hydrogen *except* for the property of combining with oxygen to form water would enable us to predict the formation and qualities of water," or (the more usual formulation) what is similar but not the same thing, "A complete knowledge of the properties of hydrogen and oxygen in isolation, i.e., *not* including their relational properties (what they combine with to form compounds) would enable us to predict the properties of water."

If we apply this to the case of living organisms, the question becomes, "If we had a complete knowledge of the physical and chemical properties of every cell (including that of every molecule composing these cells) within a living organism, except the relational properties of combining in certain ways to form organisms, would we be able to predict what all the properties of the organism would be?" In the case of some properties, we already can; the weight of the organism, for example, is merely the weight of its constituent cells, which are in turn the aggregate weight of their constituent molecules. Similarly, much of the digestive behavior of organisms is predictable on the basis of a knowledge of the chemistry of the extremely complex compounds involved in the digestive process. What is *not* predictable on the basis of our present knowledge of physics and chemistry is the *teleological* (purposive) behavior of the organism—for example, red blood cells going "in case of emergency" to parts of the body where they are needed to keep the organism alive. How in a million years, one may ask, would a phenomenon like the complex and intricate group behavior of wasps and bees—such as scouting around through a neighborhood to familiarize themselves with the terrain, so as not to forget the location of the nest or hive—be predictable on the basis of even a complete knowledge of the physical and chemical properties of these organisms?

Even at this point we should not rest content with a definite yes-or-no answer, not because the empirical sciences have far from completed their investigation of the properties of organisms (though this is true enough), but because there is still a further source of unclarity to be removed: What is meant by "predictable"?

When we say that a certain property, say of water or of a living organism, is predictable on the basis of a knowledge of the properties of its constituents, what do we mean? When we say it is predictable we surely do not mean merely that someone can volunteer a prediction about it; we mean at least that he is in a position to volunteer a prediction that will turn out to be correct. Probably or certainly correct? Doubtless we can mean either one, but probability is not usually what is intended in discussions about this issue. For example, if we know the properties of sodium chloride (salt), sodium iodide, and sodium bromide (chlorine, bromine, and iodine are all members of the halogen family of elements), would we be able to predict, without observing them, what the properties of sodium fluoride (fluorine being also of the same family) would be? We might volunteer a prediction, and say that it was probable on the basis of previously observed similarities in the properties of the compounds formed by these elements. But we might well be mistaken: we sometimes are in such matters. We could say, "The other compounds of fluorine have turned out to be like the corresponding compounds of chlorine, and so forth, so *probably* this one will be too," but even if such a prediction turned out to be correct, the participants in the mechanism-vitalism controversy would not be inclined to say that this constituted predictability, thus proving that the mechanist was right. What is wanted is certainty, specifically logical certainty: the issue is whether, from propositions about the constituents, we are able to *deduce logically* propositions about the wholes which they form. *"If* such-and-such physical and chemical properties, *then* such-and-such behavior."[7] If the propositions about the wholes cannot be so deduced, the properties of the whole are emergent; if they can, these properties are not emergent.

3. Reducibility.   But if this is so, the controversy about emergence has become one with the controversy about *reducibility,* which is another form which the mechanism-vitalism dispute may take.

[7] This, of course, in no way affects the issue of certainty and empirical statements discussed in Chapter 2. *"If* this is salt, it contains sodium" is certain, for it is analytic, even if "This substance is salt" is never certain.

One science is said to be reducible to another science, or one part of it reducible to another part, when all the statements in the one science can be logically deduced from statements in the other. The mechanism-vitalism question, in this guise, is: "Is biology reducible to physics and chemistry?" If it is, mechanism is true, and if it is not, vitalism is true.

This sounds like an outright empirical question; but our formulation is not yet quite accurate. If it is taken as it stands, the answer is definitely in favor of vitalism, for the simple reason that the biological laws we now have cannot possibly be deduced from laws of physics and chemistry; and they cannot be so deduced because biological laws contain references to entities such as cells which are never mentioned in physics and chemistry, and of course a statement about cells cannot be logically deduced from any number of statements that do *not* contain any reference to cells. This is true not only of the relation of biology to the other physical sciences; it is also true within physics itself. For example, the laws of thermodynamics are not reducible to those of mechanics, because thermodynamic laws involve the use of concepts such as heat, while in mechanics no reference to heat occurs. In this strict sense, then, neither the sciences nor the various branches of the sciences are reducible to each other; the irreducibility is by no means peculiar to statements about living things.

Yet it is usually agreed among physicists that thermodynamics, for example, *is* reducible to mechanics, and in fact has already been so reduced, while it is not yet certain whether biology is reducible to physics and chemistry. What then is meant? The answer is that *by introducing as premises* hypotheses which permit us to omit all references to heat and to substitute only references to things which *are* a part of the subject-matter of mechanics (such as the motion of molecules), we *can* deduce all the statements in thermodynamics from statements of mechanics. In this example, the hypothesis is the kinetic theory of heat; once this is used as a premise in the deduction, the laws of thermodynamics are deducible from those of mechanics, and thus thermodynamics is reducible to mechanics.

Similarly, there are good grounds for saying that all of chemistry is reducible to physics, and that in the course of time a complete reduction will have been achieved. Propositions about the color, weight, melting-point, and other chemical properties of elements and compounds can be deduced (again, together with certain hypotheses, usually involving molecular structure) from propositions about the intra-molecular properties of these elements and compounds.

Now, in this sense, is biology reducible to physics and chemistry? If this means, "Has it now, at the present time, been reduced?" the answer is no. If it means, "Will it ever?" the answer is that of course we do not know, but that it is quite possible that it will. A great deal of it already is. The part that resists reduction is chiefly the part having to do with the teleological behavior of organisms. What further reductions can be made as biological science advances is something that only time can tell. Here, then, we shall leave the matter to the empirical sciences.

Whatever be the outcome of this controversy, vitalism in the sense of irreducibility is a far different thing from vitalism in the sense of a special nonmaterial Life-force which we considered earlier. There is nothing unscientific about irreducibility. It may well be that the laws of some sciences will never be reduced to the laws of other sciences at a "lower" level; yet each will continue to operate thoroughly and systematically. The only persons who will be disappointed at irreducibility will be those who are monists by temperament and have a burning desire to "reduce everything to unity." Such are those who say that fundamentally there is only one science, physics, and that all the others are only more complicated special cases of this one basic science. In other words: basic laws (p. 247) are found only in physics, not in chemistry or biology. The hopes of such persons may in time be dimmed by our continued failure to work biology into this neat scheme; and if they are dimmed by biology, they may well be dashed to the ground when we consider a still "higher" level of existence, namely mind. To this we now turn.

Exercises

1. "Organisms are just complex machines." But what is meant by "machine"? Try to think of a list of conditions, the fulfillment of which would entitle a thing to be called a machine. Then, in the light of this definition, assess the view that organisms are machines.

2. Evaluate the following assertions:

a. Biology is reducible to physics and chemistry.

b. No one would be able to predict the properties of H_2O (water) if he knew all the properties of hydrogen and oxygen in isolation.

c. No one would be able to predict the teleological behavior of living organisms (for example, the embryonic development of the eye, as if it were *in order to* enable the organism to see) if he knew all the properties of the organic materials constituting those organisms.

d. On the basis of what was taking place on the earth two billion years ago (before life existed on the earth), the advent of life could not have been predicted.

e. What's the vitalism dispute all about? Everyone knows that organisms behave differently from rocks and rivers.

f. Evaluate this argument: "All organisms can reproduce themselves. But no machine can reproduce itself. Therefore, organisms are not machines."

g. What's meant by all this talk about predictability? Whether something is predictable depends on (1) who is doing the predicting and (2) what is the basis on which he makes the prediction—what his prediction is based on. Thus, one can't give a general answer to the question whether this or that event is predictable.

3. Are all empirical sciences reducible to one science, physics? (Why select physics here instead of another science such as chemistry?)

4. Discuss the mechanism-vitalism controversy as set forth in one of the following: (a) Morris R. Cohen, *Reason and Nature*, pp. 241–282, and (b) C. D. Broad, *The Mind and Its Place in Nature*, Chapter 2.

20. Mind and Body

A. Mental and Physical Events

In historical succession, mind follows upon life. Just as life did not occur on our planet until inorganic matter assumed forms of great complexity, so mind did not arise until organic matter had reached a still further degree of complexity, involving sense-organs, nerves, and brains.

It is often said that within the realm of the empirical we find three levels: matter, life, and mind. Living things, though remarkably different from non-living things, are still material, or physical, things: they are composed of matter, albeit organic matter. But now we come to something that, in the opinion of most philosophers at least, is not material at all: the organic bodies which are apparently necessary conditions for the occurrence of minds are material, but minds themselves are not. If this is so, we have a wider "gap" between life and mind than we had between inorganic matter and life.

Our first task will be to show that there is such a thing as the mental as opposed to the physical. Not everyone will agree with the distinctions we are now about to draw, but every student should at least be thoroughly familiar with them, not only because most persons who have spent considerable time with the subject would assent to them, but because without them one is apt to commit some easily detectable errors.

Mental events. What happens when you hear a noise? Unless you are just "hearing things," in which case the auditory sensation is generated from within the brain itself, something first happens outside your body: sound-waves, alternate condensations and rarefactions of the air, cause air-particles to strike repeatedly on your eardrum, so that it vibrates. The eardrum is connected by three small bones to a membrane that covers one end of a spiral tube in the inner ear. The vibration of your eardrum is transmitted through this chain of three bones to the membrane at the end of the tube. The tube is filled with a liquid, perilymph, so that the vibration in the membrane attached to these bones causes a corresponding vibration to pass through this liquid. Inside the first tube is another one, filled with a liquid called endolymph; vibrations in the perilymph cause vibrations in the membranous wall of the inner tube and waves in the endolymph. Small hairs stick out from the membranous walls into the endolymph, which are made to vibrate by the vibrations in the endolymph. The auditory nerve is joined to the roots of these hairs. The vibration of the hairs causes impulses to pass up the auditory nerve to a part of the brain called the auditory center. Not until the auditory center is stimulated do you hear a sound.

So far all the events described have been physical; they have been minute changes going on inside your head. They are extremely difficult to observe, even with cleverly devised instruments, since people's heads are not transparent and it is difficult to open a person's head while the person remains alive with his brain functioning as usual. Nevertheless, many such minute physical changes have been observed and measured. (Even if this were not so, it would still be logically possible to observe them; the impossibility would be merely technical.)

The entire process just described takes only a small fraction of a second; but now, when the auditory nerve has carried the stimulus to the appropriate portion of the brain, something new and different occurs: you *hear a sound*, you have an *auditory sensation*. This is "something new under the sun." It is something quite different from anything that went on earlier in this brief but complex process. The auditory sensation is a *mental event*, not a physical event like the preceding ones. It is an *awareness*, a state of *consciousness*. The same holds for visual sensation and all other kinds of sensation: kinesthetic sensations, smell-sensations, taste, touch, heat, cold, pain, and so on; and also for states of consciousness not directly associated with the senses, such as thoughts memories, images, emotions. Let us see in what ways they are different from physical events.

1. We can always locate physical things, events, and processes in space. They take place some*where*. The sensory and neural processes associated with sensation take place inside the person's head. But where is the sensation? Suppose you hear a bell ringing; where then is your auditory sensation? It is not in the physical sound-waves—these are in space outside your body, between the bell and your ears. Still less is it in the bell, which is a physical object which you can locate in space. But the auditory sensation—where is it? Inside your head somewhere? Would a surgeon cutting open your head ever find it? If your skull were transparent and a surgeon with a powerful microscope could see what was going on inside it, he might see the stimulation of the auditory nerve, but would he see or hear your *sensation?* (And if he did would it not be his sensation rather than yours?)

Or take the case of vision. Light-waves impinge upon the retina of your eye, producing there an inverted image of the object seen. This is physical; the inverted image can be observed (though it is not what *you* are seeing). The optic nerve is stimulated, a chemical-electrical impulse passes along it, and finally, in a very small fraction of a second, the occipital lobe of the brain is stimulated; then a *visual sensation* occurs. Up to the occurrence of the sensation, every step of the process can be located in space, somewhere inside your head. But supposing you are looking at a solid green wall, where is your sensation of green? Is it in your head, inside your brain somewhere? If so, where? Would someone opening your head or looking at it through a super-X-ray microscope find the green you were seeing? Would it make sense to say that the green was 4 inches behind your eyes? It *would* make sense to say of a neural process that it was going on 4 inches behind your eyes.

Similar considerations apply if the sensation is not caused by objects outside your body. Suppose you are, as we say, seeing red spots before your eyes. Where are the spots? Before your eyes, literally? Six inches in front of your eyes perhaps? You cannot locate them there, and neither can anybody else. These spots do not exist in space at all. You may say, "They aren't real; they don't really exist at all." But don't they? They do not exist as physical spots, like the spots on a dog, but you *do* see spots and that is an inescapable fact of your experience, just as inescapable as your visual sensation of the dog's spots. By saying that they are not real you may mean that they do not form part of the physical world, but they do certainly exist—you are seeing them right now. Perhaps they exist only as mental events, but they still exist. Because they are not physical, however, you cannot locate them in the physical world, in front of your eyes or behind your eyes *or anywhere else.* Mental events are non-spatial; physical events are spatial. It makes no more sense to ask "Where (in space) is this mental event occurring?" than it does to ask "Where is the number 4?" (as opposed to the *numeral* "4" which I have just written on the blackboard and which certainly *is* located in space). Do not assume that because it is false that a mental event occurs outside one's head it therefore occurs inside one's head. A physical event or process would have to go on in the one place or the other, but not a mental one: the category of space, or spatiality, just does not apply to them at all. That is one thing that distinguishes them from physical events and processes.

If mental events (states of consciousness), then, are not locatable in space, then neither are they *extended* in space. You cannot meaningfully ask how much space they occupy. How much space do the red spots before your eyes occupy? Two inches? Three feet? (And if you did make some such assertion, how would you go about verifying it?) Suppose you form an image of the Empire State Building, or, more precisely, an image shaped to represent the Empire State Building. How tall is, not the Empire State Building itself, but your image of it? What is the tallness of the image as compared with the tallness of the Empire State Building itself? Is it one-tenth as tall, perhaps? If so, how could it possibly be squeezed into your brain, whose dimensions are only a few inches? If you constructed a *model* of the Empire State Building , you could meaningfully say that your model was one-tenth as tall, or one-thousandth as tall, as the building itself, for your model is a physical object located at a definite place in the physical world. But the image you have in your mind is not like the model you have before you on the table: the image is not inside your head (no one opening your head or looking at it from the outside would ever find it there), but neither is it outside your head, say on the table. It is not in space at all, and consequently it has no extension in space either.

2. Physical objects, physical events, and physical processes are publicly observable; but mental events (states of consciousness) can be experienced by only one person.

It may be technically impossible now (though possibly not fifty years from now) for me to observe what is going on inside your head, say at the midpoint of a straight line connecting your two ears. But whatever it is, it is some physical process taking place in your brain.

Indeed, we might imagine a machine, called an "auto-cerebroscope," by means of which you yourself could see what was going on in your own brain. With an ingenious series of mirrors you could see the surgeon cutting away at the cerebral cortex of your brain, while you were under a local anesthetic. You could see just which nerve-pathways were stimulated when you had each experience; for example, you could see exactly what happened in the occipital lobe of your cortex when you experienced the green of the tree. There is nothing absurd about such a possibility, and it may some day become actual. What the example illustrates is that the green you see, and whatever is going on in your brain when you see the green, are two different things. Your brain is available to the surgeon's inspection as well as your own through the auto-cerebroscope; but the experience of green is yours. If a law of psychophysical correlation could be established about what was going on in your brain whenever you had the experience of seeing green, the surgeon would be able to say, "Aha! You must be seeing green, for that little ganglion is wiggling in that funny way again," but he would never be able to have your experience of green. Doubtless he could have an experience of green by looking at something green himself, but that green would be correlated with *his* brain-state, not yours. You and the surgeon could observe one another's brain-states, but you could not have one another's experiences.

Is it *logically* possible for me to feel your pain, or you mine? In ordinary life we sometimes say "I feel your pain," by which we only mean that we empathize very strongly, sometimes so strongly that we too may feel a pain, but then of course our pain and the other man's pain are two different pains. But we are not asking here whether a person can empathize strongly with another person; we are asking whether two persons can feel literally *the same pain*, the way they can see the same head or the same house. Is it logically impossible, or is it logically possible but not actual?

Suppose that the world were different from the way we now find it, with biological laws quite different from the ones that now describe it. Suppose, specifically, that every time your finger was pricked with a pin, I felt a pain, but you felt none; and that every time I was hit, you felt a blow, and so on. This is a logically possible state-of-affairs. It is not actual; for in actual fact, my pains are dependent on the state of my organism; your pains are dependent on yours. As far as we know, it is empirically impossible for the situation we have just described to occur; but it is logically possible and easily imaginable. Suppose that this state-of-affairs occurred; would we then say that I felt your pain and that you felt mine?

It would all depend on what we meant by the phrases "your pain" and "my pain." We might mean by "your pain" the pain that occurs when your body is injured; and by "my pain," the pain that occurs when my body is injured. ("Injured" here does not carry any connotation of *feeling* the injury, but labels only the physical state of the body, as does "damaged" when we speak of damaged luggage.) In that case the answer is yes, I do feel your pain: I feel the pain that occurs when your body is injured.

We *could* use the phrases "your pain" and "my pain" in this way. But even if we did, there would still remain another and more fundamental sense, in which it would *not* be the case that I felt your pain, or you mine. If I felt it, even though it occurred when your body was injured, it would still be my pain. This is the way we always speak now, since the pain I feel is causally dependent on injury to my body and not to yours, and we would still speak that way in the causally different universe just described when we wished to identify the ownership of the pain rather than the causal conditions under which it was experienced. If I feel the pain, it is my pain regardless of where the injury is. In this sense, it is logically impossible for me to feel your pain. If I feel it, it is *ipso facto* my pain, and if you feel it, it is your pain. If we both feel pain, it is not the same pain we feel: you feel your pain and I feel mine. If there are two pain-experiences, there are two pains, since the word "pain" is the label for an experience, and has no existence apart from being experienced.

In short, in the sense now under discussion, "my pain" means the same as "the pain I feel," and this statement is necessarily true. It is not a necessary truth that I feel pain, but it is a necessary truth that whatever pain I feel is my pain. It is also, of course, analytic: it becomes "the pain I feel is the pain I feel." Whether or not this analytic statement reflects a fundamental feature of reality, we may leave it to rationalists and empiricists (pp. 198–207) to dispute.

Our knowledge of other minds.   I can see the outside of your head, and some day I may be able to see what is going on inside it even while you remain alive and continue having experiences; but even then I shall not be able to *have* your experiences—your sensations of green, your pains, your thoughts, and so on. I may be able to have experiences in some ways like yours, but I cannot literally have yours. My knowledge of your experiences is always based on *inference*: I cannot experience your pain, I only infer that you have a pain from watching your behavior, your facial expressions, and listening to your words. But in my own case I do not have to *infer* that I am having a pain: I know this in the most direct way I can ever know anything—I feel the pain, and this by itself entitles me to say that I have it. (See pp. 124–27.) I do not have to look in the mirror and say, "My brows are furrowed, my facial expression is such-and-such, so I must be having a pain." (I *would* have to go through such a procedure in diagnosing that I had a certain illness: I would have to examine my eyes, my skin-texture, my tongue, and so on, in order to make a diagnosis, just as a physician would do. But having an illness is not a state of consciousness, as having a pain is. It usually *involves* "feeling ill," but there is much more to having an illness than feeling ill: it also involves saying that I have certain germs inside me, that such-and-such symptoms will be progressively occurring, and so on.) There is, then, an enormous difference between my way of knowing that I have a pain and my way of knowing that you have a pain. I don't have to observe myself carefully to infer whether I am in pain; I do not have to infer it at all.

But I do infer that you are having a pain, and this is a peculiar kind of inference. In ordinary cases of inferences it is at least logically possible (and usually empirically and technically possible as well) to check directly whether the inference is correct. If I see smoke, I infer that there is a fire, but I can go directly to the building and see whether there is a fire. If all the cars coming into town have mud on them, I infer that the road leading into town is muddy but I can travel the road myself to see whether it is muddy. But when I infer from your symptoms that you are in pain, there is no logically possible way I can check the correctness of this inference: all I can do is observe more symptoms—I can never feel your pain. I can check one symptom against another one: I can observe whether in addition to exhibiting a pained facial expression you also withdraw your hand from the pain-causing fire. But I cannot in any way verify the target proposition ("You have a pain") by experiencing it *independently* of observing the symptoms, as I do with myself.

Indeed, one might go further: How do I know you are in pain at all? How do I know that you experience pain or pleasure or have sensations or thoughts or feelings of any kind? Could you not be a cleverly rigged-up automaton, wound up like a top every morning to go through certain complicated motions every day, but all the while experiencing nothing at all? True, you give answers to mathematical questions faster than I do; but so do computers, when they have been programed to do so. How do I know that you are not a fancy computer, having no more feelings or thoughts than the computers we build? If you were one, programed to go through just the motions that you do, how would I ever know the difference? You would do the same things, say the same things, every bit of your behavior would be the same—so how could I tell? I can tell that you feel pain only from the symptoms from which I make the inference—but what if the symptoms were the same? If I don't believe that a computer has feelings, and if you behaved just as a computer does (the computer too can exhibit pain behavior and say that it is in pain), what reason would I have for saying that you experience pain but the computer doesn't?

This issue has been argued so extensively in the literature of contemporary philosophy that it would require many hundreds of pages merely to summarize its main contents. But a few relevant observations may be made at this point:

1. There is one solution that would short-circuit the whole controversy, but it will not suffice: one could say that when I talk about my pain I am talking about my pain, but that when I talk about your pain I am talking only about your behavior. But this, as we saw in discussing verifiability (pp. 264–66), will not do. It's true that your behavior is all I can *verify,* but it is not all I *mean.* When I say that you are having a toothache, I mean that you are feeling an *ache,* not merely that you have a decayed tooth (which is a cause of your pain, not the pain itself) or that your face is contorted (this is an effect of your pain, not the pain itself). If this fact cannot be reconciled with the testability criterion, so much the worse for the criterion: it is a plain fact that when I say that you have a pain I mean to attribute to you the same kind of feeling I attribute to myself when I say that I have a pain.

2. Nowhere is the ambiguity of the word "knowledge" more misleading than here. *Knowing that* you have a pain is not the same thing as *experiencing* your pain. True, I can know it only by inference in your case, but still this doesn't prove that I don't know it. I can know that there is radioactivity in the vicinity by using a Geiger counter, though I don't feel the radioactivity; similarly, one might argue, I can know that you are in pain from the way you behave, even though it is logically impossible for me to experience your pain.

Thus the skeptic who argues "I can never know that you are in pain, because I can never feel your pain" is offering a bad argument; he is simply confusing *knowing that* with *experiencing.* He is confused about the meaning of the word "know." But though his argument is poor, our question remains: Since I cannot experience your pain, how do I *know that* you have one? Isn't it logically possible for you to exhibit all kinds of pain-behavior and still feel no pain? Perhaps you are a clever actor; the question still remains: How can I tell the difference?

3. Strictly speaking, I do have more to go on than your behavior, if by your behavior we mean your bodily movements, your facial expressions and gestures. We also have neuro-physiological evidence: the stimulation of your nerve-endings, the state of your brain (all of which is empirically possible for us to discover, but not in every case technically possible at present). This neuro-physiological evidence would show whether you were play-acting or not. But the skeptic, of course, could still argue, "That doesn't prove anything; you may know that when *you* feel pain your nerve-endings are stimulated, but how do you know that when other people's nerve-endings are stimulated in the same way, *they* feel pain? How do do you know that the correlation between physiological and mental states exists in any case except your own?"

Is there any answer to the skeptic? If he insists that the only way to *know* that another person is in pain is to experience that other person's pain, then we must admit that we cannot fulfill this requirement: indeed, its fulfillment is *logically* impossible, for it would require that we literally *be* someone else (and not ourselves) in order to fulfill it. But we can also point out to the skeptic that he has an unduly narrow conception of human knowledge. We cannot observe electrons directly, yet no physicist would admit that we know nothing about electrons. The knowledge is inferential, to be sure, but inferential knowledge is still knowledge. We might even admit that it is something less than knowledge: perhaps it is well-grounded belief, belief for which we can adduce very considerable evidence without its being *complete* evidence. Scientific theories have come and gone, and perhaps we cannot be as sure of electrons as of this table. I can be absolutely sure that I am feeling pain, but perhaps I cannot have the same grounds for certainty about anyone else's pains. But even so, I have *very strong* grounds for the belief: I see your hand in the fire, I see it getting burned, I hear your screams, and I can also obtain physiological evidence by measuring the stimulation of nerve-endings and the state of your brain. If we do not grant that all these things together provide good evidence that you are in pain, then we will have to deny what seems to be an obvious uniformity in the way natural processes occur: we shall have to say that whereas a stimulation of nerve-endings, etc., is correlated with pain in my case, it is not so correlated in your case. We can then turn the skeptic's technique back upon him and ask him *what reason* he has, in the face of all this, to suppose that other people do *not* really have pain, when they exhibit all the signs of having it.

But assuming that other people do have experiences, how do I know that their experiences are qualitatively similar to mine?

How do we know that we're seeing the same color? When I look at the grass, I see green. How do I know that you see green when you look at the grass? I ask you what color you see, and you say "green," of course; and I ask whether you see the same color as you do when you look at the tree, and you say yes. But how do I know? I can't get inside you and find out what you see; perhaps where I see green you really see red, but of course you have always called it "green" because you have been taught to do so. Perhaps you are the victim of the "inverted spectrum": perhaps where I see green you see red, where I see red you see green, where I see yellow you see blue, and so on, with you seeing the complementary color of what I see on all occasions. If this were so, how could it ever be discovered? Perhaps you have been suffering from an inverted-spectrum vision all the time and don't even know it. How could we ever know?

Cases of ordinary color-blindness, of course, can be easily discovered. Color-blindness is the failure to make certain color *discriminations*. The person who is red-green blind can't tell the difference between a red tie and a green tie, as long as they are equally light or dark. That is how we discover that he is different from the rest of us, for we can. To a person who was completely color-blind, everything would look the way a black-and-white movie does to us. Moreover, we have ways of knowing that he is color-blind, for he cannot make the required discriminations, no matter how high a reward he is offered for making them. Not only do we know that he is color-blind: *he* can easily know it himself. He cannot imagine the colors he is unable to see, but he can easily know *that* there are discriminations that others can make that he can't. Suppose we offer him a bunch of cards, half of them green and half of them red. He says they all look alike to him, and that we are lying when we say they are not all alike. We then separate the cards into red and green piles and return them to him; he marks them in a way known only to himself. He then shuffles the cards and presents them to another person, who arranges them in exactly the same way that we have. Before this process has been many times repeated, with the same cards always in the "red" and "green" piles, our man must realize that there is *something* we are seeing that he is not.

In short, there are *ways we can tell* whether or not a person is color-blind Color-blindness is an inability to make color-discriminations, and we can tell whether or not another person is able to make these discriminations. But the case before us does not admit of such empirical resolution. A person who saw green where you saw red and vice versa throughout the entire spectrum would be making all the color-discriminations you are: every time you saw two colors, he would see two colors; only he would see different colors from the ones you saw. So how would you ever know that he was seeing different colors? Would not the difference be forever undetectable?

"Well, what difference would it make? He would pass all the color-blindness tests. He would give the same verbal responses you would, such as 'green' on pointing at the grass. So who cares?" True, it would make no practical difference at all. But the issue does not on that account lack philosophical interest: could it be true that there is a difference that is forever impossible to discover?

"But wouldn't the difference come out in the way the person describes things? For example, he would call the flames yellow and orange just as we do; but if he actually saw them as blue and violet, wouldn't he say that the fire had cool color, whereas grass, which he saw as red, would have a warm color?" No, for if he saw the flames as blue, then the color blue would be associated for him with warmth, and so quite naturally he would say that blue (which he called yellow) was warm in color. The difference would be undetectable as long as it was systematic.

"Couldn't the difference be detected if you and he exchanged eyes?" This is not now technically possible, but suppose it were possible, as it some day may be, to exchange eyes as we now exchange glasses. Suppose your eyes were grafted into his optic nerve, and vice versa. Then if you looked at the grass and saw red instead of green, and so on, you would say, "Aha! He did have the inverted spectrum after all, for what I see through his eyes is the complementary color to what I saw through mine." But suppose you continued to see green as before: would this disprove the inverted-spectrum hypothesis? Perhaps the difference in color-vision is not a function of any difference in the structure of the eye, such as the rods and cones of the retina, but of some difference in the two *brains*.

Suppose then that both parties exchanged brains. But if you had his brain, you would have his memories, his dispositional traits, his personality—then how could it still be *you* who was doing the seeing? It would seem that in order to carry out the decisive experiment you would have to be him and he you.

The difficulty is to set up the problem in such a way that *some* experiment (as long as it is a logically possible one) could settle it, while retaining the original meaning of the hypothesis. Or is this hypothesis one that has meaning only when a verfication procedure is specified? (See pp. 270–72.)

The reductive fallacy.   It would seem, then, that states of consciousness, however closely correlated they may be with brain-processes, are not the same thing. When any two things (or processes or events), A and B, always occur together, there is a great temptation to try to "reduce the one to the other"—to say that one of them is "nothing but" the other. To do this is to commit the reductive fallacy (or nothing-but fallacy).

"Thoughts are nothing but electro-chemical impulses through neural pathways to the brain." "Pain is nothing but (a certain kind of) stimulation of the nerve-endings." "Sounds are nothing but alternating condensations and rarefactions of air (or some other medium)." "Colors are nothing but wave-lengths of light." "Heat is nothing but the motion and molecules." Let us reflect for a moment on statements such as these.

When thoughts occur, neural processes are going on in the brain; indeed, it seems to be the case that thoughts never occur in the absence of neural processes; in other words, the neural brain-processes are a necessary condition for the occurrence of thoughts. But if A is a necessary condition for B, A and B are not one and the same thing; A could hardly be a necessary condition for itself. If B is causally dependent on A, then *ipso facto* there are two things, A and B. In general, it seems to be an empirical fact that mental life is utterly dependent on brain-activity. If certain parts of the brain are damaged or removed, certain aspects of conscious life never occur. But to say that consciousness is utterly dependent on brain-activity is a far cry from saying that consciousness *is* brain-activity. It may be, for example, that the occurrence of the sensation of pain is causally related to the stimulating of nerve-endings, but again this is not to say that it *is* this stimulation. You can know that you feel pain without knowing anything about your nerve-endings, or even that you have any. You do not need to study physiology to know that you feel pain, though you do in order to know the causal conditions of pain.

In the case of colors, there is not even a perfect correlation between the wave-lengths of light and the color-sensations we have. In general, we see red when the wave-lengths of light are between 550 and 700 Angstrom units.

However, if you are blind, or have your eyes shut, or are color-blind, you do not see red at all, even in the presence of light of this wave-length. And if you are having the hallucination of a red dragon, or seeing red spots before your eyes, or seeing red objects in your dreams, you are having the experience of red in the absence (at that moment at least) of light of the required wave-length. If there is any correlation between seeing red and some physical state, it is between the sensation and a certain specific brain-state (we do not yet know which)—the brain-state which normally (but not always, as we have seen) follows upon the stimulation of the retina of the eye by light of the required wave-length.

The physicist, of course, *defines* color-words in terms of wave-lengths. This he has every right to do, since he has freedom of stipulation (p. 7). But this does not for a moment imply that the experience of red does not exist. No definition can subtract a jot or a tittle from what exists (pp. 30–31). The physicist is merely ignoring the sensation; it is his business to study physical conditions, not experiences, so he defines "red" in terms of the physical conditions under which we normally see red. The wave-lengths, of course, are not what we see; red is what we see, and the physicist is giving us a useful bit of information when he tells us that we normally see it under such-and-such circumstances. What he is defining is not the word naming the experience, but the word naming the *conditions* under which the experience normally occurs. (The word naming the sensation may be verbally indefinable—see pp. 59–64). We knew what the experience was like, and people knew it for centuries, before we knew that it usually occurs under these specific physical conditions. Exactly the same analysis applies in the case of sounds.

The same analysis applies also if we use the concept of heat as an example. "Heat is the motion of molecules." If this means the experience of heat, it most assuredly is not the motion of molecules; what *is* true is that, normally, when molecules are in more rapid motion we have a more intense heat-experience, and (up to a point, at any rate) the more the one increases the more the other increases. But this is not to say that the experience is the same thing as the motion.

To complicate the matter further, suppose now that someone says that heat is the degree of expansion of a column of mercury in a tube. Again, he can define "heat" in this way if he likes; but it legislates out of existence neither the motion of molecules nor the sensation of heat. Since we cannot examine molecules directly, we use the height of the mercury column as a *measure* of the rapidity of the motion of molecules; we do this because, for good empirical reasons, we believe that there is a close and reliable correlation between the rapidity of this molecular motion and the height of the mercury column. At very high temperatures we no longer use the mercury column as an indicator of molecular motion because (we believe) the correlation breaks down. In other words, no one, on reflection, would *identify* heat with the height of the mercury column; he would use the latter as an *indicator* of the former. *Both* of these, of course, are physical, and are not the heat-experience. Between the molecular motion and the experience, and also between the mercury column and the experience, the correlation is far less reliable: for example, if you have a fever you may feel boiling hot in a room even though the thermometer registers less than 60° F.

Which is *the real meaning* of "heat"? What is heat itself? The foolishness of such questions should be apparent after our study of language and meaning. The word "heat," like any other word, has no more meaning than its users have given it; and the meaning which is first chronologically is the sense in which "heat" stands for a certain kind of experience familiar to all of us; this is still the sense we use most in daily life, the one we use before we know anything about thermometers or molecular motions. The sense in which "heat" means molecular motion arose only after the rise of modern science in the seventeenth century. Neither is "the real" meaning; both are legitimate meanings, harmless enough as long as we do not try to use the word to deny the existence of anything in the world. This is precisely what happens in the case of the reductive fallacy, particularly with people who know a little about physics and nothing whatever about semantics: "Heat just *is* molecular motion; that's all there is, there is nothing more to it." As if people could not talk meaningfully about heat for centuries before anyone had ever heard of molecules! No one denies that there are such things as molecules; no one denies (or should deny) that there are such things as heat-experiences. *Both* these things exist, and it appears that there is a causal relation between them. No amount of defining can put either of these things out of existence.

The fallacy, however, in our century at least, is as widespread as it is simple. It shows up again in the view known as *materialism*.

Materialism. The word "materialism" is often used to stand for the view that everything is material, and that there is nothing mental at all: "All matter, no mind." Here again the familiar question arises: what exactly does this mean?

1. If "mind" is defined as something more than the totality of mental events, or as some substance in which mental events inhere, then some philosophers would be inclined to agree that there is no such thing. (We shall discuss this issue later in this chapter.) Still, such persons would not be materialists, for they would still believe in mental events. Let us turn, then, to another meaning.

2. One could mean that there really are no mental events: no thoughts, no sensations, no emotions—no states of consciousness at all. But this view is so preposterous that it is difficult to believe that anyone could ever have held it. Imagine a person who thinks that there are no thoughts: does he not think

that his view is true? But then there is at least one thought after all, namely the thought that this view is true. If this is what is meant by "materialism," materialism is self-refuting.

3. A more likely meaning, then, is this: thoughts, sensations, and so forth do occur, but they are physical in nature, not mental at all. Here, of course, everything depends on how broadly one is going to use the word "physical": if he uses it so broadly as to cover every phenomenon, no matter what it is like, then he has won an easy but empty triumph in concluding that everything is physical—like that of a person who says that everything is blue in color, using the word "blue" so broadly as to cover not only what we now call "blue" but also what we now call "red," "green," "white," and so on. The relevant question, then, is this: Are there not some events that are different enough from events which we ordinarily call "physical" to deserve another name? Is it not true that some events and processes, such as thoughts, are not publicly observable, not locatable in space? And do we not have public observability and spatial location in mind when we call something "physical"? But if this is so, it is mere verbal obstinacy for us to keep calling them "physical" even though they do not possess the distinguishing characteristics by virtue of which we now call something "physical." To call these things physical would be just as misleading as to call a person a humorist if he tells one joke every twenty years.

In common parlance, however, the word "materialism" is not used to name the view that denies the mental in any of these senses. It is used to name either the view that mental life is *dependent upon* physical conditions and would not exist without it—this will be discussed further when we take up the theories of mind-body relationship—or, more popularly still, the view that human beings either *are* or *should be* exclusively interested in material things, such as money or possessions; this in the one case is a psychological doctrine and in the other case an ethical one, and in either case is not relevant here.

Behaviorism.   Behaviorism in psychology is often thought of as the twin or counterpart of materialism. As a rule, however, those who call themselves behaviorists do not wish to deny the mental in any of the three senses listed in the paragraphs above. (If they do, the same remarks made in connection with materialism will apply here.) Rather, the word "behaviorism" generally names a kind of *method* employed in psychology, a method characterized chiefly by the refusal to use introspection of one's own mental states as material for arriving at laws in psychology. Its chief data consist of overt and publicly observable behavior, introspection and even introspective reports being considered too misleading and insecure to constitute data of the required scientific exactness. With behaviorism as a method of procedure in psychology, of course, we are not here concerned.

Even here, however, we should be on our guard not to define "behavior" so broadly as to include consciousness, lest the word lose all distinctive meaning; nor should we identify behavior with the consciousness that goes along with it.

Wherever there is consciousness there is behavior. Even in thinking, or in dreaming, we are reacting, though merely in slight, tentative ways, not visible to a spectator. Whatever we are conscious of (whether in perception or in conception, with our eyes open or in a brooding reverie) we are reacting *to*. The behaviorists have dragged to light these multitudinous, minute, incipient reactions, and shown us that all organisms, and especially the higher organisms, are incessantly performing these delicate reactive movements, and, in that way, keeping in touch, as it were, with their world. Since all definition is, at bottom, arbitrary, we might be content to call this incessant play of reactions, incipient and overt, the organism's consciousness of things, *except that we need the term "consciousness" for something else!*

When I look at a red flag, my head turns, my eyes focus themselves at the proper distance, certain tensions and inhibitions are produced which I call "paying attention" to it, incipient reactions of various sorts are engendered, according to what the flag means to me, and what thoughts, or esthetic feelings, or purposes, or emotions it arouses. All this is grist for the behaviorist's mill. But *in addition* to all this, I have the sensation *red*. The behaviorist who is studying my reactions cannot find that sensation red anywhere in me. He may have a similar sensation himself if the flag is within his field of vision; but we are talking, not about his sensation of red, but about mine. The completest possible account of my bodily reactions leaves out of account what I *see,* my sense-data; and, likewise, what I *hear,* and so on. Nor can the behaviorist discover my feelings and emotions, my thoughts and dreams. He can guess at them, from studying my reactions; but the quality of my feeling eludes him. He may see me writhing, but he cannot feel my pain. He may see my smiles, measure my muscular tensions, count my heartbeats, discover what my glands are doing, but he cannot feel my happiness. That, and all the rest of my conscious experience, is private.[8]

B. The Relation Between Mental and Physical

Physical events and processes occur, and mental events and processes occur, regardless of how we may interpret substance-words about the physical and the mental. What, then, is the relation of these events and processes to each other? Do they affect each other, and if so, how? Let us consider the principal traditional theories on this question:

1. *Interactionism.* Interactionism begins as a simple "common-sense" view. What could be more obvious than that physical events cause mental events and that mental events in turn cause physical events? You receive a blow on the head (physical event) and you feel pain (mental event); light-waves impinge upon your retina (physical event) and you experience a visual sensation (mental event). Every time a physical stimulus causes something

[8] Durant Drake, *Invitation to Philosophy,* pp. 329–30.

to register in consciousness, we have proof positive that physical events cause mental events. It is equally clear that mental events cause physical events: you feel frightened (mental event) and your heart beats faster (physical event); you decide to step outdoors (mental event) and you step outdoors (physical event). Every time a volition (act of will) results in your doing what you willed to do, we have proof positive that mental events cause physical events. In other words, mind and body *interact*. True, as far as we know body never acts on mind except by means of the brain, nor does mind affect body except through the intermediary of the brain. The brain, which itself is physical, is the connecting link between other physical states and mental states. Thus the interaction takes place only under very specialized conditions; but it does take place.

The chief defect that has traditionally been found with interactionism can be put as follows: How does the body affect the mind, or the mind the body? When we become aware of a light flashing, what happens? Most of the story is plain enough, even though its details are extremely complex: it is the old story of retina, optic nerve, brain. We can trace a continuous series of physical impulses. But now what happens when we get to the brain? As long as we stay in the brain, there is no difficulty: what happens in the brain is extremely difficult to discover, of course, but this is a technical difficulty only. But what of the mental event which is supposed to occur *as a result* of a brain-event, say the last (or terminal) brain event before the mental event occurs? It cannot even be spatially located. How does the brain-state bring it about?

This difficulty is even more keenly felt when we consider a mental event (such as a volition) causing a physical event (such as a bodily movement). Nerve pathways are stimulated from the brain; but how do the brain-centers get stimulated by the volition? The volition, being a mental event, can hardly *touch* any physical particles in the brain to give them the appropriate stimulation; but how else can they be caused to move? "By the mental event," the interactionist says; but the critic who tries to visualize this state-of-affairs (volition, non-spatial, affecting a spatially locatable part of the brain) finds himself baffled. "Of course," the interactionist reminds him, "you can't visualize it because mental events are not spatial, not extended, hence not visualizable to begin with!" But the critic remains dissatisfied. He wants to know more of the *how* of this relation; how could a mind act upon a body to produce a physical event?

Much of the difficulty doubtless stems from an unduly narrow concept of causality. If you assume that C cannot cause E without C *acting on* E, you will remain uncomfortable about mind-body and body-mind causality because one thing cannot literally act on another unless they are both physical things. But why must all causality be of the acting-on variety? (1) Even in the physical realm, there are cases of causality in which it is difficult or impossible for us to see how the one entity acts upon the second. In gravitation, how does the sun *act upon* the planets? This example is already a far cry from the classical billiard-ball case, in which the first billiard ball causes the second to move by bumping against it. In other words, there does seem to be "action at a distance" (the action of gravitation, magnetism, cosmic rays, etc.): causality without one body acting upon another. We know that the first causes the second, but we cannot point to any kind of contact between them (unless, of course, we invent *ad hoc* the hypothesis that there is: see pp. 319–20). (2) There are many cases in which all we can say is that the causal relation *does* occur—that C is a sufficient condition for the occurrence of E—*without* being able to indicate *how,* or by what mechanism, the causation occurs. But knowing *that* C causes E is different from knowing *how* the causation occurs. We can know the first without knowing the second. All we can say in these cases, as in that of the gravitational influence of the sun upon the planets, is "It just happens, that's all." The same could be true of the mind-body relationship.

Perhaps we feel uncomfortable about this. "After all," we may say, "the relation between the physical and the mental hasn't been *explained*—it is simply left hanging in the air, with nothing to account for it." But what does it mean to explain (pp. 240–42)? An event is explained when it has been subsumed under a law (or set of laws), and a law is explained when it has been shown to be a consequence of some other, more basic, law (or theory). But when we arrive at an ultimate, or "really basic," law of nature, we can do no further explaining (what would it mean to explain a basic law? what would we explain it by?); we can only assert the uniformity. The peculiarity of the mental-physical relations seems to be that the laws concerning these are all basic laws. We cannot, for example, say *why* this particular physical state should be invariably associated with this particular sensation (which we call "red") rather than with another one (which we call "yellow," or "pain," or "pungent smell"); we know of no other law from which we could derive this one: we can only assert the uniformity.[9]

There may, however, be another source of worry. Doesn't the interactionist thesis run head-on into a well-established principle of physics, the Law of Conservation of Energy? According to this law, the amount of energy in the universe always remains constant. Now, when stepping on a nail (physical event), together with other occurrences in muscles, nerves, and brain, causes me to feel pain (mental event), is physical energy *lost?* And when I decide to leave the room, and as a result my body starts to move, is physical energy *created?* But no such gains and losses have ever been detected. How then can the interactionist theory be true, if it is incompatible with a law of physics that is certainly better established than it is?

First let us see what the Law of Conservation of Energy says.

[9] See John Stuart Mill, *A System of Logic,* Book 3, Chapter 14, Section 2. In Mill's opinion, all laws stating correlations between physical states and states of consciousness are basic laws.

It is found that, if we take certain material systems, e.g., a gun, a cartridge, and a bullet, there is a certain magnitude which keeps approximately constant throughout all their changes. This is called "energy." When the gun has not been fired it and the bullet have no motion, but the explosive in the cartridge has great chemical energy. When it has been fired the bullet is moving very fast and has great energy of movement. The gun, though not moving fast in its recoil, has also great energy of movement because it is very massive. The gases produced by the explosion have some energy of movement and some heat-energy, but much less chemical energy than the unexploded charge had. These various kinds of energy can be measured in common units according to certain conventions. To an innocent mind there seems to be a good deal of "cooking" at this stage, i.e., the conventions seem to be chosen and various kinds and amounts of concealed energy seem to be postulated in order to make the principle come out right at the end. . . . Now it is found that the total energy of all kinds in this system, when measured according to these conventions, is approximately the same in amount though very differently distributed after the explosion and before it.[10]

In other words, the bullet, gun, and charge together are a "conservative system," in which the total amount of energy remains constant (each of these three items alone would *not* be a conservative system). The human body may also be a conservative system, though the evidence for this is inconclusive. But assuming that it is, what happens to the physical energy when matter affects mind, and whence does the physical energy appear when mind affects matter? No such loss or sudden appearance of energy has been recorded.

But why need there be any? The conclusion—that mind never affects matter or matter mind—

. . . does not follow from the Conservation of Energy and the experimental facts alone. The real premise is a tacitly assumed proposition about causation: viz., that, if a change in A has anything to do with a change in B, energy must leave A and flow into B. This is neither asserted nor entailed by the Conservation of Energy. What *it* says is that, *if* energy leaves A, it must appear in something else, say B; so that A and B together form a conservative system.[11]

Since the Law of Conservation of Energy says nothing about any "transfer" of energy, there is nothing in it that is incompatible with interactionism.

According to another view, however, there is no causal relation at all between the physical and the mental:

2. *Psychophysical parallelism.* Parallelists contend that there is no causal relation between mind and matter: it is as if the two kinds of events occurred along two parallel tracks without ever touching one another. For every mental event there is a physical event corresponding to it (its "physical correlate") in the brain. But the reveres is not true: there are many physical events, like the digestion of food, for which there is no mental correlate at all.

[10] C. D. Broad, *The Mind and Its Place in Nature*, pp. 103–4.
[11] *Ibid.*, p. 107.

How can any theory deny that physical stimuli have mental effects, and vice versa? Isn't this going flatly contrary to the most obvious empirical facts that we experience thousands of times a day? No: parallelism is not denying any fact of experience; it does not deny the truth of a statement such as that the strong light caused you to get a headache; it only says that strictly speaking the relation is not a causal one, and that common-sense is using language loosely when it talks as if the relation were causal. What causes a physical event, according to parallelism, is always another physical event, and this in turn is caused by another physical event, and so on, the chain of physical events being unbroken. When physical events of a certain highly specific nature occur, however (namely, events in the cerebral cortex of a brain), then mental events occur as a kind of *running accompaniment* to them. But the physical does not *cause* the mental. Rather, there is a *one-to-one correlation* between them. Between certain physical states of the brain and mental events there is a one-to-one correlation, so that if a certain brain-state were repeated exactly, the corresponding mental event would be repeated exactly; and the physical brain event and its corresponding mental event always occur simultaneously.

What, then, according to parallelism, is the true account of what happens in the process of sensation? Light-waves impinge upon the retina (in the case of vision); an impulse is carried along the optic nerve to the brain. All this is physical. Does this not *cause* a mental event to occur? No. What is caused is always another physical event. In this case what is caused is a brain-event, which in turn causes another brain-event, and so on. But, along with these brain-events, events in consciousness (mental events) now occur, and invariably occur; but they are not *caused* by them.

Neither does a mental event ever cause a physical one. Suppose the visual sensation referred to in the preceding paragraph is one of seeing the words in a recipe book, "Add a pinch of cinnamon"; don't you then *will* to walk over to the spice cabinet? And don't your legs move in that direction as a *result,* an *effect,* of your volition? Again the parallelist's answer is no. Your legs move—granted. What causes this motion is not a mental event at all but a series of brain-events (the last ones in the series described in the preceding paragraph), which in turn stimulate certain nerves (efferent nerves) going all the way from the brain, through the spine, to the feet; these in turn affect the muscles, and you walk. *The entire series of causes and effects can be traced in the physical realm.* For a complete causal account of what happened from the time of stimulation of the retina to the time of walking (perhaps just a fraction of a second) you can trace an unbroken series of causes and effects in the physical realm, A causal account need include nothing more. A complete description of what happened, of course, would include more; it would have to include the mental events, since of course parallelism does not deny that they occur. It is only their acting as causes and effects that parallelism denies.

According to parallelism, is not the mind in the position of a mere passive spectator of the physical, unable to *do* anything in the physical world? No, says the parallelist, not if the situation is properly understood. For suppose that the chain of physical events described in the previous paragraphs is labeled P-1, P-2, P-3, and so on. This chain of physical events is uninterrupted. Now, at a certain stage, namely when brain-events of a certain kind occur, mental events occur simultaneously with them. Suppose this starts at P-12. Then corresponding to P-12 we have M-12; corresponding to P-13 we have M-13; and so on. The relation between M-12 and P-12 is invariable: if P-12 were to occur again, M-12 would occur again simultaneously with it. (Probably this outright repetition would never occur, because memory-traces in the brain would make the second brain-state different, even if the external stimulus were exactly the same; and the consciousness of previous occurrences of the same kind of event—memory— would make the mental event different the second time.) Now let us assume that P-25 is the legs moving, or more precisely one event in that process; and that M-15 is the volition (act of will) and P-15 its corresponding brain-event, about which at present we really know nothing. Now P-15, a brain-event, *is* in the causal chain of events leading up to P-25, and without it P-25 would not have occurred. M-15 is not in this causal chain; P-15 is M-15's *representative*, as it were, in the causal order; it is only by means of P-15 that any effect is caused in the world. Nevertheless, *M-15 is essential to the process: P-25 would no more have occurred without M-15 than it would have occurred without P-15.* In other words, M-15 is just as much a *necessary condition* (and part of the sufficient condition) of P-25 as P-15 is.

No house was ever built, no book was ever written, without the occurrence of mental events. The parallelist does not deny this. He only insists that what did the actual *work* in the physical world was never the mental event itself but its representative in the physical realm, not M-15, but P-15.

If this is so, what is the difference between saying that M-15 is a necessary condition but *not* a cause, as the parallelist does, and saying, as the interactionist frankly does, that it *is* a cause, at least *one* causal factor in the occurrence of P-25? There does not seem to be any. If M-15 always occurs before P-25, and P-25 never occurs without M-15, then is not M-15 just as much a cause of P-25 as P-15 is? Is not the difference between parallelism and interactionism a difference of language—in other words, a verbal difference, the one applying the word "cause" in a situation where the other refuses to do so? According to both views, a physical stimulus is part of a sufficient condition (and in most if not all cases, a necessary condition as well) of a mental effect; and according to both views, a mental event such as a volition is part of a sufficient condition (and in most cases at least, a necessary condition as well) of a physical effect, or series of physical effects such as building a house. The interactionist calls this a *causal* relation, as indeed we do in ordinary life. Is not the parallelist then being merely obstinate in refusing to call it causal? Seeing red depends on a multitude of factors in the physical world, including the brain; what is the point, or even the sense, in saying "It's dependent all right, but not causally dependent"? Perhaps the parallelist still has "in the back of his mind" the idea of causality as necessarily involving action of one physical entity upon another—and since this is not present in the physical–mental case, he refuses to call the relation causal. But we have already seen that this stricture is unwarranted: there are many events and processes, even in the physical world alone, in which causation does not involve one thing acting upon another. Why then insist upon it here? The main reason that parallelism has tended to drop out in 20th century discussions of the mind–body relation is that once the dispute over the meaning of "cause" has been straightened out, there does not appear to be any difference between it and interactionism. The kind of relation that exists between the mental and the physical would be called causal in any other context, and there appears to be no good reason for refusing to call it so here.

But now another view of the mental-physical relation awaits us:

3. *Epiphenomenalism.*   According to this view, the mind is nothing but an "epiphenomenon" of the body. Its relation to the body is like that of the smoke to the locomotive, or shadow to the person. The motions of the person cause the motions of his shadow, but the motions of the shadow do not in turn cause the motion of the person. Similarly, the physical causes the mental, but the mental never in turn causes the physical. It is strictly a one-way causal relationship.

The great disadvantage of this view, once we get the interesting bits of picture-thinking out of it, is that it combines whatever difficulties can be found in both the previous views. Whatever reason can be found for saying that the physical causes the mental (physical cause and mental effect) will *also* hold good for saying that the mental causes the physical, as in volitions causing bodily movements. And whatever reasons can be found *against* saying that the mental causes the physical, as the parallelist does if he interprets causation as implying contact, can *also* be found against saying that the physical causes the mental, such as "How do motions in particles of matter bring forth mental events?" Thus, caught between the two other views (which do remain two different views if the interactionist means to imply contact, as he traditionally does), epiphenomenalism tends to drop out of the picture.

The feature that makes epiphenomenalism most difficult to accept is that, since mind never affects body, one is committed to the belief that the entire course of events in the physical world would have been exactly the same as it now is, *even if there had been no minds at all*. But how, one might ask, could cities have been built, books and symphonies written, colleges attended and courses taught, if human minds were not causally efficacious in the world?

Surely if any fact of reality is obvious, it is that the world is different because minds exist. But the epiphenomenalist accepts this conclusion with composure. Just as your body can exist on cloudy days when it casts no shadow, so (he says) the brain-activity could occur without any mental activity accompanying it. Cities could not have been built or books written without the enormously complex activity of cells in the human *brain*, but this is far different from saying that these things could not have been accomplished unless *consciousness* existed, and it is only the existence of consciousness that he denies as causally necessary to the process. Now, strictly speaking, in order to prove this, we would have to re-enact the entire history of the universe, *with* human brains and *without* human consciousness, in order to see what would occur in such a situation. But to conduct such an experiment successfully we would have to circumvent what seems to be a law (or series of laws) of nature, that whenever a physical brain-event P occurs, a corresponding mental event M also occurs, and vice versa. This latter fact, if it is a fact, would make the experiment not only technically but empirically impossible.

4. *The double-aspect theory.* According to this view, mental and physical events are merely two aspects of the same underlying *substance*. The substance itself is generally conceived to be unknowable by human beings, but two of its aspects, the mental and physical, are known. It is as if one is passing down a corridor with a mirror on both right and left, and one's body is reflected in both mirrors. One mirror is the physical and the other the mental, and they both simultaneously reflect different aspects of the same substance, you. This is easy enough to see in the case of the mirror, but not so easy to see in the case of the mental-physical relation. We can speak glibly enough of "two aspects of the same thing," "two sides of the same coin," and so on; but precisely what is it of which the mental and the physical are two aspects? It would seem that in attempting to get rid of one mystery (or at any rate one ultimate fact), we have got stuck with another. Instead of saying that mental-physical correlations are ultimate laws of nature, we attempt to explain them by saying that they are two aspects of some underlying substance—a substance with which, however, no one has any acquaintance, and of which no one has any knowledge.

It is probable that most persons whose use of language suggests the double-aspect theory actually wish to hold that in some sense or other the mental and the physical are *identical*. But this takes us to our final theory.

5. *The identity theory.* According to this theory, mental states are identical with certain physical states of the brain. To say that you are in a certain mental state is to say that a certain event is going on in the cerebral cortex of your brain; you may not know what it is, but the two are identical nevertheless. It is not merely that physical brain-states and mental states are correlated with one another ("whenever P then M") but that they are literally *the same event*.

What meaning of "identical" is involved here? (1) When you say that this marble is identical with that marble, you mean that the two marbles have exactly the same characteristics. There may not be two identical marbles in the world, but if there were they would have exactly the same characteristics: "identical" here means *exactly the same.* Of course, if occupying the same portion of space and the same segment of time is to count as a characteristic, then it would be logically impossible for two marbles to be identical, for if they were at the same place at the same time they would be one marble, not two. When we say that two things are identical, we usually mean that they have exactly the same properties *except* for their spatio–temporal properties. But there is another meaning of "identical" as well (2) When you say that A is identical with B, you may mean *numerical* identity—that they are, quite literally, *one and the same thing.* The ancients thought that the morning star and the evening star were two stars, but we now know that they are one—the planet Venus. The morning star and the evening star are identical: they are one and the same object. Similarly, two explorers may be mapping unknown territory, and each one, approaching a mountain from the opposite direction, may give a different name to what turns out (after they have compared maps) to be the same mountain. The supposedly two mountains are numerically identical: they are one and the same mountain. The identity theory of mind-body says that mental states and physical brain-states are numerically identical: they are literally the same thing.

When I say that a sensation is a brain process or that lightning is an electric discharge, I am using "is" in the sense of strict identity. (Just as in the—in this case necessary—proposition "7 is identical with the smallest prime number greater than 5.") When I say that a sensation is a brain process or that lightning is an electric discharge I do not mean just that the sensation is somehow spatially or temporally continuous with the brain process or that the lightning is just spatially or temporally continuous with the discharge.[12]

But how can this be? If we accept any such identity, aren't we going back on the very distinction between mental and physical that we laboriously introduced on pp. 378–82? In the light of these considerations, it would appear that the identity theory is open to the objection that mental and physical events cannot be the same:

However completely the behavior of an external body answers to the behavioristic tests for intelligence, it always remains a perfectly sensible question to ask: Has it really got a mind, or is it merely an automaton? It is quite true that we have no available means of answering such questions conclusively. It is also true that, the more nearly a body answers to the behavioristic tests for intelligence, the harder it is for us in practice to contemplate the possibility

[12] J. J. C. Smart, "Sensations and Brain Processes," *Philosophical Review*, 1959, p. 145. It should be noted, however, that "lightning" and "electric discharge" are not strictly identical: lightning is only *one kind* of electric discharge.

of its having no mind. Still, the question "Has it a mind?" is never silly in the sense that it is meaningless. At worst it is silly only in the sense that it does not generally express a real doubt, and that we have no means of answering it. It may be like asking whether the moon may not be made of green cheese; but it is not like asking whether a rich man may have no wealth. . . .

Let us suppose, for the sake of argument, that whenever it is true to say that I have a sensation of a red patch it is also true to say that a molecular movement of a certain specific kind is going on in a certain part of my brain. There is one sense in which it is plainly nonsensical to attempt to reduce the one to the other. There is a something which has the characteristic of being my awareness of a red patch. There is a something which has the characteristic of being a molecular movement. It should surely be obvious even to the most "advanced thinker" who ever worked in a psychological laboratory that, whether these "somethings" be the same or different, there are two different *characteristics*. The alternative is that the two phrases are just two names for a single characteristic, as are the two words "rich" and "wealthy"; and it is surely obvious that they are not. If this be not evident at first sight, it is very easy to make it so by the following considerations. There are some questions which can be raised about the characteristic of being a molecular movement, which it is nonsensical to raise about the characteristic of being an awareness of a red patch; and conversely. About a molecular movement it is perfectly reasonable to raise the question: "Is it swift or slow, straight or circular, and so on?" About the awareness of a red patch it is nonsensical to ask whether it is a swift or a slow awareness, a straight or a circular awareness, and so on. Conversely, it is reasonable to ask about an awareness of a red patch whether it is a clear or a confused awareness; but it is nonsense to ask of a molecular movement whether it is a clear or a confused movement. Thus the attempt to argue that "being a sensation of so and so" and "being a bit of bodily behavior of such and such a kind" are just two names for the same characteristic is evidently hopeless.[13]

Strong though this argument appears to be, the identity theorist denies that it is valid. Being identical, the mental and the physical event are not two different events; but to believe that the phrases are "just two names for the same thing"—which is also false—is not the only alternative. Let us first consider this objection, and how the identity theorist replies to it. (The first four objections are very similar, and indeed might be considered variations of the same basic objection.)

1. "How can words describing mental events and words describing physical events have the same meaning? They obviously have very different meanings. When I say that I have an after-image, I mean something *different* from saying that my brain is in a certain state. And if they don't mean the same, how can the two possibly be identical?"

The identity theory, however, does not say that mental words *mean* the same as physical words. The phrase "human being" does not mean the same

---

[13] C. D. Broad, *op. cit.,* pp. 614, 622–23.

as the phrase "featherless biped," and yet the two phrases do, or at any rate may, *denote* the same things. The phrases "Vice-president of the United States" and "president of the United States Senate" do not have the same meaning, but they do denote the same individual. The word "lightning" does not mean the same as "electrical discharge," though every flash of lightning is in fact an electrical discharge. That this is so is of course an empirical discovery unknown before the rise of modern physics. But so is the identity theory, if true, an empirical discovery—the discovery that what we previously thought were two events are in fact one.

"I see lightning" does not *mean* "I see an electrical discharge." Indeed, it is logically possible (though highly unlikely) that the electrical discharge account of lightning might one day be given up. Again, "I see the Evening Star" does not *mean* the same as "I see the Morning Star," and yet "The Evening Star and the Morning Star are one and the same thing" is a contingent proposition. . . .[14]

Nor do the words "somebody" and "the doctor" mean the same, but the somebody whose office I was in this morning is nevertheless numerically identical with the doctor. Similarly, when I say "I have an after-image" I do not *mean* the same thing as when I say "I have such-and-such a brain-process." The ordinary man when he reports an experience is reporting that something is going on, but he leaves it open as to what sort of thing is going on. Yet what is going on is a brain-process just the same.

2. "But A cannot be numerically identical with B if there are things you can know about A without knowing them about B, or vice versa."

But this is not true, says the identity theorist. We believe that a flash of lightning is an electrical discharge, and yet we may know that something is a flash of lightning without knowing that it is an electrical discharge. We may know that someone is Vice-president of the United States without knowing that he is also president of the Senate; yet the person who is Vice-president is the same person who is president of the Senate. I may know that the object I see is red but not know that it is a balloon; yet it is a fact that the red object I see is a balloon: the object I see and the balloon are the same object. You may know that X has characteristic A and that Y has characteristic B but not know that X and Y are the same object; but if they are, then we have found that the X that has A is the same object as the Y that has B. Thus a person may be able to talk about his thoughts, feelings, and sense-experiences without knowing anything about his brain processes, just as he can talk about lightning without knowing anything about electricity. X may be identical with Y, although we may not know that it is, and therefore we may not know that the qualities we attribute to X are also qualities of Y.

[14] J. J. C. Smart, *op. cit.*, pp. 147–48.

3. "But isn't it *logically* possible for mental events to occur without physical events, even if they never do? And how can it be logically possible according to the identity theory?"

It can, and it is. *If* there were conscious states without bodies—a possibility we shall examine in the next section—this would at once disprove the identity theory, for according to this theory every state of consciousness is numerically identical with a brain-state, and this would obviously be false if one ever occurred without the other. The occurrence of mental states without physical ones would disprove the identity theory, just as the occurrence of a flash of lightning that was not an electrical discharge would disprove the empirical hypothesis that flashes of lightning are electrical discharges. But let us remember that, though numerical identity, the identity that is claimed is still an *empirical* entity, and that the discovery of such an identity would be an empirical discovery—not a *logical* identity, or identity of meaning. It is still *logically* possible for mental states to occur without physical ones. What is *not* logically possible, because self-contradictory, is for mental states to occur without physical ones *and* for the identity theory nevertheless to be true.

4. "If X and Y are identical, then we cannot utter any true statement about X that is not also true about Y. And in this case we can. I can say that I expect a certain after-image when I have looked at an intense color on a screen, but this is not the same as expecting that my brain will be in a certain state: I have no knowledge, and hence no expectations, about that."

This is perfectly true; but the identity theory does *not* claim that when we use a mental word, "after-image," we can substitute a physical word describing a brain-state without change of meaning. The two do have different meanings. It is not a *meaning*-identity between two sets of *words* that is claimed but an *empirical* identity between two *things*. I can expect a flash of lightning without expecting an electrical discharge, if I know nothing about electrical discharges; but when lightning flashes, it is an electrical discharge just the same. I can expect an after-image without expecting a brain-process, since I know nothing about brain-processes; but what is happening is a brain-process just the same. It is possible for two things, A and B, to be numerically identical, and yet for a person to *expect* A without expecting B. This peculiarity arises because the words "A" and "B" may have different *meanings* even though they have the same *denotation*, and our expectation is directed toward a certain meaning (I may expect the Vice-president but not the president of the Senate). Thus the fact that I can expect a certain experience without expecting a brain-process does not prove that the two are different things but only (what was already granted) that the *meaning* of the words "experience" and "brain-process" are not the same.

But another objection arises out of this that is more difficult for the identity-theorist to answer:

5. "We agree that the phrases 'morning star' and 'evening star' do not mean the same, although they both denote the same object. But now I would remind you that *if* the morning star has any characteristics that the evening star does not have, or vice versa, then they cannot be numerically identical (the same object). We can, of course, *believe,* or even know, that the evening star has them without knowing that the morning star has them (we may not even know that the morning star exists), but if they are *in fact* numerically identical, then it must *in fact* be true that every characteristic of the first is also a characteristic of the second, and vice versa. Now, the mental has characteristics that the physical does not have, and vice versa; and if this is so, they cannot be numerically identical." Thus:

(a) "A brain-process always occurs at a certain place—in the brain. Does the mental event occur there?"

No. B-processes [brain-processes] are, in a perfectly clear sense, located where the brain is, in a particular region of physical space. But it is not true that C-states [conscious states] occur in the brain, or inside the body at all, for that matter. To be sure, I may have a pain in my leg or in my head; we do locate sensations in the body. But that is not to say that we give location to the *state of consciousness* that I have when I am having a sensation. The pain is in my leg, but it is not the case that my state of being-aware-of-a-pain-in-my-leg is also in my leg. Neither is it my head. In the case of thoughts, there is no temptation to give them location, nor to give location to the mental state of being aware of a thought. In fact, it makes no sense at all to talk about C-states as being located somewhere in the body. We would not understand someone who pointed to a place in his body and claimed that it was there that his entertaining of a thought or having of an after-image was located. It would make no more sense than to claim that his entertaining of a thought was cubical or a micrometer in diameter.

The fact that it makes no sense to speak of C-states occurring in a volume occupied by a brain means that the Identity Theory cannot be correct. For it is a necessary condition for saying that something is identical with some particular physical object, state, or process that the thing be located in the place where the particular physical object, state, or process is. If it is not there, it cannot be identical with what *is* there. Here we have something that distinguishes the mind–body case from such examples of identity as men with featherless bipeds, Morning Star with Evening Star, water with H_2O, lightning with electrical discharge, etc.[15]

(b) "A brain-process is a publicly observable event; difficult though it may be to get at for technical reasons, different surgeons could observe it. But a pain or a thought is a private event: nobody can have your pain or your thought but you. (You and I can have the same thought in the sense that we

[15] Jerome Shaffer, "Could Mental States Be Brain Processes?" *Journal of Philosophy,* LVIII (1961), pp. 815–16.

can think *about* the same thing, but when we do so there are two occurrences, two acts of thinking, yours and mine.)"

It may be replied that this is only a temporary matter owing to our comparative ignorance of brain-states, and that if I had a complete knowledge of neurology, I could, by looking into your brain, know that you were having a pain and even what you were thinking about. This last remark is true, but of course it does not meet the objection: the fact still remains that even if I *know* what you are thinking, I do not *have* your thought, and knowing that you are in pain is different from experiencing your pain. (Even believers in telepathy do not claim that I can *have* your pain but only that I can *know that* you are in pain, without observing you.) The experience of the mental event is still private, though the knowledge that you have it may be publicly available. The perfect neurologist could be just as sure as you are that you are experiencing a pain, but he still would not be having it.

The identity theorist may reply, "Until brain-process theory is much improved and widely accepted, there will be no *criteria* for saying 'Smith has an experience of such-and-such a sort' *except* Smith's introspective reports. So we have adopted a rule of language that (normally) what Smith says goes."[16] But even if there *were* criteria other than Smith's introspective report, such as examining Smith's brain at that moment, and even if everyone by taking a peep at Smith's brain could tell exactly what Smith was thinking, it would still be the case that Smith alone is *having the experience;* and it is the having of the experience that is private, not the *knowledge* that Smith is having it.

It is not easy to see how the identity theory can convincingly meet this objection. Until it does, we must conclude that it does not provide a satisfactory account of the mental–physical relationship. The analogy that it presents with *other* cases of identity is more convincing than the conclusion that the mental and the physical are identical.

When we say the Morning Star and the Evening Star are identical, we mean that both names refer to one physical object at different times in different places. When we say that the president and the commander-in-chief of the armed forces are identical, we mean that both roles are assigned, by law, to the same person. What do we mean in the case of the Identity Theory? Do we mean (1) that certain *brain states are mental,* that they can be directly known by introspection, that someone without the slightest training in neurology can know without observation that certain incredibly complex events are going on in his infero-temporal cortex? Do we mean (2) that *mental events are physical,* that the thought that today is a holiday, for example, has a shape, a size, a charge, or a color, that it can be photographed, or perhaps smelled? Both of these interpretations seem most paradoxical.[17]

[16] J. J. C. Smart *op. cit.,* p. 152.

[17] Jerome Shaffer, "Recent Work on the Mind–Body Problem," *American Philosophical Quarterly,* II (1965), p. 94.

C. The Self, Personal Identity, and Immortality

We have now discussed the distinction between mental and physical events, and described some theories about the relation between the two. The terms "mental" and "physical" should now be quite familiar to us, but thus far little has been said about the correlative nouns, "body" and "mind."

The body. In general, physical events occur in the history of physical *things:* when you repaint the table, different events occur in the history of this thing, the table; a description of these events is a description of changes that are occurring in the history of this table. Molecular changes are constantly going on, and they take place in the history of the things of which the molecules are parts. Sometimes the changes are not, strictly speaking, *in* the object: light-waves and sound-waves *emanate* from objects, enabling us to see and hear them, but it is still physical things or objects from which they emanate. There are, however, physical events that do not seem to be part of the history of physical *objects* at all: for example, a flash of lightning, a clap of thunder, a rainbow, disturbances in a magnetic field, cosmic rays. These are still physical events, or phenomena, because they have a definite spatial location and their existence is publicly verifiable; but if you ask, "What is the object in whose history the flash of lightning is an event?" the answer seems to be "None."

But the physical events we are concerned with in the mind–body problem are all events in the history of a physical object, the body. The body is a physical thing, like chairs and trees, occupying space, having mass, etc., like every other physical thing. Physical objects are collections of molecules, and so is an organism, though the molecules constituting it are primarily organic molecules.[18]

What is it that distinguishes the body I call mine from all the other bodies in the world? These features at least: (1) It is the only body I cannot get away from—it is always there whenever I am conscious, and I can never see it walking away in the distance. (2) I can see it, unlike other bodies, only from certain perspectives: I cannot see its face except in a mirror, or the back of its head except in two or more mirrors, and its chest and shoulders (for example) always appear in about the same place in my visual field, at about the same apparent distance. (3) It is the only body of which I have kinesthetic and other somatic sense experiences; of other bodies I can have visual and tactile experiences, but not kinesthetic. (4) Most important, it is the only body I can directly control. I can decide to raise its arm (the arm of the body I call mine), and the arm rises; the act follows upon the decision. I cannot control any other body in this way, but only indirectly via command or physical force. I can also alter the position of things in the physical world,

[18] There are problems about body also: see Douglas C. Long, "The Philosophical Concept of a Human Body," *Philosophical Review*, 1964, pp. 321–37.

as in moving a chess piece from this square to that, but I can move these other things only by moving this body: my influence on the outside world is always by means of this body.

The mind.   Now what of mental events? What of sense-experiences (sight, hearing, smell, and so on), feelings, thoughts, dreams? These all fulfill the requirements—described earlier—for being mental. But to what do *they* belong? The traditional answer seems obvious enough. Just as physical events occur in the history of physical objects (including human bodies), so mental events occur in the history of *minds*. The mind is that in which mental events occur, just as the body is that in which physical events occur. Physical events are parts of the history of physical bodies, and mental events are parts of the history of minds.

But what *is* the mind? On this question there has been no end of disagreement. We use the word "mind" as a noun, and we tend to assume that "for every substantive there is a substance." Thus it is quite natural that throughout the history of philosophy from Plato on, the prevailing view has been that the mind is some kind of substance. The mind is the locus, or center, or owner of thoughts, feelings, sense-experiences, just as the body is the locus of physiological changes. A human being consists of two different substances, a mind and a body, which, however they may be connected (see the various theories above), are as irreducibly different as the kinds of events occurring in each. This view is the *mental-substance* theory of mind.

The self.   According to the mental-substance theory, the human being consists of two separate kinds of thing or substance, a mind and a body; but it is the mind that is the more intimately connected with what I call "myself." I *have* a body—the body whose movements I am able to control to some extent; but the I that does the controlling is not a body but a mind. It is true that we sometimes say "I have a mind," just as we say "I have a body"; but it would be more correct according to this view to say "I *am* a mind," whereas it would be quite mistaken to say "I am a body."

It is true that sometimes, when I am discussing physical characteristics only, I can identify myself with my body: "I am six feet tall" means the same as "My body is six feet tall," and to say "I am six feet tall, but my body is not six feet tall" would be self-contradictory; and the same for "I weigh 150 pounds, but my body does not weigh 150 pounds." But when I say "I am thinking," I am referring to the mind, which thinks, and not my body, which cannot think, though doubtless a body (particularly a brain) is required if I am to do any thinking—the body is a necessary condition for thinking, but it is not what thinks. Similarly, when I believe, wonder, dream, perceive, feel pain and pleasure, and so on, it is not the body that *does* any of these things but the mind; the mind is "my essential self." The body is, at the most, the invariable accompaniment of the mind, and, at the least (in the view of Plato, which was taken up by St. Augustine and the early Christian Fathers), the prison in which the mind is "housed" and to which it is "chained" in this earthly life. According to some the existence of mind without body is only a logical possibility, whereas, according to others, it is actually the case—but of this more presently when we discuss immortality.

What kind of substance is the mind? Since it is not a physical substance like lead or salt, it cannot be seen or touched or even visualized; nor is it a tenuous or ethereal substance like fog or smoke, since these are after all as physical as lead. No, it is non-material, and as such it has no spatial location at all. The mind cannot be in the body, nor can it be in the brain (no one opening a brain could ever discover it). Events occurring in the mind's history are causally connected with events in the brain's history, but this does not imply that the mind is in the brain. This of course does not mean that it is *outside* the brain: it just has no spatial location at all. Anyone who said that it was either inside or outside the brain would be guilty of a category-mistake, just as he would if he attributed spatial location to the number 2.

The nature of this mental substance, then, seems increasingly to be quite mysterious. How could its existence ever be known or verified? What would we say to someone who denied its existence? The mental-substance theory seems indeed to be a kind of substratum theory. We have already seen reason to be suspicious of physical substratum (pp. 351–54), and we could make analogous criticisms of the concept of mental substratum. Indeed, many would allege that we have no such *concept* at all but that what we take for a concept is only a meaningless string of words.

Yet we do not willingly part with the conviction that there must be a mind, an owner-of-experience. We may feel dubious enough about any form of substratum theory, yet we remain convinced that there must be *owners* of all the mental events that occur. My thoughts, my wonderings, my sense-experiences are all connected in that they are a part of the history of *me*, their owner. There can't be just the experiences—there must be an owner to tie the experiences together. Since the body does not have the experiences (although the experiences may be *of* the body), it must be the mind, and there must be as many minds as there are owners-of-experience. We may not like to talk of mind in the sense of "mental substance," but we still want to say that there are such things as minds, and whatever the nature of these may be, they are at least owners of experiences. As the Scottish philosopher Thomas Reid (1710–1796) expressed it,

My personal identity implies the continued existence of that indivisible thing which I call *myself*. Whatever this self may be, it is something which thinks, and deliberates, and resolves, and acts, and suffers. I am not thought, I am not action, I am not feeling; I am something that thinks, and acts, and suffers. My thoughts, and actions, and feelings, change every moment; they have no continued, but a successive, existence; but that *self*, or *I*, to which they belong, is permanent, and has the same relation to all the succeeding thoughts, actions, and feelings which I call mine. Such are the notions that I have of my personal identity.[19]

[19] Thomas Reid, *Essays on the Intellectual Powers of Man* (1785), Essay III, Chapter 4.

Whatever we may think of "mental substances," the words expressed here seem to be eminently sensible: experiences must be distinguished from experiencers, and mental events from the minds that have them.

Nevertheless, there have been opponents of this view. David Hume, who was one of the critics of the doctrine of physical substratum, was also critical of mental substrata; he was in fact skeptical about the ownership-view in any form:

> There are some philosophers who imagine we are every moment intimately conscious of what we call our *self;* that we feel its existence and its continuance in existence. . . . For my part, when I enter most intimately into what I call *myself* I always stumble on some particular perception or other, of heat or cold, light or shade, love or hatred, pain or pleasure. I never can catch *myself* at any time without a perception, and never can observe anything but the perception.[20]

Hume thus gets rid of the mental substratum, which leads to so many puzzling questions, and leaves us with only successive states of consciousness. According to this view, the self is merely a *bundle of experiences:* from birth to death, the experiences occur in temporally successive order, and this whole series constitutes the bundle; there is no self beyond the bundle of experiences, and the bundle simply *is* the whole series of experiences. We may call this the *bundle theory* of the self.

Yet it may seem that Hume, in order to get rid of all unobservable entities, has left us with *Hamlet* without the Prince of Denmark. Here are some questions that can be asked of his view:

1. How can there be thoughts and feelings without owners, without any person or self to have them? No thought occurs without a thinker, and no experience without an experiencer. There are no free-floating thoughts and experiences. But in that case, must there not be a something, *I,* to whom these events belong? Every mental event must in some way or other belong to some individual, some center of consciousness. But in that case the "I" must be more than the collection of mental events themselves.

Hume might well reply that he was not denying the existence of the self but attempting to give an *analysis* of what a self is (just as he was not denying the existence of causality but giving an analysis of causality as we saw in Chapter 5). But can any analysis of the self that does not include specific reference to ownership of experience be satisfactory?

2. There surely is a difference between my experiences and your experiences. But if the self is simply a bundle of experiences, how does one distinguish the ingredients of one bundle from the ingredients of another? What makes this experience that I am now having *mine,* and the one you are now having yours? If, like sticks in various bundles, the experiences could be

[20] David Hume, *Treatise of Human Nature,* Book I, Part 4, Chapter 6.

mixed up, how in sorting them into their proper bundles could you tell which experiences belonged in which bundle? If the ownership-thesis is abandoned, what is the *principle of individuation* by means of which one could tell which experiences belonged in which bundle?

3. Hume's own analysis seems to be self-contradictory. He writes, "I never catch myself . . ." but what or whom does the word "I" refer to? An owner of experiences? But Hume has already ruled this out. He is aware only of certain states of consciousness (Hume calls them "perceptions" in this passage) but not of the *self* that has them. But what then makes them his? That they occur in a certain temporal succession? But so do yours and mine. Whose states of consciousness does he find? No one's, presumably—just states of consciousness. But how is this possible? Surely it is *his own* experiences that he finds. In that case, however, we seem to be driven back to the view that the "I" is something more than the series of states of consciousness.

4. We might ask, further, whether it is even true that I am not aware of *myself* as a continuing entity beyond the series of experiences. When I have an experience, am I aware only of the experience or also of myself as the owner or "haver" of the experience? One might say, against Hume, that I don't experience it just as an experience but as *my* experience. Can't the ownership of the experience be a part of the total experience? And thus we seem to be forced back to the conditions of selfhood stated by Reid in the earlier quotation.

Yet we remain troubled. If the mind is not a mental substance (and what is that?), then what is it? If it means simply ownership or possession of experiences, what does *that* mean?

Possession . . . is essentially a social concept, and sometimes a strictly legal one. Something counts as one of my possessions by virtue of my title to it, and this is something conferred by men, in accordance with conventions and laws fabricated by men themselves. Thus does a field or a building count as one of my possessions.[21]

But it is not in this way that I own or possess my experiences, for this possession does not arise from human conventions or laws, and cannot be changed by conventions or laws. Perhaps then the use of "ownership" or "possession" is nothing but a bad metaphor, and should be dropped. But what then *is* the relation of myself to my experiences? One might allege that it is not like any other relation there is; but this, if true, is not very helpful, for it leaves the questions raised about it just where they were. Indeed, the question of the nature of the self and its relation to its experiences is one of the most perplexing in philosophy. The question "What am I?" sounds simple enough until we go about trying to answer it. When we do, we encounter nothing but difficulties and perplexities.

[21] Richard Taylor, *Metaphysics*, p. 11.

Personal identity. If we seem to be baffled at every turn in trying to answer the question "What is the self?" we may be able to make more headway if we change the focus of the question somewhat and ask instead "Under what conditions is X the *same* self, or the same person, as before?" That is, what mental or physical changes can occur in Mr. X without his ceasing to be Mr. X? We already examined this question when the X was a physical thing, such as a table or a car (pp. 38, 63); let us now examine it in a far more complex case, when the X is a human being.

We might first suggest a straightforward physical criterion, the possession of *the same body*. A person's body can change a great deal and still be the same body: you have the same body as you did when you were a child, but it is now much larger, and so different in general appearance that someone who had not seen you since you were three years old would probably not recognize you today. Still we say, "It's the same person, all right," and at least a part of what we mean by this seems to be that it is the same physical body that you had then, however much it may have grown or changed. This one human body has continuously existed during the entire interval. If someone had followed you around day and night with a motion-picture camera, the recorded film would have been that of one continuously existing body. There was not a split second in that entire time-interval during which this body did not exist, although some changes were doubtless occurring in it at every moment. And so one might say: It's the same person as long as it's the same body. No matter what mental characteristics may change, it's still you as long as it's the same continuously existing physical body. You may suffer from total amnesia and not recognize anyone ever again or even know your own name, but it's still you, because the same body continues to exist. Even if you suffer a sudden personality-change, and turn from a thief into a saint without apparent cause, we will say it's the same person: we may say "How he's changed!" but it is still the same *he* that has undergone the change, since the same body continues to exist. (We may, indeed, view him with sadness as he lies on his hospital bed, and say, "He isn't the same person any more," but this usage is clearly figurative. We already presuppose that he *is* the same person when we say that *he* isn't the same person. He isn't the same person as himself? What we mean, literally, is that he is very much changed—which is quite compatible with being the same person.)

Let us turn, however, from the actual to the logically possible. Here is Mr. Smith, whom we all know. Suddenly, before our eyes, mysterious physical changes start to occur in him; and just to be sure they are really occurring we use our motion-picture camera again. Smith's limbs begin to change their size and their spatial relations to one another, his face undergoes a swift transformation, hair sprouts all over him, and in a minute we see before us not a human body but a chattering monkey. In other respects, however, there is no change: he talks to us as before, tells us how shocked he is at his sudden transformation, and just to let us know that he's still the same person he tells us things he remembers about his life prior to his transformation, and shows that he has an excellent memory of his pre-monkey state; indeed, aside from an understandable trauma at his sudden transformation, his personality-traits remain as before. Would we not say that it's still Smith who, though now a monkey (more accurately: though now having the body of a monkey), still exists, albeit in a transformed state? Precisely this sort of thing happens in Franz Kafka's story *The Metamorphosis,* in which a human being changes into a beetle and yet remains the same person he was, with memories of his previous state untouched and his habits and personality-traits unchanged. (If a human being had simply been *replaced* by a beetle, his state would not have been so terrifying: he would have died and never known the difference; the terrible fact is that it is still the same person, though now in—or occupying, or possessing, or animating—the body of a beetle.) The transformation described is, so far as we know, empirically impossible and contrary to all biological laws; but it is logically possible, and in fact it is easily imagined. Our question remains: If this happened, wouldn't we still say "Here is the same person"?

Yet we cannot say it is the same body: It was originally a human body, and now it is the body of a monkey (or a beetle). Thus our original criterion, having the same body, is not fulfilled. Nevertheless there is a *physical continuity* between the earlier and later state: the motion-picture camera would record all the biological transformation, without one moment during which no organism at all existed. Nothing suddenly popped out of existence, only to be replaced a moment later by something else. Our original criterion, then, must be liberalized somewhat: there must be physical continuity, but not necessarily a continuity of the same body. The point at which we would say "It's no longer the same body" is vague, as in the case of "the same table" and "the same train," (pp. 38–39). The *degree* of difference and the *suddenness* of the transformation would both be criteria here.

Now let us consider a further logical possibility. Couldn't a person successively inhabit different bodies, like the hero of the motion picture *Here Comes Mr. Jordan* who begins as a prizefighter, dies at a nonpreordained time owing to some mixup in the files of heaven, and then occupies the body of an industrialist, with his memory and personality-traits intact? Or consider this logical possibility:[22] Professor Smith attends a convention in New York and there suddenly disappears from everyone's view; at that very moment he turns up in the midst of a convention in Australia. New Yorkers are as mystified by his sudden disappearance as Australians are by his sudden appearance there. Our first hypothesis, strange as it is, would probably be that a person has mysteriously disappeared in New York and another one mysteriously appeared in Australia. But after checking one another's date, the New Yorkers and the Australians might conclude that the one

[22] Taken from John Hick, "Theology Today," in *Body, Mind, and Death,* ed. Antony Flew (New York: The Macmillan Company, 1964), pp. 271–72.

who disappeared and the one who appeared are really *the same person:* both had the same clothing, the same birthmarks, the same fingerprints, the same manuscript in their hands, the same notes and doodles on the paper in their pocket, and so on. What would clinch the matter is that, though Smith had no memory of traveling from one place to another and was as mystified as anyone else by the sudden switch in locations, he clearly remembered being in New York up to the moment of his disappearance and could recite the whole of his life history. On the basis of such evidence we would surely say that the person who disappeared in New York was the same person who appeared on Australia.

But in this case the physical continuity has been broken: there would be a slight break in the motion-picture record. If he appeared in Australia one second after disappearing in New York, there would be a one-second gap in the record even if a motion-picture camera happened to be present and in use at the appropriate location in Australia. If he appeared in Australia at the very instant he disappeared in New York, there would be a continuity break in the fact that, unlike any physical body ever known, he got from one place to another without having traversed the space between. Yet in spite of this we would still probably say that it was the same person. If he returned to New York, rejoined his family, and went on living as before, could we have any doubt of it? What is it that would make us so sure? It is partly the similarity of the body, but this is not decisive because we would say it was the same person on the basis of the other evidence even if many bodily characteristics had changed; it is mainly the continuity of his states of consciousness, so far as we could determine these from hearing him talk and recite memories and from watching his behavior with care—the same tone of voice, the same uh's and ah's, the same manifestations of selective generosity combined with ill-concealed self-centeredness, and so on; nothing is different except the one sudden shift in the location of his body.

Let us try one more case. Professor Smith dies in New York, many people attend the funeral and view the body in its casket, and the body is buried. But at the moment of his death a body just like the one he had prior to his death suddenly appears in Australia—a body so much like the one in New York that anyone who knew him there would recognize him in Australia and say "It's the same person." The personality-traits and memories are the same, as in the previous case. This example provides more of a conceptual jolt than the previous one, for there are now two bodies instead of one—the dead one in New York, the live one in Australia—and we might wonder, "Which body is Smith's? Or does he have two bodies?" But in spite of this jolt, we would soon came to identify this live person in Australia as the same person who died in New York, and would speak of this live body as "Professor Smith's new body." As those who knew him before came to see him now, in the new body, and conversed with him exactly as they had in New York, they would not doubt that this was really Professor Smith. And even if they were skeptical because of the strangeness of the case, Professor Smith himself would know, would he not? If he remembered being in New York and having a heart attack there, would he not know that he had survived the death of his body in New York?

The discussion thus far has shown that, though we take it as a criterion of personal identity in ordinary life, bodily continuity is not the *only* criterion. Every believer in immortality must deny that it is the only criterion, for he knows that the body disintegrates in the grave yet believes that the *person* continues to exist, either with a new body or without any body at all. The believer in immortality holds that consciousness survives after the body dies; even disbelievers in immortality do not deny that consciousness-surviving-bodily-death is logically possible. More often this point is expressed by saying that the *soul* survives—but what is this supposed to mean, if not simply that consciousness survives? Is the soul a non-material substance of some sort? We can avoid that quicksand of confusions by saying simply that (at least as a logical possibility) *consciousness* survives.

But what ensures that the consciousness that survives is the consciousness *of the same person?* Why not just say that one bit of consciousness was snuffed out when the body died, and another bit of consciousness suddenly arose thereafter, without its being the consciousness of the same person? The fact of consciousness itself does not provide the link, for the two might be quite different, with no evidence that they are both conscious states of the same person. What then does provide the link? One obvious answer is *memory*. If a person survives his death, he must have some memory of his state before death. The memory would not have to be complete, but if there was *no* memory at all of his previous state, what would entitle anyone, including the alleged survivor himself, to say that the being who exists now and the one who died earlier are the same person? It seems that without some memory of the former state, there would be no reason for calling this the same person.

Persons who claim to be a reincarnation of someone else run into this difficulty without usually being aware of it. "In my previous incarnation I was Johann Sebastian Bach!" exclaims a music student. He knows well enough that Bach's body is no more, and he does not claim to have any of Bach's memories. He has to take classes in harmony and counterpoint with the other music students, and the enormous musical skill that "he" had as Bach is of no use to him now. What good is it to him now, we might ask, that he was once Bach? In fact, what does it mean to say that he *was* once Bach? What would be the difference between saying (1) that he was once Bach and (2) that Bach died and now he, the student, lives? The second formulation is the one we would all use; the first would mislead people into thinking that Bach's genius was continuing in him, that he had Bach's creative talents (not only talents *like* Bach's, but the very same ones—that is, those of the very same person), and so on. Since no such new and surprising phenomenon has occurred, it is preferable to describe the situation in the familiar and ordinary way, since it is indistinguishable from the situation we already describe in this way. Such reincarnation-hypotheses contain no "difference that makes a difference."

What progress have we made thus far in our search for criteria of personal identity? (1) In daily life we use the criterion of bodily continuity. Here it does not matter whether one's memories are totally destroyed, or how many abrupt personality-changes there may be; there is bodily continuity, and as long as this condition is met, we say that the changes are all occurring to the same person. (2) But once we start thinking about post-mortem existence, there is no longer a body to establish the continuity: the body is dead in the grave, or burnt to ashes, or eaten by sharks. What then is left? We have suggested that even if consciousness in some way survives bodily death, it could not, in the absence of *memory*, be called consciousness of the same person; the person would have to remember his existence prior .o his bodily death. It might seem as if we could let the matter rest here. But memory will prove troublesome if it is the *only* criterion. In the absence of a body, memory is *necessary,* but is it alone *sufficient?* We may well doubt that it is:

1. If memory is not only necessary but sufficient, we get the curious result

. . . that a man may be, and at the same time not be, the person that did a particular action. Suppose a brave officer to have been flogged when a boy at school for robbing an orchard, to have taken a standard from the enemy in his first campaign, and to have been made a general in advanced life; suppose, also, which must be admitted to be possible, that, when he took the standard, he was conscious of his having been flogged at school, and that, when made a general, he was conscious of his taking the standard, but had absolutely lost the consciousness of his flogging. These things being supposed, it follows . . . that he who was flogged at school is the same person who took the standard, and that he who took the standard is the same person who was made a general. Whence it follows, if there be any truth in logic, that the general is the same person with him who was flogged at school. But the general's consciousness does not reach so far back as his flogging; therefore . . . he is not the person who was flogged. Therefore the general is, and at the same time is not, the same person with him who was flogged at school.[23]

As long as we have bodily continuity of some kind, the situation Reid depicts need not trouble us: bodily continuity assures the continued existence of the same person even if there are lapses in memory. But the situation becomes most troublesome when everything is made to hinge upon memory alone. If memory alone is made to insure personal identity, it seems that the memory-experiences will have to be continuous and infallible—something we need not insist on in bodily life, where we still have one criterion to spare, but which we cannot do without when memory becomes the one slender reed upon which personal identity rests.

[23] Thomas Reid, *Essays on the Intellectual Powers of Man* (1785), Essay VI, Chapter 5.

2. Memory cannot occur in isolation. Memory presupposes someone to do the remembering—an enduring *self*. The memory-experiences must be some*one*'s experiences. And thus we are led back to the question "What is the self?" Memory-experiences must refer to previous occurrences in the history of the same self—and thus memory, as a criterion of personal identity, presupposes a self, or haver of experiences. The problem of the self is with us once again, with all its perplexities.

3. "Memory itself, by tying present experiences to past ones, provides the *experience* of personal identity," we may say. At any rate, without it there would be no such experience. But here is a consideration so simple that it may surprise us: doesn't there have to *be* personal identity before there can be *experience* of personal identity?

But though consciousness of what is past does thus ascertain our personal identity *to ourselves,* yet to say, that it *makes* personal identity, or is necessary to our *being* the same persons, is to say, that a person has not existed a single moment, nor done one action, but what he can remember; indeed none but what he reflects upon. And one should really think it self-evident, that *consciousness of personal identity presupposes, and therefore cannot constitute, personal identity;* any more than knowledge, in any other case, can constitute truth, which it presupposes.[24]

All these difficulties came upon us the moment we started to ask questions about personal identity in a post-mortem existence. It is time, then, that we asked a few questions about this form of existence.

Immortality. Is it possible for mind to exist without body? If this means "Is it *logically* possible?" most philosophers would doubtless reply in the affirmative. Some, however, would not, and we shall consider their reasons for this later in this section. First, however, let us assume the logical possibility and see where it takes us. Let us try to imagine ourselves dying and then waking up in an entirely different environment, surrounded, let us say, by angelic hosts playing harps. *If* you died and then awoke again, you would know that you had survived the death of your body. (If you didn't awake again, then you would never know that you had *not* survived. This was one of our problems with the testability criterion: if true, the proposition can be verified, but if false, it cannot.)

Would we have to wait until dying to know? It would, indeed, provide the decisive test, but there might be indirect evidence available to us even now to lend some probability to the view that others have survived their bodily deaths. Suppose that before your grandfather died he said to you, "After I die, if my consciousness survives I'll try to get into contact with you. I'll sound middle C three times on the living-room piano the day after my funeral, and if I can I'll speak a few words." You are skeptical, but you sit in the living-room the day after the funeral, with other observers and tape-

---

[24] Bishop Joseph Butler, "Of Personal Identity," in *Works,* I, as quoted in Antony Flew (ed.), *Body, Mind, and Death,* p. 167. Italics mine.

recorders ready. Suddenly you hear middle C sounded on the piano three times; the others hear it too, and it is recorded on the tape. Then you hear a voice that is unmistakably your grandfather's: if it is not his, it is exactly like it. Moreover, he says things to you that you said to him some months ago and that you never told to anyone else. If this occurred—plus as many other bits of evidence as one might care to add—would it not be at least a plausible hypothesis that your grandfather was still alive, even though you could no longer see or touch him? If he predicted when he would talk to you next, and he (or the voice) always fulfilled the prediction, could you still say that this series of events was a run of coincidences, or did not constitute even the slightest evidence of your grandfather's continued existence? Some evidence of this kind has actually been presented, and although the results of it are inconclusive and many are quite skeptical of it, it is worth considering.[25] In any case, the *failure* of such events to occur—for example, the failure of your grandfather to keep his prediction—would not disprove immortality: he might still exist but be unable to communicate with you, or unwilling to do so, etc.

In what way might a person survive his bodily death? He might live in another body, or he might lead an entirely disembodied existence. Let us examine both these possibilities.

1. Life in another body. When they attempt to picture a person's post-mortem existence, most religious traditions imagine the person as having a new and resurrected body. There is disagreement about what term would be most appropriate here: possessing another body? inhabiting another body? animating another body? Or does the dead person simply have his mental states causally related to the physical states of another body? In any event when we try to imagine people now dead continuing to exist, we usually imagine them as having bodies similar to the ones they had when we knew them, as well as memory, intelligence, and other features sufficiently similar to the ones they had in this life for them to be recognizable by others as the same person. The widow who wants to be reunited with her dead husband imagines him as being very much as he was before he died: doing similar things, looking as he did (if his face and form were very different she might not care for him any more), caring for her and showing affection, sitting at the dinner table, and so on. It is in this way that she wants to rejoin him, not as a disembodied spirit or as having a body so different from the one she knew that she could not recognize him. Of course there would be problems: if he was a cripple in this world, would he still be one in a better world? What if he

---

[25] See, for example, C. D. Broad, *Human Personality and the Possibility of Its Survival* (1955), and also his *Lectures on Psychical Research* (New York: Humanities Press, 1962); C. J. Ducasse, *Nature, Mind, and Death*, chapters 20 and 21, and, by the same author, *A Critical Examination of the Belief in a Life after Death* (Springfield, Ill.: Charles C Thomas, Publisher, 1960); Gardner Murphy, "An Outline of Survival Evidence," *Journal of the American Society for Psychical Research*, 1945; R. H. Thouless, "The Empirical Evidence for Survival," same journal, 1960; H. H. Price, "Survival and the Idea of 'Another World,'" *Proceedings of the Society for Psychical Research*, 1953.

was irritable, or alcoholically inclined: would he now lack these tendencies? Would he be without fault (if that can be imagined), even the faults she loved him for? Would he still belong to the male sex? How much of the man she loved would still exist? This might well make some difference in her attitude toward him. Presumably he would no longer be the family provider, since the need for such activity would no longer exist; but this too might make a considerable difference in her attitude: one kind of need for him would be gone. Change enough characteristics, and she might not even care to rejoin him: what she wants is a continuation—with improvements, of course—of her present existence with him. If this would include having and raising children, it would present further problems; nor, presumably, would the children appear *as* children in an afterlife, if they grew to maturity in this life.

Moreover, if he has a *new* body, presumably that body will also have a brain, and his personality in his new form would depend to a very large extent on the nature of this brain—whether he was quick-witted or slow, whether he was lethargic or mercurial, and so on. Would he still have that mole on his cheek? Would he still prefer his steak rare? Would he still have that stomach disorder, for which she had to prepare a special diet? Would he still be cheerful yet sometimes depressed? (This would depend on things like the supply of oxygen reaching his brain-cells.) Would he have the body of a man of a certain age, say the age at which he died, and remain forever at this age? Or would his new body grow older and die in turn, to be replaced perhaps by still another? Most people have not made at all clear to themselves what kind of immortality they have in mind, even when they fix all their hopes on the truth of this hypothesis.

2. Disembodied existence. Let us try now to imagine an entirely disembodied existence—consciousness continuing entirely in the absence of a body. You have no physical body, but you still think thoughts, have feelings and memories, even sense-experiences (if you like) of seeing, hearing, etc., but (since you lack a body) *without* the sense-organs that in this life are the empirically necessary condition of having these experiences. Let us try to imagine what it would be like, even in this present life, to awaken and find that you no longer have a body. You go to bed one night, turn out the light, go to sleep and then wake up some hours later to see the sunlight streaming in the window, the clock pointing to eight, the mirror near the foot of the bed. You see the bed, but you do not see your own body in it—in fact, you see the sheets directly under the places where you thought your limbs were. Startled, you look into the mirror, but your face and body are not visible there either; you see reflected there the entire uninterrupted expanse of the headboard behind you. "Have I become invisible?" you ask yourself; and thinking of H. G. Wells's invisible man, who could not be seen but could still be touched, you try to touch yourself, but there is nothing there to be touched any more than to be seen. A person coming into the room would not be able to see you or touch you: he would not know you existed unless you could utter sounds (though you have no organ to utter them with) or communicate with him in some other way. He could run his hands over the entire bed without ever coming in contact with a body, visible or invisible. You are now thoroughly alarmed at the idea that no one will know you exist. You try to walk toward the mirror, but of course you have no feet. Nevertheless you find the objects near the mirror increasing in apparent size and the objects behind you apparently becoming smaller, just *as if* you were walking toward the mirror: all the experiences are the same except that of seeing and touching your body. You might even have the experience of bodily strain and effort, kinesthetic experiences of balance and uprightness, etc., without actually having a body, which is (empirically speaking, in the world we now know) a prerequisite for having the experiences.

Now, it may be thought, we have imagined a clear case of disembodied existence. But have we? There are some implicit references to body even in this brief description. You see—with eyes? No, you have no eyes, since you have no body. But we may let that pass, as long as you have experiences such as you *would* ordinarily have by means of eyes. But if you *look* in one direction and then in another, how do you do this? By turning your head? But you have no head to turn. Let us say that you have the experience you *would* ordinarily get by turning your head. This may not pass muster, but let us try the next step. You find that you can't touch your body because no body is there, just the bed and the covers. How do you find this out? Do you reach out with your fingers to touch the bed? But you have no fingers, since you have no body. What would you touch (or try to touch) with? You move, or seem to move, toward the mirror—but what moves? Not your body, since you have none. Nevertheless things seem to get larger in front of you and smaller behind you, as if you were moving. In front of and behind what? Your body? But once again you have none. So how is this apparent motion to be conceived?

Every step along the way is riddled with difficulties. It is not just that we are accustomed to think of people as having bodies and can't get out of the habit. This makes things more difficult, but it is only part of the story. The fact is that you can't imagine doing things like looking in a different direction without turning your head, which is usually the result of a decision to do this—and of course you can't turn your head if you have no head to turn; and if you *decide* to turn your head, you can't carry out this decision in the absence of a head, so how can the fact that you see now the mirror and now the window be the result of your decision? There seem to be many difficulties, not merely technical but logical, constantly embedded in the attempted description.

There is no necessary, conceptual, connection between the experience we call "seeing" and the processes that physiologists tell us happen in the eye and brain; the statement "James can still see, although his optic centers are destroyed," is very unlikely on inductive grounds but perfectly intelligible—after all, people used the word "see" long before they had any idea of things happening in the optic centers of the brain. It therefore appears to be clearly conceivable that seeing and other "sensuous" experiences might go on continuously even after the death of the organism with which they are now associated, and that the inductive reasons for doubting whether this ever happens might be outweighed by the evidence of Psychical Research.

I think it is an important conceptual inquiry to consider whether *really* disembodied seeing, hearing, pain, hunger, emotion, etc., are so clearly intelligible as is supposed in this common philosophical point of view. . . .

"The verb 'to see' has its meaning for me because I *do* see—I have that experience!" Nonsense. As well suppose that I can come to know what a minus quantity is by setting out to lose weight. What shows a man to have the concept *seeing* is not merely that he sees, but that he can take an intelligent part in our everyday use of the word "seeing." Our concept of sight has its life only in connection with a whole set of other concepts, some of them relating to the physical characteristics of visible objects, others relating to the behavior of people who see things. (I express exercise of this concept in such utterances as, "I can't see, it's too far off—now it's coming into view!" "He couldn't see me, he didn't look round," "I caught his eye," etc., etc.) It would be merely silly to be frightened off admitting this by the bogy of behaviorism; you can very well admit it without also thinking that "seeing" stands for a kind of behavior. . . .

To have the concept *seeing* is not even primarily a matter of being able to spot instances of a characteristic repeatedly given in my ("inner-sense") experiences; *no* concept is primarily a recognitional capacity. And the exercise of one concept is intertwined with the exercise of others; as with a spider's web, some connections may be broken with impunity; but if you break enough the whole web collapses—the concept becomes unusable. Just such a collapse happens, I believe, when we try to think of seeing, hearing, pain, emotion, etc., going on independently of a body.[26]

If this is true—and the case here presented is merely a strong one—then it *is* after all logically impossible for minds to exist without bodies. This does not, of course, rescue the identity theory from the objections that have been brought against it: in no sense does it "reduce" mental events to physical any more than color and shape are reduced to one another by the fact that the first never occurs without the second. If the objection quoted is sound, the identity theory may still be mistaken, but any theory of disembodied existence can no longer be accepted.

Exercises

1. In each of the following sentences, certain mental events or operations are described through the use of physical models. Substitute for the figurative

[26] P. T. Geach, *Mental Acts: Their Content and Their Objects* (London: Routledge & Kegan Paul, Ltd.), pp. 112–13.

expression a literal expression, without (as far as possible) changing the intended meaning of the sentence.

 a. You didn't really see it—it's all in your mind.

 b. She has too many silly ideas in her head.

 c. This strange idea kept cropping up in the back of her mind.

 d. She was a scatterbrain—her thoughts just went flitting this way and that through her mind.

 e. Having so many responsibilities put too much pressure on his mind.

 f. He changes his mind so frequently that no one knows what he really believes.

 2. Evaluate each of the following assertions:

 a. Mental events are nothing but brain events.

 b. According to psychophysical parallelism, mind exerts no influence on matter.

 c. The brain secretes thought as the liver secretes bile.

 d. What I see is always something going on in my own brain.

 e. Mental events and physical events are logically interconnected.

 f. If mental telepathy is a fact, I can experience your pain directly.

 g. If mental telepathy is fact, one's experiences are not really private, for other people can share them.

 h. Mental events are not really private even now (without telepathy), since I can share your experiences (such as your suffering) by being with you and empathizing with you.

 i. Some mental events *are* locatable in physical space; for example, I have a pain in my finger, or my tooth, or my leg (I can even have a pain in an amputated leg).

 j. It is true that no surgeon, on opening someone's brain, has ever found any mental events, but perhaps that's because he has never looked hard enough.

 3. According to Descartes (*Traité des passions de l'âme*, p. 34 ff.), an interactionist, the point of contact between mind and body lies in the pineal gland of the brain, by which physical stimuli cause states of consciousness and volitions are carried into action. "Let us . . . conceive of the soul as having her chief seat in the little gland which is in the middle of the brain, whence she radiates to all the rest of the body by means of the spirits, the nerves, and even the blood, which, participating in the impressions of the spirits, can carry them through the arteries to all the members . . ." Evaluate this view.

 4. "It is not the mind that survives death, it is the *soul* which survives death." What could be meant by "soul" if the word is not synonymous with "mind"? Is the soul a substance? a mental substance? Would a theory of the soul be different (and if so, how) from a theory of the mind?

 5. Do you consider it logically possible, and why,

 a. for one mind to affect another mind without the intermediary of matter?

 b. for a mind to exist without a body?

 c. for a mind to touch a body?

 d. for one person to have two bodies?

 e. for one person to have two minds?

 f. for one mind to control two bodies directly? (e.g. by willing to raise its arm)

 g. for one body to be controlled by two minds?

In each case, try first to describe a situation which would count as an instance of the kind of thing mentioned.

6. Do you consider the hypothesis of life after death to be compatible with the testability criterion of meaning? First read A. J. Ayer, *Language, Truth, and Logic*, p. 198, for a negative answer to this question; then, for an affirmative answer, see Moritz Schlick, "Meaning and Verification," and Virgil C. Aldrich, "Schlick and Ayer on Immortality," both in H. Feigl and W. Sellars, *Readings in Philosophical Analysis* (New York: Appleton-Century-Crofts, 1949).

7. Is it logically possible to witness one's own funeral? (See two articles on this by Antony Flew: "Can a Man Witness His Own Funeral?" *Hibbert Journal*, 1956; and "Sense and Survival," *The Humanist* (London), 1960.

8. What would you say about personal identity if the existence of the body was *intermittent?* Two minutes out of every three there is a body—you see it moving and hear words come from its lips—and the other minute there is nothing there at all: nothing that can be seen, touched, photographed, X-rayed, nothing fulfilling any of the tests for a physical object. What meaning (if any) would you attach to the hypothesis that he existed during the one-minute intervals? What (if anything) would entitle us to say that what reappeared after the one-minute disappearance each time was *the same* person as the one who existed before the disappearance? (Would he have to reappear in the same place, or have the same physical characteristics that he had prior to his disappearance? By what criteria would you decide whether it's "really the same person"?)

9. Which of the following ways of speaking would you find preferable, and why?

"I am a mind" or "I have a mind"? "I am a body" or "I have a body"? Can you give some basis for the preference? Which do you consider preferable, "I am a mind which has or is associated with a body" or "I am a body which has or is associated with a mind" or "I am a person who has a mind and a body" or "I am a person who is both a mind and a body"—or some other formulation?

10. Would you still say "It's the same person" if

    a. he loses his memory, completely and permanently, but his body persists?

    b. he turns into a monkey, but retains his memories as a human being?

    c. he turns into a monkey, and also loses his memories as a human being?

    d. his body disintegrates before your eyes, but his voice (or one that sounds exactly like his) continues to speak?

    e. his body disappears before our eyes, returning (or another body just like it) ten years later, complete with the man's memories and personality-traits?

11. If you opened someone's body and instead of finding blood, muscles, and bones, you found wires and electrical circuits, would you be entitled to say that the body was a robot or automaton incapable of thinking or feeling? If so, what would entitle you to say this? (If someone opened *your* body and found wires and circuits instead of blood and muscles, would he be entitled to say that you had no thoughts or feelings?)

12. Defend one of the following views: (a) that you can know that others have pains and can give evidence; (b) that you can have well-founded belief that others have pains, but belief short of knowledge; (c) that you do not have even well-founded belief in this matter.

Selected Readings for Chapter 6

The problem of universals:

Aaron, R. I., *The Problem of Universals.* Oxford: Clarendon Press, 1952.

Blanshard, Brand, *Reason and Analysis.* LaSalle, Ill.: Open Court Publishing Co., 1962.

Bochenski, J. M., Alonzo Church and Nelson Goodman, *The Problem of Universals.* South Bend, Ind.: University of Notre Dame Press.

Brandt, Richard, "The Languages of Realism and Nominalism," *Philosophy and Phenomenological Research,* 17 (1956-1957).

Locke, John, *Essay Concerning Human Understanding.* Book III. Many editions.

Pap, Arthur, *Elements of Analytic Philosophy.* New York: The Macmillan Company, 1949. Chapter 4.

Pears, David, "Universals," *Philosophical Quarterly,* 1950-1951.

Plato, *Parmenides; Phaedo.* Many editions.

Price, H. H., *Thinking and Experience.* London: Hutchinson & Co. (Publishers), Ltd., 1953. Chapter 1.

Quine, Willard V., *Word and Object.* New York: John Wiley & Sons, Inc., 1960.

Rand, Ayn, "The Objectivist Theory of Knowledge," *The Objectivist,* July-Dec. 1966.

Russell, Bertrand, *The Problems of Philosophy.* London: Oxford University Press, 1912. Chapters 9 and 10.

Ryle, Gilbert, "Abstractions," *Dialogue,* June-July 1962.

Woozley, A. D., *Theory of Knowledge.* London: Hutchinson & Co. (Publishers), Ltd., 1949. Chapter 4.

Matter and Life:

Bergson, Henri, *Creative Evolution.* London: Macmillan & Co., Ltd., 1911.

Broad, C. D., *The Mind and Its Place in Nature.* London: Routledge & Kegan Paul, Ltd., 1925. Chapter 2.

Cohen, Morris R., *Reason and Nature.* New York: Harcourt, Brace & World, Inc., 1931. Book 2, Chapter 3.

Drake, Durant, *Invitation to Philosophy.* Boston: Houghton Mifflin Company, 1933. Chapter 18.

Driesch, Hans, *The History and Theory of Vitalism.* New York: The Macmillan Company, 1914.

Haldane, John Scott, *Materialism.* London: Hodder & Stoughton, Ltd., 1932.

————, *Mechanism, Life, and Personality.* New York: E. P. Dutton & Co., Inc., 1923.

McDougall, William, *Modern Materialism and Emergent Evolution.* London: Methuen & Co., Ltd., 1929.

Meehl, Paul and Wilfrid Sellars, "The Concept of Emergence," in *Minnesota Studies in the Philosophy of Science,* Vol. 1. Minneapolis: University of Minnesota Press, 1956.

Needham, D., *Man a Machine*. London: Routledge & Kegan Paul, Ltd., 1926. Psyche Miniatures.

Needham, Joseph, *Order and Life*. New Haven, Conn.: Yale University Press, 1936.

Rignano, Eugenio, *Man Not a Machine*. London: Routledge & Kegan Paul, Ltd., 1926. Psyche Miniatures.

Schubert-Soldern, Rainer, *Mechanism and Vitalism*. South Bend, Ind.: Notre Dame University Press, 1962.

Simpson, George G., *The Meaning of Evolution*. New York: New American Library, 1951. Mentor Books paperback.

Scriven, Michael, *Primary Philosophy*. New York: McGraw-Hill Book Company, 1966. Chapter 5.

Woodger, J. H., *Biological Principles*. New York: Humanities Press, 1966.

Mind and Body:

Anderson, A. R. (ed.), *Minds and Machines*. Englewood Cliffs, N. J.: Prentice-Hall, Inc., 1964. Paperback.

Aune, Bruce, "The Problem of Other Minds," *Philosophical Review*, 1961.

Ayer, Alfred J., "One's Knowledge of Other Minds," in *Philosophical Essays*. London: Macmillan & Co., Ltd., 1955.

————, "Privacy," *Proceedings of the British Academy*, 1959. Reprinted in *The Concept of a Person and Other Essays*. London: Macmillan & Co., Ltd., 1964.

Blanshard, Brand, *The Nature of Thought*, Vol. 1. London: George Allen & Unwin, Ltd., 1939.

Brain, W. Russell, *Mind, Perception, and Science*. Oxford: B. H. Blackwell, Ltd., 1951.

Broad, C. D., *The Mind and Its Place in Nature*. London: Routledge & Kegan Paul, Ltd., 1925.

Descartes, René, *Meditations*, 1621. Many editions.

Ducasse, Curt J., *Nature, Mind, and Death*. LaSalle, Ill.: Open Court Publishing Co., 1951. Parts 3 and 4.

Ewing, Alfred C., "Professor Ryle's Attack on Dualism," *Proceedings of the Aristotelian Society*, 1952–3. Reprinted in H. D. Lewis (ed.), *Clarity Is Not Enough*. London: George Allen & Unwin, 1963.

————, *The Fundamental Questions of Philosophy*. New York: Crowell-Collier & Macmillan, Inc., 1962. Paperback.

Feigl, Herbert, "The Mental and the Physical," in *Minnesota Studies in the Philosophy of Science*, Vol. 2, ed. H. Feigl and M. Scriven. Minneapolis: University of Minnesota Press, 1957.

Feyerabend, H., and Grover Maxwell (eds.), *Mind, Matter, and Method*. Minneapolis: University of Minnesota Press, 1966.

Flew, Antony (ed.), *Body, Mind, and Death*. Crowell-Collier & Macmillan, Inc., 1962.

————, "Can a Man Witness His Own Funeral?" *Hibbert Journal*, 1956.

Fullerton, G. S., *A System of Metaphysics*. New York: The Macmillan Company, 1904. Part 3.

424   SOME METAPHYSICAL PROBLEMS

Laslett, Peter (ed.), *The Physical Basis of Mind*. Oxford: B. H. Blackwell, Ltd., 1951.

Lewis, H. D., "Mind and Body," in *Clarity Is Not Enough*. London: George Allen & Unwin, Ltd., 1963.

Reeves, J. W. (ed.), *Body and Mind in Western Thought*. Baltimore: Penguin Books, Inc., 1958. Paperback.

Ryle, Gilbert, *The Concept of Mind*. London: Hutchinson & Co. (Publishers), Ltd., 1949.

Scriven, Michael, "A Study of Radical Behaviorism," in *Minnesota Studies in the Philosophy of Science,* Vol. 1, ed. H. Feigl and M. Scriven. Minneapolis: University of Minnesota Press, 1956.

Shaffer, Jerome, "Can Sensations Be Brain-Processes?" *Journal of Philosophy,* 1961.

———, "Persons and Their Bodies," *Philosophical Review,* 1966.

———, "Recent Work on the Mind-Body Problem," *American Philosophical Quarterly,* II (1965), 81–104.

Shoemaker, Sydney, *Self-Knowledge and Self-Identity*. Ithaca, N. Y.: Cornell University Press, 1963.

Strawson, P. F., *Individuals*. London: Methuen & Co., Ltd., 1959. Also in paperback.

Vesey, G. N. A. (ed.), *Body and Mind*. London: George Allen & Unwin, Ltd., 1964.

Wisdom, John, *Other Minds*. Oxford: B. H. Blackwell, Ltd., 1949.

7

The Philosophy of Religion

21. The Existence of God

There are many problems in the field of philosophy of religion: What kind of belief is belief in God? What is the evidence for belief in God? What is the evidence against such belief? What alternative beliefs are open to us? What can we say not only about God's existence but about God's nature—God's power, goodness, intelligence, purposive behavior, government of the world, and so on? How, if at all, can we discover such beliefs to be true or false? Is the language we use to describe God to be taken literally? What conclusions about human behavior can we draw from the existence or non-existence of God? In this section, we shall be primarily concerned with arguments for and against the existence of God.

Many facets of religion will not concern us here. Religion is concerned not only with belief in God but with prayer, ritual, ecclesiastical organization, and other matters of more interest to ecclesiastical authorities than to philosophers. Philosophy in the field of religion is concerned, as always, with the justification of belief by means of argument.

The word "religion" itself needs clarification. A belief in God does not by itself constitute a religion: as the word is commonly used, the belief must be institutionalized, and contained in the doctrines of a religious body, such as a church or synagogue. Moreover, according to some definitions, at any rate, religion *need* not involve belief in God. Buddhism is usually considered to be a religion, but it contains no belief in a God such as is clearly found in Judaism and Christianity. The word "religion" indeed has been stretched almost beyond recognition: some have said that belief in the fundamental goodness of man is a religion, and that an ideology such as communism is (or can be) a religion, because it is the highest value to those who hold it. In this sense, one's religion is whatever value one holds highest in life, or whatever is one's ultimate concern. Religion has even been defined as "what one does with his leisure time." In these loose senses, everyone has a religion, since everyone has something he values highly and everyone does something with his leisure time. But if the meaning of the word is stretched so far, it is doubtful whether it any longer serves a useful purpose, and it may be positively misleading: "Everyone has a religion," someone may say, but this does not mean that everyone believes in God, but merely that everyone has some ideals. Instead of saying that communism *is* a religion, it would be preferable to say that communism has some features *in common with* religion: it involves beliefs about many things, amounting to a pervasive world-view; it evokes fierce loyalties, being something that people die for (and against); and so on. It would be pointless, as well as misleading, to define "religion" in such a loose way that the statement "Everyone has a religion" becomes true by definition.

Whether or not religion always involves belief in God, we are led next to the question "What kind of belief is belief in God?" What does the word "God" mean? There is an enormous range of things that people have meant by "God" (or "gods"). At the very least, we can say that belief in God is belief in some kind of *supernatural* being: supernatural not in the literal sense of being *above* nature but in the sense of being *other than* or *more than* the totality of things and processes to be found in the physical universe (including human minds). Sometimes it is held that God and nature are identical; but if this were so, the word "God" would be superfluous and the word "nature" would suffice alone. Whatever is to be called God, it is not nature; it must be something beyond the totality of natural processes.

But the term "supernatural" in turn calls for clarification. God is thought to be at least a *mind,* an intelligence capable of purposive behavior. God's intelligence need not be infinite, as Christianity holds: it might indeed be quite limited, like that of many of the Greek gods. But in addition to intelligence, God must possess a certain *power;* the power need not be infinite, as in the God of Christianity, but there must be enough to execute at least some of his purposes. Usually the power must be greater than human power—it would include the power to create matter (but not in the ancient Greek religion), the power to suspend laws of nature, the power to intervene in the course of events (even if this power is not always exercised), sometimes the power to create a world—power to do things which are superhuman (that is, which no human being can do). He may or may not also be benevolent: some gods are conceived as being evil in the extreme, such as those who demand human sacrifices or demand the plunder of entire nations to appease their wrath. In some religions, God has not only a mind but a physical body, like Zeus on Olympus, though in other religions God is a mind unattached to any physical body—a "pure spirit," without taint of matter.

One can believe in many gods (polytheism) or one (monotheism). One can believe in a God who created the world and then left it to run by itself in splendid isolation (deism) or one who continues to exercise his influence over the course of the world at every stage of its history (theism). One can believe that there is no God at all (atheism), or that we are not entitled on the basis of evidence either to believe God exists or that he does not exist (agnosticism, literally "I-don't-know-ism").

The God of the Judaeo-Christian tradition is conceived to be the only God (monotheism); to continue to be actively engaged in the life of human beings, such as hearing prayer and answering it (theism); and to be all-knowing (omniscient), all-powerful (omnipotent), and good (benevolent). In the early stages of this religious tradition, God is conceived as having a physical body: he walks with Adam in the cool of the evening, appears to Moses on Mt. Sinai, and so on. But in the later stages, God is an incorporeal spirit, without the limitations of a physical body: he sees everything, hears everything, knows everything, which would be impossible if he had just two eyes and could look only in one direction at a time. He is, in short, a disembodied mind: a consciousness divorced from body but able to think and feel and plan, and also with the power to execute these plans: although not a body himself, he is able to move bodies at his command, to will things into existence, to create things merely by a fiat such as "Let there be light." It is primarily at a God thus conceived that the major arguments for God's existence are directed.

A. The Ontological Argument

Most of the arguments for the existence of God attempt to show that there is some *evidence* for God provided by aspects of the nature of the world or of human experience. The ontological argument is the only one that attempts to prove God's existence from "pure reason" alone—by deducing the proposition that God exists from premises that, it is believed, we must accept. Not many philosophers or theologians believe that this proof is valid, but nevertheless the ontological argument is one with which we should come to grips, and without which our examination of arguments for God would be incomplete.

The argument proceeds as follows: God is a being than which no greater can be conceived. Now, we have the idea of such a thing (we understand what it is for there to be such a being). But existence is necessary to the concept of such a being: if he did not exist, he would not be as great as if he did exist, and by definition he is the greatest being that can be conceived. Therefore, such a being exists.

1. The most obvious remark that will occur to us in criticism of this argument is that you cannot define anything into existence. You can define "God" as "the greatest (most perfect) being conceivable," but it doesn't follow that such a being exists. You can define a perfect island as an island that has ideal temperature, climate, natural resources, etc., or in any other

way that you wish, but it doesn't follow that such an island really exists. If it did, you could define a perfect island, a perfect university, a perfect razor-blade, and countless other things, and prove that they all exist. But unfortunately they do not, since you cannot prove the existence of anything by simply giving a definition. Nothing can be defined into existence; from a definition of X, nothing follows about the existence of X. (See p. 30.)

The point is sound, but a defender of the ontological argument would admit it in general yet deny it in the special case of God. For, he would argue, the perfect island and the other things are not beings that are the greatest conceivable: they are only the greatest (or most perfect) *of their kind*. But God is not merely the greatest X (X being any class of objects) but the greatest conceivable being of *any* kind. And he wouldn't be the greatest conceivable being unless he existed; without existence, he would lack one of the prerequisites of perfect greatness (or perfection). Suppose you conceive of such a perfect being (just as you can conceive of a unicorn), and that he does *not* exist; then you can conceive of a perfect being who *does* exist. Your second conception will be of something greater than your first one, because the second being exists and the first one does not. Without existence, the being would not be as perfect as if he did exist—and by definition we are talking about the most perfect being that is conceivable. In the case of the most perfect conceivable being, his existence is necessary to his perfection—he would not be really perfect if he did not exist. If he did not exist, it would not be the most perfect conceivable being that we were thinking of.

But this leads us directly into a second objection:

2. Existence is not a property of anything. Suppose that we do have the idea of a being than which no other could be greater. (Greater in what respect? What is the meaning of "greater" here? This could be argued at length.) Assuming that we have the concept of such a being, the concept of the *existence* of such a being adds nothing to the concept of the being itself. What we conceive of is the same whether we conceive it as existing or not existing. If I imagine a horse and then imagine the horse as existing, *what* I imagine is no different in the two cases; if it were different, if something were added in the second case, then I would not be imagining as existing *the same thing* that I had previously imagined.

By whatever and by however many predicates we may think a thing . . . we do not make the least addition to the thing when we further declare that this thing *is*. Otherwise, it would not be exactly the same thing that exists, but something more than we had thought in the concept; and we could not, there-fore, say that the exact object of my concept exists. If we think in a thing every feature of reality except one, the missing reality is not added by my saying that the defective thing exists. On the contrary, it exists with the same defect with which I have thought it, since otherwise what exists would be something different from what I thought. When, therefore, I think a being as the supreme reality, without any defect, the question still remains whether it exists or not.[1]

If we say that a horse has a mane, a tail, four legs, and hoofs, we are attributing *properties* to the horse; but if we go on to say that the horse *exists,* we are not adding another property: we are saying that the thing we conceived as having these properties *also exists.* We are not adding to our concept of the thing: we are asserting a relation between the concept and the world.

The difference between saying that X has certain properties and saying that X exists can be illustrated as follows: "Unicorns have one horn" means "If there is (exists) anything that is a unicorn, then it has one horn." And so on for any other property of unicorns. According to this same analysis, "Unicorns exist" would mean "If there is (exists) anything that is a unicorn, then it exists"—and this flat tautology is certainly not what we would mean if we said that unicorns exist. Worse still, "Unicorns do not exist" would become "If unicorns exist, then they do not exist"—which is self-contradictory. But the proposition that unicorns do not exist is certainly not self-contradictory. In this way we see that "Unicorns have one horn" and "Unicorns exist," though they are grammatically similar, are very different in type: the analysis that works for the first will not work for the second. Having one horn is a property, having four legs is a property, being white is a property, and so on; but existing is not a property. To say that something exists is to say that there is a something that has the properties.

The argument, then, does not prove that there is a greatest conceivable being. We can safely say that *if* there is a greatest conceivable being, then he exists—but this is a tautology, and it in no way proves that there is such a being.

B. The Causal Argument

The *cosmological argument* proceeds from the fact that the universe, or cosmos, exists. From this initial premise the argument can proceed in either of two directions, of which the first is the causal argument, sometimes called the argument from origins. Look around you at the universe, one might say—the millions of stars and galaxies, the vast array of living things, the panorama of human life. It all must have come from somewhere. Some being must have produced all this—and who or what could have produced it but God? More succinctly stated, the argument says: Everything has a cause. If this is so, then the universe itself must have a cause. That cause is God. Therefore, God exists.

[1] Immanuel Kant, *Critique of Pure Reason,* Norman Kemp Smith trans., pp. 505–6.

1. "Everything has a cause." Different people have given different interpretations of that dark saying, which we examined in detail in Chapter 5, and we need not go into this vexed controversy again. But let us suppose, for the sake of argument, that the statement is true (whether a priori or not we need not stop to decide). But even if true, it applies only to events, or things happening. Do things as well as events have a cause? It would doubtless be better to say that a-thing-coming-into-existence has a cause rather than that the thing itself has a cause: it is always some temporal event or process that *occurs* in the history of things that has the cause. When we ask for the cause of a thing, such as an egg, we ask for the cause of its coming-into-being, which is an event or process. But of course we might ask this same question about the universe.

But is the universe a thing? One would be more inclined to say that the word "universe" is a collective noun, and that the universe is a collection of things—the collection of every thing that there is. Must an entire collection have one cause, or may not each member of the collection have a different cause? As Hume wrote, "Did I show you the particular causes of each individual in a collection of twenty particles of matter, I should think it very unreasonable, should you afterwards ask me, what was the cause of the whole twenty. This is sufficiently explained in explaining the cause of the parts."[2]

This point can be dramatized in the following way:

Suppose I see a group of five Eskimos standing on the corner of Sixth Avenue and 50th St. and I wish to explain why the group came to New York. Investigation reveals the following stories: Eskimo No. 1 did not enjoy the extreme cold in the polar region and decided to move to a warmer climate. No. 2 is the husband of No. 1; he loves her dearly and did not wish to live without her. No. 3 is the son of Eskimos 1 and 2; he is too small and too weak to oppose his parents. No. 4 saw an advertisement in the New York Times for an Eskimo to appear on television. No. 5 is a private detective engaged by the Pinkerton Agency to keep an eye on Eskimo No. 4.

Let us assume that we have now explained in the case of each of the five Eskimos why he or she is in New York. Somebody then asks: "All right, but what about the group as a whole, why is *it* in New York?" This would plainly be an absurd question. There is no group over and above the five members and if we have explained why each of the five members is in New York, we have ipso facto explained why the group is there. A critic of the cosmological argument would claim that it is just as absurd to ask for the cause of the series as a whole, as distinct from asking for the causes of individual members.[3]

2. Let us, however, assume that we can admit the question "Does the universe as a whole have a cause?" Now suppose we answer "God." Then

[2] David Hume, *Dialogues Concerning Natural Religion*, Part IX.
[3] Edwards and Pap, *A Modern Introduction to Philosophy*, p. 380.

comes the inevitable next question: "But what caused God?" Many children ask this question, to the great embarrassment of their parents. But the question is perfectly legitimate: After all, we have just been told that everything has a cause, and if that is true, then God too must have a cause. And if God does *not* have a cause, then it is not true that everything has a cause. Yet that was the first premise of the argument—that everything has a cause.

It would seem, then, that the causal argument is not merely invalid but self-contradictory: the conclusion, which says that something (God) does not have a cause, contradicts the premise, which says that everything does have a cause. If that premise is true, the conclusion cannot be true; and if the conclusion is true, the premise cannot be. Many people do not at once see this because they use the argument to get to God, and then, having arrived where they want to go, they forget all about the argument. As Schopenhauer pointed out, they use the argument as they would a taxicab—they use it to get to their desired destination, and then dismiss it without thinking any further about its fate. But consistency requires us to think further: if the conclusion contradicts its own premise, we have the most damning indictment of an argument that we could possibly have: that it is self-contradictory.

"But," one might object, "I don't mean that *everything* has a cause—I mean that everything *except God* has a cause." But why do we stop at just this point? If we stop somewhere, why not stop with the universe itself? At least that is something of which we have some experience and some knowledge.

If we stop, and go no farther, why go so far? Why not stop at the material world? How can we satisfy ourselves without going on ad infinitum? And after all, what satisfaction is there in that infinite progression? Let us remember the story of the Indian philosopher and his elephant. It was never more applicable than to the present subject. If the material world rests upon a similar ideal world, this ideal world must rest upon some other; and so on, without end. It were better, therefore, never to look beyond the present material world. By supposing it to contain the principle of its order within itself, we really assert it to be God; and the sooner we arrive at that Divine Being, so much the better. When you go one step beyond the mundane system, you only excite an inquisitive humor, which it is impossible ever to satisfy.[4]

3. In any case, it does not seem that we are justified in tracing causes beyond the empirical realm in which alone we have any evidence for causality. Our knowledge of causes lies entirely within the realm of spatio-temporal things, processes, and events. Beyond that, we have no reason to speak of causes at all, for experiences tell us nothing about any such causality. To extend the principle into some trans-empirical realm is to desert the empirical evidence in which the principle is grounded. Indeed, one might

[4] David Hume, *Dialogues Concerning Natural Religion,* Part IV.

well ask what *meaning* the word "cause" has apart from any references to events and processes going on in the universe. As Kant pointed out, "The principle of causality has no meaning and no criterion for its application save only in the sensible world. But in the cosmological proof it is precisely in order to enable us to advance beyond the sensible world that it is employed."[5]

4. Yet in the minds of many persons there lingers the idea that in some way the actions of conscious agents, as manifested in their volitions, have a unique place in the sphere of causation. We do not see sticks and stones coming together of themselves to form mechanical objects: we contrive them, plan them, then arrange the matter of which they are composed into certain complex structures (in making houses, watches, wrenches, and so on), and they would not have existed in this form but for our mental activities. And so, we reason, it must be the same with the universe.

The conception of the universe as the result of plan or design will be discussed under the heading of the teleological argument. But while we are discussing the causal argument, it may be worth our while to pause for a moment to ask: Proceeding on the basis of *empirical evidence alone,* are we entitled to say that volitions are ultimate causes? It would seem that they are not: (1) Many movements of matter, such as arranging pieces of wood into a house, are indeed the result of will, and without volition they would never occur. (2) But in no case are we entitled to say that the will *creates,* or brings into being, the matter; it merely changes the position of particles of matter which already exist. (3) Neither does volition create force or energy. The will does originate motion, for example when a bodily movement follows upon an act of will; but it does so only by means of innumerable brain-events, in which one form of energy is converted into another (energy of motion); energy itself the will does not create. Far from creating energy, the behavior of the brain-particles (which must occur if consciousness is to occur at all) is itself an instance of the law of Conservation of Energy, and presupposes it. In all cases of which we have had experience, energy is prior to volition and not the other way around; volition (or its bodily concomitant, depending on one's theory of mind) is just one of thousands of manifestations of energy. So volition is hardly in a position, in an empirical argument, to be an ultimate cause. (4) It seems quite certain that volition did not come into being for countless ages—during all of which the law of Conservation of Energy was nevertheless in operation—until during the long evolutionary process it finally arose. Matter and energy are, so far as we know, eternal; volitions are not, for we can trace their beginning in time.

A first cause in time.   It is often assumed that the series of causes and effects cannot go on backward in time forever but must come to a stop. Three billion years ago the earth was formed, but the sun was already there. And

[5] *Critique of Pure Reason,* Norman Kemp Smith trans., p. 511.

before that? The sun was thrown off by the spiral arms of the cooling galaxy, along with millions of other stars. And before that? The galaxy itself was formed—and here the history becomes obscure, and controversy is rife among cosmologists about just what happened and when, but they do not doubt that *something* happened before that. But, it is sometimes said, we must nevertheless ultimately come to a stop. There was a time when the series of event *began*—that is, there must be a *first cause* of events.

Perhaps this means that there was a first *event*. If so, that idea is shrouded in obscurity and replete with difficulties. When did the first event occur? Since we can speak of time only in the context of the succession of events themselves, is this a meaningful question? What made the first event occur when it did or have the nature that it had? Nothing, apparently: since it was the first event, it could have no cause; it had no predecessors, nothing to cause it to be as it was—it just popped into existence with no cause at all (if it had a cause, then it was not the first event). In any case, God could not be the first event, since God is not an event at all.

Perhaps, then, God caused the so-called first event: history had a beginning in a mind—God—and God then created the universe out of nothing and thus caused the first event (or series of events) to occur; his will alone is the reason why the first event, and all the succeeding events as well, were what they were and occurred as they did. The series of events reaching into the past comes to a stop with God.

But this, of course, again raises the question of what caused God. It will not do to say that God caused himself. If God was already there, he would not need to cause himself since he was already on the scene. If God was not already there, he was not on the scene to do any causing: nothing cannot cause something. So either way, the existence of God would have to be accounted for. We could, of course, simply take God's existence as a given, a fact requiring no explanation—but then we could do the same for the universe as well.

An infinite series of causes. But why need there be a First Cause, or a God who preceded the "First Cause" and set the series going from a point earlier in time? Why may not the series of events go back infinitely? This has, in fact, often been suggested:

There need not have been a first event; we can imagine that every event was preceded by an earlier event, and that time has no beginning. The infinity of time, in both directions, offers no difficulties to the understanding. We know that the series of numbers has no end, that for every number there is a larger number. If we include the negative numbers, the number series has no beginning either; for every number there is a smaller number. Infinite series without a beginning and an end have been successfully treated in mathematics; there is nothing paradoxical in them. To object that there must have been a first event, a beginning of time, is the attitude of an untrained mind. Logic does not tell us anything about the structure of time. Logic offers the means of dealing with infinite series without a beginning as well as with series that have a beginning. If scientific evidence is in favor of an infinite time, coming from infinity and going to infinity, logic has no objection.[6]

Nevertheless, we may feel some difficulty about an infinite series of causes, which we do not feel in the case of numbers. When we say that the series of integers is infinite, we mean that no matter how large a number you think of, you can always get a bigger one by adding 1, and that the number series *has no* last member. When we say that the series of events in the history of the universe is infinite, we are committed to saying that the series had no beginning (not merely that we can't find one). Since there is an infinite series of events, they will take an infinite time to get through. How is this different from saying that they *never* get through? If an infinite series of events has preceded the present moment, how did we get to the present moment? How could we get to the present moment—where we obviously are now—if the present moment was preceded by an infinite series of events?

Let us suppose that this difficulty is overcome (the issue is still in dispute); what are we left with? An infinite series of events stretching infinitely into the past; but where does God fit into this picture? Not as a being existing temporally prior to the first event, since there was no first event. Nor, since the universe has always existed, did God create it at a certain point in time. Indeed, whatever may be said for this view, it no longer falls under the Causal Argument at all, since it is no longer an attempt to answer a question about the *origin* of the universe in time.

Where did the universe come from?   Let us consider what meaning questions about the origin of the universe have. We often ask questions of the form "Where did X come from?" If we investigate what meanings this question can have in daily life, we may shed some light on what meaning (if any) it has in the special case of the universe.

"Where did X come from?" (1) Sometimes, when we ask this question, we mean, In what previous place was it? and an answer such as "It came from Africa" or "It came out of my pocket" would suffice. (2) Or it may mean, How did it get from its previous place to its present one? How did that package get there? The mailman brought it in. This is considered a satisfactory answer to the question, without pursuing further where it was before it was brought in. (3) Sometimes we are after a different bit of information: *Who* performed the activity that resulted in this product? For example, (a) "Where did that painting come from?" "My brother painted it." (b) "Where did that contraption come from?" "Junior put it there." This sense of "come from" of course presupposes the existence of a sentient being to create it or put it there. (4) Sometimes we want to know in what previous state or condition X existed. If a native of the tropics is flown to a cold

[6] Hans Reichenbach, *The Rise of Scientific Philosophy,* pp. 207–8.

climate and sees a peculiar solid substance in his canteen (he has never seen ice before), he may ask, "Where did it come from?" which is answered not by saying "It came from Africa" (though the very same molecules of H_2O that are now frozen were in Africa 24 hours before), but by explaining that the substance in question has undergone a change of state. (5) Sometimes the information sought is how it got from its previous state to its present state: for example, "It got colder and froze"—a process which we could show the native himself by (for example) placing water in the ice-tray of the refrigerator and inviting him to watch it at various stages of its transformation into ice.

But none of these meanings of "Where did X come from?" is applicable to the universe as a whole. "The universe" includes all places and times, and all the things that exist in space and time. Thus the first sense of the question does not apply: the universe, unlike a material object, could not have been in some previous place prior to being where it now is; it already includes all places. Since the first sense is not applicable to the universe as a whole, neither is the second: if the universe could not have been in a previous place, it could not have come from that place to this one. The third sense is question-begging in the present context: it presupposes that there was a conscious being who "put it there," which is the very thing in question. And the phrase "put it there" also presupposes that there are other places—at least one into which the X was put, and another from which it was put—which again does not apply to the universe as a whole. Neither does the fourth sense apply to the universe: since the universe includes within itself all times as well as all places, it could not have arisen out of a previous state that was *not* part of the history of the universe. Nor, of course, could the fifth sense apply (how it got from its previous state), since this too presupposes a previous state.

It is true, of course, that we can meaningfully ask about the causes of the *present* state of the universe (or some aspect thereof); then we cite causal factors occurring in the past. And we can ask about the causes of these in turn, and can list causes occurring still further back; and so on ad infinitum. This is what cosmologists do when they write books with titles such as *The Origin of the Universe*. They mean, not the "original origin" of the universe, but the origin of its present state: "Stars condensed out of vast whirling nebulae," and so on for states of the universe prior to that. But if someone says, "I don't mean today or a million years ago or a trillion years ago, I mean from the beginning of time," his last phrase is meaningless: there could not be a moment earlier than the history of time, nor any time when there was no time. Thus the trouble with the question "Where did the universe come from?" is similar to other questions we have already examined (pp. 85–88): a word or phrase has a clear enough meaning in one context, but it is then used uncritically and placed in a very different context in which it has no meaning at all.

However, one may object, there is still another sense in which the question "Where did X come from?" might be construed. It may be taken as a request for an *explanation,* not for a cause or origin. We have already considered explanation (pp. 240–47); we explain an event by bringing it under a law or theory, and we explain a law by bringing it under other laws or theories. If someone asks why the radius vectors of the planets cover equal areas in equal intervals of time, we can answer by showing that this is a consequence of Newton's laws of motion. But to ask why *all* the laws (or total state-of-affairs in the universe) are as they are is to go outside the context in which the question has meaning—or so, at least, it would seem.

God as explanation.   Nevertheless, it is as explanation, not as cause, that God is invoked in the next argument we are to consider. God, so the argument runs, should not be conceived of as a cause of temporal events, for causes occur in time, but as the *explanation* for the fact that there is any series of causes existing at all, finite or infinite. God is not the first member of a causal series, but the reason why there is any series at all.

On this view, God is timeless; we might also say "eternal," except that the word "eternal" is ambiguous: it may mean *everlasting* (temporal but lasting throughout all time—such as energy or, perhaps, matter); but it may also mean *timeless* (non-temporal, not in time at all). Mathematical entities, such as the number 2, and universals, such as blueness and triangularity, are timeless: they have no history, there is no before and after, and it would be neither true nor false but meaningless to say "The number 2 started to exist yesterday." That to which no temporal attributes can meaningfully be ascribed is timeless. According to this view, God is not a cause, for causes are thoroughly embedded in the time-stream; rather, God is the non-temporal (timeless) explanation for the existence of everything else, both laws and particular events in time. This being so, we are no longer speaking of the Causal Argument: God is not suggested as a cause, but as the explanation of the existence of the entire series of events. This takes us into the second version of the Cosmological Argument:

C. The Argument from Contingency

The argument can be formulated in this way: Every thing and every event in the universe is *contingent;* it depends for its explanation on something outside itself. But not everything can be contingent: since every contingent existence requires an explanation outside itself, there must be something in reality that is not contingent but is a reason for its own existence, and that something is God.

First of all, we know that there are at least some beings in the world which do not contain in themselves the reason for their existence. For example, I depend on my parents, and now on the air, and on food, and so on. Now, secondly, the world is simply the real or imagined totality or aggregate of individual objects none of which contain in themselves alone the reason for their existence. There isn't any world distinct from the objects which form it, any more than the human race is something apart from its members. Therefore, I should say, since objects or events exist, and since no object of experience contains within itself the reason of its existence, this reason, the totality of objects, must have a reason external to itself. That reason must be an existent being. Well, this being is either itself the reason for its own existence, or it is not. If it is, well and good. If it is not, then we must proceed farther. But if we proceed to infinity in that sense, then there's no explanation of existence at all. So, I should say, in order to explain existence, we must come to a being which contains within itself the reason for its own existence, that is to say, which cannot *not* exist.[7]

How, according to this argument, is the existence of God to be explained? (Not caused, for causes are prior conditions, but explained, accounted for.) God needs no explanation, the proponent of the argument replies: God is a necessary being, and a necessary being contains the explanation of its existence within itself. God is not self-caused in the sense already criticized (God does not bring himself into existence); he is self-caused only in the sense that he exists "by his own nature," not contingently, not in dependence on something else. And God's existence is necessary: God is a necessary being.

A being that depends for its existence upon nothing but itself, and is in this sense self-caused, can equally be described as a necessary being; that is to say, a being that is not contingent, and hence not perishable. For in the case of anything which exists by its own nature, and is dependent upon nothing else, it is impossible that it should not exist, which is equivalent to saying that it is necessary.[8]

And if God is a necessary being, we can even speak of God as *creating* the universe, though not in any causal sense. Creation here does not mean creation *in time;* since the universe had no beginning in time, it was not created by God as an event in time. It can be said to have been created only in another and quite different sense of "create":

If one thing is the creation of another, then it depends for its existence on that other, and this is perfectly consistent with saying that both are eternal, that neither ever came into being, and hence, that neither was ever created at any point of time. Perhaps an analogy will help convey this point. Consider, then, a flame that is casting beams of light. Now there seems to be a clear sense in which beams of light are dependent for their existence upon the flame,

---

[7] F. C. Copleston, in "The Existence of God—a Debate," by Bertrand Russell and F. C. Copleston, in P. Edwards and A. Pap, *A Modern Introduction to Philosophy,* p. 474.

[8] Richard Taylor, *Metaphysics,* p. 93.

which is their source, while the flame, on the other hand, is not similarly dependent for its existence upon them. The beams of light arise from the flame, but the flame does not arise from them. In this sense, they are the creation of the flame; they derive their existence from it. And none of this has any reference to time; the relationship of dependence in such a case would not be altered in the slightest if we supposed that the flame, and with it the beams of light, had always existed, that neither had ever *come* into being.[9]

What shall we say of the argument as thus propounded?

A: I think the entire argument is a nest of confusions. First of all, I don't know what's meant by "necessary being." We speak a great deal in philosophy of necessary *propositions*. I know what a necessary proposition is, but I don't know what a necessary *being* is.

B: A necessary being is one that depends for its existence upon nothing but itself. Not being contingent, the explanation of its existence does not lie in something outside itself but within itself alone.

A: Words, words, words! I still don't understand what a "necessary being" could be. I understand what it is to explain something in terms of something *else:* for example, to explain the rusting of iron in terms of the oxygen in the air, which combines with the iron to form iron oxide. But to say that something can be explained in terms of *itself alone* seems to me either a contradiction in terms or pure gibberish. To explain *is* to explain in terms of something else; what else could explanation be?

B: That's what explanation is in every case *other* than that of God. In the case of a necessary being, its explanation is to be found within itself only—that's part of what we mean by calling it a necessary being.

A: We are back with that again. I still don't know what you mean by "necessary being." It sounds intelligible because we already have the phrase "necessary proposition," but it seems to me that you are trading on the admitted meaningfulness of this last phrase in order to give meaning to the first one.

B: Not at all. There must be a necessary being if the totality of things is to have any explanation. Look: in all the physical universe, including human minds, there is no necessary being but only contingent beings. Of every single one of them we can say that they *might* not have existed; indeed, they *would* not have existed if certain conditions had been different. If your parents had not met you wouldn't be here; if certain other things had been different—collocations of matter in our galaxy—the earth would not have existed; and so on. We can and do explain the existence and nature of some contingent beings in terms of other contingent beings. But we have not really explained any of these things until we have traced them back to some necessary being, which is the explanation of why any of them exists and is what it is.

[9] *Ibid.,* p. 89.

A: I don't see why. Every phenomenon in nature can be explained in terms of others—laws plus particular conditions. (See pp. 241–42.) If there were a God who created everything there is, you could explain the existence of the created things by saying that God decided to create it; but even so you would not have explained the existence of God.

B: But God requires no explanation; God, alone among all things, contains the explanation of his existence within himself; that is, God is not contingent, as everything else is.

A: There we go again: I don't see how anything can be explained in terms of itself; explanation is always in terms of something else. That's what "explanation" means. You say, "But not in the case of a necessary being"; but this doesn't help me, since I don't know what a necessary being is—that is, I cannot attach any meaning to that mysterious phrase.

B: I don't see any difficulty about it at all. We all understand what is meant by an *impossible* being—one that by its very nature *cannot* exist; for instance, a square circle. So why is it any more difficult to understand what is meant by a *necessary* being—one that by its very nature *must* exist?

A: Square circles are not logically impossible *beings*. The phrase "square circle" contains two words with incompatible definitions, and hence is *self-contradictory;* accordingly the proposition that there are square circles is self-contradictory. And conversely, "Squares are four-sided" is analytic, and the proposition that squares are four-sided is logically *necessary*. Please note that I don't say that a square is a necessary being, or that it's logically necessary that there be any squares; the sentence means only that *if* there are squares, *then* (necessarily) they are four-sided. All such necessary statements are hypothetical (if . . . then . . .). None of them makes any existential claim; they do not say that anything *exists,* much less that it necessarily exists. Indeed, I just don't know what you mean by saying that anything necessarily exists. There is certainly no X of which it could be said that the sentence "X exists" is a necessary truth.

B: But that is just what I claim for God: being the explanation of everything that exists, God necessarily exists himself. If his existence were not necessary, it would be contingent, like the existence of everything else in the universe, and we would still want an explanation of why it is.

A: If by "contingent existence" you mean simply that it could (logically) have been other than it is (or non-existent), and would have been so if certain conditions had been different, then I am perfectly content to say that every existent thing in the universe is contingent. I certainly won't buy the idea (if indeed it is an idea and not just a meaningless string of words) that there is such a thing as a necessary existent.

B: But if you won't admit that there is a necessary existent, you are left with a problem. You will admit, I assume, that there are various possible worlds. (Let us say "possible universes," since "world" often means the same as "earth.") For instance, it is logically possible that the universe might have been just as it is except that your parents never met, and consequently you wouldn't be here now. That is one possible universe. Another possible universe is that in which there were galaxies and a sun but no system of planets, no earth, hence no life on earth. Another possible universe—far more different from this one—is one in which certain laws of nature were not as they are now: for example, one in which particles of matter attract one another not inversely as the square of the distance between them (as now) but inversely as the cube. And so on. We could exercise our imaginations endlessly by plotting out possible universes. Now the question arises: *Why, of all the infinity of possible universes, do we have just the one we have?* Why does this one exist, among all the logically possible ones? Why, indeed, does *any* universe at all exist—why is there a universe at all rather than simply nothing? For this you have no explanation at all. But I do. I hold that there is a necessary being, God, and that since he exists necessarily, all contingent existents (and that includes everything in the universe) owe their existence to this necessary being and are explained by the fact that this necessary being exists.

A: I don't see how your so-called explanation is any explanation at all. I don't claim to have an explanation for everything, but neither do I appeal to God—that "asylum of ignorance," as Spinoza says—every time I can't explain something. Assume for a moment that I can't explain why the world is as it is or has the laws that it has. I don't see how you have explained it either. "God is the explanation," you say. But this won't do. That doesn't explain why the world has these laws or particular existents rather than some other. And even if it did, it still leaves the questions of what explains God's existence, why God is there at all, and why God has the nature he has and makes the decisions he does (including the decision to have just this universe). If you now tell me that God *necessarily* has the nature that he has, I can't make sense out of that either, and I don't think anyone can.

B: On the contrary, I believe it to be the only explanation of why things are as they are, and why there is anything at all.

A: Including God?

B: No, for God necessarily exists, and his explanation is to be found within himself alone. But the existence of God does explain why everything else is as it is and why there is a material universe.

A: How does the existence of God explain it? Do you want to say that God *chose* to have this particular universe, and that since he had the power, he brought it into existence?

B: Yes, I do hold that God's choosing it explains it. Let me make myself clear: There are *mechanical* explanations (in terms of events and processes antecedent to the event to be explained), and there are also *purposive,* or *teleological,* explanations. We are familiar in daily life with both kinds, and we constantly use them both. Why is the ice cream in the refrigerator melted? Because the current was off for some hours during the night. (Mechanical.)

Why are there no houses in that city block? Because the Housing Authority had these properties condemned and razed in order to make room for a public park. (Teleological.) Now, I want to insist that the universe as a whole cannot have a mechanical explanation, for these explanations are always in terms of laws plus antecedent events. Besides, mechanical explanations won't tell us why *this* universe with its laws exists, of all logically possible universes: mechanical explanations will simply *use* the laws we know to tell us why, *assuming* these laws, certain things are as they are. But such explanations can't tell us why the universe is as it is, with just the laws that it has, or even why it exists at all.

A: And you think that teleological explanations must be invoked to explain this?

B: Precisely. After all, there must be *some* reason why there is a universe, with the laws that it has. And if mechanical explanations won't tell us, we must appeal to teleological explanations. God, a necessary being, chose this particular one among all the infinity of logically possible universes. Why did he do so? Perhaps because of all possible universes this one is the best.[10] Or perhaps his reasons are inscrutable to man. But I am sure that the question "Why just *this* universe, or any universe at all?" is one that demands an answer, and that since we cannot use mechanical explanations in this case, we must give a teleological explanation. And this we can do, in terms of a choice by a supreme being, God.

A: Very ingenious. But there are several things wrong with it. To begin: I don't see how a teleological or purposive explanation is even meaningful here; for remember that God is not being conceived now as first cause, or as any kind of temporal being antecedent to the series of causes in the history of the universe. God in our present context is a *timeless* being (like the number 2), and thus not something that *acts in time* at all. Indeed, I don't see how God thus conceived could have any personality; with him there is no before-and-after, no creation-in-time of a universe, no "Let there be light" followed in time by the existence of light, and so on. On this interpretation, God cannot be the kind of entity that most religions believe in, for they believe in a being who created the world at a moment of time, hears and answers prayer, will later fulfill his promises to us and judge us at a tribunal at the end of the world, and so on. All such conceptions go out the window once you have God as a timeless being; such a being, or entity, cannot be a personality, can have no analogy at all with human beings. Indeed, I don't see why such an entity would be called God. It seems to me dishonest to call this "God" while taking away all the characteristics that people have always associated with the word "God." In any case, such a being cannot *choose* to have this or that world, or any world at all, for choosing *is a temporal activity:* it can take place only in time. You choose X or Y at this or that particular time; what would it mean

---

[10] We shall postpone discussion of this point until we discuss the problem of evil, under the heading "The Teleological Argument." (See pp. 455–78.)

to choose X or Y not at this or that particular time, not at any time at all, but somehow timelessly? Can you really make any sense of the alleged concept of a non-temporal choice? It seems to me that at points like these religions have to fish or cut bait; but they don't. On Monday, Wednesday, and Friday they say that God is timeless, with God there is no before and after, no changing or shadow of turning, and so on; but on Tuesday, Thursday, and Saturday they say that God created us, that he will one day judge us, that he will fulfill his promises to us, and so on—all of which places God's activity in time. But this is just double-talk. Theologies are caught in a contradiction: they want to say each of two opposite things—one to answer arguments from philosophers, the other to give comfort to their people. Give theologies enough rope, and they will all hang themselves, for if you listen a while you find them saying absolutely incompatible things. This, then, is one objection: the alleged concept of a timeless choosing, or a timeless "act of creation," or any other timeless act or process, is simply unintelligible; it contains within itself a blatant contradiction.

B: You still haven't told me how you would answer the question "Why, of all possible worlds, do we have just *this* universe, or any universe rather than simply nothing?"

A: That is my second point. My first impulse is to say "I don't know"; this is just a "brute fact"—the universe has such-and-such laws, and if these are ultimate (underived), we can't derive them from any other ones; that's it, that's as far as we can go. Perhaps this is satisfactory, but I want to probe one step deeper: I want to suggest to you that the question is meaningless or, to be more precise, self-contradictory. If we have once arrived at a basic or underived law (not that we ever know that we have), then it is self-contradictory to ask for an explanation of it. If we don't see this, it's because we ordinarily operate in the context of why-questions that can and do have answers, because we have not yet reached the level of basic laws. But we should remember that when we explain, we always explain *in terms of something* (something *other* than the thing to be explained, otherwise we have no explanation at all). And if *ex hypothesi* there is no longer any something for it to be explained in terms *of,* then the request for an explanation is self-contradictory. It demands on the one hand that you explain X in terms of Y while insisting on the other that there is no Y.

I conclude, then, that (1) the question "Why is the universe as it is?" (including "Why are its basic laws as they are?") is self-contradictory if there is nothing other than it in terms of which an explanation can be provided. (It only *seems* to be meaningful because it is so similar in formulation to other questions that are.) (2) But *if* there is a being, God—I don't say a necessary being, for I still don't know what that is—who has purposes and fulfills them by doing things like creating a universe (all of which must be in time—for the concept of a non-temporal choosing or creating is self-contradictory), *then* one could answer the question "Why is the universe as it is?" by saying "Because there is a God who chose to make it as it is." We have then answered *that* question, but only at the price of having another one on our hands: "What is the explanation for God's existence, and for his having the nature he has, including his motives and wishes?" So we have answered one question, in theological terms, only by bringing down on our heads another one that is more troublesome than the first. And if you say, "But in the special case of God, we don't need an explanation, for God is a necessary being, and a necessary being is one who doesn't need an explanation outside of himself," I submit that this provides no answer at all, for (a) explanation *is* always in terms of something else, and (b) that something else is never a "necessary being."

B: You beg the question by insisting on this one sense of "explanation," the sense that is ordinarily used in daily life and in science. In that sense, of course, nothing is its own explanation. But in the special case of a necessary being, it is.

A: It is not that I am arbitrarily sticking to the ordinary sense of "explanation" when there is another one. As far as I can see, there isn't. As the word is here used, it has no meaning. "Its full explanation lies within itself." What does that mean? Moreover, even if you *could* show me that you had a distinct and intelligible sense in mind, you would be playing on words by using the same word, "explanation," to cover both of such utterly different things. "The universe demands an explanation, doesn't it?" you say, and your question gains a misleading plausibility because you use the same word that we all do in asking "The broken windows require an explanation, don't they?" In this latter case we all assent, and we are inclined to in the former also only because the same word, "explanation," is used—but as you admit, they aren't used to mean the same thing in the two cases. I don't see, therefore, that your so-called special sense has any meaning.

B: That is a pity—I have no difficulty with it at all.

A: And let me add one point: even if I did grant that you have a meaningful sense of "explanation" here, I need not grant that there exists a necessary being. I have to grant this *only* if I also grant another suppressed premise of your argument, that there really are explanations in your special sense of the word. Even if you succeeded in convincing me that you have a special sense, I would not have to admit that anything *has* an explanation in this sense. I could say that perhaps the universe *has* no explanation. Your argument apparently consists of these three propositions:

Things have not really been explained without reference to a necessary being.
There are explanations in this sense.
Therefore, there is a necessary being.

Even if I accepted the first premise (which I don't, since I don't know what "necessary being" means, nor understand your sense of the word "explanation"), I would not have to accept the second premise; and consequently I would not have to accept the conclusion.

D. The Argument from Religious Experience

The argument from religious experience is not always clearly stated, and it is more often not stated at all but is held implicitly as a kind of unspoken proof that never reaches the stage of outright verbal presentation. This is approximately what it comes to: I (and other persons) have experiences of a peculiar nature, which are so profound, so meaningful, so valuable, that they cannot be explained on any natural hypothesis; they must then be due to the presence of a Supernatural Being, God, who inspires such experiences.

Let us first consider the expressions "God" and "religious experience." The word "God" *may* be used synonymously with "religious experience," simply as a label for the experience itself. There are those who would accept this meaning of the word "God"; and in this sense, of course, it is simply a tautology to say "If there are religious experiences, God exists," for it is no more than saying "If there are religious experiences, there are religious experiences." In this sense, it would be self-contradictory to say that God exists even when religious experiences do not, just as it would be self-contradictory to speak of a pain existing unfelt. For a pain to exist is simply for it to be felt, and for God to exist (in this sense) is simply for religious experiences to occur.

Most persons, however, would not attach this meaning to the word "God." They would not say that when they assert that God exists they are asserting merely that religious experiences exist. They would say, rather, that the experience is merely an *indicator* of something beyond itself, namely of a Being who exists just as objectively as the tree out there exists. The religious experience points to a Deity, but it is not the same thing as a Deity.

What of the term "religious experience"? Why not simply define it as "an experience of God"? Thus defined, the occurrence of religious experiences would prove the existence of God, since by definition a religious experience *is* an experience of God. In this case again the existence of religious experiences proves that God exists; indeed it is analytic to say so. But, as in cases we have already considered, it hardly establishes what people may want it to establish; it only shifts the question. The original question was, "Religious experiences exist; does God exist?" whereas the question now becomes, "On this definition of 'religious experience' (on which God must exist in order for the experience to be a *religious* experience), *are* there any religious experiences?" We cannot, after all, define anything into existence (see pp. 30–31).

Usually when we talk about religious experiences we mean experiences (whose precise quality is hard to describe, partly because of lack of words for describing what it is like, partly because the quality of the experience itself varies so much from person to person) which cause those who have them to attribute them to a god and increase one's tendency to worship, adore, reverence, or fear the god allegedly revealed in the experience. Conceived in this way, religious experiences are, as the name implies, simply experiences of a certain special kind (admittedly difficult at times to mark off from other kinds), and the question then remains, "Can we infer from the occurrence of these experiences that a deity or deities exist to cause these experiences?"

Let us see what happens if the inference is granted. It seems that if the argument proves anything it proves far too much. There are multitudes of religious experiences, and if in one case we can infer from a religious experience a deity of which it is the experience, we can do the same in another case. If the religious experience of A, a Christian, proves the existence of the Christian God, it would seem that the religious experience of B, a Moham-medan, would prove the existence of Allah, the Mohammedan God. People use the argument from religious experience in support of their own religious experiences, being unaware perhaps that the same argument, if admitted, would permit the same inference for the religious experiences of persons embracing different religious faiths. If we admit one, we must admit all.

Why not admit them all? Because, of course, they contradict each other and cannot all be true. Each religion claims to be the only true one, and it is logically impossible to have a number of religions each of which is the only true one.

In order to ameliorate this situation, the following argument is sometimes used: All religious experiences are of the same Being; people disagree only in the way they *describe* the object of these experiences, for this depends on their particular environment and upbringing; they are at a loss for words and use language in loose, misleading, and even contradictory ways when they talk about it. The god experienced is the same in every case; only the historical, "accidental" features are different. Purge the religions of their historical features, in which Mohammedanism and Christianity for example do contradict each other, and take only the essence or kernel common to them all, and they do not contradict each other because they are one.

This may seem an easy way out of the situation; but there are several points that should be considered before it is adopted. (1) In this process you have taken away the God of every *particular* religion. Christianity declares, for example, that God is revealed in the Holy Scriptures, and manifested in Christ, and that any view which denies this is false. Remove these beliefs and you do not have "the essence of Christianity" left; you have something left that can hardly be called Christianity at all, whatever else it may be. Purge Christianity of its "historical features," and you have purged away virtually all of Christianity. Some may consider this all to the good, but let us not then say that we have "true Christianity" left when we have done this. (2) Let us try to imagine such a being as the God who is supposed to possess only the features shared by all religions, and none of the peculiarities of any particular religion. Such a God could not be loving (for the gods of some religions are not), or brutal (for the gods of some religions are not so), and so on; such a

God could hardly possess any characteristics whatever, so few are the characteristics which the deities of all, or even a small fraction, of the religions of the world possess in common. About all such a God would have left is power. Strictly speaking, he would not even possess unity, for many religions are polytheistic—but at the same time he could not be multiple either, for some religions are monotheistic. What kind of God would it be that is neither one nor more than one? (3) Neither could such a God be given "more character" through the *addition* of certain characteristics—he could not be the God of various specific religions "all rolled up into one," as has sometimes been suggested; for then he would be loving like the Christian God, vengeful like Yahweh, demanding human sacrifice like Baal, prohibiting it like the God of Christianity, and so on. These characteristics are logically incompatible with each other. Clearly *some* of these beliefs must be wrong; hence it would appear that religious experience alone cannot guarantee the truth of the God of any religion.

"But some religions must be excluded—the obviously barbaric ones, such as Baal-worship . . . ." Where, in this case, are we to draw the line? What kinds of religious experiences are going to establish the God in question, and which are not? What is the criterion? More important still, how is this criterion to be justified and defended against others? If the occurrence of one religious experience really establishes the existence of the Deity believed in by this person, what is to exclude another from doing so? One may, indeed, employ some question-begging use of the term "religious experience," so that only the experiences of one religion or denomination are "truly religious," the others being "mere deceptions." But the opponent of one who argues thus can simply return the compliment. Logically there is nothing to choose between them. Each side can use its own persuasive definition (see pp. 53–54) of the word "religious"; and there, perhaps, ends the argument and begins the fight.

It would seem, then, that having a certain kind of experience is not *by itself* a guarantee that an objective thing corresponding to that experience exists. Let us compare the present situation for a moment with a situation encountered in perception. Suppose a person were to argue, "Of course ghosts exist; how else could I have seen one last night?" One need not deny that the person had a *visual experience* of a certain kind, which led him to declare the existence of ghosts; but having the ghost-experience is perfectly compatible with having a hallucination. A traveler in the desert may "see" an oasis in the sense of having a visual experience which leads him to judge that there is an oasis not far off; but of course he can judge wrongly. The existence of the experiences is not denied—the persons in question are not deliberately deceiving others when they report thus, but what can be denied is that an objective ghost or oasis exists which is the object of these experiences. If the occurrence of these experiences were sufficient to insure the existence of the alleged objects of these experiences, we would have to say that every dream-object or hallucination which anyone ever experienced had an objective existence.

Religious experiences are, of course, very different from these ghost-experiences and oasis-experiences. They are far more intense, more deep-seated, more valuable, and they "mean more" to the experiencers. As far as the inference from experience to object is concerned, however, the same consideration applies: one cannot, merely on the basis of having the experience, admit any one of the alleged objects of the experience without admitting them all. The fact of religious experience alone cannot guarantee the truth of a religious belief. When we assert that something objective exists, the mere fact of having a (subjective) experience is not enough; there must be some *criteria of objectivity* for distinguishing what has objective existence (as opposed to existence merely as an experience, like the oasis in the hallucination) from what does not have objective existence.

In the case of perceiving physical objects, we do have such criteria; here we do bridge the gap between subjective and objective. Here we not only have experiences, we can tell by means of them (not always right away) whether or not there is a real oasis, a real unicorn, and so on. How do we do this? The criteria by means of which we distinguish cases of "truly perceiving" from "falsely perceiving" (veridical and non-veridical perception) will be discussed on pp. 509–14. It must suffice here to note that there are such criteria and that in fact we use them every day of our lives. In most cases, at any rate, a hallucination does not deceive us very long; in general, we know how to distinguish a real oasis from an oasis-hallucination. A single experience does not suffice for this, but a number of them, of a certain variety and in a certain order, do.

Why can we not do this in the case of religious experiences? There is no reason in principle why we cannot; but in fact *no set of criteria* in this field has ever been set forth which enables us to distinguish veridical from non-veridical religious experiences. No matter what criteria have been suggested—such as number of people having the experiences, repetition of the experiences, intensity, duration—various conflicting religious views are admitted by these criteria. There is no means, at least not by the argument from religious experience alone, of admitting any one religious hypothesis while rejecting the rest.

In one sense of "see," when we say we see an oasis we are asserting no more than that we are having a certain kind of visual experience; but in another sense of "see," we are asserting in addition that a real physical oasis exists, and in this second sense, having the visual experience does not ensure that the oasis exists. When we say that we experience God, in one sense of "experience" we are asserting only that we are having a certain (indescribable) kind of feeling; in another sense, we are asserting in addition that an objective being, God, exists, and in this second sense, having the feeling does not ensure that such a being exists. We should not confuse these two senses; else we may slip from the first sense to the second and make an inference from experience to object which we are not entitled to make. When a statement which seems to be simply about an experience asserts, however covertly, the existence of something beyond the experience itself, then the occurrence of the experience alone can never guarantee that the thing beyond it exists.

E. The Utility Argument

The argument which often goes by the name of "the utility argument" is strictly irrelevant to the present discussion, and is not much used in philosophical circles. But since it is an extremely popular one in the public mind, perhaps it should be mentioned here. The argument runs somewhat as follows: Belief in God is a great and indispensable moral influence. Without it, human beings would not live good lives. Therefore, it must be true. (The argument is not usually stated in this bald fashion, but its validity is often assumed in popular reasoning.)

If this is intended as a serious argument, several obvious considerations present themselves:

1. Of which religious belief is the argument intended to establish the truth? All of them? But they contradict one another and cannot all be true. If only one of them is established by the argument, why not the others?

2. Is it really the case that religion is indispensable to good conduct? To determine this, of course, we would have to conduct a detailed survey of the mores of all tribes and nations in order to know whether there were fewer murders, acts of deceit, and so on, and more kindness, fair play, and honesty (or whatever we had in mind in speaking of "good conduct"), when religious belief was present than when it was not. We would have to make sure whether all moral acts that were done in the *name* of religion were done *because* of religion; whether the effects of early religious training were the result of being religious rather than of merely being early; whether the influence of religion was more powerful in shaping a moral life than the influence of parental authority or public opinion, even when these were divorced from religion.[11] Such an investigation, however interesting, would hardly belong in philosophy; it would be a purely empirical investigation: in this case, whether religious belief was correlated with a marked increase in good conduct and a decrease in bad, independently of other possible influences, such as law and public opinion.

3. More relevant here, however, is the question "What does the utility argument prove?" Let us assume for the moment that people live better lives if they possess religious beliefs and worse ones if they do not. Would this show that the beliefs were *true?* If people could be made to behave only if

---

[11] John Stuart Mill's essay, "The Utility of Religion," in his *Three Essays on Religion,* is a classic study of this question.

they believed in ghosts, would this make the belief in ghosts true? The moment this question is asked there seems little doubt about the answer. Beliefs are not rendered true or false by the fact that people want to believe them, or are persuaded to believe them, or need to believe them. Belief in Santa Claus or in "good luck just around the corner" does not make such beliefs true, however much they may buoy up one's spirits; and refusal to believe in any unpleasant facts does not make them any less facts. You might, of course, have a "moral right" to hold to a belief, whether true or not, if highly desirable consequences resulted from believing it (this is a moral question), but saying that a belief is true and saying that you will be better off for believing it are, nevertheless, two different things. If a particular religious belief has a good moral influence, this does not prove it true, and if it has a bad moral influence, this does not prove it false; it is simply irrelevant either way. Saying "If people believed it, however questionable, this would be a good thing" is very different from saying "The belief is true." And in daily life this is ordinarily accepted—we all store in our minds many true but useless bits of information, like obsolete telephone numbers. When a belief is widely accepted as true, no question ordinarily arises about whether it is also useful, certainly not about whether its usefulness is a reason for believing it to be true. John Stuart Mill said:

An argument for the utility of religion is an appeal to unbelievers, to induce them to practice a well-meant hypocrisy, or to semi-believers to make them avert their eyes from what might possibly shake their unstable belief, or finally to persons in general to abstain from expressing any doubts they may feel, since a fabric of immense importance to mankind is so insecure at its foundations, that men must hold their breath in its neighborhood for fear of blowing it down.[12]

And Bertrand Russell has said in our own day:

I can respect the men who argue that religion is true and therefore ought to be believed, but I can feel only profound reprobation for those who say that religion ought to be believed because it is useful, and that to ask whether it is true is a waste of time.[13]

Many persons, indeed, have been much concerned to disengage morality from any dependence on religion. They have felt that it is a dangerous thing for religion and morality to be closely intertwined in the public mind, the survival of morality being made dependent on the survival of religion; for in that case, if the religious belief should ever collapse, the morality which has been made dependent upon it may collapse with it.

[12] *Ibid*, p. 70.
[13] *Why I Am Not a Christian* (London: George Allen & Unwin, Ltd., 1957), p. 172.

F. The Argument from Miracles

One of the most popular arguments for the existence of God has always been the occurrence of miracles. The argument runs as follows: Miracles have occurred at various times in human history. (There is much disagreement, however, over which events were miraculous and which were not.) And how could you account for a miracle in any other way than by saying that God intervened in the natural course of events (took nature into his own hands, so to speak) and made the miraculous event occur? The occurrence of miracles, then, proves that God exists.

But what *is* a miracle? Suppose that at this moment a solid iron bar is thrown into water and floats. Many persons see this happen, and the event is photographed. Is it a miracle? What must an event be like in order to be miraculous?

1.   Everyone would probably agree that a miracle must be an unusual event; something that happened all the time or even once a year would not be considered miraculous, unless we extended the word to include such uses as "the miracle of sound," "the miracle of the new Chrysler," and so on. A miracle can hardly be just any unusual event. The earth passing through a comet would be an unusual event, but it would not be considered·miraculous as long as it could be accounted for (as it could) by known laws of nature. Perhaps an object may drop from an airplane and in falling strike a telephone wire outside your window and sever the wire, and the segment of wire on its way to the ground may strike a passing cat and electrocute it. This is surely unusual—"it wouldn't happen again in a million times"—but it would not be considered miraculous, since everything that occurred in this unusual sequence of events is explainable by known laws.

2.   It would seem, then, that no event would be called a miracle as long as it is an instance of some known law or laws of nature. But is this enough? Suppose that an event occurred which could not be accounted for on the basis of any *known* laws of nature. Would it then be a miracle? Probably it would make us suspect that there were some laws of nature we did not yet know, or that some of those we were already familiar with had been inaccurately formulated and must be revised or qualified in such a way as to admit the new occurrence. When it was first noticed that photographic plates were exposed although they had been in complete darkness all the time, this could not be accounted for on the basis of any known law of nature; but men soon came to realize that there were other laws they had never suspected which did account for this curious phenomenon, and in so doing the science of radioactivity was founded. When comets' tails were found to be repelled by the sun, it was not assumed that the universal attractive power of matter stated in the Law of Gravitation had gone berserk; new laws were discovered which accounted for cases like these.

3. Under what conditions *would* an event be considered miraculous? We cannot now say "when it isn't an instance of any *known* law"; shall we say "when it isn't an instance of *any law at all,* known or unknown"? This would seem to be more satisfactory; at least it escapes the objection to the previous view. Of course, on this conception of a miracle, we could never definitely state that any event was miraculous. For how could we ever know that the event in question could never, even in millions of future years of scientific investigation, be explained on the basis of some law of nature, however complicated and elusive? We could not, and therefore we could never know an event to be miraculous. If the iron bar suddenly floated, we would indeed be surprised; but who knows after all exactly what complicated sets of circumstances may cause matter to behave as it does? We judge what is probable or improbable by the kind of behavior Nature has exhibited in the past; but there may be a good many springs in Nature's depths which only occasionally, or under very special conditions, bubble up to the surface. The surprising behavior of the iron bar might turn out to have something to do with the moisture in the air, or some law of radioactivity not now known, or even the mental state of observers. Such things would be unexpected because they are not in accordance with the way Nature generally works (as far as our present knowledge goes), but they would certainly not be without precedent in the history of science. It was a surprise to learn that profuse bleeding could result from a mental condition and not from any of the physiological causes so earnestly sought for, or that a perpetual hand-tremor could result from a forgotten aggressive act committed in early childhood in which no physiological damage was done. Many persons are still suspicious of such phenomena because they feel that "Nature just doesn't work that way"; but we should have learned enough by now in the hard school of scientific experience to know that Nature has a few tricks up her sleeve that we never suspected, and which will certainly seem strange as long as we judge "how Nature ought to behave" by laws which are already familiar to us.

The important point here is that, on this definition of "miracle," we could never be sure that any event, no matter how bizarre or unusual or contrary to the regular course of our experience, was a miracle; we could never know that the event could not be subsumed under some laws. However, let us *suppose* that we could be absolutely sure that some such event was *not an instance of any law at all, known or unknown.* Would this show that God must be invoked to account for it? The answer seems almost inevitable: of course it wouldn't; it would only prove that some events are not instances of laws. But to establish this and to establish the existence of God are, of course, two entirely different things.

4. According to others—for example, John Stuart Mill—an event cannot be considered a miracle no matter how strange it is, if it would occur again if the same set of conditions were repeated. (This comes to much the same thing as the preceding sense.) In order to constitute a miracle, an event must take

place *without* having been preceded by a set of conditions which are sufficient to make it happen again. The test of a miracle is: Were there present conditions such that whenever these conditions reappear the event will recur? If there were, the event is no miracle. Once again, of course, we could never be sure that an event was a miracle in this sense—we could never know for sure that if the same conditions were to recur, the "miracle" would not recur; at best we could only know that when the conditions were the same as *far as we knew* (and taking into account only those conditions which we thought to be causally related to the event, we have to add this provision or else the conditions to be included might be extended to cover the entire state of the universe, which of course can never repeat itself), the allegedly miraculous event did not occur. But there might always be other conditions that never occurred to us to consider, which were yet causally relevant, and if added to the set of conditions to be repeated, the event *would* recur.

Moreover, just as on the preceding definition of "miracle," even if somehow we *could* know that we had all the relevant conditions, and that they were all the same, but the event did not recur, what would this prove? Only indeterminism—that is, that two identical sets of conditions may yet be followed by non-identical events. This might be a surprise, but would it force us to invoke God to account for it, any more than a completely deterministic state of affairs would do so? After all, one might ask, why shouldn't the universe be indeterministic rather than deterministic?

5. There is still another meaning of the word "miracle," according to which a miracle would be *defined* as an intervention of God into the natural course of events. Now if it is asked whether a miracle in this sense would entail (logically imply) the existence of God, the answer of course would be yes—an intervention of God would indeed entail (logically imply) the existence of a God that could intervene! But this definition, of course, begs the whole question. The question would now become *"Are* there any miracles in this sense? *Is* there in fact anything to correspond to this definition?" *If* there are miracles in the sense we are now considering, then of course God exists, but to say this is only to utter a crass tautology; it is only to say "If God intervenes, there is a God." But what would establish the statement that God intervenes? The existence of unusual events, as we have just seen, would not prove it.

Thus the argument from miracles encounters the following dilemma: if miracles are defined in any of the ways other than the last one, their occurrence could at most prove indeterminisim, but not God; while if miracles are defined in the last way, they do require a God to cause them (indeed it is analytic to say so), but there is no way of showing that any event exists to correspond to the definition.

The existence of unusual events would not *prove* it to be a miracle; but couldn't the existence of such events give it a high credibility, make it extremely probable? In other words, is there any evidence that such events occurred that might reasonably be interpreted as divine intervention into the course of events?

Many such events have been alleged. It has been alleged that the sun stood still for Joshua in ancient Israel, and that it stood still once again before the citizens of the Portuguese village of Fatima in 1917. It has been alleged that water was turned into wine, that a small number of loaves and fishes was multiplied into enough to feed thousands, that people were raised from the dead, healed of their diseases, and so on—all through miraculous intervention. Of course, if these events can be explained by natural means, no recourse to miracles is required; this is often the case with the healing of diseases, for example, in which cures are often possible by psychological means such as hypnotism, combined with a certain mental set on the part of the patient. But there is no known way events like the multiplication of loaves and the sun standing still can be accounted for by natural means. So, it is argued, if they occurred, it must be miraculous: an intervention of God.

But did they occur? In his famous essay "On Miracles," Hume argued that our only guide to estimating the probability of these alleged events is our total experience of the existing order of nature. "No testimony," he wrote, "is sufficient to establish a miracle unless the testimony be of such a kind that its falsehood would be more miraculous than the fact which it endeavors to establish." And in virtually every miracle ever recorded, it is more congruous with the course of our experience to believe that the miracle did not occur. That people are deluded (or even that they lie), that rumors spread and are wildly exaggerated when they have spread even a small distance from their source, that people will believe almost anything and broadcast it as true when it is something they *want* to believe and are already strongly conditioned toward believing—these are all facts well known to all of us and require no miracles for us to believe; we are acquainted with all these things in our everyday experiences. Most alleged miracles were reported by people in bygone times whose stories we can no longer check, people moreover who were ill-trained in reporting exactly what they saw and were usually wishing for the occurrence of the miracles; and the wish was father to the belief. Even when the miracle *was* attested by many people, as was the case in Fatima, our reason for doubting it is much greater than our reason for believing it, since we know what would have to happen in nature in order for the account to be true. For the sun to stand still in the sky—that is, for the earth to stop revolving about the sun—would be contrary to the entire course of nature as we know it, and it would have many other consequences, such as objects flying off into space, which did not occur. It is more probable, then, that the people were deluded in their reports of what happened than that the miraculous event actually occurred.

None of this, however, *proves* that the events reported did not occur. We may have no decisive evidence that they did; but neither have we (at least in many cases) decisive evidence that they did not. We are rather in the position of a Sherlock Holmes who has to solve a crime that was committed many years ago and in which most of the clues once available have now vanished. The fact is that people who *already* believe in God on other grounds will tend to believe in miracles as an added manifestation of God's handiwork but that people who see no reason to believe in God do not find in the evidence about miracles anything sufficient to convince them on these grounds alone. The argument from miracles does not constitute a strong enough argument by itself, but if one is already convinced by one or more of the *other* arguments for God's existence, he may accept this one as supplementary to it.

Belief or disbelief in miracles—in the events occurring *as being* manifestations of God—depends not nearly as much on the evidence in the particular case (in most cases we have no evidence one way or the other) as on our antecedent beliefs or disbeliefs about God's nature. We believe that most of the alleged miracles are in some way unworthy of an omnipotent being. If God wanted people to believe in him, why perform a few miracles in a remote area where few people could witness them? Would it not be just as easy for an omnipotent being to issue proclamations in loud tones emanating from the sky and simultaneously intelligible to all people in all languages? If the latter had occurred, many more people would be convinced of God's existence than they would from any present accounts, where most people have to go by hearsay. Instead of healing a few people of their disease, why not all sufferers? Instead of performing a miracle in Fatima in 1917, why not put an end to the enormous slaughter of World War I, which was occurring at the same time, or keep it from starting? Or, if this is tampering with man's free-will, why not perform another kind of miracle that would also save lives, such as stopping the earthquake in Lisbon that killed 30,000 people as they were gathered in their churches to worship (the example repeatedly employed by Voltaire in *Candide*)? Why not stop or prevent a major catastrophe instead of a minor one, instead of an event like turning water into wine, which made little difference one way or the other compared with the vast misery of human beings at the same time and place, none of which was alleviated?

It is interesting to observe, also, that people are quick to accept as a miracle any unusual event, or an event that goes contrary to natural probabilities, as long as it works in their favor. A hundred people are killed in an airplane accident, but one survives. "It's a miracle!" say the survivor and his family. What the families of the non-survivors had to say about the matter is usually not recorded. Now suppose, instead, that there is an airplane accident in which one person dies but a hundred survive. The family of the one non-survivor does not say, "It's a miracle!" although the survival of a hundred when one dies is on a par with the survival of one when a hundred die. In general, people who already have some kind of theistic belief are apt to call miraculous any event that is unusual, whose causes they do not fully know, and that works in their favor. Those who reflect on this fact are not likely to put much stock in the argument from miracles—not because they have an alternative explanation for the event (though sometimes they do) but because they see that what people call a miracle depends very much on what they *want* to believe, more than on what the facts of the case are. One would not call a miracle the sudden death of all one's friends, no matter how much the event defied a natural explanation, though some might say it of the death of their enemies; the enemies, of course, would simply reverse the classification. Moreover, each religion has its own set of miracles; and the events that are classed as miracles by one religious group are denied to be miracles by the others.

G. The Teleological Argument (Argument from Design)

The most popular of all the arguments for the existence of God is the teleological argument, or argument from design. This argument attempts to arrive by empirical means at the conclusion that God exists, by examining the world and trying to show that it points to the existence of a God. Look out upon the world, says the argument, and you will find that it shows many evidences of order and design. If you reflect on the way the universe is arranged, you will find it difficult to avoid the conclusion that there is a purpose in it, that a Master Architect has been at work. Not blind chance but purpose governs the universe. And where there is a purpose, there must be a purposer; where there is design, there must be a designer.

But what kind of designer? What kind of being must the designer of the universe be? Is he (or it) a person, a personality? Does he have intelligence, wisdom? Does he have unlimited power? Is he benevolently disposed toward his creation, or malevolently, or indifferently?

And how are we to know? Since the being never appears in person, how are we to infer his existence? Assuming that we can infer that he exists, how are we to determine his nature? What evidences have we to go by?

To a greater extent than any of the previous arguments, the teleological argument takes its cue from the specific features of the universe. The universe has such-and-such features, therefore a divine designer exists: that is the structure of the argument. Just as we can infer the nature of the changes in the earth's crust during the past millions of years on the basis of geological evidence, so we can infer the existence and nature of a designer on the basis of certain features of the universe in general. Presumably if the evidences in nature were different, our conclusions about the nature, or even the existence, of the designer would be different.

The arguments here are *only* for a cosmic designer. The teleological argument, if successful, does not prove the existence of a necessary being, a first cause, or even a creator-of-the-universe-out-of-nothing. At best, it could only give evidence that the universe is the product of design, which requires a being with intelligence and enough power to shape the materials of the universe in accordance with a plan. Thus it is questionable whether a designer, if he exists, should be called "God." The first-cause argument, had it been successful, would have yielded us only a first cause; the contingency argument, had it been successful, would have yielded us only a necessary being; the teleological argument, if it is successful, will yield us only a cosmic designer. Traditionally we give the name "God" to *all* these things, but this is a confusion. A first cause need not also be a designer nor a source of religious experience nor a source of moral precepts. We should not say that they must all be the same being just because we use the word "God" for them all. At any rate, if we do say that what we get as the upshot of all these arguments is the very same being, in fact as well as in name, we would require additional arguments to prove this. When Plato discussed the hypothesis of a Designer (or Artificer) in his dialogue *Timaeus,* he never assumed (nor did any of the Greeks) that the cosmic designer was a first cause or that he created the universe *ex nihilo:* he took the materials that were already to hand and shaped them in accordance with a plan, much as a builder takes materials that are already in existence and uses them to build a house.

Let us see, then, what forms the teleological argument can take, what kind of designer it can make a case for, and what evidence it can adduce. When we have done so, we shall examine the general structure of the argument in all its varying forms.

The universe, the argument begins, is *orderly,* and order is the result of design. The millions of stars in the heavens behave in an orderly manner, all exhibiting certain physical laws that hold equally for all of them; and so do the millions of species of life on the earth. How could all these things have come into existence except as the result of design? Pieces of clay do not come together of themselves to make bricks, or bricks to form a house; this requires the designing activity of man. In the same way, particles of matter cannot come together of themselves to form living cells, or cells to form the complex living organisms that inhabit the earth; such a result can be brought about only by a designer who fashions the materials in such a way as to form them.

But such arguments are subject to several objections: (1) The word "order" is not very clear: that which seems orderly to one person will not seem so to another. A painting that appears orderly to one observer will appear chaotic to another. (2) Nor is it clear that the universe is orderly in any specific sense. If galaxies are orderly, but drifting nebulae in the universe are not, then it must be pointed out that there are many nebulae in the universe; and so on for anything that might be considered not to be orderly. Yet if *anything* that the universe contains is orderly, no matter what, then what are the limits on the term "orderly"? What could count *against* a thing or arrangement of things being orderly? If you throw a bag of marbles on the floor, they must fall out in *some* order or other. In this sense, every arrangement of things must be orderly, so the statement that *this* universe is orderly tells us nothing distinctive about it. (3) Most important, what is the guarantee that order is always the result of design? Some examples of order are indeed the result of design, as in the case of mechanical objects (watches, wrenches, automobiles); we know this because we ourselves (or other human beings) have taken the materials and put them together in certain ways to form objects that we can use and enjoy. The order is there as a result of designing minds—*ours*. But as Hume said, order is evidence for design *only* to the extent that order has been *observed* to result from design. And the order we find in plants and animals has *not* been observed to result from design. We have never seen any beings who form plants or animals, or for that matter stars, as a result of their design, and therefore we are not entitled to conclude that these things do exist as the result of design.

"But that's just the point," the defender of the teleological argument will reply. "We have never *seen* plants and animals being designed the way architects design buildings and watchmakers design watches, but we must *infer* that they were designed, for how else could we account for their existence? Once again, stones don't come together on their own to form cathedrals, and neither can particles of matter come together to form organisms. This requires intelligence, and since the intelligence in the case of organisms is not human, it must be divine."

This comment, however, invites still another objection. What if the phenomenon in question can be explained without assuming the existence of a cosmic designer? Then we shall not, strictly speaking, have disproved the hypothesis, but we shall have shown that it isn't required in order to account for the facts. Can this be done, specifically in the case of organisms, which are the most striking example of order that invites the hypothesis of design?

In a universe composed chiefly of inorganic matter, the existence of life and mind seemed a mystery that could be explained only on the hypothesis of a cosmic designer. But for many thousands of years there have been theories of organic evolution attempting to explain the existence of organisms without recourse to the hypothesis of a designer. The early Greek philosopher Anaximander (611–547 B.C.), for example, argued that organisms originally sprang from the sea and evolved into land-creatures. But no comprehensive theory with the full weight of detailed and painstaking empirical observation behind it arose until the publication of Charles Darwin's *The Origin of Species* in 1859. Darwin set forth a hypothesis according to which organisms gradually evolved, from the simplest amoebas to the most complex primates, through the struggle for existence and the survival of the fittest. As a result of his pioneering and the work of many biologists since then, the hypothesis of organic evolution has become so well confirmed as to be universally accepted among biologists. It did not, to be sure, explain everything: it explained the *survival* rather than the *arrival* of organisms. But this gap too has been virtually closed, beginning more than a century ago with the synthesis in the laboratory of uric acid (the first organic compound to be produced from non-organic ones) to the latest experiments with the protein molecule today. Gradually, by bits and pieces, the formation of life (under conditions occurring during the pre-Cambrian era of the earth's history) has come to be explained without any recourse to design.

The designer-hypothesis has not thereby been shown to be false. If a person believed in design before, he could do so after Darwin as well as before, even accepting all of Darwin's conclusions. He could say that, whereas it had previously been thought that God had created all the species instantaneously, he now believed that God had chosen the slow and gradual process of evolution as a means of executing his design. The method of design would have changed, but not the fact. Nevertheless, the teleological argument has lost most of its currency (among scientists, at any rate) since Darwin—not because Darwin disproved design, for he did not, but because there no longer seemed to be any necessity for having such a hypothesis. If you believed that a knock on your door was caused by the ghost of a departed spirit, you no longer need to believe this if you find that the knock was caused by a salesman making a call (though it is still possible for you to hold that the knock was caused by the salesman *and* a departed spirit).

But the impact of Darwin's theory cut somewhat deeper: it did not refute design in general, but it did appear to refute, or at any rate seriously to impair, belief in a *benevolent* design—yet the belief in a benevolent designer, one who cared about his creatures and did not wish them to suffer, has always been the mainspring of belief in design. People would not be so likely to be attracted to the argument from design if they thought that the cosmic designer was malevolent. Yet it was precisely the belief in a benevolent designer that was difficult to sustain in the face of belief in the evolutionary process, for the evolutionary process is a scene of continuous and endless strife, pain, and death. Life is a struggle for existence, in which many species die out and every individual inevitably dies—most often in direct agony, through starvation, cold, disease, or being eaten alive by other animals. The individual life is expendable: millions of individuals of every species die every day (usually before they have lived out a full life), but life continues through their offspring, who in their turn die in pain and suffering. Does the designer inflict all this suffering merely to preserve the species, at the expense of the individual? If so, it is not much consolation to the individual; and of what value is a species if all the individuals in it must live a life of constant threat and insecurity and finally die in pain and suffering? Besides, nature is no more careful of the species or type than of the individual: thousands of species have perished through starvation, changes in climate, being attacked by other animals, or because some new mutation arose that was swifter or more adaptable. Nature throughout is red with blood.

> "So careful of the type?" but no.
> From scarped cliff and quarried stone
> She cries, "A thousand types are gone:
> I care for nothing, all shall go.

. . . . .

> [Shall] Man, her last work, who seem'd so fair,
>   Such splendid purpose in his eyes,
>   Who roll'd the psalm to wintry skies,
> Who built him fanes of fruitless prayer,
>
> Who trusted God was love indeed
>   And love Creation's final law—
>   Tho' Nature, red in tooth and claw
> With ravine, shriek'd against his creed—
>
> Who loved, who suffer'd countless ills,
>   Who battled for the True, the Just,
>   Be blown about the desert dust,
> Or seal'd within the iron hills?[14]

Through countless ages innumerable species of creatures evolve; those that are able to adjust themselves to changing conditions, to find sufficient food and drink and shelter and safety, survive for a time; the rest are blotted out in the struggle for existence. Most living things, including all the carnivorous animals, can continue to live only by catching other living things as prey and devouring them as food. Even when they are successful in this (at the expense of the creatures they kill), the environmental conditions are so undependable, and the life of the organism so dependent on a vast multitude of conditions (they can live only within a narrow range of temperature, moisture, and nutritional supply), that even a comparatively small change in the environment or disorder in the functioning of the organism may cause their extinction. If nature is designed, the plan of the designer is not merciful.

In sober truth, nearly all the things which men are hanged or imprisoned for doing to one another, are nature's every-day performances. Killing, the most criminal act recognized by human laws, Nature does once to every being that lives; and in a large proportion of cases, after protracted tortures such as only the greatest monsters whom we read of ever purposely inflicted on their living fellow-creatures. . . . Nature impales men, breaks them as if on the wheel, casts them to be devoured by wild beasts, burns them to death, crushes them with stones like the first Christian martyr, starves them with hunger, freezes them with cold, poisons them by the quick or slow venom of her exhalations, and has hundreds of other hideous deaths in reserve, such as the ingenious cruelty of a Nabis or a Domitian never surpassed. All this, Nature does with the most supercilious disregard both of mercy and of justice, emptying her shafts upon the best and noblest indifferently with the meanest and worst; upon those who are engaged in the highest and worthiest enterprises, and often as the direct consequences of the noblest acts; and it might almost be imagined as a punishment for them. She mows down those on whose exist-

---

[14] Alfred, Lord Tennyson, *In Memoriam*, LVI.

ence hangs the well-being of a whole people, perhaps the prospects of the human race for generations to come, with as little compunction as those whose death is a relief to themselves, or a blessing to those under their noxious influence. Such are Nature's dealings with life. Even when she does not intend to kill, she inflicts the same tortures in apparent wantonness. In the clumsy provision which she has made for that perpetual renewal of animal life, rendered necessary by the prompt termination she puts to it in every individual instance, no human being ever comes into the world but another human being is literally stretched on the rack for hours or days, not infrequently issuing in death. Next to taking life . . . is taking the means by which we live; and Nature does this too on the largest scale and with the most callous indifference. A single hurricane destroys the hopes of a season; a flight of locusts, or an inundation, desolates a district; a trifling chemical change in an edible root, starves a million of people. The waves of the sea, like banditti seize and appropriate the wealth of the rich and the little all of the poor with the same accompaniments of stripping, wounding, and killing as their human antitypes. Everything, in short, which the worst men commit either against life or property, is perpetrated on a larger scale by natural agents. . . .[15]

The facts of biology, then, lend no plausibility to the hypothesis of a benevolent designer. Yet arguments for design persist: (1) "Consider what a variety of conditions are required for life to exist at all. There must be a basic minimum of elements—oxygen, nitrogen, carbon, and hydrogen —without which life cannot exist at all; there must be certain conditions of moisture, temperature, and soil that must be fulfilled; and just these conditions do exist on the earth. How could such a concatenation of conditions have come about except by design?" But on the other hand, one could argue, "Life requires a delicate combination of conditions in order to exist at all—true. But on the many planets that do *not* support life (and ours is the only one we know that does), this combination of conditions does not exist—is this to be taken as evidence against design? Moreover, the variety of conditions required for life on this planet works against us; when one such condition, such as sufficient moisture, is not met, the creature dies of thirst. The organism is an enormously complex structure, admirable to behold, and according to you a proof of design. But this complexity means that when one thing goes wrong, the organism does become ill and often dies; heart disease, cancer, fibrosis of the liver—any of a number of things can extinguish his life; if life did not depend on such a delicate balance of conditions, it might not be so hedged on every side by threats to its existence and dangers of its extinction." (2) "What a marvelous design exists in living organisms: consider a young kitten, leaping and playing; its body, a vast network of tiny nerves and muscles and bones, regenerates with smooth efficiency. Surely such a complex system must have been designed." But on the other hand, "With what wonderful craftsmanship the pit viper is designed: it can both see

---

[15] John Stuart Mill, "Nature," in *Three Essays on Religion,* pp. 28–30.

its prey and sense it directionally in the dark by means of the heat that the victim's body emits; its tongue darts out, and with lightning-like speed its fangs with their deadly poison are infixed in the body of its victim, who swells up, goes blind, undergoes the most indescribable pain, and within half an hour is dead." (If the victims were always rats or other creatures we do not like, we would probably not mind, but human beings are equally the victims. People want the design to be not only benevolent but benevolent toward *them*. A design that kept vipers going at the expense of people or even dogs is not one likely to appeal to people.) (3) "What wonderful forces are at work in the human body, so complex that centuries of biological investigation have not yet enabled us to understand its workings fully. Every part is interdependent with every other part, one part assisting another when the organism's life is threatened, each part working together with others to maintain the health of the entire organism." "Ah, but not always. Because of this very interdependence, things are constantly going wrong, and often no cure is possible. Moreover, surgeons (not supplied by nature but by man's ingenuity) have to get at our internal organs as one would open a can of sardines, since the designer, if there is one, has seen fit to put these complex and vulnerable organs inside us without the convenience of a zipper-like opening for easier access. Would it have been much trouble for the designer to make our arteries out of durable elastic tubing so that they would not harden with age? Wouldn't people be better off if brain-power and energy-drive lasted throughout a lifetime instead of reaching a peak at about 40 and then declining? Why should so many people, before they even start in life, be condemned by incipient weaknesses and congenital diseases, to physical agony or chronic illness or idiocy? Nor are the parts replaced in the course of nature when they go wrong; what would you think of a car-manufacturer who failed to supply new parts even though his automobiles were constantly needing them? Observe too how a cancer works away at a vital organ, silently and unnoticed, as if to escape detection by anyone who wants to discover it before it is too late, making the victim suffer unremitting torments for weeks or months, passing through every stage of intense pain until death comes as a relief."

The problem of evil. The principal objection to the teleological argument, if that argument is intended to prove the existence of a *benevolent* designer, is the problem of evil. In ancient times Epicurus (342–270 B.C.) put the problem as follows: "Is God willing to prevent evil, but not able? Then he is not omnipotent. Is he able, but not willing? Then he is malevolent. Is he both able and willing? Then whence evil?" Hume put the argument in the form of a dilemma: "If the evil in the world is from the intention of the Deity, then he is not benevolent. If the evil in the world is contrary to his intention, then he is not omnipotent. But it is either in accordance with his intention or contrary to it. Therefore, either the Deity is not benevolent or he is not omnipotent."

We should notice first that the problem arises only if the hypothesis is that of a designer who is both omnipotent and benevolent. If he is not omnipotent, then the evil in the world can be attributed to the fact that he doesn't desire it but is unable to prevent it. If he is not benevolent, then the evil can be said to arise from the fact that he is able to prevent it but doesn't wish to. But if he is both benevolent and omnipotent (which most religions say that he is), then the problem arises in full force: why evil?

Hume's dilemma is valid, as every student of elementary logic can work out for himself. But are its premises true? There have been a number of attempts to escape from it by questioning one or more premises in some way or other.

1. There is no evil in the world. One might deny that there is any evil at all and thus undercut the presupposition of the problem. But this solution is so implausible that it would take considerable gall to suggest it. People may not entirely agree on what things are evil (it would require a long excursus into ethics in order to become clearer about this), but they do agree that some things are. Who does not believe that some things are bad and to be avoided? Ordinarily, for example, we believe that pain and suffering are evil, and we exhibit this belief in our practice when we try to avoid them or to minimize them as much as possible; for example, we try to alleviate the pain of those who suffer from terminal diseases. And surely this suffering does occur—just walk through the wards of any hospital. Nor is the suffering illusory: people do not merely *think* they are suffering, they *are* suffering. The fact of such suffering is, indeed, one of the principal reasons many persons find it difficult to believe in a God who is both all-powerful and benevolent. *We* would alleviate these sufferings if we could; yet God, who is supposedly all-powerful and benevolent, fails to do so.

2. Evil is a negative thing. St. Augustine advanced the idea that evil is not a positive thing but a lack, a privation, a negative. There is no evil, but only the comparative absence of good; evil is simply non-being. Sometimes it is added, as Augustine did, that to be real is to be perfect, and thus only God can be wholly real; his creation, being necessarily finite and limited, must necessarily involve incomplete goodness, and thus involve evil to some degree or other.

But to say that evil is negative seems to be primarily a play on words. Is war negative, the absence of peace, or is peace negative, the absence of war? Whichever way we classify it, the one is as real as the other—there is war and there is peace; there is happiness and there is suffering; there is good and there is evil. The facts of reality are not changed by being classified as negative or positive. Suffering exists, and is not alleviated in the slightest by the consideration that "it is only negative."

It may console the paralytic to be told that paralysis is mere lack of motility, nothing positive, and that insofar as he *is,* he is perfect. It is not clear, however, that this kind of comfort is available to the sufferer from malaria. He will reply that his trouble is not that he lacks anything, but rather that he has too much of something, namely, protozoans of the genus *Plasmodium*.[16]

3. *Evil is necessary to the greatest good.* "Granted that there is evil in the world. But there *has* to be, since that is the only way good can be achieved. We are all familiar with instances of this: you cannot get back to full health without painful surgery, but you undergo the surgery (which is not a good when considered by itself—that is, you wouldn't do it *except* thereby to achieve an end) to achieve a goal. The pain and suffering incurred are worth it as long as they are the only means by which you can achieve recovery. And so on for countless situations. Even war is sometimes the only way a better world (or the prevention of a worse one) can be attained. Thus, though there *is* evil in the world, it is compatible with the goodness of God, since the evil that there is is the least possible required to get the greatest possible good. This is not a perfect world, but it is the *best* of all *possible* worlds."

It is true that people often have to suffer pain in order to recover health, our medical knowledge being what it is, and the laws of nature (particularly of biology in this case) being what they are. But this consideration, which does justify a physician in inflicting pain on a patient in order that the patient may recover, applies only to limited beings who can achieve the end *in no other way*. Once we suspect, however, that the physician could achieve the goal *without* inflicting suffering on his patient, and that he is inflicting it anyway, we call him a cruel and sadistic monster. Now God, unlike the physician, is omnipotent; he could bring about a recovery without making the patient go through the excruciating pain. Why then does he not do this? If it is objected that this would require a miracle and that it would upset the orderliness of nature to continually perform miracles, it can be replied that the laws of nature could have been so set up that no miracle would be required in each case. After all, who is the author of the laws of nature? Why did God set up the causal order in such a way as to require his creatures to die in pain and agony? There is not the excuse in the case of God that there is in the case of the surgeon, who can bring about his patient's recovery *only* by causing suffering; for God, being omnipotent as well as benevolent, could easily bring about the recovery without such means; indeed, he could have kept the patient from being sick in the first place. What would we think of a surgeon who first infected his child's leg and then decided to amputate it, although a cure was within his power to give and the infection was of his own giving to begin with? But this would be precisely the position of an omnipotent God. A physician who is benevolent but not omnipotent can be excused for causing suffering only because the end can be achieved in no other way; but this is precisely what is not the case with an omnipotent God, for, being omnipotent, he does not need to use evil means to bring about a

[16] Wallace I. Matson, *The Existence of God*, pp. 142–43.

good end. Indeed, it is a mistake to use means-end terminology in talking about omnipotence at all: an omnipotent being could bring about the end directly, without embarking upon means to do it. Means toward ends have to be taken only by beings who are not omnipotent.

When I was in India, I was standing on the veranda of an Indian home darkened by bereavement. My Indian friend had lost his little son, the light of his eyes, in a cholera epidemic. At the far end of the veranda his little daughter, the only remaining child, slept in a cot covered over with a mosquito net. We paced up and down, and I tried in my clumsy way to comfort and console him. But he said, "Well, padre, it is the will of God. That's all there is to it. It is the will of God."

Fortunately I knew him well enough to be able to reply without being misunderstood, and I said something like this: "Supposing someone crept up the steps onto the veranda tonight, while you all slept, and deliberately put a wad of cotton soaked in cholera germ culture over your little girl's mouth as she lay in that cot there on the veranda, what would you think about that?"

"My God," he said, "what would I think about that? Nobody would do such a damnable thing. If he attempted it and I caught him, I would kill him with as little compunction as I would a snake, and throw him over the veranda. What did you mean by suggesting such a thing?"

"But John," I said quietly, "isn't that just what you have accused God of doing when you said it was His will? Call your little boy's death the result of mass ignorance, call it mass folly, call it mass sin, if you like, call it bad drains or communal carelessness, but don't call it the will of God. Surely we cannot identify as the will of God something for which a man would be locked up in jail, or put in a criminal lunatic asylum."[17]

Of course, if God too is limited in power, as the physician is, then the outcome may be the result of his inability to do better in spite of his good intentions. But such an excuse is not available in the case of a God who is both benevolent and omnipotent.

. . . did I show you a house or palace, where there was not one apartment convenient or agreeable; where the windows, doors, fires, passages, stairs, and the whole economy of the building were the source of noise, confusion, fatigue, darkness, and extremes of heat and cold; you would certainly blame the contrivance, without any further examination. The architect would in vain display his subtlety, and prove to you that if this door or that window were altered, greater ills would ensue. What he says, may be strictly true: the alteration of one particular, while the other parts of the building remain, may only augment the inconveniences. But still you would assert in general, that if the architect had had skill and good intentions, he might have formed such a plan of the whole, and might have adjusted the parts in such a manner, as would have remedied all or most of these inconveniences.[18]

[17] Leslie D. Weatherhead, *The Will of God* (Nashville: Abingdon Press, 1944), quoted in Harold Titus, *Ethics for Today,* 3rd ed., p. 539.

[18] David Hume, *Dialogues Concerning Natural Religion,* Part XI, Norman Kemp Smith edition (Edinburgh: Nelson & Sons, 1935), p. 204.

A good architect would have designed the house in such a way as to avoid these disadvantages, so that one would not have to choose between a design that was bad and one that was worse. And if an architect was so incompetent that he could devise no such house, perhaps he should refrain from any more house-designing. If the best universe that God could bring about is one as full of pain and suffering as this one, perhaps he should have refrained from universe-designing and chosen instead some activity in which he had greater competence.

"But doesn't good often come out of evil? Out of hardship and adversity comes achievement. Out of suffering comes appreciation of the feelings of others. Out of poverty comes thrift. And so on. How else can these things come about?"

"In the first place, if God could not bring about any other outcome, he is not omnipotent. *We* perhaps cannot bring about another outcome, conditions being what they are, and the laws of nature being what they are; but an omnipotent God could. In the second place, the good that comes out of evil is often hardly sufficient to justify it. The causal order is so complex that there is probably no disaster to one person that does not work to the advantage of another. A hurricane kills a hundred people and destroys a hundred buildings, but it provides work for builders. Is it worth it? If you were God, would you be justified in bringing about all this death and destruction in order to provide this work? Don't you consider the bombing of cities evil, in spite of the fact that some old buildings are destroyed, which enables new and better ones to be built on their site? Would *you* feel justified in bombing a city to bring about this result? And in the third place, if good sometimes comes out of evil, evil also sometimes comes out of good—probably just as frequently. For everything we thought evil at the time and later changed our minds about in the light of later developments, there is probably another event we thought good or beneficial at the time that in the light of later events we now consider disastrous or regrettable. The fact is that the most usual tendency is for good to produce more good and evil to produce more evil."

Health, strength, wealth, knowledge, virtue, are not only good in themselves but facilitate and promote the acquisition of good, both of the same and of other kinds. The person who can learn easily, is he who already knows much; it is the strong and not the sickly person who can do everything which most conduces to health; those who find it easy to gain money are not the poor but the rich; while health, strength, knowledge, talents, are all means of acquiring riches, and riches are often an indispensable means of acquiring these. Again, *e converso,* whatever may be said of evil turning into good, the general tendency of evil is towards further evil. Bodily illness renders the body more susceptible of disease; it produces incapacity of exertion, sometimes debility of mind, and often the loss of means of subsistence. All severe pain, either bodily or mental, tends to increase the susceptibilities of pain for ever after. Poverty is the parent of a thousand mental and moral evils. What is still worse, to be injured or oppressed, when habitual, lowers the whole tone of the character. One bad action leads to others, both in the agent himself, in the bystanders, and in the sufferers. All bad qualities are strengthened by habit, and all vices and follies tend to spread. Intellectual defects generate moral, and moral, intellectual; and every intellectual or moral defect generates others, and so on without end.[19]

"But the purpose of evil is not to make us happy but good, or virtuous. The world is a moral training-ground for the building of character. Evils are put there to discipline and improve us rather than to punish us."

"But the order of nature is such as to frustrate the goal of making people virtuous as much as or even more than the goal of making people happy. Here is a person who, we believe, needs to know what suffering is like, so that he will not be so insensitive to it in others; and what happens? He is never made to experience it; but a person who already is borne down by the weight of suffering only has more of the same heaped upon him—the person who already has one disease, let us say, contracts another. This is the way of things in the actual world. Sufferings occur hit-or-miss: they miss the person who (if anyone) should have them, and come constantly to others who already have more than they can bear, rendering them miserable and perhaps embittered for life. This is quite inconsistent with the behavior of a being who is both omnipotent and benevolent. Or to take a specific case: Here is a man who drives his car carelessly so as to be a danger to others on the highway. Short of changing his nature, the best way to make him more careful would be to have him involved in an accident in which he was slightly injured, just enough to scare him; but what actually happens, more often than not, is that he escapes scot-free while others are injured or killed, until that one last time when he himself is killed in an accident, when it is too late to improve him. If moral improvement was his aim, any reasonably intelligent 15-year-old who was benevolently disposed and had the power could effect a better distribution of good in the world than now exists."

If the Creator of mankind willed that they should all be virtuous, his designs are as completely baffled as if he had willed that they should all be happy; and the order of nature is constructed with even less regard to the requirements of justice than to those of benevolence. If the law of all creation were justice and the Creator omnipotent, then in whatever amount suffering and happiness might be dispensed to the world, each person's share of them would be exactly proportioned to that person's good or evil deeds; no human being would have a worse lot than another, without worse deserts; accident or favoritism would have no part in such a world, but every human life would be the playing out of a drama constructed like a perfect moral tale. . . . The world we live in is totally different from this; insomuch that the necessity of redressing the balance has been deemed one of the strongest arguments for another life after

[19] John Stuart Mill, "Nature," *Three Essays on Religion*, pp. 35–36.

death, which amounts to an admission that the order of things in this life is often an example of injustice, not justice. . . . Every kind of moral depravity is entailed upon multitudes by the fatality of their birth; through the fault of their parents, of society, or of uncontrollable circumstances, certainly through no fault of their own. Not even on the most distorted and contracted theory of good which ever was framed by religious or philosophical fanaticism, can the government of Nature be made to resemble the work of a being at once good and omnipotent.[20]

4. *Man's freedom as the cause of evil.* "The evil in the universe is caused by man's wickedness. Man is free, which means free to do evil as well as good. Even an omnipotent being could not make man free and yet not free to do evil. Evil is thus an inevitable consequence of man's freedom."

This is probably the most serious attempt to get round the problem of evil. Its first point, however, is factually mistaken: there is a distinction between *natural* and *moral* evils. Natural evils are those that occur in the course of nature without man's intervention: earthquakes, volcanic eruptions, floods, hurricanes, plagues, and so on. These catastrophes are not caused by man's activity. Moral evils, however, are those inflicted by men upon other men, such as mental and physical torture, plunder, killing, war. The latter is the only class of evils that could be said to be the result of man's wickedness. Even if the argument we are now considering is a valid one with regard to this class, it does not explain the existence of the natural evils.

But let us now concentrate on the moral evils.

A: Man, you will surely agree, is created a free being, which means that he is free to choose good or evil. His often choosing evil, then, is the result of his freedom. There is no way for man to be free except by having choices open to him, and the moment choices are open to him he may choose the worse instead of the better alternative. From this fact very great evils may indeed follow: one man in a position of power may order millions of other men to be killed in concentration camps. But all this is a part of man's freedom: once you grant that man is free, you must go along with it *all the way*. If man is free, he is free to perpetrate the most monstrous horrors upon other men.

B: But if this is so, is man's freedom worth such a price? If one man's freedom involves the power to have millions of other people exterminated, I'm quite sure the victims would wish the freedom of the dictator to be somewhat more limited. In order that *he* may have his freedom, *they* must be massacred. Isn't that putting rather too high a premium on *his* freedom, since his freedom requires that they give up not only their freedom but their lives? Is it any comfort to them, as the gas in the chamber is turned on, to reflect that this is the price they are paying for the dictator's freedom of decision? Could not that freedom be possible at a lesser price?

[20] *Ibid*, pp. 37–38.

A: No, it couldn't. If man is free, he is free to do the most atrocious evils. Otherwise freedom is a delusion.

B: But there are many things that man is not free to do now, such as fly like a bird or eat sticks and stones. I don't see why a few further limitations would not be beneficial. For instance, man might have a protective shell so that he would be immune to attack by other men, thus making murder impossible. Man would still be free to make countless decisions, and he would still have many choices open to him, but at least he would not be free to take away the lives (and with them the freedom) of *other* men. There would still be many choices available that did not carry in their train the destruction of other free agents. One of the greatest areas in which man can exercise his choice is in scientific or artistic creativity. There would be a large area of free choices here, without choices going so far as to involve murder. I would think that that would be a much better basis for the exercise of choice than we have now, for as things are now one man's choice may involve another man's destruction. And I would remind you that if God could *not* devise a system without evil in which man is free, then God is not omnipotent.

A: I don't believe this. Let's see what is involved in believing that God is omnipotent. I don't think it would make sense to say that God could do what is logically impossible. For example, God couldn't make a square circle, since if it was a circle it wouldn't be a square. Nor could God change the past, for this too would involve a contradiction: the past has already happened, and even omnipotence could not make what has happened *not* have happened. God could not make the past *not* have existed. When we say that God is omnipotent, then, we must mean that he can do anything *except* what is logically impossible.

B: I agree that divine omnipotence does not mean that God can do what is logically impossible. But why isn't it logically possible for God to create man free and yet not free to kill other men, for example? Man is not free in many other ways, and yet you don't say that man is not a free being because of these other limitations.

A: But God did create *human beings,* and if these human beings were not free in certain crucial respects—which includes the possibility of doing harm to one another—they would not be *human* beings but automata.

B: Then I would say that the price that is paid for making *human* beings, in your sense, is too great; the result is not worth it. But I would add, once again, that man could still be free in countless ways—free to exercise his power of choice in many directions—without causing the evil that exists now. Indeed, if God had made the world somewhat different, man could have been free to exercise his choice in much more fruitful and creative ways *without* the unfortunate consequence that such choices may have now—for instance, that one person may pay with his life (or a million persons may) for the free choices of other men. That this is possible seems to be an enormous blot on the nature of things. It removes some people from existence in order to secure the freedom of others. If I said to you, "God has made me free, so I am going to kill you now; that is part of my divine gift of freedom," you would, I suggest, not be deeply impressed by my reasoning.

A: It is only in the context of such a world as we have now that man's character and all his nobler attributes can be formed:

Suppose, contrary to fact, that this world were a paradise from which all possibility of pain and suffering were excluded. The consequences would be very far-reaching. For example, no one could ever injure anyone else: the murderer's knife would turn to paper or his bullets to thin air; the bank safe, robbed of a million dollars, would miraculously become filled with another million dollars (without this device, on however large a scale, proving infla-tionary); fraud, deceit, conspiracy, and treason would somehow always leave the fabric of society undamaged. Again, no one would ever be injured by acci-dent: the mountain-climber, steeplejack, or playing child falling from a height would float unharmed to the ground; the reckless driver would never meet with disaster. There would be no need to work, since no harm could result from avoiding work; there would be no call to be concerned for others in time of need or danger, for in such a world there could be no real needs or dangers.

. . . . . .

. . . [In] such a world . . . our present ethical concepts would have no meaning. . . . If, for example, the notion of harming someone is an essential element in the concept of a wrong action, in our hedonistic paradise there could be no wrong actions—nor any right actions in distinction from wrong. Courage and fortitude would have no point in an environment in which there is, by definition, no danger or difficulty. Generosity, kindness, the *agape* aspect of love, prudence, unselfishness, and all other ethical notions which presuppose life in a stable environment, could not even be formed. Consequently, such a world, however well it might promote pleasure, would be very ill adapted for the development of the moral qualities of human personality. In relation to this purpose it would be the worst of all possible worlds.[21]

B: An omnipotent God could still create man in such a way as to have him develop moral qualities without massacring one another. It's true that the moral qualities are very valuable, the world being what it is *now:* courage is valuable when one goes to war, but wouldn't a world without war be bet-ter? And couldn't human virtues still be exercised in other ways, for example in the self-discipline required to complete some worthwhile creative activity? Besides, we have already seen (pp. 466–67) that the world is not a very effi-cient training-ground of moral virtues—that if *that* is God's purpose, the pur-pose is as much frustrated as if it were to make men happy. Many of the things we call virtues now are so only because of the evil of the world we live in, and I would gladly do without them if the world were ever so much better—then

---

[21] John Hick, *Philosophy of Religion*, pp. 44–45.

we wouldn't need them. Those virtues that are contingent upon having an evil world we could well do without if the world were no longer evil. Besides—and this is very important—the distribution of these evils is far from what justice would demand. If the moral evils of the world are a punishment for man's wickedness, what of the innocent victims? The aggressors sometimes get away with what they do, but the victims never. For what is a child being punished when he is left alone in a room and burns to death on a hot stove, or when he is stricken with poliomyelitis or spinal meningitis? For what is a whole people being punished when their country is invaded by a powerful foreign army and they must give thousands or millions of their best men to fight the invader? Is *this* your idea of a justly governed universe?

A: All these injustices will be rectified in another world, the hereafter.

B: This of course you would have to prove to me separately, and I don't see how you could; that the present world is evil doesn't prove that there is another one that is better any more than the fact that people are hungry proves that they will always have food. But even if I grant you the belief in an after-life, it still would not remove the evils of this one. In one of Dostoyevsky's many examples of the evil inflicted on human beings by one another, he considers a sadistic army officer who has a child torn to pieces by wolves. But all is well, you say, the officer will suffer in hell. But what good does hell do, since the child has already been tortured? That evil *has* occurred, and even omnipotence cannot make what has happened *not* have happened. Nothing that could ever happen in the future would be just recompense for this monstrous act. It remains a stain, a blot, on the history of the world, a blot that *nothing* can remove, not even eternal punishment for the person who committed the deed. The world is put together in such a way that this thing not only could have happened but *did* happen. And nothing that will ever happen can make it otherwise.

5. *God's goodness different from ours*. But now a different solution may be suggested: "Perhaps what we call evil is really good; what seems evil to us is in fact good when seen from the vantage point of omniscience. The goodness of everything is perceived only by God, but he after all sees everything while we see very little: that everything is good is seen by his infinite intelligence but is beyond our finite comprehension."

But considering the spectacle of the world as we find it, there is no judgment of which we are more certain than that it is not perfectly good. If we distrust this judgment, we have no reason to trust *any* moral judgment, including the judgment that what is evil to us is good to God. Even if everything we think is evil is really good, the fact is that we still *think* it is evil—and this would be an error, an error hiding from us the perfect goodness of the universe. And since it would surely be better if we did not commit this error, the existence of this error would be an evil.

But in fact the view that what seems evil to us is all good in God's eyes would require us to take a very curious view of God. This world is full of pain and suffering, cruelty and death, wars, plagues, floods, and droughts, and human beings who suffer and die when they occur. If there is a powerful being who considers all this to be *good,* what view must we take of the morality of such a being? Is such a being worthy to be worshiped? Would he not rather be like a dictator whom we might obey because of his power but whom we would never for a moment think of as *good?* We would not think of a physician as good who failed to prevent suffering of his patient even if he had the power to do so and yet effect a cure; but an omnipotent God would be in precisely this position: why then should we call him good when we would call the physician who did this a sadistic monster? Yet we are supposed to believe that a God who could prevent needless suffering and yet refuses to do so is good. But as Mill said:

> When I am told that I must believe this, and at the same time call this being by the names which express and affirm the highest human morality, I say in plain terms that I will not. Whatever power such a being may have over me, there is one thing which he shall not do: he shall not compel me to worship him. I will call no being good, who is not what I mean when I apply that epithet to my fellow creatures; and if such a being can sentence me to hell for not so calling him, to hell I will go.[22]

Mill adds that so many of the things we are supposed to attribute to God are incompatible with anything we can possibly call goodness that we try to change the meaning of "good" to accommodate the discrepancy. We are told that God is good, but infinitely good, and that of course we cannot understand infinite goodness. But, of course, the same argument could support the view that either God or the world is infinitely *bad:* if some things look to us as if they were good, never fear, in the light of infinite knowledge we could see that they are all bad after all—the universe is the perfect epitome of evil. This argument is exactly on a par with the view that, although it sometimes seems evil, everything is really good.

Moreover, if God is infinitely good, the fact remains that infinite goodness must still be *goodness,* just as infinite space must still be space.

> Among the many who have said that we cannot conceive infinite space, did anyone ever suppose that it is *not* space? that it does not possess all the properties by which space is characterized? Infinite space cannot be cubical or spherical, because these are modes of being bounded; but does anyone imagine that in ranging through it we might arrive at some region which was not extended; of which one part was not outside another; where, though no Body intervened, motion was impossible; or where the sum of two sides of a triangle was less than the third side? The parallel assertion may be made respecting infinite goodness. What belongs to it as infinite I do not pretend to know; but I know that infinite goodness must be goodness, and that what is not consistent with goodness, is not consistent with infinite goodness.

[22] John Stuart Mill, *An Examination of Sir William Hamilton's Philosophy,* p. 131.

If in ascribing goodness to God I do not mean what I mean by goodness; if I do not mean the goodness of which I have some knowledge, but an incomprehensible attribute of an incomprehensible substance, which for aught I know may be a totally different quality from that which I love and venerate . . . what do I mean by calling it goodness? and what reason have I for venerating it? If I know nothing about what the attribute is, I cannot tell that it is a proper object of veneration. To say that God's goodness may be different in kind from man's goodness, what is it but saying, with a slight change of phraseology, that God may possibly not be good? To assert in words what we do not think in meaning, is as suitable a definition as can be given of a moral falsehood.[23]

The power of the Deity, by contrast, is always interpreted in a completely human way: it is never thought to mean that we could not be killed or thrown into hell-fire, in spite of the fact that the power of the Deity is conceived of as far greater than ours. Greater power means more of the same thing that we experience and call "power." Does not the same remark apply to "good"? But this is often spoken of, unlike the power, as inconceivable, perhaps because so many of its manifestations conflict so strongly with anything we would ever call goodness.

Alternative versions of the teleological argument. It would seem, then, that the teleological argument, in the form that holds to the existence of an omnipotent and benevolent being, is done in by the problem of evil. But this is not the only kind of cosmic hypothesis that can be held. Here are a few others:

1. An omnipotent being who is malevolent. This view has not been as popular as the belief in a benevolent being, perhaps because one's desire for justice to be done in an after-life is not fulfilled by belief in a malevolent being. Such a being would be like a powerful but tyrannical dictator, different only in that he is all-powerful and one would be completely and forever in his clutches: no act, no thought could escape his attention, and non-compliance with his will, however evil his dictates, would result in endless torture. Many critics of Christian fundamentalism have believed that the Christian God is something like this in that he has devised hell—a place of never-ending torment for non-believers in him. Even the most hardened prisoner in an earthly jail may be released or paroled for good behavior after serving a sentence, but not so with the God who punishes his creatures forever without any hope of reformation, pardon, or parole. Such punishment would seem to be utterly pointless, since it could never lead to any good result, and, one might wonder, what crime could possibly deserve *endless* punishment, particularly since the primary offense—non-belief in God and his goodness —could often be held for very cogent reasons and by very conscientious people.

Or perhaps the Christian Devil (Satan) comes closer to being omnipotent and malevolent. It could be argued that Satan has some virtues, such as

[23] *Ibid.,* p. 101.

persistence and patience, but even if he has none, at any rate he is not omnipotent. But if he were the perfect epitome of vice, and if he were omnipotent, he would be the kind of being suggested by the teleological argument in the present form. The support for this hypothesis would be found in the very facts that were difficulties for the previous view: the prevalence of pain and suffering, the helplessness of many people to face obstacles that they have to face, the facts of dying and that life can live only on other life, and so on. All such things could be easily explained on the hypothesis of a sadistic being who designed the whole scheme of things so as to maximize the torment of his creatures.

On this view, the problem of evil would not exist, since the world was designed by a being whose sole interest was the creation and promotion of evil. Rather, there would be a "problem of good"; why is there any good at all when God is both evil and omnipotent? Then there could be various unsuccessful theories to get rid of the problem of good: good is really nonexistence; good is a negative; everything is really evil, but some good is required to achieve evil ends; and so on.

2. *A benevolent but not omnipotent designer.* There might be a cosmic designer who was benevolent but limited in power, like human beings only less so. On this view, there is no problem of evil: there is evil because God is limited in power and cannot help the evil that there is—he has to work with material over which he lacks complete control. It has sometimes been suggested that God is merely a fellow-worker with human beings in the attempt to minimize the evil in the universe. This view not only encounters no problem of evil but also has inspired many persons to work for the elimination of evil, since it is now up to them; their efforts can make a difference. Yet the view has not been very popular, doubtless because people desire a God who can present them with certain guarantees: particularly that if they deserve their reward he will be able to deliver it, and that there will be no hitches in his plan. They want security more than incentive. (One difficulty for this view: If there is but one God, who or what could limit his power? Whence would come the competition?)

3. *Ditheism.* Since ancient times it has often been suggested that there are two cosmic intelligences, each planning and executing his plans in the world, but whose plans work at cross-purposes. Obviously neither is omnipotent (if one were, the other would not be God), but one is benevolent and the other not. Thus the ancient Zoroastrians and Manicheans argued that the world is a battle-ground for conflicting deities, not the work of a single designer; that is why some things in the world really are good and others really are bad (they do not merely appear to be so). Nor is there any problem of evil: the evil is easily explained by the existence of the evil deity. (On one doctrine, the physical universe was designed by the good god and man was designed by the bad one—a doctrine perhaps better in accord with observable facts than any other we have thus far encountered.)

Sometimes, in Christian theology, it is as if there were two gods, Jehovah and Satan. But Christianity is not ditheistic, since one of the two is all-powerful. Hence the conflict between them is a sham-battle, since Jehovah created Satan in the first place, is guaranteed to win over him in the end, and could destroy him any time if he so desired (which raises the question why this has not happened). In a genuine religious ditheism, both deities must be limited in power, and the outcome of the struggle must be genuinely in doubt.

4. *Polytheism.* If two, why not more than two? Why not revive the polytheism of the Greeks, who believed in many gods, each with his separate sphere of influence, and each interacting with the rest? To be sure, Zeus was the kingpin; but he was by no means omnipotent, for his best-laid plans could be thwarted by other gods, and particularly by his wife Hera. Since the laws of nature operate uniformly and impartially, there must be a certain degree of cooperation among the gods, or perhaps Zeus reigns supreme in one department; but there is still much room for diverse influences, even for gods working at cross-purposes. Why, indeed, should there be only *one* cosmic planner? In the cases of design known to human beings, a plan usually was devised in a rather crude form by one person, then certain rough edges were removed by someone else, and further improvements made by a third, and so on through many generations, as in the case of shipbuilding:

If we survey a ship, what an exalted idea must we form of the ingenuity of the carpenter, who framed so complicated, useful, and beautiful a machine? And what surprise must we feel, when we find him a stupid mechanic, who imitated others, and copied an art, which, through a long succession of ages, after multiplied trials, mistakes, corrections, deliberations, and controversies, had been gradually improving? Many worlds might have been botched and bungled, throughout an eternity, ere this system was struck out; much labor lost; many fruitless trials made; and a slow, but continued improvement carried on during infinite ages in the art of world-making.[24]

And, one might add, even at the present moment the art of world-making has been far from perfected; perhaps if the cosmic world-designers pooled their efforts and got at the job more conscientiously, a world might be brought about that is a considerable improvement over the present one.

5. *A cosmic organism.* Thus far we have considered only teleology in the form of design, or plan, in the mind of a designer. A being possessing a mind plans, and carries out his plan; this is the most familiar type of teleology known to us, since it goes on in ourselves: we design something, and it comes into existence as a result of our plan. But organisms also exhibit teleological behavior: the sunflower deepens its roots in the life-giving soil and turns its face to the sun, thereby making its continued existence possible. True, the sunflower does not consciously do this *in order* to preserve its existence, but

[24] David Hume, *Dialogues Concerning Natural Religion,* Part V.

(pp. 244–46) its behavior is teleological nonetheless: it acts in such-and-such a way, thereby making it possible for a goal to be achieved that would not have been achieved without this activity. Instead of saying, then, that the universe is the result of a plan in a mind (which would require us to believe in minds without bodies), why not say instead that the universe is the result of teleological activity on the part of a huge cosmic organism?

In like manner as a tree sheds its seed into the neighboring fields, and produces other trees; so the great vegetable, the world, or this planetary system, produces within itself certain seeds, which, being scattered into the surrounding chaos, vegetate into new worlds. . . .[25]

Or why not consider the ancient Brahmin hypothesis:

. . . that the world arose from an infinite spider, who spun this whole complicated mass from his bowels, and annihilates afterwards the whole or any part of it, by absorbing it again, and resolving it into his own essence. Here is a species of cosmogony, which appears to us ridiculous; because a spider is a little contemptible animal, whose operations we are never likely to take for a model of the whole universe. . . . But . . . were there a planet wholly inhabited by spiders (which is very possible), this inference would there appear as natural and irrefragable as that which in our planet ascribes the origin of all things to design and intelligence. . . . Why an orderly system may not be spun from the belly as well as from the brain, it will be difficult . . . to give a satisfactory reason.[26]

"But this is ridiculous!" we may exclaim. Aren't these hypotheses absurd? Are they *all* wildly improbable? Must we admit them all as possibilities, and a thousand others like them? "What wild, arbitrary suppositions are these? What *data* have you for such extraordinary conclusions? And is the slight, imaginary resemblance of the world to a vegetable or animal sufficient to establish the same inference with regard to both?"[27] But this, says Hume, is just the point: they are all vastly improbable; there is no justification for believing any of the forms of the teleological argument.

We have no *data* to establish any system of cosmogony. Our experience, so imperfect in itself, and so limited both in extent and duration, can afford us no probable conjecture concerning the whole of things. But if we must needs fix on some hypothesis, by what rule, pray, ought we to determine our choice? Is there any other rule than the greater similarity of the objects compared?

[25] *Ibid.*, Part VII (p. 177 in the Norman Kemp Smith edition).
[26] *Ibid.*, pp. 180–81.
[27] *Ibid.*, p. 177.

And does not a plant or an animal, which springs from vegetation or genera-
tion, bear a stronger resemblance to the world, than does any artificial machine,
which arises from reason and design?[28]

Argument from analogy.   All the arguments in this group are arguments
from analogy, and it is important that we be aware of the structure of this
kind of argument. An analogy is simply a comparison, and an argument from
analogy is an argument from comparison. An argument from analogy begins
with a comparison between two things, X and Y. It then proceeds to argue
that these two things are alike in certain respects, A, B, C, and concludes that
therefore they are also alike in another respect, D, in which they have not
been observed to resemble one another. For example, a man (X) and a dog
(Y) are alike in numerous respects: they have hearts that pump blood, they
consume and digest food, and so on (A, B, C). Therefore, it is concluded,
since a man has a liver (D), the dog will also have a liver. (Assume that the
argument is presented before it has been discovered through dissection of
dogs whether they have livers.) Since man and the dog are alike in numerous
respects, the argument runs, it is likely that they will resemble one another in
the other respect in which no such similarity has yet been discovered.

It will be apparent at once that an argument from analogy is never
conclusive. That two things are alike in numerous respects never proves by
itself that they will also be alike in other respects that have not yet been
examined. They may be, but even if they are, the argument from analogy
does not prove it; only an investigation of the two things will enable us to
discover whether they are alike in the new respect. Of course, if the two
things are very similar in a large number of respects, it will in general be more
likely that they are similar in the new respect; thus, since lions and leopards
are very similar in most respects, a characteristic of lions is quite likely to be
true also of leopards—but not all characteristics: if all of them were the same,
lions would be indistinguishable from leopards. Thus, even in cases where the
two things are very much alike, the argument from analogy is still
inconclusive.

The teleological argument in its various forms has usually been presented
as an argument from analogy. Thus, there is a watch and a human eye. They
have some characteristics in common: particularly, the same apparent
adaptation of means to ends. If we came across a watch without knowing
what it was for, we would conclude that it had been designed by someone, for
every part is linked to every other part in such a way as to fulfill one function,
that of keeping time. Similarly, in the human eye there is the same complex
interconnection of parts, all serving one function, that of seeing. Since the
watch is the result of design, we infer that the eye is also the result of design.
(And since a design presupposes a designer, a designer must exist.)

---

[28] *Ibid.*

There is precisely the same proof that the eye was made for vision, as there is that the telescope was made for assisting it. They are made upon the same principles; both being adjusted to the laws by which the transmission and reflection of rays of light are regulated. . . . These laws require, in order to produce the same effect, that the rays of light, in passing from water into the eye, should be refracted by a more convex surface than when it passes out of air into the eye. Accordingly we find that the eye of a fish, in that part of it called the crystalline lens, is much rounder than the eye of terrestrial animals. What plainer manifestation of design can there be than this difference?[29]

The analogy between the eye and a manufactured object like a watch or telescope may seem very close. There is in both cases a complex structure that fulfills a function. (We must say "function" and not "purpose," for to say that the eye fulfills a purpose would assume the point at issue; opponents of the teleological argument would say that the eye, while it fulfills a function, seeing, was not the result of design, and hence not of a designer's purpose.) But in the case of the eye, as well as of organisms in general, no designing activity has ever been observed, whereas in the case of manufactured objects it has; and in addition, there is considerable other evidence that the eye, along with the entire organism of which it is a part, is the result of a slow and gradual process of evolution.

To discover that certain forms and formations are adjusted for certain action has nothing to do with design. None of these developments are perfect, or anywhere near so. All of them, including the eye, are botchwork that any good mechanic would be ashamed to make. All of them need constant readjustment, are always out of order, and are entirely too complicated for dependable work. They are not made for any purpose; they simply grew out of needs and adaptations; in other words, they happened.[30]

The teleological argument does not prove what it sets out to prove, for the analogy between a watch and an eye (or between any manufactured object and any natural one) is far from perfect. But even if it did, it would prove far too much: for the very same argument can be used, as we have seen, to prove the existence of two designers, many designers, a cosmic organism, and so on. If we start with ships instead of watches, we get the hypothesis that the universe was the result of many centuries of accumulated experience in world-making. If we start with desert wastes, we get the hypothesis that besides being sloppy and inefficient, the designer did not have man's well-being in mind. It all depends on what features of the universe we start with.

[29] Bishop William Paley, *Evidences of the Existence and Attributes of the Deity* (1802). Passage reprinted in P. Edwards and A. Pap, *A Modern Introduction to Philosophy*, p. 412.

[30] Clarence Darrow, "The Delusion of Design and Purpose," in *The Story of My Life* (New York: Charles Scribner's Sons, 1932), p. 413.

The universe contains so many things, with so many characteristics, that there is virtually no argument from analogy that we cannot construct, depending on what features we select at the outset; yet each of the arguments would yield a different kind of designer (or designers). If one argument is valid, so are the others—yet the conclusion of one argument contradicts the conclusions of the others. Thus we end with a *reductio ad absurdum* of the teleological argument. As Hume said, the argument provides no basis for any designer-hypothesis.

Is the teleological argument, defective as it is, an empirical hypothesis at all? Granted that it is inconclusive, even a total failure, it seems to be a hypothesis that is in the empirical domain. But is it? Initially, the argument was presented as if it were a scientific hypothesis, which could be confirmed or disconfirmed by facts about the physical universe. But as more and more facts turned up that seemed to disconfirm it and yet the hypothesis of a cosmic designer was not withdrawn, it gave more and more the impression of a hypothesis that *no* facts could disconfirm. But in that case, how could any facts confirm it either? What kind of a hypothesis is it that nothing can count either for or against? What can such a hypothesis even mean? It is time that we gave some further scrutiny to the meaning of the God-hypothesis.

Exercises

1. Discuss the considerations in favor of the ontological argument in either of the following: (a) Charles Hartshorne, *The Logic of Perfection,* or (b) Norman Malcolm, "Anselm's Ontological Arguments" *(Philosophical Review,* 1960; reprinted in his *Knowledge and Certainty).*

2. To what extent is the argument from contingency the ontological argument over again? Explain.

3. What observable features of the world might lead you to accept (a) polytheism, (b) ditheism, (c) monotheism? Explain.

4. Evaluate the following assertions:

 a. God was the first event.

 b. God caused the first event.

 c. There was no first event, but God is the explanation of why there was a first event as well as any subsequent events.

 d. God was present before time began.

 e. God created time.

 f. God created time, then the world.

 g. The universe came from God.

 h. First there was a conscious being (God), a mind without a body, who then created matter (including bodies).

 i. God created space before creating the matter which would occupy the space.

 j. Only if one believes in God can one solve the mystery of why anything exists at all.

 k. If you don't believe in a God who created and designed the universe, you must believe that everything that happens and ever has happened is one vast *accident.*

1. Since the innocent often suffer and the guilty go unpunished in this life, there must be another life in which these wrongs are righted and each person judged by an impartial God according to his deserts.

5. Which of the following are valid deductive arguments? Explain. In which ones do you consider the premises true?

a. Religious experience (psychological events of a certain kind) exist; therefore God exists.

b. Religious experiences (experiences of God) exist; therefore God exists.

c. Miracles (events not explainable by laws of nature) occur; therefore God exists.

d. Miracles (interventions of God) exist; therefore God exists.

e. Organisms are constructed in a certain way; but construction implies a constructor; therefore a Constructor of Organisms (God) exists.

f. If the earth stopped rotating on its axis, it must have been a miracle.

g. If the earth stopped rotating on its axis, and there was no natural explanation for it, it must have been a miracle.

h. Every possible configuration of matter must have a certain order. Order implies (presupposes) an orderer. Therefore an orderer (God) exists.

i. There is a certain benevolent (or good, or desirable) order of things observable in the universe. But such order presupposes an orderer. Therefore, an orderer (God) exists.

6. Describe the kind of universe (if any) which would make the following hypotheses (each in turn) probable.

a. There are two gods (one good, one evil) fighting for control of the world.

b. There are many gods, each with his own sphere of· influence.

c. Everything in the universe tends toward good.

d. Everything in the universe tends toward evil.

e. Everything that appears to be bad in the world, will in the end turn out for the best.

f. Everything that appears to be good in the world, will in the end turn out for the worst.

g. There is one God, both omnipotent and benevolent.

h. There is one God, omnipotent but not benevolent.

i. There is one God, benevolent but not omnipotent.

7. Are there any occurrences, or series of occurrences, which if they were to happen would lead you to say "It's a miracle"? If so, describe them and indicate why you would label them miracles.

8. "My sick child recovered, and I take this fact as evidence for a benevolent God." "But my sick child did not recover, so I take this fact as evidence that there is not a benevolent God." Does either alleged fact confirm the hypothesis for which the fact is given as evidence? Justify your answer.

9. "Two hundred years ago the average human life-span was only half what it is now. This increase is directly traceable to the advances in medical science. Medical science, not God, is the cause of the greater longevity today." "No, the facts you cite equally confirm another hypothesis: that God used medical science (perhaps even implanting ideas in the minds of medical experts) to fulfill his plan, that of lengthening the span of human life." Discuss.

10. We all know what it is to create a poem, or a disturbance, or an idea. But what is it to create out of nothing? Imagine yourself a conscious being, and no material universe exists. You say, "Let there be stars," and suddenly stars come into existence where there were none before. How would you know

that your sentence, "Let there be stars," was what created the stars? How would you know there was a causal relation between your utterance and the event? How would you know it wasn't a coincidence that you uttered the sentence and the stars appeared at the same time?

11. *Why* would belief in a cosmic designer require belief in a mind without a body (pp. 415–18, 475)?

22. Religious Concepts and Meaning

Anthropomorphism. People say that God is intelligent, wise, benevolent, powerful; that he commands, hears our prayers, desires our welfare, forgives us our trespasses, and so on. But how can the properties that people attribute to God literally apply? It is difficult if not impossible to imagine all this occurring without any kind of organism—and almost no one today would wish to say that God is a physical organism having eyes, nose, hands, feet, and so on. All kinds of personal characteristics are attributed to God, yet how can any being have these characteristics but not have a body of any kind? (Remember pp. 418–19.) Consider this simple example: Virtually all traditional religions refer to God as "he." Do they really mean that God is of masculine gender? If they believe that God is not or has not a body, and also that masculine gender can be distinguished only with reference to organisms (what would "masculine gender" mean outside that context?), they must necessarily conclude that the pronoun "he" is not intended literally. Some worshipers doubtless do intend it literally: they would say that God is male, and they imagine him sitting on a throne, wielding a scepter, with flowing white robes, and so on. But this, it would soon be admitted, is only accompanying imagery; perhaps the use of the pronoun "he" is a relic of the days when the man was undisputed head of the household. In any case, if God is not an organism, he cannot be a male organism. By the same token, God is not female. But if God is nevertheless a personality, though a disembodied one, it would seem that God cannot be neuter either; the pronoun "it" seems to be even less appropriate than "he" or "she" since it seems to imply an inanimate thing without personality. Yet masculine, feminine, and neuter are the only personal pronouns we have. If they are all inapplicable, what word shall we use? And if we must use one, what criterion underlies our choice, since none of the three is applicable?

This example illustrates as well as any other the problem of anthropomorphism (*anthropos*, "man," and *morphe*, "form"), "conceiving God in the form of man." We conceive God as a human being—a bigger and better human being, perhaps, but human nevertheless, if not in physical characteristics (since God has no body) then in mental ones. Believers hold that God is not literally a human being, yet they all impute to God many characteristics of human beings. "Well, what else can we do?" one might ask. In what other way can we conceive of God? Perhaps we have no more conception of God's qualities than a child has of mature sexual love, but these are the only words we have, and however inadequately they enable us to conceive God's nature, they are the best we can do. We must conceive God anthropomorphically or not at all. We need not conceive God in the *crudely* anthropomorphic way that primitive religions do—as a big superman up in the skies or atop the highest mountain, hurling thunderbolts; but even if we outgrow the physical anthropomorphism we cannot escape the mental anthropomorphism, the likening of God's mental processes to our own. If we abandon this, we seem to abandon any concept of God at all.

The problem is not really diminished when we consider God's alleged personality-characteristics. We speak of God as thinking, willing, desiring, planning, and many people take this quite literally. God plans as human beings plan. Nevertheless, when we reflect about these activities, they give us pause: for example, how can someone desire something unless there is something that he does not have? Yet in the next breath we say that God, being infinite, has everything or even *is* everything. Or why is it necessary to have plans, and to find ways of accomplishing things in the world, when the being in question is omnipotent and would never need to cast about for means to accomplish his ends? (See pp. 463–67.) (God created the world in order to glorify his name, people say; but as Mill pointed out, this is to attribute to God one of the lowest of human attributes, a restless appetite for applause.) Whatever difficulties we are led into by attributing these human characteristics to God, there is one shared by all of them: thinking, willing, desiring, planning, and so on are all *temporal processes*. Does not thinking necessarily take place in time? Would it make sense to speak of thinking of something but not for a definite length of time, indeed not in time at all? Isn't deciding on a plan an event, and do not all events necessarily occur in time? But if it is really true, as theologians often assert, that God is a timeless being (see pp. 436, 441–42), how can we escape contradiction when we attribute these mental processes to a timeless being?

Yet it is precisely of such temporal events and processes that a *mind* is constituted.

A mind, whose acts and sentiments and ideas are not distinct and successive; one, that is wholly simple, and totally immutable; is a mind which has no thought, no reason, no will, no sentiment, no love, no hatred; or in a word, is no mind at all. It is an abuse of terms to give it that appellation; and we may as well speak of limited extension without figure, or of number without composition.[31]

Yet if we speak of a mind *without* thoughts, feelings, volitions, and other events in its history, and yet call it a mind, is this not to take away with one

---

[31] David Hume, *Dialogues Concerning Natural Religion*, Part IV (p. 159 in the Norman Kemp Smith edition).

hand what we give with the other? It does not help to say that it is still a mind, but a mind of a very different kind from ours, such that we cannot really conceive of it; for if we cannot conceive of it, what entitles us to call it a mind at all? What entitles us to say that it is a *mind* rather than something else, or even to say that there is an "it" that we can call a mind? It is much as if we were told that there exists a very special and unusual kind of book that has no pages, no cover, no print—in fact, it is a red liquid. But whatever it is, this is not what we mean by "book" when we use the word; it cannot be a book, since it lacks the defining characteristics of books. Just as surely, it would seem, does "timeless mind" lack the defining characteristics of mind, and land us in a contradiction. If something lacks the defining characteristics of X, we are not entitled to call it an X; as Hume says, "It is an abuse of terms to give it that appellation."

One could, of course, escape these meaning-difficulties by holding that God is finite, limited, and temporal—and we would probably have to end up believing that if God is a personality he must also be a biological organism. But this is a step that very few believers have been prepared to take.

Mysticism.   We reach an impasse like this every time we think anthropomorphically about God. At this point enters the *mystic*, who opposes all anthropomorphism. The moment we attribute a characteristic to God, says the mystic, we are *conceptualizing* God, for we have a *concept* of something and attribute to God the characteristic of which we have the concept. And this, according to the mystic, is just what we cannot do, for God *cannot be conceptualized*. To refer to God as masculine is to bring God under a concept, but to speak of God as a mind, or as having wisdom, power, or goodness, is to do so not a whit less. All of these are conceptualizations, and as such all of them are equally illegitimate.

Where then does this leave us? What *can* we say truly about God? According to the mystic, nothing at all. Indeed, to say anything about God is to *limit* God. To say that God possesses characteristic A is to say that God lacks the characteristic not-A, and to say this is already to limit God, who transcends all such distinctions. Since God is limitless, it is a mistake to say anything that would limit God's nature; and any characteristic we attribute to God does precisely this.

But if this is so, must we not carry the same reasoning on to its full conclusion? Can we even speak of God as *limitless*? for surely to say this is to attribute a characteristic. The same reasoning which would prevent calling God a mind would prevent calling him limitless. Could we even speak of God as *existing*? Would not this limit God in the same way? Even if existence is not an attribute (see pp. 428–29), it is still true that to refer to God as existing is to say something about him, to use a concept to refer to him, and thus to fall prey to the mystic's objection. If God transcends all description, this would seem to include describing God as *existing*. Indeed, to be rigidly consistent we would have to take the ultimate step: we would have to cease even to use the word "God," for to use the word and to mean something by it is already to conceptualize.

Having come to this impasse, one might well ask, "How is mysticism to be distinguished from agnosticism or skepticism? The consistent mystic must be silent—he says that God is beyond any description, that no words can be used to characterize God, including ultimately, even the word 'God' itself. Is this not, if anything, more radical than the position of the skeptic, who doubts that God exists, or of the agnostic, who says that he does not know?"

At this point the mystic offers an answer: he says that the religious statements that he utters—such as "God is the ultimate Unity of all things," "God's goodness is an infinite outpouring from an infinite vessel," "God overflows all existence, transcends all distinctions, obliterates all boundaries"—are *not literally true at all*, and not intended to be so; rather, they are *symbolically* true. On the literal level, these statements (as well as more traditional and orthodox religious statements, such as "God is benevolent," "God is powerful, wise, and so on") are all vulnerable, and justly so, to the criticisms of the skeptic: he has an easy time refuting the literalist and exposing his fallacies and contradictions. Nevertheless, if taken symbolically rather than literally, many religious statements may be true.

How can such a claim be justified? Let us recall our discussion of figurative language (see pp. 15–16). When we say "She is but a walking shadow," we are using figurative language, for we do not literally mean that she is a shadow; nevertheless we are able to back up the check of figurative language with the cold cash of literal fact: we can say "What I mean is that she is very thin, she is pale, she looks anemic. . . ." The same can be done for most of the figurative expressions we employ in ordinary life; we can produce a literal meaning when we are called upon to do so. But what is the literal meaning when we say "God is the ultimate Unity of all things," "I am *one with* God," "God overflows all boundaries," and the like, if these are not intended to be literally true? What *are* the literally accurate expressions into which we could translate them? We cannot produce any. Then what could justify us in using such expressions, seeing that we cannot say what they mean? What, indeed, justifies us in saying what we do say rather than something else, for example the opposite?

Analogy.   The only answer that seems possible is that there is a certain *analogy*[32] or *resemblance* that is felt to exist between the things referred to in the symbols and the inexpressible, non-conceptualizable X which the symbols are said to be symbols *for*. If this were not so, there would be no grounds for saying that the expression "God is love" is a better symbol for an inexpressible truth than the expressions "God is hatred" or "God is pink fortitude."

---

[32] "Analogy" is synonymous with "resemblance" or "basis of comparison." It is not to be confused with an argument from analogy (see pp. 476–78)—that is, an argument from resemblance.

To say even this much, however, is already to compromise the purity of the mystic's position. Using one expression, X, is a symbolic way of referring to an inexpressible, non-conceptualizable X′, and using another expression, Y, is a symbolic way of referring to an inexpressible, non-conceptualizable Y′. Now why—on the basis of what—is X a better symbol for X′ than Y is? Surely it is because there is some *likeness* of X to X′ that X does not bear to Y′. If there were not some affinity between X and X′, however tenuous, the use of one expression rather than another, even symbolically, would be indefensible. Even if the statement made is not literally true, and what *is* literally true is inexpressible, one statement is taken as a better symbol for the inexpressible than another one is; and if one knows this, does not one already know something about the inexpressible? And if one knows nothing about it, then one is not entitled to say anything about it, not even that X is a better symbol for X′ than Y is. It would seem that the genuine mystic must be silent.

In any case, the majority of theologians have taken a middle road: while acknowledging the difficulties of anthropomorphism at one extreme, they have rejected at the other the way of mysticism, with its inexorable logic leading to utter silence. They have, rather, held that the words used to characterize God are used *analogically,* and their view is called "the doctrine of analogical predication."

. . . when a word, such as "good," is applied both to a created being and to God, it is not being used *univocally* (i.e., with exactly the same meaning) in the two cases. God is not good, for example, in identically the sense in which human beings may be good. Nor, on the other hand, do we apply the epithet "good" to God and man *equivocally* (i.e., with completely different and unrelated meanings), as when the word "bat" is used to refer both to the flying animal and to the instrument used in baseball. There is a definite connection between God's goodness and man's, reflecting the fact that God has created man. According to Aquinas, then, "good" is applied to creator and creature neither univocally nor equivocally but *analogically*. What this means will appear if we consider first an analogy "downwards" from man to a lower form of life. We sometimes say of a pet dog that it is faithful, and we may also describe a man as faithful. We use the same word in each case because of a similarity between a certain quality exhibited in the behavior of the dog and the steadfast voluntary adherence to a person or a cause which we call faithfulness in a human being. Because of this similarity we are not using the word "faithful" equivocally (with totally different senses). But, on the other hand, there is an immense difference in quality between a dog's attitudes and a man's. The one is indefinitely superior to the other in respect of responsible, self-conscious deliberation and the relating of attitudes to moral purposes and ends. Because of this difference we are not using "faithful" univocally (in exactly the same sense). We are using it analogically, to indicate that at the level of the dog's consciousness there is a quality which *corresponds* to what at the human level we call faithfulness. There is a recognizable likeness in structure of attitudes or patterns of behavior which causes us to use the same word for both animal and man. Nevertheless, human faithfulness differs from canine faithfulness to all the wide extent that a man differs from a dog. There is thus both similarity within difference and difference within similarity of the kind that led Aquinas to speak of the *analogical* use of the same term in two very different contexts.[33]

As the dog's properties are to man's, so man's are to God's, with the gap between ours and God's being greater than the gap between the dog's and man's. Thus, though God's goodness is far greater than ours and very different from ours, there is still enough of an analogy between the two to entitle us to call them both "goodness." The word "goodness" is more appropriate than any other word, although it gives only an inadequate conception of the quality possessed by God.

So runs the doctrine. But it is riddled with difficulties. *In what way* are the properties of human beings and the properties of God supposed to be analogous? On this question the entire problem turns.

1. It is sometimes held that there is a kind of *proportionality* between the two: God's properties are to God's nature as man's properties are to man's nature. But how are these two proportions to be linked? Are the two relations identical? The closer we come to saying that God's goodness is just like man's, the more the difference or "otherness" of God from man is thereby compromised. But if the identity between the two relations is replaced by some other relation—if, for example, it is said that the relation of God's properties to his nature is, in some unknown or entirely unspecified way, only "like" the way man's properties are related to man's nature—then the "otherness" of God is preserved, but having knowledge, or even a concept, of God seems to be impossible: we can only speak, as Mill said, of "an incomprehensible attribute of an incomprehensible subject."

2. It has also been held that properties (goodness, wisdom, etc.) can be attributed to God in some full and non-derivative way and applied to other things, such as human beings, in a derived sense that is analogous to but not identical with the original sense. Thus we speak of an organism as healthy (underived sense) but also of certain foods as healthy (or more correctly, healthful): the second sense means only that eating them makes you healthy in the first sense. The second sense is derivative from the first one but clearly analogous to it. Similarly, it has been suggested, the original and underived sense of "goodness" and "wisdom" apply to God alone—God alone is good and wise in the full sense—and that these words are applicable only in a derived and analogous sense to human beings.

But whatever concept people have of God is surely derived from their acquaintance with human beings and their properties. To the extent that God is supposed to have some property utterly different from ours, how could we know *that* he had it or *what* the property was? We could know it only if we could observe God's properties and man's properties *independently* of one

[33] John Hick, *Philosophy of Religion*, pp. 79–80.

another, and only then would we be entitled to assert or deny some analogy between the two. But this of course is precisely what we cannot do. Knowledge of such an alleged fact about God is cut off by the epistemological fact that we can speak meaningfully about something unknown only to the extent that it is like, or analogous to, the known. And it is surely man and his properties that we know and from which we try to make some meaningful assertion about God and his properties—not the other way round.

Such are the problems that confront us when we try to make a case for "knowing God by way of analogy."

What difference does the belief make to experience?   If God exists—as first cause, or designer, or necessary being, or source of religious experience, or any of the outcomes of the other arguments—what difference would it make to anything we could verify empirically? How indeed *could* we verify it? Since God unlike trees and stones cannot be observed by means of the senses, how could we verify the existence of such a being, assuming that he exists?

Suppose someone asked, "How do you know there aren't lots of invisible elephants in this building, only you can't see them because they are invisible?" We might reply, "Well, we could touch them or bump into them, as we do invisible glass." "No, suppose they are intangible also—they can no more be touched than seen." "And they don't affect instruments like X-ray machines and radar?" "No, not a trace." We might first be tempted to ask: What's the difference? What does it matter whether there are such elephants in the building or not? But on second thought we might ask a more probing question: What does it even *mean* to say that there are such elephants in the building—or that there are not? What would it mean to say that they are invisible elephants rather than invisible horses or stones? Indeed, what would be the difference between saying that there are only invisible elephants in the building and saying that there is *nothing at all* in the building? To say that there is an elephant in the building is surely to say that there is a perceivable thing in the building. If there is nothing perceivable (visible and tangible), then there are no elephants, since what we *mean* by saying there are elephants in the building is that there are perceivable things in the building. We can learn the meaning of "elephant" only by having a perceivable thing pointed out or described to us. An unperceivable elephant would be a contradiction in terms.

Now, God is (according to all but the most anthropomorphic accounts) unperceivable by means of the senses. Does this condemn us to talking nonsense if we say nevertheless that such a being exists? Not by itself. Even in the empirical sciences we speak of unobservable entities such as electrons (pp. 236–38), and although there are many problems about these peculiar entities, scientists do not doubt that in some sense or other they exist. Of course, there are differences between God and electrons: the electron-hypothesis has a mass of supporting evidence with which every physicist is familiar, whereas such evidence, in view of our discussion of the arguments, appears to be lacking in the case of God. But evidence or no, it would seem at any rate that we we have the concept: however difficult it may be to give an account of personal characteristics in the absence of an organism, it seems to many people that we can conceive of a mind without a body. Since mind and body are distinguishable, they could, it is said, be conceived to occur separately, even if never in our entire experience do we encounter the one without the other. And if this is so, we can conceive of a mind existing without a body, although many have raised very searching questions about this. In any case, there remain problems about how such a mind could affect the physical universe, and we must beware not to fall into contradictions by speaking of the mind as timeless.

But if such a mind exists—and none of the arguments thus far considered has shown that it does—how would we ever know it? What difference would it make to our experience whether it does or does not? If the teleological argument had been successful, we could have expected the perceivable universe to be different because of the existence of such a mind: if the divine mind were benevolently disposed toward the universe, we would expect to find clear evidences of this benevolence in the universe, particularly in the life of sentient beings, and, as we have seen, we fail to find it. This does not, of course, show that a malevolent designer exists but only that (so far as we can tell) there is no evidence that any designer exists at all.

But perhaps a mind can exist even though we lack any evidence that it does. The ancient Epicureans believed that there were many gods but that they had nothing to do with human life—they sat in the garden and chatted and drank ambrosia, but they had nothing to do with this world, and the fact of their existence made no difference to human experience. If human beings had wished to devise the hypothesis that such beings existed, and then looked to experience for confirmation of the hypothesis, they would have found none, since the gods had left no traces in the world. Still, one could urge, they might exist even though people looked in vain for traces of their existence.

It has been suggested by a contemporary philosopher, John Wisdom, that the difference between an atheist and a believer may lie not in what he believes exists "out there" but in his way of *looking at* the world that we all experience.

Two people return to their long neglected garden and find among the weeds a few of the old plants surprisingly vigorous. One says to the other "It must be that a gardener has been coming and doing something about these plants." Upon inquiry they find that no neighbor has ever seen anyone at work in their garden. The first man says to the other, "He must have worked while people slept." The other says "No, someone would have heard him and besides, anyone who cared about the plants would have kept down these weeds." The first man says "Look at the way these are arranged. There is purpose and a feeling for beauty here. I believe that someone comes, someone invisible to mortal eyes. I believe that the more carefully we look the more we shall find confirmation of this." They examine the garden ever so carefully and sometimes they come on new things suggesting that a gardener comes and sometimes they come on new things suggesting the contrary and even that a malicious person has been at work. Besides examining the garden carefully they also study what happens to gardens left without attention. Each learns all the other learns about this and about the garden. Consequently, when after all this, one says "I still believe a gardener comes" while the other says "I don't" their different words reflect no difference as to what they have found in the garden, no difference as to what they would find in the garden if they looked further and no difference about how fast untended gardens fall into disorder. At this stage, in this context, the gardener hypothesis has ceased to be experimental, the difference between one who accepts and one who rejects it is now not a matter of the one expecting something the other does not expect. What is the difference between them? The one says "A gardener comes unseen and unheard. He is manifsted only in his works with which we are all familiar," the other says "There is no gardener" and with this difference in what they say about the gardener goes a difference in how they feel towards the garden, in spite of the fact that neither expects anything of it which the other does not expect.[34]

On such a view, there is no empirically discoverable difference between the universe as conceived by the atheist and the universe as conceived by the believer. There is no verifiable fact about the world that the one would grant but the other would not. (It does seem from the account, however, as if they disagree about one thing: whether there is or is not an "invisible gardener." There is no *verifiable* difference between them, but still (one might contend) a difference. A difference that was purely subjective, in the "way of looking at the world," would not involve even this difference.)

Some writers[35] have gone even further and suggested that belief in God is merely a disguised ethical belief, that uttering sentences like "God is good" is merely a way of stating one's commitment to a certain way of life, plus (perhaps) belief in certain historical events such as the life of Jesus. But if this is all the belief involved, it would better be considered under the heading of ethics. It smacks of intellectual dishonesty to take religious language, which most people employ to express genuine theistic belief, and use it to express something entirely different—moral views—especially if one continues to leave his hearers with the impression that he still intends the words in the former religious sense. We shall not dignify this mode of speaking by calling it *religious* belief.

Another possible view, however, is that although there is no verifiable difference *in the here and now* between the belief of the atheist and that of the

[34] "Gods," *Proceedings of the Aristotelian Society*, 1944–45. Reprinted in Antony Flew (ed.), *Logic and Language*, First Series, pp. 192–93. Also reprinted in John Wisdom, *Philosophy and Psychoanalysis*.

[35] For example, R. B. Braithwaite, *An Empiricist's View of the Nature of Religious Belief* (London: Cambridge University Press, 1955).

theist, there is the expectation of a difference to be discerned later, after death:

Two men are travelling together along a road. One of them believes that it leads to the Celestial City, the other that it leads nowhere; but since this is the only road there is, both must travel it. Neither has been this way before; therefore, neither is able to say what they will find around each corner. During their journey they meet with moments of refreshment and delight, and with moments of hardship and danger. All the time one of them thinks of his journey as a pilgrimage to the Celestial City. He interprets the pleasant parts as encouragements and the obstacles as trials of his purpose and lessons in endurance, prepared by the king of that city and designed to make of him a worthy citizen of the place when at last he arrives. The other, however, believes none of this, and sees their journey as an unavoidable and aimless ramble. Since he has no choice in the matter, he enjoys the good and endures the bad. For him there is no Celestial City to be reached, no all-encompassing purpose ordaining their journey; there is only the road itself and the luck of the road in good weather and in bad.

During the course of the journey, the issue between them is not an experimental one. They do not entertain different expectations about the coming details of the road, but only about its ultimate destination. Yet, when they turn the last corner, it will be apparent that one of them has been right all the time and the other wrong. Thus, although the issue between them has not been experimental, it has, nevertheless, been a real issue. They have not merely felt differently about the road, for one was feeling appropriately and the other inappropriately in relation to the actual state of affairs. Their opposed interpretations of the situation have constituted genuine rival assertions, whose assertion-status has the peculiar characteristic of being guaranteed retrospectively by a future crux. . . . The theist and the atheist do not (or need not) expect different events to occur in the successive details of the temporal process. They do not (or need not) entertain divergent expectations of the course of history as viewed from within. However, the theist does and the atheist does not expect that when history is completed it will be seen to have led to a particular end-state and to have fulfilled a specific purpose, namely, that of creating "children of God."[36]

This possibility, were it to materialize, would not of course solve all our problems, as its author is well aware. If someone survived his bodily death, it would constitute no proof of theism; it could be just another fact about the universe, perhaps a surprising one. It would constitute proof of immortality, but what would constitute proof of God? "Seeing God directly" is the answer given by most believers in immortality. But this runs up against a difficulty if God is not a being perceivable by the senses. "But might he not be perceivable by the senses in an after-life?" In a resurrected body we might indeed have senses and perceive many things, but would anything that we perceived *be* God? would it not just be another organism, perhaps bigger and better than other organisms but an organism still, with all the limitations of

[36] John Hick, *Philosophy of Religion*, pp. 101–2.

organisms (perceiving the world only from a particular place and perspective, unable to be omnisentient, and so on)? "Perhaps then the perceivable creature would not *be* God but a *manifestation* of God." But how would one ever know, of any perceived being, that it was a manifestation of an unperceived one? And if God himself is not perceivable, what would constitute proof of his existence, even in an after-life? It would seem that whatever evidence there could be would have to be indirect, like our present evidence for electrons. But what would constitute such evidence in the case of God? This is a question to which believers have not paid the attention it requires. Until they do, we shall have to conclude that there is no evidence for an "unobservable divine being" the way there is for unobservable protons and electrons—and that, in fact, no clear meaning has thus far been given to the alleged hypothesis. Not only is there no evidence for X, but those who say that there is have not given us a clear account of what the X is which the evidence is supposed to support.

Exercises

1. "No scientific argument—by which I mean an argument drawn from the phenomena of nature—can ever have the slightest tendency either to prove or to disprove the existence of God." (W. T. Stace, *Religion and the Modern Mind,* page 76.) Do you agree with this statement, and why? Discuss the general question of the relevance of empirical facts to religious belief. (Read Chapter 5 of Stace's *Religion and the Modern Mind,* the chapter from which the above quotation was taken, for more material on this question.)

2. Which of the following statements could be taken, in your opinion, as literally true? When words or phrases in them cannot be taken literally, try to translate the sentences in which they occur into sentences which *can* be taken literally. Examine those that can be taken literally, for internal consistency.
    a. God is above the stars.
    b. God is above human concerns.
    c. God existed before time began.
    d. "And God said . . ."
    e. God exists throughout all space and all time.
    f. The earth is God's footstool.
    g. God caused the world.
    h. God is love.
    i. God is truth.

3. Discuss the criteria for the use of the word "exist" with reference to each of the following:
    a. "Tables exist."
    b. "Headaches exist."
    c. "Magnetism exists."
    d. "Ghosts exist."
    e. "God exists."

4. "God does not really possess the properties we attribute to him (masculine gender, existing in time, having will and intellect and feeling, and so on),

but he possesses something *like* each of these things; the words we use to characterize God apply only *analogically.*" Evaluate this view.

5. Which of the following would you accept, and which would you reject, and why?

a. There is an elephant in this room, invisible and intangible.

b. There are radio waves in this room, invisible and intangible.

e. There are atoms in every bit of matter, invisible and intangible.

f. There is a God in the world, invisible and intangible.

6. If the following events were to occur, what would they show? Would they prove the existence of God? (What meaning of "God"?)

a. Someone who is about to kill another human being suddenly dies of a heart attack.

b. A voice appears out of the clouds and says, "Those who kill others will be struck dead by a lightning-bolt on the spot." And starting at this moment, this actually occurs: everyone who kills another human being is struck by a lightning-bolt and killed.

c. You die, and then wake up again, with a different body but all of your memories of earthly life. You see around you a city of gold, a radiant sky, and white creatures with wings flying about. Someone in a long white robe approaches you and says, "You are in heaven now."

d. Someone appears on earth and says, "God is invisible, but I, who am visible, am God's representative." To show his credentials he changes water into wine and raises people from the dead.

Selected Readings for Chapter 7

Alexander, Samuel, *Space, Time, and Deity.* 2 vols. London: Macmillan & Co., Ltd., 1918.

Alston, William (ed.), *Religious Belief and Philosophical Thought.* New York: Harcourt, Brace & World, Inc., 1963.

Baier, Kurt, *The Meaning of Life.* Canberra, Australia: Commonwealth Government Printer, 1957. Paperback.

Dewey, John, *A Common Faith.* New Haven, Conn.: Yale University Press, 1934.

Ducasse, Curt J., *A Philosophical Scrutiny of Religion.* New York: The Ronald Press Company, 1953.

Findlay, John N., *Language, Mind, and Value.* London: George Allen & Unwin, Ltd., 1963.

Flew, Antony and Alasdair MacIntyre, *New Essays in Philosophical Theology.* London: SCM Press, 1955.

Hartshorne, Charles, *The Logic of Perfection.* LaSalle, Ill.: Open Court Publishing Co., 1963.

————, and William L. Reese, *Philosophers Speak of God.* Chicago: University of Chicago Press, 1953.

Hepburn, R. W., *Christianity and Paradox.* London: C. A. Watts & Co., Ltd., 1958.

Hick, John (ed.), *Classical and Contemporary Readings in the Philosophy of Religion.* Englewood Cliffs, N. J.: Prentice-Hall, Inc., 1964.

————, *The Existence of God*. New York: The Macmillan Company, 1964. Paperback.

————, *Faith and Knowledge*. Ithaca, N. Y.: Cornell University Press, 1957.

————, *Philosophy of Religion*. Englewood Cliffs, N. J.: Prentice-Hall, Inc., 1962. Paperback.

Hook, Sidney (ed.), *Religious Experience and Truth*. New York: New York University Press, 1961.

Hume, David, *Dialogues Concerning Natural Religion*. First published 1779. Many editions.

James, William, *The Varieties of Religious Experience*. New York: David McKay Co., Inc., 1902.

Lewis, C. S., *The Problem of Pain*. New York: The Macmillan Company, 1962. Paperback.

Lewis, H. D., *Our Experience of God*. London: George Allen & Unwin, Ltd., 1959.

Macpherson, Thomas, *The Philosophy of Religion*. Princeton, N. J.: D. Van Nostrand Co., Inc., 1965. Paperback.

McTaggart, J. E., *Some Dogmas of Religion*. London: Edward Arnold & Co., 1906.

Martin, C. B., *Religious Belief*. Ithaca, N. Y.: Cornell University Press, 1959.

Matson, Wallace I., *The Existence of God*. Ithaca, N. Y.: Cornell University Press, 1965.

Mill, John Stuart, *An Examination of Sir William Hamilton's Philosophy*. London: Longmans, Green & Company, Ltd., 1865. Chapter 7.

————, *Three Essays on Religion*. "Nature," "The Utility of Religion," and "Theism." London: Longmans, Green & Company, Ltd., 1874.

Mourant, J. A., *Readings in the Philosophy of Religion*. New York: Crowell-Collier & Macmillan, Inc., 1954.

Munz, Peter, *Problems of Religious Knowledge*. London: SCM Press, 1959.

Pike, Nelson, *God and Evil: Readings on the Theological Problem of Evil*. Englewood Cliffs, N. J.: Prentice-Hall, Inc., 1964. Paperback.

Ramsey, Ian T., *Religious Language*. London: SCM Press, 1957.

Santayana, George, *Reason in Religion*. New York: Charles Scribner's Sons, 1905.

Scriven, Michael, *Primary Philosophy*. New York: McGraw-Hill Book Company, Inc., 1966. Chapter 4.

Smart, Ninian (ed.), *Historical Selections in the Philosophy of Religion*. New York: Harper & Row, Publishers, Inc., 1962.

————, *Philosophers and Religious Truth*. London: SCM Press, 1964.

Stace, W. T., *Religion and the Modern Mind*. Philadelphia: J. B. Lippincott Co., 1952.

————, *Time and Eternity*. Princeton, N. J.: Princeton University Press, 1952.

Taylor, A. E., *Does God Exist?* New York: The Macmillan Company, 1945.

Wisdom, John, "Gods," in *Logic and Language,* First Series, ed. Antony Flew. Oxford: B. H. Blackwell, Ltd., 1952.

8

Our Knowledge
of the Physical World

Thus far we have assumed that our sense-experiences enable us to have knowledge of the physical world. When we asked whether we could ever be certain of the truth of empirical statements, we suggested that if we saw the book, touched it, etc., we could not doubt its existence—but we did not then question that we could actually know of the existence and nature of objects around us by means of sight and touch. When we asked how laws of nature such as "Water boils at 212° F." could be verified, we suggested that they might be reduced to singular statements such as "This sample of water boils at 212°," "That sample boils at 212°," and so on, never doubting that we could know these singular statements to be true on the basis of sense-experience. When we analyzed the meanings of statements about unobservable entities such as electrons, we inquired whether such statements could be reduced to statements about the things we can see and touch, such as laboratory instruments and pointer-readings—again never doubting that these could be known through sense-experience. But it is time now to question these assumptions.

But why on earth, one might ask, should they be questioned? True, philosophy is devoted in large measure to the questioning of our beliefs, but isn't the belief in a world of trees, hills, and stars unquestionable? At least, if we questioned this belief, what is there left that we could not question? If we doubt not only causality and induction but the simple belief in a physical world, are we not reduced to sheer insanity? Don't we all, every moment of our lives, have an unshakable belief in a physical world—and not merely as a prejudice but for good reasons, since we see and touch the objects in the physical world constantly? What could be more certain than this? When I survey the scene before me, I would describe it by saying that I see a desk with some papers on it, books on a shelf, several chairs, walls, and a window, and, outside the window, houses and trees in the distance. I see these things, and can touch them if I want to. So if one asked, "How do you know that these things exist?" I could reply, "I see and touch them, of course. How could I see and touch them if they weren't there ?" In all of this, what is there that could possibly constitute a problem? Nevertheless, many of our common-sense beliefs about the reality of the physical world have been doubted and questioned by many persons who have given considerable thought to the matter.

23. Realism

Naïve Realism

The man in the street who has not reflected very much about the problems of perception and the physical world is a realist (in one sense of that highly ambiguous word): he believes that a physical world exists and is there whether we perceive it or not, and that we can know various things about it. The following five beliefs seem to be shared by virtually all human beings, and the first four of them together constitute the view that has sometimes been called " naïve realism":

1. There exists a world of physical objects (trees, buildings, hills, etc.).
2. Statements about these objects can be known to be true through sense-experience.
3. These objects exist not only when they are being perceived but also when they are not perceived. They are independent of perception.
4. By means of our senses, we perceive the physical world pretty much as it is. In the main, our claims to have knowledge of it are justified.
5. The sense-impressions we have of physical things are *caused* by those physical things themselves. For example, my experience of the chair is caused by the chair itself.

Yet there is not one of these propositions that has not been called into question by people who have thought about them systematically. What could possibly be the basis for such a doubt? Here are a few considerations that have led to such doubt:

1. Isn't what we perceive dependent, at least in part, on the nature of our organs of perception? If our eyes were different, what we see would be different; if our taste-buds were different, so would be the tastes we have. What right then have we to assume that we see or taste things the way they really are? In fact, how could we possibly know "how things really are," or "what they are really like in themselves"? Suppose our two eyes did not focus into one image and we saw everything double. Or suppose we had one eye on each side of our heads, like horses, so that we could see almost 180° of an arc but (probably) no spatial depth. Or if the rods and cones in the retina

were different or nonexistent, we would not have the color-vision we now have—indeed, most mammals do not have color-vision, and cannot distinguish one color from another, only degrees of lightness and darkness (as in a black-and-white movie); bees, on the other hand, can see ultraviolet, which we cannot even imagine. Or suppose we had a thousand eyes, like some insects; would not the world look very different to us?

Similarly, our senses of hearing, smell, taste, and touch might be quite different from what they are. We might have other senses, too, the nature of which we cannot now even imagine, which would reveal to us things we cannot now imagine either. Would not the world then look very different to us? (We can't even say "look," for this implies vision; and we have no names for the hypothetical other senses we are now discussing.) How would things look—or shall we say appear—to the inhabitant of Mars, for example to the "very intelligent cuttlefish" that H. G. Wells conceives as inhabiting that planet? As long as the content of our perceptions depends so much on the nature of the perceiving organ, and as long as we are unable to shed our perceiving organs as we do spectacles to try out other ones, how can we be so sure that we are perceiving things as they are? (We use the general word "perceiving" to cover hearing, seeing, smelling, etc., the "etc." covering also whatever senses there may be available to living creatures elsewhere is the universe.) Indeed, do we have any right to say what the physical world is *really* like at all?

2. Even with our present organs of perception, there are perfectly familiar cases of not perceiving things as they are. These we call *illusions*. The stick looks bent when it is half immersed in water, though it is really straight. The trees on the distant mountainside look grayish-blue, though ordinarily we would say they are dark green. The two lines in the Müller illusion (one with arrows pointing inwards, the other with arrows pointing outwards) look different in length, though they are equally long. In yellowish artificial light the blue dress looks black. The train whistle seems to be higher in pitch as the train approaches and lower as it recedes, though the pitch (so we believe) is the same all the time. The vessel of lukewarm water feels cold to one hand (which has just been near a hot stove) and hot to the other (which has just been in ice water) although the temperature of the water is the same throughout the vessel. Surely it is a matter of common knowledge that in sense-perception we are sometimes deceived. Everybody makes the distinction between how things seem, or *appear,* and how they really *are.* We often "perceive things the way they aren't." (Sometimes the causes of such phenomena lie within us, sometimes without; but they are all classed together here as illusions.)

3. Indeed, often there is an appearance when there is no reality at all; we "perceive things that aren't even there." This is a more radical way in which we may be misled. The drunken man sees pink rats going up and down the wall, but there are no pink rats there. Press your eyeball and you will see two

candles, but only one is there. If you are anxiously waiting for someone you may hear a knock on the door ten times throughout the evening, though no knock has really occurred. A man may feel intense pain in his leg although that leg has been amputated some time before.

This is a more misleading kind of perceptual error than illusion. So far we have assumed that, although we perceived certain things wrongly, and that the nature of our perceptions depended on the nature of the perceiving organ, there were nevertheless things to be perceived. In hallucination, however, we seem to perceive what does not even exist, at least not at the time and place we perceive it.

4. Having thus prepared the ground, we can be much more radically skeptical than this. Our senses sometimes deceive us. Very well; how do we know they don't deceive us all the time? If sometimes, why not always? Maybe the whole world is one gigantic hallucination; maybe it isn't there at all; maybe we are constantly being deceived. A much more skillful deception, no doubt, than pink rats, or oases in the desert when you are thirsty and they suddenly disappear; but isn't it possible? How do we know that it isn't so?

Descartes (1596–1650) told himself that perhaps there was an evil demon at work, arranging things in such a way that he would *believe* there was a world of real physical objects, when in fact there were no such objects at all. It would be just *as if* there were—so much "as if" that he could never tell the difference. Thus, Descartes decided that he could never know that what was before him was really a table, that there were real trees outside, and so on. All these things he could doubt. What could he *not* doubt? Only that he, the doubter, existed, at least while he was doubting.

What then about the physical world? How do we know that the demon is not constantly deceiving us? Descartes tried to show that God is not a deceiver and therefore would not play us false on so important a matter as this. But, beginning with only oneself and one's doubt, how does one get to God? And how can one prove that God is not a deceiver? Doubts about the physical world could also take the form of suspecting that it is all a dream—that perhaps we shall even awaken the next minute and find it so.

Such possibilities will be explored in this chapter. But let us begin with a milder one. For the moment let us leave Propositions 1, 2, and 3 unquestioned, and look more closely at 4 and 5. It will not take much extension of our common-sense thinking to put both these propositions in serious doubt.

Representative Realism

The principal exponent of representative realism, John Locke (1632–1704), believed that there are physical objects existing independently of perception, but that the way these objects appear to us is in many ways different from the way they really are. In daily life we say that a tree has a certain size, shape, weight, color, hardness, and so on; but, said Locke, not all these qualities are of the same kind. He divided the qualities of things into primary and secondary.

The *primary* qualities of an object are those qualities it has "in itself" quite apart from any perception, qualities it would have even if there were no sentient being to perceive them. These are, in general, the qualities that can be dealt with in science—those that can be measured. Whether or not it is perceived, an object has a certain size, shape, weight. These qualities are intrinsic to the object. But there are also *secondary* qualities, such as color, smell, taste, and tactile quality, which are not really qualities of the object at all. Consider color, for example: the color that an object appears to have varies considerably—in a bright light a thing looks one color, in the twilight another, and in the dark it looks black. It depends on the light, but also on the condition of the observer: a color-blind person will not perceive certain colors at all (though he will perceive their shape), and to a person with jaundice everything will look yellowish. They will also look different colors when seen through different instruments: in an ordinary light blood looks red, and we say it *is* red; but look at it through a microscope and it looks transparent with a few red flecks. With greater microscopic power it would probably look still different. In view of all this, can we really say what its true color is, or that it has any?

The same kind of observation can be made regarding smell, taste, and tactile qualities. A piece of cake will taste sweeter if you have just eaten something sour than it will after eating cookies. How something smells will depend on the nature of your olfactory organs and on what, if anything, you have smelled just before. What smell or taste has the thing really? Has it any at all? Is there any such thing as the real smell, color, taste, etc. of a thing?

Locke held that color, smell, taste are not qualities inherent in a thing. They are merely "ideas" we have, produced by the *secondary qualities* of the object. According to Locke, a secondary quality is not really a quality of the object at all; the object only contains within itself a *power* to produce in perceivers certain sense-experiences ("ideas" in Locke's sense). The object itself has no color; it has, somewhere in its "insensible parts"—that is, the arrangement of molecules within it—only the *power* to produce in perceivers a certain kind of sense-experience. Objects we call red have no redness themselves: they have only the power to produce in us the sense-experience we call red; and the objects we call blue, having somewhat different "insensible parts," have the power to produce in us the sense-experience we call blue. The power is in the object, but the red and blue exist only as ideas in my mind. What these sense-experiences are will depend on circumstances: the object we call red has no power to produce red sense-experiences in the dark, or in color-blind people, or in people with jaundice.

The experiences produced in us by secondary qualities, then, are qualities of an *object* only in a derived sense, for the object does not really have them:

it has only the power to produce in us certain sense-experiences, which we then (mistakenly, on Locke's view) take to be the real qualities of the object. The object has the quality only in the sense of power to produce in us the idea.

What then of primary qualities? We have sense-experiences ("ideas") of these too, so what is *their* relation to the object that causes them? Here, said Locke, the relation is one of *resemblance:* an object really is square, and it also looks square; another is round, and looks round; this one is larger than that, and so it appears to our senses. Our sense-experiences of the primary qualities resemble the qualities that the object has.

This, briefly, was Locke's view of the distinction between primary and secondary qualities and the sense-experiences caused by them. Before we turn to his views on the causation of sense-experiences, let us see what more can be said about Locke's distinction. George Berkeley, Bishop of Cloyne (1685–1753), of whom we shall hear more presently, was Locke's sharpest critic; he believed that there was no basis whatever for holding a distinction between primary and secondary qualities. His main reasons were these:

1. Inseparability. Secondary qualities, Berkeley argued, are inseparable from primary ones: if the object does not have the one, it cannot have the other. For example, color and shape are inseparable. Consider any shape you please, such as you might draw on the blackboard or paint on a canvas. What can fill the shape except a color? Shape, said Berkeley, is simply the boundary (or "limit") of a color. You can't even imagine a shape without a color. Whether it's a square shape, a circular shape, or any other, what fills it up must be some color or other. (Black and white of course count as colors; it is only when we consider the physical explanation of them that we say, for instance, "Black is not a color but the absence of colors.") But then, if shape is a primary quality of objects, so is color; and if color is not, neither is shape.

2. Variability. A thing may indeed, said Berkeley, appear to have different colors, depending on the conditions of the environment and the internal condition of the observer. But if variability proves subjectivity—that is, if it proves that the object does not itself possess these qualities—then Locke's argument proves too much, for it applies not only to colors and smells but to shapes and sizes and other so-called primary qualities as well. A thing will appear to have different shapes when viewed from different angles: the coin looks circular seen from above and elliptical from various angles, the degree of ellipticity depending on the obliqueness of the angle. And things look different sizes, depending on one's distance from them. Shape and size are variable no less than color and smell.

Thus far, we might be able to counter Berkeley's move by making an added distinction: we might say that things really do have certain shapes and sizes, but that a thing has a certain shape and size *from a place*. A coin *is* round from a perpendicular and *is* elliptical from an angle; a thing *is* larger when seen from five feet away than from ten feet away; and so on. But this suggestion is of doubtful value. Why not continue to say, as common sense does, that it continues to *have* the same shape and size as before but only *appears* to have a different shape and size? But then the same consideration will apply to color also: the object continues to be red but only looks gray when seen through green glasses; the trees on the distant hillside continue to be green but only look purplish-gray when seen at a great distance. In both cases equally, the change in appearance owing to change in the conditions of perception is predictable and regular. Moreover, saying that it *has* a different size from a different distance clearly breaks down when we pin it down to some definite size. The object is, say, four feet by six feet; what would be meant by saying that it *is* (not just looks) a different size at a different distance? Apparently it either has this size or it doesn't. The only way to avoid this would be to say that the object *changes* its size, depending on the position of the viewer. But what then of its size when different observers see it at the same time?

It would seem, in fact, that apparent shape and size and other primary qualities vary as much as color, smell, and taste. One thing may just "look bigger" than another one to us, whether it is or not, and for no reason that we can assign. This may happen with color too, but it only shows that the same variability affects both. A bucket of water feels heavier than it did an hour before if we are now tired. The wind feels colder if we are already cold. If you hold your hands in lukewarm water, the water will feel colder to the hand that has just been near the spout of a boiling teakettle than it will to the other hand. You see one candle, but if you press your eyeball you will see two candles. And so on. All this, of course, is "common sense": we constantly distinguish between the way things are and the way they appear. We don't hesitate to say that things appear (look, feel, smell, taste, sound) a vast variety of ways, but we believe too that in spite of all these variations they still *have* a definite size, shape, weight, temperature, *and* color. We believe as strongly that a thing is really red as that it is really round. How we distinguish between the real and apparent shape or color will concern us in the following pages. But we do make the distinction (whatever our criteria are), and—the point that concerns us at the moment—we make it of the so-called secondary qualities as much as of the so-called primary qualities.

If the variability of an object's appearance under varying conditions of perception proves that the object does not have a certain quality, then *all* the qualities we perceive must be denied of the object, and not just the secondary ones. Yet we do distinguish between the real and apparent ("seeming") qualities of things (by whatever means), so it seems that we must do so in some other way than by means of variability, which equally affects them all.

In the light of all this, what are we to say of the distinction between primary and secondary qualities? So far, it does not hold up very well. If the argument from variability shows that an object can't have a certain color, it shows equally that it can't have a certain shape. But what about another criterion for distinguishing primary from secondary that Locke sometimes used: the *measurability* of primary qualities? If the distinction hinges upon the possibility of *quantitative* treatment of the qualities in question, there may have been some excuse in Locke's day for distinguishing them, since physical science had not advanced so far. In Locke's day sizes and weights could be measured, but not colors. But this is no longer the case. As determined by wave-lengths of light, colors are as subject to quantitative treatment as sizes are. Smells, too, occur in a certain serial order: though less is known even today about this, there are measurable differences among smells, just as there are among colors and shapes. Hence this criterion (quantitative treatment) will not provide us with a distinction between primary and secondary qualities any more than the others.

In the light of this fact about quantitative treatment, we can now make one important point. The word "color" is ambiguous: it can refer to the *color-experience* we have (the sense in which "color" is indefinable except ostensively), and it can refer to the *physical basis* of our color-experience (the different wave-lengths of light emanating from the object to our eyes, or color in the physicist's sense). Color-experiences have a physical correlate, and so do smell-experiences. (We already noticed on p. 37 that "sound" can mean either the auditory experience or the vibrations of air that are its physical correlate. This ambiguity of "sound" was one of our first examples of verbal ambiguity.) The same occurs with "pain": as used in daily life the word refers to a certain type of experience, but as used by the physiologist it refers to the stimulation of nerve-endings that is the physical correlate of the pain-experience.

Exactly the same thing occurs in the case of the so-called primary qualities: there is the experienced (or "sensible") shape and size, and there is the physical shape and size that can be measured. There is the physical shape of the coin (round), which can be measured with a compass, and the physical size, which can be measured with a ruler; and there is the sensible or experienced shape (round if seen from a perpendicular, elliptical if seen from other angles) and the sensible or experienced size (smaller if one recedes from the object).

In all this there is no distinction between primary and secondary qualities: both sets of qualities, we might say, have both their primary (physical) and secondary (experienced) aspects. Let us call the physical shape "p" and the experienced shape "e." Then we have shape$_p$ and shape$_e$, we also have size$_p$ and size$_e$; and let us note, we also have color$_p$ and color$_e$, and even smell$_p$ and smell$_e$. Shape$_p$, size$_p$, and color$_p$ are all qualities of the object, and shape$_e$, size$_e$, and color$_e$ all characterize our sense-experiences (Locke's "ideas"). All these words are systematically ambiguous; so if you take only the p sense of some of them (shape, size) and only the e sense of the rest of them (color, smell), then naturally you end up with a distinction between shape$_p$, a property of the object, and color$_e$, which is not. But you might as well put this the other way round: shape$_e$ is not a property of the object, and color$_p$ is. The fact is that *both* sets of terms can be used in *both* ways. Instead of a distinction between primary qualities (for example, shape) and secondary qualities (for example, color), we end up with a distinction between *physical* qualities and *sensible* qualities, which extends throughout the range of *both* the Lockean primary and secondary qualities.

Beginning with Locke's primary v. secondary qualities, we have now been led to a different distinction, between physical and sensible properties. Virtually everyone who knows a little physical science would agree with it; indeed, it might be described as plain common sense enlightened by a certain degree of scientific knowledge. But now let us return to Bishop Berkeley, for his most important arguments against Locke have not yet been presented.

3. Resemblance. Locke says that our sense-experiences ("ideas") of primary qualities are *resemblances* of these same qualities, as they really do characterize the object in the outside world. But our experiences of the secondary qualities do not resemble any quality in the object, for there is in the object no such quality: there is only the power to produce certain sense-experiences of color, sound, smell, etc. But now, says Berkeley, *how could we ever know* that our experience of primary qualities resembles those qualities in the object itself? How could we ever compare them to discover this? We can speak of comparing only when we are in a position to compare: we can compare two colors—for example, say that this one is lighter than that one—because we can see them both. But how can we compare our *experience* of shape or size with the allegedly *real* shape and size the object has independently of our experience? We could not possibly do so—it would in fact be logically impossible to do so—because to do so we would have to be able to experience both of the items to be compared. And this we cannot do. We are acquainted only with *our own experiences,* and we cannot experience anything other than them. Try to compare these two: (1) the desk and (2) your sense-experience of the desk. The feat is impossible, for you have no two things available to compare. All you know about the desk is your desk-experiences, the total of your experiences of sight and touch with regard to what you believe to be the desk. You cannot tell whether your desk-experience is *like* the desk itself, because you cannot compare your desk-experience with the desk-as-it-is-apart-from-experience. So even if your experiences of the primary qualities did resemble the qualities as they exist in the object itself, neither Locke nor anyone else could ever know that they do.

"An idea," said Berkeley, "can resemble nothing but another idea." Translated into 20th century language, this means that sense-experiences can be compared with other sense-experiences but not with the supposed causes of these sense-experiences. What would it even mean to say that the experience of size is like the object's real size? Not only couldn't you compare them for resemblance, since you couldn't experience both of the items to be compared, but you couldn't discover whether they had any relation *other* than similarity either. There is simply nothing that you could say about them at all. We can say many things about our sense-experiences, but we cannot say anything at all about the physical world "as it is in itself" that the sense-experiences are supposed to resemble. Thus, on the question of whether the experiences we have of shape and size resemble (or have any other relation to) the real shape and size of the object, Locke is condemned to a total and incurable skepticism.

4. Causality. This skepticism must extend to every property that the object "as it really is" is supposed to have, including its causal properties. Since all we can know is our own experiences—and Locke had admitted this himself when he said that "the mind hath acquaintance with only its own ideas"—we can have no way of knowing whether our experiences resemble the objects themselves, or whether the objects *cause* the experiences either. What could possibly entitle us to say "Our sense-experiences are caused by physical objects"? If A causes B, we must be able to experience both A and B and observe some correlation or regularity between them in order to prove that the causal relation exists. But in the present case, though we have access to B (the experience), we have no possible access to A (the object-as-it-is-apart-from-experience). It lies forever beyond experience, and nothing whatever can be known about it.

It would be easy to reply "But we couldn't have any sensations if there were no real physical objects outside of us to cause them!" If we are acquainted only with our own sensations, how can we know this? By being acquainted with physical objects too, namely things that are *not* sensations? But this, on our present hypothesis, is impossible. If you are acquainted only with your own sensations, you cannot smuggle in something which is *not* sensations in order to prove that something other than sensations exists to cause the sensations.

The analogy of the telephone exchange.   The following analogy has sometimes been used to illustrate the situation: The mind is like a telephone exchange; you are the telephone operator, or clerk; messages come in to you along the wires (nerves) from the outside world. You do not see the people who do the telephoning; you do not even hear them as you would if you were in the same room with them; you hear only the sounds of their voices as they reach your end of the wire. You receive their incoming calls via the incoming wires (afferent nerves) and you connect them with their proper parties via other wires (efferent nerves), but you yourself never get outside the exchange.

This situation was put very vividly by the scientific writer Karl Pearson, in the late 19th century, in his book *The Grammar of Science:*

We are accustomed to talk of the "external world," of the "reality" outside us. We speak of individual objects having an existence independent of our own. The

store of past sense-impressions, our thoughts and memories, although most probably they have besides their physical element a close correspondence with some
physical change or impress in the brain, are yet spoken of as *inside* ourselves.
On the other hand, although if a sensory nerve be divided anywhere short of the
brain, we lose the corresponding class of sense impression, we yet speak of many
sense-impressions, such as form and texture, as existing outside ourselves. How
close then can we actually get to this supposed world outside ourselves? Just as
near but no nearer than the brain terminals of the sensory nerves. We are like
the clerk in the central telephone exchange who cannot get nearer to his cus-
tomers than his end of the telephone wires. We are indeed worse off than the
clerk, for to carry out the analogy properly we must suppose him *never to have
been outside the telephone exchange, never to have seen a customer or any one
like a customer—in short, never, except through the telephone wire, to have
come in contact with the outside universe*. Of that "real" universe outside himself
he would be able to form no direct impression; the real universe for him would
be the aggregate of his constructs from the messages which were caused by the
telephone wires in his office. About those messages and the ideas raised in his
mind by them he might reason and draw his inferences; and his conclusions
would be correct—for what? For the world of telephonic messages, for the type
of messages that go through the telephone. Something definite and valuable he
might know with regard to the spheres of action and of thought of his telephonic
subscribers, but outside those spheres he could have no experience. Pent up in
his office he could never have seen or touched even a telephonic subscriber *in
himself*. Very much in the position of such a telephone clerk is the conscious
ego of each one of us seated at the brain terminals of the sensory nerves. Not a
step nearer than those terminals can the ego get to the "outer world," and what
in and for themselves are the subscribers to its nerve exchange it has no means
of ascertaining. Messages in the form of sense-impressions come flowing in from
that "outside world," and these we analyze, classify, store up, and reason about.
But of the nature of "things-in-themselves," of what may exist at the other end
of our system of telephone wires, we know nothing at all.

But the reader, perhaps, remarks, "I not only see an object, but I can *touch* it.
I can trace the nerve from the tip of my finger to the brain. I am not like the
telephone clerk, I can follow my network of wires to their terminals and find
what is at the other end of them." Can you, reader? Think for a moment whether
your ego has for one moment got away from his brain exchange. The sense-
impression that you call touch was just as much as sight felt only at the brain
end of a sensory nerve. What has told you also of the nerve from the tip of your
finger to your brain? Why, sense-impressions also, messages conveyed along
optic or tactile sensory nerves. In truth, all you have been doing is to employ
one subscriber to your telephone exchange to tell you about the wire that goes
to a second, but you are just as far as ever from tracing out for yourself the telephone wires to the individual subscriber and ascertaining what his nature is in
and for himself. The immediate sense-impression is just as far removed from
what you term the "outside world" as the store of impresses. If our telephone clerk
had recorded by aid of a phonograph certain of the messages from the outside
world on past occasions, then if any telephonic message on its receipt set several
phonographs repeating past messages, we have an image analogous to what goes

on in the brain. Both telephone and phonograph are equally removed from what the clerk might call the "real outside world," but they enable him through their sounds to construct a universe; he projects those sounds, which are really inside his office, and speaks of them as the external universe. This outside world is constructed by him from the contents of the inside sounds, which differ as widely from things-in-themselves as language, the symbol, must always differ from the thing it symbolizes. For our telephone clerk sounds would be the real world, and yet we can see how conditioned and limited it would be by the range of his particular telephone subscribers and by the contents of their messages.

So it is with our brain; the sounds from telephone and phonograph correspond to immediate and stored sense-impressions. These sense-impressions we project as it were outwards and term the real world outside ourselves. But the things-in-themselves which the sense-impressions symbolize, the "reality," as the metaphysicians wish to call it, at the other end of the nerve, remains unknown and is unknowable. Reality of the external world lies for science and for us in combinations of form and color and touch—sense-impressions as widely divergent from the thing "at the other end of the nerve" as the sound of the telephone from the subscriber at the other end of the wire. We are cribbed and confined in this world of sense-impressions like the exchange clerk in his world of sounds, and not a step beyond can we get. As his world is conditioned and limited by his particular network of wires, so ours is conditioned by our nervous system, by our organs of sense. Their peculiarities determine what is the nature of the outside world which we construct. It is the similarity in the organs of sense and in the perceptive faculty of all normal human beings which makes the outside world the same, or *practically* the same, for them all. To return to the old analogy, it is as if two telephone exchanges had very nearly identical groups of subscribers. In this case a wire between the two exchanges would soon convince the imprisoned clerks that they had something in common peculiar to themselves. That conviction corresponds in our comparison to the recognition of other consciousness.[1]

It looks as if the picture of the world we get from science à la Pearson has painted itself into a corner. Our sense-experiences, it says, are the last item in a long chain of events starting with the physical object and going by way of the eyes, optic nerve, and brain to the sense-experience. At the same time, according to the account, all we can really know in our experience is this terminal event—the nature of the sense-experiences we have. But if these sense-experiences (strictly speaking: propositions about these sense-experiences) are all we can know, then how can we know anything at all about the alleged causes of these sense-experiences, or even whether there are any? If they have a cause, we can never know what it is, for we are confined within the circle of our own sense-experiences and cannot break out; and if we cannot through sense-experience know that anything beyond sense-experience exists, then we have no reason to *say* that it does, much less to say that it *causes* the sense-experiences we have. We seem to be blocked at every turn. We have given a "scientific" account of the conditions of

[1] Quoted from Everyman Library edition, pp. 56–58.

perception, and yet if this very account is true, we could never know that it is true!

In this theory, the sense-organs, nerves, and brain are the connecting links between the physical objects outside and the sense-experiences that occur after the brain has been stimulated by way of the sense-organs. But brain, sense-organs, and nerves are just as much physical objects as are tables, trees, and rocks. If we are acquainted with them, then *they* must be sense-experiences also. But a sense-experience can hardly be the connecting link between physical objects and sense-experiences. On the other hand, if we are *not* acquainted with them, how can we know that the sense-organs, nerves, and brains exist? At this point the analogy of the telephone exchange breaks down. The telephone operator can be acquainted with nothing except the sounds that come in along the wires of the exchange; but how can he then know that there are wires, or that he is in an exchange at all? It would appear that the entire telephone exchange has now collapsed into the operator.

What has happened? The telephone-exchange theory proceeds on the assumption that it itself is not true. In the very process of trying to show that we have no knowledge of an outside world but only of our own sense-experiences (messages at the end of a wire), it has assumed that there is an outside world and that we have knowledge of it—at least enough to be able to say that there are things in the outside world that stimulate sense-organs, which in turn stimulate nerves and send messages to the brain. Only if we know these things can our analogy get into operation; but if the telephone-exchange theory is true, we can never know these things. The sounds we hear at the end of the wire are causally related to the exchange; later the very possibility of knowing that there is such a thing as an exchange has to be denied, but meanwhile it has played an indispensable part in the analogy. Once we are clear about this, we shall have to reject the analogy: we cannot both know that there is an exchange (as the theory requires us to) and also not know it (as the theory also requires, since we know only the sounds at the end of the wire). A self-contradictory account cannot be a true one. So let us look elsewhere—back to Berkeley.

Exercises

1. "How do I know that physical objects (trees, stones, tables, and so on) exist?" "Because I see them and touch them!" Do you consider this a satisfactory answer? Why?

2. What line of thought would lead anyone to the conclusion that a person can be acquainted only with his own states of consciousness (for example, not the table, but certain table-experiences)? Assess the validity of this line of thought.

3. What inconsistencies are there in the analogy of the telephone exchange? Can you construct an analogy of your own which is less defective?

4. Assess Berkeley's argument from inseparability (against Locke's primary v. secondary qualities). Do you consider it valid, and why? Then assess his argument from variability.

5. Here are six suggested ways of distinguishing primary from secondary qualities. Try each of them in turn. Is there a distinction in each case, and when there is, does shape become primary and color secondary (that is, does the distinction into "primary" and "secondary" yield the Lockean denotation)?

a. Primary qualities are present in the world even when they are not being perceived; secondary qualities are not.

b. Primary qualities are perceived by more than one sense; secondary are not.

c. Primary qualities have not the variability of secondary qualities: for example, color may change, while shape remains constant.

d. Primary qualities are those left in the object after we break it down physically. (Descartes said that if we melt wax it loses its solidity and shape—both of which Locke called primary qualities—but never loses its extension, and accordingly Descartes considered extension the only "primary" quality of matter. Note: Does the wax lose shape, or only a particular shape?)

e. Primary qualities are those left after we remove as many properties from things by abstraction as we can and still have objects. (Something without color or smell would still be an object, but not without shape or size.)

f. Primary qualities are those that correspond with the "insensible parts" of objects. If we understood the molecular arrangement of an object completely, we could predict the color and smell, for example, but we could not predict the shape and size from a knowledge of the color and smell.)

6. "Do atoms have color?" "Of course not." "You mean they are colorless —transparent?" "No, they have no color at all." "How then is one to imagine them?" "One can't imagine them; they are not visualizable, the way macroscopic objects (such as marbles and planets) are." "So the popular belief that atoms are like tiny solid marbles is mistaken?" "Of course." "Atoms then have no color; do they have no other of the qualities of macroscopic objects, such as size and shape and weight?" "Yes, they do; physicists can tell us how many of them there are per cubic centimeter, and what their mass is." "So then they *do* have some of the qualities of macroscopic objects." "Yes, they do have some of them—the primary qualities." "But now I don't understand—size, shape, and mass, but no color. Now I run into Berkeley's objection: isn't a shape the limit (boundary) of a color? How can something have shape but no color (not even transparent)?" Can you escape this objection? Can you give a coherent account of the physicist's description of sub-microscopic "particles"?

7. Is there, in your opinion, any basis at all for the distinction between primary and secondary qualities? If so, state it as clearly as you can. (Would a physicist uphold the distinction as applied to atoms?)

8. State whatever difficulties you can find in the view (a) that physical objects cause sense-experiences, (b) that our sense-experiences resemble (are like) the physical objects they are of or about.

24. Idealism

Thus far, we have not stated Berkeley's positive view. We have only shown why, according to Berkeley, Locke had no reason for holding to his view about the existence of a physical world. Locke, said Berkeley, is committed to skepticism regarding a physical world: he cannot know that it exists, even if it does; and he is inconsistent, because he assumes that it exists and makes claims concerning it yet cuts himself off from the possibility of knowing it—which invalidates the arguments about physical objects and their qualities that he had given just before.

Now Berkeley takes his positive step. We have followed him to the point where he says we have *no good reason*, and can have none, for saying that a physical world outside our minds exists. Now comes the next step: *no such world exists at all*.

"But," we may object, "this is the very height of insanity! No world at all! No trees, no sun and moon, no tables and chairs! No books either—and what does Berkeley think he's writing?"

Let us be quite clear, however, about what Berkeley is and is not saying. He is not denying that there are trees and books and tables, but he *is* denying that there are any physical things in the sense of objects that exist *independently* of minds. In short, he is an *idealist* (idea-ist: "all that exists is minds and their ideas"—but, again, "idea" in the 18th century sense, which is much broader than ours, and covers any content of consciousness). There are not, as Locke thought, first trees and then sense-experiences-of-trees that "copy" or resemble the trees; there is just one thing, the sense-experiences-of-trees. Even if the trees did exist apart from sense-experiences, we could not know this; they would do us no good anyway, so we might as well do without them. All that exists are minds and the experience-of-minds (including book-experiences, tree-experiences, etc.), but there are no independently existing physical objects to cause the experiences. Why should we have first our-experience-of-the-chair and then the-chair-itself-as-it-exists-unexperienced? The first is enough; the second is excess baggage.

But if we speak of our-experience-of-the-chair, aren't we implying that there is a chair for our experience to be *of*? No; our language here is misleading. It happens that there is no convenient way to describe the contents of our sense-experiences other than by mentioning the name of the physical object we believe the experience to be of. There is no way in words to describe these particular sense-experiences and mark them off from all other sense-experiences other than to use the physical-object-word itself, but *without* any implication of a physical object existing to cause the experience. We would do better to speak of "chair-ish experiences" than "experiences of a chair." So we shall use this terminology, keeping in mind (what for non-philosophical purposes we do not need to keep in mind) that we are using the term merely to describe the qualitative nature of the sense-experiences themselves. We all know what chair-ish sense-experiences are like, else we would not be able on having a few of such experiences to say "There's a chair." But we could still have the chair-experiences without there being any chairs. If we are having a hallucination and think we see a chair when there isn't any, it is still true that we are having chair-*experiences*—not experiences *of* a chair, but chair-experiences.

Berkeley did indeed believe that there are chairs, but *not* that our chair-experiences are caused by chairs—that is, by physical objects existing outside us and independently of us. He believed, rather, that "chair" and all other physical-object words are names for *recurring patterns,* or complexes, of sense-experiences, and nothing else. Berkeley would say, "If by 'physical objects' you mean things existing outside us and causing our sense-experiences, I insist that they do not exist, nor could we know that they existed even if they did. But if by 'physical objects' you mean groups or complexes of sense-experiences, then they undoubtedly *do* exist—indeed, we are aware of them every waking moment of our lives, since we are constantly having sense-experiences that fall into ordered patterns or groups."

What exactly is meant by saying that a chair, or any other physical object, is a pattern, or complex, of sense-experiences? This is somewhat difficult to convey in a few words; let us first take an example. Consider this table, which we believe to have a rectangular top. Now as I look at this table-top (ordinarily speaking), I find that my experience has the following characteristics:

1. The appearance of the table-top varies in systematic ways. If I move away from it, it appears to get smaller, and when I approach it it appears to become larger again. When I view it from above, it looks rectangular, but if I look at it from any other angle, it looks more like a trapezoid, with the acute angles on the nearer side. The apparent shape and size vary systematically with the angle of vision.

2. As I stand still, it continues to look the same; but when I move, the apparent shape changes, and when I get back to my former position, it looks as it did before. After I have had a little experience of the way the apparent shape changes, I can predict how it will look after my next change of position: the whole series of sense-experiences is systematic and predictable.

3. As I move, the visual sense-experiences from moment to moment resemble one another: shape A shades into shape B, B into C, C into D, etc., though A may not greatly resemble D. Apparent shape 1 may not resemble apparent shape 50, but the two are connected by a series of apparent shapes, each of which closely resembles the one on each side of it. Again, the change is gradual and regular.

4. There is no discontinuity in the series. As I look, or walk while looking, there is no moment at which I do not have the sense-experience (unless I turn my head or blink). The shape does not jump out of my field of vision and then pop back into it again somewhere else.

5. The series of apparent shapes has a center from which the others deviate in a progressive *distortion-series.* The round apparent shape of the penny is the center around which all the elliptical ones congregate.

6. My visual experiences act as *signs* of my tactual ones: if I go up to what I believe (on the basis of my visual sense-experiences) to be the table, I have tactual sense-experiences. My visual experiences are highly correlated with

tactual ones. Occasionally they are not, to be sure: if I don't know I am looking in a mirror I may approach what I believe to be the table, only to bump into the mirror—there will be no tactual sense-experience corresponding to the visual one: the tactual experience will be of the mirror, not of the table; there is no table beyond the mirror.

In short, the table-top sense-experiences form an *orderly series*. The entire series of shapes constitutes, as it were, a *family:* they all "belong together" in a different way from the way the series of shapes we see looking at a coin do—these constitute another, and very different, family. A physical object is nothing more or less than a *family of sense-experiences*.

Hallucinations.   Among our innumerable sense-experiences, the vast majority are members of families. One family constitutes the chair, another the table, another the coin, another this book before me, and so on. But when we have hallucinations, the sense-experiences are not members of any family: they are unattached, or "wild." If in a state of intoxication I see pink rats going up and down the wall, they may behave in all sorts of peculiar ways: their apparent shape and size may not vary in the regular ways just described; and even if they do, the visual experiences are not followed by any tactual experiences (that is, even if I reach out I can't touch them).

It is a fortunate contingent fact about the universe that the vast majority of our sense-experiences belong to families, thus making them, on Berkeley's analysis, real things—what we would call "physical objects." We could easily imagine a state-of-affairs in which this would not be so. Imagine for a moment that all our sense-experiences occurred hit-or-miss, with visual sense-data hopping all about our visual field, changing shapes and sizes in chaotic and unpredictable ways, each visual sense-experience discontinuous with the next one, coming and going and changing character every moment, visual sense-experiences not being followed by tactual ones, and tactual ones occurring unpredictably without visual ones having occurred to warn us. You could easily imagine most or even all of your sense-data being "wild," and in this case there would be no such things as physical objects, since there would be no such things as families of sense-experiences. One might say that there would be at least one family present, your own body. But that could also be otherwise: you might have the chaotic series of sense-experiences without even having any of the sense-experiences you now attribute to your own body (as we saw in Chapter 6). But fortunately, our experiences are not like this: most of our sense-experiences belong to families.

The criterion we actually use in determining whether something is a hallucination, says Berkeley, is to observe whether the sense-experience in question belongs to a family. In doing this, we relate our sense-experiences *to one another*. We do not do what Locke's view would seem to require: relate our sense-experiences to a reality outside our sense-experience to see whether they correspond. According to Locke, if we have a table-experience and there's no table there, it's a hallucination; and if there is, it's not (it is then "veridical"—a "true" perception). But we could never apply such a correspondence test, for we could never get outside our sense-experiences to discover whether or not there is something outside them to correspond to something within them. We never in fact even attempt to apply such a test: we compare our sense-experiences with one another, not with something else that isn't sense-experience.[2] It is true, of course, that in hallucination "there is no table there"; but this means, according to Berkeley, only that in hallucination there is no family of table-experiences. It takes only a little time to discover whether or not the experience we are having is "wild." The distinction between veridical perception and hallucination is always to be found in the relation of sense-experiences *to one another*—specifically, in whether or not they belong to a family. Those that don't belong to a family we call hallucinations.

Much misinterpretation of Berkeley has occurred on this point. Some have alleged that according to Berkeley everything is imaginary. But there is plenty of difference between a real table and an imaginary table. I can't sit on an imaginary table, or place books on it, nor will it hold my weight if I try to step on it: the sense-experiences don't cohere as a family. Asked to refute Berkeley's view, Samuel Johnson kicked a stone and exclaimed, "I refute it thus!" But Berkeley, of course, did not deny the existence of the stone: he would have said merely that a stone is a family of sense-experiences (not at all a hallucination), and that kicking the stone only confirmed his point: visual stone-experiences are followed by tactual stone-experiences, just as they could be expected to do in any well-ordered family of sense-experiences.

Berkeley laid almost exclusive emphasis upon touch as a criterion for the existence of "real" objects. If no touch-experience can be obtained, he believed, there is no physical object, even though the visual part of the family might be quite orderly. Thus, if you have visual tree-experiences and go up to touch the tree but have no touch-experiences, you must admit that what seemed to be a tree was a hallucination. On the other hand, if you should stumble into something invisible, but its tactual shape was like that of a tree, you would have to say it was an invisible tree, and not a hallucination. (This is our situation regarding invisible glass.) Or: If you thought you saw two iron bars side by side, but on touching them found that there was only one continuous surface, you would have to conclude "It was one bar, but it looked like two" (never "It was two bars, but it felt like one"). But if you thought you saw one bar and on touching it found two separate tactual series (you could put your hand between them), then you would have to admit that it was two bars that looked like one (never one bar that felt like two). Our ultimate criterion

[2] According to Locke, all we can actually do in this situation is apply the test of "vivacity" (the real thing is more "lively" or "vivid" than the hallucination) and "coherence" (the real things fall into patterns, as in Berkeley's account). But what we *can* do, and what we would *have* to do to prove Locke's theory of independently existing objects, are two different things. (Locke, *An Essay Concerning Human Understanding*, Book IV, Chapter IV, sections 3–4.)

for concluding whether our experiences are veridical or hallucinatory is whether there is a "touch-member" of the family. Visual experiences are merely the signs, or harbingers, of touch-experiences.

Illusions. Sometimes the sense-experiences we have belong to a family—hence are not hallucinatory—but the qualities of some parts of the family are at variance with those of other parts; then we say that the object "really has quality A" but "only appears to have quality B." For example, a straight stick looks bent in water: there is a touch-experience, but when we look at the stick in water we are inclined to say "It's bent" and the moment it is out of water we are inclined to say "It's straight." Why do we say that the stick was really straight all the time and only *looked* bent while in the water, rather than that it became bent while in the water and only felt straight at that time? Once again, we take the touch-experience as decisive. But this is not the only relevant fact in the situation. If we place a measuring-rod in the water alongside the stick, we find that it too looks bent, and yet they both feel straight all the time. We can explain, by laws of refraction, why the stick looks bent in water; and for this reason also we say that it really is straight all the time, rather than that it becomes bent in water while continuing to feel straight. We thus have a coherent scientific system, with no facts unaccounted for, by holding that it is straight but looks bent, instead of holding that it is bent but feels straight.

The coin looks elliptical from most angles, yet we say that it only looks elliptical but really *is* round. It is true that it feels round, but even without touch, we could (and doubtless would) say that it is round, on the basis of sight alone. The round appearance that the coin presents us when seen from a perpendicular is the center of the distortion-series, from which all the other appearances "radiate"; it is, so to speak, the nucleus of them all. And thus we say "The coin really is round; it only looks elliptical from this angle" rather than "It becomes elliptical when viewed from an angle" (what if someone continued to look at it from above, saying "It doesn't become elliptical at all—it still looks round to me"?) or "It is elliptical all the time; it only looks round when seen from above" (but it feels round all the time; besides, we can explain the elliptical appearance by means of optical laws, as in the case of the straight stick that looks bent).

Not everyone would agree on the criteria that are to be employed in each case: some would say that we take the round appearance as "the real shape" and the elliptical one as "mere appearance" because we can use the round shape as a basis of prediction: if we assume that it is round we can predict how it will look from various angles (varying degrees of ellipticity). But are we quite sure that we couldn't equally well predict the round appearance from above on the basis of the varying elliptical appearances?

It is important to remember that we do not always use the same criteria for distinguishing "reality" from "appearance." In the case of shape, we have both sight and touch to go by, but color can be discerned by vision only. How do we distinguish what we call "the real color of the object" from the colors that it appears to have in varying conditions of light and distance?

We say that a certain dress is dark blue, although most of the time (and under almost all artificial light) it looks black. If someone were to say that the dress is really black, we would say he is mistaken, though we do not deny that it now looks black, both to him and to us. What criterion then do we apply in this case? Clearly we cannot perform a Lockean comparison of the-appearance-of-the-dress with the-dress-itself: we have only the varying appearances to go by. But we select, among the totality of appearances, *some* as "standard": we say that the dress really has the color it appears to have under certain standard conditions. Specifically, we say that the dress really has the color it appears to have when viewed in sunlight. In sunlight it looks dark blue, and accordingly we say that it *is* dark blue.

Why, however, do we say that it is dark blue because it appears so in sunlight, rather than that it is black because it appears so in artificial light? Why this prejudice in favor of sunlight? Is it because human beings first used sunlight as a standard, and just never got out of the habit? Or is it because sunlight is the light we encounter most often? No, neither of these facts has anything to do with the matter. Even if sunlight were not the most frequently encountered kind of light—and it is not for those who sleep during the day and are awake at night—it would still be considered standard, because sunlight is the light that affords us the *maximum possible discrimination* of colors. Two dresses look the same (black) in artificial light, but when we see them in sunlight one looks dark blue and the other looks black, and consequently we say that the one *is* dark blue and the other black. If we took artificial light as our standard (in which both dresses look black) we would not be able to predict what colors they would appear to have in sunlight, whereas having seen them both in sunlight we can easily predict that both of them will look black in artificial light. Thus we are back with maximum predictability: we take maximum discrimination as a criterion because the conditions of maximum discrimination are also the conditions in which maximum predictability of color-appearances occurs.

The real color of the object, we say, is the color it appears to have under conditions of maximum discrimination—that is, in sunlight. The real color is a selection from the totality of apparent colors, guided by a criterion. It may be that sunlight is more frequently encountered, but this fact is of no relevance in selecting the color-appearances that we call "the real color": the real color is the color it appears to have in such-and-such conditions, no matter how frequently encountered such conditions may be. If we found some source of light that could systematically reveal distinctions within what we thought was a uniform dark blue, we would say, "It looks a uniform blue in sunlight, but wait until I shine this other light on it and you'll see that the dress really has various colors."

So much for the difference between sunlight (condition of maximum color-discrimination) and other types of light. When the difference in color-experience depends on the light, we can appeal to the principle of maximum discrimination. But not all the variety of our sense-experiences, even with regard to color, depends on this difference. Three people may be looking at the curtain in sunlight; the first person may see blue; the second may see a purplish shade because he is looking through red glasses, and a third, person looking through yellow glasses, may see green. We say that the curtain really is blue, not the other colors. Why? Each of the others is a member of a distortion-series, beginning with blue.

Blue is the color upon which they all *converge*. Blue is, as it were, the common theme, and they are the different sorts of variations which may be made upon it, each series of variations being ordered in degrees of increasing oddness. And if instead of putting on spectacles we progressively alter the illumination in various ways, or take various drugs in increasing doses, we get another group of progressively increasing variations. And here, too, blue is the common theme.

Thus although all these different colors are alike in being sensed, and hence are all equally actual, blue does enjoy a peculiar and, as it were, privileged position among them. It is not enough to say "All these colors are equally real or equally unreal, equally 'right' or equally 'wrong.' Quite so. But what is the structure of this 'all'? When we reflect upon that, we find that it is not a mere aggregate, like a heap of stones, but a *system* of a peculiar sort: it is an ordered group of variously increasing divergencies, having a certain single quality for its center.

This is the fact that common sense is trying to state when it says that blue is the real color of the curtain. But the statement is infelicitous, owing to the ambiguity of the term 'real.' It is apt to suggest that the blueness is actual and the other colors (say the purple sensed by the man with red spectacles) are not actual: which is plainly not the case, for all of them are actually given. But this is a misinterpretation. The meaning of 'real' here is more like the one it bears in such statements as 'The real way to do it is this' or 'The real authority on the subject is Smith'; it means something like 'superior to others of the same kind.' Now there is a very good sense in which the color blue is superior to, and more important than, the many other colors which are also exemplified when we look at the curtain. They are no less actual than it, but the fact remains that in the case of the curtain it is the one by reference to which alone all the others are ordered; were it not for their common relation to it, the group would fall to pieces, and would not be the sort of ordered group that it is. And it is more important than the rest not only ontologically but also epistemically: it is, so to speak, the key to the group, and if we know what it is, we can infer what the other members must be. Let us sum all this up by calling it the *standard color* of the curtain, thus avoiding the ambiguity of the word 'real.' What common sense maintains, then, is that blue is the standard color of that particular curtain, and moreover, that any material thing has its own standard color. If so, it is clear that common sense is perfectly right. And we may observe that neither the analysis nor the justification of its statement requires any appeal to causal considerations at any point.[3]

[3] H. H. Price, *Perception,* pp. 211–12.

We see, then, that different criteria are used for different situations. To find the "real color" amidst different appearances, we employ one criterion when the difference in appearance depends on differences in illumination, and another when it depends on differences in perspective or abnormalities of vision. To complicate the matter further, we sometimes speak of "the real quality" as being one thing when we are speaking in one context, and another in another context: for example, blood is red, just as the curtain is blue, and for the same reasons given above: red is the color you will see when you look at blood in sunlight, and it is the nucleus of any distortion-series. On the other hand, if we are biologists in a laboratory we will say that blood is not a uniform red (though that's the way it looks) because when viewed under a microscope it presents greater differentiations of color: in this "scientific" sense, it really *is* red-and-transparent (not all red), since this is the color you will regularly see when you look at it through a microscope. In every case, it is the appearance we get under certain privileged conditions that is decisive. Our last consideration was merely that the set of conditions we take as privileged may vary somewhat with the context in which we are speaking.

Dreams. We have now given an account of hallucinations and illusions; but there is still another kind of experience we have not considered, dreams. Hallucinations and illusions at least occur during our waking life, but dreams do not even do that; since there is virtually no limit to what we can dream, dreams constitute a more radical departure from the daily regularity of experience than do the other two. How shall we distinguish dreams from waking-life experiences?

Are waking-life experiences more vivid than dreams? Not necessarily; sometimes dreams are as vivid as any waking-life experience could be. Are the dreams less orderly in content? Sometimes, but not necessarily—colors and shapes, sounds, smells, tastes, and feelings may all occur in dreams in an orderly manner, as they do in waking life, so we cannot take "failure to follow the laws of nature" as distinctive of dreams: the table in your dream may not suddenly vanish or be levitated or disappear from one place and reappear in another any more than waking-life tables do. It seems impossible to distinguish dreams from waking-life experiences on the basis of any qualitiative dissimilarity between dream-experiences and waking-life experiences.

One might suggest: "The difference is that if we draw inferences from dream-experiences the inferences are false, but not if we draw them from waking-life experiences. You dream that your wife is dead, but if you infer that she really is dead, you are mistaken, for when you awaken you find her right there." There is, to be sure, this discrepancy between your inference from dream-experience and your inference from waking-life experience; but so far there is nothing to tell us which inference is correct. Perhaps what you experienced in the dream was what really happened and it is the waking-life experience that misleads you. We do believe that the waking-life experience entitles us to say what really happened, and that if we make similar inferences from dreams we are deluded; but why don't we say it the other way round? Why not say "The dream shows that what I thought happened in waking life didn't really happen"? ("In waking life I can not only see things but touch them, and so on," But so can you in your dream.)

"There are real physical objects to correspond to the waking-life experiences but not to the dream-experiences." But this worn argument will not work: for how do you know that there is a correspondence between experience and something else in one case but not in another, if you have access only to the experiences? Here we have Locke's problem once again. However we may distinguish dream-experiences from other experiences, this is not the way.

The difference, it would seem, depends not on the nature of the experiences considered by themselves but on the total *context* in which they occur. The table in the dream may be just as vivid, just as shining, just as black, and just as tangible as the one in waking life; but the one in waking life is set in a huge and pervasive pattern of interconnecting experiences that does not occur in the dream. You awaken, you find yourself in bed, there are the same furniture and windows you have seen a thousand times, and you remember going to bed, getting drowsy, turning off the light. And suddenly the gap is bridged—the experience you had of being in the South Seas must be a dream, for it doesn't fit anywhere into the context of all the other experiences.

Consider how we recognize dreams or delusions for what they are. When we are suddenly roused from a vivid dream, we may be momentarily dazed, not knowing the dream from the actuality. How do we establish which is which? Mere vividness does not decide the matter; the dream may be of nightmare intensity while the perception of our familiar surroundings may be comparatively dim. The deciding factor in the battle is what may be called the mass and integration of the household troops. The bureau and windows of our familiar bedroom and the sound of a familiar voice throw out innumerable lines of connection that bring our everyday world around us again in irresistible volume. Against the great bulk of this world, and without any lodgment in it, the figures of our dream appear unsubstantial and fugitive, quickly dissolving for want of support; and it is just the recognition that what we have been experiencing will not fit into our common-sense world that we mean when we say wake from a dream. The power to measure such fancies and phantasms against the ordered mass of experience is the logical meaning of sanity; its disappearance is insanity.[4]

That is what is distinctive of dream-experiences—*not fitting in*. Our Waking-life experiences form an ordered pattern, shown by the shaded lines in the diagram: in waking-life experience we find certain objects and certain people; the objects behave in predictable ways (laws of nature); and when

[4] Brand Blanshard, *The Nature of Thought*, II, 278–79.

the sensory environment changes we can assign a cause, such as "I walked from here to there." During sleep we have other experiences, dreams—D_1, D_2, etc. Then we wake again, and experience resumes the character it had before we had the dreams, proceeding as if the dream-experiences had never occurred. The "world" of D_1 doesn't fit in with the steady and constant world W.L. (waking life); for that matter, D_1 doesn't fit in with D_2 or D_3 either. We call them dreams precisely because they don't fit in. And we say that the waking-life experiences are "real," not because the dream-experiences aren't real experiences (both types of experiences obviously *occur*) but because, as with illusions, we confer the adjective "real" upon a privileged class of experiences—in this case those that have the pervasive orderliness and coherence that waking-life experiences do have.

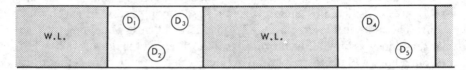

But how do we know that it isn't *all* a dream? Perhaps the whole of our experience is a dream. This may sound like a profound suggestion, but in fact it is only a verbal maneuver. The word "dream" is now used in our language to designate a certain class of experiences—D_1, D_2, etc.—and to distinguish them from all other experiences. The dream-experiences are those that don't fit in with the regular everyday order of our other experiences. Now, if we said of *every* experience we ever had that it is a dream, our assertion would be strictly meaningless. It doesn't fit in with what? "Fitting in" has meaning only in relation to a context or background of *other* things into which this fits. You can't say of everything that it fails to fit in; what could it fail to fit in with? We would be using a word or phrase outside of the only context in which it had a meaning.

Or we could put the matter this way: Say, if you like, that it's all a dream. You are then using the word "dream" to cover not merely D_1, D_2, etc., but the entire range of experience (the whole diagram). Very well, it's all one big dream. But within that one big dream that we are all in all the time, there is still a distinction to be made between those "islands" of experience that don't fit in with the others and the vast remainder that are uniform. That distinction will still be valid, only now we won't be able to use the word "dream" to distinguish the islands from the rest, since we have already pre-empted this word to apply to the totality of all experience. So we shall have to invent a new word to talk about exactly the same thing that we used the word "dream" to talk about before. What possible gain is there in this? We would not be changing any of the features of our experience by doing this; we would only be substituting a new word for one that is already in current usage and that everyone already understands.

There is, in fact, very little difficulty in distinguishing dream-experiences from waking-life experiences. A few moments at most after we awaken, we perceive that the South Sea Island experiences don't fit in with any of our other experiences. But it is logically possible that there could be much more difficulty in making the distinction than there now is; one can imagine logically possible conditions in which we wouldn't know *what* to say. Suppose that the totality of your experience is divided into two equal parts: one period of one type of experience, T_1 (house, books, classrooms, one group of people), followed by an equal period of an entirely different type of experience, T_2 (tropical palms, ocean, native tribes), and that these two sets of experiences alternated throughout your lifetime. Neither set of experiences has any relation to the other set, but each one is complete and coherent within itself. You could ask yourself, "Was I dreaming when I experienced the tropical ocean and the palm trees?" But in the next span of experience you could ask yourself, "Was I dreaming when I experienced bedroom, kitchen, familiar persons, etc.?" And since both sets of experiences were equally ordered and coherent, there would be no way for you to distinguish them. Your experiences would be split into two groups, with no qualities of the one group privileged over the other to enable you to say "This is reality; the other was only a persistent dream."

Esse est percipi.   We must now consider another aspect of idealism. According to idealism, physical objects are families of sense-experiences. But obviously experiences do not exist unexperienced. Physical objects, then, do not exist unexperienced either.

This last assertion certainly conflicts sharply with our common-sense beliefs. We believe that physical objects continue to exist whether they are experienced or not. Idealism is committed to denying this. According to idealism, *esse est percipi* ("to be is to be perceived") as far as physical objects are concerned. Idealism says about physical objects the same thinig that common sense says about experiences of all kinds: that they do not and cannot exist unexperienced; and if they cannot do so singly, combinations of them (by which idealism defines physical objects) cannot do so either. There can be no reality apart from experience, says idealism. Tables, trees, and other physical objects are families of experiences. They have no other existence than as experiences; and even if they did, we could not know that they did, since our knowledge is limited to the range of our experiences.

But surely the table doesn't cease to exist when I go out of the room! No, not if you stay in the room and continue to perceive it. But suppose we both leave the room; does the table then cease to exist? Yes, if no one is having table-experiences. If we think no one is in the room, and we leave for 15 minutes and then go back, we may find our friend Jones saying, "It existed all the time; I was looking through a peephole in the wall, and I can assure you that I had table-experiences while you were gone exactly as I did when you were here." No idealist would deny this. But now suppose that *no* one is in the room—no person, no organism of any kind that could have table-experiences. Does the table exist during that period? No; *esse est percipi*, and there is no *esse* because there is no *percipi*.

"Well, what difference does it make?" one might ask. "As long as the table is always there when we get back, what do we care? The question whether it exists during intervals between perceptions can make no difference whatever to our actual experiences." The idealist, of course, would not deny this. Still, whether it is a practical question or not, it would be interesting to know what the answer is, and how it can be known to be true.

"Physical objects do exist during inter-perceptual intervals, and I can easily prove it," one might suggest. "Bring a motion-picture camera into the room, set it going, and then have everyone leave. Come back a few minutes later, develop the film, and project it on the screen. We will then all witness the exciting drama of table-continuing-to-exist-during-our-absence." But the idealist would not be convinced by any such experiment. The motion-picture camera is itself a physical object, and is also, according to idealism, a family of sense-experiences that also ceases to exist when not experienced. The camera, the table, and indeed the room itself and the building it is a part of are all in the same boat: *esse est percipi* applies equally to all of them. Moreover, our account of the entire series of events is all given in terms of experiences: we have table-experiences, then table-and-camera experiences, then other-room experiences, then table-and-camera experiences again, and later table-projected-on-a-screen experiences. No one, certainly not the idealist, doubts that we have this sequence of experiences. And that is all there is—just this sequence of experiences. Nothing apart from the series of experiences exists, and we wouldn't know it even if it did.

Our frustration at this point may be similar to that of the boy who was told by his brother that the street light went out whenever his eyes were shut. He watched the street light intently, studiously shut his eyes, then furtively opened them again for a moment; the street lamp was shining as usual. "But you told me it went out!" "Yes," said his brother, "when your eyes are shut; but when you peeked, they were open." How could the boy ever prove otherwise? Is idealism, as one 18th century critic remarked, "utterly absurd, and utterly irrefutable"?

"We have to believe that physical objects exist unperceived in order to account for what we see when we perceive them again." You light a fire in the fireplace, watch it burn for a time, then leave the room for half an hour. When you return, nothing is left in the fireplace but a pile of glowing embers. Surely the fire must have burned down even though no one was perceiving it; how else can you explain the fact that there were burning logs on the fire when you left and only embers when you returned? The wood must have burned while you were gone, and in order to burn, it must have existed while you were gone. Or: Many times you have seen a house and also its shadow; this time you see the shadow but are not yet in a position to see the house. But surely the house must be existing at this moment even though neither you nor anyone else is perceiving it, else what would be casting the shadow?

In these examples we are appealing to well-established laws of nature about the behavior of fire and shadows. But, the idealist reminds us, we have known these laws to hold true only for cases we could observe; we have no justification for extending them to unobserved cases. "Every time I have observed X I have observed Y; therefore, it is inductively probable that this time when I observe X I shall observe Y." But this says nothing whatever about what happens when I do *not* observe X. No observation can possibly tell me what exists when nobody observes it. Even if physical objects continue to exist when no one perceives them, how can we have any good reason to believe that they do, since no one can observe them existing unobserved?

It is true that I may have watched a fire burning down many times, and I can argue inductively that if I light a fire this time I can watch it burn down again. But I cannot argue, from present or past experience, anything whatever about what happens or will happen when neither I nor anyone else is observing it, for I have no observational basis on which to make any such assertion. *Esse est percipi* applies to laws of nature as well as to physical objects. The only laws we are in a position to state are those connecting experiences with each other; we can state nothing about what exists apart from experience.

How, indeed, could we possibly know that physical objects exist unperceived? (1) We cannot know it by experience, since of course no one can observe them existing unobserved. (2) So we could know it only by *inference*. But (a) we cannot infer it *deductively*. We cannot deduce any statement about any unobserved state of a physical object from observational premises that refer only to the observed states of that object; we cannot deduce a conclusion about what is unobserved from premises about what is observed—such a conclusion would not logically follow from the premises. (b) Nor can we refer it *inductively:* to establish a conclusion inductively (which at best gives probability, not certainty), we have to argue from instances we observe. We observe X followed by Y once, twice, a thousand times, and infer inductively that the next time we observe X we will observe Y also. But we cannot infer that a thing, or event, or uniformity among events, in addition to existing when observed, *also* exists when unobserved. Of any correlation between two events—the first observed and the second unobserved—*we cannot observe even a single instance,* and hence we have no observed basis for even getting an inductive argument started.

How, then, could we possibly know anything about objects existing unobserved? We could know it only by observation or by inference. We cannot know it by observation. Inference is either deductive or inductive. We cannot know by deduction, and we cannot know it by induction; therefore we cannot know it by inference. Since we cannot know it by observation or by inference, we cannot know it at all. Q.E.D.[5]

Weak v. strong idealism.   Such is the view of one version of idealism, which we may call weak idealism, not because it is less plausible but because it makes a smaller claim than does strong idealism. Weak idealism says: Even if physical objects do exist unperceived, we have no reason whatever for believing that they do—we could not know it even if they did but it is still logically possible that they do. Strong idealism says: It is not logically possible that they do; physical objects existing unperceived is a contradiction in terms. This is what Berkeley said, except that he usually spoke of "repugnancy" rather than "contradiction." It is not (said Berkeley in effect) that there is no *evidence* that physical objects exist unperceived—how could there be evidence for what is logically impossible?—it is that if you say a physical object exists unperceived you are contradicting yourself. Why is this? Let us examine the reasoning.

1. We do have acquaintance with physical objects.
2. All we can have acquaintance with is experiences.
Therefore, 3. Physical objects are experiences (that is, families of experiences).

That is the first step. Statement 1 is one we all believe, and must believe if we are not to avoid complete skepticism; we will not wish to tamper with this statement unless we absolutely have to. Statement 2 is held not only by Berkeley but by his opponent Locke. And the two together yield the conclusion, statement 3. Now statement 3, the conclusion of the first argument, is made a premise of a second argument:

3. Physical objects are experiences.
4. Experiences can't exist unexperienced. (Can't = logically impossible.)
Therefore, 5. Physical objects can't exist unexperienced. (Can't = logically impossible.)

We have already arrived at 3; 4 is surely true—indeed, it is analytic; and it yields the conclusion, statement 5, which we appear to be stuck with whether we like it or not. If we assert that physical objects do not exist unexperienced, we are uttering an analytic statement, and if we deny it we contradict ourselves.

Why then is the conclusion so surprising? No one wants to deny an analytic statement or to assert a self-contradictory one. The idealist says it is surprising only because we have never really digested the initial premise of idealism, that physical objects *are* families of sense-experiences. Digest this premise, and none of these objections will arise. We are surprised and

[5] See W. T. Stace, "The Refutation of Realism," *Mind*, LIII (1934).

bewildered by the conclusion only because we still have lurking in the back of our minds the idea of tables and trees as inhabiting a world of things that are independent of minds and keep on existing regardless of perceivers: in other words, of tables and trees as *not* being families of sense-experiences at all. Accept the equation "Physical objects = families of sense-experiences," and there is no more basis for complaining about the discontinuity of physical objects (no longer existing when unexperienced) than there is about the discontinuity of pains and pleasures, which everyone already accepts. We have thrown the concept of physical objects as independent existents out the front door, but we have sneaked them in again through the back door. Once we really grasp the fact that physical objects are families of sense-experiences, and really master this statement of identity, we shall never bring up any question of their existing unperceived, any more than we do now in the case of pains or pleasures, thoughts or ideas.

"But what is logically impossible can't even be conceived or thought of." And don't we constantly think of physical objects as existing unexperienced? Whether they do so exist or not, surely we can think of them as so existing? So how can their existence unexperienced be logically impossible? But Berkeley replies:

But, say you, surely there is nothing easier than to imagine trees, for instance, in a park, or books existing in a closet, and nobody by to perceive them. I answer you may so, there is no difficulty in it; but what is all this, I beseech you, more than framing in your mind certain ideas which you call books and trees, and at the same time omitting to frame the idea of anyone that may perceive them? But do not you yourself perceive or think of them all the while? This therefore is nothing to the purpose; it only shows you have the power of imagining or forming ideas in your mind; but it does not show that you can conceive it possible the objects of your thought may exist without the mind. To make out this, it is necessary that you conceive them existing unconceived or unthought of, which is a manifest repugnancy.[6]

The causation of sense-experiences. Another problem arises, however; what is the cause of our sense-experiences? Locke said that physical objects, existing apart from experience, cause them; but Berkeley attempted to refute this view. If physical objects are families of sense-experiences, as Berkeley held, this option is not open to him, for he would have to go back on his entire account of physical objects. Still, must our sense-experiences not have a cause? Surely their occurrence has some cause or other.

One might have thought that Berkeley would have to say that sense-experiences are caused by physical objects if he was to believe in the possibility of empirical science. But Berkeley does not agree; science is possible, he said, but when you consider what science is, you will find that it

⁶ George Berkeley, *Principles of Human Knowledge,* paragraph 23.

only correlates sense-experiences with one another. "If there is lightning, there is thunder," says science, making no reference to our sense-experiences. But, as we have just argued, neither science nor anything else is in a position to say anything about what happens when no one is observing it; the scientist can only report what he observes, and thus he cannot say, any more than anyone else can, anything about events occurring unobserved. According to Berkeley, all scientific statements are really statements of uniformity among sense-experiences: thus, "If you have a lightning-experience, it will be followed by a thunder-experience." The scientist, to be sure, makes no explicit reference to the observations but only to the events observed. Yet, says Berkeley, the *observed* events are all he has any right to talk about. Scientists frame inductive generalization of the form "If A, then B"; but they *should*, if they were quite accurate, be saying instead "If A-experience, then (regularly) B-experience." Every statement about events can be translated into statements about experiences, and every correlation of events is a correlation of experiences. If we are to be able to say anything about causes, these causes (and effects) must be experienced ones. We can make causal generalizations only about what we experience, else we have no basis for making them. We state causal regularities connecting some items in our experiences, A's, with some others, B's. Thus we can make causal statements, but they are statements of correlations of experience ("constant conjunctions" within experience) and nothing more. We can thus make a place for causality without appealing to any such doctrine as that physical objects exist unobserved.

Still, we are not satisfied. Even if there is a causal relation among sense-experiences (we shall examine this point later), isn't there also a causal relation among our sense-experiences and whatever causes them? And what could cause them but (in some sense or other) physical objects? How else can we explain that we have similar sense-experiences, if not by the fact that there are physical objects causing them? Surely we have to account somehow for the fact that when we look in the same direction we both have table-experiences rather than, say, elephant-experiences. And surely the most straightforward way of accounting for this similarity of our sense-experiences (without which communication would be impossible) is that we both experience the same physical object, and the physical object causes the experiences. True, Berkeley said that "physical objects existing unobserved" is a contradiction is terms. But if we do need physical objects as the causes of sense-experiences, doesn't this show that Berkeley's analysis of "physical objects existing unobserved" is mistaken somewhere along the line?

Berkeley *might* have said simply, "Physical objects are families of sense-experiences, as I have shown in my arguments. In any other sense, they do not exist; indeed, to say that they did would involve self-contradiction. Causality is a relation among sense-experiences; the concept of cause cannot be employed to connect sense-experiences with anything besides other sense-experiences. Therefore, it cannot be used to connect sense-experiences with non-observable causes-of-sense-experiences. Period."

But Berkeley did not say this. Instead, good bishop that he was, he argued that all sense-experiences *are* caused—by an infinite spirit, God. God, not physical objects, causes our sense-experiences. The reason the sense-experiences occur in an orderly way—barring hallucinations and so on—is that God gives us our sense-experiences, and he does so in an orderly way so that we can make predictions on the basis of them and thus guide our actions accordingly. God *could* have made our experiences so chaotic that there were no families-of-sense-experiences at all, and hence no regularities of experience that we could call physical objects. But God, being good, has chosen instead to give us orderly sets of sense-experiences. He plants these in our minds directly: he does not need the intermediary of the realist's physical objects. (Since we could not know the existence of these physical objects anyway, they wouldn't do us any good even if they did exist.) He feeds us our experiences directly, without mediation. Reality thus consists of *minds* and *their experiences*. God is an infinite mind, and you and I finite minds. There are minds (God's and ours) and their experiences (God's and ours). Experiences are events in the history of minds. That is all there is—there is no more. God causes us to have our experiences in the order that we have them. There is no need for anything else.

Why is it that when we both look in the same direction we have similar sense-experiences? Because God feeds us similar sense-experiences in similar contexts, so that we may communicate with one another. If you saw a tree where I saw an elephant, and the next moment you saw in that place a sofa and I a bushel of apples, we would not be able to communicate. But by correlating the series of your experiences with mine, God makes prediction and communication possible. God works in an orderly manner: so orderly, indeed, that God not only enables different minds to communicate but also regulates the course of various persons' sense-experiences, so that by noting what regularly follows what in their experience they can establish correlations within the total series. Thus is science made possible. The laws of nature are the will of God manifested in the orderly series of sense-experiences that we have.

Criticisms.   Once we have introduced God into the picture as cause and correlator of our sense-experiences, objections start to rain down on Berkeley's view.

1. Berkeley began with the premise he inherited from Locke, "The mind has acquaintance only with its own experiences." This is what led Berkeley to deny physical objects as anything other than experiences, so that he might still retain physical objects as knowable. But now Berkeley has introduced something other than experiences—God as the cause of them. If we can know only our own experiences, however, how can we know that there is a God who causes them? If our knowledge (empirical knowledge, at any rate) is

limited to what sense-experience gives us, and if God is not a sense-experience (or family of such experiences), how can we know anything about God, by Berkeley's own premises? If we say that such a God exists, and that we can know this, then we *do* know something other than our own sense-experiences after all. And if we can know one thing—God—beyond our sense-experiences, why not also a second thing, physical objects? If Berkeley can bring in something other than sense-experiences, why can't we bring in something else? Berkeley brought in God; most of us would bring in physical objects. But then, of course, we run into Berkeley's argument that the concept of physical objects is self-contradictory. If this charge is true, we are not entitled to bring in physical objects—but what entitles him to bring in God?

Many readers who have followed Berkeley thus far, and either agreed with him or felt unable to refute him, believed that his introduction of God as the cause of experiences was an unfortunate error. It laid him open to precisely the kind of objection that he himself gave of Locke and the realists. In saying that we can know only our sense-experiences, and also that we can know that God exists to cause them, the second statement contradicts the first, and one of the basic tenets of Berkeley's epistemology has been betrayed. There is scarcely a reader of Berkeley who, when God is suddenly injected into the scene, does not feel that this is cheating.

But suppose, now, that we leave God out of it. Assume for a moment that Berkeley has never introduced God into his epistemology. Are there other objections we might make to his view?

2. Let us carry our first objection further: If Berkeley really believes that all we are acquainted with is our own experiences—and consequently that all the propositions we can have knowledge of are about our own experiences—what reason have we to believe that not only God but other *minds* exist? I have the same evidence for believing that your *body* exists that I have for the table and the books: they are all, according to Berkeley, families of sense-experiences. I can observe your body, but I cannot observe your thoughts and feelings and sense-experiences. What reason have I then to believe that your body has a mind connected with it at all? Indeed, we can go further: what reason have I to believe that your body, the table, and other physical objects are anything more than sense-experiences of mine?

Solipsism (myself-alone-ism), in its weaker form, holds that I am the only mind that exists—that there are physical things (including other bodies) apart from myself, but that my mind is the only one there is. In its stronger form, solipsism holds that not even physical objects (including other bodies) exist; they are only sense-experiences of mine, and have no other existence than as the contents of my mind. In either case, I have no reason for believing in the existence of minds other than my own, and so I assert that mine is the only one. "The mind hath acquaintance only with its own ideas," so that is all that exists—my mind and its ideas.

No one in fact is a solipsist; we all believe there are other people, who think and feel and have sense-experiences as we do. A person would be in a curious position who said "I am so convinced of solipsism that I believe everyone ought to be a solipsist!" And if a solipsist writes books to prove his view, to whom is he addressing them, since he believes there is no one who can read and understand them? Moreover, solipsism seems to break down into as many different views as there are people: if Jones is a solipsist, he believes that only Jones exists; but if Smith is a solipsist, he believes that only Smith exists, which is a very different view and in fact conflicts with Jones's view.

Our question at the moment, however, is not about the difficulties of solipsism but about Berkeley. Our question was: How, on Berkeley's premises, could he avoid solipsism? Isn't solipsism the consequence of his own premises? It is true that Berkeley tried to avoid this conclusion by saying that *"Esse est percipi"* applies only to physical objects, not to minds: minds exist regardless of whether or not they are experienced; it is only physical objects that do not. For minds *"esse est percipere"* ("to be is to perceive"—that is, to experience). So far so good; but on Berkeley's own premises how could he know this? If human minds have no windows to observe anything but the course of their own sense-experiences (which does *not* include other minds or *their* sense-experiences), it would appear that Berkeley's mind must have had at least a door.

3. Now let us try another line of attack: that "Physical objects exist" (in Locke's sense, not as "bundles of ideas") is not just false, Berkeley said, but self-contradictory. This is a strong statement. One might reply to it: "One can always make a statement self-contradictory by defining one's terms so as to make it turn out that way. If I define 'circle' as 'a large octagon,' then the statement 'circles have no corners' is self-contradictory—but only because I have defined 'circle' in that peculiar way. You are welcome to define it thus if you wish, but there is no reason why I should accept such a stipulative definition, and hence its implication that 'Physical objects exist unperceived' is self-contradictory."

Berkeley, of course, says that there *is* good reason for defining "physical object" in that way: if you do not, you are left with complete skepticism about the existence and nature of physical objects. The only non-analytic propositions we can know are about our own sense-experiences, so if physical objects aren't sense-experiences (or families of them), they are unknowable. This premise can be questioned, and will indeed be questioned later in this chapter; but this can best be done in the context of the theories that question it. Meanwhile, let us make a simple distinction that may put a chink into Berkeley's armor:

"Physical objects cannot be thought of as existing apart from a thinking mind," Berkeley believed. (The moment you try to think of books in a closet existing without a mind, you are thinking about them.) But there is an ambiguity in this. If you mean that

    1. Physical objects cannot be thought-of-as-existing apart from a thinking mind,

this is doubtless true. You cannot think of them or of anything else as existing or doing anything else without first having a mind to think with. This statement is so obviously true that it is hardly worth making. (Perhaps it is analytic, but we need not take time at this point to investigate this.) But it should not be confused with a very different statement,

    2. Physical objects cannot be thought of as existing-apart-from-a-thinking-mind,

which is not trivial at all, and in fact is false: we do so think of them all the time. I cannot think without a mind, but I can think of something as *existing* without a mind. Thoughts cannot exist without minds, but this doesn't prove that tables and trees cannot exist without minds. Whether they do exist or not—and perhaps we can't know whether they do or not—at least we *think* of them as existing without minds. Doesn't the realist think of them thus—even if, as Berkeley said, the realist is wrong? And the same with perception as with thought: you can't perceive without a mind any more than think without a mind, but it doesn't follow that *what* you perceive can't exist without a mind. Maybe it doesn't, of course, but at least we cannot prove that it doesn't by Berkeley's argument. *Perception* can't occur without a mind, but *that which you perceive* can—at least it is logically possible. Whether there is some positive way of defining "physical object" other than as a family of sense-experiences remains to be seen. But if the logical barrier is removed, we may go further:

    4. Even if we have cast some doubt on Berkeley's assertion that "Physical objects exist unperceived" is self-contradictory, we have not yet dealt with the milder assertion that even if they do exist unperceived, we can have no good reason for believing that they do, since "no one has ever observed them existing unobserved."

    In daily life we do not hesitate to believe that physical objects exist unobserved. If I leave the tub running in the bathroom and come back later and find that it is full of water, I assume that water flowed into the tub during my absence—how else, I believe, could I explain how the water got there? And so on. The idealist (weaker version) argued, however, that there is no way of proving this (pp. 519–20): I cannot perceive it existing unperceived, no deductive argument will enable me to conclude anything about the unobserved when all the premises are about the observed, and no inductive argument will be able to get off the ground because we have not even observed one case of A (something existing observed) being accompanied by B (something continuing to exist unobserved). Thus the view that physical objects exist unobserved, even if not self-contradictory, is one for which there is and can be absolutely no evidence.

But is this true? Is there *no* evidence? Isn't the fact that the bathtub is full of water when I return evidence that water flowed into it during my absence? According to Berkeley it is one big "as if": the series of my sense-experiences is just what it would be *if* the tub and the water had existed during my absence. But why resort to this circuitous "as if" if we can say just as well that it *did* exist during my absence? (It is true that Berkeley says "It wasn't unobserved, for God was observing it all the time," but we have already seen reason to object to Berkeley's introduction of God into the matter.) Well, we can *say* it, but what evidence can we adduce? We can't perceive its existence unperceived, nor can we deduce it from statements about what we observe. Our evidence must be *inductive*. It can be argued that the idealist's concept of induction is too narrow. Our evidence for the existence of protons and electrons is inductive, in spite of the fact that no one has ever observed these entities. We cannot argue "Every time we have been in perceptual conditions C, we have seen electrons," for we never have seen them. Instead, we argue from some very special features of our sensory experience (exactly what they are could be stated precisely only by trained physicists) to the existence of entities that would explain these features. Electrons are incapable of being observed, but they are the best explanation of what we do observe. Now it would seem that we can argue the same way for the existence of physical objects when unobserved. If we assume that they exist unobserved, we have the best *explanation of certain facts of experience*, for instance that the shadow continues even when we don't see the house, that the tub is full of water when we return to the bathroom, and so on. Science is constantly postulating entities on the basis of reasoning of this kind, and there seems to be no reason why we should not avail ourselves of it here as well.

This hypothesis—that physical objects exist unobserved—is possible only *provided* that it is logically possible for physical objects to exist unobserved; a hypothesis must always be a logical possibility. But if Berkeley is right, that physical objects exist unobserved cannot be even so much as a tentative hypothesis, for it is logically impossible—a contradiction in terms. Physical objects, according to him, are families of sense-experiences, and sense-experiences of course can't exist unexperienced. Our first task, then, must be once and for all to break the back of this definition of "physical object" so that it will never rise to haunt us again.

To accomplish this task, another theory now enters the arena. While agreeing with idealism on many points, such as the analysis of perceptual error (hallucinations, illusions, dreams), *phenomenalism* emphatically disagrees with idealism on *"esse est percipi."* It offers a different account of physical existence that enables us to say without contradiction that physical objects exist unperceived. Let us now turn to this theory, to see what alternative account it has to offer.

Exercises

1. Assess Berkeley's view that "the real object is the touch-object." Can you think of any exceptions to this? (Note: We have not yet touched any of the planets besides the earth. Why nevertheless do we consider them to be real physical objects? What about flashes of lightning? rainbows?)

2. It is sometimes said that we take our touch-experiences as decisive because "experience has shown that we have more visual illusions and hallucinations than tactual ones." What is wrong with this reasoning?

3. If we had no visual or tactual sense-experiences but only experiences of hearing and smell, would we have been able to form the concept of a physical object? If you had never seen or touched a bell but only heard the ringing, would you be able to say "The sound comes from a bell" or even "The sound comes from a physical object"?

4. What are our criteria in making the following distinctions?

   a. We say that the trees on the distant mountaintop are really green, although they look purplish-gray in the distance.

   b. We say that a certain area in a pointillist painting looks green but really is dots of blue and yellow side by side.

   c. We say that the curtains are blue, although they don't look blue when seen through red spectacles. (H. H. Price, *Perception,* pp. 210–13.)

   d. We say that the whistle of the railway engine has a constant pitch, although if you are moving away from the engine the pitch appears to be falling and if you are approaching it the pitch appears to be rising. (Price, *op. cit.,* p. 214.)

   e. We say the orange really has a certain taste-quality, although we have one kind of taste experience if we eat it without anything preceding, another if we eat it after eating a lemon, and still another if we eat it after eating a lump of sugar. (Price, *op. cit.,* pp. 214–15.)

   f. We do not say "The after-image I had was really red, though of course it appeared yellow to me at the time." Why not?

5. We approach an object that appeared to have one uniform color, say green, and on closer approach find that it consists of small blue and yellow squares. This closer view is more differentiated—has more specific detail—and so we consider it the preferable view. But what if I see double? I see two things and you see only one. Is that not more differentiated? Or when I "look through uneven glass, is not my view more differentiated than usual? . . . I see a kinked object of complex shape when you see only a homogeneous straight-sided one. Then ought not my view to be called the better one of the two? But of course everyone holds that it is the worse." (Price, *Perception,* p. 224.) Explain why this is. (Price suggests an answer on pp. 224–25.)

6. If we can never "get beyond" sense-experiences—can never compare sense-experiences with anything that is not sense-experiences to discover whether they "correspond"—how can we preserve the distinction between appearance and reality in perception, between how things appear or seem and how they really are? Or can we never know "how they really are"?

7. State as precisely as you can (a) how we know whether a certain sense-experience is hallucinatory, (b) how we know when a certain sense-experience is illusory, (c) how we know when we are dreaming (or have been dreaming), (d) how we know that all of our experience isn't one big long dream.

8. Could the idealist reply successfully to the following? If so, how?

a. I place a tablecloth over the table, so that no part of the table can be seen. The idealist must then say that the table does not exist, but only the table-cloth. What, then, supports the tablecloth? Is it simply suspended in the air, contrary to laws of gravity?

b. I am the only perceiver about, and I see only the top half of a build-ing. But the bottom half must be there even if I don't see it; how could it continue to stand there without the bottom half existing to support it?

c. I leave the room while the fire is burning in the fireplace; half an hour later I come back and there are only glowing embers left. Doesn't this show that the fire existed and went on burning while I was out? But if it burned while I was out, it must have existed while I was out.

d. I'll prove to you that the table exists even when no one is perceiving it. We'll all go out of the room, but before doing so we'll set a motion picture camera going, focused on the table. Later we'll come back, remove the film, develop it, and project it on a screen. We will then witness the exciting drama of "table-continuing-to-exist-while-we-are-all-gone"—which, if not exactly high drama, at least proves that the table did exist unperceived.

9. How would (or might) an idealist respond to the following? Satisfactorily, in your opinion?

a. If idealism is true, science is impossible. And since science is not only possible but actual, idealism must be false.

b. Sense-experiences can't just exist by themselves. We have to believe in the existence of physical objects, even if for no other reason than that we must give some *explanation* of the fact that sense-experiences do occur in the order they do. For example, table-experiences occur because there is really a table there causing them.

c. If you can bring in God to explain the orderly occurrence of sense-experiences, I can bring in physical objects much more plausibly to explain the same thing.

d. If *esse est percipi,* I must not even exist when I'm asleep. (Note: Of physical objects, Berkeley said "Esse est percipi," and of minds Berkeley said "Esse est percipere." What is the implication of this distinction with regard to the present question?)

e. Idealists admit, in fact they insist, that there are sense-experiences. Now how can there be sense-experiences unless there are sense-organs, nerves, and brains? But sense-organs, nerves, and brains are physical objects. So there are physical objects after all!

10. Examine the following deductive arguments in defense of idealism. (The conclusion of the first argument is a premise of the second.) Do you accept the conclusion in each case? If not, can you find any flaw in the reasoning? any premises that you would not accept?

We do have acquaintance with physical objects.

All we can have acquaintance with is experiences.

Therefore, Physical objects are experiences.

Physical objects are experiences.

Experiences can't exist unexperienced.

Therefore, Physical objects can't exist unexperienced.

11. Do you think that the following lines of argument would give any diffi-culty to idealism? Why?

a. Physical objects are experiences (or complexes of experiences); experi-ences are private; yet physical objects are public.

b. Physical objects are extended; experiences are unextended; therefore physical objects can't be experiences.

12. What would you say to someone who declared that he was a solipsist? Do you think that solipsism can be disproved?

13. Set forth arguments either defending or attacking each of the following views:

a. ("Weak" idealism:) Even if physical objects do exist when no one is observing them, we can have no reason to believe that they do, for no one can observe them existing unobserved.

b. ("Strong" idealism:) The proposition that physical objects exist unobserved is not only without supporting evidence: there *could* be no evidence for (or for that matter against) it, for it is *self-contradictory*.

14. First read G. E. Moore's essay "The Refutation of Idealism" (in his book *Philosophical Studies);* then read W. T. Stace's essay "The Refutation of Realism" *(Mind,* 1934). Outline the main arguments in each essay. Which do you find the more convincing, and why?

15. Would the following help in determining which is dream and which is waking life?

a. Just before experiencing the series T_2 I remember going to bed, becoming drowsy, and trying to sleep; so T_2 must have been a dream.

b. As Freud has shown, a person's dream-experiences are a good basis for inferring what his waking-life experiences (especially conflicts) are; but his waking-life experiences provide no basis for inference about his dreams. So we can tell which is which by discovering from which group inference is the more successful.

c. All the people in a given locality have very similar waking-life experiences (seeing the same buildings, etc), but the dreams of each person will be wildly discrepant with those of every other person. I can distinguish the waking-life experiences from the dream-experiences by checking with other people to see if they had experiences similar to mine.

25. Phenomenalism

Phenomenalism agrees with idealism that our knowledge of physical objects comes entirely from our sense-experiences; but it does not follow, says the phenomenalist, that when we talk about physical objects we are talking only about our sense-experiences—at least not about *actual* sense-experiences. We are also able to talk about *possible* sense-experiences —sense-experiences that we *would* have if certain conditions were fulfilled. Physical objects are families of actual *and possible* sense-experiences. When I look at the tree I am having actual sense-experiences; but when I am not, the tree still exists, for I *could* be having the tree-experiences even though I am not: they are still *available* to me. If the tree is cut down and burned, the tree no longer exists, and the tree-experiences are no longer available; but as long as it is possible to have the tree-experiences, the tree still exists. One must simply specify the conditions in which the experiences can be obtained. I am not in the hall now, but I believe that the drinking-fountain there still exists: that is, if I were to go out into the hall I would have visual and tactual fountain-experiences. If I went out into the hall and to my great surprise saw no fountain where I had seen one only a few minutes before, I would have to admit that my statement "There is still a fountain in the hall" was false.

The claim that a physical object exists is, therefore, testable: it is not required that the object be actually perceived but that it be *perceivable*. "To be is to be perceivable," at least when it is physical objects we are talking about. If I claim that there is a diamond in my desk drawer, I need not be perceiving it; but if I open the drawer and it is empty, I must withdraw my claim—not because the diamond was not perceived when I made the claim, but because it was not perceivable at all (that is, not perceived when the conditions in which the claim could be put to the test were fulfilled but the requirement of perception was not met). In some cases, of course, meeting the conditions of perception is difficult or even technically impossible: there are doubtless flora and fauna at the bottom of the ocean that no one has ever perceived, but we could rightly claim they are not there only if we went down there and, having fulfilled the perceptual conditions, still didn't find any. There were long geological ages in which there were no sentient beings to perceive the changes taking place on the earth's surface; yet we can say that those changes took place, because we can say "*If* someone had been there (though no one was), then he *would* have observed these changes." What those changes were is of course a matter for geologists to investigate on the basis of the present fragmentary evidence; but at least we can say that they did occur, and our statements will not be self-contradictory though they may sometimes be false. We do not need God perceiving them all the while to give meaning to our assertion that they took place. It is enough to say "*If* a perceiver had been there, with the appropriate sense-faculties (not blind, etc.), then he would have observed the changes taking place."

As John Stuart Mill, one of the early phenomenalists, put it, "Matter is the permanent possibility of sensation." The possibility of sensation exists even when the actual sensation does not. But now we must introduce a point of terminology that, however trivial it may seem at first, is of some importance. Locke and Berkeley used the word "ideas," but this has such a different meaning in the 20th century that we have not used it here; we have employed instead the comparatively self-explanatory term "sense-experiences." Mill used "sensations," but the use of this word is apt to be misleading. If someone asked you, "What is it that you see?" you might at first reply, "A table with some books and papers on it." But if you were asked not to read anything into the experience but just to report what you saw—what you immediately (non-inferentially) were aware of—you might say, "Colors and shapes in certain patterns." You would not say, "I see certain sensations." The word "sensation" is usually reserved for *the having of* the experience, but the sensations are not *what* we experience; what we immediately experience are certain colors and shapes (which we usually interpret without conscious effort to be the colors and shapes of tables, books, etc.). It is by *having* sensations, no doubt, that we experience the colors and shapes; but the latter are what we experience, not the sensations. (What would it mean to say "I am seeing certain visual sensations"?)

We see (immediately) certain colors and shapes, and this remains true even if we are the victims of a hallucination or are dreaming. You see red spots before your eyes. There are, you believe, no red spots in the physical world, say 18 inches before your eyes. Still, there is *something* red that you see; it may exist only in your visual field, and have no existence before or after you have the experience, but still there is a red spot there now—which need not be a *physical* spot, for if it were physical other people could see it too, but it is still true that you see it even if no one else does. There is *something present to your consciousness*, a red spot, whether or not that spot is a part of physical reality. It may not be real in the physicist's sense (a part of the physical universe, located at a definite place in space), but it is real in the sense of being a real experience of yours: you really do have the experience of seeing a red spot in your visual field. *What* you see (not your seeing of it) directly—that is, non-inferentially—is called a *sense-datum* (more frequently used in the plural, sense-data).

But we need not turn to hallucinations and dreams in order to explain what is meant by "sense-datum."

I hold up this envelope: I look at it, and I hope you all will look at it. And now I put it down again. Now what has happened? We should certainly say (if you have looked at it) that we all *saw* that envelope, that we all saw *it, the same* envelope: I saw it, and you all saw it. We all saw *the same* object. And by the *it,* which we all saw, we mean an object, which, at any one of the moments when we were looking at it, occupied just *one* of the many places that constitute the whole of space. . . .

But now, what happened to each of us, when we saw that envelope? I will begin by describing *part* of what happened to me. I saw a patch of a particular whitish color, having a certain size, and a certain shape, a shape with rather sharp angles or corners and bounded by fairly straight lines. These things: this patch of a whitish color, and its size and shape I did actually see. And I propose to call these things, the color and size and shape, *sense-data,* things *given* or presented by the senses—given, in this case, by my sense of sight. Many philosophers have called these things which I call sense-data, *sensations.* They would say, for instance, that that particular patch of color was a sensation. But it seems to me that the term "sensation" is liable to be misleading. We should certainly say that I *had* a sensation, when I saw that color. But when we say that I *had* a sensation, what we mean is, I think, that I had the experience which consisted in my *seeing* the color. That is to say, what we mean by a "sensation" in this phrase, is my *seeing* of the color, not the color which I saw: this color does not seem to be what I mean to say that I *had,* when I say I *had* a sensation of color. It is very unnatural to say that I *had* the color, that I *had* that particular whitish grey or that I *had* the patch which was of that color. What I certainly did *have* is the experience which consisted in my seeing the color and the patch. And when, therefore, we talk of *having* sensations, I think what we mean by "sensations" is the experiences which consist in apprehending certain sense-data, *not* these sense-data themselves. I think, then, that the term "sensation" is liable to be misleading, because it may be used in two different senses, which it is very important to distinguish from one another. It may be used either for the color which I saw or for the experience which consisted in my seeing it. . . .

Part, at least, of what happened to me, I can now express by saying that I saw certain sense-data: I saw a whitish patch of color, of a particular size and shape. And I have no doubt whatever that this is part, at least, of what happened to all of you. You also saw certain sense-data; and I expect also that the sense-data which you saw were more or less similar to those which I saw. You also saw a patch of color which might be described as whitish, of a size not very different from the size of the patch which I saw, and of a shape similar at least in this, that it had rather sharp corners and was bounded by fairly straight lines. But now, what I want to emphasize is this. Though we al¹ did (as we should say) see *the same* envelope, no two of us, in all probability, saw exactly the *same sense-data*. Each of us, in all probability, saw, to begin with, a slightly different shade of color. All these colors may have been whitish; but each was probably at least slightly different from all the rest, according to the way in which the light fell upon the paper, relatively to the different positions you are sitting in; and again according to differences in the strength of your eye-sight, or your distance from the paper. And so too, with regard to the size of the patch of color which you saw: differences in the strength of your eyes and in your distance from the envelope probably made slight differences in the size of the patch of color, which you saw. And so again with regard to the shape. Those of you on that side of the room will have seen a rhomboidal figure, while those in front of me will have seen a figure more nearly rectangular. . . .

Now all this seems to me to show very clearly, that, *if* we *did* all see the same envelope, the envelope which we saw was not *identical with* the sense-data which we saw: the envelope cannot be exactly the same thing as each of the sets of sense-data, which we each of us saw; for these were in all probability each of them slightly different from all the rest, and they cannot, therefore, *all* be exactly the same thing as the envelope.[7]

Indeed, it would seem that there are as many sense-data as there are observers. The envelope has a slightly different appearance to each observer, hence the sense-data in every case are different: the language of sense-data is the language of appearance. A description of your sense-data is a description of how the things appear to you—and even if there is no physical thing at all, as in hallucination, you can still describe the sense-data you are experiencing. Physical objects need not be as they appear; but sense-data are, for the sense-datum language was introduced precisely in order to describe the appearances, with no strings attached as to reality.

[7] G. E. Moore, *Some Main Problems of Philosophy* (London: George Allen & Unwin, Ltd., 1952), pp. 30–33.

"I can understand how sense-datum descriptions are simply descriptions of what I see, hear, etc. These are direct—not arrived at by inference. But I don't understand how one can say that we arrive at our knowledge of physical objects by inference. I don't remember ever seeing certain patterns of colors and shapes and then *inferring* that this was a pile of books on a table. I see the books and the table as directly as I see anything, and not by any inference, the way I might infer that the dog has been here from seeing muddy tracks on the floor. I see the books and touch them; what's inferential about that?" Here the phenomenalist would answer that one must distinguish the *logical* from the *phychological* meaning of inference: psychologically we are not aware of going through any such process in the case of books and tables, any more than we are aware of moving our legs in every step we take going from the kitchen to the parlor. But logically your claim about physical objects is an inference, for the claim is based upon the kind of sense-data you experience and their relations to one another: it takes much more to defend the claim that you are seeing an envelope than it does to defend the claim that you are seeing a whitish rectangular shape. The former is a stronger claim, and requires more to back it up than simply saying that you see in your visual field a whitish rectangular shape, which is all that you *directly* (non-inferentially) experience.

We can best grasp what phenomenalists have had in mind in distinguishing the *sensing* of sense-data (immediate) from the *perceiving* of physical objects (inferential) by asking ourselves, in a typical perceptual experience, *what we can doubt;* or in other words, what we can, and what we cannot, be mistaken about. The position is that we cannot be mistaken about the data we sense (though we can describe them mistakenly), but we *can* be mistaken in our claim about the existence and qualities of physical objects.

When I see a tomato there is much that I can doubt. I can doubt whether it is a tomato that I am seeing, and not a cleverly painted piece of wax. I can doubt whether there is any material thing there at all. Perhaps what I took for a tomato was really a reflection; perhaps I am even the victim of some hallucination. One thing however I cannot doubt: that there exists a red patch of a round and somewhat bulgy shape, standing out from a background of other color-patches, and having a certain visual depth, and that this whole field of color is directly present to my consciousness. What the red patch is, whether a substance, or a state of a substance, or an event, whether it is physical or psychical or neither, are questions that we may doubt about. Whether the something persists even for a moment before and after it is present to my consciousness, whether other minds can be conscious of it as well as I, may be doubted. But that it now *exists*, and that *I* am conscious of it—by me at least who am conscious of it this cannot possibly be doubted. And when I say that it is "directly" present to my consciousness, I mean that my consciousness of it is not reached by inference, nor by any other intellectual process.[8]

[8] H. H. Price, *Perception*, p. 3.

In saying "There is a tomato" (physical-object report), we can easily be mistaken. Physical-object reports are not indubitable. We see the red bulgy patch, and infer that there is a tomato—an inference that *may* be mistaken. True, we are not conscious of making an inference; but at any rate in saying that it *is* a tomato we are bringing more into our description of the experience than the experience itself warrants. The first time we opened our eyes on the world and saw, say, a tomato, we were aware, probably, only of a "round bulgy patch" (though we could not have described it in this way or any other way, for we knew no language) in our visual field, and were in no position to conclude that it was a tomato or anything else. But after a while, when we continued to have similar experiences, and they fell into orderly patterns (*families,* we have called them), and after we found our visual sense-data to be good indices of touch sense-data, then we needed only to sense the red round patch in order to conclude (without being conscious of any steps of inference between) "There's a tomato"—but logically it was an inference just the same, for we were using the sense-data we experienced as evidence for claims about the existence and qualities of a physical object.

This is not to say that sense-datum reports can never be false. (1) We may be lying—we may say we see red when we really see green. (2) We may make a slip of the tongue and get the wrong words out. (3) Most important, we may be making a *verbal* error: we may see red but not know that "red" is the word used in English to describe that shade of color; or we may not be clear about the boundary-lines of application of the word, and call something "red" that we would later have called "orange" when we acquired a better knowledge of established language-usage. But, if we are not lying or making a slip of the tongue or committing some verbal error of misdescribing what we see, then (says the phenomenalist) our sense-datum reports are *indubitable*. They simply report what we are directly aware of in sense-experience, and no more. These sense-datum reports are the rock-bottom of all empirical knowledge. Without them we could never go beyond them to make statements about the existence and nature of physical objects. If we experienced no sense-data of sight, touch, hearing, etc., we would never know anything about a physical world; our sense-data are our sole access to that world.

To experience sense-data—such as red round spots when you are seeing "spots in front of your eyes"—is not, of course, the same as to *know* anything. You can experience the sense-data without knowing *that* these are called spots or red or round. You can obviously have the experience without knowing anything about these words in our language; presumably animals have sense-experiences without calling them anything. Sensing is not knowing; but sensing is a prerequisite (necessary condition) for knowing— for instance, for being able to say that you know you are seeing red. Without sensing, you would not be in a position to know even this. The claim to know that there is a real tomato in front of you is a far more complex claim still (we shall see in a moment what complexities are involved in it), but it, too, could not be made unless we experienced sense-data.

Sensing is different from perceiving. We sense sense-data; we perceive physical objects. Perception is impossible without sensing (without something given to sense), but it involves more. When we open our eyes we have certain visual experiences—sense-data; in this we are passive, and cannot help what we see. But in addition to this passive intake of sense-data there occurs an activity that we may call *interpretation*: no sooner are sense-data present to sense than the process of interpretation sets in (consciously or unconsciously). Even when we say we are seeing something red and round (sense-data, not necessarily a physical thing) we are interpreting: we are in effect saying that the words "red" and "round" are correctly applicable to the sense-data; we are classifying our present experience into molds already established by previous experiences. To use language at all is already to interpret our experience. But this is only the beginning. Once we have looked enough to notice that the tomato-sense-data constitute a family, and experienced tactile sense-data as well, we interpret the "red round bulgy patch" as a real physical object: we make the leap from sense-datum claim to physical-object claim. This is a more far-reaching piece of interpretation. Every time we see a tomato (or what looks like one) in the future, we will come to this experience with all this "apperceptive background" and thus read into what we directly sense many qualities that this experience has not yet exhibited—for example, hardness or softness, before we have touched it.

Usually this leap from sense-data to physical object is justified, for in most cases in which we see the "red bulgy something" it turns out that our statement ("That's a real tomato") was true; hallucinations are the exception, not the rule, in our experience. But if we have any reason to suspect that our initial sense-data are misleading, we can make a more guarded claim: "I see what looks like a tomato," "That appears to be a tomato," "I seem te see a tomato," and so on. We do not say "I sense round reddish sense-data," since the term "sense-data" is a technical one devised by epistemologists; we *can* do without this technical term, but we cannot do without an appearance-language of some sort ("This looks like a tomato," "There appears to be a tomato there," etc.), which enables us to distinguish the full physical-object claim from the milder claim about the momentary sensory presentation, or sense-datum. If you said "There's a tomato" and there was none, you would have to withdraw your statement; but if you merely said "I seem to see a tomato" or something of that sort, then the fact that there is no tomato would not require you to withdraw your statement—even if there is no tomato there, it would still be true that you seemed to see one, or saw something that looked like one. When you make only a sense-datum claim, your statement cannot be proved false by subsequent sense-experience, as it can when you make a physical-object claim.

We can now understand more precisely why statements about sense-data are indubitable—with the provisos listed on p. 535—whereas statements asserting the existence and qualities of physical objects are not. Physical-object claims are subject to one kind of error that sense-datum reports are not: *empirical* error. A physical-object claim can be doubted or even refuted by subsequent sense-experience, but a sense-datum report cannot. The claim that I am seeing a real tomato may prove dubious or even false, but even if it does, it still remains true that I had certain sense-experiences that led me to believe that a tomato was there. No future experiences can cast doubt on the fact that I did at this moment have this experience. Even if the alleged tomato disappears into thin air the next moment and is never seen again, it is still true that at this moment I did have this sense-experience. In making the sense-datum report I am making no claim whatever beyond the moment on which I am reporting; I am just saying that I'm having such-and-such an experience, and no more. But—and this is where the possibility of empirical error comes in—when I claim that there is a real tomato out there, I *am* making a claim beyond the present moment. I am, in other words, making an *implicit prediction*. I am implying, for example, that if I continue to look in that direction I shall continue to have similar sense-experiences, that if I reach out to touch it I shall experience certain tactile sense-data (a certain degree of hardness or softness), and so on—the features we have already mentioned in discussing the concept of a *family* of sense-data. If my experience of a tomato is veridical (a true report), many other sense-data—those constituting a family—will be forthcoming. And this, of course, is a prediction about my future sense-experience. Every physical-object statement is an implicit prediction, and, as with all predictions, this one may go wrong. Other sense-data of the family *may* not occur.

How great is the range of predictions of future sense-experience involved in every claim about the existence or nature of a physical object? How many sense-experiences are required before I am fully entitled to say "That definitely *is* a real tomato before me"? Can I ever make such a statement with as great a certainty as I can say "I am now having such-and-such sense-experiences"? Opinions differ on this point, and we shall describe briefly two opposing views on the matter.

1. According to one view, no physical-object statement can ever be known with certainty; at best we can get only increasing degrees of probability. Why is this? Because there is an *infinite* range of sense-data, the sensing of which would be relevant to determining the truth of the physical-object statement. Consider vision alone: from how many angles can the table be viewed? An infinite number; and between any two angles from which you might view it there is an infinite number of others. In practice we are confident that it's a table after a few brief glances; but if we ask "At what point do you really *know* beyond doubt that it's a real table? At what point is the claim forever immune to doubt, so that no future sense-experience could

possibly overthrow it or even cast the slightest doubt on it?" the answer is: "Never." You would have to sense an infinite number of sense-data, for the family of table-sense-data is infinitely large; and of course you could never sense them all. At first glance the coin looks somewhat elliptical; a split second later, from a more acute angle, it looks somewhat more elliptical; but if you hadn't blinked for a tiny fraction of a second between you *might* have experienced, instead of a sense-datum of an ellipticity between these two, a visual sense-datum that was shaped like a cow. And in that case you would have had reason to doubt your original assumption that you weren't having a hallucination. But this sort of thing is always a possibility: you can never be absolutely sure that this won't happen, no matter how many favorable sense-data (members of the sense-datum family) you have experienced. You would have to experience the *whole family* in order to be sure; but the whole family is infinite. You cannot know that a statement is true until it is completely verified; and complete verification would require the sensing of an infinite series of sense-data.

I believe there is a piece of white paper now before me. The reason that I believe this is that I see it: a certain visual presentation is given. But my belief includes the expectation that so long as I continue to look in the same direction, this presentation, with its qualitative character essentially unchanged, will persist; that if I move my eyes right, it will be displaced to the left in the visual field; that if I close them, it will disappear; and so on. If any of these predictions should, upon trial, be disproved, I should abandon my present belief in a real piece of paper before me, in favor of belief in some extraordinary after-image or some puzzling reflection or some disconcerting hallucination.

I do look in the same direction for a time; then turn my eyes; and after that try closing them: all with the expected results. My belief is so far corroborated. And these corroborations give me greater assurance in any further predictions based upon it. But theoretically and ideally it is not completely verified, because the belief in a real piece of white paper now before me has further implications not yet tested: that what I see could be folded without cracking, as a piece of celluloid could not; that it would tear easily, as architect's drawing-cloth would not; that this experience will not be followed by waking in quite different surroundings; and others too numerous to mention. If it is a real piece of paper before me now, then I shall expect to find it here tomorrow with the number I just put on the corner: its reality and the real character I attribute in my belief imply innumerable possible verifications, or partial verifications, tomorrow and later on. . . . Even if the mentioned tests of the empirical belief about the paper should have been made, the result would not be a theoretically complete verification of it because there would be further and similar implications of the belief which would still not have been tested. . . .

If we now ask ourselves how extensive such implied consequences of the belief are, it seems clear that in so simple a case as the white paper supposedly now before me, the number of them is inexhaustible. . . . They presumably will never come to an end in point of time: there will never be a time when the fact—or non-fact—of this piece of paper now lying on my desk will not make some trivial difference. . . .

If the result of any single test is as expected, it constitutes a partial verification of the judgment only; never one which is absolutely decisive and theoretically complete. This is so because, while the judgment, so far as it is significant, contains nothing which could not be tested, still it has a significance which outruns what any single test, or any limited set of tests, could exhaust. No matter how fully I may have investigated this objective fact, there will still remain some theoretical possibility of mistake; there will be further consequences which must be thus and so if the judgment is true, and not all of these will have been determined. The possibility that such further tests, if made, might have a negative result, cannot be altogether precluded; and this possibility marks the judgment as, at the time in question, not fully verified and less than absolutely certain. To quibble about such possible doubts will not, in most cases, be common sense. But we are not trying to weigh the degree of theoretical dubiety which common-sense practicality should take account of, but to arrive at an accurate analysis of knowledge. This character of being further testable and less than theoretically certain characterizes every judgment of objective fact at all times; every judgment that such and such a real thing exists or has a certain objectively factual property, or that a certain objective event actually occurs, or that any objective state of affairs actually is the case.[9]

2. But other philosophers do not share this view. It is, they would say, *logically* possible that the future sense-data may not occur as expected, but this is only to say that it is not self-contradictory to say so—which is true enough, but irrelevant. "It is not certain that I am now looking at a piece of paper, because it is logically possible that I might be" is an invalid argument. Anything that isn't self-contradictory is, of course, logically possible; but that something is logically possible does not even begin to show that the statement is not true, in fact certainly true. Indeed, we have already agreed that sense-datum reports (if no verbal error is committed, etc.) are certain, and yet it is *logically* possible that they might be false, for the simple reason that they are not analytic statements: there is no contradiction involved in denying them. Thus the *logical* possibility that something might not be true does not in the slightest degree affect the certainty of a statement. If a statement is not certain, it must be for reasons *other* than that it is logically possible that it might be false. Logical possibility is simply irrelevant here: what *is* relevant is the question "Is there any reason to believe that the statement is not certain? Specifically, is there any evidence against it, or any consideration you could adduce to show that it is anything less than completely certain?"

According to this view, there are many statements—including physical object statements—that are completely certain in spite of the irrelevant fact that it is *logically* possible that they might be false. For example:

[9] Clarence I. Lewis, *An Analysis of Knowledge and Valuation*, pp. 174–76, 180.

Suppose I think that *Paradise Lost* begins with the words "Of Man's first disobedience," but that I am not sure and wish to verify it. I take from the shelf a book entitled *Milton's Poetical Works*. I turn to the first page of verse and under the heading *Paradise Lost, Book I,* I see that the first four words of the first line of verse are "Of Man's first disobedience." It would ordinarily be said that I had verified it. The proponents of the Verification Argument would say that I had not "completely" verified it. They would say that I had not even "completely" verified the fact that the first four words of verse on *the page before me* are the words "Of Man's first disobedience." What shall I do to *further* verify this latter fact? Shall I look again? Suppose that I do and that I see the same thing. Shall I ask someone else to look? Suppose that he looks and that he sees the same thing. According to this philosophical theory it is still not "completely" verified. How shall I further verify it? Would it be "further verification" if I were to look *again* and *again* at this page and have more and more other people look again and again? Not at all! We should not describe it so! Having looked once carefully, if I then continued to look at the page we should not say that I was "further verifying" or "trying to further verify" that the first four words of verse on that page are "Of Man's first disobedience." Carnap declares that although it might be foolish or impractical to continue "the series of test-observations" still one could do so "theoretically." He implies that *no matter what the circumstances* we should describe certain actions as "further verifying" or "further confirming" this fact. That is a mistake. Suppose that I continued to look steadily at the page and someone wondered why I was behaving in that way. If someone else were to say "He is trying to further verify that those are the first four words," this would be an absurd and humorous remark. And this description would be equally absurd if my actions consisted in showing the book to one person after another. In those circumstances there is nothing which we should *call* "further verification." To suppose that "the process of verification" can continue "without end" is simply to ignore the ordinary usage of the word "verify." It is false that "there is always the theoretical possibility of continuing the series of test-observations." It *is* possible that I should continue to *look at the page*. It is *not* possible that I should continue the verification of that fact because, in those circumstances, we should not describe *anything* as "further verification" of it. The verification *comes to an end*.[10]

Those who deny that physical-object statements can be known for certain to be true do not deny that they can be "practically certain" (which normally means "almost certain"); they only deny that such statements can be "theoretically certain." But this too is a mistake:

How are they using the expression "theoretical certainty"? What state of affairs, if it could be realized, would they call "theoretical certainty"? In what circumstances, supposing that such circumstances could exist, would it be "theoretically certain" that a given statement is true? The answer is clear from

---

[10] Norman Malcolm, "The Verification Argument," in *Knowledge and Certainty,* pp. 53–54. The full reasons for Malcolm's conclusion cannot be understood without reading the entire essay from which this passage is quoted.

the context of their arguments. It would be "theoretically certain" that a given statement is true only if an *infinite* number of "tests" or "acts of verification" had been performed. It is, of course, a *contradiction* to say that an infinite number of "tests" or acts of any sort have been performed by anyone. It is not that it is merely impossible in practice for anyone to perform an infinite number of acts. It is impossible *in theory*. Therefore these philosophers *misuse* the expression "theoretically certain." What they call "theoretical certainty" cannot be attained even *in theory*. But this misuse of an expression is in itself of slight importance. What is very important is that they identify what they mean by "theoretically certain" with what is ordinarily meant by "absolutely certain." If this identification were correct then the ordinary meaning of "absolutely certain" would be contradictory. The proposition that it is absolutely certain that a given statement is true would *entail* the proposition that someone had performed an infinite number of acts. Therefore, it would be a *contradiction* to say, for example, "It is absolutely certain that Socrates had a wife." Statements of this sort are often false, or they are often unjustified on the strength of the evidence at hand. But to say that such statements are one and all *self-contradictory* is perfectly absurd. A philosophical theory that has such a consequence is plainly false.[11]

At this point many would be prepared to leave the issue, believing that between absolute certainty and the near-approach to it that is "practical certainty" (enough to base your actions on, and indeed your life) there is not enough difference to argue about. At any rate, we must leave the matter here, except to make one point that, if true, is somewhat startling: a statement that simply reports one's immediate experience—a sense-datum statement—may indeed be absolutely certain, but, one may add, no pure sense-datum statement can ever be made. Even when you say "I see red spots," without the slightest implication that you are perceiving any physical object at all, you are going beyond the momentary experience you are allegedly reporting: even when you describe your sense-datum as "red," you are not saying something that applies only to this particular sense-datum. Like all descriptive words, "red" not only describes this experience but many others as well. When you say it is red, you are *relating* this experience to many other experiences you have had before (and will probably have again): you are lumping this experience together with other experiences, past and future, saying that they belong in the same category, that they are all describable by this same word; that this present experience is *like* other experiences you have had, enough like them to have the same descriptive word, "red," applied to them all. And in saying this, might you not be mistaken? In calling this experience red, you are relying on *memory*, which is fallible. Yet memory is involved in calling this sense-datum "red": in calling it "red" you are in effect saying that it is like other sense-data you have experienced before, at least enough like it to deserve the same word to describe it.

[11] *Ibid.*, pp. 55–56.

In calling it red you are not *naming* this sense-datum; if you were, you could never use the word again, for this sense-datum disappears forever; rather, you are *describing* it, saying what it is like. And that is just the point: you are saying what it is *like*, that it is like other data for which you have used the same descriptive word. If you could give every sense-datum a different proper name, you could get round this difficulty, though it would require an infinite number of proper names, none of them repeatable. But, as language is, it remains a fact that when you use language for any purpose other than to assign proper names, you inevitably go beyond the sense-datum of the moment and relate your present sense-data to past ones. In the very act of trying to report this momentary sense-datum only, you use words that connect it (through a relation of similarity) to *other* sense-data and commit you to saying that this is like those. And in doing this, of course, you go beyond the sense-data of the moment, with all the possibilities of error pertaining thereto. It is certain, of course, that you sense what you sense, and that you experience what you experience—but this is analytic; the moment you try to *describe* the experience in words, even using a simple sense-datum word like "red," you are going beyond the momentary sense-datum that you are attempting to report. A possibility of error thus arises in the very act of using language.[12] Sense-datum reports are certain, but no pure sense-datum report can be made: every report uses words, and words connect the experience reported with other experiences that at that moment are not present.

Whatever we may think of this point, we should be quite clear that the kind of error to which even sense-datum statements are subject—and which, it would seem, is shared by all statements using descriptive terms—is quite different from the *additional* kind of error (empirical error) to which physical-object statements are subject (some would say finitely subject, some would say infinitely). The important kind of error is one that characterizes physical-object statements but not sense-datum statements.

Sense-data and physical objects. Regardless of what we may believe about the certainty of physical-object statements, let us now return to the main thesis of phenomenalism: that all statements about physical objects can be translated into statements about phenomena—that is, about what is immediately (non-inferentially) present to consciousness, namely sense-data. "Matter is the permanent possibility of sensation," said Mill; but in the light of our discussion of sense-data we can now revise this to read, "Matter is the permanent possibility of sense-data." The sense-data are actual when you are perceiving the object, and possible when you are not. So far so good. But what is the status of possibilities in Mill's analysis? That which is actually

---

[12] Some philosophers would say that calling a sense-datum "red" implies only acquaintance with a *linguistic rule* specifying under what conditions a symbol (in this case the word "red") is to be used. This may be so. But the net result is the same. For in this case also, error is possible; one may misapply a rule.

before me exists, but in what way can *possibilities* exist? The mountain that no one is perceiving exists—that is, it would be perceived if anyone came within viewing range; but what at this moment exists, assuming that no one is perceiving the mountain? A possibility? But what is that? Can a possibility-of-sense-data hold a tower on top of it, which we may see even if we don't see the mountain? Surely there is something wrong here. There is something that exists *now*, not just a mere possibility of something, whatever that may be.

The contemporary phenomenalist attempts to formulate his answer more carefully than did Mill: It is not true that mere possibilities exist now: physical objects—the mountain—exist now, although unperceived. But how can we express this proposition—that the mountain exists unperceived—in sense-datum terms? This, after all, is the phenomenalistic program: Everything that can be said about physical objects can be translated into statements about sense-data. Yet there are no mountain-sense-data when no one is observing the mountain; how then is the translation possible? The phenomenalist replies: Statements about physical objects existing un-perceived *can* be translated into statements about sense-data, but not into statements about sense-data that are being sensed now. They must be translated into *hypothetical* (if–then) statements: "The table exists now, though unperceived" is translatable into *"If* someone fulfilled certain perceptual conditions (were in the same room as the table, with sufficient light, etc.), *then* he would perceive the table." This hypothetical proposition can be true even though the if-clause remains unfulfilled. But the table, not a mere set of possibilities, does exist now: that is, it is true *now* that if anyone were to go into the next room he would perceive the table. Do not say that hypothetical sense-data exist now (what would the phrase "hypothetical sense-data" mean?); say rather that hypothetical *propositions* about sense-data are true now. It is the proposition, not the sense-data, that is hypothetical; the adjective "hypothetical" modifies the noun "proposition," not the noun "sense-data." We are not translating physical-object propositions into propositions about hypothetical sense-data; we are translating physical-object propositions into hypothetical propositions about sense-data.

If we are supposed to be translating physical-object statements into sense-datum statements, however, the above translation has not succeeded. "There is a table in the next room, unperceived" becomes "If I (or some observer) were'in the next room, I would perceive it"; but this is not a translation into sense-datum terms, for there are at least three physical-object references in the proposed translation: first, the reference to the observer who is doing the perceiving; second, the reference to a physical location where he would have to be to perceive it ("in the next room"); and third, to that which would then be perceived, the table. If the phenomenalist is to carry out his program of translating all physical-object propositions into sense-datum propositions, he will have to eliminate all these physical-object references in favor of references exclusively to sense-data. If he does not, he will not have justified his assertion that "everything that is say-able about physical objects is sayable exclusively in terms of sense-data."

The third reference is the most easily taken care of. "I would see the table" would be translated into "I would experience table-sense-data (sense-data constituting the table-family)." It would not be sufficient to have one or two fleeting table-experiences, for this would still be compatible with having a hallucination. There would have to be enough sense-data of the table-family to ensure that one's experience was veridical, not a hallucination or a dream. (Whether this would be an infinite number we need not take up again.)

The first reference—to the observer—is more difficult. "If *I* were . . ."—but whether the I is myself or any other person, the difficulty is the same: I am at least a body, and a body is a physical object. The phenomenalist can easily reply that statements about bodies, being physical-object statements, are themselves reducible to statements about sense-data; and that therefore the original physical-object statement requires two reductions: the physical object referred to (the table), and the observer's body. The table is one family of sense-data, the body another. (If it is *my* body, it is distinguished by certain special features described on pp. 405–6, but it is a physical object in any case.) This may complicate things, but, says the phenomenalist, the principle is no different: if phenomenalism can take care of one physical object, the table, it can surely take care of a second, the observer's body, by simply repeating the translation.

But the issue is more difficult than this, for the reference to an observer is not merely a reference to a body. A body does not by itself experience sense-data: *I*, a person, experience sense-data, and let us grant that without a body I could not do this. But perceiving requires consciousness, a mind; and then the troublesome question of what is the true account of the nature of the self (pp. 406–9) rises to haunt us again. Propositions about minds cannot be reduced simply to propositions about bodies. Perhaps, however, it is quite acceptable to retain a reference to minds: it was only references to physical objects that had to be eliminated in favor of references to sense-data. The reduction will then be into propositions about "minds and their sense-data."

The second reference—to physical location—is the most difficult to handle. "If I (or some other observer) were in the next room, I would sense table-sense-data." "If I were at the South Pole, I would be experiencing ice-sense-data." And so on. But the South Pole and the next room are physical places, located in physical space (not simply in perceptual space like the spots before your eyes); and how can you locate a place in space except by reference to physical coordinates? Let us grant that you can translate physical-object statements into sense-datum statements as phenomenalism says; but when you are talking about physical objects existing unperceived, you have to specify a place at or from which the sense-data *could* be experienced, and this, it seems, requires a reference to a physical coordinate-system. It would appear that the phenomenalistic physical objects must at least exist in a non-phenomenalistic physical frame.

This difficulty is not easy to remedy. A reference to physical location is clearly contained in the hypothetical statement that is offered as the translation of the physical-object statement. If the phenomenalist is right, all references to physical things must be eliminated in favor of references to sense-data alone. But how is it to be done in this case? "If I were in Paris now . . ." How can one translate such a clause as this into sense-datum terms?

If it can be done at all, the procedure would be so complicated as to baffle the imagination. The phenomenalist would reply that phrases like "so many miles from here" and "in such and such a direction" will have to stand for the *sense-datum route* that anyone would have to travel if he were to pass from where he is to the other place (Paris). This is to be done as follows: I am now visually aware of a certain sense-datum field. If I walk a step, I am aware of a similar and mostly overlapping sense-datum field. The same happens if I walk a third step. Finally none of the sense-data I began with are in my visual field any more. But they do not change suddenly, only gradually, in an *overlapping series of sense-fields*. Let us call these S_1, S_2, S_3, etc. Then, *if* I replaced S_1 by S_2, S_2 by S_3, S_3 by S_4, and so on, I would finally be sensing the visual field of sense-data belonging to Paris. Of any place, P, P will have to be defined in terms of the sense-datum route that leads from my present sensory field to the sensory field that includes P.

This complicates matters enormously. But even this is not all. By "If someone were at place P . . ." we mean "If someone were *really* at place P . . ." He might dream he was there, or have a hallucination of being there; but this would not do. And so for the sense-datum route: he must really travel it, not dream that he was doing so. Thus the sense-datum route (the series of sense-data between the experience of being here and the experience of being at P) is more complicated than we indicated above. We require still more ifs. If the sense-datum route is S_1, S_2, S_3 . . . , in saying that I am at any stage—let's say S_3—I must be able to sense *further* S_3-ish sense-data, enough to establish that I am not dreaming or having a hallucination. The same must be possible at the next stage, S_4, and at every stage along the way. At every stage of the series leading to P, there must be the possibility of another sense-datum series branching off from the main one, so that *if* I had obtained sense-data belonging to this branch, I would have verified the existence of a physical object located at that place. I may not experience any of these branch-series; for that matter, I need not experience the main series. But it must be *possible* for me to experience both: once again, *if* I were in these sense-datum circumstances, then I would have experienced such-and-such sense-data. After all, if it is *not* possible, then it isn't true that I might have had the experience of really moving from here to P.

The same problems arise about *time*. "*If* an observer had been at that place at time *t*, he would have experienced such-and-such sense-data."

"Time *t*" will mean so many days or seconds or centuries ago. And this in turn the phenomenalist will have to analyze in terms of a sense-datum route by which someone could have been *going to* sense the sense-field that is being sensed by the speaker; so again it will contain a whole battery of "ifs" inside itself. "Caesar sensed X 2,000 years ago" would have to be something like this: "Caesar sensed a sense-field such that *if* he had been going to sense a later one temporally adjacent to it, and *if* he had been going to sense a still later one temporally adjacent to that one, and so on, then eventually he *would* have been going to sense the sense-field that is now being sensed by the speaker."

Nor is this all. He must *really* be at time *t*—he must not dream it or hallucinate it. "Caesar was in Rome in 50 B.C." must be translatable into the sense-datum routes in time, through successive sense-fields connecting the two times; and it must *really* connect them. Some could dream of the whole series of events filling the interval between 50 B.C. and now. The sense-datum route from 50 B.C. to now must consist of normal or veridical sense-data; and again this means that there must be the possibility of experiencing innumerable branch-series, just as in the case of space.

The completion of this whole series would be a staggering task. And the question that haunts us before we even begin to attempt it is: How could the phenomenalist even begin with it if he had not already before his mind the thought of a physical world, ordered in space and time, conceived to be already there, waiting to be sensed? What else could guide us in our choice of the right if-clauses, and enable us to know which should come after which?[13] Yet the concept of physical space and physical time is not a priori; somehow we begin with the raw data of sense-experience and from it arrive at the idea of a physical world ordered in space and time—that is, with spatiotemporal coordinates. However complex this process is, we do succeed in performing it.[14]

Causality. A similar problem arises for phenomenalists when they consider sense-data in relation to causality. Let us ask our old question: What causes sense-data? Phenomenalists do not avail themselves of Berkeley's God to answer the question. If they said, "Sense-data are caused by physical objects," they would be reminded that references to physical objects are to be eliminated (by their own program) in favor of references to sense-data only, so we are back with sense-data again. If they say, "Sense-data cause other sense-data," the question again arises, "But what causes the sense-data themselves?" One can, of course, say that sense-data are simply the ultimate and irreducible data of experience, which are capable of no explanation; but this is more like throwing in the towel than giving a positive answer.

[13] See H. H. Price, *Hume's Theory of the External World*, pp. 188 ff.

[14] Phenomenalists have, indeed, attempted to show, at least in outline, how the concepts of physical space are "constructed" from the given sense-data. See A. J. Ayer, *Foundations of Empirical Knowledge*, pp. 260–63.

At this point the phenomenalist, at least the 20th century variety, will contend that the whole issue has been misconceived and misstated. The question is posed as if there were two kinds of things in the world, sense-data and physical objects, the only question being to discover what relation there is between them. But the issue should be cast not in terms of relation between two types of entity in the world but in terms of the relation between two kinds of propositions, sense-datum statements and physical-object statements. Causation takes place among physical objects, and the propositions about these physical objects can then be translated into statements about sense-data. When the physical objects (and processes attending them) are observed, the translation is easy: "C causes E" becomes "C is regularly followed by E," which becomes "C-sense-data are regularly followed by E-sense-data." But what if the C and E are not observed? Then the phenomenalist's favorite device, hypothetical propositions, comes into play once more. The first billiard ball hits the second one (C), and the second one moves (E). We believe that this happens when we do not see it as well as when we do. We can now render this into phenomenalist terms as follows: C may not be observed, but we *could* observe it if we chose, and the same with E. Even though we do not see C and E, we can say that *if* we were in a position to observe C (let us call this P_1), we would observe it, and if we were in a position to observe E (call this P_2), we would observe it. Thus we get a hypothetical within a hypothetical:

If (if we were in P_1 we would observe C), then (if we were in P_2 we would observe E).

The whole thing can be stated in terms of the sense-data we *would* be sensing if we were in circumstances of perception in which we are not at the moment placed.

The same analysis applies if the effect is observed but the cause is not. A magnetized bar is concealed in someone's pocket, and although no one is experiencing bar-sense-data, a compass-needle is nevertheless seen to be deflected, and the deflection is the effect of the presence of the magnetized bar. No actual sense-data of the magnet-family exist. Nevertheless they are *available;* and now our hypothetical statement goes into operation once again. "Needle-sense-data occur" (this part is categorical, since the needle is actually perceived), "*and* if the pocket were to be emptied, the bar would be seen." This hypothetical proposition we have every reason to believe is true, along with countless similar hypothetical propositions.

So much for causal relationships among physical objects; propositions about these, according to phenomenalism, can be translated into hypothetical propositions about sense-data. But now what about the special case of the causation of sense-data themselves? We believe that the presence of a physical object, say a tomato, plus light-waves from it impinging on the retina, etc., causes a person to experience a reddish roundish sense-datum. I cannot, of course, observe this in my own case: I cannot first observe the tomato and then observe my tomato-sense-data; I am aware only of the latter. What then entitles me to believe that, were it not for the presence of a tomato, I would experience no tomato-sense-data? This is due, no doubt, to our observation of other organisms. I cannot experience your sense-data, but I can observe that when a tomato is placed in front of you (that is, when I experience certain tomato-sense-data and your-body-sense-data), you say "Tomato" (I have this auditory experience), and when an apple is placed in front of you (again, when I experience apple-sense-data), you say "Apple," and so on; also that if your eyes are closed or your optic nerve cut or your brain damaged, you cannot regularly give the right answers. From this I infer—and it is only an inference—that the sense-data you experience (indeed, whether you experience any at all) depend on certain conditions: the presence of certain physical objects and of certain physiological conditions (all of which I can, and indeed must, describe in sense-datum terms). As a further inference, I conclude that if this is true in your case, and in as many other cases as I care to observe, it is probably true in mine also: that the occurrence of sense-data in my own consciousness depends on the prior fulfillment of similar conditions. I can also note that when I close my eyes I can see nothing, etc., but I still cannot observe two separate things, (1) the tomato and (2) my tomato-sense-data. If (1) precedes (2) in time—as scientists say it does, by a very small fraction of a second—I cannot observe the time-lapse in my own case.

Phenomenalism and laws of nature.   What is the status of laws of nature if phenomenalism is accepted? Suppose we have a law of nature asserting some kind of invariant relation between A and B. Shall we translate it into "Whenever A-sense-data occur, B-sense-data occur," or "There is an invariant relation between A-sense-data and B-sense-data"? This, however, will not do, for there *is* no invariant relation among sense-data. We believe that "If there is lightning there is thunder" is true, but certainly "If I see lightning, I'll hear thunder" is *not* true—suppose that I am deaf, or the thunder is too distant for me to hear, or I have my eyes averted and do not see the lightning. A strange law, that can be violated by a mere turning of one's head! Or consider this simple law (or situation that exemplifies a law): "When you strike an elastic ball against a wall, the ball rebounds." But suppose that when the ball hits the wall you close your eyes and don't see it rebound, or that the wall is concealed by darkness; then the law does not hold. In the past the one sense-experience was followed by the other, but this time (because of closing your eyes, or the wall being beyond range of your flashlight) the second sense-experience does not occur. Even the blink of an eye can dash the most secure generalization against the rocks. The fact is clear: there is *no invariant relation* to be found among sense-data. Experiences are fragmentary, but the application of laws of nature is not. And in fact the laws of nature refer to the occurrence of events, but not to one's perceiving of them. Friction causes heat; the volume of a gas varies inversely with the pressure; bodies fall at a constant rate—and all with no reference to perceivers or the conditions of perception. Laws of nature have to with things, events, and processes in the world of nature, not with our perception of them.

Does this imply that science is impossible if phenomenalism is correct? It does, if the above analysis is correct; but the phenomenalist will declare that this analysis is entirely in error. The law involved in the rebounding-ball case does not say that if you see the ball moving toward the wall you will also see it hit the wall—this depends on many conditions of perception and on your decision whether or not to turn the other way. But it *does* say something about what sense-data you *would* sense *if* you were in the appropriate circumstances, and these circumstances too can be described phenomenalistically. The story is now a familiar one:

If (if conditions of perception$_1$, then A-sense-datum), then (if conditions of perception$_2$, then B-sense-datum).

And once again, this conditional statement (including its two sub-conditionals) can be true even though the if-clauses are unfulfilled.

The stone wall continues to have the causal characteristic of impenetrability even when no one is observing any phenomena of the kind described. What then is involved in this? No more, surely, than that if anyone were to observe any "foreign" family prolonging itself up to the family that constituted the stone wall, he would observe that it prolonged itself subsequently in a different direction. In other words, the existence of the causal characteristic is, in such cases, a matter of the truth of a hypothetical proposition about sense-data; and it is not in the least necessary for the validity of this hypothetical proposition, though it may be necessary for its actual verification, that the protasis [if-clause] should be realized.[15]

Exercises

1. Explain why phenomenalists consider the term "sense-data" preferable to (a) "ideas," (b) "sense-experiences," (c) "sensations."
2. Discuss these objections to Mill's phenomenalism ("Matter is the permanent possibility of sensation"):

a. How can a possibility do anything? Either a thing exists unobserved (in which case no possibility is needed) or it does not (in which case there is nothing to do or cause anything, and no reference to possibilities will help).

b. We have sensations (mental), and matter is possible sensations (again mental); so in Mill's phenomenalism the entire physical world is part of the mental. (Is this feature overcome when the term "sense-data" is substituted for the word "sensations"?

[15] A. J. Ayer, *Foundations of Empirical Knowledge*, p. 227.

3. If there were no hallucinations, no illusions, and no dreams, would the introduction of sense-data be required? Would the distinction between sense-data and physical objects become unnecessary, pointless, or meaningless? Explain.

4. How is the verb "see" used differently in each of the following sentences?
a. I see green.
b. I see an oasis. (Assume that there is no oasis.)
c. I see a tree. (Assume that there is one.)

5. "Nobody knows what physical objects are like really; we only know how they *appear* to us, not how they really *are,* what qualities they really have." What would phenomenalists say about this view, and why?

6. "Provided one is not making a verbal error or lying, sense-datum statements are certain." "But no pure sense-datum statements can be made." Evaluate both of these assertions. Do they have any bearing on the acceptability of phenomenalism?

7. Since, according to phenomenalism, all physical-object sentences are translatable into sense-datum sentences, why has no such translation been achieved? Cite as many reasons as you can. Does this failure show that phenomenalism is false?

8. In the light of our discussion of phenomenalism, write a brief essay on the subject "Are Any Non-analytic Propositions Certain?"

9. Defend one of the following views: Some physical-object propositions are (a) absolutely certain; (b) practically certain but never theoretically certain; (c) relatively certain (near enough to certain to be a basis for action) but never absolutely certain.

10. Explain the meaning of the assertion that every physical-object proposition is an implicit prediction. Prediction of what? Is the series of predictions involved in "That's a table over there" infinite or finite? Justify your answer.

11. Attack or defend the view that laws of nature can be expressed entirely as regularity-relations among sense-data. (Actual or possible sense-data? And if possible sense-data, what kind of propositions would this involve, and why?)

26. Alternatives

Some objections to the phenomenalistic program have now been given, but the phenomenalist claims to have answered them. There are, however, other objections to phenomenalism that are not so easy to answer. Some fundamental objections have been made by various philosophers, not concerning the details of the phenomenalistic program (such as those presented above), but attacking it at its very foundations. Let us begin by probing a bit more deeply the point just made about laws of nature in relation to phenomenalism.

On that view, to say that the bursting of the pipes is caused by the formation of ice in them is to say that whenever one observes or could observe sense-data of the set constituting a burst pipe, one either has or could have previously observed sense-data of the set constituting a lump of ice inside that pipe. But quite clearly, in practically every instance of this rule, nobody does actually observe the ice; the sense-data of the ice are possible, not actual. That is to say, causality in such a case is a relation between something and nothing, between an actually observed burst, and a hypothetical proposition to the effect that if something had happened which did not happen and in practice could not have happened, then something else would have happened which also did not happen. This interpretation flouts our usual assumption that what might have happened but did not happen can have no effects. The actual material agents of physics and common sense must be replaced by a set of hypothetical facts relating to unfulfilled conditions. If this is so, it is difficult to see why we should suppose that these hypothetical propositions are true. If I leave a fire in my room, I expect it to be warm on my return; but is this not because I believe that the fire is still now burning, a real present fire exercising an influence on a real present atmosphere? I cannot see what reason can be given for expecting the room to be warmed, independently of my reasons for supposing that the fire *is* burning *now* (and not that, *if* I went and looked, I should see flame). I can see reason for believing in regularities in nature holding between one event and another; but no reason at all for believing in regularities holding between one event which happened and another which might have happened but did not.[16]

The phenomenalist will reply that he has already answered this charge—that the relation is between real (not hypothetical) ice in the pipe and the real bursting of that pipe, but that when one or both members of this pair is not observed its meaning must be rendered by means of hypothetical statements about what one *would* have observed. But at this point the critic pursues the offensive: he says that it won't do to say that *if* you had observed A you *would* have observed B. Of course it *is* true that you *could* have observed both, and that if you had been in the appropriate perceptual circumstances you *would* have observed both—this the critic admits. But what he does not admit is that "There is a fire burning now" *means* the same as "If I went and looked, I would see flames." He does not accept the very basic tenet of phenomenalism, that the first sentence is translatable into the second one. They have, he says, very different meanings: the first is about events in nature that occur regardless of perceivers, and the second about what perceivers would perceive if certain conditions were fulfilled. The meanings of these two are irreducibly different. If the first one is true, the second is doubtless true also—if there is a fire, then you could go and look at the flames—but the second is a *consequence* of the first, not a translation of it. The phenomenalistic translation, with its hypotheticals within hypotheticals, has to make reference to the conditions of perception, whereas the physical law itself never makes any reference to the conditions of perception. This alone, says the critic, should be enough to show that the two sentences have different meanings, and that the first (the physical law) cannot be translated into the second (the hypothetical proposition about what we would observe

[16] C. H. Whiteley, *An Introduction to Metaphysics,* pp. 94–95.

if . . .). I believe that the table next door is *there,* and that its being there has nothing to do with the occurrence of sense-data (actual or possible), or with the fact that if I went next door I would perceive it:

> The question of the . . . existence of the table next door, is one thing, and the question of the presence or absence, even hypothetically, of an observer, is another. The statement that if there had been (and there was not) any observer, he would have observed (and no one did observe), certain data, seems . . . not equivalent to asserting the past existence of material objects. Categorical propositions about material objects are replaced by unfulfilled "counter-factual" hypothetical propositions about observers, and what troubles the plain man is the thought that if the hypotheticals are unfulfilled, if no observers were in fact observing, then if the phenomenalist analysis is correct, there was—in a sense-datum sense—*nothing at all;* and, moreover, that this sense of "existence" is basic: because the alleged material object sense in which the non-existence of actual sense-data nevertheless can be "translated into" the existence of material objects, is not a sense in which the word "exist" is commonly understood. If he is then told that to say there was a material object . . . is to say something about the data there would have been if . . . he feels cheated. For these data appear to depend on the activity of observers; so that the material object becomes analyzed into a series of either purely hypothetical, i.e., non-existent, or at best, intermittent data occurring and disappearing as the observer observes or ceases to observe. And this seems empirically a different picture of the world from that which he started by believing; and in no sense merely a description of the old picture though in different words. . . .
>
> Existential propositions expressed categorically—in indicative sentences—tend, as it were, to "point" towards their "objects"; and demonstratives which appear in existential propositions, like, "this is," "there is," "here we have," etc., often function as substitutes for such acts of pointing to things or persons or processes. The characteristic force of the categorical mode of expression is often exactly this—that it acts in lieu of a gesture, of an "act of ostension," "Here *is* the book," I say to someone looking for it, or I could point to it and say, "The book," and convey roughly the same information by both methods. But hypotheticals normally do the opposite of this. Hypotheticals, whatever they describe or mean, whatever they entail or convey or evince, in whatever way they are verified or fail to be verified, do *not* as a general rule directly assert that something has been, is being, or will be occurring, or existing, or being characterized in some way: this is precisely the force of the conditional mood. . . . Thus, "Anyone who was there at 3 o'clock saw the meteor fall," because it is compatible with "And no one in fact was," *can* be translated into "If anyone was there, or had been there, etc., then he saw, or would have seen, etc."; whereas, "He gave away his books to anyone who asked for them," is *not* equivalent to "If anyone asked for, had asked for, etc., his books he was, or would have been given, etc.," but needs in addition, *"and some persons did ask."* It seems quite clear that in this last sentence a conditional or hypothetical sentence by itself tells us nothing about what in fact happened, and

an indicative or categorical one is therefore required by ordinary usage to convey "existential import"—to refer to actual events which are believed to have taken place.[17]

Phenomenalism, the critic continues, provides a good account of how we *verify* the existence and characteristics of physical objects: we can verify that physical objects exist only because we experience sense-data. This is not denied. But we should not confuse what something is with how we know it: we should not confuse the *evidence* for *p* with *p*'s *meaning*. Only by means of sense-experience can we know that there are physical objects, but this does not make sentences about sense-experience equivalent to (and therefore translatable into) sentences about sense-data. The meaning of the target-sentence is different from the meaning of the evidential sentence. Phenomenalism is, in a way, simply the verifiability theory of meaning applied to the special problem of perception, and as such it is open to all the objections to which that theory is subject (pp. 263–73).

What, then, is the status of physical objects if the above criticisms are acceptable? The immediate data of experience are still sense-data: only by the sense-datum route can we know anything about physical objects. But what are these physical objects that are known by means of sense-data? Must we go back to the causal-correspondence theory of Locke, which resulted in total skepticism concerning our knowledge of physical objects? Is there an iron curtain between sense-data and physical objects that nothing can penetrate? Berkeley at least got rid of any such curtain by insisting, however un-common-sensically, that physical objects are families of sense-data and no more. Phenomenalism too involves no curtain, since according to it physical-object sentences are translatable into sense-datum sentences, with the proviso that some of these sentences be hypothetical. But if idealism and phenomenalism are rejected in the light of the above criticisms, what happens to physical objects? Are they merely, as Hume thought, a product of the imagination that extends through inter-perceptual periods the same phenomena that we experience during the perceptual periods? And is this product of the imagination anything more than our own invention, a convenient fiction with no rational basis?

One answer that has been given to this question is that physical objects are *hypotheses* to account for the order among our sense-data. Our sense-data possess a certain order that permits them to be classified into families, but they are also fragmentary and intermittent, and there are no laws of invariant relation, or regularity, among our sense-data. If we do want to hold that there is such an order of nature—and without this we have no basis for prediction of future events—then we must believe that there are unperceived as well as perceived events. We do not *discover* through sense-perception that there are

[17] Isaiah Berlin, "Empirical Propositions and Hypothetical Statements," *Mind*, 1950, pp. 296, 299–300.

invariant regularities in the physical world even when the events are unperceived; what we do discover is that there are imperfect regularities *among* our sense-data. That there *is* a physical world in which the sequences of events are really invariant (unlike the sequences of perceptual events) is a hypothesis—a hypothesis invoked for purposes of explanation and, through explanation, prediction. "That there are physical objects is a supposition, not a datum. The use of the supposition is to account for the regularities of sensory phenomena, to enable the course of events to be set in a framework of regular sequences and concomitances.[18]

But if the belief in physical objects is a supposition (hypothesis), not a datum, why adopt it? Is the hypothesis well-founded? According to the view we are now considering, it is: "It is confirmed by the success we achieve in ordering our experiences by its aid, in making our generalizations continually more extensive and more exact."[19]

We can and do make a vast number of predictions on the basis of our natural belief in an independent physical world. These predictions are usually fulfilled. In view of the fact that the probability of an unfounded guess that an experience will have a certain character being fulfilled is immensely small owing to the vast number of logically possible alternatives, and in view of the vast number of predictions that have been fulfilled, it is immensely improbable that these predictions would have all turned out right if the belief were not true. . . .

Practically no scientific or even merely common-sense predictions about our future perceptions can be made without introducing as an intermediate link between the prediction and the direct observations on which it is based the notion of a physical object existing unperceived, and practically no casual laws can be stated in terms only of actually perceived states of objects. We have thus in order to make predictions to assume at least that our experience will go on *as if* there were physical objects existing independently of us in the realist sense. This at least we must admit, even if we say that independent physical objects are only methodological fictions. But this itself is a very strong argument for their really existing. That experience should persistently go on as if something were true is the strongest empirical argument we can have for its really being true.[20]

The existence of physical objects (to conclude this line of thought) is a hypothesis to account for the order of our sense-experiences. This we may call a *first-order hypothesis*. Once we have accepted physical objects, including of course the belief in their existence during inter-percepetual intervals, we notice many features of these too that in turn require explaining,

[18] C. H. Whiteley, "Physical Objects," *Philosophy*, XXXIV (1959), 142–149.

[19] *Ibid.*, p. 149.

[20] Alfred C. Ewing, "The Causal Argument for Physical Objects," *Proceedings of the Aristotelian Society*, Supplementary Vol. XIX (1945), 35, 37.

and this physicists do by invoking invisible entities such as atoms and electrons; and the existence of these is a *second-order hypothesis*. Sentences about electrons, etc., are no more translatable into sentences about visible and tangible things like instrument-panels and cloud-chambers than sentences about physical objects in their turn are translatable into sentences about sense-data. These are, so to speak, different orders of being. In the *metaphysical* order—of "how things are"—physical objects come before sense-data: if there were no physical objects there would be no human beings to have sense-experiences. But in the *epistemological* order—of "how things are known"—sense-data come first: it is only by the experiencing of sense-data that we can justify our beliefs about physical objects (just as it is our beliefs about physical objects that justify our second-order hypotheses about the "ultimate particles" of physics). Epistemologically speaking, "it all goes back to sense-data": there is no belief about the existence or properties of physical objects that must not find its verification in sense-experience, just as there is no belief about ultimate particles that does not find its verification in the properties of physical objects and, through them, in sense-data. The verification must always occur in sense-experience. If there is a difference between two hypotheses, whether first- or second-order, it must be shown by the difference it makes to immediate experience, sense-data. No matter how riddled the statement of it is with reference to unobservable or abstract entities, no hypothesis can fail "to make some difference to the given"—there must be some observable difference between its being true and its not being true: that is the "cash value" of the hypothesis. No matter how high the hypothesis may fling its superstructure into the sky, its substructure must be firmly anchored in the subsoil of sense-experience; when it is not, it must be rejected as cutting no ice with experience. Any empirical proposition, it may be suggested, must meet this requirement.

The attack on sense-data.   But we have not yet concluded our critique of phenomenalism: a more fundamental one is yet to come. How could any criticism, one may ask, be more fundamental than the attack on its main premise, the translatability thesis? There is one form of attack still more basic, since it is involved in the very concept of a translation, and that is the attack on the concept of sense-data itself.

How can anyone doubt that there are sense-data? Every time you see a color or hear a sound, aren't you experiencing sense-data? Aren't sense-data the most indubitable of all the allegedly indubitable things in the furniture of heaven and earth? It may come as something of a surprise that the very existence of sense-data has been attacked, and not only that but the meaning of the term itself—it has been alleged that phenomenalism breaks down (even if for no other reason) because its own basic concept, or alleged concept, is meaningless.

1. We introduced the term "sense-data" in order to preserve the distinction between *what* I sense (sense-data) and the *sensing* of it

(sensation). I sense the red spot, but the sensing is not red. The distinction between sensation and sense-datum is the distinction between act and object-of-the-act. But in the present case this distinction leads to an embarrassment: if there is a distinction between act and object here, why should the object (the red spot) cease to exist when the act ceases? Why, if it is distinguishable from my act of sensing it, should the red spot not persist *after* I cease to sense it? No one wants to say that the red spot exists after I sense it; we want to say that, like pleasures and pains and thoughts, its existence *consists* in its being experienced—that just as it is self-contradictory to say that a pain exists unfelt, so it is self-contradictory to say that the red spot or after-image persists after I experience it. If it is an experience, it can't exist unexperienced. Yet if the act-object analysis that led to introducing sense-data in the first place is accepted, shouldn't it at least be an open question whether the object (the sense-datum) persists after my experience thereof has ceased?

The act-object analysis has, in fact, been often rejected in the sense-data case. There are cases in which the act and the object of the act can be distinguished: when I hit a ball, the hitting of the ball is distinguishable from the ball, and the ball (we believe) persists after I have hit it. But there are other cases in which no such distinction can be made: when I dance, what do I dance? A dance. Is there the activity of dancing, and besides that the thing danced—the dance itself—which may continue after I have stopped dancing? In this case the act-object analysis is, to put it mildly, less plausible: it would seem that there is here no object apart from the activity itself—the dance I dance *is* simply the dancing; that which I do is exhaustively described by my doing of it.[21] But if the act-object analysis is rejected in the sense-data case, there seems to be no reason left why we should introduce the term "sense-data" at all. The supposed precision of this term was based on an invalid distinction.

Does this fact, if it is a fact, invalidate everything we said about sense-data since we introduced the term in this chapter? Not at all: though we may reject the technical term as resting on an act-object distinction that does not apply here, at any rate we do have sense-experiences, and we could go back to the old term "sense-experiences," which is not theory-laden as "sense-data" is. And the same question would still confront us: What is the relation between our sense-experiences and the physical reality that we believe to exist independently of the occurrence of these sense-experiences? But let us continue:

2. The sense-datum language is an appearance-language, as we said: if the coin appears elliptical, then we see an elliptical sense-datum regardless of what the real shape of the coin may be. For sense-data, the "is" is the same as

---

[21] See Curt J. Ducasse, "Moore's Refutation of Idealism," in *The Philosophy of G. E. Moore,* ed. P. A. Schlipp (Evanston, Ill.: Northwestern University Press, 1942), pp. 225–252.

the "appears": the coin appears elliptical, so the sense-datum *is* elliptical. It is logically impossible for sense-data to have properties they do not appear to have, since the term "sense-data" was introduced to describe the appearance only, regardless of whether there was a physical object present to do the appearing.

So far so good. Now a puzzle arises: What if the conditions of perception are not favorable, or if for some other reason the appearance is hardly characterizable at all? Suppose the coin doesn't appear round but doesn't appear elliptical either—it's nearly dark in the room, and I just can't make out *how* it looks. Or suppose the optician asks me not what letters there *are* on his chart but what letters there *appear* to me to be (that after all is what he wants to know, since he is testing my vision; he knows very well what the letters *are*), and I can't tell him whether it appears to me to be an E or an F. What is it then that I am directly aware of? An E-sense-datum, an F-sense-datum, or neither? The law of Excluded Middle says "Either A or not-A"; and since this applies to all propositions, it applies to propositions about sense-data too. Well, which is it—an E-sense-datum or not-an-E-sense-datum? It must be the one or the other. But the trouble is we can't say which it is.

Why should this fact be bothersome? There are plenty of occasions when we can say, for example, "This is a gnu or not a gnu, but I don't know which, for I am not expert at recognizing gnus." But in these cases there are more properties of the creature that we could discover if we wished to do so. In the case of sense-data, however, this possibility is excluded: a sense-datum is what it appears, and can have no properties it does not appear to have; our knowledge of its properties is exhaustive at the moment we have the experience. So we can't say of sense-data, "It really *does* have an E-shape or it doesn't, but I can't be sure which." Not only must it be either, but we must know which, because, for sense-data, what is is what appears, and I know how it appears (though I may not be able to describe it in words).

This problem has been given some notoriety in "the problem of the speckled hen." When I glance at the hen I notice that it has numerous speckles on it, but I don't know how many. The real physical hen has, of course, a definite number of speckles, though no one may have counted how many. But if I am talking now not about the number of speckles it *has* but about the number of speckles it *appears* to have (sense-datum speckles), how many speckles are there? It doesn't appear to have any definite number at all: since I didn't notice a definite number, there does not *exist* a definite number of appearance-speckles (sense-datum speckles). But this is most peculiar: either there are, say, 1,047 sense-datum speckles or there are not. It must be one or the other, though we don't know which. But the trouble with the sense-datum speckles is that it *isn't* the one or the other: the hen doesn't appear to have 1,047 or not to have 1,047. We could count the physical speckles to find out how many it really has, but this doesn't help us answer the question

"How many did it appear at that moment to have?" It appeared to have—well, an indeterminate number. But how can there *be* an indeterminate number, and no definite or determinate number, of speckles? Can there be "numerosity without number"?

We are, then, caught in a bind: if there is *no* definite number of sense-datum speckles, then there is "numerosity without number"—which is extremely paradoxical. Could there ever be such a thing?[22] On the other hand, if there *is* a definite number, the fact remains that we don't know what that number is, so sense-data can have properties that they don't appear to have, just as physical objects can. But this contradicts the definition of "sense-data" on an extremely fundamental point—that the term "sense-data" refers to appearance only.

This problem arises because we *notice* features of things that we did not take in at first. We didn't notice that the rose looked red; we saw a whole garden of roses and noticed this rose only as dark, not as dark red or dark purple or any other color. The rose itself of course has a determinate color; but the sense-datum of the rose didn't, because it didn't *appear* to have, and for sense-data what appears *is*. It appeared only to be dark. Was the rose-sense-datum then dark, but of no determinate color? This is just as strange as numerosity without number. We believe that physical objects have absolutely determinate properties, such as a definite number of speckles and a definite shade of red; but that doesn't describe the momentary appearance, which is describable only as "very numerous," "dark." We are barred from saying that we can notice features of sense-data that we didn't notice earlier, for that would mean that sense-data really had features that they didn't at first appear to have; we can say only that the indeterminate sense-data are replaced (as we look more carefully) by determinate sense-data, but that leaves the puzzle about the initial indeterminate sense-data just where it was. Saying that the sense-data had features it didn't appear to have violates our definition of "sense-data," so we turn to the alternative, that it didn't *have* the more determinate feature (a definite number, a definite color)—but this alternative is just as puzzling as the other one.

3. Another puzzle arises about sense-data. Earlier phenomenalists spoke of sense-data *and* physical objects, as if they were two kinds of entity: as if, were we to make a complete inventory of the universe and include in it everything there is, we would have to include physical things and also sense-data, since they are both existents, though of a different kind. Later phenomenalists avoided this way of talking, and spoke not of the relation of two kinds of thing or entity in reality but of the relation between two kinds of sentences: hence the phenomenalistic program of translating physical-object sentences into sense-datum sentences.

---

[22] Some say there can, and that the puzzle arises only because we think of sense-datum speckles as if they were physical speckles. See A. J. Ayer, *Foundations of Empirical Knowledge*, pp. 123–35.

The problem of specifying the relationship of material things to sense-data . . . is apt to be obscured by being represented as a problem about the inter-relationship of two different classes of objects. There is, indeed, a sense in which it is correct to say that both sense-data and material things exist, inasmuch as sentences that are used to describe sense-data and sentences that are used to describe material things both very frequently express true propositions. But it would not be correct to infer from this that there really were both material things and sense-data, in the sense in which it can truly be said that there really are chairs as well as tables, or that there are tastes as well as sounds. . . .

It is commonly said that material things are nothing but collections of actual and possible sense-data. But this is a misleading formula and one that provokes objections which a more accurate way of speaking might avoid. Thus, it is sometimes argued, by those who reject this "phenomenalistic" analysis of the nature of material things, that to conceive of such things as houses or trees or stones as mere collections of actual and possible sense-data is to ignore their "unity" and "substantiality," and that, in any case, it is hard to see how anything can be composed of so shadowy a being as a possible sense-datum. But these objections are founded upon the mistaken assumption that a material thing is supposed to consist of sense-data as a patchwork quilt consists of different colored pieces of silk. To remove this misconception, it must be made clear that what the statement that material things consist of sense-data must be understood to designate is not a factual but a linguistic relationship. What is being claimed is simply that the propositions which are ordinarily expressed by sentences which refer to material things could also be expressed by sentences which referred exclusively to sense-data; and the inclusion of possible as well as actual sense-data among the elements of the material things must be taken to imply a recognition that some of these statements about sense-data will have to be hypothetical. . . .[23]

But this too generates a problem: what are sense-datum statements *about*? Presumably they are about sense-data. But then sense-data are existents after all, and *are* to be included in the complete inventory of the universe. Yet many phenomenalists wish to deny that sense-data are, like watches and trees, a part of the furniture of earth, and that they are "just a convenient way of talking." Talking about what? About immediate experience? Fine; but then immediate experiences do occur and *are* to be included in the inventory of existents, along with physical objects.

There is much vacillation on this important point: sometimes sense-data are spoken of as if they were a separate class of existents, and sometimes as if they were merely ingredients in propositions, or "ways of talking." This vacillation is made all the more curious by the fact that writers speak as if they could *stipulate* what characteristics sense-data have; for example, "Sense-data by definition have no properties other than those they appear to have." But if something exists, you don't stipulate its properties, you have to *discover* what they are.

[23] A. J. Ayer, *Foundations of Empirical Knowledge*, pp. 229, 231–32.

4. There are other puzzles too, which we need not dwell on separately. Aside from whether sense-data can enter into causal relations—which we have already discussed—we can ask, for example, (a) whether they are mental or physical. Or perhaps they are neither, but the raw material out of which both the mental and the physical are "constructed"? (This view is called "neutral monism.") (b) Do they occur in space? Not in physical space, it is said, but in phenomenal space (physical space is constructed out of phenomenal space). Very well, but (c) do they occur in time? Physical time? Or is there phenomenal time out of which physical time is "constructed," as in the case of space? But couldn't you clock, in physical time, how long a sense-datum lasts, for example how long you see a red spot before your eyes? Isn't its duration physical duration? (d) Then how long do they last? If you continue to see the red spot, is it one sense-datum spot, or many different identical spots replacing one another continuously? If the spot increases in size in your visual field, is it the same sense-datum as before or a different one (has the smaller sense-datum spot been replaced by a larger sense-datum spot)? Can the same red sense-datum move across a screen, or is it a different sense-datum at every moment of its journey because the spatial position is different? And does it remain the same sense-datum as long as it doesn't move or vary its size? (e) Can different people sense the same sense-data? Some say, "No, sense-data are by definition private." Others say, "Yes, if you and I stand in the same place we can both see (for example) the same after-image, not two after-images similar to each other." And so on.

How do we determine the duration of a sense-datum? If I blink my eyes while looking at a red patch, are there two sense-data separated in time, or is there only one interrupted in its career? If a change occurs in my visual field, has the sense-datum changed or been replaced by another? If the latter, is there any reason why, when no change is observed, a sense-datum should not be replaced by another exactly like it? It may be said that to answer these questions is not important. I am inclined to agree that it is not; but the only reason I can see for this is that, sense-data being wholly fictitious entities, we can attribute to them what qualities we please.[24]

Puzzles are followed by puzzles, with no apparent way of resolving them. The conclusion that many writers have drawn from this is that either (a) sense-data don't exist at all (they are a myth), or that (b) it doesn't make sense to say that there are sense-data or that there aren't, since the word has no discernible meaning to begin with—much as, if you were asked "Are there flubjubs or aren't there?" you would say "I can't understand the meaning of your question until you tell me what 'flubjub' means." Either of these conclusions, of course, would be fatal to the sense-datum theory.

[24] Winston H. F. Barnes, "The Myth of Sense-data," *Proceedings of the Aristotelian Society*, XLV (1944–45), 100. The author's term "sensum" has been replaced by the word "sense-datum" to preserve consistency of terminology.

There is one argument that has been used to clinch the case against sense-data—an exposure of one central fallacy that, in the opinion of the critics, if it had been avoided, would have prevented the term "sense-data" from being introduced in the first place. Sense-datum philosophers have argued as follows:

1. I see the coin.
2. The coin is round.
3. The coin appears elliptical to me.

Therefore, 4. I see an elliptical sense-datum.

But (so runs the criticism) this argument is fallacious. That the coin appears elliptical to me is no reason whatever for concluding that there is anything (a sense-datum) that *is* elliptical. There is just *nothing* in the situation described that *is* elliptical; there is nothing elliptical to be sensed. There *is* something—the coin—however, which, though it *is* round, *appears* to be elliptical. It is the coin that (a) *is* round and (b) *appears* elliptical. We don't need a sense-datum in the picture at all. There is no elliptical existent, only a round existent, the coin, which, however, appears elliptical from this angle. I am seeing the coin; in fact, I am seeing a round coin; but from this angle the coin does not appear round but elliptical. I cannot infer, from the fact that I am seeing something, and that it is round and looks elliptical, that there *is* an elliptical something (an elliptical sense-datum) at the place in my visual field where the round thing is (which appears elliptical).

"But no!" one may object. "The coin is round, granted; the coin from this angle appears elliptical, granted. So there *is* something elliptical—there is *an elliptical something* in my visual field, and that elliptical something is what we call a sense-datum. How could I see something elliptical unless there were an elliptical something to be seen?"

But this is just what the critic denies: there is no elliptical something at all, he says. There is only a round something, the coin, which appears elliptical. There is no reason why something should not have one property while appearing to have another: the distant trees look purplish but are green, the object looks small but is large, and so on endlessly. There are, to be sure, *ways of appearing* that an object has: but "modes of appearance are clues to the nature of what exists"; they are *not existents themselves*. It is improper to ask whether the elliptical mode of appearing (which is how the coin appears to me) *exists*. You can ask whether the coin exists, and whether it is round or elliptical, and in doing so you must consider how it appears under different conditions. But modes of appearance are not themselves existents; they are only evidence-providing material that we use to discover the nature of existent things.

What has happened? We have dispensed with sense-data entirely. There are no sense-data to appear: physical objects appear, and they have varying appearances depending on varying conditions of perception. This at any rate is the thesis of the *Theory of Appearing*. Physical objects appear, and their appearances are various. (How else would one expect it to be? Would you expect something to look equally large no matter how far away from it you were, or the same shape no matter what your angle of vision?) But there is no such thing as a sense-datum that *is* the appearance.

> *Objects themselves* appear to us in sense-perception. . . . When I see a circular penny as elliptical I am seeing the circular surface of the penny, not some elliptical substitute. This circular surface, it is true, appears elliptical to me, but that fact has no tendency to show that I am not directly aware of the circular surface. Aeneas was none the less in the presence of his mother Venus though she concealed from him the full glory of her godhead.[25]

Or again, when I see a red balloon, I may not see red (if I see it through a fog, or in twilight), but what I see is still a red balloon. I may not even know that it is a balloon at all—just as I don't know that the animal I'm watching at the zoo is a gnu—but it *is* a balloon just the same, and it *is* also a balloon that I am seeing even though I may not know *that* it is a balloon that I am seeing.[26]

Now let us try a more difficult case. I see double: I see two pennies when there is only one. Surely one of them must be only an *apparent* penny (a sense-datum penny?), since there are not two physical pennies. There appear to be two things, yet only one penny exists to do any appearing. It is not as if there were one penny, which looks one way from one angle and another from another: it is one penny that *looks* two. And twoness is not a property of one penny.

But the reply would be substantially the same as before: Being double can't be a property of one penny, but *looking* double can be. One penny can't be two pennies, but one penny can (under certain circumstances) appear to be any number of things, including two pennies.

We may feel a bit uncomfortable with this reply. When we see double, there are two apparent extended expanses. Are both expanses the surface of an object? If so, of what object, since *ex hypothesi* there is only one penny? Which is the real penny, and what is the status of the other one if we cannot bring in sense-data? But let us turn to a still more difficult case:

What of hallucinations? What happens when there is no coin there at all? Then what is it that appears? Apparently there is nothing to do the appearing. What of the dagger that Macbeth thought he saw?

> It is misleading . . . to say that there exists "a dagger-like appearance," though we need not be misled by such a use of the word "appearance" if we

[25] *Ibid.,* p. 112.

[26] Cf. G. J. Warnock, "Seeing," *Proceedings of the Aristotelian Society* 1954–55, and Roderick Chisholm, "The Theory of Appearing," in Max Black (ed.), *Philosophical Analysis* (Englewood Cliffs, N.J.: Prentice-Hall, Inc., 1963).

are careful. Strictly speaking, however, there are no such things as appearances. To suppose that there are would be like supposing that because Mr. X put in an appearance, there must have been something over and above Mr. X which he was kind enough to put in. "Mr. X appeared"; that is the proper mode of expression if we are to avoid difficulties.[27]

Whether this kind of reasoning is satisfactory has been disputed. It is true that there is nothing over and above Mr. X, for Mr. X himself appears—here there *is* something to do the appearing. But when there is no physical object at all, what does the appearing? It would seem that there is nothing at all, and that therefore the analogy between the situation of Mr. X and the hallucination does not hold. What, then, are we to do? Perhaps we must resort to sense data again—or, if this term is too theory-laden or immersed in invalid distinctions, we must resort to something we admittedly do have, and that is sense-*experiences*. And so the dispute continues.

Exercises

1. Is belief in Berkeley's God just as satisfactory an explanation of the order of our sense-experience as is the belief in enduring physical objects? Defend your opinion.

2. According to phenomenalism, "There is ice at the South Pole now" becomes, "If I were there, I could perceive . . ." etc. But no one is there now, so how do I know? Of course I could fly there and see; but then I would have verified the statement for a *later* time, t_2, when I arrive there—not for the original time, t_1, at which the statement was made. But at t_1 when I say the ice is there, I mean that it is there *now*, not later when I verify it.

Do you think this objection is fatal to phenomenalism? What do you think, and why, of the following reply? "It's true that I can't verify it until later, but nevertheless when I say the ice is there I mean that if someone were there *now* he would experience ice-data. And I *now* have reason to believe that this is true. I won't have direct evidence (seeing it) until later when I go there, but I have indirect evidence now—indirect, but evidence just the same."

3. What do you think of the following suggested way of eliminating the contrary-to-fact hypotheticals involved in phenomenalism? "By definition, sense-data exist only when sensed; but there are also *sensibilia*, which are just like sense-data except that they exist unsensed: sensibilia are sense-data that *would* be sensed if a person were in the right position, etc. Assume I am looking at the coin from an oblique angle and sensing an elliptical sense-datum; no other sense-data (of the coin) now exist. If I were to look at it from above, I would sense a round sense-datum; if from another angle, a sense-datum of a different ellipticity; etc. Now, all these potential sense-data are *actual sensibilia*, existing unsensed, waiting (as it were) to be sensed. To become aware of these sensibilia I would have only to fulfill certain conditions (change my position, get in a good light, etc.) required for sensing them. Only a small number of these sensibilia become actual sense-data; but they are all there, in an infinite array, all part of reality, and many sensibilia exist that will never be sensed at all because no one will be in the exact condition required to sense them."

[27] Winston H. F. Barnes, *op. cit.,* pp. 113–14.

4. Sometimes, when you have three shades of color, you can't detect any difference between A and B or between B and C, but you *can* detect a difference between A and C. Since for sense-data what appears is, you will say accordingly that (speaking of appearance only) A was identical with B and B was identical with C, but that A was not identical with C. But isn't it a necessary proposition that things identical to the same thing are identical to each other? (See A. J. Ayer, *Foundations of Empirical Knowledge*, pp. 131–34.)

5. Are any of the objections to phenomenalism based on mistakes or misunderstandings? If so, state them.

6. Do the objections to the use of the term "sense-datum", in your opinion, show that the term is meaningless, or that it should be deleted from the vocabulary of epistemology? Does it render phenomenalism untenable?

Selected Readings for Chapter 8

Armstrong, D. M., *Perception and the Physical World*. London: Routledge & Kegan Paul, Ltd., 1961.

Austin, John L., *Sense and Sensibilia*. London: Oxford University Press, 1962.

Ayer, Alfred J., *Foundations of Empirical Knowledge*. New York: The Macmillan Company, 1940. Chapters 1, 2 and 5. ·

———, "Phenomenalism," "Basic Proportions," and "The Language of Sense-data," in *Philosophical Essays*. New York: The Macmillan Company, 1955.

———, *The Problem of Knowledge*. New York: The Macmillan Company, 1956.

Barnes, Winston H. F., "The Myth of Sense-data," *Proceedings of the Aristotelian Society*, 45 (1944-1945).

Berkeley, George, *Three Dialogues between Hylas and Philonous*, 1713. Many editions.

———, *A Treatise Concerning the Principles of Human Knowledge*, 1710. Many editions.

Broad, C. D., *The Mind and Its Place in Nature*. London: Routledge & Kegan Paul, Ltd., 1925. Section B.

Chisholm, Roderick, *Perceiving: A Philosophical Study*. Ithaca, N. Y.: Cornell University Press, 1957.

———, "The Theory of Appearing," in Max Black (ed.), *Philosophical Analysis*. Englewood Cliffs: Prentice-Hall, Inc., 1963.

Ewing, Alfred C., *Idealism: A Critical Survey*. London: Methuen & Co., Ltd., 1934. Especially chapters 6 and 7.

———, (ed.), *The Idealist Tradition*. New York: Free Press, 1957.

Firth, Roderick, "Radical Empiricism and Perceptual Relativity," in *Philosophical Review*, 59 (1950).

———, "Phenomenalism," *American Philosophical Association, Eastern Division*, Vol. 1 (1952).

Hirst, R. J., *The Problem of Perception*. London: George Allen & Unwin, Ltd., 1959.

Hume, David, *A Treatise of Human Nature*, 1739. Book I. Many editions.

Lean, Martin E., *Sense-Perception and Matter*. London: Routledge & Kegan Paul, Ltd., 1953.

Lewis, Clarence I., *An Analysis of Knowledge and Valuation.* LaSalle, Ill.: Open Court Publishing Co., 1946. Especially chapters 7 and 8.

Locke, John, *Essay Concerning Human Understanding,* 1690. Book 2. Many editions.

Malcolm, Norman, *Dreaming.* London: Routledge & Kegan Paul, Ltd., 1959.

————, *Knowledge and Certainty.* Englewood Cliffs, N.J.: Prentice-Hall, Inc., 1963.

Marhenke, Paul, "Phenomenalism," in *Philosophical Analysis,* ed. Max Black. Ithaca, N. Y.: Cornell University Press, 1950.

Mill, John Stuart, *An Examination of Sir William Hamilton's Philosophy.* London: Longmans, Green & Company, Ltd., 1865. Chapters 11 and 12.

Montague, William P., *The Ways of Knowing.* London: George Allen & Unwin, 1925.

Moore, G. E., *Philosophical Papers.* London: George Allen & Unwin, Ltd., 1959. Chapters 2 and 7.

————, "The Refutation of Idealism," in *Philosophical Studies.* London: Routledge & Kegan Paul, Ltd., 1922. Also paperback.

Paul, G. A., "Is There a Problem about Sense-data?" in *Logic and Language,* First Series, ed. Antony Flew. Oxford: B. H. Blackwell, Ltd., 1959.

Pearson, Karl, *The Grammar of Science.* London: J. M. Dent & Sons, Ltd., 1892.

Price, H. H., *Hume's Theory of the External World.* London: Oxford University Press, 1940.

————, *Perception.* London: Methuen & Co., Ltd., 1933.

Prichard, H. A., *Knowledge and Perception.* London: Oxford University Press, 1950.

Quinton, A. M., "The Problem of Perception," *Mind,* 64 (1955).

Reichenbach, Hans, *Experience and Prediction.* Chicago: University of Chicago Press, 1938.

Russell, Bertrand, *The Problems of Philosophy.* London: Oxford University Press, 1912. Chapters 1–5.

————, *Our Knowledge of the External World.* London: George Allen & Unwin, 1914.

Ryle, Gilbert, *Dilemmas.* London: Cambridge University Press, 1954, Chapter 7.

Santayana, George, *Scepticism and Animal Faith.* New York: Charles Scribner's Sons, 1923.

Sellars, Wilfrid, *Science, Perception, and Reality.* London: Routledge & Kegan Paul, Ltd., 1963. Chapter 3.

Stace, Walter T., *The Theory of Knowledge and Existence.* Oxford: Clarendon Press, 1932. Chapter 6.

————, "The Refutation of Realism," *Mind,* 43 (1934). Reprinted in P. Edwards and A. Pap, *A Modern Introduction to Philosophy,* and in H. Feigl and W. Sellars, *Readings in Philosophical Analysis.*

Urban, Wilbur M., *Beyond Realism and Idealism.* London: George Allen & Unwin, 1949.

Warnock, Geoffrey, *Berkeley.* Baltimore: Penguin Books, Inc., 1953.

Whiteley, C. H., *An Introduction to Metaphysics.* London: Methuen & Co., Ltd., 1950.

9

Ethical Problems

Most of the statements we make in daily life are reports of some kind of fact or alleged fact: "There are five persons in this room," "Water boils at 212° F.," "4 × 4 = 16," "The helium atom has two electrons," "God exists," "I have a toothache," "She is conscientious"—these already are quite a diverse assortment. Some are particular, some general; some are about states of consciousness, some about external situations; some are about occurrent states, some dispositional; some are about observable entities, others can only be inferred from what is observed; some are empirical, some not. But they all purport to be statements of fact of one kind or another.

But now we come to statements that seem, at least, to be of a very different kind. If we say "The atomic bomb can kill millions of people," we are making a statement of empirical fact; but when we say "The use of the atomic bomb ought to be outlawed," we are making a statement not about what is but about what ought to be. If we say "That painting is in oils, with predominantly blue and green hues," we are making a statement of fact about the painting; but if we say "That painting is *good*," we are making a judgment of value about painting. It is easy to see how we would test the truth or falsity of the first statement in each pair, but how would we go about finding out whether the second one in each pair is true? There are similar differences between "This has gone on for three weeks" and "This has gone on too long," between "She has red hair" and "She is gorgeous," between "Health is desired" and "Health is desirable." What are we to say about the meaning of the latter sentence in each pair?

Not all propositions that ascribe value to something are ethical propositions, though ethical ones are the only ones we shall be concerned with in this chapter. The two fields of value-theory that have come to have a place in philosophy are ethics and aesthetics. In ethics we are concerned with matters of good and bad, right and wrong, duty and obligation, and moral responsibility. In aesthetics we discuss matters of aesthetic value (expressed sometimes by "this painting is good" and sometimes by "this painting is beautiful"), and also concepts such as aesthetic expression, the nature and function of critical judgment, artistic symbolism, meaning, truth, and aesthe*ic experience (all of these chiefly in the context of works of art). But many evaluative utterances, such as "That policy is economically sound," "She is gorgeous," and "This hat is worth keeping," seem to fall outside both these areas.

Even sentences containing the word "good," which is the central word in ethics, do not in the majority of cases express moral judgments. "I hope we'll have good weather today," "He is a good swimmer," "It's a good thing that he harvested the crops before the rains came," "He played a good game of baseball"—in these and countless other instances we use the word "good" without entering the sphere of morality at all. In general, when we say "This is a good X" we usually mean that X fulfills, to a higher degree than most X's, the criteria (whatever they are)for X's—whether the X is a tennis-player, an apple, a desk, an automobile, a road, or a college. The criteria differ from case to case, but the meaning of "good" does not.

But the word "good" is also used in moral discussions, and it is here that many problems arise. We use "good" in describing someone's *character:* "He is a good man." We also say that a person's *motives* and *intentions* are good or bad. We also speak of the *consequences* of a person's actions as good or bad. Most important, we speak of a person's ideals, goals, and *ends* as good or bad: "That is a good thing for him to aim at." On the other hand, we speak of what he does, his acts, as *right* or *wrong:* "He did right to return the money, though his motives in doing it may not have been good."

The main moral words we use in ethics are "good," "bad," "right," and "wrong." Concerning the meaning of these terms there has been no end of controversy. (1) The field of inquiry that considers the meaning (and inter-relations of meaning) of ethical words is called *meta-ethics.* Thousands of pages have been written in our century on meta-ethical questions; the problems often become extremely technical, and the inexperienced reader, who is after more appealing quarry, is apt to be left cold by these controversies. In any case, (2) the other main division of ethics, which has been prominent since the time of Socrates, Plato, and Aristotle, is *normative ethics,* which is the attempt to discover some acceptable and rationally defensible view concerning what kinds of things are good (worth aiming at) and what kinds of acts are right, and why (not to mention further topics, which we shall have no time to consider in this chapter, such as the conditions of moral praiseworthiness and blameworthiness, and of moral responsibility). To condense this enormous field into one brief chapter without being guilty of gross oversimplification will doubtless be impossible.[1] After an extremely cursory survey of meta-ethical problems in the first section of the chapter,

[1] Having written a book (*Human Conduct*) of almost half a million words that barely skims the surface of these problems, I am painfully aware how little can be accomplished in one chapter.

we shall consider two questions of normative ethics, "What is good?" and "What is right conduct?" in the remaining two sections.

27. Meta-ethical Theories

The principal meta-ethical theories are (1) ethical naturalism (or definism), according to which all ethical sentences (containing "good," "right," or other ethical words) are translatable without loss of meaning into non-ethical ones; (2) ethical non-naturalism, according to which at least some ethical sentences cannot be translated into any other kinds of sentences but constitute an autonomous class; and (3) ethical non-cognitivism, according to which ethical sentences do not express any propositions at all.

1. **Ethical naturalism.** According to all forms of ethical naturalism, ethical sentences can be translated into non-ethical ones; when you utter an ethical sentence your sentences can be translated without change of meaning into another sentence or series of sentences that do not contain any ethical terms. If such an analysis is successful, ethical terms can be eliminated from the vocabulary, leaving only non-ethical ones—just as "yard" can be replaced by "three feet" each time it occurs, with no sentences left containing the word "yard." The difficulty is to find any analysis of ethical sentences by means of which they can all be replaced by non-ethical ones without any change of meaning. Let us make a few attempts.

a. The autobiographical definition.   According to this theory, when I say that a certain act is right, I am only saying that I approve of it; saying that it is right and saying that I approve of it are the same thing. When I say it is right I am not really saying anything about the nature or quality of the act itself—I am only saying that I have a certain attitude toward it, the attitude of approval (or of moral approval, if indeed there is a distinct kind of approval that can be called "moral").

But this view is vulnerable to a number of objections. (1) If it is true, then no acts are right or wrong in themselves; there are only favorable or unfavorable attitudes toward them. Thus, if I want to know whether an act is wrong, I have only to introspect and see whether I approve it; if I do, it is right, and if I don't, it is wrong. If I approve it one day and disapprove it the next, then it is right one day and wrong the next. And if I approve it and you don't, then it is right for me and wrong for you. Anything, even killing, will become right for me if I can work myself into a state of approval toward it. This is surely the reverse of the procedure people ordinarily employ. A person may say "I approve this because it's right," but he will not say "It's right because I approve it." Indeed, might not one's approval be misplaced, unenlightened, or mistaken? Can I not know whether I approve something without knowing that it is right? And if I am in doubt whether to approve it, is this not because I am in doubt whether it is right? But if A is based on B, A is not the same as B. If I could convince myself that X is right, then I would approve it, but belief that it is right is not the same thing as the belief that I approve it. The attitude of approval is consequential upon the belief, not vice versa. What I want to know is not whether I approve something but whether my approval is justified. (2) If the view under consideration is true, there is never any disagreement about matters of ethics—and this is quite a conclusion to swallow, for nothing seems more patently true than that people do constantly disagree about these matters. Yet there can be no ethical disagreement on the present view: for if Mr. A says that act X is right, he means only that he, A, approves it; and if B says that X is wrong, he means only that he, B, disapproves it; and, far from contradicting one another, these two propositions (that A approves X and B does not) can both be true simultaneously. Indeed, both A and B usually know before the argument starts that they are both true (A knows that B disapproves X, and B knows that A approves), for that is why there is an argument in the first place.

The truth seems rather to be this: Ordinarily I do not say something is right *unless* I approve it, but it doesn't follow that what I *mean* by saying it is right is merely that I approve it. I don't talk about philosophy unless I am breathing, but when I talk about philosophy I am not talking about my breathing. Breathing is simply a necessary condition for talking about philosophy or about anything else.

b. The sociological definition.   According to this definition, "X is right" means the same as "The majority of people approve X." This has many variations: it may be the majority of people in my social group or in my country, or in the world now, or in the world during all the eras of history put together. How do you find out what is right? You take a poll. You find out how many approve the act in question, and once you know this, you know whether it is right.

But why should majority approval make an act right any more than it makes a scientific theory true? Cannot the majority be stupid, unenlightened, mistaken? Why should the majority view prove that an act is right any more than that the earth is flat? That the majority approves something is an interesting sociological fact, but it is of very little interest for ethics; in ethics we still want to ask whether or not the majority view is mistaken. Moreover, there must be something for the majority's belief to be about; and presumably what their belief is about is whether or not the act is right, not whether or not the majority of them approve it. There is genuine disagreement possible about what the majority approves, so that objection to the autobiographical theory is overcome, but unfortunately the belief is about the wrong thing. A minority who knew that the majority approved X would not conclude that X was wrong; they would conclude instead that the majority was mistaken.

c. The theological definition.   According to this definition, to say that X is right is to say that God approves it (or commands it): "X is right" is not an empirical statement, as in the two definitions above, but a theological statement. But even the theologically committed would do well to be aware of the implications of saying that "X is right" just means that God approves X. It implies that all ethical statements are disguised theological statements: that if a person says that something is right but does not believe in God, his statement is not only false but *self-contradictory,* for he would be saying that something is right (God approves it) but God does not exist—and surely nonbelievers have views about right and wrong, even if their views are all mistaken. To define "right" in this way is arbitrarily to legislate out of existence all views of nonbelievers in, or skeptics about, God's existence. It may be that everything that God approves is right, and vice versa, but is God's approval of it what is *meant* by saying that it is right? Socrates, in Plato's *Euthyphro,* would seem to have disproved that doctrine once and for all.

d. The ideal-observer definition.   To say that X is right, according to this definition, is to say that not you or I or the majority but an ideal observer would approve X. What is an ideal observer? Briefly, an ideal observer (or ideal judge) is one who (a) is impartial (unbiased) in regard to the question facing him (we shall have more to say about impartiality later), (b) has full knowledge of the facts of the situation being judged, and (c) can imaginatively identify with every person involved in the situation. If a person possessed these characteristics, he would be a perfect moral judge of any situation, being able infallibly to say what was right and what was wrong. Not only this, the ideal observer's pronouncement would tell the *meaning* of "right" and "wrong" (as long as this theory is considered meta-ethical). Knowing that the ideal observer approves X is the same as knowing that X is right.

This theory is doubtless an improvement over the previous ones; whereas it was not at all plausible to identify the rightness of an act with your or my approval of it, or indeed that of any individual or group, it might be reasonable enough to identify the rightness of X with what an ideal observer or judge would approve. Probably no such observer exists, since no one in the world is completely impartial, fully knowledgeable, and capable of full imaginative identification; but the theory does not require the existence of such a being—it says only that if there were such a being, his judgment would infallibly be correct. But the theory goes further: it says not only that the ideal observer's judgment would be the correct one in every case but that this would be so by definition—that this is the very meaning of the sentence "X is right." And here we may well object. "Perhaps," we may say, "what such an ideal judge would say would in fact always be correct (if it weren't you wouldn't call him an ideal judge), but this is surely not the meaning of saying that act X is right."

If the point of the objection is that the ideal-observer definition does not tell us what we consciously meant when we said that an act is right, the objection is surely justified: we probably never before heard of the ideal-observer theory, so we could not have meant any such thing when we said that an act was right. But, as we saw in Chapter 1, that we did not consciously mean something is no proof that a definition is inadequate; we may have been using a criterion for deciding whether something is an X without having formulated it to ourselves: it is enough that we used it as a criterion. But in the present case, does the ideal-observer definition suffice even in this sense? It would not seem that it does. The definition, indeed, tells us nothing about the nature of the act, X—it tells us what a perfect judge would say about X, but this tells us more about the judge than about the act that is judged. Sometimes we may be overwhelmed by the complexity and difficulty of a moral issue and say "If Mr. A, whose judgment I respect, and who has wider knowledge and a steadier mind than I, were here to judge it, I would accept his judgment as right"; but even though we might accept his judgment as the true one, we would not accept it as what we meant by "X is right" all along, or as the criterion we had been using all along for determining whether X was right. We have not all along used the verdict of the hypothetical ideal judge as a criterion, the way we used equidistance of all points from the center as the criterion for deciding whether a certain plane figure is a circle. If we already believe an act to be right, we shall then assent to the proposition that an ideal observer would approve it, but hardly the other way round: when we say that an ideal observer would approve it, we may then believe it is right, but not that this is what is meant by saying that it is right. When we say that X is right, we mean (or so it seems) that *X itself* has some property. The simplest of these views is:

e. The utilitarian definition. According to this definition, "X is right" means the same as "X will promote the maximum happiness" (in the long run, to all concerned). We shall examine the utilitarian theory in due course, as a theory of normative ethics; we are concerned with it here only as an attempt to render the meaning of "right" as a meta-ethical theory. It has at least the merit of defining "right" in terms of some property of the act itself (its tendency to produce happiness): an act is right if it has such-and-such consequences, those producing the maximum possible happiness for all concerned. (If we said "maximum possible *good,*" we would be defining one ethical term, "right," through the use of another, "good," and our definition would not be naturalistic.) But whatever may be said of this as a theory of normative ethics, it is very doubtful whether it will suffice as a *definition* of "right." Many ethical philosophers, for example, are not utilitarians; is their view not only false but self-contradictory? When they say that a certain act is right but does not produce maximum happiness, are they saying that it produces the maximum happiness but does not produce the maximum happiness? Even if non-utilitarian views of normative ethics are mistaken, they can hardly be ruled out by *definition*. Utilitarians may stipulate this definition, but non-utilitarians will simply reject it. Whatever the definition of "right" (if one can be found), it will not do to define it in such a way as to prejudge the truth of some special theory of what is right. One cannot make any special theory true simply by defining his terms in such a way as to make it analytic. This consideration would apply to utilitarianism and, it would seem, *any other* theory of normative ethics. If they can be defined at all, ethical terms must be defined in such a way as to leave the merits of one or another theory of normative ethics an *open question*.

   2.   Non-naturalism.   We are led, then, to a consideration of ethical *non-naturalism* (sometimes misleadingly called "intuitionism"). According to this view, at least some ethical terms are verbally indefinable. Even if (as seems unlikely in view of the preceding paragraph) "right" can be defined, say as "productive of the most good," at least "good" in its turn cannot be defined. There is no combination of non-ethical terms that will suffice as a translation of this term (or probably of "right" as well). As Henry Sidgewick said in his classic work *The Methods of Ethics*:

What definition can we give of 'ought,' 'right,' and other terms expressing the same fundamental notion? To this I should answer that the notion which these terms have in common is too elementary to admit of any formal definition. . . . The notion we have been examining, as it now exists in our thought, cannot be resolved into any more simple notions: it can only be made clearer by determining as precisely as possible its relation to other notions with which it is connected in ordinary thought, especially those with which it is liable to be confounded.[2]

   If you say that something has such-and-such consequences, you are making an empirical statement about it; but if you say that having such-and-such consequences is good, you are saying something quite different, and not translatable into any empirical statements at all. To say that X has such-and-such characteristics (is enjoyed, is desired, is approved by the speaker or by God or by the majority, etc.) is to say one thing; to say that X is good is quite another. To say that X is good is, indeed, roughly synonymous with saying that X is (not desired but) *desirable;* but then "desirable" is synonymous with "ought to be desired," and "ought" is again an ethical term. Non-naturalism does not say that ethical terms cannot be defined by means of *other* ethical terms—for example, "desirable" can be translated into "ought to be desired," and "right" might be translated into "ought to be approved" (which is very different from saying that it *is* approved); but this is only to define one ethical term by using another. What non-naturalism says is that one cannot define ethical terms exclusively by means of non-ethical ones—any more than one can define temporal words by means of others that make no reference to time, or words about magnitude by means of words making no reference to magnitude. "You can't get an ought out of an is" is the motto of

   [2] London: Macmillan & Co., Ltd., 1878, p. 23.

non-naturalism. Such words as "good," "right," and "ought" are so fundamental in ethics that there are no other words by means of which to define them: their own synonyms will not do, since these are ethical terms as much as the ones we are attempting to define.

G. E. Moore (1874–1958) attempted to refute all naturalistic theories by a famous device known as the "open-question technique." Regardless of what property of a thing you suggest as the meaning of an ethical term, he said, you are always open to the following objection: someone can always meaningfully grant that X has the property, A, in question and yet deny, or doubt, that it is good. One can always say "I grant that X has this property (by which you endeavor to define 'good'), but nevertheless, *is* X good?" I know that this person is supremely happy, but nevertheless, is happiness (always and everywhere) good? I know that this man is honest, but is honesty good? Perhaps the answer is yes; but even if it is, one cannot answer this simply on the basis of a preferred definition of "good" with which others might strongly disagree.

Indeed, says Moore, "good" is verbally indefinable, just as other words in our language, such as "yellow" and "pleasure," are verbally indefinable. To identify "good" with any "natural object" Moore calls the *naturalistic fallacy*.

Suppose a man says, "I am pleased"; and suppose that it is not a lie or a mistake but the truth. Well, if it is true, what does that mean? It means that his mind, a certain definite mind, distinguished by certain definite marks from all others, has at this moment a certain definite feeling called pleasure. "Pleased" *means* nothing but having pleasure, and though we may be more pleased or less pleased, and even, we may admit for the present, have one or another kind of pleasure; yet in so far as it is pleasure we have, whether there be more or less of it, and whether it be of one kind or another, what we have is one definite thing, absolutely indefinable, some one thing that is the same in all the various degrees and in all the various kinds of it that there may be. We may be able to say how it is related to other things: that, for example, it is in the mind, that it causes desire, that we are conscious of it, etc., etc. We can, I say, describe its relations to other things, but define it we can *not*. And if anybody tried to define pleasure for us as being any other natural object; if anybody were to say, for instance, that pleasure *means* the sensation of red, and were to proceed to deduce from that that pleasure is a color, we should be entitled to laugh at him and to distrust his future statements about pleasure. Well, that would be the same fallacy which I have called the naturalistic fallacy. That "pleased" does not mean "having the sensation of red," or anything else whatever, does not prevent us from understanding what it does mean. It is enough for us to know that "pleased" does mean "having the sensation of pleasure," and though pleasure is absolutely indefinable, though pleasure is pleasure and nothing else whatever, yet we feel no difficulty in saying that we are pleased.[3]

[3] *Principia Ethica* (London: Cambridge University Press, 1903), pp. 12–13.

But here emerges a difficulty: It is true that "pleasure" cannot be defined verbally, but it *can* be defined ostensively, and that is how it enters our language and its meaning is understood by many people. The word stands for a certain kind of experience that virtually everyone has. But "good," apparently unlike "yellow" and "pleasure," does not stand for an experience; one may indeed have an experience that we call "feeling good" (as when we are healthy, happy, and brimming with vitality), but that is not what "good" means in ethics.

One may object that "good" too can be defined ostensively: one may point to things that have this property. One may point to this honest person, to that kind deed, and so on. Perhaps so; but what is the property common to all those things being pointed to, wherein their goodness consists? Will not people disagree enormously on what this property is (or what these properties are)? One may point to kindness, another to indifference or hostility (or to things or situations in which these properties occur). And if one pointed to instances of honesty and so on, how would one show that these were also instances of goodness? There is, then, a difficulty about "good" that there is not about "yellow" and "pleasure": people agree on the meaning of "yellow" and "pleasure" even though they cannot define them, but this is notoriously not the case with "good" as used in discussions of ethics.

But if ethical sentences have a meaning that is not reducible to non-ethical ones, what is that meaning? It is just *different* from the meaning of any other kind of sentence. Sentences using "time," "event," "before," and other temporal words cannot be reduced to (translated without change of meaning into) sentences that do not contain any temporal words: temporal predicates are unique and not reducible to any other ones. Sentences in mathematics using terms like "number," "plus," and "equals" are similarly not reducible to any non-mathematical sentences (some of these terms can be translated into other ones within the realm of mathematics, but not into non-mathematical ones). And so on for many other sentences. In the same way, ethical sentences have a meaning different from any non-ethical sentences, and it would do violence to that meaning to attempt to translate them into any other sentences—whether empirical, theological, or any other. They are simply unique, and only by leaving the ethical terms alone (not trying to eliminate them in favor of non-ethical terms) can we preserve that uniqueness.

This is all very well, one may object; but still, isn't there a problem about ethical sentences (and of other value-sentences as well) that doesn't arise in the case of the others? What are the ethical sentences about? They are not about the speaker's feelings of approval toward the X in question, nor about any other feeling or attitude, nor about God's attitude toward X, nor about the consequences of X, nor about any other property of X that we can think of. True, says the non-naturalist, they are not about any of these things: they are about what is good, what is valuable, what is right, what one ought to do, what one should be commended for, what one is morally responsible for, and so on. "A thing is what it is and not another thing," said Bishop Butler 200 years ago; goodness is goodness and not anything else whatever. Ethics is autonomous, and not reducible to any other discipline.

Still, one remains puzzled. Taking a new tack, we may ask, how is one to know whether ethical propositions are true? We know how we discover whether propositions about time are true, such as "He arrived before she did." We know how we discover whether mathematical propositions are true, such as "$6 \times 3 = 6 + 6 + 6$." But how are we to discover whether ethical propositions are true? When people disagree about them, how is such disagreement to be resolved?

At this point some non-naturalists have said, in effect, "There is no empirical observation and no mathematical or logical calculation which would enable us to discover the truth of ethical propositions. All we can do is to distinguish them carefully from all other propositions (especially some empirical ones with which they are apt to be confused), and then reflect upon them and see whether, after this reflection, we believe that they are true.[4] Some have gone further and said that we can know by means of intuition that they are true (hence the title "ethical intuitionism" has become attached, mistakenly, to all forms of non-naturalism). But both these attempted answers are full of difficulties. Both "reflection" (whatever exactly this is supposed to involve) and "intuition" are extremely dubious as roads to knowledge, as our discussion of intuition (pp. 136–39) has shown, and open the way to all kinds of conflicting intuitions the correctness or incorrectness of which can never be determined. Must we leave the matter at that? Perhaps we can do nothing else, but is this not the counsel of despair?

Others, while remaining non-naturalists, have said that while ethical sentences cannot be reduced to or translated into any other kind of sentence, one can yet give good *reasons* for accepting some of them and rejecting others.[5] But this position too is not without its difficulties. What is the criterion for deciding what is a good reason? If "Because it will cause him needless suffering" is a good reason for saying "It is wrong to steal his wallet" but "Because you might get caught" is not (at least not a moral reason), why is this so? And how does one know this? Indeed, how can we know that p is a good reason for believing q unless we already know what q means? We cannot pursue this line of thought further here, but perhaps enough has been said to show that the problems of non-naturalism (whatever may be its merits in opposing the naturalist analysis) have not been disposed of by this new turn of argument.

3. Non-cognitivism. There is still another analysis of ethical sentences, non-cognitivism (sometimes called "the emotive theory"), according to

[4] See G. E. Moore, *op. cit.*, Chapter 1.
[5] See, for example, Stephen Toulmin, *The Place of Reason in Ethics.*

which the main function of ethical sentences is not to express propositions at all. When one says "X is good," one is not asserting anything, although the sentence looks like an assertion. But whereas the sentences "Snow is white" and "Jones is happy" are used to assert something (they express propositions that are either true or false), the sentence "Lying is wrong" does not express any proposition at all, and is not used by the speaker to assert anything. It does not even express the proposition that the speaker disapproves of lying. One can speak of ethical sentences (sentences that use ethical words) but not of ethical propositions, for no ethical sentences express propositions.

What then do ethical sentences do, if they do not express propositions? What is their function? Their function is to express the speaker's feelings and attitudes. In this respect they are not unlike screams, groans, and cries of joy—these too are human utterances, but they do not express propositions and are not used to assert anything. One uses them to vent one's feelings but not to say anything (not even about one's feelings). I use the sentences to purr or to snarl, and from this people may sometimes infer how I feel about the thing in question, without my having asserted anything—just as I may infer how you feel from your groans, or that a dog is pleased from his wagging tail. The utterance provides an "inference-ticket," but not by means of any assertion. One can make inferences from many things other than assertions.

This view should not be confused with the autobiographical version of ethical naturalism. To express an attitude or feeling is not the same as to state that you have one. "Hurrah!" expresses joy, but "I am feeling joyous" is an autobiographical sentence asserting that one has the feeling. The speaker uses the second to state a proposition, but not the first. But a listener could use either set of words to make an inference about how the speaker feels.

If I say to someone, "You acted wrongly in stealing that money," I am not stating anything more than if I had simply said, "You stole that money." In adding that this action is wrong I am not making any further statement about it. I am simply evincing (expressing) my moral disapproval of it. It is as if I had said, "You stole that money," in a peculiar tone of horror, or written it with the addition of some special exclamation marks. The tone, or the exclamation marks, adds nothing to the literal meaning of the sentence. It merely serves to show that the expression of it is attended by certain feelings in the speaker.[6]

A non-cognitivist need not, however, limit himself to the view that ethical utterances serve only to *express* the feelings or attitudes of the speaker. He may also hold that they can be used to *evoke* feelings or attitudes in the listener, as when the mother says to her child "Telling lies is wrong," not so much to express her own attitude toward lying as to instill in the child an unfavorable attitude toward lying. The propaganda use of ethical words and

[6] Alfred J. Ayer, *Language, Truth, and Logic,* p. 158.

sentences is usually evocative rather than expressive—indeed, the speaker himself may not even have the attitude (toward the thing in question) that he is trying to evoke in his hearers. Nor need ethical utterances be construed on the analogy with screams, cries, and groans: they may be construed as *commands*. Thus "Stealing is wrong" could be construed as equivalent to "Don't steal!" which, being a command, is neither true nor false. Ethical utterances may be used to express, to evoke, to command, to suggest, to entreat, to cajole, and a vast variety of other things—all of them equally compatible with the non-cognitivist theory, for what these functions all have in common is the negative characteristic, distinctive of non-cognitivism, that they are not used to state any propositions.

This, then, is the pure or unmixed non-cognitivist theory. But virtually no one today is a pure non-cognitivist. Non-cognitivism has been combined with the other meta-ethical theories that we have already described. Thus a person might say that ethical sentences are used to express and evoke attitudes but also to state certain facts. For example, "X is right" might be translated as "I approve of X; do so as well."[7] The first is a naturalistic definition (the autobiographical one), according to which the sentence is used to state a fact about the speaker; the second is non-cognitivist, a command (which is neither true nor false).

Indeed, once the fact is pointed out, it is difficult to deny that ethical sentences are used to express the speaker's attitudes, to evoke attitudes in the hearer, and so on; one has only to observe parents using ethical sentences in the education of their children to be convinced that this is how they are being used (at least on these occasions)—and the same is true of adults talking with one another ("I don't feel that you should do this—it's wrong," etc.), persuading and counter-persuading, attempting to influence and counter-influence, using the ethical sentences as counters in the game of expressing their own attitudes and influencing those of others. That ethical sentences are often so used seems obvious indeed; that they are typically so used seems almost as obvious. When a child learns how to use ethical words and sentences, he does not learn anything about the properties of the thing, X, that is called good or bad, right or wrong; he knows only that what is called "bad" is something he's not supposed to do, and that the sentence is to be uttered with the appropriate expression of revulsion or condemnation.

Must we all then be non-cognitivists? No; granting that ethical sentences are used in this way does not commit us to non-cognitivism, but only to the conclusion that there is a non-cognitive component in the meaning of ethical sentences. Whether one is a non-cognitivist or not (not a pure but a mixed or modified one) depends not on whether one believes that ethical sentences are used expressively or evocatively at all, but on whether one believes that this non-cognitive function is *primary*. One is still a non-cognitivist if one believes

[7] C. L. Stevenson, *Ethics and Language* (New Haven, Conn.: Yale University Press, 1944), p. 21.

that the primary function of ethical sentences is non-cognitive, even though the sentence may also function in an auxiliary manner to describe certain features of X. You may believe that "Stealing is wrong" (1) expresses the speaker's attitude toward stealing *and* also (2) describes certain consequences of stealing; but in spite of the cognitive component (the second), you would still be a non-cognitivist as long as you believed that the first function is primary: that is, if you believed that the speaker would withdraw his sentence if he were no longer using it to express his disapproval of stealing, even though his view of the consequences of stealing (the descriptive component) had not changed.

One such view is that of R. M. Hare in his book *The Language of Morals*. The primary function of the sentence "X is good," according to this view, is to *commend*. When we hear someone utter the sentence "X is good," we do not yet know anything about the properties of X, but we do know that the speaker is commending X (for whatever reason). This commendatory meaning of "good"—which is reflected in dictionaries, which call "good" the "most general term of commendation in the language"—is the primary one: when we use it we are always commending the thing we call good. But the thing we commend also has certain properties, and it is in virtue of these features that we commend it. Saying that X is good, then, is (1) commending X (this part is non-cognitive) and (2) saying that it has certain properties (this part is cognitive). But the first one is the primary one; we may later commend Y rather than X, or commend X for having properties other than those for which we originally commended it. The *descriptive* (or cognitive) meaning of "good" thus varies from case to case, while its *evaluative* (or commendatory) meaning remains the same.

When we call a motor-car or a chronometer or a cricket-bat or a picture good, we are commending all of them. But because we are commending all of them for different reasons, the descriptive meaning is different in all cases. We have knowledge of the evaluative meaning of "good" from our earliest years; but we are constantly learning to use it in new descriptive meanings, as the classes of objects whose virtues we learn to distinguish grow more numerous. . . .[8]

Since the non-cognitive part (the commending) remains constant even while the cognitive part (the descriptive) changes,

. . . we can use the evaluative force of the word in order to *change* the descriptive meaning for any class of objects. This is what the moral reformer often does in morals; but the same process occurs outside morals. It may happen that motor-cars will in the near future change considerably in design (e.g., by our seeking economy at the expense of size). It may be that then we shall cease giving the name "a good motor-car" to a car that now would rightly and with the concurrence of all be allowed that name. How, linguistically speaking,

[8] R. M. Hare, *The Language of Morals*, p. 118.

would this have happened? At present, we are roughly agreed (though only roughly) on the necessary and sufficient criteria for calling a motor-car a good one. If what I have described takes place, we may begin to say "No cars of the 1950's were really good; there weren't any good ones till 1960." Now here we cannot be using "good" with the same descriptive meaning as it is now generally used with; for some of the cars of 1950 do indubitably have those characteristics which entitle them to the name "good motor-car" in the 1950 descriptive sense of that word. What is happening is that the evaluative meaning of the word is being used in order to shift the descriptive meaning; we are doing what would be called, if "good" were a purely descriptive word, re-defining it. But we cannot call it that, for the evaluative meaning remains constant; we are rather altering the standard. This is similar to the process called by Professor Stevenson "persuasive definition."[9]

The same process, of course, occurs in ethics. In ethics as well as elsewhere, "good" is a term of commendation, of favorable evaluation; a person would not use the word "good" if he were not commending or favorably evaluating. But the word also carries a descriptive meaning—a very general one, but a descriptive meaning nevertheless. When we say that X is good, we are (1) commending X (if we ceased to commend it we would cease to call it good) and (2) saying, at least implicitly, that anything else exactly like X, or like it in the relevant respects, would also be good—that is, we could not say that X was good and yet say that something exactly like X was not good. If we did, we would be guilty of self-contradiction; for to say that X is good is implicitly to say that other things exactly like X (or like it in the relevant respects) are also good: we could not without contradiction hold the one and withhold the other.[10] To say that X is good is implicitly to utter a universal proposition about all things of a certain kind; there is a universalizability built into the very meaning of "good." We shall have more to say about universalizability later in this chapter.

Exercises

1. Can you think of any naturalistic theories of the meaning of "right" (or "good") which are more plausible than those we have considered in this chapter?

2. Are the following theories naturalistic (definitions of ethical terms in non-ethical terms)? Do you consider them satisfactory? Explain.

    a. What's good is what I feel good after.
    b. The good is the desirable.
    c. The good is what a rational person would desire.
    d. A right act is one that is approved by God.
    e. A right act is one that my conscience says "yes" to.
    f. A right act is an act which one ought to perform.

[9] *Ibid.*, p. 119.

[10] See Hare, *Freedom and Reason,* Chapter 2. (We have discussed persuasive definitions on pp. 53–54.)

g. A wrong act is one that violates someone's rights.

h. The good is that at which all men aim.

3. Do you agree with non-naturalists that ethical terms must be defined (if at all) in such a way as to leave open the question of whether a given view of normative ethics is correct?

4. What kind of assertion is "The infliction of needless pain and suffering is evil"? Is it analytic or synthetic? a posteriori or a priori? Is it a proposition at all? Justify your answer.

5. If "good" and other ethical words are verbally indefinable (into non-ethical terms), what follows? That they mean nothing? that they must be definable ostensively? that they refer to non-sensible qualities? that they have emotive meaning only and do not stand for qualities at all?

6. "If a person first believes that killing is never right (strict pacifism), and later comes to believe that it is sometimes right (however rarely), he has surely changed his mind about the wrongness of killing. His present belief is incompatible with his former belief. This alone is enough to prove that the sentence 'Killing is always wrong' expresses a *proposition*—and thus that the pure emotive theory is false. If he had one belief, and now has another which is logically incompatible with it, he must have believed a proposition to be true which he now believes to be false. The emotive theory cannot account for so simple and ordinary a fact." Comment on this argument.

7. "Suppose a person once believed in strict pacifism, and then changes his mind. His view about the facts of the matter need not have changed at all: he may still have the same views about (for example) the consequences of killing that he did before. All that need have changed is that he now approves of killing (in some circumstances, at least) whereas previously he did not. So he now uses the ethical sentence 'Killing is sometimes right' to express his present approval of killing in some circumstances, whereas he formerly said 'Killing is always wrong' to express his disapproval of killing under all circumstances. This shows, then, that the emotive theory is true: we use ethical sentences to express (and evoke) certain attitudes toward the thing in question." Comment on this argument.

8. Evaluate Mill's argument: "The only proof that a thing is visible is that people see it. The only proof that a thing is audible is that people hear it. In the same way, the only proof that a thing is desirable is that people desire it."

28. Theories of Goodness

Whatever our meta-ethical conclusions may be, let us turn now to normative ethics. Instead of inquiring about the meanings of ethical terms, let us consider to what things these terms are applicable. Philosophers appear to disagree much more on the designation of the word "good" (and other ethical words) than they do on at least some of the denotations of the word. (We have encountered this situation before, p. 47.)

In this section we shall consider some views on the question "What kinds of things are good?" (theories of goodness), and in the next section we shall consider some views on the question "What kinds of acts should one perform?" (theories of conduct). But before we inquire what things can be called good and bad, and why, it may be helpful at the outset to ask a few questions about *value*. The attempt to give a satisfactory definition of "value" is an unexpectedly difficult and tricky business, which space does not permit us to enter upon here; it belongs to the domain of theory of value, of which ethics and aesthetics are special branches.

There would be no judgments about what is good and bad if people did not *value* certain things above others. In the simplest sense, I value something if I like it or if I prefer it to something else. The dog values the bone more than he does the grass, but the cow values the grass more than the bone. Some people value excitement more than security; others, security more than excitement. To value something it is not necessary that a *judgment* of value be made: the cat values the cream but presumably makes no judgment about the value of the cream. But valuing does presuppose being conscious, since liking or caring about something is a conscious state. Thus the concept of value would have no application on an uninhabited planet; it arises only when there are conscious beings who have interests—likings and dislikings, pro-attitudes and anti-attitudes. In its most primitive sense, "I value this" is approximately synonymous with "I like this," "I prefer this."

However, we also speak of value in another sense, when no conscious state such as liking or preferring is present. We say that a man's health is of value to him, even though he acts in such a way as to undermine or destroy it. We say that continuance in alcoholism is of disvalue to him, though the man continues to prefer it. We say to a student "It would be of value to you to buckle down and study instead of wasting your time," though the student's felt preference is for loafing. What *is* of value to you in the attainment of some goal is not necessarily what you prefer. That which one values (subjectively) is one thing, and that which is (objectively) of value to him is another. Thus far, then, we have isolated two senses of "value": (1) a liking or preference, and (2) that which promotes a goal (end) independently of one's liking or preference. (Exactly the same ambiguity can be found in the word "interest": what we take an interest in is one thing, and what it is to our interest to pursue is another. The main task of Plato's moral philosophy was to discover what kind of life is to our interest$_2$ to lead, so that we might thereby take an interest$_1$ in pursuing it.)

Is the concept of value applicable to plants? In the second sense, yes: soil and moisture and warmth are of value to the plant in the preservation of its life, since without these things the plant would die; plants exhibit teleological behavior even though they do not, presumably, envision any goals. But in the first sense, no: unlike animals, plants do not (so far as we can tell) have consciousness, hence they do not have likings and preferences.

Plants and non-human animals act *as if* they were concerned that their activity . . . should maintain itself. Even atoms and molecules show a selective bias in their indifferencies, affinities and repulsions when exposed to other events. With respect to some things they are hungry to the point of greediness; in the presence of others they are sluggish and cold. It is not surprising that naïve science imputed appetition . . . to all natural processes. . . . In a genuine although not psychic sense, natural beings exhibit preference and centeredness.[11]

But the story is not yet over. Certain things are of value to one's health, others to success in one's work, still others to one's peace of mind. What things are of value in each context varies somewhat from one individual to another, but in each case they are facts of reality independent of our preferences. But, one may object, we still haven't shown that these things (health, success in one's work, etc.) are *themselves* valuable: all we have shown is that certain things are *means* toward the achievement or attainment of certain other things. But what about those other things? Proper diet is a means toward health; but is health valuable? We all tend to assume that it is, but how could we prove this? Health may indeed be valuable as a means toward something else, such as happiness or peace of mind; but then how do we prove that these things in turn are valuable? The "objective" sense of "value" we considered thus far—A is valuable in the attainment of B—simply reduces to the empirical statement that A is a means to B (a necessary condition for B or at least conducive to B). If you aim at B, then A is a means toward it, and therefore of value in the pursuit of it; but if you aim at D, then a different set of things, C, will be of value in the pursuit of D. But aren't there things that are of value regardless of what we are aiming at? Is the valuableness of something always relative to some end? It would seem that we are here using "value" in yet another sense: (3) that which has value or worth in itself, without reference to any end. If something is of value in this sense, it is not valuable merely in the sense that it is conducive to something else but is valuable, period, not merely relative to the end in question. But *is* anything valuable in this sense? Most philosophers have answered this question in the affirmative, although they have not always agreed on what things possess this kind of value.

Intrinsic and instrumental good.   Some things, these philosophers have held, are valuable, desirable, worthwhile, worth having, *good* for their own sakes, whereas other things are good only insofar as they lead to these things. (They need not be *morally* good—that is a later question.) If you were to compile a list of things you considered desirable, worthwhile, or good, you might include such things as security, peace, money, pleasure or enjoyment or happiness, knowledge, honesty, kindness, intelligence, affection, beauty. But not all these things would be of the same kind. You might desire all these things, but not in the same way: some of them you want for their own sakes alone (not as a means toward anything else), and some you want because

[11] John Dewey, *Experience and Nature* (New York: Dover Publications, Inc.), p. 208.

having them is a means to the attainment of the things you desire for their own sakes. If you think money is good, it is good only for other things that it will help to bring: material comforts, release from drudgery, freedom from certain fears for the future, a measure of peace and happiness. If money could not bring you any of these things, there would be no point at all in having it. To the extent that it is good at all, money is clearly an *instrumental* good; we do not desire it for its own sake but only for the sake of other things that it will enable us to have. It was of no use to Robinson Crusoe.

Are all these things that money brings worth having for their own sake? What about the material comforts that money can buy—are they desirable in themselves? Surely not: if we are asked "But why do you want these things?" we can give an answer, such as "Because if I have them I will be happier." We still want them for the sake of something else. What about happiness? This seems to be the one thing we value for its own sake—we want other things in order to be happier, but happiness is something we desire for itself. If someone were to ask "But what do you want to be happy for?" we would feel that the question was strange, and we might hardly know what to answer. We don't want happiness *for* anything else at all—we just want to be happy, that's all. We don't aim at it in order to get other things—we aim at other things in order to get *it*.

By contrast, when you endure the pain of the dentist's drill, you do not consider it worth enduring for its own sake: you bear it only because you believe it will lead to certain results, such as health and cessation of pain. If you didn't think it would have this effect, you would not go. (Even the masochist doesn't enjoy pains in general such as headaches—he enjoys only those physical pains that bring him the experience of pleasure.) In general, you go to doctors and dentists to sustain or restore your health. "But why do you desire health?" This question too may sound strange, because we usually assume without question that health is a desirable state; but if asked you *could* doubtless give an answer, such as "Because if I am constantly having aches and pains, I can't enjoy life, I can't be happy, or at least not as happy as if I am not bothered by these things." But then we are back to happiness again, as something worth having itself, for its own sake.

Pleasure and happiness.   Sometimes we speak of pleasure, and sometimes of happiness; what exactly is the difference? Pleasure is a certain kind of state of consciousness (not verbally definable), a psychological state with which we are all acquainted in our own experience. We speak of the pleasures of eating, drinking, sexual experience, taking a walk in the country, reading a good book, contemplating works of art, mastering a new concept, engaging in conversation with friends. All these things are *sources* of pleasure, but the pleasure that results from each of these activities is somewhat different in each case; yet they are all similar enough to be called "pleasure." "A life of pleasure" need not mean (as when this phrase is used by the puritan) a life of sensual abandon; the pleasures of acquiring understanding, of solving mathematical problems, of religious experience, of listening to music are sometimes not as intense at the time but are usually longer lasting than the purely physical pleasures, such as eating and drinking. The opposite of pleasure can best be called *displeasure* rather than pain, since pain is ordinarily a *source* of displeasure (but not to the masochist, for whom some pains are sources of pleasure), and not the only source at that: the irritations we encounter in our daily life (such as being caught in a traffic jam) can hardly be called pains, but they cause considerable displeasure nonetheless.

Now what of happiness? We do not use the word "happiness" synonymously with "pleasure." We speak of an intense pleasure lasting for a few seconds and then ceasing, but it would be strange to speak of being happy for a few seconds and then becoming unhappy and then happy again a few seconds later. And a person may experience many such pleasures without being happy. The relation of pleasure to happiness is rather like that of part to whole: happiness consists of a *sum* of pleasures. A person may experience numerous pleasures without being happy, but he cannot be happy without experiencing pleasure from some source or other: a happy person is one who has many pleasures, usually from diverse sources. A person may enjoy books and not be happy, and have many pleasant sex experiences and yet not be happy; but if he has these things *and* a benevolent attitude toward life, and if he does not expect the impossible of reality, and if his behavior is guided by knowledge (so that he is not constantly in danger of unexpected catastrophes that he could have avoided), and so on, then he is probably happy. Some sources of pleasure, of course, count much more toward happiness than do others; one's basically healthy attitude toward life and a sunny disposition, which are with one from day to day throughout the years, are much more conducive to happiness than are fame and glamour or the pleasures of Lothario.[12]

Hedonism.   According to the ethical philosophy of hedonism (from the Greek *hedone,* "pleasure"), (1) all pleasure is intrinsically good, and (2) *only* pleasure is intrinsically good—that is, worth having for its own sake. In view of our conclusion about the relation of pleasure to happiness, we can extend the hedonistic doctrine to include happiness, since it consists of pleasures (the sum of pleasures), and thus say that according to hedonism happiness is the sole intrinsic good.

This doctrine, however, is easily misinterpreted. The word "pleasure" carries a somewhat unfavorable secondary meaning, and the phrase "a life of pleasure" has come to signify something more appropriate to pigs than to men. It is important, therefore, to remember that "pleasure" includes *any* kind of satisfaction, not merely that which comes from food, drink, and sex. Hedonism simply says that the more pleasure there is in the world the better,

[12] For a fuller account of the relation between pleasure and happiness, see John Hospers, *Human Conduct,* pp. 111–16.

and that the life containing the most intrinsic good is the one that contains the most pleasure and the least displeasure. But we must be careful here: (1) It doesn't mean that one should consciously aim at pleasure during all one's waking life. Very often "Happiness to be got must be forgot," and if one goes about one's daily work without thinking particularly about happiness, one is much more likely to find it (to be happy) than if he goes about consciously seeking it. (2) Often many activities must be engaged in that are sources of considerable displeasure, as a necessary *means* toward the achievement of greater pleasure in the end. Sometimes one's work may be unpleasant, but if one sticks with it he has the satisfaction of financial security, of being able to buy with his income certain things he would enjoy having, of having performed a task well, and so on. Sometimes one must endure great displeasure in order to make certain necessary conditions for happiness possible: one must discipline oneself and learn to study hard and efficiently in order to acquire the knowledge and skill required for becoming a physician; one must often endure a certain unpleasantness at the outset in order to enjoy throughout one's lifetime certain kinds of music; one may even have to fight for the preservation of liberty, in the conviction that without liberty life is not worth living. (3) Sometimes indulging in a pleasure will decrease the chances of being able to enjoy pleasure later. Eating the tasty dessert may bring indigestion, and knowing this, one does without this pleasure. Nor would one recommend that thieves and murderers be given a great many sources of pleasure in prison, since this would make prison attractive enough to many others to lead them to commit crimes in order to enjoy the pleasures possible in prison. Shipping all prisoners to Tahiti might start a crime-wave (not to mention its effect upon the Tahitians). It is the maximum pleasure in the long run, over an entire life-span, that one should try to achieve (one's own pleasure if one is an egoist, the pleasure of everyone if one is a utilitarian—this will be discussed in the next section when we consider theories of conduct).

According to the hedonist, then, pleasure and happiness are always intrinsically good. They may not, however, always be instrumentally good. By saying that they are intrinsically good we mean that they are always good as ends in themselves, without considering their effects. Even the pleasure the ax-murderer gets from killing his victim is *intrinsically* good: it is good when considered alone, simply as an instance of pleasurable experience. But since such pleasurable experiences, if encouraged, would lead to considerable extinction of human life (and hence of all possibility of the victims' future happiness), every measure should be taken to make sure that no such pleasures are enjoyed, *not* because they are not intrinsically good but because they are instrumentally so catastrophic in the extreme displeasure to all concerned that they cause in the long run. In the light of the ideal, of maximizing the total amount of happiness in the world, such pleasures tend to inhibit this ideal rather than to promote it—they are like getting a penny (which *is* money, just as the ax-murderer does have pleasure) when if one had not taken the penny one could have had a hundred dollars. Another example: Suppose that the amount of pleasure one person gets out of reading Shakespeare's *King Lear* is the same as another person gets from breaking a roomful of crockery. Then the two pleasures are equally intrinsically good. Yet the first is far preferable to the second, because the first is conducive to more intrinsic good in the future than the second: the crockery must be paid for by someone, and the breaking of it may reinforce the pleasure of doing it, thus leading to more breaking or other forms of destructiveness; while the reading of *King Lear* reinforces the pleasures of reading great works of art (which, unlike breaking the crockery, harms no one) and may also increase one's wisdom in the art of living, which may well increase one's long-term happiness. The potential of the two events for *future* happiness is, thus, far different.

There are many other things that the hedonist would consider good, but only pleasure and happiness would be considered *intrinsically* good. Works of art are good in that they provide the possibility of pleasant aesthetic experiences: works of art are not intrinsically good, only the pleasurable *experience* of them is. (Works of art experienced·by nobody would have no intrinsic value—only experiences have intrinsic value. They are sometimes said to have a special kind of instrumental value, *inherent* value, since the contemplation of them is itself pleasant; hammers, by contrast, have no inherent value because the contemplation of them is not itself pleasant, but they have instrumental value in that they have a utility for human purposes, such as building houses, which in turn leads to greater happiness.) Money is instrumentally good if it adds to the sum of human happiness, though it can also be instrumentally bad, depending on what it is used for. Productive work is instrumentally good, not only for the satisfaction the work itself may bring (inherent value) but for the income it makes possible, which in turn can be used in the furtherance of one's happiness. Many things, of course, are instrumentally good in some situations and not in others; each situation would have to be evaluated on its own for its long-term happiness-potential.

Among the things that are instrumentally good (in the hedonist view) are *moral qualities*—honesty, benevolence, industriousness, and so on. In general, moral qualities are those that tend to make oneself or other people better human beings; but there is no sharp line between moral and non-moral qualities. (Is thrift a moral quality?) But the main point of the hedonist with regard to these desirable qualities is that their good is exclusively *instrumental*. Courage is not good in itself but only because it leads (sometimes) to situations in which the world's happiness is increased (or a threat to it is removed). Honesty is good, but not in itself: a world in which people can trust one another in their financial and other dealings is a better world (a happier world) than one in which no one could trust anyone else. Conscientiousness is often an instrumental good, though in the case of the conscientious Nazi it is an instrumental evil, since it tends to promote the evils of the system in whose behalf one is conscientious; in any case, its value is not intrinsic—there is nothing good about conscientiousness in itself—it is good (when it is) only because it leads to more intrinsic good. The acquisition of knowledge is in general good, but it can also be evil, depending on the purposes for which it is used; in any case, when it is good, its goodness is instrumental—knowledge that adds to the sum of happiness is good, knowledge that does not is not. Whether it is or is not is often impossible to tell at the time the knowledge is acquired: knowledge of principles of physics has been of enormous value in human life, yet withuot it hydrogen bombs could not have been made.

What about undeserved happiness—the happiness (such as it is) of the criminal who gets away with his crime, or of the person who wins a contest by cheating? Like all happiness, it is intrinsically good—good when considered alone, apart from its consequences. If such happiness had no ill consequences, it would be just one more bit of good in the world. But of course it does have ill consequences: the person who deserved to win (by the standards of the contest) did not win and is deprived of the satisfaction; and every criminal who gets away with his crime paves the way for the robbery or death of many other innocent victims.

Ethical pluralism. Most opponents of hedonism do not deny that pleasure and happiness are intrinsically good, but they would accept other candidates for this position as well. Let us examine two of the main ones:

a. Knowledge. It is not truth but knowledge for which intrinsic goodness is sometimes claimed. True propositions are of no value unless someone knows that they are true. But once they are known to be true, we can act on this knowledge. If you know that a certain disease is contagious, you can avoid exposing yourself; if you know that the exhaust fumes of a car contain carbon monoxide, and that carbon monoxide is poisonous, you will avoid excessive use of the motor when the garage door is shut. Knowledge makes the difference between the Stone Age and a civilized society. The value of knowledge in human life is inestimable. But is it intrinsic value?

"Yes," replies the pluralist. "Knowledge is not only an instrument in the advance of human civilization, it is also worth having for its own sake. Knowledge is a good thing to have, even if it does not add to your happiness or that of the world. You may study philosophy or mathematics or one of the empirical sciences simply to acquire knowledge, not in order to increase your or the world's happiness (though it can be used to promote this also). Perhaps those who have studied one of these subjects are no happier than those who haven't; still, the subject was worth studying, simply because it represents an addition to human knowledge. The more one knows, and the more knowledge there is in the world, the better—provided it is genuine knowledge and not pure assumption or superstition. It is good to have knowledge, even if that knowledge leads to no increase of happiness for oneself or for anyone else."

But the hedonist is not convinced. "Though a great good," he says, "knowledge is still only instrumental, like liberty; it is not good in itself, it only makes certain intrinsic goods possible. When knowledge is good at all, it is instrumentally good; nor is it even that under all circumstances. Should the incurably ill person be told that he is incurably ill? Most people would doubtless prefer to know, but every case should be judged on its own merits. Should a person who is too old to change be told that he is a stupid hypocrite, whose desperate rationalizations are believed by nobody? It would make him unhappier than he is already, with no good purpose being served by such a reminder, even though the reminder is true. Should a man whose life revolves around his love for his wife be told the truth, that she doesn't love him but loves someone else instead? Perhaps, if this will help prepare him for her absconding with the other man, or if it will help him make himself more lovable to her. But perhaps not, if there's nothing he can do about it; at least while he is working on his important project he should not have this knowledge, for it would tear him apart and render him incapable of completing it. There are circumstances in which knowledge, far from being an intrinsic value, is not a value at all; and whether it is depends on its happiness-potential. It is the happiness that is intrinsically good, not the knowledge. The goodness of knowledge depends on its happiness-potential. Even when it is good, it is not intrinsically good."

"But consider this situation," says the pluralist. "Here is a man with a true belief, and there is a man with a false belief; each belief provides the man who has it with equal happiness. Surely the situation of the first man is *better* than that of the second. Indeed, I would go further and say that it would be better if the second man were made so unhappy by his false belief that he would investigate it and discover it to be false than that he would be satisfied with his belief."

"In *intrinsic* worth the two do not differ at all," replies the hedonist; "but they differ enormously in their potential for *future happiness* (and avoidance of unhappiness). The man who is made happy by a false belief is playing a dangerous game with reality; the facts of reality are against him and may trip him up. If he believes he is the world's greatest chemist (assuming that he is not), he will feel unjustly treated when he doesn't get the best jobs, and finally will believe that everyone is persecuting him and not recognizing his greatness. If he believes falsely that his wife loves him, he will be in for a shock when she leaves him or reveals the truth. But it is only because false beliefs, unlike true ones, are like an unexploded time-bomb with respect to future happiness that they are so much to be deplored. All this, however, can be perfectly accounted for by hedonism."

"But of course you haven't proved your case. I could still be right in saying that knowledge is an intrinsic value, but believe at the same time that sometimes this intrinsic value is more than counterbalanced by the negative intrinsic value of the unhappiness it causes, especially when the situation is one that cannot be remedied by telling the person the truth."

"Nor have you proved yours. I have adequately accounted for the facts by my simple hypothesis that only happiness is intrinsically valuable; there is no need to add that knowledge also is an intrinsic value, and moreover I believe it is a mistake to do so, for if we do we shall give undue reverence to knowledge, even when such knowledge does not add to the sum of human happiness."

b. Moral qualities.   What about kindness, honesty, benevolence, loyalty, generosity, good-will, fidelity? What makes these qualities valuable? According to the hedonist, their value is entirely instrumental: a world in which people are honest, kind, and generous is happier than one in which these qualities are not present. But there is nothing good about them in themselves: if industry and hard work did not make for a happier world (both in making the benefits of civilization possible and inculcating in people a degree of self-discipline and character-building that will enable them to perform other tasks that are in turn conducive to happiness), they would have no value. Digging ditches has no value in itself but only in relation to the end that it serves. Indeed, all these qualities can be used for either good or ill and are not always even instrumentally good: loyalty, generosity, and honesty are evil when used in a bad cause, as exemplified by the fanatic loyal to his party, ready to slaughter thousands rather than give up his belief; the person who is generous to lazy and shiftless people, when the generosity only perpetuates their parisitism; and the person who tells the truth always, even to dictators and their secret police, and thus enables them to count on his truthfulness to pursue their evil ends.

But the pluralist attaches to these qualities an intrinsic value; even when they have bad consequences, they are still of intrinsic value, though this intrinsic value may sometimes be outweighed by the unhappiness they cause when misused. Indeed, their value may often be more important than the happiness they cause or accompany.

Even if it should happen [wrote Immanuel Kant about the good will] that owing to a special disfavor of fortune, or to the niggardly provision of a step-motherly nature, this will should wholly lack power to accomplish its purpose, if with its greatest efforts it should yet achieve nothing, and there should remain only the good will . . . then, like a jewel, it would still shine by its own light, as a thing which has its whole value in itself, its usefuness or fruitlessness can neither add to nor take away anything from its value.[13]

It is the moral virtues that we should keep our eyes fixed on, and let happiness take care of itself. Try to imagine a world with people who lack these qualities, and you see the enormous value of these qualities.

"Of course," replies the hedonist, "but this value is still instrumental. It is better to keep an eye on the cultivation of the virtues, because they are the sure *way to* happiness. Sometimes happiness to be got must be forgot. But if

[13] *Fundamental Principles of the Metaphysics of Morals*, Part I, p. 11.

you cut the virtues off from the goal of happiness in which their (instrumental) value resides, you are faced with the question, what are all these virtues *for?* Why cultivate them at all? What end do they serve? No end at all, you say—they are ends in themselves. But here I cannot agree. What is there valuable in itself about loyalty, conscientiousness, industry? They have certain desirable consequences when used in a good cause, and their cultivation requires a certain self-discipline that is a valuable asset in countless situations we confront throughout life—self-discipline being again an instrumental value. But what is intrinsically good about them?"

"You can see what is intrinsically good about them if you try to imagine what happens when they are absent. Even if happiness could exist without the exercise of moral qualities, what good would it be without them? The exercise of desirable character-traits is not merely an instrument for the achievement of greater human happiness in the long run (though it is this too); these traits are desirable in themselves, and people usually value them for themselves. The more kindness, generosity, wisdom, etc., there are in the world, the better, quite apart from what they lead to; if they lead to greater human happiness (as they normally do), then the resultant happiness constitutes an *additional* good. But the total good is only increased by the presence of happiness as the consequence of virtue; it is not constituted entirely of this happiness. Much that is worthwhile for its own sake has already occurred when these virtues have been exercised, even before we know that they will have any favorable hedonic result. If you are kind to someone (at least to someone who deserves to be kindly treated), this is already a good in the world, and an intrinsic good, even if no happiness resulted from this act. It is true that we do not call a human trait (such as kindness) a virtue if it fails to promote human happiness in the long run as its usual result. But this does not in any way show that the exercise of the virtue is not itself intrinsically good. I hold that it is, and that if happiness results from its exercise, then we have a *second* intrinsic good. The exercise of moral virtue, then, is not merely instrumental to the achievement of happiness but has a value of its own, independent of its happiness-potential."

At this point we must leave the controversy. One further alternative, however, should be mentioned.

Self-realization.   According to the "self-realizationist" view, the only thing that is worthwhile for its own sake is a person's development of his best capacities as a human being. Every human being has many capacities, or potentialities, most of which he never realizes; indeed, he could not possibly do so, for the pursuit of one (his capacity for being a skilled physician, for example) will eliminate the development of many other capacities that were also possible to him. A thousand lifetimes would not be enough for a person to realize all his capacities. Moreover, everyone has many potentialities that doubtless *should* not be developed: for being a psychopath, for being a parasite, for becoming a murderer or a bank-robber. That is why the advice

"Realize your capacities" tells us very little and is made to read instead "Realize your *best* capacities." But immediately the question arises what the best ones are.

Aristotle argued that "exercising one's best capacities" meant exercising the capacity that is unique to man, the rational faculty, or reason. Man shares his capacities for growth and nutrition with all living things, and his sentience (the capacity for having sense-experiences) with the other animals, but reason is the faculty that man shares with no other species. This is the faculty that is unique to man, and accordingly it is the one that should be realized—not to the exclusion of the others (that is biologically impossible) but with the others subordinate to it: man's reason must be in the driver's seat, and all his other faculties held in control by it. However, one might remark, the fact that reason is unique to man is no proof that the exercise of this is best: uniqueness does not prove desirability. Besides, are all manifestations of this faculty desirable?

A more recent doctrine, closer in some respects to the self-realization view than to other ethical theories, is the ethical philosophy of the contemporary philosopher and novelist Ayn Rand. According to this view, the good is that which is proper (appropriate, conducive) to the life of man as a rational being. This formulation requires considerable unpacking.

Ayn Rand's ethics begins with an analysis of the concept of "value." She maintains that values arise from and are necessitated by the distinctive nature of living organisms. Briefly, the argument is this: A value is that which one acts to gain and/or keep. A value is the object of an action; it is that which can be secured only by action. Values presuppose the existence of an entity to which things are a value, an entity capable of acting to achieve values, an entity capable of initiating goal-directed behavior. Values further presuppose the existence of *alternatives,* in the face of which action is *necessary.* If there are no alternatives, then no goals and hence no values are possible.

There is only one fundamental alternative in the universe: existence or non-existence—and it pertains to a single class of entities: to living organisms. The existence of inanimate matter is unconditional, the existence of life is not: it depends on a specific course of action. Matter is indestructible, it changes its forms, but it cannot cease to exist. It is only a living organism that faces a constant alternative: the issue of life or death. Life is a process of self-sustaining and self-generated action. If an organism fails in that action, it dies; its chemical elements remain, but its life goes out of existence. It is only the concept of "Life" that makes the concept of "Value" possible. It is only to a living entity that things can be good or evil.[14]

Thus it is the existence, nature, and needs of living organisms that make the existence of values possible and necessary. It is the requirements of a living organism's survival that must set the standard of its values.

[14] Ayn Rand, *Atlas Shrugged* (New York: Random House, 1957), pp. 1012–13.

Adherence to its life as the standard of value is automatic for plants and animals; the standard is innate: all living species except man are programmed by nature to perform the actions and pursue the values required for their survival (given an appropriate environment in which this is possible to them). There is no question of their *choosing* a code of values.

But man faces just this issue. Man is not born with an automatic, innate knowledge of what is good for him or evil, what will serve his life or destroy it. He must discover, by a process of thought, the goals and actions on which his life and well-being depend. To acquire this knowledge, man must think. But to think is an act of choice. The exercise of man's mind, of his rational faculty, is *volitional*.

Consciousness—for those living organisms which possess it—is the basic means of survival. For man, the basic means of survival is *reason*. Man cannot survive, as animals do, by the guidance of mere percepts. A sensation of hunger will tell him that he needs food (if he has learned to identify it as hunger), but it will not tell him how to obtain his food and it will not tell him what food is good for him or poisonous. He cannot provide for his simplest physical needs without a process of thought. He needs a process of thought to discover how to plant and grow his food or how to make weapons for hunting. His percepts might lead him to a cave, if one is available—but to build the simplest shelter, he needs a process of thought. No percepts and no instincts will tell him how to light a fire, how to weave cloth, how to forge tools, how to make a wheel, how to make an airplane, how to produce an electric light bulb or an electronic tube or a cyclotron or a box of matches. Yet his life depends on such knowledge—and only a volitional act of his consciousness, a process of thought, can provide it.[15]

Thus, if man is to live, he must *choose* to think, he must *choose* to hold life as his standard of value, he must *discover* the specific values that his life requires. A code of values accepted by *choice,* says Rand, is a code of ethics or morality.

Since reason is man's basic means of survival, the life appropriate to man is the life appropriate to man as a rational being. Reason is the faculty that identifies and integrates the material provided by man's senses. According to this system of ethics, *rationality* is man's foremost virtue and the source of all his other virtues. Accordingly, evasion, the refusal to think, the suspension of his consciousness, is man's basic vice. Since man must produce the things his life requires, productive work is a cardinal virtue of this ethical code. Since the achievement of values involves an effort and a struggle, man must consider himself a worthy beneficiary, must consider his life worth preserving—hence another cardinal virtue of this code: *pride*.

Some men attempt to live without thought or productive work, but their survival is made possible only by those who do think and produce. The existence of those who are living a life proper (appropriate) to man is

[15] Ayn Rand, *The Virtue of Selfishness*, p. 21.

required for the survival of those who are not, the irrationalists, the parasites, the looters.

The men who attempt to survive, not by means of reason, but by means of force, are attempting to survive by the method of animals. But just as animals would not be able to survive by attempting the method of plants, by rejecting locomotion and waiting for the soil to feed them—so men cannot survive by attempting the method of animals, by rejecting reason and counting on productive *men* to serve as their prey. Such looters may achieve their goals for the range of a moment, at the price of destruction: the destruction of their victims and their own. As evidence, I offer you any criminal or any dictatorship.[16]

"Man's survival," then, means his survival as a specific *kind* of biological organism—that is, as a human being; that is, as a rational being. The good-for-man is that which is required for his survival as a rational being. Accordingly,

It does not mean a *momentary* or a merely *physical* survival. It does not mean the momentary physical survival of a mindless brute, waiting for another brute to crush his skull. It does not mean the momentary physical survival of a crawling aggregate of muscles who is willing to accept any terms, obey any thug and surrender any values, for the sake of what is known as "survival at any price," which may or may not last a week or a year. "Man's survival *qua* man" means the terms, methods, conditions and goals required for the survival of a rational being through the whole of his lifespan—in all those aspects of existence which are open to his choice.[17]

Man's life as man, then, is the *standard* of value of this code of ethics. But for each individual man, his own life is its *purpose*. What is the role of happiness, in this ethical system? It is seen as an emotional reward of life-serving action—as a concomitant of successful life. Life requires the achievement of values; happiness is the emotional consequence of achieving the values proper to man—that is, appropriate to his nature and needs. Thus the maintenance of one's life and the achievement of one's happiness are seen as two aspects of a single achievement. To the extent that a man holds contradictory values, values that are incompatible with his nature and inherent needs and with the facts of reality, both his life and happiness are placed in jeopardy. Thus, in this system of ethics, man's life (and the enjoyment thereof, which is its concomitant) is the ultimate value that all other values serve. This is the one thing that is an end in itself.

Does it follow from the above that it would be wrong for a man ever to risk his life or actually to commit suicide? Not at all: if, for instance, a man were trapped in a dictatorship, where freedom of thought and action were suppressed and proper human conditions of existence were made impossible,

[16] *Ibid.*, pp. 23–24.
[17] *Ibid.*, p. 24.

he might very well risk his life in the fight to escape or to overthrow the dictatorship; but his act would be motivated by loyalty to the life proper to man and by his refusal to exist in a *sub*human state. Or if a man were dying in agony of some incurable disease, he might decide that he had nothing to gain by prolonging his agony and might seek to end his life. But he would be rebelling against the improper state of his own organism; he would be rebelling against a state that was neither death nor the state proper to the life of a human being. The point here is not, of course, that his suicide would be mandatory but simply that it would not necessarily be irrational or in conflict with the principle of man's life as the standard of value.

Suppose someone said, "Prove to me that life is valuable." Rand would hold that this request contains an inconsistency. It is, she holds, the existence and nature of life that sets the conditions for what is valuable; it is the distinctive nature of life that gives rise to the need for values. In saying this, one is saying much more than simply that man must be alive in order to pursue values: one is saying that man must pursue values in order to remain alive—and that this is the base of ethics and of all questions of moral value. Just as (Rand would say) it is only the concept of life that gives rise to such concepts as health and disease—just as it would be meaningless to talk of health and disease except with reference to the standard and goal of life, and talk about health is meaningful only in that context—so it is meaningless to speak of values, of good and evil, except with reference to *the needs of a living organism*. The concept of value, Rand maintains, is genetically and epistemologically dependent on the concept of life, just as the concepts of health and disease are genetically and epistemologically dependent upon the concept of life. Thus to say "Prove that it is morally obligatory to value life" is similar to saying "Prove that it is medically obligatory (that is, necessary for health) to value life."

Exercises

1. How might a hedonist reply to the following charges?

a. A life of nothing but pleasure would soon become intolerable. In every life there must be change, variety. Yet a life filled with nothing but pleasure is the hedonist's ideal.

b. The hedonist is wrong: not all pleasure is intrinsically good (worth having for its own sake), only certain pleasures—the pleasures of companionship and good music, but not the pleasures of destructiveness and sadism.

c. In general, happiness is good, but not without exception: happiness is good only when it is deserved. (Intrinsically? instrumentally?)

d. If hedonism is true, then a lifetime of enjoyment by a person of cultivated tastes and inherited wealth is a better life than the life of a genius who was alone, ignored, and misunderstood in his own lifetime (the life of a Galileo or a Beethoven), even though such a life conferred immeasurable good on mankind for generations to come.

e. The hedonist would say that happiness is preferable to productive work. But isn't happiness good only if it is the result of productive work?

2. What is your view on the following assertions? Is your answer favorable to hedonism, unfavorable to it, or neither? Explain.

a. Should we encourage a bright young physics student to go ahead with a career in his subject because he will thereby acquire valuable knowledge? or because he will be happier in this career? (What if he wouldn't?) or because his knowledge will increase the happiness of others? or simply because "knowledge is a good thing to have"?

b. "Let him work hard for a while, it will make a man out of him."

"But it won't make him any happier, now or later. If you agree with this, shouldn't you change your mind about making him work hard?"

c. "If the early Romans had had happiness as an ideal, instead of the simple virtues such as hard work, thrift, honesty, and integrity, they would never have achieved greatness."

d. "Hard work is needed so that people will have something to enjoy. But in between times they should have as much enjoyment as possible. What else is life for? The Puritan takes the means to be the end."

e. "Living the life proper to a rational being is the only thing worthwhile in itself. Happiness will be a consequence of living in that way, but it is only a consequence, not what the good consists in."

3. What precise meanings does Ayn Rand attach to the terms (a) value, (b) man's survival *qua* man, (c) the life proper to a rational being, (d) standard v. purpose?

4. Schopenhauer believed that human desires are one and all doomed to frustration, and that the continued existence of life under these circumstances is not a thing to be valued. Does this contradict Rand's theory of value? (If the frustration of desire is bad, would its fulfillment if it is possible—be good? Is life *per se* an evil in Schopenhauer's account, or only a life in which all desire is doomed to frustration—which he believed was true of human life?)

5. Why would an advocate of Ayn Rand's theory of goodness object to each of the following assertions?

a. Life at any cost, life under any conditions, is valuable; it's always better to be alive than dead.

b. Animals in the jungle survive by killing and eating one another. So should human beings.

c. Under no circumstances should a person lay down his life for a cause he believes in, for it is never to one's interest to give up one's life.

d. People should exercise their rational powers because reason is the faculty that distinguishes man from the other animals.

e. The rational self-interests of human beings often conflict, and when they do a person should promote his own interest at the expense of the interests of others.

29. Theories of Conduct

Whatever things we may believe to be valuable or worthwhile, the obvious next question arises: What should we do about it? So what? we might ask, as far as our consequent actions are concerned. How should we act as a result of these considerations? It is here that ethical views are most at variance.

Most of us were brought up to follow certain *moral rules*. But the moral rules followed by different people, particularly in different cultures, often differ sharply. The following are examples of moral rules that different people at different times have thought it incumbent upon them to follow:

> Never take a human life.
> Never take a human life outside one's own tribe.
> Never cause needless pain and suffering.
> Do not gamble or wager.
> Do not engage in sexual activity outside marriage.
> Do not eat pork or shellfish.
> Always turn the other cheek when you have been injured.
> Always take revenge upon the party that has injured you.
> Do not steal from others.
> Do not get caught stealing from others.
> Kill your parents when they are too old to travel with the caravan.
> Honor your father and your mother.
> Never tell a lie.
> Never tell a lie except to an enemy (or a stranger).

But no theory of conduct can rest content with a listing of such moral rules for several reasons: (1) None of them is a complete guide to conduct—each covers only a certain type of activity but says nothing about what one should do in other contexts or situations. (2) Many of the rules contradict one another, and it would be logically impossible to follow them all. Telling a lie to an enemy violates one rule, not doing so violates another. If one is never to cause needless or avoidable suffering, presumably one should put incurably ill people to sleep (forever) painlessly, with their consent; yet this violates the rule that forbids taking human life. (3) The rule tells you what to do, but it does not say *why* you should follow the rule. What we need is a moral *principle*, or set of moral principles, from which such rules follow, and that is what we attempt to find in ethics. Are there, then, any general principles of conduct, which prescribe what one should do in all circumstances? There are several theories of conduct (of right and wrong, or of obligation) that do attempt to state such principles, from which in turn certain rules of conduct would follow as special cases.

A. Universalizability

The Golden Rule.   One precept of ethics is contained in the Golden Rule of Christianity, "Do unto others as you would have them do unto you." If you want to be fairly treated, you should treat others fairly; if you want help in time of trouble, you should help others when they are in trouble; and so on. The main force of this precept is not to make an exception out of yourself: don't expect treatment from others that you are not willing to give, and don't do things to others that you are not willing to have done to you. It is thus a rule of *impartiality*: don't treat yourself as a special case; be as impartial in considering what you should do as you would be in deciding what someone quite unknown to you (in whom you have no special interest) should do. There are, however, a few problems with the Golden Rule as stated.

What if you desire something that other people don't? I enjoy receiving chocolate bonbons for Christmas, so I should give all my friends chocolate bonbons (even though they hate them)—I am only giving to them what I would like to have given to me. As Bernard Shaw said, "Don't do unto others as you would have them do to you—their tastes might be different."

Perhaps, however, the rule is being too narrowly interpreted. Perhaps it should be construed to mean not that you should give others candy if you like candy given to you but that if you want to be given things useful or pleasing to you, you should give things useful or pleasing to them. (And, of course, different things might please them than please you.) And perhaps this is an improvement. But we have still not come to the heart of the difficulty.

Suppose that you are perfectly content to "do as you would be done by" in certain criminal activities: you would like other people to help you in safe-cracking or bank-robbing activities, and, since you enjoy it, you are perfectly willing to help them in their similar activities. Presumably the Golden Rule is not supposed to sanction such activities. But why not, since they are all cases of doing to others as you would have them do to you?

It seems that the chief defect in the rule here is in the reference to *wanting*. If you happen to want something badly enough (whether it is good or bad), you might very well be willing to help others in such activities in exchange for their helping you. But does this make them right? The rule should be more carefully stated: "If something is right for you to do, then it is also right for others; and if it is wrong for them to do, it is also wrong for you." It can't be right for you to kill other people indiscriminately and cheat in your financial transactions yet wrong for others to do so, or wrong for them to assault you without its being also wrong for you to do this to them. Thus construed, the Golden Rule is quite simply a rule of impartiality, telling each person not to treat himself as a special or favored case.

But of course, it doesn't tell you what is right or wrong; it just tells you that *if* a certain thing is wrong for others to do, it is also wrong for you to do. Yet is even this apparently harmless statement true? What if your special circumstances are different? If you decide that your neighbors should not get a divorce, are you committed to believing that therefore you shouldn't either? No, for your circumstances may be different: they may have children whereas you and your spouse are childless, and your difficulties may be remediable but theirs irreconcilable. The rule only tells you that if an act done by someone else is wrong (or right), it is also wrong (or right) if done by you, *provided* that you are *in exactly the same circumstances*. But, of course, you are never in exactly the same circumstances as other people; so the rule seems to be useless. To make it useful, it would have to be relaxed somewhat: If something is wrong for them, it is also wrong for you, provided your circumstances are sufficiently similar, or similar in the relevant respects. But this introduces a new set of problems: When are the circumstances sufficiently similar? And when are they similar in the relevant respects? What constitutes a relevant respect? Until these difficult questions are answered, the rule gives us no clear guidance.

The Categorical Imperative.   Immanuel Kant set forth a moral principle in some ways similar to the Golden Rule, but designed to overcome its defects: "So act that you could wish the maxim of your action to become a universal law of human conduct." If you decide to break an agreement because it is no longer convenient for you to keep it, the maxim (or "private rule") of your action is "Break an agreement when keeping it is no longer convenient"; is this a rule that you would wish everyone to follow, particularly in their dealings with you? You may wish to break an agreement (or promise, or contract) when it has become a nuisance to you, but would you also wish other people to break their agreements with you when it is to *their* convenience, especially when you count heavily on the agreement being kept? Clearly you would not want them to behave in that way to you, and therefore (not being a special case) you should not behave in that way to them.

Thus far, the Categorical Imperative is very similar to the Golden Rule. But now a few distinctions must be made. There are maxims that *could not* be universalized, which are in fact logically impossible to universalize. "Be a parasite" could not be universalized, for if everyone were a parasite, living off someone else, there would be no one left for the parasites to live off. "Don't buy a newspaper, read one over someone else's shoulder" cannot be universalized for a similar reason. For that matter, "Be a teacher of philosophy" could not be universalized: if everyone were a teacher, who would be the students? And how would food and shelter be provided, and so on? Surely it will not do to say that unless everyone should do it, no one should do it.[18]

But there are other maxims that it is *possible* to universalize but that it might not be *desirable* to universalize. You may decide never to help anyone else in time of trouble: "I'll leave others alone, provided they leave me alone," you may say, and there is nothing in this that it is impossible to universalize. An entire society might well live in that way. But the society might also live by the rule "You should help others in trouble, and they should help you when you are in trouble." Both are possible alternatives, and the Categorical Imperative does not tell us which of these two rules should be followed. The requirement of impartiality is perfectly compatible with both of them. The same for "It's right for me to steal from others, and for others to steal from me" and "It's right for me to keep my neighbors awake all night by

---

[18] On this point see Marcus Singer, *Generalization in Ethics*.

playing my hi-fi set loudly as long as I would consent to their doing the same." All these rules could be applied universally; yet surely some such rules are more desirable than others? In any case, it is logically impossible to universalize them all, for they contradict one another (although each one *singly* can be universalized).

Could one remedy this situation by saying not that the maxim of your action could be universalized but, as Kant said, that you could *wish* the maxim of your action to be universalized? One could indeed make this change in the formulation, but would it be an improvement? It would make the application of the rule extremely subjective, since what one could wish universalized depends on who is doing the wishing. A person who likes to live dangerously may be content to have few or no traffic laws—he doesn't feel obliged to stop at red signals, nor does he feel it incumbent on others to stop at red signals for him (if this latter requirement were not met, he would not be wishing the rule to apply impartially). Or a person may think it noble and daring to steal if he is not caught in the act; we may suspect that he wants to be free to steal but doesn't want others to steal from him—and if so, he is again not willing to apply the rule impartially. But suppose that he is willing to be stolen from as well; he may say, "I should get by with it unless I'm caught in the act, and anyone who steals from me should get by with it too unless he is caught in the act. If he can get by with it, I've got to hand it to him." The world that this person would like to see realized is more chancy and daring than the one that prohibits all stealing, but it is a logically possible one, and one that many may quite impartially wish to have realized. What a person of one temperament and set of desires would wish to have universalized, a person with a different temperament or set of desires would not.

By what criterion, then, are we to tell which maxims should be universalized? Granted that whichever these are, they should be applied impartially; but since many rules that contradict one another can be applied impartially, we are left with the question of which ones it is desirable to apply, and how we are to tell. Impartiality may be a necessary condition for moral rules, but it is not a sufficient condition, since we need other principles to tell us which rules should be applied. And this consideration takes us to other theories of conduct.

But first a word of clarification about moral rules. Are all moral rules universal, in the sense of applying to everybody? Is the rule "All those who kill should be punished" applicable to everyone, or only to those who kill? The rule is indeed universal, for it is hypothetical: "*If* someone kills, he should be punished." As such it applies to everyone—it holds true of everyone that if he kills he should be punished. Moreover, the rule can contain qualifications within itself and still be universal: "All those who take human life except in self-defense should be punished" is also universal: it is true of every person (if the rule is accepted) that if he kills other than in self-defense he is liable to punishment.

To say that a rule applies universally is not, however, to imply that it is a good or acceptable rule. "All persons whose names begin with the letter B should be exempt from the penalties for embezzlement" is surely not a good rule (we shall see why later), though it is universal in scope. Indeed, one could frame a rule, without using proper names, in such a way as to exempt only himself from punishment: "All persons shall be punished for stealing unless they are of 5'11" height, 160 pounds in weight, have blue eyes, etc., etc." until the qualifications became so specific that only oneself is exempted from the punishment. (Yet the rule is universal, for it says that *if* anyone fulfills the following requirements, then . . . .) Moreover, each person could frame the rule in such a way as to exempt himself from penalty or blame. Clearly one must ask the reasons for such strange and arbitrary exclusions; but this takes us into conditions other than the universalizability of the rule itself, for the rule itself is universal as long as it applies to everyone fulfilling the conditions described in the "if" clause.

B. Ethical Egoism

By what rules should a person guide his conduct? According to all forms of ethical egoism, the goal of a person's actions should be his own self-interest: the promotion of whatever is to his own long-term advantage should be the end at which he aims. Different ethical egoists may disagree over which courses of action will have this result, but once it is known that a certain action will contribute more than any other to the long-term advantage of the agent (the person acting), he should do it.

At first it might seem that doing what is to my interest is equivalent to doing whatever I want to do. But this is not so: what a person wants may be to get drunk every day, but to do so would not promote his long-run interest, for it would be inconsistent with other things, such as having a long life, a life without aches and pains later on, and a reliable source of income, all of which he also wants. Taking care of one's health is a necessary condition for achieving such long-term ends, and so for egoistic reasons he should do so even though he may not want to do some of the things required to make it possible. He may not want to be honest in his dealings with other human beings, but he will have to if he wants to get a favorable reputation in the community, and he needs this if he is to have continued dealings with them. Doing what you want, then, is not at all the same as doing what is to your own long-range interest. A life of "eat, drink, and be merry" may be what a person wants, but it is seldom if ever to one's long-run advantage to live in this way, so even from the point of view of egoism he should not do it.

Epicureanism. Egoists, however, have differed greatly from one another with regard to what kind of life one should live. In ancient times the principal exponents of ethical egoism were the *Epicureans*. They held that each person should conduct his life in such a way as to bring himself the most pleasure (they considered pleasure the sole intrinsic good, so "that which is my good" becomes "that which is conducive to my greatest pleasure"). And they had definite ideas about how each person's maximum pleasure could be achieved: each person should live an abstemious life, not given to excessive food and drink or involvement in personal relationships. He should eat and drink only what is necessary for the maintenance of his life, and should not accustom himself to expensive dishes to which he might become habituated and which in any case would result in indigestion and subsequent illnesses. He should not involve himself in close relationships with others, for others may betray him, or desert him, or die, and the jealousy and bitterness of a love-relation are not worth the transitory pleasure experienced at the height of such a relation. Indeed, one should not become attached to any-thing—whether material things or people—that one is likely to lose and that is *outside one's control*. One should live life coolly, calmly, always emotionally reconciled to any sudden change of fortune that may come. Just as one should not become involved in intense personal relationships, thus enslaving oneself to the changing whims of other human beings, so one should not participate in political and other civic activities, since (they argued) doing so very seldom makes one happier and only leads to frustration when his idealistic dreams are not fulfilled. One should turn away from all these things and gain solace from oneself alone (whom else can one ultimately depend on?). Indeed, the Epicurean ethics is not so much a formula for achieving pleasure as for avoiding displeasure.

One could, of course, easily be an ethical egoist and yet deny the tenets of Epicureanism. One could believe in pursuing one's own good without believing that this good consists in one's own maximum pleasure. And even if one is a hedonist and believes that good consists in pleasure, one could deny that the Epicurean recommendations for achieving it are the best ones: one could say that the Epicureans' statements of the form "Such-and-such actions will lead to one's maximum pleasure" are not true. One could hold that a life of involvement in human affairs and personal relationships results in more happiness than a life of calm withdrawal and disinterested observation à la Epicureanism. One could hold that the Epicurean view is one of "no hits, no runs, no errors" and that the best life is one lived with a certain involvement (combined perhaps with a certain detachment), and that even if one's money is lost or one's loved ones die, it is better to have loved and lost than never to have loved at all. Indeed, all the specific tenets of Epicureanism—about how to maximize one's own long-run pleasure—could be questioned on empirical grounds. One could question all these and still be an ethical egoist.

Even though Epicureanism claims to be a long-term egoism (acting in ac-cordance with a long-range plan for the conduct of one's life), one could question whether the Epicurean is not a short-sighted egoist. He plans long-range, but he is so afraid to get involved in things not within his control that he needlessly sacrifices many experiences that would afford him his greatest satisfaction if he only permitted himself to have them. In the 18th century many views of "enlightened self-interest" were advanced; but to show how different a view can be included under the heading of ethical egoism, let us consider briefly a 20th century view: the theory of conduct of Ayn Rand, whose theory of goodness we have already described.

Rational self-interest. We have already seen (pp. 591–93) that according to Rand's view the standard by which one judges what is good or evil is man's life—that which is required for man's survival as man; and that since reason is man's basic tool of survival, that which is proper to the life of a rational being is the good, that which opposes or tends to destroy it is the evil. Since life is an attribute of individual organisms, for each individual man his own life is the *purpose* of ethics. Thus this doctrine is a species of ethical egoism.

The distinction between a *purpose* and a *standard* is already familiar to us in a medical context: the purpose of a physician's treatment of an individual patient is to restore him (not others, but *that* patient) to health. To achieve that purpose, the physician must be guided by his knowledge of man's physical nature and needs, of the conditions of human health and disease. Thus *man's* life and health (and all the medical knowledge relevant to this subject) is the *standard* by which the physician is enabled to achieve the specific *purpose* of securing this particular patient's physical well-being.

Man, says Rand, is an end in himself, not a means to the ends of others. An individual life is an end in itself. Man's moral purpose is the achievement of his own rational self-interest. In social relationships, one should neither sacrifice himself to others nor sacrifice others to himself; he should deal with others by trade, by the exchange of values, by voluntary consent to mutual advantage.

Does it follow from this that there are no circumstances under which a man should wish to help another human being? Not at all:

Concern for the welfare of those one loves is a rational part of one's selfish interest. If a man who is passionately in love with his wife spends a fortune to cure her of a dangerous illness, it would be absurd to claim that he does it as a "sacrifice" for *her* sake, not his own, and that it makes no difference to him personally and selfishly, whether she lives or dies.

Any action that a man undertakes for the benefit of those he loves is *not a sacrifice* if, in the hierarchy of his values, in the total context of the choices open to him, it achieves that which is of greatest *personal* (and rational) importance to *him*. . . .

If one's friend is in trouble, one should act to help him by whatever non-sacrificial means are appropriate. For instance, if one's friend is starving, it is not a sacrifice, but an act of integrity to give him money for food rather than buy some insignificant gadget for oneself, because his welfare is important in the scale of one's personal values. If the gadget means more than the friend's suffering, one had no business pretending to be his friend.[19]

[19] Rand, "The Ethics of Emergencies," in *The Virtue of Selfishness,* pp. 45–46.

On a larger scale, but by the same principle, the kind of government one lives under is of enormous personal and selfish importance to one's life. A rational egoist would do everything in his power to prevent a dictatorship from being established in his country, since a dictatorship, depriving him of his rights, his freedom, and possibly his life itself, institutes conditions of existence in which the pursuit of rational self-interest becomes impossible.

In order to understand the distinctive nature of Rand's doctrine of self-interest, one must consider the theory of *human rights* that is basic to her ethics, and which sharply differentiates it from other species of egoism. Each man possesses certain basic rights, not as a gift from God or by permission of society (permissions can always be revoked) but by virtue of his nature as a rational being. Rights define the conditions of survival proper to a rational being in a social context.

A "right" is a moral principle defining and sanctioning a man's freedom of action in a social context. There is only *one* fundamental right (all the others are its consequences or corollaries): a man's right to his own life. Life is a process of self-sustaining and self-generated action; the right to life means the right to engage in self-sustaining and self-generated action—which means: the freedom to take all the actions required by the nature of a rational being for the support, the furtherance, the fulfillment and the enjoyment of his own life. (Such is the meaning of the right to life, liberty and the pursuit of happiness.)[20]

The question of rights never arose for Robinson Crusoe—not, that is, until Friday came along, since until then there were no other human beings of whose presence he had to take account. But in all other situations, when men interact with one another in society, the question "What rights does each man have vis-à-vis other men?" becomes pressing. This is why Rand speaks of rights as principles pertaining to man's freedom of action *in a social context*.

Now if the standard of action, of good and evil, is man's life (as described in the preceding section), then man—every man as an individual—has the right to live and to take the actions that his life as a rational being requires. He has the right to further his life by his own thought and effort; he has the right to work, and to keep the results of his effort, which is the right of property; he has the right to choose his own values and to pursue them—that is, the right to liberty and the pursuit of happiness. All these are required for the long-range living of his life as a rational being.

But every individual has these rights, since they derive from man's nature as man; so no man has the right to violate the rights of others. There can be no right to violate rights. A man does not have the right to murder, rob, or enslave other men. He has no right to seek values from others by resorting to the *initiation* of physical force.

No one has any obligations to other men other than those he has voluntarily undertaken by his own actions. He does not bear from birth any

[20] "Man's Rights," *ibid.*, pp. 93–94.

burden of guilt for the suffering of all mankind; he is not responsible for that which he did not cause, and he is not born into serfdom to the needs of others. If he has made a contractual agreement with someone, he is morally bound to keep it; if he has children, he is morally bound to support them, since it is by his action that they were brought into the world. But he has no *unchosen* obligations, imposed on him by anything but his own actions. The obligation to respect the rights of other men—which is a purely negative one, since it consists of not violating their rights—is chosen in that it is morally entailed by the choice to deal with other men at all.

If each man's rights are to be preserved, any undertaking that involves more than one man requires the *voluntary* consent of every participant, since each one of the people involved has the right to make his own decision. The right to life does not mean that others must provide you with the necessities of life; they have no such obligation toward you, and to force them to do it would be a violation of *their* rights. The right to property means that one may take the actions necessary to earn property, and that one may use it or dispose of it as one wishes, not that others must provide you with it; if it meant the latter, then those who had to provide it would be forced to forfeit *their* rights—they would be your slaves. The right to free speech does not mean that others must provide you (without their consent) with a lecture hall or radio station; to insist that this is owed to you by someone is again to imply that someone is your slave, that someone's rights are to be sacrificed to your desires. Nothing can be a right that requires for its implementation the non-voluntary participation of other human beings, since their rights would necessarily be violated in the process.

Thus this theory of ethical egoism must be sharply distinguished from all other egoistic doctrines. Rational self-interest can be defined only by reference to the objective requirements of one's life as a rational being. Rational self-interest does not consist of doing whatever one pleases. It consists of assuming the responsibility of discovering, by a rational process of thought, what one's self-interest actually consists of, and of being guided in one's actions accordingly. It does not consist of trampling on the rights of others. It consists of respecting the rights of others and demanding that one's own rights be respected. It does not consist of regarding other human beings as sacrificial objects. It consists of refusing to regard any human being—oneself or others—as a sacrificial object.

C. The General Good

Utilitarianism. Whatever kind of world we find to be most valuable—a world containing the maximum pleasure or happiness, or this plus the most knowledge, or the most rational beings functioning in their proper capacity—one answer to the problem of conduct, or "What should we do about it?" is that given by utilitarianism, and its answer is very simple: "Act so as to bring about the greatest good possible." Not just your own good, but the good of *everyone* affected by the action, is what you should try to produce. If your action affects ten people, consider its effects on each one of these ten, yourself included (you count as one, but only as one); it is not only the effects on you, but the *total* effects of your action, that you should consider. Among the alternative actions open to you, the one you should choose is the one that produces the most total good—or, in other words, the one that has the best total consequences. If, for example, happiness is the good to be aimed at, then our acts should be such as to produce the most all around, not just my happiness or yours but the happiness of everyone concerned. The calculation of this may be difficult, and to do it mathematically is impossible: I cannot say that you or I will be two or five times as happy if I do this than if I do that. Still, we can give good approximations: I know that the gift of a philosophy book will make A happier than it will B; that eating the watermelon will cause more pleasure than letting it rot; that more happiness will result from my visit to a friend's house than from my setting fire to it. And I have good evidence for believing that more total happiness will result from saving my neighbor's life or helping him in distress than from leaving him in his present condition, even though I am greatly inconvenienced by helping him.

In acting so as to promote the maximum happiness to all concerned, it is the *net* happiness I must consider, not the *gross*. I may make someone happy by providing him with a diet of lamb curry and martinis, but if he has stomach trouble he will (when he arrives at the hospital with bleeding ulcers) curse me for my benevolence; the happiness (or pleasure) he enjoyed from his repast is more than counterbalanced by the pain, distress, and all-round displeasure of its aftermath. I should consider the total happiness which will be caused by my actions *after* the unhappiness has been subtracted from it. In some cases the unhappiness may be preponderant no matter which alternative I choose; I then choose "the lesser of the two evils"—the alternative in which the negative (unhappiness) has the smallest excess over the positive (happiness) of any alternative action open to me. For example, if I am a company commander in wartime and no matter which alternative I choose there will be some loss of life among my men, I choose the alternative that (as far as I can foresee, to the best of my knowledge) will result in the largest gain combined with the smallest loss of life.

It is often very difficult, and sometimes in practice impossible, to know which alternative this will be; but all I can do is act according to my best knowledge, the best information available at the time. My duty is to act in accordance with the best available evidence; omniscience is not required. Since "ought implies can," I cannot be expected to do what is impossible for me. I cannot be expected to jump into the air 500 feet, or to digest stones, nor to know exactly how the battle will go (this depends on countless factors unknowable to me at the time I must make my decision). It may even happen that my act results in disaster: I may pick up a group of walking children in my car, and two minutes later through no fault of mine a careless driver may crash into my car, killing some of the children. But at the time I could not have foreseen this consequence as anything but extremely unlikely, so my act of picking them up (which ordinarily would have helped them) was not wrong. Similarly, it would be wrong for me to drive recklessly in traffic, thus endangering my life and the lives of many other motorists, even though I might avoid an accident and get to my destination somewhat earlier. I might get by, but the risk is too great. In short, I should perform that act which, of all the alternatives available to me, will (on the basis of the best evidence available to me at the time) produce the most good for all concerned.

The utilitarian ethics can thus be stated very simply. The proposition that a certain act is right follows as a conclusion from two premises:

> The act that will (on the basis of the best evidence available at the time of acting) produce the greatest total good is right.
> This act will produce the greatest total good.
Therefore, this act is right.

The second premise—that this act will have such-and-such consequences—is often difficult or even impossible to determine. But this is only because the sequence of causes and effects in the world is extremely complex, and it is very difficult indeed to know, or even to estimate with probability, especially in complex cases, what all the far-flung consequences of one's actions will be. If one did know that this act would produce the most total good, however, then according to the utilitarian one should do it. Doubt about what you should do stems more from the second premise—whether this act will have the best consequences—than from the first, which is of course the statement of the utilitarian theory of conduct.

Nevertheless, utilitarianism has been challenged in many ways: it has seemed to many philosophers that it is *not* always one's duty to perform that act which will produce the greatest good. Let us consider a few examples: (1) Suppose I promise to perform some service for you. Should I keep this promise only when I believe (with good evidence) that doing so will do the most good? Should I keep this promise only because doing so will do the most good (if it will)? Shouldn't I keep the promise *because I made it?* If I were asked "Why did you keep that promise?" the normal reply would not be, "Because I thought that by doing so I would be producing the most good." If the promisee thought that the latter was my reason, he would be suspicious of future promises: he would think, rightly, that the next time I might break the promise if I believed I could do more good by doing something else. This is not to say that one should *always* keep his promises—if I've promised to meet you at 4 P.M., but can save a life in a traffic accident along the way, I would doubtless be justified in being late for my appointment. Nor should I keep a promise to help you rob a bank. But neither (so runs the objection) is my duty to keep the promise based entirely on the good consequences of keeping it: it is based also (and primarily) on the fact that I made it. (2) This becomes especially pressing in the case of promises that no one knew were made. If two explorers are lost in the Arctic, and there is only enough food to keep one of them alive until the supply ship is scheduled to arrive, the first explorer may express his willingness to die if the second one promises to educate the first man's children after he (the second man) reaches civilization. Would the second man be justified, on returning to civilization, in reasoning thus: "No one knows that the promise was made; there will be no bad consequences of breaking it. Since I consider my children more worth educating than the dead explorer's, and since I can't afford to educate both, I shall educate my own and forget about my promise to the dying man"? (3) A man ordinarily feels obliged to provide for his family, not his neighbor's family. What if, however, on a given occasion, he could do more good by helping his neighbor's family than by helping his own? Should he do it? Would he be just as obliged to do it as to help his own? (4) Suppose a prisoner were to argue, "I admit that I committed an armed robbery. But that is over and done with. I would be happier if I were released. My family, which depends on me for support, would also be much happier if I were released and could earn money for their support. You, Judge, would be no worse off: it would be no skin off your back if I were released. Nor would it encourage other people to commit crimes in the hope of getting a similar release, because no one outside my family (who aren't going to talk) knows I committed this crime, and I am certainly not going to advertise it. Nor am I going to commit any crimes again; I've learned my lesson on that score. I have a job waiting for me. So everyone would be better off if I were released. Therefore, I beg you to release me." Still, we would be inclined to be suspicious of this appeal; we might not be able to formulate exactly why, but we would be inclined to say that justice is not done if this man is released without paying some penalty for his crime. Or consider: (5) The district attorney, after attempting without success on numerous occasions to convict a man for crimes he committed, has finally obtained a conviction for his latest alleged offense. Then he comes upon unimpeachable information that the man did not commit this last offense. Suppose at that point he were to reason: "I'll just sit on the evidence. No one else knows or will know that the man is innocent this time; if he is released now he will only commit other crimes and be a danger to life and property; by being convicted this time he will only be paying for crimes that he committed earlier for which he was not convicted (but for which he admitted guilt after the trial was over). It would be better all round if he were not released, as he surely would be if I made this information public. Therefore, I am justified in keeping back this evidence." Yet would we not be quite uneasy about this reasoning? Our conviction would persist that if he has not committed *this* crime, then he should not be imprisoned for it, even though more good might be produced in this case by letting the conviction stand. (6) If your father and a famous physician were both trapped in a burning building, and you had time to rescue only one of them, should you rescue your father or the physician? Assume that the physician, if he lived, would save many lives by performing operations that very few physicians can perform. The utilitarian would surely say that you should rescue him. Far more good could be done by rescuing the physician. Yet most people would believe that you should rescue your father first.

Rule-utilitarianism. In order to take care of cases such as these, utilitarianism now takes another turn. The traditional version of utilitarianism, which we have been considering thus far, is *act-utilitarianism:* the act that should be performed is the act that has the best consequences. But the change is suggested by *rule-utilitarianism*, which holds that we should not judge the rightness of the act by *its* consequences but by the consequences of adopting the *rule* under which the particular act falls. For example, one important rule in law is that a person who is known to be innocent should never be found guilty. Sustaining the conviction of the man even after we know that he is innocent would clearly violate this rule. Whatever the consequences may be of *this* particular conviction, the consequences of adopting any *rule* that permits conviction of people who are known to be innocent is very bad indeed—and it is the rule that we wish to preserve. Even if no one (except the D.A.) knew that the rule has been violated in this case, the fact is that the rule *would* have been violated, and the rule is a good one. What makes it a good rule? Consider the consequences of *not* having such a rule: a person's conviction would not be based on evidence, or on whether he was (according to the best available evidence) innocent or guilty; people would become rightly suspicious of all law, and there would be great public demoralization, as there is in any country in which evidence can be manufactured against someone and people known by the authorities to be innocent can be railroaded to prison or death because the officials want to get rid of them. Such a system would be so horrible that we must preserve at all costs the rule "The known innocent shall not be convicted," even when in an individual case the following of the rule may not have the best consequences. We go by the consequences that the rule has, not by the consequences of the individual act.

Finding the best rule (a rule whose adoption would have the best consequences) is often difficult. Most such rules will be far from simple. For example: Should we adopt the rule "Never take a human life"? Is killing so horrible that we should never do it? Is the rule against killing so important to preserve that we should consider killing wrong under all circumstances? So the strict pacifist believes. But the simple rule "Never kill" may not be the best rule. What about killing in self-defense, for example? If someone is attempting to kill you, should you simply allow yourself to be victimized? What would be the effects of following the rule "Never kill under any circumstances"? It would be an open invitation to anyone who wished to commit aggression against you; and the adoption of such a rule would result in the death of the innocent and the survival of thieves and murderers. A far more desirable rule would seem to be "Never kill except in self-defense" (or a similar rule, "Never *initiate* aggression against other human beings"). This would put would-be aggressors on guard that you would not take their attempts passively, and at the same time would make others feel secure that you would not *start* any use of force against them. The phrase "except in self-defense" would not be an exception *to* the rule; it would be a qualification *within* the rule: the rule would apply impartially to all acts of non-defensive killing. Whether the rule should have further qualifications (for example, capital punishment) would take too long to argue here. The point is that we must get the best rule we can about killing and then stick to it without exceptions (though the rule may contain numerous qualifications within itself), and the best rule is that rule whose adoption would result in the best consequences.

"Never break a promise" would not be as good a rule to follow as "Never break a promise unless it was made under duress," and perhaps (this could be argued) even this latter, qualified rule would not be as good a rule as "Never break a promise unless it was made under duress or unless some *very great* good would be achieved, or evil prevented, by breaking it"—this last provision, though vague, would take care of cases like breaking the promise to meet somebody because of giving help to the victim of a car accident along the way. But "Never break a promise unless it was made in secret" would *not* be a good rule: there are times when promise-keeping is of value even when no one besides the promiser and the promisee knows that the promise was made (as in the case of our Arctic explorers), but if this rule were adopted, promises made in secret or without witnesses could not be relied on. Among the circumstances that would excuse you from breaking your promise, the fact that no one knew about the promise is *not* one of them, for if this class of exceptions were incorporated into the rule, the adoption of the rule would have worse consequences than if the rule did not contain such a qualifying clause. Even "Never break a promise except when breaking it will do the most good" would not be a desirable rule to follow (though this would be the rule the act-utilitarian adopts), because the promisee would not know under what kind of condition the promiser would feel himself justified in breaking his promise—there would be no rule under which he was operating specifying the kinds of conditions in which he would break the promise, and the promisee would have very little idea when he could trust the promiser's word and when he could not, thus resulting in a lessening of reliability of promises.

Rule-utilitarianism also endeavors to provide an answer to the problem that troubled us earlier: When are two situations relevantly different? "What you shouldn't do I shouldn't do either, unless our situations are relevantly different"—but when are they? In rule-utilitarianism, the question becomes one of following the best rules—that is, the rules that produce the most good. The rule "Never get a divorce" would be a bad one, since it would keep many couples tied together for a lifetime of misery; but the rule "Always get a divorce after a marital quarrel" would be a bad one also, for many quarrels can be patched up. The rule "Never tell lies" would be a bad one, since, as we have seen, it would enable evildoers to use our commitment to truth to further their ends. But "Always tell lies when it is convenient to do so" would also be a bad rule, since even trustworthy people would not be able to rely on our truthfulness. Finding the best rule about lying is difficult: different qualifications of the rule against lying occur to us, and each one would have to be checked out to discover whether or not it would (if added) improve the rule. But at least rule-utilitarianism provides a test for relevance. Suppose I tell a lie at 11:30 P.M. on Tuesday in full moonlight, while wearing a blue suit; and suppose that someone who disapproved of my action (but perhaps not lies of his own) were to propose the rule "Never tell lies at 11:30 P.M. on Tuesdays when the moon is full, when you're wearing a blue suit." We all believe that these circumstances are irrelevant, but why? Because there is *no difference* between the consequences of telling lies on Tuesdays and the consequences of telling them on any other day, no difference whether the moon is full or not, and so on. The rule about lying has been made more specific by the mention of these additional circumstances, but not *relevantly* more specific, since there is no known difference between the effects of lying whether these conditions are present or absent; in other words, it is simply an empirical fact that its being a Tuesday, or one's wearing a blue suit, has nothing to do with the consequences of lies that one tells. (If lies told on Tuesdays, but not those told on other days, had good effects, then its being a Tuesday *would* be relevant in deciding what should be included in the rule.) When a rule can be made more specific by the mention of various types of circumstances, but *irrelevantly* more specific, then the irrelevant circumstances should not be included in the rule. By contrast, when a rule can be made *relevantly* more specific, it should be considered, and only those circumstances that would improve the rule should be included in it. For example: The pacifist says, "I should never use physical force against another human being." But there are various kinds of activities included in the category of "the use of force," and their consequences differ markedly from one another. There is using force to defend oneself against attack; there is the use of force that is entirely unprovoked; there is the use of force by a policeman in catching a lawbreaker, or by a drunkard in response to an imaginary affront. Using force against someone who is trying to kill you has the good effect of preserving your life, whereas using force if no one has threatened you has the bad effect of possibly killing or injuring an innocent person, as well as setting an example of the initiation of force to settle conflicts. Thus, in arriving at the best rule about the use of force, the spelling out of different kinds of use of force *is* relevant: that is, the rule is made relevantly more specific by the mention of these types of cricumstances.

Rule-utilitarianism also endeavors to solve the problem (which we can only mention here) of *ethical relativism*. Ethical relativism should be sharply distinguished from *cultural relativism*, which is not an ethical doctrine at all but the report of an anthropological-sociological phenomenon. It says merely that different moral rules are operative in different societies. And in this sense cultural relativism is clearly true. If, however, it says (as cultural relativists sometimes do) that different societies operate from different basic moral principles, then its truth is not so obvious. Many widely differing rules in different places and times are special cases of the moral principle "That action is best that is most conducive to the survival of the tribe." Sometimes, moreover, the differences among tribes are *non-ethical* differences. Among some Eskimo tribes it is considered one's duty to kill one's parents when they have become too aged to travel (indeed, the parents expect it); for if the parents lived it would be impossible for the tribe to reach the summer quarters, where their animals can graze, from the winter quarters, where they can be protected against the elements, in sufficient time to enable the tribe (including the parents, if they lived) to survive. In a situation so different from our own, where it is a matter of some surviving or none at all, might not we too approve such a rule? In certain South Sea Island tribes, parents are also disposed of by the age of 60 and no rigors of climate are there present to justify such a procedure. But in this case there is a difference of metaphysical belief: the islanders believe that they will survive in the next world with the body they had in this world at the time of their death, and they do not wish to go into the next world wrinkled and feeble. Does this prove cultural relativism, or only that different rules of conduct will be prescribed when certain non-ethical beliefs are different?

But *ethical* relativism is concerned with the question whether there is one basic moral principle (or set of principles) that *should* (not does) operate in all societies. According to rule-utilitarianism, there is only one basic moral principle, that of rule-utilitarianism, but when this moral premise is combined with certain empirical premises about the conditions existing in various societies, it may well yield differing moral *rules:* whether a given rule is the best one in a society depends on the conditions existing in that society. Thus in a desert society it may rightly be considered a capital crime to waste water, since the lives of many others may depend on water not being wasted; but in a water-affluent society, there need be no rule prohibiting the extensive use of water (provided that future needs are considered), since more harm than good would result from having such a rule. In a society in which the ratio of men to women is approximately equal, monogamy may well be the best system (at least regarding rules of marriage, whatever may be said of sexual encounters outside of marriage), but in a society depleted by war, in which women outnumber men ten to one, monogamy may not be the best rule; at any rate, it depends upon the conditions. In an industrial society, keeping contracts and being punctual are important virtues, since the smooth functioning of industry depends on these things; but in a nomadic or agrarian society, these virtues may (in some respects at least) be less important. On the other hand, some rules—such as that prohibiting killing except in self-defense (and perhaps in a very limited number of other kinds of circumstances)—are so vital to the functioning of a society and the preservation of the individuals within it that this kind of prohibition should be universal. According to rule-utilitarianism, then, ethical relativism applies to rules but not to the moral principle (or principles) from which the rules are derived.

Theories of conduct not based on consequences.   According to both types of utilitarianism, what we should do depends entirely on consequences—on the consequences of the particular act in act-utilitarianism, on the consequences of the rule that the act exemplifies in the case of rule-utilitarianism. But not every theory of conduct relies exclusively on consequences as the "right-making" feature of acts.[21] "Why am I against killing? Well, killing is just wrong, that's all." "To break one's word is a bad thing—I can't give you any reasons, it's just that I believe one shouldn't do it except perhaps in circumstances of extreme distress." These rather naïve but often encountered expressions of moral belief may leave something to be desired, but they show that those who utter them think of certain types of act as wrong quite apart from (or at any rate in addition to) the bad consequences that may result from doing the things in question. According to such views, we should consider not only the probable consequences of the act (which lie in the future) but also the conditions in which the act was performed (which lie in the past).

Following this line of thought, it has been alleged that there are various types of moral obligation that the utilitarian does not sufficiently recognize, or of which he does not give a satisfactory account. (1) There are duties of *gratitude* to those who have helped us. We owe a duty of gratitude to our parents, who supported us for all those years, in a way that we have no such duty to strangers. I owe a duty of gratitude to my father and not to the physician, so it is my father whom I should rescue from the burning building. This duty is not based on any probable future consequences; if it were, I should rescue the physician, for he will do much more good in the world. But I have a special duty to my father that I do not have to the physician, because of the past; my duty to him is past-looking, not future-looking. Moreover, it has a personal character—I have the duty to my father, and you do not

---

[21] Theories of conduct that base the rightness of an act entirely upon consequences (whether of the act or of the rule) are sometimes called "teleological" theories, whereas those that base the rightness of the act on other considerations (sometimes including consequences, but never exclusively) carry the barbarous name of "deontological" theories.

(you have it to *your* father); duties have a personal character: they are to certain people and not to others, because of their special relation to you. (2) There are duties of fidelity. I have made a promise, and therefore I should keep it. My duty to keep it rests on the fact that I have made it, and making it is something that occurred in the past. This duty is past-looking, not future-looking—it is not based on the probable good consequences of keeping the promise, but simply on the fact that the promise was made. It is also personal, for the person to whom I owe it is the person to whom I made the promise, not just anyone. It is, again, a because-of duty, not an in-order-that duty. (3) There are also duties of *justice*. The word "justice" does not always carry the same meaning, and space does not permit an analysis of it here.[22] In one sense "justice" means *equal treatment:* if the judge sentences a stranger to the full penalty under the law but lets off his friend or political crony for exactly the same offense, an injustice is done because the treatment is unequal: justice says there should be equal treatment for equal offenses (as well as equal reward for equal achievements). But equal treatment does not exhaust the meaning of "justice." Suppose the judge sentenced everyone, friend and stranger alike, to life imprisonment for a minor traffic offense (assuming this were in his power), including himself if he later committed the same offense. He would thus be severely impartial in his sentences, not exempting even himself from the rule guiding his decisions. But still, we would say, such a sentence would be unjust—not because it was not administered equally to all the guilty but because such a sentence was unjust to begin with: it was not in accordance with what the offenders *deserved*. Justice, in this very important sense, means *treatment in accord with desert*. It may be very difficult to figure out what a person deserves in a particular case (does the armed robber deserve only a fine, or a year of imprisonment, or ten years?), but once we are convinced that a person is getting a more severe (or for that matter a less severe) penalty than he deserves, we believe that his punishment is not just. Justice has to do with desert, and an appeal to desert is *not* an appeal to future consequences. The man deserves a punishment because he has killed someone, or embezzled, or robbed, and so on—and these are things that, like promises, occurred in the past. His punishment should not depend on probable future consequences of his being punished but simply on his desert in the light of his past actions.

The *utilitarian* theory of punishment is entirely future-looking: one should punish in-order-to, not because-of. According to the utilitarian, punishment is justified because it may (a) improve the offender, perhaps "teach him a lesson" so that he will not repeat his offense; (b) deter other people from committing similar offenses; and (c) protect other people (potential victims) from such offenders by isolating them from the rest of society. But the

---

[22] See John Hospers, *Human Conduct,* Chapter 9 ("Justice"). On the different kinds of non-utilitarian duties, see W. D. Ross, *The Right and the Good.*

retributivist view of punishment is that all such possible good effects are merely by-products and do not constitute the reason why punishment should be administered. Punishment should be administered simply because an offense *has been* committed, for which the offender deserves to be punished.

According to act-utilitarianism, if the results of keeping this promise, or of punishing this offender, are not good in the particular case, then the promise should not be kept or the man punished. But the rule-utilitarian does not consider the consequences of the particular act but the consequences of the rule. Both types of utilitarian place exclusive emphasis upon consequences, but the consequences of the particular act are not the same as the consequences of following a certain rule, and the rule-utilitarian would say that the rightness or wrongness of the act depends on the good or bad consequences of the rule under which it falls. *Why*, he would say, should a person be punished in accord with his desert? Why should we do good to those who have benefited us, more than to others? And so on. The answer, he says, is to be found in the consequences of having the rule: beneficent acts among human beings should be encouraged, and therefore we should have a rule whereby those who have benefited us have first claim on our beneficence. Again, why punish? Why not just ignore the offense entirely? Because the consequences of not punishing would be very bad indeed—people would commit countless crimes, knowing that they could get by without being punished. And why should some punishments be more severe than others? "Because the offenses are more serious, and the person who commits the more serious offense deserves the more severe punishment." But why punish in accord with desert rather than in accord with some other criterion? Because in more serious crimes more deterrence is needed, and more protection on the part of society against the persons who commit them. It all comes down to consequences after all, says the rule-utilitarian—not the consequences of the particular act but of the adoption of the rule. What makes one rule better than another is always the consequences of having it—and this is future-looking, not past-looking.

We shall not attempt here to settle this controversy in general; each side can make a powerful case for its own position. Let us concentrate rather on one type of case, which will bring the two positions sharply into focus and will try rule-utilitarianism to its utmost. Let us consider the case of an innocent man who has been condemned to death by the authorities, who know perfectly well that he is innocent (or at any rate have no evidence that he is guilty) but convict him nevertheless. They believe, perhaps with good reason, that much good would result, or harm be prevented, by having him out of the way; moreover, there is a crime-wave and people are impatient with the police for not finding the culprit—they will rest more securely if they believe that the guilty party has been found, and this will in turn create more respect for law and order, letting would-be criminals know that they will not escape punishment for any crimes they may commit. Let us assume also that the real culprit is dead, and that no one but the authorities know who he is or that he committed the crime, so the fact will never come out to embarrass them in the future. Why not, then, railroad an innocent man for this crime, especially if he is a public nuisance who has committed many crimes before, even though he has not committed this one? There would be many good consequences of doing so, and no bad ones that can be foreseen—so why not do it?

The retributivist would say at once that the man should not be punished for this offense, for the simple reason that he has not committed it. To punish him for something he didn't do would be a clear example of injustice. He should not be punished, even though the consequences of punishing him in this case might be very good, because punishment is justified by considerations of desert and not of the future consequences of punishing. But neither would the rule-utilitarian be in favor of punishing him, though his reasons would be different: he would say, as we saw before, that the consequences of having such a rule (permitting on occasion the punishing of those known to be innocent) would be disastrous in a society: it would make everyone feel insecure, it would undermine the foundations of law, and so on. Thus both parties would agree on the issue, though for different reasons.

But now the retributivist can start to put the squeeze on the rule-utilitarian. "Just as you included in your desirable rule about promise-keeping the clause 'unless by breaking the promise a very great good would result,' wouldn't you have to include the same proviso in your rule about not punishing the innocent? Wouldn't you have to say 'Don't punish the innocent, unless some very great good could be thereby achieved—such as restoring public morale, or stopping a crime-wave, or building a greater society? If preserving public morale was one of your reasons for having such a rule as 'Don't punish the innocent,' it would surely seem that in a case where public morale *could* be restored by punishing the innocent, your rule should provide for this type of exception, and should read 'Don't punish the innocent unless some very great good could thereby be attained.' I think you are committed to this, since you assess the desirability of rules entirely in terms of their consequences—and the consequences of having such a revised rule might well be better than the consequences of having no provisions in your rule for this exceptional type of case. I think that if you proceed on the basis of consequences alone, you need such a built-in qualification to the rule, just as you introduced it in the case of the rule about promise-keeping. But although you are committed to this, since yours is entirely an ethics of consequences, I believe that here you are mistaken. I say that it would be wrong to punish an innocent man no matter how many good consequences would result from doing so. The fact is that the man is innocent, and this *alone* is perfectly sufficient to justify us in saying that he should not be punished—no, never, not in any circumstances, not even to stop a crime-wave or to quell a riot. I believe that the 'social engineers' of Soviet Russia in the 1930's could well have given a utilitarian (yes, even a rule-utilitarian) justification for their deeds. Many people were condemned to death though known to be innocent of the crimes charged against them; but a perfectly good utilitarian reason could have been given for sentencing them: a Great Society was being built (or so the leaders may have thought), and of what value is an individual life, or even a few thousand individual lives, in comparison with so great an ideal? The individual life, they could reason, is just a chip on the current; and if the continuation of that individual life would destroy, or even compromise, the attainment of the great ideal, why then it should be snuffed out, on the basis of manufactured charges if necessary, rather than stand in the way of the ideal designed to benefit millions for generations to come. I don't see why the perpetrators of these atrocities couldn't have been good and conscientious utilitarians, giving utilitarian reasoning to justify their acts. True, the acts didn't have the envisioned consequences—the killing only led to more killing, the terror and violence to more terror and violence, and the ideal never did become realized, and is today as far from realization as ever—and perhaps in the light of historical evidence about past tyrannies the leaders should have known this. But at any rate, they *could* have given just as plausible a defense of their acts, on utilitarian grounds, as most utilitarians do now of their day-to-day actions, in terms of their probable consequences. This is the fate of utilitarianism when it is not embedded in principles of justice to which no exceptions can be made."

But must not justice in turn be embedded in the concept of human rights? We are thus led back again to the topic of rights. If each man has a right to his life, the products of his labor, and his own free and independent judgment, one could argue, justice will not be violated provided that these rights are recognized in the legal system of the nation and no exceptions made. A nation's constitution must place individual rights outside the reach of public authorities, even beyond the power of vote, else an intolerant majority may legally persecute or kill or send to concentration camps any unpopular minority. With the political power thus delimited, the lives and property of minorities are not at stake; they cannot be taken away by majority vote, and no man by achieving political power can take them away. A just society is one that recognizes individual rights and so embeds them in its constitutional structure that no would-be tyrant or group of commissars, no matter how much they may proclaim "the greatest happiness of the greatest number," can take them away. "The greatest happiness" is the happiness of each individual, and cannot be achieved by the sacrifice of one individual to another individual or group of individuals. A theory of conduct that includes no explicit doctrine of human rights is a theory without a vital center, and no theory that assesses the rightness of acts in terms of consequences alone can ever provide it.

Exercises

1. Are the following maxims universalizable? Of those that are, would you consider it desirable for them to be universalized? Explain.
   a. Don't depend on yourself for a living—beg and steal from others.
   b. Never start a fight, but defend yourself if you are attacked.
   c. Give half your income to the poor.
   d. Don't take help from others, and don't give it.
   e. Receive help from others, and also give it.
   f. Love your enemies.
   g. Be more charitable than anyone else is.
   h. Keep your promises unless it is inconvenient for you to do so.
   i. Take as much of everything as you can get.

2. Evaluate the following rules. Can you improve any of them by building certain qualifications into them? State the qualifications, in each case, and show why the rule would be improved by having them.
   a. No one should take another human life except in self-defense.
   b. People should always be honest and trustworthy in their dealings with one another.
   c. People should always try to help one another in emergencies.
   d. One should never discriminate against applicants for a job because of their race.
   e. Married couples who have children should never be divorced.
   f. Corporal punishment should never be used against children.
   g. One should never take anything that belongs to another without the owner's consent.
   h. A person charged with a crime should always be considered innocent until he is proved guilty.

3. The opposite of egoism is altruism: egoism says that one's self-interest should be the goal of one's activities, and altruism says that the interests of others (not of oneself) should be. Is utilitarianism altruistic? is Kant's ethical view? is the ethics of Christianity? Explain.

4. Comment on the following expressions of opposed points of view:
   a. "The only life worth living is a life devoted to the service of others." "Greater love hath no man than this, that a man lay down his life for his friend." "Sell all that you have, and give to the poor."
   b. "If enjoyment is a value, why is it moral when experienced by others, but immoral when experienced by you? If the sensation of eating a cake is a value, why is it an immoral indulgence in your stomach, but a moral goal for you to achieve in the stomach of others? Why is it immoral for you to desire, but moral for others to do so? Why is it immoral to produce a value and keep it, but moral to give it away? And if it is not moral for you to keep a value, when you give it, are they not selfish and vicious when they take it? Does virtue consist of serving vice? Is the moral purpose of those who are good, self-immolation for the sake of those who are evil?" (Ayn Rand, *Atlas Shrugged,* p. 1031.)

5. In what respects does the egoism of Epicureanism differ from that of Ayn Rand?

ETHICAL PROBLEMS

6. Would an advocate of Ayn Rand's theory be opposed, and why, to (a) Kant's universalizability criterion? (b) act-utilitarianism? (c) rule-utilitarianism? (d) rule-utilitarianism supplemented by a separate principle of justice?

7. In which (if any) of these ways do you interpret rule-utilitarianism? Which do you consider preferable, and why? Can you think of a specific rule which should be adopted under interpretation (a) but not interpretation (b), or vice versa?

a. One should adopt, now, those rules which would produce the most good *if* they were adopted universally.

b. One should adopt, now, those rules which, in the *present* context of social customs, will bring about the most good.

8. How might the rule-utilitarian differ from the act-utilitarian on the solution to these problems?

a. The student goes to his professor at the end of the term and asks for a change of grade. "But you don't deserve a better grade," says the professor. "I admit that," says the student, "but if I don't get that grade I won't be able to get into medical school, which I want very much to do. Not getting that grade may mean the difference between getting into the profession that I want and having to put up with a life-work that I like less. The consequences for my happiness would be enormous. As to your happiness, surely giving me that A couldn't make very much difference to that. Every utilitarian consideration, then, should lead you to change the grade."

b. A man has been sentenced to prison for armed robbery, and admits guilt for the deed. "But," he reasons, "I'll never do anything of the kind again. I'm not insane, or a danger to society. I would be happier out of jail than in. My wife depends on me for support, and she and the children would be far happier if I were able to be the family breadwinner again. As to the influence on others, almost no one would ever know about it; you can keep the matter out of the newspapers and no one except you will even know that the crime was committed. Therefore, you should release me."

9. Do you consider rule-utilitarianism to be adequate to decide the following cases, or must it be supplemented, for example by some separate principle of human rights?

a. The sheriff in a southern town is guarding the courthouse against a mob that is about to storm it by force, in order to capture a Negro prisoner and lynch him even before his trial. If the mob is frustrated, many people may be killed in the ensuing riot. Should the sheriff deliver the prisoner to the mob, thus sacrificing one life instead of many?

b. May a hundred men get together and kill one man in order thereby to live a more peaceful life (assuming that the man they eliminate is a wastrel, a public nuisance, and a chronic trouble-maker)?

c. Should the wealthier members of society be forced to pay, through taxation, for the poorer members (the sick, the unemployed, and those who refuse to work)?

10. Do you consider it a violation of anyone's rights (and why)

a. for a government to censor newspapers and radio-television programs?

b. for a college administration to prevent the circulation of a campus magazine?

c. for a parent to open his 12-year-old son's mail?

d. to reveal to others certain facts about a friend's private life, which he told you in confidence?

e. for a government to own all the means of production within a nation?

f. for government agents to use wire-tapping to discover what is being said in your home?

g. for an organization of gangsters to control the appointments in a city government?

h. for a government to require involuntary military service?

i. to have capital punishment for certain crimes?

j. to have a law of eminent domain (requiring you to vacate your property if a bridge or freeway or other construction sponsored by government is to be built there)?

k. for a government to nationalize private property (factories, etc.)?

l. for a political candidate to demand free broadcast time on a television station?

Selected Readings for Chapter 9

Anthologies of readings:

Abelson, Raziel (ed.), *Ethics and Metaethics*. New York: St. Martin's Press, Inc., 1963.

Brandt, Richard B. (ed.), *Value and Obligation*. New York: Harcourt, Brace & World, Inc., 1961.

Edwards, Paul and Arthur Pap (eds.), *A Modern Introduction to Philosophy* (rev. ed.). New York: Free Press of Glencoe, Inc., 1965. Chapter 4.

Katz, Joseph, Philip Nochlin and Robert Stover (eds.), *Writers on Ethics*. Princeton, N. J.: D. Van Nostrand Co., Inc., 1962.

Melden, A. I. (ed.), *Essays in Moral Philosophy*. Seattle, Wash.: University of Washington Press, 1958.

————, *Ethical Theories* (2nd. ed. with revisions). Englewood Cliffs, N. J.: Prentice-Hall, Inc., 1967.

Munitz, Milton K. (ed.), *A Modern Introduction to Ethics*. New York: Free Press of Glencoe, Inc., 1958.

Oldenquist, A. (ed.), *Readings in Moral Philosophy*. Boston: Houghton Mifflin Company, 1964. Paperback.

Selby-Bigge, L. A. (ed.), *British Moralists*. Oxford: Clarendon Press, 1897. Paperback, Bobbs-Merrill Company, Inc., 1964.

Sellars, Wilfrid and John Hospers (eds.), *Readings in Ethical Theory*. New York: Appleton-Century-Crofts, 1952.

Primary sources:

Aristotle, *Nicomachean Ethics*. Many editions.

Ayer, Alfred J., "On the Analysis of Moral Judgments," in *Philosophical Essays*, London: Macmillan & Co., Ltd., 1955.

Baier, Kurt, *The Moral Point of View*. Ithaca, N. Y.: Cornell University Press, 1958.

Bentham, Jeremy, *The Principles of Morals and Legislation*. Many editions.

Binkley, Luther J., *Contemporary Ethical Theories*. New York: Citadel Press, 1961.

Blanshard, Brand, *Reason and Goodness*. London: George Allen & Unwin, Ltd., 1961.

Brandt, Richard B., *Ethical Theory: The Problems of Normative and Critical Ethics*. Englewood Cliffs, N. J.: Prentice-Hall, Inc., 1959.

Dewey, John, *The Theory of Valuation*. Chicago: University of Chicago Press, 1939.

Edel, Abraham, *Ethical Judgment*. New York: Free Press of Glencoe, Inc., 1955.

Edwards, Paul, *The Logic of Moral Discourse*. New York: Free Press of Glencoe, Inc., 1955.

Ewing, Alfred C. *Ethics*. New York: The Macmillan Company, 1953.

———, *The Definition of Good*. New York: The Macmillan Company, 1947.

———, *Second Thoughts in Moral Philosophy*. London: Routledge & Kegan Paul, Ltd., 1959.

Frankena, William K., *Ethics*. Englewood Cliffs, N. J.: Prentice-Hall, Inc., 1963. Paperback.

Hall, Everett W., *What Is Value?* New York: Humanities Press, 1952.

Hare, R. M., *The Language of Morals*. Oxford: Clarendon Press, 1950. Paperback.

———, *Freedom and Reason*. Oxford: Clarendon Press, 1963. Paperback.

Hartland-Swann, John, *An Analysis of Morals*. London: George Allen & Unwin, Ltd., 1960.

Hazlitt, Henry, *The Foundations of Morality*. Princeton, N.J.: D. Van Nostrand Company, Inc., 1964.

Hospers, John, *Human Conduct*. New York: Harcourt, Brace & World, Inc., 1961.

Hume, David, *A Treatise of Human Nature*. Book 3. Many editions.

———, *An Inquiry Concerning the Principles of Morals*. Many editions.

Kant, Immanuel, *Fundamental Principles of the Metaphysics of Morals*. Many editions.

Ladd, John, *The Structure of a Moral Code*. Cambridge, Mass.: Harvard University Press, 1957.

Mill, John Stuart, *Utilitarianism; On Liberty*. Many editions.

Montefiore, Alan, *A Modern Introduction to Moral Philosophy*. New York: Frederick A. Praeger, Inc., 1959.

Moore, G. E., *Principia Ethica*. London: Cambridge University Press, 1903. Also in paperback.

———, *Ethics*. London: Oxford University Press, 1912. Also in paperback.

Nowell-Smith, P. H., *Ethics*. London: Penguin Books, Inc., 1954. Paperback.

Perry, Ralph Barton, *General Theory of Value*. Cambridge, Mass.: Harvard University Press, 1926.

———, *Realms of Value*. Cambridge, Mass.: Harvard University Press, 1954.

Plato, *Republic; Philebus; Meno; Euthyphro; Crito*. Many editions.

Pratt, James B., *Reason in the Art of Living*. New York: The Macmillan Company, 1949.

Rand, Ayn, *The Virtue of Selfishness*. New York: New American Library, 1964. Paperback.

Ross, W. D., *The Right and the Good*. London: Oxford University Press, 1931.

———, *The Foundations of Ethics*. Oxford: Clarendon Press, 1939.

Russell, Bertrand, *Human Society in Ethics and Politics*. London: George Allen & Unwin, Ltd., 1955.

Sesonske, Alexander, *Value and Obligation*. New York: Oxford University Press, Inc., 1964. Paperback.

Singer, Marcus, *Generalization in Ethics*. New York: Random House, 1961.

Smart, J. J. C., *Outlines of a Utilitarian System of Ethics*. London: Cambridge University Press, 1961. Paperback.

Stace, Walter T., *The Concept of Morals*. New York: The Macmillan Company, 1937. Paperback.

Taylor, Paul, *Normative Discourse*. Englewood Cliffs, N. J.: Prentice-Hall, Inc., 1961.

Toulmin, Stephen E., *The Place of Reason in Ethics*. London: Cambridge University Press, 1950.

Von Wright, G. H., *The Varieties of Goodness*. London: Routledge & Kegan Paul, Ltd., 1963.

Warnock, Mary, *Ethics Since 1900*. London: Oxford University Press, 1960.

Zink, Sidney, *The Concepts of Ethics*. New York: St. Martin's Press, Inc., 1962.

Index